RACE AND INTELLIGENCE
Separating Science From Myth

RACE AND INTELLIGENCE
Separating Science From Myth

Edited by
Jefferson M. Fish

LAWRENCE ERLBAUM ASSOCIATES, PUBLISHERS

2002   Mahwah, New Jersey   London

Lawrence Erlbaum Associates, Inc., Publishers
10 Industrial Avenue
Mahwah, NJ 07430

Cover design by Kathryn Houghtaling Lacey

Library of Congress Cataloging-in-Publication Data

Race and intelligence : separating science from myth / edited
    by Jefferson M. Fish.
        p.   cm.
Includes bibliographical references and index.

ISBN 0-8058-3757-4 (cloth : alk. paper)
1. Intellect. 2. Race. 3. Intelligence levels—Social aspects
    4. Intelligence tests—Social aspects.   I. Fish, Jefferson M.

BF431 .R27   2001
305.9'082—dc21   00-033164
                                                                  CIP

Books published by Lawrence Erlbaum Associates are printed on
acid-free paper, and their bindings are chosen for strength and
durability.

Printed in the United States of America
10   9   8   7   6   5   4   3   2

*To Dolores
and Krekamey*

Contents

Part I

Homo sapiens has no extant subspecies: There are no biological races. Human physical appearance varies gradually around the planet, with the most geographically distant peoples generally appearing the most different from one another. The concept of human biological races is a construction socially and historically localized to 17th and 18th-century European thought. Over time, different cultures have developed different sets (folk taxonomies) of socially defined "races."

Part II

Racial categories are developed to serve social ends, including the justification and perpetuation of inequality. IQ testing has been a part of this process of stratifying groups.

Part III

Cultural content, values, and assumptions are an inherent part of IQ tests. Formal schooling teaches people new ways of thinking, which are then measured by the tests. Access to schools, school quality, modes of instruction, attitudes toward formal education, and educational values vary cross-culturally.

Part IV

Biological-sounding concepts, especially heritability, have been misused to imply a genetic basis for group differences in IQ scores. There are many cognitive abilities—a single general factor of intelligence is inadequate to account for current knowledge in psychological measurement or cognitive science.

Part V

A wide variety of data, including reanalyses of data presented in *The Bell Curve*, imply that group differences in IQ are social in origin and can change as the result of changing social circumstances or social interventions.

Preface

Race and Intelligence: Separating Science From Myth is a comprehensive response to claims of differences in innate intelligence between the races. It differs in two important ways from other works on the topic, which tend to be limited to a discussion of IQ in the United States. First, this book discusses in great detail the concept of race, shows why it has no biological basis, explains the nature of human physical variation, and discusses the history and cross-cultural variability of conceptions of race. Second, in addition to discussing the United States in detail, it considers the measurement of intelligence and the use of IQ tests from a global perspective.

Race and Intelligence shines the light of science on a number of widespread but false beliefs and presents a more accurate picture in their place. Taken together, these beliefs constitute a coherent but inaccurate ideology that has a long and unfortunate history; this work confronts the ideology in its most recent incarnation. Fortunately, what is known about the subject matter is fascinating and it forms a coherent alternative vision that can be presented in this single wide-ranging volume.

The beliefs that this book responds to and that form a kind of syllogism, are the following:

1. Over time, *Homo sapiens* evolved into different subspecies or races—principally Mongoloids, Caucasoids, and Negroids.
2. In addition to biological differences in physical appearance, these races also manifest biologically based differences in behavior.
3. Human intelligence is an important form of behavior that can be measured by IQ tests. Intelligence is best understood as comprised of a single factor, g (general intelligence); and g has been shown to be largely (40%–80%) inherited.
4. There are racial differences in intelligence, with Mongoloids somewhat more intelligent than Caucasoids, and Caucasoids significantly more intelli-

gent than Negroids. These differences are in large measure genetically based.

5. Because racial differences in intelligence are genetically based, not much can be done to change them; and it is pointless, if not counterproductive, to waste money on social policies that attempt to do so.

There are so many errors of fact, false assumptions, misunderstandings, and other distortions in these widely held assertions that it requires a wide-ranging work to clarify matters. Because American cultural beliefs with significant time depth make these assertions seem reasonable, it is important at the outset to contrast them with an alternative set for which extensive scientific evidence is presented in this volume. These are:

1. *Homo sapiens* has no extant subspecies: there are no biological races. Human physical appearance varies gradually around the planet, with the most geographically distant peoples generally appearing the most different from one another. The concept of human biological races is a construction socially and historically localized to 17th- and 18th-century European thought. Over time, different cultures have developed different sets (folk taxonomies) of socially defined "races."

2. Racial categories are developed to serve social ends, including the justification and perpetuation of inequality. IQ testing has been a part of this process of stratifying groups.

3. Cultural content, values, and assumptions are an inherent part of IQ tests. Formal schooling teaches people new ways of thinking that are then measured by the tests. Access to schools, school quality, modes of instruction, attitudes toward formal education, and educational values vary cross-culturally.

4. Biological-sounding concepts, especially heritability, have been misused to imply a genetic basis for group differences in IQ scores. There are many cognitive abilities—a single general factor of intelligence is inadequate to account for current knowledge in psychological measurement or cognitive science.

5. A wide variety of data, including reanalyses of data presented in *The Bell Curve*, imply that group differences in IQ are social in origin and can change as the result of changing social circumstances or social interventions.

Because these five assertions are so important and lay out the overall structure of the argument of the book, they are repeated as the headings of its five parts.

To discuss such wide-ranging issues, this volume brings together leading scholars from a range of disciplines—anthropology, biology, economics, history, philosophy, psychology, sociology, and statistics. As might be expected given the terms *race* and *intelligence*, anthropology and psychology are the most heavily represented.[1]

---

[1]Disciplines, languages, and chapter authors differ on the capitalization of race terms (e.g., Black vs. black in English, but only *preto* in Portuguese) for a variety of reasons. Rather than insist on an arbitrary consistency, I made the editorial decision to allow each chapter to follow its own capitalization preferences.

In addition to its overall mission, a secondary goal of the book is to promote informed communication about the topics of race and intelligence—between its covers, among readers from different academic disciplines, and among the general public. Because knowledge is highly specialized, scientists and scholars often rely on "common sense" or "common knowledge" when going beyond the bounds of their expertise. Unfortunately but unavoidably, and within every culture, people's fund of common experience is heavily invested with inaccurate ethnocentric assumptions. Thus, a book like this can help to develop a shared body of knowledge that can form the basis for more productive future discussions.

For this reason, although all the chapters are intellectually rigorous, the use of specialized terminology and technical language has been limited as much as possible to cases where they are necessary, and an attempt has been made to offer explanations in those cases. This editorial policy not only facilitates interdisciplinary communication—especially between psychology and anthropology—but also helps to make the work accessible to the public at large. Although the book is about understanding race and intelligence, and not about public policy, the issues it discusses have long been raised in policy debates, so citizens deserve to be informed in ways that are clear without being overly technical.

Because the authors of the various chapters discuss race and intelligence from so many different perspectives, they sometimes make points that are relevant to other parts of the book in addition to the one in which their presentation is situated. Furthermore, because the chapter authors come from a wide range of disciplines, not all can be expected to agree on the policy implications of a scientific understanding of race and intelligence. They do, however, agree that science forms a better basis for public policy than ethnocentric assumptions.

It is one thing to argue that a particular government program (or, for that matter, a privately funded program) might not work, or is too expensive, or is a less efficient use of limited resources than some alternative, or is an inappropriate use of funds, or stigmatizes minority groups by singling them out, or to make some other argument based on evidence or political philosophy. It is quite another to say that such programs are doomed to failure because Negroids as a group[2] have a racially based biological inferiority to Caucasoids, and—adding insult to injury—that the programs are counterproductive because they make the inferiority of Negroids excruciatingly obvious and thereby demoralize them. The latter argument is not science, but racist myth masquerading as science, and deserves to be unmasked as such.

---

[2]The term *group* illustrates differences in the use of language between psychology and anthropology. Psychologists use the term in contrast to *individual*; group has multiple meanings that are rarely defined explicitly. Among these are (a) people with some face-to-face contact or a sense of themselves as belonging to a particular entity that is different from other comparable entities, and (b) a social category that arbitrarily includes people who lack these affective ties (e.g., group data). Anthropologists routinely make these distinctions, referring to the former as "group" or "social group" and to the latter as "category" or "social category."

Here and in the chapters I have written I follow psychological usage. Readers from the other social sciences should be aware that, for example, the reference to "Negroids as a group" does not imply that people who have been classified together think of themselves that way or share any historical or territorial connection.

I am a psychologist, so it is easy to understand how upset I was when I heard that articles by well-known psychologists arguing for racial differences in intelligence were appearing on racist web sites and seeming to give intellectual legitimacy to them. (These web sites are referred to in chap. 3.) Although I have no reason to believe that the authors gave permission for use of their work, this state of affairs does raise disturbing questions about the social responsibilities of scientists in the information age.

The process of learning about race and intelligence is one of challenging inaccurate assumptions and ultimately of coming to better understand ourselves as a species, as a variety of cultures, and as individuals. It is an intellectual journey well worth taking, and it is a pleasure to invite readers along for the ride.

ACKNOWLEDGMENTS

Any large-scale work requires the cooperation of many individuals. I would like to begin by thanking the chapter authors for their dedicated work. They are all extremely busy people, and their contributions to this project are greatly appreciated. I would also like to thank those individuals who assisted chapter authors by commenting on drafts or otherwise affecting their chapters, for their indirect contributions to *Race and Intelligence: Separating Science From Myth*. In addition, I regret any inconvenience to others whose work had to be put on hold so that chapter authors could do their part for this volume.

I want to thank those who reviewed drafts of chapters or the entire manuscript—the book is a stronger one for their suggestions. Because of the book's interdisciplinary nature, I was fortunate that a number of contributors were willing to review chapters in their areas of expertise. Their input also enhanced the cooperative spirit of this volume. Reviewers included Frank A. Biafora, Jr., Mark Nathan Cohen, Robert Ghiradella, Joseph L. Graves, Jr., Jeffrey Long, Jonathan Marks, Dolores Newton, Michael Palij, Alan Templeton, and Robert Tillman. Their contributions enhance the book, and responsibility for its shortcomings remains with me.

I would like to thank Michael Moskowitz for his support of this project during its initial stages, and Louis R. Franzini and Jerome M. Sattler for their helpful advice as it neared completion. In addition, research reductions in my teaching load at St. John's University, along with a research leave, provided time to work on this and a number of contemporaneous projects.

The idea for this book grew out of a conference at the New York Academy of Sciences, organized by Michael Palij and me, on the more restricted topic "*The Bell Curve* Reconsidered: Multidisciplinary Perspectives on Race and IQ." The conference was supported in part by a grant from Yeshiva University, and the following scholars made presentations: Gwyneth Boodoo, Ned Block, Jefferson M.

Fish, John L. Horn, Jonathan Marks, John U. Ogbu, Michael Palij, Eugenia Shanklin, Andrea Tyree, and Kimberly C. Welch. Michael Palij deserves special thanks for his contributions to that conference; in addition, it was he who came across the racist web sites referred to earlier.

These acknowledgments would be incomplete without special mention of the multiple direct and indirect influences on this volume by my anthropologist wife Dolores Newton. If we had never met, I would probably still be a monolingual, monocultural American psychologist. I would never have had the exposure to the other side of the American "racial" divide. I would never have lived in Brazil and learned its very different way of understanding human physical variation, nor, as a result, would I have developed a curiosity about other cultures' "racial" folk taxonomies. I would not have discovered physical anthropologists' understanding of human variation, nor probably—like other psychologists—would I have realized that my basic assumptions about race were simply wrong.

As an intellectual companion, Dolores has explained concepts, debated ideas, and referred me to sources I would not otherwise have encountered. For example, I did the research for and wrote chapter 5, but it is impossible for me to apportion its ideas into hers, mine, and ours. That chapter, and in some ways this book, can best be seen as the most recent product of three decades of ongoing dialogue. Furthermore, in addition to reviewing several chapters and the manuscript as a whole, she has also done much more than her share on the home front to enable me to make this book happen.

This book says things that need to be said; Dolores more than anyone else has helped it to become a reality.

—Jefferson M. Fish

Contributors

W. Steven Barnett, PhD, is Professor of Economics at the Rutgers University Graduate School of Education in New Brunswick, NJ.

Ned Block, PhD, is Professor in the Departments of Philosophy and Psychology and in the Center for Neural Science at New York University.

Gregory Camilli, PhD, is Associate Professor and Chair of the Department of Educational Psychology at the Rutgers University Graduate School of Education in New Brunswick, NJ.

Mark Nathan Cohen, PhD, is Distinguished Teaching Professor of Anthropology at the State University of New York at Plattsburgh.

Bernie Devlin, PhD, is Director of the Computational Genetics Program and Assistant Professor in the Department of Psychiatry at the University of Pittsburgh.

Stephen E. Fienberg, PhD, is Maurice Falk University Professor of Statistics and Social Science at Carnegie Mellon University in Pittsburgh.

Jefferson M. Fish, PhD, is Professor and former Chair of the Department of Psychology at St. John's University in New York City.

Joseph L. Graves, Jr., PhD, is Associate Professor of Evolutionary Biology at Arizona State University West in Phoenix.

John L. Horn, PhD, is Professor of Psychology at the University of Southern California in Los Angeles.

Michael Hout, PhD, is Professor of Sociology at the University of California, Berkeley.

Jonathan Marks, PhD, is a biological anthropologist in the Department of Sociology and Anthropology at the University of North Carolina at Charlotte.

John U. Ogbu, PhD, is Chancellor's Professor in the Department of Anthropology at the University of California, Berkeley.

Daniel P. Resnick, PhD, Is Professor of History at Carnegie Mellon University in Pittsburgh.

Kathryn Roeder, PhD, is Professor of Statistics at Carnegie Mellon University in Pittsburgh.

Eugenia Shanklin, PhD, is Professor of Anthropology at the College of New Jersey in Ewing.

Audrey Smedley, PhD, is Professor of Anthropology at Virginia Commonwealth University in Richmond.

Alan R. Templeton, PhD, a past President of the Society for the Study of Evolution, is Professor of Biology and Genetics at Washington University in St. Louis.

Kimberly C. Welch, PhD, is Assistant Professor of Latin American Studies at the University of Redlands in Redlands, CA.

A Scientific Approach to Understanding Race and Intelligence

Jefferson M. Fish

PSYCHOLOGISTS, ANTHROPOLOGISTS, AND RACE

Anthropologists long ago began investigating the observation that peoples who live at great distances from one another look different; speak different languages; and have different customs and ways of experiencing, relating to, and understanding the world. It took a great deal of effort and investigation to conclude that these apparent relationships are socially, rather than biologically based. That is, language, customs, and worldviews result from the ways individuals are socialized by their groups and are unrelated to their physical appearance. Healthy newborns from anywhere in the world can be equally well socialized into any distant society, learn to speak its language(s), and become a part of its culture and show no linguistic or behavioral traces of the culture of their faraway biological parents.

The discipline of anthropology incorporated this understanding into its very structure, known as the *four-field approach*. The primary division is between the field of physical (or biological) anthropology and the three subdivisions of cultural (or sociocultural) anthropology—the fields of ethnology (the description and comparison of cultures), archaeology (the study of cultures through time), and linguistics (Ember & Ember, 1988).

Unfortunately, this understanding of the independence of culture from biology seems never to have reached most psychologists or other social scientists. Lacking cross-cultural knowledge, they have often seen the world through the filters of current American folk categories and presented data on contemporary American behavior as representative of human behavior in general.

Let me give an example from a heated discussion about race that I had with my African American wife nearly 30 years ago. We were each frustrated with the other's inability to reach certain obvious conclusions about particular populations. It turned out that, as a psychologist, I was using the term *population* to mean statistical population, whereas she, as an anthropologist, was using it to mean breeding population. In other words, our cultural misunderstanding was due not to differences in black versus white assumptions but in anthropologist versus psychologist assumptions.

The cultural gap between anthropologists and psychologists—in this case illustrated by linguistic differences in the meanings of technical vocabulary—seems not to have been bridged over the decades. For example, I have never met a psychologist who has heard of a breeding population—members of a species that breed among themselves more than they do with other members of the species—except for those to whom I have explained the concept. (To my dismay, with the decline of the four-field approach in anthropology, paralleling increased specialization in psychology, I have discovered in recent years that many anthropologists seem not to have heard of the concept either.[1])

From my point of view as a psychologist, one key reason that cultural misunderstandings and mutual ignorance between psychology and anthropology are problematic is that they permit psychologists to take seriously statistically intelligible but otherwise absurd research. Because knowledge is unitary, studies based on ethnocentric assumptions that are contrary to what is known about human evolution can only lead to false conclusions and a self-perpetuating confidence in those assumptions.

Psychologists generally view race as a biological classification, like sex—assuming that there are two sexes (male and female) and three races (Caucasoid, Mongoloid, and Negroid). Despite the existence of hermaphrodites and transvestites, the sexual classification is generally accurate, and categorizing experimental

---

[1]As I have worked on this multidisciplinary book and spoken with experts in a variety of fields, I have become increasingly aware of and distressed by the extent to which disciplinary specialization has prevented scholars from getting the big picture about race, even as they see their own pieces of the puzzle with great clarity. Not only are psychologists unaware of anthropologists' knowledge and vice versa, but cultural anthropologists are often uninformed about physical anthropologists' knowledge and vice versa. Similarly, whereas the nonexistence of biological races in the human species is common knowledge among evolutionary biologists, other biologists often have not heard of it. Hence, in addition to fostering communication among disciplines, this book aims at promoting communication within disciplines among their various specialties.

participants by their physical appearance or self-designation leads to few problems. In contrast, the question "How do you know what race your participants are?" has not been understood by psychologists to be unanswerable. Meanwhile, the classification of people into biological races has long been known by anthropologists to be scientifically inaccurate, but reflective instead of American folk beliefs, which differ from folk beliefs in other cultures. Because psychologists in the United States are culturally American they take these scientifically inaccurate beliefs for granted. When they assume that human races exist, and categorize their experimental participants by their physical appearance or self-designation, they unwittingly create much mischief.

Many psychologists, as part of their general education, have been exposed to the broad outlines of human evolution. Anatomically modern members of our species first appeared in Africa about 200,000 years ago. After about 80,000 to 100,000 years, small groups that were biologically unrepresentative of the continent's diversity began leaving Africa through the Middle Eastern land bridge and spread out across Eurasia, while the large and varied populations in Africa continued to evolve (although some genetic interchange between Africa and Eurasia also continued over time). About 15,000 years ago, when the Ice Age lowered the sea level enough to create a land bridge across the Bering Strait, small and biologically unrepresentative groups of Asians entered and spread out across the New World. Thus, rather than three races, we have three geographical regions of human variability: The preponderance of human physical variation is in Africa, a much lesser range of variation can be found in Eurasia, and relatively little variability exists among indigenous populations of the Americas. If biological races did exist, they would be found only in Africa, although psychologists in their research persist in acting to the contrary.

Psychologists' (and other social scientists') lack of awareness of the basics of physical anthropology is illustrated by *The Bell Curve*'s evaluation of the scientific status of the work of the developmental psychologist J. Philippe Rushton. Rushton actually asserts that Negroids have small brains, large genitals, and lots of sex; that Mongoloids have large brains, small genitals, and little sex; and that Caucasoids fall in between. In Herrnstein and Murray's (1994) words, "According to Rushton, the average Mongoloid is toward one end of the continuum of reproductive strategies—the few offspring, high survival, and high parental investment end—the average Negroid is shifted toward the other end, and the average Caucasoid is in the middle" (pp. 642–643).

Herrnstein and Murray (1994) evaluated Rushton's work as follows:

> Setting aside whether his work is timely or worthwhile—a judgment we are loath to make under any circumstances—it is plainly science. He is not alone in seeking an evolutionary explanation of the observed differences among the races. As science, there is nothing wrong with Rushton's work in principle; we expect that time will tell whether it is right or wrong in fact. (p. 643)

This evaluation makes it clear that they view such work as serious science meriting serious consideration. I hope that *Race and Intelligence: Separating Science From*

Myth will help interested readers—including psychologists and other social scientists—to understand why it is that races do not exist, and to distinguish between culturally constructed labels for people's physical appearance and what is known about human evolution.

The notion that the human species has no races in the biological sense is not a new one in anthropology. Montagu (1941) made the point six decades ago, and it was commonly accepted in anthropology by the 1960s, although the relevant knowledge seems never to have diffused to other disciplines. Perhaps the publication of *The Bell Curve* served to legitimize the discussion among scientists of views about race and eugenics that have remained dormant since the end of World War II and the discovery of the Nazi death camps.

SOME RECENT BOOKS DEALING WITH RACE AND INTELLIGENCE

Before discussing the content of this volume in detail, I should mention that it was prepared over a period of several years. During this time, a number of other books have appeared that have dealt with the same topic as a main or secondary focus of attention. These books have been written from a variety of perspectives and have made a variety of claims. As I see it, their appearance has only confirmed the need for this book; a number of them are discussed or alluded to in other chapters. Suffice it to say at this point that none of them showed an understanding of the facts of human physical variation. Several showed an ethnocentric misunderstanding of the evidence, and in others the question was not even dealt with.

Perhaps even more disturbing was the fact that many of these books displayed no awareness that there was something to be known. That is, because the authors did not know what they did not know, there was no way that relevant information could have an impact on the arguments they were making. In particular, the key issue of the irrelevance of data concerning differences in performance between categories of Americans labeled as "races" to the question of whether those differences are the result of innate biological differences could not be adequately addressed.

Part of the problem is the naive notion among many researchers in psychology, sociology, education, and other fields that one can operationally define "race" in terms of American categories, as self-reported by Americans or rated by American judges, without reference to the knowledge of evolutionary biology or physical anthropology—and then make inferences about biological causation from the data obtained. It is the biological ethnocentric counterpart to the psychological ethnocentric practice of operationally defining a dimension of American personality and then imposing it on other cultures for which it may be irrelevant. By measuring it cross-culturally and then comparing (or even ranking) cultures, one winds up with quantitative ethnocentric nonsense. (As is mentioned in chap. 5, cross-cultural psychologists refer to such a concept as an *imposed etic* [Berry, 1969].)

Books Claiming Innate "Racial" Differences

Several recent books define race ethnocentrically (in terms of American folk categories) and misunderstand, misrepresent, or ignore evidence concerning human physical variation. The scientific way to go about the matter is to ask what we know about human physical variation, then to ask whether the evidence suggests the existence of biological races, and only if the answer is "yes" to proceed to investigate differences between the races. Because the answer is "no," the discussion is pointless, and scientists can go on to investigate other matters.

Instead, these authors appear committed to investigating IQ differences between unscientific, nonbiological, American folk categories. Their goal seems to be to demonstrate that—despite centuries of slavery, segregation, and discrimination as alternative explanations—African Americans really are inferior. Thus, Rushton (1997) never really defined what races are; assumed the existence of Mongoloids, Caucasoids, and Negroids as biological entities; blithely lumped together widely varying groups of individuals and data of uneven quality into these three categories; and referred to resulting numbers as racial differences.

Levin (1997) also assumed the existence of Mongoloids, Caucasoids, and Negroids. Although he does give a definition of race, it is an unashamedly ad hoc one —"letting 25 years mark a single generation, a 'Negroid' may be defined as anyone whose ancestors 40 to 4,400 generations removed were born in sub-Saharan Africa" (p. 20). As is discussed briefly in this chapter, and at length in Parts I and II of the book, Americans have long used ancestry, in the form of the folk concept of blood, as their own cultural criterion for race. In this way, the definition is ethnocentric. However, 110,000 years ago (25 × 4,400) all anatomically modern humans were in Africa. Hence, by this definition, all humans are Negroids. Clearly, what Levin was trying to do was create a biological definition that corresponds to American folk categories. As he said, "One hundred randomly chosen individuals sorting passers-by on an urban street would, without hesitation or collusion, almost always agree on who is black, white, or Asian" (p. 19). Evidently, he was assuming that the generic humans who are randomly chosen are Americans on an American street. They are not, for example, Brazilians in Brazil or Haitians in Haiti who, as I point out in chapter 5, have very different systems of "racial" classification. And what of the billion people in India? What race are they? There seem to be quite a few people who do not fit into these purportedly universal categories. Finally, studies of race and intelligence make no effort to trace the ancestry of individuals back even 4 generations, let alone 40 or 4,400, nor are genetic tests routinely run on children even to verify that their socially designated fathers are their biological fathers. So what we are left with is that socially designated race in the United States today is race.

Eysenck (1998) did not define race, but assumed that races exist and used terms like "the white (Caucasian) race" and "mongoloid races" (p. 10). He made it clear that he believes these are biological entities, and that a significant part of differences in IQ scores between the races is biological in origin.

Jensen (1998) wrote that "virtually every living species on earth has two or more subspecies. The human species is no exception, but in this case subspecies are called races" (p. 425). This statement is simply false; *Homo sapiens* has no subspecies, as Templeton demonstrates in detail in chapter 2.

Jensen (1998) went on to write:

> A race is one of a number of statistically distinguishable groups in which individual membership is not mutually exclusive by any single criterion, and individuals in a given group differ only statistically from one another and from the group's central tendency on each of the many imperfectly correlated genetic characteristics that distinguish between groups as such. (p. 425)

This is an example of the kind of ethnocentric operational definition described earlier. A fair translation is, "As an American, I know that blacks and whites are races, so even though I can't find any way of making sense of the biological facts, I'll assign people to my cultural categories, do my statistical tests, and explain the differences in biological terms." In essence, the process involves a kind of reasoning by a converse." Instead of arguing, "If races exist there are genetic differences between them," the argument is "Genetic differences between groups exist, therefore the groups are races."

Humans have so many genes that any two groups are bound to differ from one another genetically. For example, just by chance, there are probably genetic differences between members of the local golf club and members of the local bowling league. However, one would not want to argue for the existence of golf and bowling races; nor would one want to argue if differences between the groups were found in income, education, or even IQ, that these were racial differences, rooted in biology, rather than social class differences reflecting the American cultural reality.

Genetic differences among local populations of the world's religions are also the result of social, historical, and geographical circumstances, and do not imply the existence of Buddhist, Christian, Hindu, Jewish, Muslim, or other races. It would be bizarre to hunt for the genes responsible for their differing religious thought processes.

Jews constitute an illuminating example because Hitler's labeling them a race was used as a eugenic justification for their extermination. It is true that because of culturally determined patterns of mating, there are slight genetic differences between European Jews and European Christians. For the same reason, there are slight genetic differences between North African Jews and North African Christians. However, European Jews and Christians are genetically more similar to each other than either is to North African Jews or Christians; and North African Jews and Christians are genetically more similar to each other than either is to European Jews or Christians. Local populations simply are not races.

Other Books

Jencks and Phillips (1998) produced a rather different book from the previous four. On the one hand, neither they nor their chapter authors define race or show an awareness of the facts of human physical variation. On the other, the book does not attempt to explain black–white test score differences in biological terms (although at times the book's ignorance of physical anthropology leads it to poorly formulated discussions of issues and scientifically questionable uses of the term *race*). It is an American-focused, policy-oriented, social science discussion of differences in test scores between people called "white" and people called "black" in the United States. It looks at those differences, their effects, and what might be done to ameliorate them, much as one might look at differences between rich and poor, or between recent immigrants and fourth-generation Americans. In this sense, its methodological approach is similar to that of Part V of this volume.

In contrast to Jencks and Phillips (1998), this volume's primary focus is on refuting claims of biologically based differences in intelligence between the races and offering an alternative understanding of the phenomena involved. Thus, although some of its conclusions might differ from those of their book, the most relevant way to view it is as simply concerned with different—but related—subject matter.

This is also the case for the edited book by Samuda et al. (1998), which somewhat misleadingly claims to discuss "cross-cultural assessment." Actually, the book discusses the cognitive assessment of American minorities, rather than of people from widely differing cultures around the world. This American ethnocentric perspective in a book that defines itself as cross-cultural is unfortunately an accurate reflection of the state of affairs in American psychology today. Cultures are different groups in the United States, and races are whatever Americans consider them to be. Although the book never defines race (like the previous and next book discussed) it also does not attempt to explain in biological terms test performance differences between groups called races in the United States. Interestingly, the book reports data on the Kaufman Assessment Battery for Children (Kaufman & Kaufman, 1983) showing that, "on average white children score only 7 points higher than African American children" (Samuda et al., 1988, p. 59). This is only about half the difference found elsewhere, and is an encouraging social indicator. The finding is consistent with evidence in this volume and elsewhere concerning both the social origins of and malleability of group differences in IQ.

An important instance of this malleability is discussed in Neisser's (1998) edited book on the Flynn effect—the surprising discovery that IQs around the world have been rising rapidly for decades. This finding is difficult to reconcile with a view of intelligence as a biologically fixed entity. Unfortunately, like the others, Neisser's book never defines race. Although its findings provide strong evidence for a social explanation of group differences in IQ, its uncritical use of the American concept of race detracts from the quality of its discussion. As might be expected, a number of chapters in this volume discuss the Flynn effect and its implications.

Finally, I would like to mention a book written for a general audience by the journalist Ellis Cose (1998). Although Cose's book deals mainly with the issue of affirmative action, the author—who is not a scientist—shows a clear understanding of basic knowledge regarding both human physical variation and the differing folk concepts of race found in different cultures. The fact that a nonspecialist had no difficulty discovering, mastering, and communicating this information is worth some comment. Cose deserves praise for his achievement, and he also demonstrates that the information is there for those who want to find it. That so many highly trained scientists, from a variety of fields, who have devoted decades of their life to some aspect of this issue, could remain unaware of or impervious to this knowledge is an indictment of (at least) disciplinary hyperspecialization.

OVERVIEW OF THIS BOOK

The presentation that follows is aimed at providing a bird's-eye view of the organization and structure of *Race and Intelligence: Separating Science From Myth*, as well as a sense of its overall argument. My hope is that this preview and associated commentary will make it easier to see how the points in the various chapters of this multidisciplinary work relate to the greater whole.[2]

Part I: Homo sapiens has no extant subspecies: There are no biological races. Human physical appearance varies gradually around the planet, with the most geographically distant peoples generally appearing the most different from one another. The concept of human biological races is a construction socially and historically localized to 17th- and 18th-century European thought. Over time, different cultures have developed different sets (folk taxonomies) of socially defined "races."

In chapter 2, Templeton applies the same biological methods that have been used to examine the genetic diversity in other species to human beings. He discusses the two ways the term *race* has been used by biologists—as a subspecies or a lineage—and shows that by either definition our species has no races. He compares humans to a dozen different geographically dispersed large mammals and presents data indicating relatively little genetic differentiation among humans. In contrast to the notion of different races in different places, the model that best fits the data is one of gradual genetic variation over space. That is, the degree of genetic difference between populations varies with the geographical distance between them. Furthermore, physical traits like skin color or hair texture, thought by Americans to distinguish between races, do not vary together geographically. For example, the two most genetically different populations he discusses—from Africa and

---

[2]My previews and discussions of material in the following chapters vary greatly in length and are unrelated to the length of the chapters. (Nor does the amount of space devoted to a chapter imply an evaluative judgment.) Rather, they are aimed at calling attention to important aspects of the overall argument of the book. For example, in some cases I have omitted reference to extensive and thought-provoking discussions of issues only secondarily relevant to race and intelligence, whereas in other cases I have added my own comments to expand on or restate a key point or line of thought.

Melanesia—used to be classified as belonging to the same race because of their similarity in skin color and hair texture.

If difference among human populations varies gradually around the globe, why then does it seem so evident to Americans that races exist? Marks (1995) pointed out that the substantial geographical distances separating three distinctive groups that came to the United States—the English colonists, slaves from west Africa, and the Chinese who built the railroads—made the belief in distinctive biological races easy to sustain. The absence, until recently, of large numbers of immigrants to the United States from intermediate places (e.g., Indians and other south Asians, Iranians and other southwest Asians) has allowed Americans to maintain the perception of discontinuities in the physical appearance of human beings.

As regards intelligence, the physical anthropologist C. Loring Brace (1998) pointed out that, although human physical traits and gene frequencies vary gradually along geographical dimensions known as clines, human cognitive abilities are not clinally distributed. That cognitive abilities do not follow the geographical pattern of distribution found for physical traits implies that population differences in measured abilities are cultural rather than biological in origin.

Finally, Templeton addresses the argument that, even though there are no races, the logical possibility of genetically based population differences in cognitive abilities cannot be dismissed out of hand. (Of course, the fact that it should be raised at all is of cultural, economic, historical, political, and social interest, and is discussed in detail elsewhere in the book.) Those few studies that investigated the relation between scores on cognitive tests and degree of African ancestry found no significant correlations, thereby falsifying the prediction. (In addition, other chapters explain why—even if significant correlations had been found between one or another "African gene" and IQ—simpler explanations exist than genetically based group differences in intelligence. For example, the genes in question could affect some other variable, such as health, that affects IQ.)

In chapter 3, Graves addresses the work of Rushton in some detail. He begins by pointing out that the r- and K-selection theory that Rushton claimed to have been applying in his work has been discarded by biologists because of both its vagueness and the inconsistent and disconfirmatory results it has produced when investigated experimentally. He points out that Rushton failed to review the relevant studies.

The chapter discusses Rushton's misunderstanding of r- and K-selection theory, and points out that the theory actually makes the opposite predictions about "Mongoloids" and "Negroids" from those he claims. Furthermore, the chapter shows how Rushton's assertions coincide with a biologized argument for racial inequality from the 1920s (which other chapters trace back much further in time). It then discusses Rushton's misunderstanding and misrepresentation of the reported research he does discuss, and even provides evidence that data presented by Rushton differ from those in the original sources, and that the inaccuracies are in the direction of his theory. Finally, it concludes that Rushton's data are grossly inadequate to test specific hypotheses about human evolution.

The chapter's conclusions are consistent with those of the physical anthropologist Leonard Lieberman (1999a, 1999b), who reviewed studies over the past 150 years claiming "racial" differences in the size of crania. Referring to Gould's (1981, 1996) work as well, he showed that both the magnitude of claimed differences and the order of racial hierarchy has varied over time, corresponding to changes in cultural beliefs. ("Mongoloids" only recently surpassed "Caucasoids" in purported brain size, as Asian countries, especially Japan, have grown in wealth and power. Of course, the real point of the argument is not to show how smart Mongoloids are, but to provide scientific-sounding "proof" of the innate inferiority of Negroids. As is discussed in other chapters, "scientific" attempts to justify slavery, and then segregation, and then discrimination have a long history.)

Lieberman calls attention to Rushton's dubious practice of lumping together data of varying quality and from diverse populations and then shoehorning them into the three "race" boxes. Furthermore, he shows that "racial" differences in brain size claimed by Rushton are too small to make a difference in intellectual functioning. Lieberman points out that human brains range from roughly 1,000 cc to 2,000 cc in size and normal human populations can appear anywhere along the continuum. Furthermore, the crania of Neanderthals were about 200 cc larger than those of Europeans today (1,550 cc vs. 1, 350 cc), suggesting that—if one wants to take the argument about brain size and intelligence seriously—smaller is smarter.

Rushton claims a mean difference of only 97 cc between "Mongoloids" and "Negroids"—roughly comparable to the 100 cc difference between men and women. However, women on average have smaller brains than men for the same reason they have smaller feet—because they are smaller, not because they are less intelligent. Along these lines, Lieberman (1999b) pointed out that "a greater number of neurons and dendrites can be packed into a smaller brain space … women have 4,000 more neurons per cubic millimeter in their cerebral cortex" (p. 11).

In chapter 4, Marks calls attention to differences between the science of genetics and folk explanations of heredity. He focuses on four folk beliefs about the biological inheritance of bodies and behavior that have had unfortunate effects on the scientific understanding of variation in human physical appearance and cognitive abilities. These are taxonomism, racism, hereditarianism, and essentialism.

Taxonomism refers to the scientifically invalid division of the human species into a number of purportedly distinct biological categories. *Racism*, as Marks uses the term, refers to the denial of rights to people based on their membership in a lesser category of a racial folk taxonomy. Historically, racism has often been a political accompaniment to taxonomism, as empirically invalid classifications of people into different groups have been used as a pretext for their unequal treatment. *Hereditarianism* is the belief that heredity plays an important role in human cognition and behavior. Often, for reasons of ideology or disciplinary self-interest, genes are postulated to play a significant role, when instead, variability in both behavior and genes need to be investigated in their worldwide social context. *Essentialism* involves focusing on one small aspect of the biological variation that exists, postulating it as the essence of an ideal type, and then using this essence fallaciously to explain all sorts of things.

Marks shows how the four folk beliefs pervaded the eugenics movement earlier in the century—they were part of the normal science of genetics of the era—and reached their culmination with the Nazi death camps. Now that these folk beliefs are becoming prominent once again, scientists bear a responsibility not to repeat the mistakes of the past.

In chapter 5, I begin by briefly reviewing human physical variation and showing that it does not correspond to what Americans think of as race. I then describe the American and Brazilian folk taxonomies of race in some detail to make clear that the American folk taxonomy of "blood" is just one culture-specific way of categorizing human physical variation. In other words, our understanding of race is neither biologically accurate nor cross-culturally general. I then briefly describe a number of other folk taxonomies of race, from Haiti, Martinique, Puerto Rico, Ecuador, Jamaica, and Cape Verde. Unlike the American system, which emphasizes ancestry in categorizing people according to "blood," all of the other systems give greater emphasis, in differing ways and in differing degrees, to physical appearance as the main principle determining how people are classified. These eight descriptions illustrate the wide range of cultural conceptualizations of race, based on differing principles of classification. They also illustrate that folk taxonomies in the same language (English in the United States and Jamaica, Portuguese in Brazil and Cape Verde, French in Haiti and Martinique, and Spanish in Puerto Rico and Ecuador), although differing greatly, are more similar to each other than they are to folk taxonomies in other languages. This is what one would expect from historical and cultural influences, but contrasts with supposed biological categories that would have to be universal. In other words, people can change their race by traveling from one culture to another. What changes is not their physical appearance (or, for that matter, their genes or ancestors) but rather the culture-specific category system in terms of which they receive racial labels.

Part II: Racial categories are developed to serve social ends, including the justification and perpetuation of inequality. IQ testing has been a part of this process of stratifying groups.

In chapter 6, Smedley examines the idea of race, and the involvement of science with it, over the past five centuries. She begins with the Europeans' question of whether the conquered peoples of the New World were fully human and descended from Noah, and the Church's decision that they were. The Enlightenment brought the discovery of striking anatomical similarities between humans and apes and the proposal that differences among distant groups of humans could be explained by differences in their social upbringing. By the late 18th century, however, this view was replaced by an ideology of natural inequality among groups that led to the conceptual framework of race.

As we now understand, because of the great geographical and temporal separations of the peoples of Western Europe from those of the New World and West Africa, the illusion that humans came in qualitatively different subgroups was easy to sustain, given the evident differences in physical appearance among inhabitants of the three regions. In the English colonies in particular, these differences in appearance were capitalized on to provide a biological rationale for innate differences among the groups. This in turn provided a justification for European economic exploitation of the other groups in convenient ways (rationalized as appropriate to their differing forms of inferiority), taking the labor of Africans by enslaving them and confiscating the land of Native Americans by limiting them to reservations.

The confounding of social behavior with physical appearance has been a part of the concept of race since its inception, as is evident in Linnaeus's racial descriptions. Europeans, not surprisingly, are racially characterized in positive terms as "gentle, acute, inventive, and governed by laws," whereas Native Americans are "obstinate, merry, free, and regulated by customs," and Africans are "crafty, indolent, negligent, and governed by caprice" (Slotkin, 1965, pp. 176–181). The scientific terms for the so-called races were similarly subjective—Europeans were called Caucasians because Blumenbach was struck by the beauty of a skull from southern Russia.

From the beginning of the United States as an independent country, biologized "scientific" explanations for the inferiority of the Negro race (including assertions of small brains and large sex organs) became an important part of the political debate over whether to end slavery. Claims of a racial hierarchy, with Europeans at the top, were the dominant scientific view throughout the 19th century. Darwin's theory of evolution and Spencer's social Darwinism were used to demonstrate "scientifically" the unfitness of inferior races and classes.

Once the concept of race had become scientifically legitimate and politically institutionalized, it was used against former slaves and also provided a justification for laws against intermarriage. The concept was also used against a variety of immigrant groups—the Chinese, Irish, Jews, and Italians among others—all of whom were viewed as racially different.

The eugenics movement became central to biology and genetics, as well as psychology. There it played an important role in the IQ testing movement, providing "proof" that northern European whites were intellectually superior to blacks, immigrants (including southern and eastern Europeans), and poor people, thereby justifying their mistreatment and creating a "problem" out of their higher birthrates. In the United States, this manifested itself in lynchings and other racist, anti-Semitic, and anti-immigrant acts, and in Europe Hitler made explicit use of eugenicist arguments as a rationale for genocide.

Following World War II, scientific advances in physical anthropology and genetics demonstrated that races do not exist in any biological sense, and eugenicist arguments lost scientific legitimacy. Although the American cultural view of race did not disappear, its scientific status was seriously undermined.

In chapter 7, Welch goes on to place the best known neo-eugenicist work, *The Bell Curve* (Herrnstein & Murray, 1994), in the context of the intellectual history of scientific racism in the United States. She discusses the eugenics movement in some detail, showing its involvement with IQ testing and its promotion of anti-immigration laws and the sterilization of minority group members.

The chapter discusses the essential continuity of thought beginning with Galton and the early eugenicists in the 19th century, continuing with Pearson and Goddard in the early 20th century, and leading to the more recent works of Jensen, Shockley, and Herrnstein and Murray. A discussion of the forced sterilization of prisoners, psychiatric patients, and the institutionally retarded earlier in this century—especially in the South—and of the disproportionate suffering of African Americans from these policies, brings home the American political implications of assertions of racial differences in intelligence. Welch goes on to point out the current use by white supremacist and neo-Nazi groups of works claiming racial differences in intelligence as intellectual justification for their mission. The possibility of history repeating itself is a disturbing implication of this chapter (and one of the reasons for the existence of this book).

Part III: Cultural content, values, and assumptions are an inherent part of IQ tests. Formal schooling teaches people new ways of thinking, which are then measured by the tests. Access to schools, school quality, modes of instruction, attitudes toward formal education, and educational values vary cross-culturally.

In chapter 8, Cohen takes an anthropologist's look at "race" and IQ testing—much as might be done in observing the multiple relations between two significant aspects of a distant culture. In so doing, he identifies seven assumptions underlying the ranking of races according to IQ. There are a variety of problems with each assumption—some are simply false—but Cohen argues that they all need to be true to uphold the reasoning leading to the ranking (a state of affairs defying rational judgment).

In discussing these seven assumptions, Cohen points out the empirical difficulties with many of them and also makes plain the ways in which a cross-cultural perspective illuminates their ethnocentric embeddedness in American culture. In particular, his extensive discussion of the content of IQ tests from a cross-cultural perspective (Assumption 6) goes well beyond similar critiques usually made from the perspective of American subcultures.

In condensed form, these assumptions are:

1. Intelligence is a single entity (g) that exists in nature and biology, and is not merely a statistical construction. All individuals in all cultures can be ranked along that single dimension.
2. Intelligence is the same thing in all cultures, and its measurement is not culture bound.
3. American IQ tests provide a valid measure of American intellectual needs.
4. Intelligence is under substantial genetic control.
5. Clearly defined "races" exist.
6. IQ tests are culture free, and scores are not affected by differences in education, language, or exposure to specific cultural content.

7. All (groups) who take the test are equally healthy, well-nourished, emotionally prepared, and intellectually motivated to do their best.

This cross-cultural discussion of IQ tests in the United States paves the way for chapter 9, in which Shanklin looks at the use of IQ tests in Africa and at Africans' reactions to them and to *The Bell Curve*. Once again, and with the distance offered by cross-cultural comparisons, we see the use of IQ tests to justify the stratification of groups, both in the European colonial powers' treatment of their African subjects and in dominant African groups' treatment of subordinate groups. Only for Europeans, however, has race served as an explanatory ideology to legitimate this exercise of power.

The chapter begins with a discussion of the ways in which European colonial powers tested their conquered subjects—both out of curiosity and to demonstrate that they were intellectually incapable of governing themselves. A key point that is developed in detail in the next chapter and discussed in several other chapters, is that formal education teaches not only specific content but also a variety of verbal, quantitative, and other reasoning and problem-solving skills. The lack of formal education of Africans in relation to European comparison groups (as well as many other important differences between higher scoring and lower scoring groups discussed at length elsewhere in this book) provided an obvious explanation for their lower test performance. Europeans, however, interpreted the Africans' test results as manifesting intellectual development that was arrested at a prelogical level.

Shanklin then describes the Internet discussion among Cameroonians living in different countries of *The Bell Curve* following its publication. Their reactions included the following: an awareness of many European and American whites' assumption that blacks were intellectually inferior and of blacks' need to cope with this; the absence of a belief in racial differences in intelligence; a recognition of ethnic prejudices about the different intellectual capacities of various groups in Cameroon; and a desire to illuminate the debate with scientific evidence. The chapter goes on to compare Cameroonian reactions to *The Bell Curve* with those of Europeans and Americans. The latter groups confuse skin color with ethnicity, whereas Cameroonians see only sociocultural information as relevant to distinguishing among groups.

The chapter concludes by pointing out that the scientific demonstration that the human species has no races in the biological sense has had little social impact and has been virtually irrelevant to combating racism. This is because misinformation is a relatively minor source of discrimination against minorities when weighed against the advantages that accrue to the favored majority.

In chapter 10, Ogbu presents a general theoretical position, and in the process responds to the question "Why do blacks score lower than whites on IQ tests in the United States?" In science, answers to general questions are more useful than answers to specific ones, so it is important to come up with good general questions. In this case, the chapter answers the broader cross-cultural questions, "As we look at IQ testing in different countries, why do some minority groups score lower than the majority group, whereas other minority groups do not? When a group is represented in more than one country are its IQ scores the same in different places?"

The chapter also addresses the issue of defining "intelligence" in a way that is not based exclusively on Western assumptions. To do so, Ogbu distinguishes among three kinds of intelligence: Intelligence A, the innate capacity or potential for intelligent behavior (presumably an inherited genotype); Intelligence B, the everyday behavior considered to manifest a culture's idea of intelligence or the lack thereof (presumably a result of both nature and nurture); and Intelligence C, IQ, or the intelligence measured by tests. It is easy to see that Intelligence B can change (e.g., as a result of the introduction of formal schooling to a nonliterate culture) and that Intelligence C is a limited example of Intelligence B.

Ogbu gives many examples of ways in which different cultures require different kinds of thinking, and shows that, when a culture changes in a way that demands new intellectual skills, its people adapt to the new demands and develop the skills. He refers to those activities in different times and places that require new intellectual skills (like the introduction of pottery making in Mexico, or computers in the United States) as "cultural amplifiers of intelligence." These amplifiers are different from and function in addition to schools, the family, and other societal institutions that transmit (preexisting) intellectual skills directly, though they do so in different ways in different cultures. The concept of a *cultural amplifier of intelligence* is in some ways analogous to Piaget's (1970) concept of *accommodation*, in which a child develops a new, more complex way of thinking when a simpler, older way confronts novel input. It is also in some ways analogous to Kuhn's (1962) concept of a *scientific revolution*, in which scientists adopt a new, more complex way of thinking (e.g., Einsteinian relativity) when a simpler, older way (e.g., Newtonian physics) confronts novel input.

The chapter goes on to make the key distinction between immigrant (voluntary) minorities, who move to a new country because they expect a better life, and non-immigrant (involuntary) minorities who were conquered or colonized by an occupying power or were taken as slaves against their will. Whereas voluntary minorities have many reasons to trust or at least cooperate pragmatically with the dominant culture and its schools and tests, involuntary minorities have many reasons to mistrust, doubt, actively or passively resist, or otherwise avoid cooperating with them.[3]

In the case of African Americans, the chapter details the contributions of both American society and African Americans themselves to their lower IQ scores. The societal contributions—segregated and inferior education, job ceilings, intellectual denigration, and cultural and language biases—are well known and are also discussed elsewhere in this book. The contributions of African Americans are not so widely

---

[3]As indicated previously, American biologize minority status into folk categories of race. For example, Native Americans, who are involuntary minorities, score low on tests, but are descended from Asians, who are supposedly the highest IQ race. Mexican Americans, who are classified as "Latino"—another low-scoring "racial" category—have on average a greater percentage of New World ancestry than Native Americans, but are not classified as such because "Indian" is a folk term that Americans only apply north of the border. In both cases, the labels applied to the groups are social constructions rather than biological categories, and the groups' performance is understandable socially (because they are minorities) but not "racially."

discussed, perhaps in an effort to avoid blaming the victim, or because behavioral scientists analyzing quantitative data have no access to the social world of African American adults and schoolchildren. These contributions include self-doubt stemming from the internalization of whites' belief that blacks are not intelligent, a folk theory of "making it" in which test scores and school credentials are not seen as important (because, historically, they have not been perceived as helping blacks to succeed), an adaptation to an ecological niche where advanced cognitive skills are not necessary for the jobs available, and an ambivalent or oppositional group identity and cultural frame of reference. With regard to the last of these, the chapter reports peer pressure against getting good grades or high test scores or taking advanced classes or speaking standard American English as "acting white."

Statistical claims that the black–white test score gap may be narrowing but will never close simply do not take into account what may appear to outsiders as a motivation on the part of many to do poorly. One is reminded of the Gypsies,[4] whose avoidance of school is legendary, who (accurately) view the schools as instruments for socializing their children into mainstream society, and who have chosen a survival strategy of group preservation through cultural isolation (Gropper, 1975; Sutherland, 1986). For Gypsies, cultural isolation depends in a profound way on individuals voluntarily distancing themselves from the norms and aspirations of the larger society. As a result, a successful Gypsy is one who has avoided the stigma of extensive formal education, as such a person would not have had the opportunity to learn the intellectual and social skills essential to his or her own culture. When a significant segment of African American youth uses low school achievement and low scores to maintain group solidarity and opt out of mainstream society, this can be seen as a similar strategy.

Gypsies can also be understood as following a strategy of provoking prejudice to confirm the need for group solidarity, thereby strengthening group boundaries. Social pressures among African American youth to limit school performance and test scores can be seen as functioning in a similar way, by confirming the intellectual prejudices of whites and demonstrating the need for solidarity in response. We can see here yet one more mutually reinforcing way in which the American black–white cultural divide continues to perpetuate itself across the generations.

After discussing the lower IQ scores of African Americans in some detail, the chapter cites evidence for a pattern of lower IQ scores among involuntary minorities around the world—in India, Europe, North America, New Zealand, and Japan. It goes on to examine in greater detail the performance of two groups, both of which are voluntary minorities in one society and involuntary minorities in another. The fact that as involuntary minorities they display poor intellectual performance but do well as

---

[4]As a unique nomadic culture that is everywhere a persecuted minority, Gypsies defy categorization even as their oppositional behavior yields fascinating insights about both them and the larger societies within which they live. Not surprisingly, they cannot be easily classified as either a voluntary minority or an involuntary minority, because they have features of both.

voluntary minorities implies that it is the nature of the groups' minority social status—not their biological inferiority—that explains their poor performance.

The Buraku outcasts in Japan, an involuntary minority who are physically indistinguishable from other Japanese, score 16 points below the Ippan majority (comparable to the American black–white gap of 13–15 points), but in the United States where both groups are voluntary minorities, the Buraku score the same as or slightly higher than the Ippan. Koreans, who are an involuntary minority in Japan, do poorly in school there, but they do well in the United States and China where they are a voluntary minority.

In short, an understanding of the low IQ test scores of African Americans, as of other involuntary minorities around the world, needs to take into account their resistance to the majority culture (including its schools and tests) and the effects of the majority culture's unequal treatment of them.

In terms of emphasis or focus, one might say that Parts I, II, and III of this book deal with race and its relation to intelligence, and Parts IV and V deal with intelligence and its relation to race. Furthermore, Parts I, II, and III are generally written from a cross-cultural perspective, whereas Parts IV and V are generally written from an American cultural perspective.

Stated in more detail, Part I shows that the concept of race is a social construction rather than a biological fact: Different cultures have come to select differing aspects of ancestry and/or physical appearance and arbitrarily combine them into biological sounding categories of "race." Part II shows that, although the categories of race are arbitrary in the biological sense, socially they exist to delineate group boundaries so that the unequal treatment of groups can be enforced—and intelligence tests have been one means for doing so. Part III shows that intelligence, like race, is a socially constructed concept in the sense that different cultures value and develop different "intelligent" abilities. In addition, the kinds of school-related intelligence measured by IQ tests are more specifically constructed through formal education—both by the kinds and quality of schooling provided to different groups and by the attitudes and motivation these groups bring to it.

In contrast, Parts IV and V are written by American social and behavioral scientists and implicitly accept American social categories of race as givens.[5] That is, they are written from a perspective that says "Whatever black, white, and race might mean, and whoever blacks and whites might be, the following is what research in the United States shows about them in relation to intelligence, especially as measured by IQ and other tests." In other words, the emphasis is on American cognitive processes, tests,

---

[5]It would be helpful if the American social and behavioral sciences would use a term with a social meaning, like *ethnicity*, instead of *race*, because that would make it clear that it is cultural differences rather than biological differences that are under discussion. Unfortunately, given the tenacity of cultural categories, many American readers (not to mention researchers) would doubtless understand ethnicity as a politically correct euphemism for race and would implicitly interpret "ethnic differences" as biological in origin anyway.

and social outcomes, and race is merely a classificatory variable in terms of which these are examined. A researcher might equally well choose social class or gender—or, for that matter, height or weight. The terms *black* and *white* are implicitly assumed to refer to *Homo sapiens* living an advanced, industrial, literate existence in the United States today, rather than to *Homo sapiens* living a hunting and gathering existence in Africa or Europe 10,000 years ago.

I call attention to this difference because it reflects a current division of perspectives in the social and behavioral sciences in the United States. This difference might be grossly characterized as cross-cultural with a significant qualitative emphasis versus American with a significant quantitative emphasis.

The reason for this difference is inherent in the methodologies. If the entities that one wishes to measure and compare—such as race or intelligence—are defined differently in different cultures, then one can do all sorts of statistical analyses within a particular culture such as the United States, but quantitative comparisons across cultures are often problematic. This is because one must gather data from the second culture along dimensions and in terms of categories that have meaning only in the first. For example, to compare black–white IQ differences in Brazil with black–white IQ differences in the United States, one would have to classify Brazilians as black or white in American terms. However, no Brazilians could be called white (even the lightest would be Latino), and the great majority of Brazilians who would be called black here would not be *preto* there. One could, of course, ask the ethnocentric question "If we pretended that Brazilians were from the United States, and did our best to classify them as black or white based on that false assumption, then how would the black–white differences on (inadequately standardized) Brazilian translations of American IQ tests compare to our black–white differences?" Such a "research question" would yield absurd results, in a manner comparable to Brazilians classifying Americans into Brazilian folk categories to study their IQ differences. (It would also have the gratuitous effect of offending Brazilians, many of whom have had the unpleasant experience of being racially misclassified when they traveled to the United States and would view such a study as a comparable affront.)

This methodological issue (referred to as *emic vs. etic comparisons*) is referred to in chapter 5. What it implies regarding black–white IQ differences is that the rhetoric of racial comparisons is implicitly biological and universal (worldwide differences between races) but the content is actually local and culture specific—differences in the United States between IQs of people called "white" and people called "black."

The inherently culture-specific nature of many of the kinds of quantitative comparisons that have been made in the United States undermines the claim that they represent differences in innate potential among groups and along dimensions that are assumed to transcend our borders. Quite apart from these limitations, such quantitative findings are often used to support arguments for one or another social policy in the United States. For this reason, and despite their specificity, they also deserve to be examined.

Although the goal of this book is to clarify thinking about race and intelligence rather than to advance a particular social agenda, some of the following chapters do address social issues, at least obliquely. Especially in Part V, the authors review a large amount of empirical evidence. At the minimum, they make clear that quantitative data from the United States also do not support the claim that black–white IQ differences result from innate racial differences in intelligence, and therefore contradict the inference that spending to overcome social inequality is doomed to fail.

To shed light on the recurrent American concern with race and intelligence, both cross-cultural data and quantitative data gathered in the United States are necessary— each type offers something missing from the other. In addition to providing comprehensive answers, I hope that this book will help the public at large as well as researchers involved with both kinds of data to transcend their differing perspectives.

Part IV: Biological-sounding concepts, especially heritability, have been misused to imply a genetic basis for group differences in IQ scores. There are many cognitive abilities—a single general factor of intelligence is inadequate to account for current knowledge in psychological measurement or cognitive science.

In chapter 11, Block discusses the concept of heritability and shows how it has been misused to imply a biologically based, inherited, intellectual inferiority of the Negroid race. Part I of this book dealt with the nonexistence of races in detail, touching on the concept of heritability only in passing. Block discusses it in greater detail.

He begins by distinguishing two ways in which the word *genetic* is used. The first, *genetic determination*, applies to individuals; for example, the notion that genes cause all humans to have five fingers or toes on each extremity under normal circumstances, so that population variations are almost all caused by the environment (e.g., accidents or prenatal thalidomide exposure). Thus, one might say, "The reason I have five fingers on each hand is genetic."

The second sense, *heritability*, applies to groups or populations. Heritability is the percentage of genetically associated variation in a population under given environmental conditions—or, in other words, the ratio of genetically associated variation to all variation (both environmentally and genetically associated). Heritability is used to refer to differences in a population, not to individual specifics (e.g., the heritability of third graders' IQs but not the heritability of Johnny's IQ). One example would be that, until fashions changed in recent years, wearing earrings was highly heritable. Women (with XX chromosomes) wore them, and men (with XY chromosomes) did not; however, the reason for wearing them was not genetic in the sense of having five fingers. An environmental change in fashion, with men wearing earrings, changed the heritability.

Block argues that IQ, like wearing earrings, may be highly heritable but is not genetically determined. Another way of putting this would be to say that heritability estimates are correlations (between genetic variation and phenotypic variation), and that one cannot infer causality from correlations. In contrast, genetic explanations are causal (e.g., XX chromosomes produce females and XY chromosomes produce males). Thus the term *heritability* sounds as if it offers a causal genetic explanation, but it does not.

In addition, the heritability of IQ within the socially constructed category of American blacks and within the socially constructed category of American whites says nothing about IQ differences between the groups. This is because heritability refers to the relative ranking of individuals within a distribution but not their actual scores: Helpful environmental effects can raise the entire distribution and harmful environmental effects can lower it. For example, imagine a group of black identical twins separated and adopted at birth in the United States, and a similar group of white identical twins. In every case, both black twins would be treated as black, and both white twins would be treated as white, creating significant environmental differences between the groups, even though each set of twins has identical genes.[6]

To give yet another example, even if the heritability of IQ were 100% for both American whites and American blacks, if the environmentally caused deficit in the average performance of American blacks were shown to be 25 points, then their observed 13 to 15-point deficit would imply that under comparable environmental conditions they would score 10 to 12 points higher than American whites.

Regarding the magnitude of the impact of the environment on IQ, Block refers to the Flynn effect (Flynn, 1987, 1999; Neisser, 1998), the worldwide rise in IQs that, in only a few decades, has exceeded the American 13 to 15-point black–white IQ gap.[7] As Flynn [1999] put it, "It is as if some unseen hand is propelling scores upward at a rate of about 6 IQ points per decade, with individual nations scattering randomly around that value" (p. 6). Thus, one way of interpreting lower IQ scores of American blacks is to view them as a function of environments equivalent to those experienced by American whites in the not-too-distant past.

---

[6]Studies of "identical twins reared apart compared to those reared together" also illustrate the much more limited view of "environment" (i.e., the United States today) that psychologists have, as compared to that of anthropologists. The studies do not compare one of each pair of twins raised by American college professors with the other raised by Brazilian Indians. Hence, in anthropological terms, such studies are of identical twins reared in very similar environments compared to those reared in extremely similar environments. By restricting the range of environments to American environments, the heritability estimate increases correspondingly. This is because the heritability statistic is a fraction—the genetically associated variation in a population under given environmental conditions divided by all variation (both genetically and environmentally associated). By limiting the environments considered, one decreases the environmentally associated variation. This makes the denominator smaller, and hence the heritability estimate larger.

[7]Substantial racial changes in intelligence test scores were similarly demonstrated in the United States earlier in this century (during segregation) by the social psychologist Otto Klineberg. He found that blacks in Northern states scored higher than whites in Southern states, and that among African American schoolchildren whose families had migrated from the South to the North, the longer they had been in the Northern schools, the higher their IQs (Klineberg, 1935, 1944, 1951).

Although this essential point—that heritability within groups is irrelevant to between-group differences—is acknowledged by all researchers, Block gives a number of examples of "yes-buts" from people using within-group heritability to argue for racial between-group differences in intelligence.

Block also discusses a number of other problems with heritability; readers who are interested in pursuing the topic further might want to consult a special issue of *Genetica* (Hirsch, 1997b) on the "Uses and Abuses of Genetics in Society." Of relevance here are two additional problems with heritability cited by the editor in his contribution to that issue (Hirsch, 1997a).

First,

> heritability estimation assumes both random mating in an equilibrium population (including the equally likely occurrence of every culturally tabooed form of incest) and the absence of either correlation or interaction between heredity and environment. In fact, when one or more of these assumptions are violated, i.e., random mating in an equilibrium population, correlation or interaction, heritability is undefined. (Hirsch, 1997a, p. 220)

Second, he reported that

> In our study of 212 nuclear families comprising 1068 people, we were able to test a subsample of 38 families for concordance on four blood groups, no less than 13% (= 5 families out of 38) had children who could not be the biological offspring of at least one of the putative parents (Hirsch, McGuire & Vetta, 1980; Johnson, 1974). In the United Kingdom, Philipp (1973) has provided evidence that 30% of husbands were not the biological fathers of their children. (Hirsch, 1997a, p. 215)

Presumably, this high number includes children (and perhaps some of their stepparents or other caretakers) who do not know they are adopted, children switched by mistake at the hospital at birth, and other kinds of nonsexual explanations—as well as children resulting from their mothers' voluntary or involuntary liaisons with men other than their socially designated fathers. Anthropologists routinely distinguish between culturally defined kin relationships and biological ones, but it appears that those who make heritability estimates of IQ may not always have been so meticulous.[8]

In chapter 12, Horn reviews the argument of *The Bell Curve*, especially as it pertains to measured intelligence and its heritability. He finds the book's claims

---

[8]Another point worth making in passing is that, to the extent to which genes are involved with IQ, there are bound to be a lot of them, with small and environmentally sensitive effects, interacting with each other in complex ways. As a result, their reshuffling over the generations to produce any population effects (raising or lowering IQ) would have to be very slow. This contrasts with eugenicist claims that higher birthrates among those with low IQs should lead to a rapid dumbing down of the population. (As we know, the Flynn effect demonstrates that the opposite is actually taking place.)

unsupported and argues that it can best be understood as advocacy for particular political policies rather than as a scientific document.

Horn begins with a discussion of the National Longitudinal Survey of Youth (Baker, Keck, Mott, & Quinlan, 1993), the data from which are the main source of *The Bell Curve*'s argument, and which is also discussed in subsequent chapters. Herrnstein and Murray (1994) used the sum of 4 of 10 subtest scores referred to as the Armed Forces Qualification Test (AFQT) from a larger battery (the Armed Services Vocational Aptitude Battery; Welsh, Watson, & Ree, 1990) as a measure of IQ, or *g*, the purported general factor of intelligence. Instead of *g*, however, the score represents crystallized knowledge (*Gc*, a measure of academic achievement), one of nine different "intelligent" abilities identified by cognitive psychology.

Horn finds serious flaws with Herrnstein and Murray's (1994) reasoning in selecting the four subtests, with their measure of socioeconomic status (SES), and with the claim that the SES score adequately accounts for environmental influences on the individuals from prenatal development through their participation in the study. As a result, the book's main findings can be summarized as follows, "a fairly reliable measure of academic achievement is a better predictor of subsequent academic achievement and its correlates than is a rather unreliable measure of social class" (p. 307, this volume).

Horn critiques Herrnstein and Murray's (1994) claim that intelligence = IQ = *g*, and argues instead that there are multiple factors. In particular, fluid reasoning (*Gf*) is closest in meaning to Spearman's *g*, but is different from Herrnstein and Murray's *Gc* measure. *Gf* and *Gc* overlap only about 25% in what they correlate with, and can be understood as different forms of intelligence. Horn discusses other forms of intelligence as well, such as short-term apprehension and retrieval (*Gm*), visual comprehension and processing (*Gv*), and auditory capabilities (*Ga*), all of which differ from one another and from *Gf* and *Gc* as well.

Horn examines the statistical assumptions underlying heritability estimates and the methodological problems involved in gathering relevant data (e.g., the similarity of environments of twins reared apart is illustrated by a heritability estimate for their religious attitudes of .49). He also argues that Herrnstein and Murray (1994) used the wrong estimate of heritability, thereby inflating their figure substantially.

Horn discusses evidence that IQ can be raised (by 8–25 points) and the increases maintained over time as a result of intensive and sustained interventions during childhood. (Much additional evidence for this point is presented in chapter 15.) In a similar manner during adolescence, intensive coaching has been shown to raise Scholastic Assessment Test scores. Finally, I would like to call attention to a study of college graduates because it used the same AFQT data set examined in *The Bell Curve*. The authors found that "it was the black students who made the largest gains between the end of high school and college graduation, with their test scores increasing more than four times as much as those of white college students" (Meyerson, Rank, Raines, & Schnitzler, 1998, p. 141).

In short, there is evidence that cognitive abilities are malleable, and as they evolve over time positive experiences along the way can lead them to improve (and negative experiences can have the opposite effect).

To combine Horn's analysis with that of Ogbu in chapter 10, one might say that individuals are born with a variety of potentials that bear varying relations to a variety of "intelligent" cognitive activities that might be displayed in varying ways and to varying degrees later in life. The varying pathways to the differing evolutions of these diverse abilities are actualized differentially both among different individuals within a culture and from one cultural group to another. Formal education is a key to developing many of these intellectual abilities.

Part V: A wide variety of data, including reanalyses of data presented in The Bell Curve, imply that group differences in IQ are social in origin and can change as the result of changing social circumstances or social interventions.

In a way, those who claim differences in innate intelligence between blacks and whites are making a nonscientific demand of their critics to prove a negative. That is, they are asking them to demonstrate that there are no differences in innate intelligence between categories of millions of people called races. Then, whatever evidence is offered is countered by an unending series of "yes-buts" and "what-ifs." For example, one cannot prove the nonexistence of ghosts because any negative experimental result could be responded to by the objection that that particular experiment might not be ghost sensitive.

This is why science is inherently skeptical and demands that those making an assertion support it with data rather than asking others to demonstrate it is false. If people want to show that there are biologically based differences in intelligence between groups then they should find the IQ-relevant genes they believe exist and demonstrate the population differences. Otherwise, the working assumption has to be that any obtained group differences are social in origin. This is because the tests measure complex learned social behavior, because the definitions of the groups are socially constructed, and because there are many substantial and well-documented social differences between the groups. The more of these social factors that are taken into account, the smaller the unexplained remaining difference. There are other variables the quantitative effects on black–white IQ differences in the United States of which have not been studied. One can only expect that taking them into account would further reduce the unexplained difference.

For example, here are three social variables of three different kinds—economic, cultural, and psychological—with effects on the black–white IQ gap in the United States that have yet to be included in multivariate analyses. Conley (1999) presented evidence that substantial black–white differences in household wealth (accumulated assets, as opposed to income differences) are related to differences in educational and other outcomes. Ogbu, in chapter 10, presents cross-cultural evidence that involuntary minorities resist the schools and tests of the majority culture, and that this resistance (in contrast to the behavior of voluntary minorities) leads to lower IQ scores. Steele (1997) showed that test performance is lowered by stereotype threat (e.g., the belief of African Americans that their academic ability is being tested or of women that their mathematical ability is being tested) and disidentification (e.g., reconceptualizing the self without academics or mathematics as a part).

In addition to such social variables, a variety of factors in the biological environment also have not been included in attempts at comprehensive analyses. These include prenatal differences in maternal diet (including alcohol consumption leading to fetal alcohol syndrome), health status, and access to prenatal care; and environmental factors in infancy and early childhood such as diet, health status, health care, and exposure to lead (leading to lead poisoning) and other environmental toxins.

These examples can hardly be exhaustive. One is tempted to ask why some investigators are so convinced that innate racial differences in intelligence exist. A few decades ago, during a previous iteration of the debate, two social psychologists examined the biographical characteristics of 83 researchers who had reached a variety of conclusions. They concluded that "investigators whose research was categorized as concluding that Negroes are innately inferior intellectually came from higher socioeconomic backgrounds" (Sherwood & Nataupsky, 1968, p. 57), suggesting that such findings may tell us more about our own society than they do about innate racial differences.

In any event, a substantial body of evidence does exist, and the three chapters of Part V examine key aspects of what is known.

In chapter 13, Hout focuses on poverty in the United States and examines *The Bell Curve*'s claim that innate differences in intelligence are its most important cause. (A modest relation between IQ-like measures and success in the labor market has long been recognized.) He begins by pointing out the decline in income of the poor and the increase in the percentage of poor Americans over the last 25 years, despite considerable economic growth. This increase in poverty at the same time as the rise in IQs (the Flynn effect) argues against a genetic explanation.

Hout reanalyzes *The Bell Curve*'s data and presents additional evidence that social factors (e.g., schools, the family, and labor markets) are the main determinants of social inequality. More specifically, poverty is much greater in families headed by a single woman, poor children attend worse schools, and gender and racial discrimination affect access to jobs.

Hout reviews the content of the AFQT, and with specific item examples, shows that it is a measure of academic achievement (see chap. 12) and that its item content assumes formal schooling (see chap. 10) and is not culturally neutral (see chap. 8). He then reviews the statistical procedures used in *The Bell Curve* and shows that they systematically exaggerate the effect of intelligence on poverty and all other outcomes (e.g., teen pregnancy or truancy) because they assume that there is no environmental component to AFQT scores. Additional analyses of the data show that—as pointed out in several previous chapters and repeated in subsequent ones as well based on a range of sources—education has an important effect on AFQT intelligence.

Separate from the question of whether the AFQT measures inherited intellectual potential is the question of how well it predicts social outcomes. By using better measures of social origins, Hout shows that they have powerful effects. African American young adults are nearly four times as likely to be poor as their white counterparts. They grew up in families with half the income, their parents had less schooling and worse jobs, and they attended inferior schools in less secure neighborhoods. The AFQT is a significant predictor of poverty, although the size of the effect is reduced substantially by controlling for several appropriate variables. Nevertheless, gender is a much stronger predictor—more than a quarter of single mothers are poor. Amidst the complexities that result in poverty, academic skills rank as a small but significant factor—far behind "race" (a social classification, as the term is used in this chapter), gender, and family issues.

In chapter 14, Devlin, Fienberg, Resnick, and Roeder report on their own and other researchers' reanalyses of *The Bell Curve*'s data. After calling attention to the intellectual roots of *The Bell Curve*'s argument in the eugenics movement, they point out flaws in the statistical methods used, leading to evidence for a much weaker effect than that claimed by Herrnstein and Murray (1994). They go on to point out difficulties with Herrnstein and Murray's use of the concept of heritability, especially as applied to IQ, as well as with their assertion that IQ is adequately represented as g.

Devlin et al. examine the logic of *The Bell Curve*'s causal model and show it to be oversimplified. In particular—and as pointed out in a variety of other ways in a number of chapters—Herrnstein and Murray omitted a consideration of the effects of formal education (as well as other potentially relevant variables) on both IQ and social outcomes. Thus, correlational effects that are claimed to be caused by IQ might well be the result (in whole or in part) of other influences. This basic logical flaw undermines the core of *The Bell Curve*'s argument.

Devlin et al. conclude by commenting on the policy implications of *The Bell Curve*. (They also discuss some recent books in the same vein by Jensen [1998] and Murray [1997], as well as their own recent book [Devlin, Fienberg, & Resnick, & Roeder, 1997] and others by Gould [1996], Neisser [1998], and Sternberg and Grigorenko [1997].) While Herrnstein and Murray (1994) expressed a libertarian ideological opposition to Head Start, affirmative action, and other government programs to reduce inequality, the scientific evidence they attempted to marshal stemmed from flawed analyses and did not support their conclusions. Devlin et al. express concern that poor social policy stems from poor statistical analyses.

I would like to add my concern that, by giving credence to Rushton's arguments because they could be mobilized to support *The Bell Curve*'s social program, Herrnstein and Murray (1994) took an unnecessary and highly questionable step. Libertarianism and eugenics are two distinct ideologies, and to the extent to which eugenicists advocate governmental action (as they did with disastrous results earlier in the century) they are in opposition. Most libertarians are antiracist and view slavery and segregation as key American examples of the dangers of governmental power. Herrnstein and Murray could have based their "meritocracy" argument solely on inherited individual differences in intelligence and could have attempted to limit debate to that issue. They made clear they understood that one could not generalize from individual differences to group differences, and yet they argued specifically for inherited group differences among people categorized into races. In so doing, they did not consider well-established knowledge in evolutionary biology and physical anthropology about the nonexistence of races. This is another important way in which the book's poor science has done real social harm.

In chapter 15, Barnett and Camilli discuss the effects of Head Start and other preschool educational programs on the cognitive development of poor children. This concluding chapter is the only one with a primary focus on policy implications, but that is not the main reason for its inclusion in this volume. Rather, because it addresses the issue of whether early interventions can have long-term effects (in contrast to the view of cognitive abilities as mainly innate) and because it examines the effects of these programs on different American "racial" groups, it is relevant to the central concerns of this volume.

Barnett and Camilli systematically review 37 long-term studies—15 model programs and 22 large-scale public school and Head Start programs that were chosen to meet a number of research criteria, critique and discuss the studies' designs and findings, and reanalyze some key data. They discuss a number of shortcomings in previous reviews of research, including (a) the failure to distinguish between IQ and achievement, and (b) a series of methodological flaws in the design and interpretation of studies that created the erroneous impression of achievement gains disappearing over time. In addition to making suggestions for future research, the authors also reach a number of important conclusions.

Barnett and Camilli conclude that both model programs and large-scale public school programs lead to substantial and long-term cognitive and educational benefits for children, and that model programs have larger effects. Furthermore, they find no evidence that the effects of the programs on cognitive development and school success differ across ethnic groups. (This contradicts assertions that long-term effects existed for Latino and white but not African American children.)

Barnett and Camilli point out that preschool programs are being asked to fill more functions outside the classroom with no increase in funding, thereby taking time and expertise away from their main mission and creating the danger of watering down their demonstrated cognitive effects. Because it appears that such programs help to lay the foundation for subsequent school learning, they also argue for investigating the effects of very early (beginning in the first year of life), very intensive programs.

CONCLUSION

With this overview of the organization, structure, and content of *Race and Intelligence: Separating Science From Myth* completed, we can go on to explore the details of human biological variability and intelligence. It is a long way from the assertion that the Caucasoid, Mongoloid, and Negroid races differ in innate intelligence to the rather different scientific conclusion that the human species has no races (although the United States and other cultures have a variety of folk concepts of race), that there is no single form of intelligence, and that formal education helps people to develop a number of cognitive abilities. It is also an intellectual journey well worth taking.

REFERENCES

Baker, P. C., Keck, C. K., Mott, F. L., & Quinlan, S. V. (1993). *NLSY child handbook (rev. ed.): A guide to the 1986–1990 National Longitudinal Survey of Youth Child data.* Columbus: Ohio State University.

Berry, J. W. (1969). On cross-cultural comparability. *International Journal of Psychology, 4,* 119–128.

Brace, C. L. (1998). Race and reason: The anthropological case for a common human cognitive condition. *General Anthropology, 5,* 1–48.

Conley, D. (1999). *Being black, living in the red: Race, wealth, and social policy in America.* Berkeley: University of California Press.

Cose, E. (1998). *Color-blind: Seeing beyond race in a race-obsessed world.* New York: Harper.

Devlin, B., Fienberg, S. E., Resnick, D. P., & Roeder, K. (1997). *Intelligence, genes, and success: Scientists respond to* The Bell Curve. New York: Springer Verlag.

Ember, C. R., & Ember, M. (1988). *Anthropology* (5th ed.). Englewood Cliffs, NJ: Prentice Hall.

Eysenck, H. J. (1998). *Intelligence: A new look.* New Brunswick, NJ: Transaction.

Flynn, J. R. (1987). Massive IQ gains in 14 nations: What IQ tests really measure. *Psychological Bulletin, 101,* 171–191.

Flynn, J. R. (1999). Searching for justice: The discovery of IQ gains over time. *American Psychologist, 54,* 5–20.

Gould, S. J. (1981). *The mismeasure of man.* New York: Norton.

Gould, S. J. (1996). *The mismeasure of man* (Rev. ed.). New York: Norton.

Gropper, R. C. (1975). *Gypsies in the city: Culture patterns and survival.* Princeton, NJ: Darwin Press.

Herrnstein, R. J., & Murray, C. (1994). *The bell curve: Intelligence and class structure in American life.* New York: The Free Press.

Hirsch, J. (1997a). Some history of heredity-vs-environment, genetic inferiority at Harvard. *The (incredible) Bell Curve. Genetica, 99*(2–3), 207–224.

Hirsch, J. (Ed.). (1997b). Uses and abuses of genetics in society [Special issue]. *Genetica, 99*(2–3).

Hirsch, J., McGuire, T. R., & Vetta, A. (1980). Concepts of behavior genetics and misapplications in humans. In J. S. Lockard (Ed.), *The evolution of human social behavior* (pp. 215–238). New York: Elsevier.

Jencks, C., & Phillips, M. (1998). *The black–white test score gap.* Washington, DC: The Brookings Institution.

Jensen, A. R. (1998). *The g factor: The science of mental ability.* Westport, CT: Praeger.

Johnson, R. P. (1974). Phenotypic variation, fingerprints, and human behavior: An application of the family-pedigree paradigm (Doctoral dissertation, University of Illinois, 1974). *Dissertation Abstracts International, 35*(1), 546B.

Kaufman, A. S., & Kaufman, N. L. (1983). *Kaufman Assessment Battery for Children.* Circle Pines, MN: American Guidance Service.

Klineberg, O. (1935). *Negro intelligence and selective migration*. New York: Columbia University Press.

Klineberg, O. (Ed.). (1944). *Characteristics of the American Negro*. New York: Harper.

Klineberg, O. (1951). *Race and psychology*. Paris: UNESCO.

Kuhn, T. S. (1962). *The structure of scientific revolutions*. Chicago, IL: University of Chicago.

Levin, M. (1997). *Why race matters: Race differences and what they mean*. Westport, CT: Praeger.

Lieberman, L. (1999a, November). *How "Caucasoids" got such big crania and why they shrank: From Morton to Rushton*. Paper presented at the meeting of the American Anthropological Association, Chicago.

Lieberman, L. (1999b). Scientific insignificance. *Anthropology News, 40*(8), 11–12.

Marks, J. (1995). *Human biodiversity: Genes, race, and history*. New York: Aldine de Gruyter.

Meyerson, J., Rank, M. R., Raines, F. Q., & Schnitzler, M. A. (1998). Race and general cognitive ability: The myth of diminishing returns to education. *Psychological Science, 9*(2), 139–142.

Montagu, M. F. A. (1941). The concept of race in the human species in light of genetics. *Journal of Heredity, 32*, 243–247.

Murray, C. (1997). *What it means to be a libertarian: A personal interpretation*. New York: Broadway Books.

Neisser, U. (Ed.). (1998). *The rising curve: Long-term gains in IQ and related measures*. Washington, DC: American Psychological Association.

Piaget, J. (1970). Piaget's theory. In P. H. Mussen (Ed.), *Carmichael's manual of child psychology* (3rd ed., Vol. 1; pp. 703–732). New York: Wiley.

Philipp, E. E. (1973). Discussion in law and ethics of AID and embryo transfer. *Ciba Foundation Symposium Vol. 17* (new series, p. 66). Amsterdam: Elsevier, Excerpta Medica.

Rushton, J. P. (1997). *Race, evolution, and behavior: A life history perspective*. New Brunswick, NJ: Transaction.

Samuda, R. J., Feuerstein, R., Kaufman, A. S., Lewis, J. E., Sternberg, R. J., & Associates. (Eds.). (1998). *Advances in cross-cultural assessment*. Thousand Oaks, CA: Sage.

Sherwood, J. J., & Nataupsky, M. (1968). Predicting the conclusions of Negro–white intelligence research from biographical characteristics of the investigator. *Journal of Personality and Social Psychology, 8*(1), 53–58.

Slotkin, J. S. (Ed.). (1965). *Readings in early anthropology*. New York: Wenner-Gren Foundation for Anthropological Research.

Steele, C. M. (1997). A threat in the air: How stereotypes shape intellectual identity and performance. *American Psychologist, 52*(6), 613–629.

Sternberg, R. J., & Grigorenko, E. (Eds.). (1997). *Intelligence, heredity, and environment*. New York: Cambridge University Press.

Sutherland, A. (1986). *Gypsies: The hidden Americans,* Prospect Heights, IL: Waveland.

Welsh, J. R., Jr., Waston. T. W., & Ree, M. J. (1990). *Armed Services Vocational Aptitude Battery (ASVAB): Predicting military criteria from general and specific abilities*. AFHRL-TR-90-63. Brooks Airforce Base, TX: Air Force Systems Command.

PART

I

Homo sapiens has no extant subspecies: there are no biological races. Human physical appearance varies gradually around the planet, with the most geographically distant peoples generally appearing the most different from one another. The concept of human biological races is a construction socially and historically localized to 17th and 18th-century European thought. Over time, different cultures have developed different sets (folk taxonomies) of socially defined "races."

The Genetic and Evolutionary Significance of Human Races

Alan R. Templeton

The life on our planet displays an amazing range of diversity at all levels of biological organization: different kingdoms of life, several millions of species, and genetic diversity within species. Some of the genetic diversity within species is present simply as allelic differences (alternative forms of the same gene) carried by a single individual (heterozygosity), some occurs as genotypic differences among individuals living in the same local area, and some exists as allele frequency differences among different local populations. All of this genetic diversity is the product of the evolutionary process. Hence, to understand the significance of genetic diversity, it is necessary to place that diversity into its proper evolutionary context. Because evolution is a biological universal, the methods of analysis for interpreting genetic diversity are applicable to all species, including our own. Unfortunately, humans have tended to interpret their own intraspecific diversity in ways that are often inconsistent with how humans analyze and interpret genetic diversity in other species. As I show in this chapter, this is certainly the case concerning "racial" variation. From a scientific perspective, the interpretation of human genetic diversity in a unique manner is indefensible: A scientific understanding and interpretation of human genetic diversity must use the same criteria that have been applied to genetic diversity in nonhuman species. My primary goal in this chapter is to examine the significance of human genetic diversity, primarily racial diversity, using the same criteria and analytical procedures applied to the remainder of life on this planet. This is not to say that humans are not a unique species—we certainly are—but it does acknowledge the fact that our genetic diversity is subject to the same basic types of evolutionary forces that shape diversity in all life.

WHAT IS GENETIC DIVERSITY?

All concepts of race are ultimately based on patterns of genetic diversity within and among the local breeding populations of a species. Therefore, the meaning of genetic diversity must be explored before addressing the concept of race. The basic units of genetic diversity are alleles, alternative forms of the same gene at a locus. Individuals generally carry two copies of each type of gene (one from the mother, and one from the father), so even an individual can display genetic diversity when the gene from the mother is of a different allelic type than the gene from the father. When this occurs, the individual is said to be *heterozygous*. If both copies of the gene are of the same allelic form, the individual is said to be *homozygous*. The combined state of both gene copies defines the individual's genotype. Genetic diversity also exists among individuals within the same local population because different individuals can have different genotypes. The genetic diversity found within a local population can also be characterized by noting all the different types of alleles that are collectively shared by the individuals and the frequencies with which those alleles occur. Finally, genetic diversity can exist between populations if some alleles are found in one population but not in the other, or if the same alleles occur in both populations but at different frequencies.

There are many ways of quantifying genetic diversity at these various levels (individual, local population, between populations). The mathematical details of this quantification are not important for the arguments to be raised in this chapter, but what is important is that genetic diversity can be objectively measured both within and among populations in a manner that can be applied to all species. Of particular importance for the concept of race is the relative amount of genetic diversity that exists among individuals within a population versus the amount of genetic diversity that exists among populations. There are many evolutionary forces that affect this balance of within to among diversity, but four forces are of particular importance. The first is *mutation*, the ultimate creator of all genetic diversity. When a new allele is created by a mutation, it obviously exists in only one local population. Therefore, mutation is both a source of genetic diversity within a local population and a source of genetic diversity among populations.

The second evolutionary force is *genetic drift* (random sampling error). The laws of Mendelian inheritance are probabilities, not certainties. If an individual is heterozygous, Mendel's first law says there is a 50–50 chance for a particular allele to be passed on to an offspring in the same sense that a flip of a coin has a 50–50 chance of being heads or tails. Note that one could flip a coin several times and by chance alone get more heads than tails (or vice versa). Similarly, just by chance alone, alleles can change their frequency in a finite population or even be lost altogether. Genetic drift therefore causes genetic diversity within local populations to decrease but at the same time causes different populations to become genetically differentiated; that is, to have different alleles or different allele frequencies.

The third evolutionary force that affects this balance is *gene flow* or *genetic exchange*, the act of interbreeding of individuals originally from different local populations. Gene flow causes genetic interchange between populations, thereby giving any local population access to alleles created by mutations occurring elsewhere. This infusion of new alleles by gene flow augments genetic diversity within local populations. Gene flow also causes alleles to be shared in common by many local populations and causes convergence to a common allele frequency, thereby diminishing genetic diversity among local populations. An important special case is when no gene flow at all exists between two populations. Such populations are said to be genetically isolated and the populations themselves are said to be *isolates*. Because there is no homogenizing force due to genetic interchange between isolated populations, mutation and genetic drift ensure that they will become increasingly different genetically. Hence, the genetic diversity between isolated populations increases with increasing time since the "split" (i.e., the time at which all gene flow was severed between them). *Admixture* occurs if the factors that caused the cessation of gene flow between the populations are altered so that genetic interchange once again commences between the former isolates. Be warned that the definitions just given are the standard definitions as used in the nonhuman literature. As will be patent soon, these same words are often applied to humans in a way that egregiously violates their standard definitions.

The fourth evolutionary force considered here is *natural selection*. If several local populations are adapting to the same environment, natural selection can be a powerful homogenizing force that maintains the same alleles at the same frequencies for those genes involved in adapting to the common environment. On the other hand, if different local populations live in different environments, natural selection will accentuate genetic differentiation among the local populations for those genes involved in the adaptations to the differing environments.

It is important to note that although natural selection can be a powerful force for either genetically homogenizing or differentiating populations, depending on the nature of the environment, selection primarily influences only those genes directly involved in the adaptation. In contrast, all genes are subject to the randomness of Mendel's laws, and when interbreeding occurs, a full complement of all the genes in the genome are interchanged. Therefore, both genetic drift and gene flow influence almost all genes, and the overall genetic diversity patterns are thus determined primarily by genetic drift and gene flow. Natural selection is only important for specific traits and their underlying genes, and these traits can and often do show patterns of genetic diversity that are inconsistent with the overall pattern of genetic diversity. Moreover, different traits that represent adaptations to different environmental variables can also be inconsistent with one another in their diversity patterns. As a consequence, traits under natural selection are not regarded as reliable indicators of taxonomic status in the nonhuman literature (Futuyma, 1986).

Note also that genetic drift and gene flow have opposite effects on the amount of genetic diversity within local populations (decreased by drift, increased by gene flow) versus genetic differentiation among populations (increased by drift, decreased by gene flow). As a consequence, the relative amounts of genetic diversity within and among local populations often reflect a dynamic balance between genetic drift and gene flow. One common method of quantifying the balance of within to among genetic diversity is the F_{st} statistic of Wright (1969) and some of its more modern variants (Hudson, Boos, & Kaplan, 1992; Lynch & Crease, 1990). F_{st} and related statistics range from 0 (all populations consist of individuals who share exactly the same alleles and at the same frequencies) to 1 (all individuals within a local population are homozygous for the same allele, but different populations are homozygous for different alleles—a phenomenon called *fixed differences among populations*). An alternative method to F_{st} for measuring the extent of genetic differentiation among populations is to convert the allele or allele frequency differences among populations into a genetic distance. There are several genetic distance measures available, and sometimes the biological conclusions are strongly dependent on the precise measure chosen (Perez-Lezaun et al., 1997). However, this problem is not discussed in this chapter because the relative distances among the major human "races" appear robust to differing genetic distance measures (Cavalli-Sforza, 1997). For the purposes of this chapter, a genetic distance is simply a number that measures the extent of genetic differentiation between two populations in terms of the alleles that are unique to each population and the extent to which shared alleles have different frequencies.

WHAT IS A RACE?

The word "race" is rarely used in the modern, nonhuman evolutionary literature because its meaning is so ambiguous. When it is used, it is generally used as a synonym for subspecies (Futuyma, 1986), but this concept also has no precise definition. The traditional meaning of a subspecies is that of a geographically circumscribed, sharply genetically differentiated population (Smith, Chiszar, & Montanucci, 1997). The problem with this definition from an evolutionary genetic perspective is that many traits and their underlying polymorphic genes show different patterns of geographical variation (Futuyma, 1986). As a result, some combination of characters will distinguish virtually every population from all others. There is no clear limit to the number of races that can be recognized under this concept, and indeed this notion of subspecies quickly becomes indistinguishable from that of a local population. One way around this difficulty is to place minimal quantitative thresholds on the amount of genetic differentiation that is required to recognize subspecies (Smith et al., 1997). A major difficulty with this solution is that there is no objective criterion for defining the threshold. A second solution is to allow races or subspecies to be defined only by the geographical patterns found for particular racial traits or characters. A similar problem is faced in defining species. For example, the biological species concept focuses attention on characters related to reproductive incompatibility as those important in defining a species. These reproductive traits have priority in defining a species when in conflict with other traits, such as morphology (Mayr, 1970). Unfortunately, there is no such guidance at the subspecies level, although in practice easily observed morphological traits (the very ones deemed not important under the biological species concept) are used. There is no evolutionary justification for this dominance of easily observed morphological traits; indeed, it merely arises from the sensory constraints of our own species. Therefore, most evolutionary biologists reject the notion that there are special racial traits. Indeed, as discussed later, using morphological traits to define races can be an impediment to understanding the evolutionary significance of morphological variation.

Because of these difficulties, the modern evolutionary perspective of a subspecies is that of a distinct evolutionary lineage within a species (Shaffer and McKnight, 1996). (However, one should note that many current evolutionary biologists completely deny the existence of any meaningful definition of subspecies, as argued originally by Wilson & Brown, 1953.) The Endangered Species Act requires preservation of vertebrate subspecies (Pennock & Dimmick, 1997), and the distinct evolutionary lineage definition has become the de facto definition of a subspecies in much of conservation biology (Amato & Gatesy, 1994; Brownlow, 1996; Legge, Roush, Desalle, Vogler, & May, 1996; Miththapala, Seidensticker, & O'Brien, 1996; Pennock & Dimmick, 1997; Vogler, 1994). This definition requires that a subspecies be genetically differentiated due to barriers to genetic exchange that have persisted for sufficient periods of time to have detectable genetic consequences; that is, the subspecies must have historical continuity in addition to current genetic differentiation. It cannot be emphasized enough that under this perspective genetic differentiation alone is insufficient to define a subspecies. The additional requirement of historical continuity is particularly important because many traits should reflect the common evolutionary history of the subspecies, and therefore in theory there is no need to prioritize the informative traits in defining subspecies. Indeed, the best traits for identifying subspecies are simply those with the best phylogenetic resolution. In this regard, advances in molecular genetics have greatly augmented our ability to resolve genetic variation and provide the best current resolution of recent evolutionary histories (Avise, 1994), thereby allowing the identification of evolutionary lineages in an objective, explicit fashion (Templeton, 1994, 1998c; Templeton, Routman, & Phillips, 1995).

The nonhuman literature therefore uses two definitions of race: (a) races as geographically circumscribed, genetically differentiated populations (the traditional definition) but now coupled with a minimum threshold of genetic differentiation that can be quantified with modern molecular genetic techniques; and (b) races as distinct evolutionary lineages within a species (the more modern definition). The fundamental question is whether human populations are genetically differentiated from one another in such a fashion as to constitute either sharply genetically differentiated geographical populations or distinct evolutionary lineages of humanity. These questions are answered with molecular genetic data and through the application of the same, explicit criteria used for the analyses of nonhuman organisms. A more detailed analysis of these questions is given in Templeton (1998a). Once the issue of race in humans has been addressed, the significance of genetic differentiation among human populations (regardless of its racial status) is examined, particularly as it relates to traits traditionally used to define races and to the question of genetic differentiation in cognitive abilities.

ARE HUMAN "RACES" GEOGRAPHICALLY CIRCUMSCRIBED, SHARPLY DIFFERENTIATED POPULATIONS?

The validity of the traditional subspecies definition of human races can now be addressed by examining the quantitative patterns and amount of genetic diversity found within and among human populations. A standard criterion for a subspecies or race in the nonhuman literature under the traditional definition of a subspecies as a geographically circumscribed, sharply differentiated population is to have F_{st} values of at least 0.25 to 0.30 (Smith et al., 1997). (Recall that F_{st} measures the relative amount of genetic diversity that is found within and among populations, with 0 indicating all genetic diversity is individual variation with no differences at all among populations, and 1 indicating that all individuals are genetically identical within a local population but that genetic diversity exists as fixed differences among populations.) The F_{st} value of humans (based on 16 populations from Africa, Europe, Asia, the Americas, and the Australo-Pacific region) is 0.156 (Barbujani, Magagni, Minch, & Cavalli-Sforza, 1997), thereby indicating that 84.4% of human genetic diversity exists as differences among individuals within populations, and only 15.6% can be used to genetically differentiate the major human populations. To put the human F_{st} value into perspective, humans need to be compared to other species. F_{st} values for many plants, invertebrates, and small-bodied vertebrates are typically far larger than the human value, but most of these organisms have poor dispersal abilities, so this is to be expected. A more valid comparison would be to the F_{st} values of other large-bodied mammals with excellent dispersal abilities. Figure 2.1 shows the values of F_{st} and related statistics for several large-bodied mammals. As can be seen, the human F_{st} value is one of the lowest, even though the human geographical distribution is the greatest.

As judged by the criterion in the nonhuman literature, the human F_{st} value is too small to have taxonomic significance under the traditional subspecies definition with the threshold values used in the recent nonhuman literature. Indeed, the levels of human racial diversity as quantified by F_{st} are modest at best when placed in a broader taxonomic context. In most other species, such an F_{st} value would be interpreted as evidence for frequent genetic interchange or much admixture among the populations. For example, as shown in Fig. 2.1, coyotes in North America have an F_{st} nearly twice that of humans, yet Lehman and Wayne (1991) concluded that this was evidence for "high rates of mtDNA gene flow continent-wide" (p. 412).

The human F_{st} value of 0.156 is an average of all 16 populations studied by Barbujani et al. (1997). However, one could argue that some particular group of

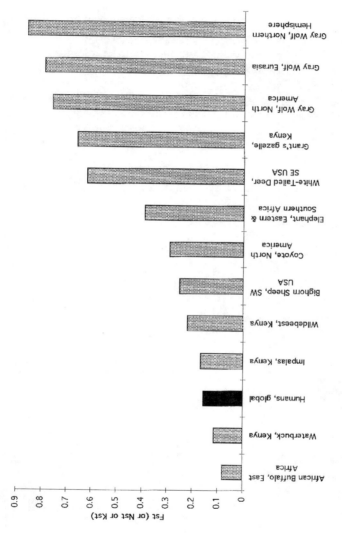

FIG. 2.1. F_{st} (or K_{st} or N_{st}) values for various species of large-bodied mammals with excellent dispersal abilities. The figure shows F_{st} (or its multiallelic analogue, G_{st}) values for African buffalo (Templeton & Georgiadis, 1996), humans (Barbujani et al., 1997), bighorn sheep (Boyce et al., 1997), elephants (Georgiadis et al., 1994, and white-tailed deer (Ellsworth, Honeycutt, Silvy, Bickham, & Klimstra, 1994); K_{st} values for waterbuck, impalas, wildebeest, and Grant's gazelle (Arctander, Kat, Simonsen, & Siegismund, 1996); and N_{st} values for coyotes (Lehman & Wayne, 1991) and wolves (Wayne, Lehman, Allard, & Honeycutt, 1992). The geographical scale of the study is indicated by the species name. Values are given in order of size, with the human value indicated in black and nonhuman values in gray.

humans does show much greater differentiation than this average and hence is a legitimate race under this definition. For example, an examination of the pairwise F_{st} values between specific pairs of human populations that are given in Cavalli-Sforza, Menozzi, Piazza (1996) reveals that the largest value of 0.265 occurs between Melanesians and some sub-Saharan Africans. Note that this is above the 0.25 lower threshold used by Smith et al. (1997). However, even in this case Melanesians and Africans would not be considered separate races by the criteria given in Smith et al. (1997) because geographically intermediate populations exist that fall well below this threshold. For example, the pairwise F_{st} value between Melanesians and Europeans is 0.148, and between Europeans and sub-Saharan Africans is 0.142. The observed pattern of genetic differentiation is not one with sharp geographical boundaries; rather, there is a continuum of genetic differentiation among the human populations that are geographically intermediate between Melanesians and sub-Saharan Africans. Hence, even in this case human populations do not satisfy the definition of subspecies as used in the nonhuman literature.

The low human F_{st} values do have evolutionary significance even though they are not consistent with the concept of subspecies. Suppose for the moment that the F_{st} values in humans truly reflect a balance between gene flow versus local genetic drift and are not due to isolated human lineages. One convenient method for quantifying this balance is Nm, the product of local effective population size (N) with m, the migration rate between demes. (Effective population size itself is a much misunderstood concept. It is not the observed population size at all, but rather says that the real population is behaving genetically like an idealized standard population of size N. This idealized standard population has many attributes that are not found in most real populations. For example, the idealized population consists solely of hermaphrodites who are capable of mating with themselves.) The product Nm measures the ratio of the strength of gene flow (measured by m) and the strength of genetic drift (which is proportional to $1/N$); that is, the ratio is $m/(1/N) = Nm$. Under the idealized population structure known as the island model, the relation between F_{st} and Nm is (Wright, 1969):

$$F_{st} = \frac{1}{4Nm + 1} \qquad (1)$$

The island model assumes that gene flow is independent of geographical distance. This assumption is violated for most real populations, so Nm is not the actual number of individuals exchanged per generation but rather an effective number of migrating individuals per generation relative to this idealized model of population structure. This allows comparisons across different species in effective amounts of gene flow with respect to a common standard. For the human F_{st} value of 0.156, $Nm = 1.35$. This result is consistent with the work of Santos, Epplen, and Epplen (1997), who examined several human data sets with a variety of statistical procedures and always obtained $Nm > 1$. With Nm on the order of 1, massive movements of large numbers of individuals are not needed to explain the modest level of genetic differentiation observed in human "races." Moreover, $Nm = 1.35$ does not mean that precisely 1.35 effective individuals migrate among the "races" every generation; rather, this is the long-term average. Assuming a generation time of 25 years, the levels of racial differentiation in humanity could be explained by interchanging 1.35 effective individuals every 25 years, or 13.5 every 250 years, or 135 every 2,500 years. Because humans often move as populations, gene flow could be very sporadic on a time scale measured in thousands to tens of thousands of years and still yield an effective number of migrants of 1.35.

Although an Nm value of 1.35 ensures that the population evolves as a single evolutionary lineage over long periods of time (Crow & Kimura, 1970), this same value of Nm also implies that at any given time human populations will show modest degrees of genetic differentiation. The island model also shows that genetically differentiated populations are not necessarily isolated populations. Equation 1 clearly shows that populations that routinely interchange genes and behave as a single long-term evolutionary lineage can nevertheless show genetic differences. This is why genetic differentiation per se is regarded as inadequate to define races in the general evolutionary literature.

The calculations made using Equation 1 were all made with the assumption that the human F_{st} value arose from the balance of gene flow versus local drift and selection rather than the accumulation of genetic differences among isolates since some time of past splitting. Unfortunately, the F_{st} statistic per se cannot discriminate among potential causes of genetic differentiation (Templeton, 1998b). Although human "races" do not satisfy the standard quantitative criterion for being traditional subspecies (Smith et al., 1997), this does not necessarily mean that races do not exist in the evolutionary lineage sense (i.e., as current or past isolates that still retain the genetic differentiation that arose while isolated). Under the lineage concept of subspecies, all that is needed is sufficient genetic differentiation to define the separate lineages. If the lineages split only recently, the overall level of divergence could be quite small. Therefore, the modest levels of genetic diversity among human populations do not rule out the possibility that human races are valid under the evolutionary lineage definition of subspecies.

ARE HUMAN "RACES" DISTINCT EVOLUTIONARY LINEAGES?

As indicated by Equation 1, even populations that experience recurrent genetic interchange can display genetic differentiation from one another, with the amount of differentiation indicating the amount of gene flow (Nm). However, genetic differentiation can also arise from populations splitting from one another (i.e., a population fragmenting into two or more isolates with no gene flow among them). In this case, the amount of differentiation reflects the amount of time since the split.

Because the F_{st} statistic is incapable by itself of discriminating between these two interpretations of genetic differentiation (Templeton, 1998b), most studies that portray human races as isolates or evolutionary lineages use pairwise genetic distance measures. Pairwise genetic distances in turn can be converted into an evolutionary tree of populations by various computer algorithms. An *evolutionary tree* is simply a branching diagram that represents the evolutionary relationships among the members of the tree. Although one normally thinks of evolutionary trees as referring to species, any biological entity that displays clear ancestral–descendant relationships through genetic continuity can be placed into an evolutionary tree. Thus, evolutionary trees can be estimated for the various alleles at a gene locus (a gene tree) if there has been little or no internal recombination within the gene. When internal recombination occurs, a new allele can be created from the parts of two different alleles, so that different sections of the new allele can have different evolutionary histories. In this case, the alleles themselves cannot be used as members of a legitimate evolutionary tree, although it may be possible to use smaller sections of the gene to define an evolutionary tree (Templeton & Sing, 1993). Similarly, an evolutionary tree can be estimated for populations if the populations are isolates. The analogue of recombination in this case is gene flow or admixture. If genetic interchange occurs among members of the populations, then populations cannot be legitimately placed into an evolutionary tree.

The computer programs that generate population trees from pairwise genetic distances do so regardless of whether or not populations are legitimate ancestral–descendant units. Assuming for the moment that human populations are true isolates, Fig. 2.2a shows such a population tree estimated from pairwise genetic distance data (Cavalli-Sforza et al., 1996). This and most other human genetic distance trees have the deepest divergence between Africans and non-Africans and interpret this divergence as accumulated genetic distance since the populations split. This split is commonly estimated to have occurred around 100,000 years ago (Cavalli-Sforza, 1997; Cavalli-Sforza et al., 1996; Nei & Takezaki, 1996). All this seems consistent with the idea that human races are valid under the evolutionary lineage concept. However, just like nonzero F_{st} values, nonzero genetic distances can also arise and persist between populations with recurrent gene flow. As shown by Slatkin (1991), recurrent gene flow results in an average divergence time of gene lineages between populations even when no population-level split occurred. Therefore, an apparent genetic time of divergence does not necessarily imply a time of actual population splitting—or any population split at all. Without a split, human "races" are not truly races under the phylogenetic definition.

Fortunately, these two interpretations of genetic distance can be distinguished. If human races can truly be represented as branches on an evolutionary tree, then the resulting genetic distances should satisfy several constraints. For example, under the evolutionary tree model, all non-African human populations "split" from the Africans at the same time, and therefore all genetic distances between African and non-African populations have the same expected value (Fig. 2.2a). When genetic distances instead reflect the amount of gene flow, "treeness" constraints are no longer applicable. Because gene flow is commonly restricted by geographical distance (Wright, 1943), gene flow models are expected to yield a strong positive relation between

A.

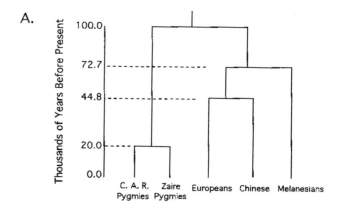

B.

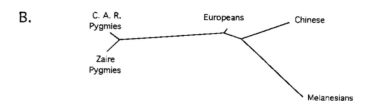

FIG. 2.2.   Genetic distances and recent human evolution: (a) An evolutionary tree of human populations as estimated from the genetic distance data given in Bowcock et al. (1991). Human population evolution is depicted as a series of splits, and the numbers on the left indicate the estimated times of divergence in thousands of years. This figure is redrawn from Cavalli-Sforza et al. (1996). (b) The same genetic distance data drawn with the neighbor-joining method but without all the constraints of a tree. This figure is redrawn from Cavalli-Sforza et al. (1996).

geographical and genetic distance. Figure 2.2b places the populations on a two-dimensional plot in a manner that attempts to reflect their genetic distances from one another, particularly nearest-neighbor distances, while otherwise attempting to minimize the total sum of branch lengths (formally, a neighbor-joining dendrogram). Figure 2.2b uses the same genetic distance data used to generate the tree in Fig. 2.2a, but without imposing all the constraints of treeness (Cavalli-Sforza et al., 1996). Note that Europeans fall between Africans and Asians as predicted by their geographical location—in contrast to the evolutionary tree model prediction of equal genetic distances of Europeans and Asians to Africans.

Statistical procedures exist to quantify the degree of fit of the genetic distance data to treeness (Templeton, 1998a). All human genetic distance data sets that have been tested fail to fit treeness (Bowcock et al., 1991; Cavalli-Sforza et al., 1996; Nei & Roychoudhury, 1974, 1982; Templeton, 1998a). In marked contrast, the genetic distance data fit well to a restricted gene flow model. For example, Cavalli-Sforza et al. (1996) assembled a comprehensive human data set and concluded that "the isolation-by-distance models hold for long distances as well as for short distances, and for large regions as well as for small and relatively isolated populations" (p. 124). Figure 2.3 is a redrawing of one of the figures from Cavalli-Sforza et al. (1996) that illustrates how well an isolation by distance model fits the human data.

Given that there is no tested human genetic distance data set consistent with treeness and that isolation by distance fits the human data well, proponents of the evolutionary tree model have postulated a complex set of "admixtures between branches that had separated a long time before" (Cavalli-Sforza et al., 1996, p. 19). The key phrase in this proposal is *between branches that had separated a long time before* (Terrell & Stewart, 1996). Admixture occurs when genetic interchange is reestablished between populations that had separated in the past and undergone genetic divergence (i.e., the gene flow patterns have been discontinuous). Proponents of the evolutionary tree model then attempt to reconcile the genetic distance data by using an admixture model that mimics some of the effects (and the good fit) of recurrent gene flow. By invoking admixture events as needed, human "races" can still be treated as separate evolutionary lineages, but now with the qualification that the races were purer in the past—the paradigm of the primitive isolate (Terrell & Stewart, 1996). However, even advocates of the races as branches model acknowledge that these postulated admixture events are "extremely specific" and "unrealistic" (Bowcock et al., 1991, p. 841). In contrast, isolation by distance fits the human data well and all that it requires is that humans tend to mate primarily with others born nearby but often outside one's own natal group (Lasker & Crews, 1996; Santos et al., 1997).

The hypothesis of admixture can be tested directly. If past isolation truly existed, the previous isolates would show many allele frequency differences. When they come into contact in an intermediate geographical area, admixture results in intermediate allele frequencies. This results in a genetic cline, a continuous shift from one allele frequency to another over geographic space. Such genetic clines are set up simultaneously for all differentiated loci, thereby resulting in a strong geographical concordance in the clines for all genetic systems. In contrast, isolation by distance may result in geographical concordance for systems under similar selective regimes (Endler, 1977; King & Lawson, 1995), but otherwise no concordance is expected. The lack of concordance in the geographical distribution of different genetic traits in humans has been thoroughly and extensively documented and has been one of the primary traditional arguments against the validity of human races (Cavalli-Sforza et al., 1996; Futuyma, 1986). This lack of concordance across genetic systems falsifies the hypothesis of admixture of previously isolated branches and the idea that races were pure in the past.

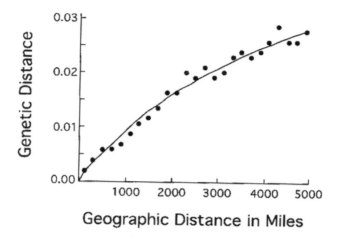

FIG. 2.3. Genetic distances and isolation by geographical distance. The global human genetic distances (the ordinate) are plotted against geographical distance in miles (the abscissa). The circles indicate the observed values and the curved line is the theoretical expectation under an isolation by distance model. This figure is redrawn from Cavalli-Sforza et al. (1996).

Another test of the hypothesis of equating races to branches on an evolutionary tree arises from phylogenetic reconstructions of the genetic variation found in homologous regions of DNA that show little or no recombination. All the homologous copies of DNA in such a DNA region that are identical at every nucleotide (or in practice, identical at all scored nucleotide sites) constitute a single haplotype class. In this sense, a haplotype is like an allele, with the main difference being that a haplotype can refer to any segment of DNA and not just a gene. A mutation at any site in this DNA region will usually create a new haplotype that differs initially from its ancestral haplotype by that single mutational change. As time proceeds, some haplotypes can acquire multiple mutational changes at several nucleotides from their ancestral type. All the different copies of a haplotype for each of the haplotypes in a species are subject to mutation, resulting in a diversity of haplotypes in the gene pool that vary in their mutational closeness to one another. If there is little or no recombination in the DNA region (as is the case for human mitochondrial DNA or for small segments of nuclear DNA), the divergence of haplotypes from one another reflects the order in which mutations occurred in evolutionary history. When mutational accumulation reflects evolutionary history, it is possible to estimate a network that shows how mutational changes transform one haplotype into another or from some common ancestral haplotype. Such a network is called a *haplotype tree*. In some circumstances, the ancestral haplotype is known or can be inferred, thereby providing a rooted haplotype tree. In practice, haplotype trees are sometimes difficult to infer from the mutational differences among a set of observed haplotypes because the same mutation may have occurred more than once or recombination may have scrambled up the DNA region so thoroughly that accumulated mutational differences reflect both evolutionary history and recombination in a confounded fashion. When they can be estimated, haplotype trees directly reflect only the evolutionary history of the genetic diversity being monitored in the DNA region under study. Haplotype trees are not necessarily evolutionary trees of species nor of populations within species. For example, suppose a species is and always has been completely randomly mating as a single population and therefore has no races or subspecies at all; yet, that same randomly mating species will have haplotype trees for all homologous DNA regions that show little or no recombination.

If a species is truly subdivided into subspecies, this should have an impact on the haplotype trees. Therefore, although haplotype trees are not necessarily population trees, they can still contain information about population history. This information in haplotype trees can be used to test the hypothesis that human races are evolutionary lineages with past purity that has been somewhat diminished by admixture. For example, to reconcile the evolutionary tree model with the genetic distance data, it is necessary to regard Europeans as a heavily admixed population (Bowcock et al., 1991; Cavalli-Sforza et al., 1996). When admixture occurs, haplotypes should coexist in the admixed population's gene pool that differ by multiple mutational events with no existing intermediate haplotypes (Manderscheid & Rogers, 1996; Templeton et al., 1995). The detection of such highly divergent haplotypes requires large sample sizes of the presumed admixed population to have statistical power. When large sample surveys have been performed on the presumed admixed European populations, no highly divergent haplotypes or evidence for admixture are observed for either mitochondrial DNA (mtDNA) (Manderscheid & Rogers, 1996) or Y (chromosome)-DNA (Cooper, Amos, Hoffman, & Rubinsztein, 1996). In contrast, isolation by distance (the gene flow model) produces local gene pools without strongly divergent haplotypes (i.e., most haplotypes differ by one or at most a few mutational steps from some other haplotype found in the same population), as is observed.

The evolutionary tree and gene flow hypotheses are models of how genes spread across geographical space and through time, and hence a geographical analysis of haplotype trees provides a direct test of these two models. Statistical techniques exist that separate the influences of historical events (e.g., population range expansions) from recurrent events (e.g., gene flow with isolation by distance) when there is adequate sampling in terms of both numbers of individuals and numbers and distribution of sampling sites (Templeton et al., 1995). This statistical approach treats historical and recurrent events as joint possibilities rather than mutually exclusive alternatives. Moreover, the criteria used to identify range expansions versus gene flow have been empirically validated by analyzing data sets with strong prior knowledge, showing that this approach is accurate and not prone to false positives (Templeton, 1998b).

Application of this statistical approach to analyzing human haplotype trees over geographic space indicates a mixture of population range expansion events and recurrent genetic exchange among the major Old World human populations for mtDNA (Templeton, 1993, 1997a, 1997b, 1998a), nuclear hemoglobin DNA (Harding et al., 1997; Templeton, 1998a, 1998b), and Y-DNA (Hammer et al., 1998). Combined, the mtDNA, Y-DNA, and hemoglobin data sets reveal that human evolution from about a million years ago to the last tens of thousands of years has been dominated by two evolutionary forces: (a) population movements and associated range expansions, and (b) gene flow restricted by isolation by distance. The only evidence for any split or fragmentation event in human evolutionary history within this time frame is one detected with mtDNA involving the colonization of the Americas (Templeton, 1997a, 1998a). However, this colonization was due to either multiple colonization events or involved movement by large numbers of people (Templeton, 1998a), resulting in extensive sharing of genetic polymorphisms of New World with Old World human populations. Moreover, the genetic isolation between the Old and New Worlds was brief (to an evolutionary biologist) and no longer exists. Other than this temporary fragmentation event, the major human populations have been interconnected by gene flow (recurrent at least on a time scale of the order of tens of thousands of years or less) during the last 100,000 to 200,000 years. Gene flow may have been more sporadic earlier, but multiple genetic interchanges certainly occurred among Old World populations more than 200,000 years ago (Templeton, 1998a). Hence, the haplotype analyses of geographical associations strongly reject the existence of evolutionary lineages of humans, reject the separation of Eurasians from Africans 100,000 years ago, and reject the idea of "pure races" in the past. Thus, human "races" have no biological validity under the evolutionary lineage definition of subspecies.

THE SIGNIFICANCE OF GENETIC DIFFERENCES AMONG HUMAN POPULATIONS

Although human populations do not define races under any of the definitions currently applied to nonhuman organisms, genetic differences do exist among human populations as already noted. These genetic differences can still have evolutionary and genetic significance, as outlined in the section on the meaning of genetic diversity Therefore, the evolutionary significance of genetic differentiation among human populations (not "races," because none exists) is still a legitimate issue, and one that I now address.

Geographical Differentiation

As the analyses given earlier in this chapter (and in more detail in Templeton, 1998a) indicate, the patterns of genetic diversity found among human populations fit well to an isolation by distance model. As mentioned previously, all finite populations, human or otherwise, have a tendency to become genetically differentiated from one another due to the sampling error associated with passing on only a finite number of gametes to the next generation, a phenomenon known as genetic drift (Wright, 1969). This tendency of all finite populations to genetically diverge from one another due to drift can be counteracted by genetic exchange among the populations, the evolutionary force known as gene flow. In many organisms, the amount of gene flow among populations is strongly influenced by their geographical proximity, with the amount of gene flow between populations dropping off with increasing geographical distance. Indeed, populations that are far from one another geographically may experience no direct genetic interchange at all, but gene flow can still occur as genes are passed on from one adjacent population to the next, a type of gene flow known as *stepping stones* (Wright 1943). Under these models of isolation by geographical distance, the genetic differentiation increases with increasing geographical distance. This expected pattern is displayed most clearly for neutral genetic variation (i.e., genetic variants that are not subject to natural selection and thereby show the effects of drift and gene flow). When variation is selected, deviations from this pattern can occur, as discussed later. Given the overall excellent fit of human genetic distances to an isolation by distance model (Fig. 2.3), the primary significance of genetic differences among human populations is that of a selectively neutral indicator of geographical origin. The primary reason "races" are genetically differentiated is that they come from different geographical regions and not because the racial classes have any significance per se. For example, consider Melanesians and Africans. As shown in Fig. 2.2b and as pointed out earlier, these two human populations have nearly maximal genetic divergence within humanity as a whole with respect to molecular markers. Moreover, note that Europeans are genetically closer to both Africans and to Melanesians than are Africans to Melanesians (Fig. 2.2b). However, Melanesians and Africans share dark skin, hair texture, and cranial–facial morphology (Cavalli-Sforza et al., 1996; Nei & Roychoudhury, 1993)—the traits typically used to classify people into races. As a result, Europeans are classified into one race, whereas Africans and Melanesians were classified into the same race in the older anthropological literature (e.g., Weidenreich, 1946). Thus, the genetic differentiation among Africans, Europeans and Melanesians is indicated by their relative geographical positions and not their "racial" classification or by racial traits such as skin color or hair texture.

Because most genetic differences among humans simply represent the balance of drift versus gene flow in a geographical context, the most extreme genetic differences between human populations are expected between those that either are the most geographically distant (e.g., Africans and Melanesians in Fig. 2.2b) or those that for some reason have had very small population sizes (which accentuates drift) or little gene flow with other, even nearby populations. Indeed, the most dramatic cases of genetic differentiation among human populations are associated with small population sizes and not "racial" categories. For example, the Old Order Amish in North America were established from relatively small numbers of founders and have had little subsequent gene flow into their population (McKusick, Hostetler, Egeland,

& Eldridge, 1964). As a consequence, the Amish have undergone extreme genetic differentiation from their neighboring populations because of powerful genetic drift. Unlike the differences among races that are primarily neutral indicators of geographical origin, genetic drift is so powerful in populations derived from a small number of founders that selected alleles can drift to highly divergent allele frequencies, even in a nonadaptive direction. As a result, the genetic differentiation found in the Amish and other small human populations does have great importance for both clinical and behavioral traits (Ludwig et al., 1997; Pericakvance et al., 1996; Polymeropoulos et al., 1996; Polymeropoulos & Schaffer, 1996). Indeed, with the advent of molecular markers scattered throughout the genome, such "founder" populations have proven to be an extremely valuable resource in mapping and identifying genetic diseases. For example, the first genetic disease gene mapped and ultimately cloned by such positional mapping was the gene for Huntington's disease (Gusella et al., 1983). The key to this original mapping effort was finding an isolated founder population in which this disease was frequent yet on a restricted genetic background. Such a founder population was discovered in Venezuela, and its discovery was critical in the identification of the Huntington's disease gene (Gusella et al., 1983). Although such founder populations do have great evolutionary and clinical significance, this drift-induced differentiation is generally not used to make racial classifications.

Adaptive Differentiation

As indicated earlier, sometimes genetic drift is so strong that it can cause human populations to become genetically differentiated, even in directions that are not favored by natural selection. Normally, natural selection tends to keep deleterious alleles rare in all human populations, thereby reducing the differentiation at such genes among human populations below that expected under isolation by distance. However, there are circumstances under which natural selection can accentuate differentiation above the levels expected under isolation by distance. Adaptive differentiation is expected to occur when a species inhabits different geographical regions that induce divergent selective pressures for some traits. Because humans are a geographically widespread species, humans have indeed adapted to local environmental conditions in a manner that does cause genetic differentiation among populations. For example, there is much evidence that the intensity of ultraviolet radiation induces natural selection on the amount of melanin in human skin, with high intensities favoring dark skins and low intensities light skins (Relethford, 1997). As a consequence, human populations have become highly differentiated in skin color in a manner that is adaptive to the area of geographical origin (Relethford, 1997). As already noted by the European, Melanesian, and African example, the pattern of genetic differentiation obtained for this adaptive trait does not reflect the overall pattern of genetic differentiation among human populations. Rather, the geographical pattern of the adaptive trait reflects the geographical pattern of the selective conditions that favor the trait in some regions but not others. Moreover, different adaptive traits show discordant patterns with one another when their selective agents are likewise distributed in a discordant fashion. For example, malaria has been a major selective influence on human populations. One of the many genetic adaptations to malaria is the allele for sickle-cell anemia at the hemoglobin beta-chain locus (Haldane, 1949; Templeton, 1982). This S allele is selected because it confers resistance to the malarial parasite when heterozygous for the most common A allele at this locus. S alleles are found in high frequencies only in populations that live now or in the recent past in malarial regions. This includes some, but not all, sub-Saharan African populations, populations in the Mediterranean and Middle East, and populations in India (Boletini et al., 1994; El-Hazmi, 1990; Oner et al., 1992 Reddy & Modell, 1996; Schiliro, Spena, Giambelluca, & Maggio, 1990). Note that sickle-cell is not cleanly associated with any "race" but rather is associated with the presence of malaria, its selective agent. Note further that its distribution is not concordant with skin color. This illustrates that it is essential to study each adaptive trait separately and relate it to its unique selective agents. When populations are interconnected by gene flow, as human populations are, locally adaptive traits are not expected to be concordant with one another or reflective of overall patterns of genetic differentiation. Hence, locally adaptive traits in populations interconnected by gene flow do not define races.

Indeed, the concept of race is an impediment to a proper understanding of adaptive polymorphism in populations interconnected by gene flow. For example, consider the water snake (*Nerodia sipedon*, previously *Natrix sipedon*) on islands in Lake Erie. These snakes have melanic and nonmelanic forms that were used to define two subspecies, *N. s. insularum* (the melanic form), and *N. s. sipedon* (the nonmelanic form that has bands; Conant & Clay, 1937). However, subsequent studies revealed that dispersal patterns and gene flow in these snakes reflected geographical distance rather than skin color category (Camin & Ehrlich, 1959). Recent molecular studies have revealed that the amount of gene flow between the skin color "races" in these snakes has Nm values of 3.6 to 9.2 (King & Lawson, 1995). Hence, strong patterns of skin color differentiation are being maintained in these snakes despite levels of gene flow that are actually greater than those observed on average between human "races." Moreover, these studies (Camin & Ehrlich, 1958; King & Lawson, 1995) indicate that skin color differences are being maintained by selection favoring melanic forms in populations inhabiting cold waters because of the thermal properties of dark skin versus selection favoring banded forms on the mainland for crypsis. Hence, these later studies revealed the evolutionary significance of melanism in these snakes. Concerning the older work that had simply placed the melanic snakes into a new subspecies, Camin and Ehrlich (1958) wrote, "the subspecies approach has tended to obscure a significant biological problem" (p. 510). Hence, subspecies in this case were actually an impediment to understanding the evolutionary significance of the "racial" variation. The same is certainly true for humans. For example, the fundamental breakthrough in our understanding of sickle-cell anemia occurred when its geographical distribution was not phrased in terms of racial categories but rather in terms of the distribution of the malarial parasite (Haldane 1949).

These examples also illustrate that even extreme differentiation for locally adaptive traits is not evidence for a lack of gene flow among populations. Local selective forces can cause strong adaptive differentiation even for populations with gene flow levels much higher than those found in humans (e.g., DeSalle, Templeton, Mori, Pletscher, & Johnston, 1987; King & Lawson, 1995, 1997; Lawson & King, 1996; Templeton, Hollocher, & Johnston, 1993; Templeton, Hollocher, Lawler, & Johnston, 1989). However, the human Nm value of about 1 is sufficient to ensure that any trait universally adaptive in all human populations will spread throughout the species (Barton & Rouhani, 1993), making humans a single long-term evolutionary lineage. Hence, there is no incompatibility between humans showing local adaptive polymorphisms and humans being a single long-term evolutionary lineage.

Differentiation in Cognitive Abilities

The premier human adaptation is our intelligence. There is no doubt that our species as a whole has had its recent evolution characterized by a large increase in intelligence, but the question still remains if current human populations are genetically differentiated with respect to intelligence either as a reflection of isolation by distance or local adaptation. Unfortunately, this question is usually muddied by two indefensible errors: (a) phrasing this question as genetic differentiation in intelligence among "races," and (b) phrasing this question in terms of the heritability of intelligence or some surrogate such as an IQ test score.

As shown previously, races do not exist in humans under any modern definition. Because different traits have discordant distributions, it is meaningless to look at "racial" differences in any specific traits, including intelligence. One can look at genetic differentiation among any two or more populations, but it would be incorrect to generalize from those specific populations to broader "racial" categories. Hence, in any discussion of intelligence, the conclusions must be limited to the specific populations under study and not generalized beyond them.

The concept of heritability is completely irrelevant to the question of genetic differentiation for any trait, including intelligence, among human populations. *Heritability* is the proportion of interindividual phenotypic variance within a population that can be attributed to genotypic differences among the individuals. Note first that heritability is defined as a within-population concept. Heritability by definition is not applicable to between-population phenotypic differences. Second, heritability examines only phenotypic variation as measured by the statistical device of variance. The first step in calculating any variance is to subtract off the mean. As a consequence, heritability is completely insensitive to the mean value of a trait in a population. A mean trait value could be shifted up or down by large amounts due to environmental factors and not have the slightest impact on the heritability of the trait. This also shows that mean differences among populations are uninformative about underlying genetic differences. Yet the literature on intelligence and race has been dominated by contrasts of mean values among populations—a contrast that lies completely outside the domain of heritability and reveals nothing about population differentiation at a genetic level. Whether the heritability of an IQ test score is 0 or 1 within any particular population is completely irrelevant to the question of genetic differentiation among populations for an IQ phenotype.

There is a way of testing if differences in phenotypic means between two populations have a genetic basis. The test was developed by Mendel and requires that the populations be crossed and that the hybrids and their descendants be raised in a "common garden" (i.e., a common environment). Despite the extreme interest in the genetic basis of between population differences in intelligence, only a handful of studies have even attempted to use this standard research design of genetics. These few studies (Green, 1972; Loehlin, Vandenberg, & Osborne, 1973; Scarr, Pakstis, Katz, & Barker, 1977) have several common features. First, they take advantage of the strong tendency of humans to interbreed when brought into physical proximity. For example, in the Americas, geographically differentiated human populations of European and sub-Saharan African origin were brought together and began to hybridize. However, most matings still occurred within populations. Given this assortative mating, the genetic impact of hybridization is extremely sensitive to the cultural environment. In North America, the hybrids were culturally classified as blacks, and hence most subsequent matings involving the hybrids were into the population of African origin. Therefore, a broad range of variation in degree of European and African ancestry can be found among North American individuals who are all culturally classified as being members of the same "race", in this case blacks (a "common garden" cultural classification). In Latin America, different cultures have different ways of classifying hybrids, but in general a number of alternative categories are available and social class is a more powerful determinant of mating than is physical appearance (e.g., skin color). As a consequence, individuals in Latin America can be culturally classified into a single social entity that genetically represents a broad range of variation in amount of European and African ancestry. Thus, these studies use a "common garden" design in a cultural sense that nevertheless includes hybrid individuals and their descendants. Second, these studies quantify the degree of European and African ancestry in a population of individuals that is culturally classified as being a single "race." Because the original geographically disparate populations do show genetic differences due to isolation by distance, the degree of European and African ancestry of a specific individual can be estimated using blood group and molecular genetic markers. Finally, the shared premise of these studies is that if a trait that differentiates European and sub-Saharan Africans has a genetic basis, it should show variation in the hybrid population that correlates with the degree of African ancestry. This is indeed the case for many morphological traits, such as skin color (Scarr et al., 1977). However, there is no significant correlation with the degree of African ancestry for any cognitive test result, either within the cultural environment of being "black" (Loehlin et al., 1973; Scarr et al., 1977) or in the cultural environment of being "white" (Green, 1972). Hence, even though these populations differ in their average test scores, there is no evidence for any genetic differentiation among these populations at genetic loci that influence these IQ test scores.

CONCLUSIONS

The genetic data are consistently and strongly informative about human races. Humans show only modest levels of differentiation among populations when compared to other large-bodied mammals, and this level of differentiation is well below the usual threshold used to identify subspecies (races) in nonhuman species. Hence, human races do not exist under the traditional concept of a subspecies as being a geographically circumscribed population showing sharp genetic differentiation. A more modern definition of race is that of a distinct evolutionary lineage within a species. The genetic evidence strongly rejects the existence of distinct evolutionary lineages within humans. The widespread representation of human "races" as branches on an intraspecific population tree is genetically indefensible and biologically misleading, even when the ancestral node is presented as being at 100,000 years ago. Attempts to salvage the idea of human "races" as evolutionary lineages by invoking greater racial purity in the past followed by admixture events are unsuccessful and are falsified by multilocus comparisons of geographical concordance and by haplotype analyses. Instead, all of the genetic evidence shows that there never was a split or separation of the "races" or between Africans and Eurasians. Recent human evolution has been characterized by both population range expansions and recurrent genetic interchange among populations. There has been no split between any of the major geographical populations of humanity.

Because of the extensive evidence for genetic interchange through population movements and recurrent gene flow going back at least hundreds of thousands of years, there is only one evolutionary lineage of humanity and there are no subspecies or races under either the traditional or phylogenetic definitions. Human evolution and population structure have been and are characterized by many locally differentiated populations coexisting at any given time, but with sufficient genetic contact to make all of humanity a single lineage sharing a common, long-term evolutionary fate. The genetic differences that do exist among human populations are explained primarily by geography under an isolation by distance model, with some extreme differentiation being due to recent founder events and local adaptations. However, all of humanity shares in common the vast majority of its molecular genetic variation and the adaptive traits that define us as a single species.

ACKNOWLEDGMENTS

I thank Dr. Robert Sussman, Dr. Erik Trinkaus, Dr. Jefferson Fish, and Dr. Joseph Graves for their excellent suggestions for improving an earlier draft of this chapter.

REFERENCES

Amato, G., & Gatesy, J. (1994). PCR assays of variable nucleotide sites for identification of conservation units. In B. Schierwater, B. Streit, G. P. Wagner, & R. DeSalle (Eds.), *PCR assays of variable nucleotide sites for identification of conservation units* (pp. 215–226). Basel, Switzerland: Birkhäuser-Verlag.

Arctander, P., Kat, P. W., Simonsen, B. T., & Siegismund, H. R. (1996). Population genetics of Kenyan impalas—consequences for conservation. In T. B. Smith & R. K. Wayne (Eds.), *Molecular genetic approaches in conservation* (pp. 399–412). Oxford: Oxford University Press.

Avise, J. C. (1994). *Molecular markers, natural history and evolution.* New York: Chapman & Hall.

Barbujani, G., Magagni, A., Minch, E., & Cavalli-Sforza, L. L. (1997). An apportionment of human DNA diversity. *Proceedings of the National Academy of Sciences USA, 94,* 4516–4519.

Barton, N. H., & Rouhani, S. (1993). Adaptation and the "shifting balance." *Genetical Research, 61,* 57–74.

Boletini, E., Svobodova, M., Divoky, V., Baysal, E., Curuk, M. A., Dimovski, A. J., Liang, R., Adekile, A. D., & Huisman, T. H. (1994). Sickle-cell-anemia, sickle-cell beta-thalassemia, and thalassemia major in Albania—Characterization of mutations. *Human Genetics, 93,* 182–187.

Bowcock, A. M., Kidd, J. R., Mountain, J. L., Hebert, J. M., Carotenuto, L., Kidd, K. K., & Cavalli-Sforza, L. L. (1991). Drift, admixture, and selection in human evolution: A study with DNA polymorphisms. *Proceedings of the National Academy of Sciences USA, 88,* 839–843.

Boyce, W. M., Hedrick, P. W., Mugglicockett, N. E., Kalinowski, S., Penedo, M. C. T., & Ramey, R. R. (1997). Genetic variation of major histocompatibility complex and microsatellite loci—A comparison in bighorn sheep. *Genetics, 145,* 421–433.

Brownlow, C. A. (1996). Molecular taxonomy and the conservation of the red wolf and other endangered carnivores. *Conservation Biology, 10,* 390–396.

Camin, J. H., & Ehrlich, P. R. (1959). Natural selection in water snakes (*Natrix sipedon* L.) on islands in Lake Erie. *Evolution, 12,* 504–511.

Cavalli-Sforza, L. L. (1997). Genes, peoples, and languages. *Proceedings of the National Academy of Sciences USA, 94,* 7719–7724.

Cavalli-Sforza, L., Menozzi, P., & Piazza, A. (1996). *The history and geography of human genes.* Princeton, NJ: Princeton University Press.

Conant, R., & Clay, W. M. (1937). A new subspecies of water snake from islands in Lake Erie. *Occasional Papers of the University of Michigan Museum of Zoology, 346,* pp. 1–9.

Cooper, G., Amos, W., Hoffman, D., & Rubinsztein, D. C. (1996). Network analysis of human Y microsatellite haplotypes. *Human Molecular Genetics, 5,* 1759–1766.

Crow, J. F., & Kimura, M. (1970). *An introduction to population genetic theory.* New York: Harper & Row.

DeSalle, R., Templeton, A., Mori, I., Pletscher, S., & Johnston, J. S. (1987). Temporal and spatial heterogeneity of mtDNA polymorphisms in natural populations of *Drosophila mercatorum*. *Genetics, 116,* 215–223.

El-Hazmi, M. (1990). Beta-globin gene haplotypes in the Saudi sickle-cell-anemia patients. *Human Heredity, 40,* 177–186.

Ellsworth, D. L., Honeycutt, R. L., Silvy, N. J., Bickham, J. W., & Klimstra, W. D. (1994). Historical biogeography and contemporary patterns of mitochondrial DNA variation in white-tailed deer from the Southeastern United States. *Evolution, 48,* 122–136.

Endler, J. A. (1977). *Geographic variation, speciation, and clines.* Princeton, NJ: Princeton University Press.

Futuyma, D. J. (1986). *Evolutionary biology.* Sunderland, MA: Sinauer Associates.

Georgiadis, N., Bischof, L., Templeton, A., Patton, J., Karesh, W., & Western, D. (1994). Structure and history of African elephant populations: I. Eastern and Southern Africa. *Journal of Heredity, 85,* 100–104.

Green, R. F. (1972). On the correlation between IQ and amount of "white" blood. *Proceedings of the 80th Annual Convention of the American Psychological Association, 7,* 285–286.

Gusella, J. F., Wexler, N. S., Conneally, P. M., Naylor, S. L., Anderson, M. A., Tanzi, R. E., Watkins, P. C., Ottina, K., Wallace, M. R., Sakaguchi, A. Y., Young, A. B., Shoulson, I., Bonilla, E., & Martin, J. B. (1983). A polymorphic DNA marker genetically linked to Huntington's disease. *Nature, 306,* 324–328.

Haldane, J. B. S. (1949). Disease and evolution. *Ricerca Scientifica, 19,* 3–10.

Hammer, M. F., Karafet, T., Rasanayagam, A., Wood, E. T., Altheide, T. K., Jenkins, T., Griffiths, R. C., Templeton, A. R., & Zegura, S. L. (1998). Out of Africa and back again: Nested cladistic analysis of human Y chromosome variation. *Molecular Biology and Evolution, 15,* 427–441.

Hammer, M. F., Spurdle, A. B., Karafet, T., Bonner, M. R., Wood, E. T., Novelletto, A., Malaspina, P., Mitchell, R. J., Horai, S., Jenkins, T., & Zegura, S. L. (1997). The geographic distribution of human Y chromosome variation. *Genetics, 145,* 787–805.

Harding, R. M., Fullerton, S. M., Griffiths, R. C., Bond, J., Cox, M. J., Schneider, J. A., Moulin, D. S., & Clegg, J. B. (1997). Archaic African *and* Asian lineages in the genetic ancestry of modern humans. *American Journal of Human Genetics, 60,* 772–789.

Hudson, R. R., Boos, D. D., & Kaplan, N. L. (1992). A statistical test for detecting geographical subdivision. *Molecular Biology and Evolution, 9,* 138–151.

King, R. B., & Lawson, R. (1995). Color-pattern variation In Lake Erie water snakes—The role of gene flow. *Evolution, 49,* 885–896.

King, R. B., & Lawson. R. (1997). Microevolution in island water snakes. *BioScience, 47,* 279–286.

Lasker, G. W., & Crews, D. E. (1996). Behavioral influences on the evolution of human genetic diversity. *Molecular Phylogenetics and Evolution, 5,* 232–240.

Lawson, R., & King, R. B. (1996). Gene flow and melanism in Lake Erie garter snake populations. *Biological Journal of the Linnean Society, 59,* 1–19.

Legge, J. T., Roush, R., Desalle, R., Vogler, A. P., & May, B. (1996). Genetic criteria for establishing evolutionarily significant units in cryans buckmoth. *Conservation Biology, 10,* 85–98.

Lehman, N., & Wayne, R. K. (1991). Analysis of coyote mitochondrial-DNA genotype frequencies: Estimation of the effective number of alleles. *Genetics, 128,* 405–416.

Loehlin, J. C., Vandenberg, S. G., & Osborne, R. T. (1973). Blood group genes and Negro-white ability differences. *Behavior Genetics, 3,* 263–270.

Ludwig, E. H., Hopkins, P. N., Allen, A., Wu, L. L., Williams, R. R., Anderson, J. L., Ward, R. H., Lalouel, J. M., & Innerarity, T. L. (1997). Association of genetic variations in Apolipoprotein B with hypercholesterolemia, coronary artery disease, and receptor binding of low density lipoproteins. *Journal of Lipid Research, 38,* 1361–1373.

Lynch, M., & Crease, T. J. (1990). The analysis of population survey data on DNA sequence variation. *Molecular Biology and Evolution, 7,* 377–394.

Manderscheid, E. J., & Rogers, A. R. (1996). Genetic admixture in the late Pleistocene. *American Journal of Physical Anthropology, 100,* 1–5.

Mayr, E. (1970). *Populations, species, and evolution.* Cambridge, MA: Belknap Press of Harvard University Press.

McKusick, V. A., Hostetler, J. A., Egeland, J. A., & Eldridge, R. (1964). The distribution of certain genes in the Old Order Amish. *Cold Spring Harbor Symposium on Quantitative Biology, 29*, 99–114.

Miththapala, S., Seidensticker, J., & Obrien, S. J. (1996). Phylogeographic subspecies recognition in leopards (*Panthera pardus*)—Molecular genetic variation. *Conservation Biology, 10*, 1115–1132.

Nei, M., & Roychoudhury, A. K. (1974). Genic variation within and between the three major races of man, Caucasoids, Negroids, and Mongoloids. *American Journal Human Genetics, 26*, 421–443.

Nei, M., & Roychoudhury, A. K. (1982). Genetic relationship and evolution of human races. *Evolutionary Biology, 14*, 1–59.

Nei, M., & Roychoudhury, A. K. (1993). Evolutionary relationships of human populations on a global scale. *Molecular Biology and Evolution, 10*, 927–943.

Nei, M., & Takezaki, N. (1996). The root of the phylogenetic tree of human populations. *Molecular Biology and Evolution, 13*, 170–177.

Oner, C., Dimovski, A. J., Olivieri, N. F., Schiliro, G., Codrington, J. F., Fattoum, S., Adekile, A. D., Oner, R., Yuregir, G. T., Altay, C., Gurgey, A., Gupta, R. B., Jogessar, V. B., Kitundu, M. N., Loukopoulos, D., Tamagnini, G. P., Ribeiro, M., Kutlar, F., Gu, L. H., Lanclos, K. D., & Huisman, T. R. (1992). Beta-S haplotypes in various world populations. *Human Genetics, 89*, 99–104.

Pennock, D. S., & Dimmick, W. W. (1997). Critique of the evolutionarily significant unit as a definition for distinct population segments under the US Endangered Species Act. *Conservation Biology, 11*, 611–619.

Perez-Lezaun, A., Calafell, F., Mateu, E., Comas, D., Ruiz-Pacheco, R., & Bertranpetit, J. (1997). Microsatellite variation and the differentiation of modern humans. *Human Genetics, 99*, 1–7.

Pericakvance, M. A., Johnson, C. C., Rimmler, J. B., Saunders, A. M., Robinson, L. C., Dhondt, E. G., Jackson, C. E., & Haines, J. L. (1996). Alzheimers disease and apolipoprotein E-4 allele in an Amish population. *Annals of Neurology, 39*, 700–704.

Polymeropoulos, M. H., Ide, S. E., Wright, M., Goodship, J., Weissenbach, J., Pyeritz, R. E., Dasilva, E. O., Deluna, R. I. O., & Francomano, C. A. (1996). The gene for the Ellis Van Creveld Syndrome is located on chromosome 4p16. *Genomics, 35*, 1–5.

Polymeropoulos, M. H., & Schaffer, A. A. (1996). Scanning the genome with 1772 microsatellite markers in search of a bipolar disorder susceptibility gene. *Molecular Psychiatry, 1*, 404–407.

Reddy, P. H., & Modell, B. (1996). Reproductive behaviour and natural selection for the sickle gene in the Baiga tribe of Central India—The role of social parenting. *Annals of Human Genetics, 60*, 231–236.

Relethford, J. H. (1997). Hemispheric difference in human skin color. *American Journal of Physical Anthropology, 104*, 449–457.

Santos, E. J. M., Epplen, J. T., & Epplen, C. (1997). Extensive gene flow in human populations as revealed by protein and microsatellite DNA markers. *Human Heredity, 47*, 165–172.

Scarr, S., Pakstis, A. J., Katz, S. H., & Barker, W. B. (1977). Absence of a relationship between degree of white ancestry and intellectual skills within a black population. *Human Genetics, 39*, 69–86.

Schiliro, G., Spena, M., Giambelluca, E., & Maggio, A. (1990). Sickle haemoglobinpathies in Sicily. *American Journal Hematology, 33*, 81–85.

Shaffer, H. B., & McKnight, M. L. (1996). The polytypic species revisited—Genetic differentiation and molecular phylogenetics of the tiger salamander *Ambystoma tigrinum* (Amphibia, Caudata) complex. *Evolution, 50*, 417–433.

Slatkin, M. (1991). Inbreeding coefficients and coalescence times. *Genetical Research, 58*, 167–175.

Smith, H. M., Chiszar, D., & Montanucci, R. R. (1997). Subspecies and classification. *Herpetological Review, 28*, 13–16.

Templeton, A. R. (1982). Adaptation and the integration of evolutionary forces. In R. Milkman (Ed.), *Perspectives on evolution* (pp. 15–31). Sunderland, MA: Sinauer Associates.

Templeton, A. R. (1993). The "Eve" hypothesis: A genetic critique and reanalysis. *American Anthropologist, 95*, 51–72.

Templeton, A. R. (1994). The role of molecular genetics in speciation studies. In B. Schierwater, B. Streit, G. P. Wagner, & R. DeSalle (Eds.), *Molecular ecology and evolution: Approaches and applications* (pp. 455–477). Basel, Switzerland: Birkhäuser-Verlag.

Templeton, A. R. (1997a). Out of Africa? What do genes tell us? *Current Opinion in Genetics & Development, 7*, 841–847.

Templeton, A. R. (1997b). Testing the out-of-Africa replacement hypothesis with mitochondrial DNA data. In G. A. Clark & C. Willermet (Eds.), *Conceptual issues in modern human origins research* (pp. 329–360). Amsterdam: Aldine de Gruyter.

Templeton, A. R. (1998a). Human races: A genetic and evolutionary perspective. *American Anthropologist, 100*, 1–19.

Templeton, A. R. (1998b). Nested clade analyses of phylogeographic data: testing hypotheses about gene flow and population history. *Molecular Ecology, 7*, 381–397.

Templeton, A. R. (1998c). Species and speciation: Geography, population structure, ecology, and gene trees. In D. J. Howard & S. H. Berlocher (Eds.), *Endless forms: Species and speciation* (pp. 32–43). Oxford, UK: Oxford University Press.

Templeton, A. R., & Georgiadis, N. J. (1996). A landscape approach to conservation genetics: conserving evolutionary processes in the African Bovidae. In J. C. Avise & J. L. Hamrick (Eds.), *Conservation genetics: Case histories from nature* (pp. 398–430). New York: Chapman & Hall.

Templeton, A. R., Hollocher, H., & Johnston, J. S. (1993). The molecular through ecological genetics of abnormal abdomen in *Drosophila mercatorum*: V. Female phenotypic expression on natural genetic backgrounds and in natural environments. *Genetics, 134*, 475–485.

Templeton, A. R., Hollocher, H., Lawler, S., & Johnston, J. S. (1989). Natural selection and ribosomal DNA in *Drosophila. Genome, 31*, 296–303.

Templeton, A. R., Routman, E., & Phillips, C. (1995). Separating population structure from population history: A cladistic analysis of the geographical distribution of mitochondrial DNA haplotypes in the tiger salamander, *Ambystoma tigrinum. Genetics, 140*, 767–782.

Templeton, A. R., & Sing, C. F. (1993). A cladistic analysis of phenotypic associations with haplotypes inferred from restriction endonuclease mapping: IV. Nested analyses with cladogram uncertainty and recombination. *Genetics, 134*, 659–669.

Terrell, J. E., & Stewart, P. J. (1996). The paradox of human population genetics at the end of the twentieth century. *Reviews in Anthropology, 25*, 13–33.

Vogler, A. P. (1994). Extinction and the formation of phylogenetic lineages: diagnosing units of conservation management in the tiger beetle *Cicindela dorsalis*. In B. Schierwater, B. Streit, G. P. Wagner, & R. DeSalle (Eds.), *PCR assays of variable nucleotide sites for identification of conservation units* (pp. 261–273). Basel, Switzerland: Birkhäuser-Verlag.

Wayne, R. K., Lehman, N., Allard, M. W., & Honeycutt, R. L. (1992). Mitochondrial DNA variability of the gray wolf: Genetic consequences of population decline and habitat fragmentation. *Conservation Biology, 6*, 559–569.

Weidenreich, F. (1946). *Apes, giants, and man.* Chicago: University of Chicago Press.

Wilson, E. O., & Brown, W. L. (1953). The subspecies concept and its taxonomic applications. *Systematic Zoology, 2*, 97–111.

Wright, S. (1943). Isolation by distance. *Genetics, 28*, 114–138.

Wright, S. (1969). *Evolution and the genetics of populations.* Chicago: University of Chicago Press.

The Misuse of Life History Theory: J. P. Rushton and the Pseudoscience of Racial Hierarchy

Joseph L. Graves, Jr.

The year 1994 saw the resurgence of psychometric theories of race and racial hierarchy with the publication of Herrnstein and Murray's *The Bell Curve: Intelligence and Class Structure in American Life*. *The Bell Curve* provided no new analysis of the original psychometrician views on race and intelligence, which can be traced back to Sir Francis Galton's (1869) work in *Hereditary Genius*. The psychometrician program consists of the following elements:

1. General intelligence can be quantified by a single metric known as *g*.
2. Standardized tests can be utilized to measure *g*.
3. *g* is mostly genetically determined.
4. Races differ consistently in their performance on intelligence tests.
5. This difference must in part be due to the genetic differences between races.
6. Races of human being can be unambiguously defined by biological means.

In addition, the program relies on the demographic argument that overreproduction of genetically deficient populations will lead to a decline in intelligence in America (called *dysgenesis*, a la Jensen, 1969). The take-home message of *The Bell Curve* is that environmental interventions such as Head Start programs and affirmative action will not alter social partitioning because innate genetic differences in racial intelligence will always fall in their way.

The Bell Curve does not, however, advance any specific evolutionary genetic rationale for how racial differences in genes related to the intelligence phenotypes they report originate. However, the authors did cite Rushton's analysis of the origin of human racial differences in the *r*- and *K*-selection as consistent with their own conclusions concerning the inferior intelligence of "blacks" (Herrnstein & Murray, 1994, pp. 642–643). The gross errors in the genetic reasoning behind the psychometrician program entailed in *The Bell Curve* have been thoroughly critiqued (e.g., Devlin et al., 1997; Graves & Johnson, 1995; Graves & Place, 1995; Templeton, chap. 2, this volume). Rushton, on the other hand, attempted to outline a specific evolutionary genetic hypothesis that tries to explain the observed differences in intelligence test scores exhibited by so-called human racial groups. Rushton relied on applying the evolutionary life history theory of *r*- and *K*- selection to human populations. This chapter examines the flaws in the general theory and specifically Rushton's application of that same theory to human data. It concludes that Rushton's theory or data could not possibly test any meaningful hypotheses concerning human evolution and the distribution of genetic variation relating to intelligence, however defined.

RUSHTON'S BIOLOGICAL DETERMINISM

It is not well appreciated that Herrnstein and Murray (1994), in *The Bell Curve*, relied heavily on the work of J. Philippe Rushton. Rushton is cited 11 times in the bibliography (it seems that only Lynn [25] and Jensen [24] were cited more often). They write in Appendix 5:

> Rushton argues that the differences in the average intelligence test scores among East Asians, blacks, and whites are not only primarily genetic but part of a complex of racial differences that includes such variables as brain size, genital size, rate of sexual maturation, length of menstrual cycle, frequency of sexual intercourse, gamete production, sexual hormone levels, the tendency to produce dizygotic twins, marital stability, infant mortality, altruism, law abidingness, and mental health.—For each variable, Rushton has concluded, the three races—Mongoloids, Caucasoids, and Negroids—fall in a certain order. (p. 642)

Rushton is a psychologist by training, and a fellow of the Guggenheim, the American Association for the Advancement of Science, and the American, British, and Canadian Psychological Associations. It appears that his "racial" work began sometime around the mid-1980s. Since that time Rushton has published more than 35 papers, predominantly in journals and edited volumes in the discipline of psychology. This work was met with great public skepticism. For example, a group of 19 students asked the Ontario Human Rights Commission to investigate charges of human rights abuses based on the 1981 Human Rights Code (Horowitz, 1995). He has received a fair amount of media attention, having made appearances on the *Geraldo Rivera Show* (NBC) and with Connie Chung (CBS). *Race, Evolution, and Behavior: A Life History Perspective*, is Rushton's (1995) major work on this topic. The paperback edition was released in 1997, and a special abridged edition was mailed free of charge to thousand of academicians in late 1999.

For many, Rushton is seen as a scientifically reputable source supporting the claims of the modern philosophers of race (e.g., DeSouza, Murray, and Levin). On the face of it, *Race, Evolution, and Behavior* presents a seamless argument for evolutionary origins of modern racial differences. Rushton summarized in this work a variety of data from human populations to support his *r*- and *K*-continuum theory of human races. The problem is that in reality Rushton reveals that he has only a rudimentary grasp of modern life history theory and has both incorrectly applied and misrepresented it to the problem of human variation.[1] Rushton is not alone in his amateurish grasp of life history evolution. Life history evolution is not simple; it concerns itself with organismal traits that figure directly in reproduction and survival. The complexity of the discipline results from the fact that organisms have evolved so many ways of dealing with this central problem in their biology. The principal life history traits are listed in Table 3.1. The central cornerstone of life history theory is the necessary existence of trade-offs in life history features. These trade-offs result from the fact that the energy input of all organisms is limited. Thus they must apportion this energy input among competing demands.

More than 130 years in the study of life history evolution has demonstrated that underlying mechanisms of any observed life trade-offs must be rigorously demonstrated, not assumed. It is on this account that Rushton's program purportedly explaining human racial variation fails. In reality it is a case study in how not to investigate evolutionary explanations concerning life history. Ironically, Rushton has attempted to seize the evolutionary and scientific high ground in defending his theories. In an article that can be currently found at the Future Generations web site (www.eugenics.net), Rushton (1998) describes how his theories are being silenced by "the new enemies of evolutionary science." In actuality, the body of modern evolutionary life history theory most vigorously opposes Rushtonism not solely because of his conclusions, but rather due to his blatant distortion of its methods.

The cornerstone of Rushton's work is his attempt to apply one component of density-dependent life history evolution theory, known as *r*- and *K*-selection, to the

---

[1]This became abundantly clear in my panel discussion on March 20, 1997, held at the John Jay College of Criminal Justice, City University of New York. The panel featured Rushton, Todd Disotell (molecular anthropologist, New York University), Walter Stafford (political scientist, New York University), and myself.

TABLE 3.1
Principal Life History Traits and Trade-Offs

Traits	Trade-Offs
Size at birth	Current reproduction and survival
Growth pattern	Current reproduction and future reproduction
Age at maturity	Number, size, and sex of offspring
Size at maturity	
Number, size, and sex ratio of offspring	
Age- and size-specific reproductive investments	
Age- and size-specific mortality schedules	
Length of life	

Note. From Stearns (1992, p. 10).

evolution of human life histories. Rushton characterizes human races along an *r*- and *K*-continuum, with African-derived people (Negroids in his language) the most *r*-selected and Asians (Mongoloids) the most *K*-selected. Caucasians are the intermediate racial group. He presents the view that fundamental genetic trade-offs between reproductive and somatic life history features are the root cause of physiological and behavioral differences between human races. These are used to explain the reported lower intelligence test scores for African-derived populations, along with other social dysfunctions (e.g., criminality). Rushton is not alone in applying *r*- and *K*-selection to describe the so-called greater African criminality. Ellis (1989) utilized the same rationale in his *Theories of Rape* to explain the supposed greater rape potential of African and African-American men as compared to men of other races.

There are grand problems with the application of *r*- and *K*-selection theory to the description of human populations. I shall describe them in detail later. Chief amongst these is Rushton's reliance on *r*- and *K*-selection. This idea was once considered a useful heuristic in evolutionary ecology. However, professional biologists who study life history evolution discarded it by the early 1990s. Indeed, throughout the 1970s and 1980s, multiple experiments failed to corroborate the premises of *r*- and *K*-selection theory. This fact would have been apparent to anyone who maintained any critical attention to progress in evolutionary genetics over this time period. Finally, even if the theory itself were reliable, Rushton and his coworkers have applied it incorrectly to describe the supposed genetic trade-offs they wish to explain. This can be demonstrated by examining the following:

1. The history and formulation of density-dependent selection theory.
2. The critical experiments that falsified the central predictions of r- and K-selection theory.
3. The attempt of Rushton to apply r- and K-theory to human life history evolution.
4. The inadequacy of Rushton's data to test any specific hypothesis concerning the evolution of human life histories.

ORIGINS OF r- AND K-SELECTION

Early Views

Darwin might be considered the originator of the study of life history evolution. For example, he spoke about the evolutionary factors involved in the molding of species life spans in chapter VII of *The Origin of Species* (Darwin, 1859), entitled "Miscellaneous Objections of the Theory of Natural Selection." The book actually deals with many topics throughout that anticipate the mature field of life history evolution. Darwin (1871/1981) also suggested that the evolution of life histories may be involved in the development of the intellectual and moral faculties of human beings:

> Thus the reckless, degraded, and often vicious members of society tend to increase at a quicker rate than the provident and generally virtuous members. Or as Mr. Greg puts the case: 'the careless, unaspiring Irishman multiplies like rabbits: the frugal, foreseeing, self-respecting, ambitious Scott, stern in his morality, spiritual in his faith, sagacious and disciplined in his intelligence, passes his best years in struggle and in celibacy, marries late, and leaves few behind him. Given a land originally populated by a thousand Saxons and a dozen Celts—and in a dozen generations five-sixths of the property, of the power, of the intellect, would belong to the one-sixth of the Saxons that remained. In the eternal 'struggle for existence' it would be the inferior and less favoured race that had prevailed—and prevailed by virtue not of its good qualities and but of its faults.' (p. 326)

Here Darwin outlined the essential argument for how life history evolution might be involved in the formulation of human intellectual and moral faculties. The hidden assumption, presented by Greg in this discussion, was that there must exist some hereditary trade-off between features that contribute to reproductive success and those that contribute to the formation of intellect and morality. Interestingly enough, during the time period in which Greg made this comparison, the demographic conditions in Ireland were exactly the opposite of what he described. The population figures for Ireland actually dropped from 8,175,000 in 1841 to 6,552,000 in 1851, and by 1911 they were only 4,240,000 (Burn, 1951–1952)! The cause of this population decline was an increase in mortality related to starvation brought on from the potato blight and emigration. This is an interesting illustration of the lack of correspondence between perception and historical reality often exhibited in simplistic models of human evolution.

Darwin himself, however, actually doubted that there was a straightforward relation between reproduction rates and the formation of intellect. Further on in this section he remarked that the awakening of Europe from the Dark Ages was problematic for the theory. He pointed out that during the Dark Ages men of "meditation and culture of the mind" had no refuge except in the bosom of the church, which demanded celibacy. In addition, during the same period, the Holy Inquisition selected with extreme care the freest and boldest men to burn or imprison them. Yet, Darwin pointed out, Europe still managed to progress at an unparalleled rate. Darwin (1871/1981) concluded:

> Judging from what we know of man and the lower animals, there has always been sufficient variability in their intellectual and moral faculties, for a steady advance through natural selection. No doubt that such advance demands many favourable concurrent circumstances; but it may well be doubted whether the most favourable would have sufficed, had not the rate of increase been rapid, and the consequential struggle for existence extremely severe. (p. 328)

Finally, he pointed out that even civilized people become indolent and retrograde when the conditions of life are very easy. This discussion can be read to mean that Darwin felt that whereas hereditary variability for intellectual and moral facilities existed within the human species, the expression of this genetic variation was strongly influenced by environmental factors. Darwin also felt that the ability to predict the subsequent intellectual evolution of human populations would be suspect for precisely this reason.

Habitat and Life Histories: Origin of the Verbal Theory

It was Skutch (1949) and Dobzhansky (1950) who first noticed that habitat, lifestyle, and life history may be correlated (Stearns, 1992). Cody (1966) reiterated this theme and Pianka (1970) cited the Dobzhansky paper in the formulation of his ideas concerning r- and K-selection (henceforth to be described as the verbal theory of r- and K-selection; after Graves & Mueller, 1993; Mueller, 1988). Dobzhansky (1950) suggested that in any lineage different life histories are found in tropical and temperate habitats because the tropics are more predictable. This would appear in r- and K-selection theory that stable habitats should be K-selecting (the tropics) and unstable habitats should be r-selected (the temperate zones). We can immediately see that Rushton utilized the theory incorrectly to explain the racial differentiation in human evolution. Rushton suggested that Negroids, who evolved under tropical conditions are r-selected. This prediction is exactly opposite the original theory.

MacArthur and Wilson (1967) presented the basic argument that became known as r- and K-selection (also called density-dependent selection). According to this theory, catastrophic weather in temperate and Arctic regions causes periodic crashes in resident populations with little regard to genotype. Population crashes are then followed by long periods of population increase, during which adaptations that increase exponential growth rate (r), including increased fecundity and early maturity, are selected. In stable tropical environments where populations fluctuate little, populations remain near the limit imposed by resources (K), and adaptations that improve competitive ability and efficiency of resource utilization are selected. The distinction between temperate and tropical patterns popularized the term r- and K-selection in the scientific lexicon (MacArthur & Wilson, 1967; Pianka, 1970). On a closer examination of the regions labeled as temperate and tropical, it is clear that there exists considerable temporal and spatial variation in climatic and biotic variables within them. For example, under contemporary conditions the region known as the tropics contains warm, moist, evergreen forest, tropical monsoon forest, tropical rainforest, savannah, semidesert, desert, and mountain biomes. The temperate zones contain desert, semidesert, temperate grasslands, chaparral, warm, moist, evergreen forest, temperate evergreen, temperate deciduous, mountain zones, taiga, and tundra (Raven & Johnson, 1996). Thus even within zones, there is room for considerable difference in habitat selection parameters.

Pianka (1970) proposed a list of traits associated with the poles of the r- and K-continuum (Table 3.2). No rationale was ever given for the assignment of these traits to either category, hence the use of the term *verbal theory* (Mueller, 1988). One immediate problem with this typology is that in ectotherms (organisms that use environmental energy to regulate their temperature) and to a lesser extent endotherms (organisms that use metabolic energy to regulate their temperature), development time, size at maturity, and fecundity are intercorrelated (Roff, 1992; Stearns, 1992). Pianka (1970) used this scheme to correlate the body length of vertebrates and insects to their generation times.

Bonner (1965) presented a similar set of correlational data and that table is reproduced in Rushton (1995) as evidence for the validity of r- and K-selection. The comparison of vertebrate and invertebrate life history features in this way is meaningless. Differences between taxa as widely separated as this are undoubtedly due to a number of causes. In addition, the statistical validity of this approach is compromised by the fact that these species are not independent observations (Garland & Carter, 1994; Harvey & Pagel, 1991; Leroi, Lauder, & Rose, 1995). That is, they

TABLE 3.2
Specific Traits Historically Associated With the r- and K-Selection Continuum

r-Selected Traits	K-Selected Traits
Rapid development	Slow development
High rate of increase	Low rate of increase
Early reproduction	Delayed reproduction
Small body size	Large body size

share common evolutionary histories, thus their genetic architecture could result from either selection or genetic drift. It is therefore literally impossible to infer a particular adaptive hypothesis by the examination of patterns of life history data alone (e.g., Resnick, 1985). A correct approach requires the genetic analysis of different genotypes or populations within a species. This point has been made both in theory and with experiment (e.g., Garland & Carter, 1994; Lauder, Leroi, & Rose, 1993; Leroi, Rose, & Lauder, 1994, Mueller, 1988; Orzack & Sober, 1994; Reznick, 1985; Roff, 1992; Rose, Graves, & Hutchinson, 1990; Stearns, 1992; Templeton 1983).

In addition to broad assumptions about environmental variability and fluctuations in population size, r- and K-selection theory depends on an implied trade-off between genes favored under conditions of high population growth rate and those favored under conditions of crowding and low resources. During its heyday in the 1970s r- and K-selection theory prompted hundreds of papers. These studies analyzed life history data, attempting to fit them into the pattern predicted by the verbal r- and K-selection theory. However, not a single study demonstrated a correlation between population fluctuation and adaptation, nor was a genetic trade-off between r- selected and K-selected traits ever proven (Ricklefs, 1977; Roff, 1992; Stearns, 1992). In the rush to apply r- and K-selection theory to real organisms, it became evident that several different definitions of r and K were employed by researchers, sometimes even within the same paper. Parry (1981) reviewed hundreds of studies and ascertained that there were four major definitions implied within the literature. The first three definitions suggested a relation between life history parameters and the environment, and the fourth definition merely described a life history parameter. Parry (1981) stated that the problem arose from the incorrect use of the variables r and K as either labels or as implied evolutionary explanations. In addition, he questioned whether there is truly a relation between total reproductive expenditure and the packaging of offspring (e.g., whether high reproductive effort actually necessitates a large progeny number; Parry, 1981). In an excellent study of the impact of K-selection on the frequency of a specific allele (abnormal abdomen in *D. mercatorum*), Templeton and Johnson (1982) showed that K-selected conditions (drought) actually increased the frequency of the abnormal abdomen allele. The abnormal abdomen allele was pleiotropically related to phenotypes that from the classic definition were r-selected. The authors concluded that due to pleiotropy (i.e., when one gene impacts several characters) an understanding of the genetic basis of the traits under selection is absolutely critical for predicting the types of life histories that will evolve under certain ecological conditions. It is precisely our grasp of the genetic basis of human life history that is missing, indicating that Rushton's program is hopelessly untestable, as it is currently formulated.

Theoretical and Experimental Tests of r- and K- life histories

By the late 1980s, r- and K-selection was clearly an antiquated paradigm. Not only were there definitional problems, but problems with the biological significance of this line of reasoning. The use of *r* and *K* as descriptors of population regulation had been confused for their use as mechanisms of selection that acted on individuals (Stearns, 1992). An examination of the best studies claiming to support *r*- and *K*-selection (Law, Bradshaw, & Putwain, 1977; Mc Naughton, 1975; Solbrig & Simpson, 1974) shows there is never a mode of population regulation established, and studies that strive to use *r* and *K* as a method of life history classification show only 50% accuracy in species from which reliable data were collected (Stearns, 1977).

The most powerful evidence dismissing the validity of the *r*- and *K*-selection paradigm has been the experimental work testing its predictions. The mechanisms of *r*- and *K*-selection by definition infer that there are costs incurred in relation to reproduction in high- or low-density conditions. Reznick (1985) outlined the criteria by which we could test any cost of reproduction argument:

1. Phenotypic correlations based on field or laboratory observations of unmanipulated situations.
2. Experiments in which organisms were manipulated to vary the amount of reproductive effort (virgin vs. mated, or manipulations of clutch size in birds).
3. Genetic correlations, obtained by sibling analysis, between reproduction and some component of fitness, such as survival.
4. Genetic correlations, demonstrated by a correlated response to selection either on the age schedule of reproduction or the correlated response of this schedule to selection on a component of fitness.

Reznick argued that because evolution can only proceed if there is genetic variation for the traits in question, only Scenarios 3 and 4 represent a definite proof of the existence of a trade-off of evolutionary significance. It is now necessary to state that Rushton's analysis only represents the evidence that one can obtain from Scenario 1 (this, of course, assumes that his observations are valid). This indicates that Rushton cannot make any definitive statements about the genetic nature of any life history features that he is postulating differ between human races. Worse, examination of phenotypic correlations indicates that they are often misleading with regard to genetic ones (Rose, 1984). For example, Roff (1992) summarized the type of phenotypic correlations that have been observed between reproductive effort and survival using Scenario 1. In unmanipulated field situations he cited 9 studies showing a negative correlation, 4 showing no correlation, and 4 showing a positive correlation. For unmanipulated laboratory situations, he cited 4 showing a negative correlation, 10 showing no correlation, and 4 showing a positive correlation. These data included a broad taxonomic sample, including vertebrates, invertebrates, and plants. This illustrates that phenotypic correlations need not show any particular form of correlation between components of survival and reproduction in any given species, let alone indicate the existence of universal genetic trade-offs as predicted by *r*- and *K*-selection theory.

An early experiment (Mueller & Ayala, 1981) gave some weak support for the type of trade-off predicted by the *r*- and *K*-paradigm. However since then, the number of experiments falsifying the form of the predicted trade-offs have been mounting like an avalanche. These are shown in Table 3.3.

These studies showed a pattern of inconsistent adherence to the predictions of r- and K-selection theory. That is, in each study, some key life history variables would conform with the prediction of the theory and others would not. For example, Taylor and Condra (1980) found that r-selected populations had a shorter egg-to-adult development time, lower preadult viability, and shorter adult life span than K-selected populations. However, contrary to theory, body size, fecundity, time to first oviposition, intrinsic rate of increase, and carrying capacity did not differ between the r- and K-populations. Similarly, Bierbaum et al. (1988) found that there was increased larval-to-adult viability, longer development time at high larval density, and larger body size of K-selected populations supporting the theory. However, there was no difference in longevity and fecundity between the stocks, and the slower development time of r-populations at low densities did not support the theory. These inconsistencies have led several authors to conclude that no simple predictions concerning the nature of life history trade-offs can be made a priori. For example,

TABLE 3.3
Some Experimental Studies Contradicting r- and K-Theory

Author	Year	Organism	Binomial
Snell & King	1977	Rotifer	A. brightwelli
Kerfoot	1977	Cladoceran	B. longirostris
Luckinbill	1979	Protozoa	P. caudatum
Luckinbill	1984	Bacterium	E. coli
Taylor & Condra	1980	Fruit fly	D. pseudoobscura
Templeton & Johnson	1982	Fruit fly	D. mercatorum
Barclay & Gregory	1981, 1982	Fruit fly	D. pseudoobscura
Mueller & Sweet	1986	Fruit fly	D. melanogaster
Mueller	1988	Fruit fly	D. melanogaster
Bierbaum, Mueller, & Ayala	1988	Fruit fly	D. melanogaster
Joshi & Mueller	1989, 1993	Fruit fly	D. melanogaster
Mueller, Guo, & Ayala.	1991	Fruit fly	D. melanogaster
Guo, Mueller, & Ayala	1991	Fruit fly	D. melanogaster
Mueller, Graves, & Rose	1993	Fruit fly	D. melanogaster
Templeton, Hollocher, & Johnson	1993	Fruit fly	D. mercatorum
Hollocher & Templeton	1994	Fruit fly	D. mercatorum

Templeton (1983) wrote that when trade-offs exist, "no general prediction can be made about which aspect of the trade-off will be favored by selection" (pp. 69–70). He further summarized:

> In summary, these results demonstrate that K-selected and r-selected regimes are not equivalent in the evolutionary sense, but neither are they dichotomies favoring mutually exclusive or opposing phenotypic traits. *Not only are the distinctions between r- and K- selection blurred in the light of this model, but they cannot even legitimately be thought of as opposite ends of a continuum.* Differences do exist, but it is impossible to specify a single phenotype that is "optimal" under one and not the other. In both cases, the exact pattern of pleiotropy and the initial conditions play a critical role in determining what is optimal. (p.70, italics added)

It is important to note that Rushton's analysis of life history theory is precisely in opposition to the reasoning of Templeton (1983). That is, Rushton relied on the validity of the *r*- and *K*-"continuum" and what it has to say about the life history features of human races. Mueller (1991) came to similar conclusions:

> The difficulty with this theory is that its very general nature precludes more detailed predictions concerning the evolution of life-history traits. For instance, even though K should increase in populations kept at high densities, it is difficult to predict precisely which life-histories will be most useful for effecting such an increase without a more detailed specification of the organisms' ecology. This does not mean that the general models of density-dependent selection, or any other general model for that matter, are unless, such models allow one to explore a variety of phenomena and determine whether certain lines of intuition are reasonable. In addition, the components of the model which are important for guiding the process of interest may be identified. However, when tests of such theories are made using a specific organism, it must be kept in mind that this specific creature may have attributes that violate key assumptions of the general model. (p. 28)

It could be argued that the limited taxonomic breadth of these studies (mostly invertebrates) is not sufficient reason to discard the theory for mammals. However, we must first understand why organisms like fruit flies, rotifers, cladocerans, and microorganisms were chosen to test hypotheses concerning life history evolution. The key to tests of theories of life history evolution is the ability to distinguish between phenotypic and genetic correlations (Stearns, 1992). Phenotypic trade-offs may exist that are not the result of genetic trade-offs, and phenotypic trade-offs may often be opposite in sign, from the underlying genetic trade-offs (Roff, 1992; Rose, 1984; Stearns, 1992). For example, Graves and Rose (1989) pointed out that much of the confusion concerning the nature of genetic correlations in *Drosophila* experiments results from factors such as gene × environment interaction, inbreeding depression, and confounded selection regimes. Organisms such as *Drosophila* have the advantage of small body size, rapid growth, ease of maintenance of large populations, and well-studied genetics. These are essential qualities for unraveling the problems described by Graves and Rose (1989), which are a prerequisite for the proper experimental investigation of population and quantitative genetic hypotheses. The *Drosophila* populations were exposed to density-dependent selection under controlled environmental conditions with large population sizes. Thus, these experiments represent our best information on the validity of the *r*- and *K*-selection paradigm. Finally, comparative data in Eutherian mammals (Harvey, Read, & Promislow, 1989; Promislow & Harvey, 1990) suggest that the *Drosophila* experiments accurately describe the inability to apply simple life history theories to mammalian diversity.

The final evidence that *r*- and *K*-selection theory has been dismissed as a useful tool to examine life history variation is evident from its declining appearance in the scientific literature. Stearns (1992) pointed out that from 1977 to 1982 there was an average of 42 references per year on *r*- and *K*-selection within the BIOSIS literature search service. From 1984 through 1989 this annual average had dropped to 16, and it continued to decline over time. Both Stearns (1992) and Roff (1992) presented *r*- and *K*-theory as being a once-useful heuristic that no longer serves any purpose in the discussion of life history theory. It is useful to note that their conclusions were arrived at 3 years before Rushton published his analysis of human racial variation, with *r*- and *K*-selection as its cornerstone. It is hard to understand how any serious student of life history evolution could have missed these developments in the theory.

THE PSEUDOSCIENCE OF APPLYING *r*- AND *K*-SELECTION THEORY TO HUMAN RACES

In his book *Race, Evolution, and Behavior: A Life History Perspective*, Rushton (1995) proposed that *r*- and *K*-selection theory accounts for the differences in IQ between the three so-called races of humans (i.e., in Rushton's terminology: Mongoloids/Orientals, Caucasians, and Negroids). As shown in Table 3.1, this theory predicts that species living in constant or predictable environments will be *K*-selected (large body size, delayed reproduction, low fecundity), whereas species living in harsh and/or unpredictable environments will be *r*-selected (small body size, rapid development, high fecundity). These traits are assumed to be genetically based. Rushton presented a modified summary of *r*- and *K*-life history features (see Table 3.4).

Rushton theorized that the survival of early human migrants from Africa, proto- Mongoloids and Caucasians, necessitated an increased cognitive ability to survive the predictable harshness of the colder climate.[2] The additional cognitive ability was achieved through selection for an increase in brain size. In Rushton's (1995) interpretation of r- and K-theory, "The racial differences in intelligence, law abidingness, health, and longevity … seem similarly ordered by r-K theory (p. 214). Rushton further claimed that these trade-offs are genetically based. He predicted that Orientals or Mongoloids (Asians) should be most K-selected (and hence have genetically greater intelligence and the lowest fecundity rates), whereas Negroids (Africans) are most r-selected (and thus should have the lowest intelligence and the greatest fecundity), and Caucasians (Europeans) should be intermediate in these traits. To this end, he reported brain size as the basal factor determining life history traits, including generation time, gestation time, rate of maturity, and body size.

---

[2]It seems that Rushton's thesis for the role of harsh winter climate playing a major role in the evolution of intelligence is an old theme. For example, Huntington (1925) presented an analysis of the role of glaciation in the acquisition of European intelligence in his chapter entitled "Glaciation and the Supremacy of Europe." Here Huntington outlined Rushton's argument:

> The contrast between the action of tropical and non-tropical environments, whether through natural selection or through stimulation of mutations, seems to be one of the most important causes of differences in racial character. It appears to be a biological law that a tropical environment, because of its uniformity, tends to perpetuate primitive, unspecialized forms. Since man split off from the apes his specialization has been in the size, complexity, and functioning of the brain. Other specializations, such as changes of complexion, stature, and hair, have been of minor importance. In equatorial regions the mental type of specialization has apparently been slow, largely because there have been no really great changes throughout man's history, not even during the severest glacial epochs. That, presumably, is one of the chief reasons why it is so difficult to impose upon equatorial people anything more than the outer husk of northern government, northern religion, northern ideals, and northern culture. (p. 50)

Huntington continued to describe the type of characters that natural selection would favor in this new climate:

> This brings us to what I believe to be another highly important step in understanding the evolution of racial character. In Northern Asia, as well as in Northern Europe, the approach of the ice age would cause three things to happen. First, some of the inhabitants, presumably the most adventurous and intelligent, would migrate to southward to milder regions. [Only begging the question, if they were so smart, why did they migrate to an ice sheet to begin with?] Second, a large percentage of the population, though not a large number as we count population, would be exterminated from generation to generation. Third, the remnant which survived would go through a process of regressive selection, whereby the survivors would be those in whom passive qualities of resistance to hunger and discomfort were most highly developed. The nervous, active types who lead the march of human progress would be at a disadvantage compared with those of a more phlegmatic constitution. (pp. 52–53)

Thus Huntington (1925) gave Rushton's entire rationale for the selection of higher intelligence in Europeans and Asians.

TABLE 3.4

From Table 10.1 in "Life History Theory" (Rushton, 1995, p. 203):
Some Life History Differences Between *r*- and *K*-Strategists

r-Strategist	*K*-Strategist
Family characteristics	
Large litter size	Small litter size
Short birth spacing	Long birth spacing
Many offspring	Few offspring
High Infant Mortality	Low infant mortality
Little parental care	Much parental care
Individual characteristics	
Rapid maturation	Slow maturation
Early "sexual" reproduction	Delayed "sexual" reproduction
Short life	Long life
High reproductive effort	Low reproductive effort
High energy utilization	Efficient energy utilization
Low encephalization	High encephalization
Population characteristics	
Opportunistic exploiters	Consistent exploiters
Dispersing colonizers	Stable occupiers
Variable population size	Stable population size
Lax competition	Keen competition
Social system characteristics	
Low social organization	High social organization
Low altruism	High altruism

Note. Modified from Pianka (1970), Wilson (1975), Eisenberg (1981), and Barash (1982).

DISMANTLING RUSHTON'S *r*- AND *K*-THEORY

Dismissal of the Concept of Human Races

The most obvious and serious flaw in Rushton's application of *r*- and *K*-selection to explain the behavioral features of human races is that there are no biologically definable "races" in the human species. This point has been appreciated since Darwin's (1871/1981) *The Descent of Man* and amplified by numerous results from biologists and anthropologists over the last century (for a recent summary see Graves, in press) Numerous authors have summarized why there do not exist any objectively definable races in the human species (Brace, 1995; Brown, 1980; Cann et al., 1987; Cavalli-Sforza, Menozzi, & Piazza, 1994; J. Diamond, 1994; Graves, 1993b; Montagu, 1974; Nei & Livshits, 1989; Templeton, chap. 2, this volume). The term *race* here is defined as a subspecies. A subspecies is considered a locally adapted population that significantly differs in average gene frequencies or chromosomal arrangements or has a distinct evolutionary history from other subspecies-level populations (see Templeton, chap. 2, this volume).

The fact that there is no biological reality to the term race is the most serious blow to Rushton's thesis. For example, given the measurement of the genetic composition of human populations, it is entirely unreasonable to expect that agents of life history evolution have acted in a consistent way to differentiate groups in the way Rushton described. For example, one could just as well search for life history variation along the r- and K-continuum within African populations. After all, they have greater genetic diversity than any of the other populations found in the human species (Cavalli-Sforza et al., 1994), and the African continent contains a wide variety of habitat regimes. There is absolutely no credible intellectual reason to suspect that genetic variation in life history characteristics should not also be distributed in a similar fashion to other human genetic variation. Note that the argument that there are only small genetic differences between human populations does not mean that there need not be phenotypic differences between them. Phenotypes for complex traits are determined by genetics, environment, gene × environment, and the covariance of genes and environment (e.g., Falconer & MacKay, 1996; Graves & Johnson, 1995; Graves & Place, 1995). The problem here is whether any examination of phenotypes alone can reconstruct the nature of the genetic variation responsible for the observed phenotype, or for the nature of the selective regimes which were responsible for the proposed genetic changes. The simple answer is no. Thus any claim to a scientific assignment of genetic determination of complex phenotypes is flawed, and in reality only rests in ideology.

Discussion of Rushton's Use of r- and K-Theory

The second fatal flaw in Rushton's (1995) thinking about the evolution of human life history patterns is that he confused the supposed pattern of phenotypic correlations engendered by a specified pattern of selection (r-characteristics, K-characteristics) with the specific patterns of selection (r-selection, K-selection). For example, in his defense of his theory in the chapter entitled "Challenges and Rejoinders: Is r-K Theory Correct?" he criticized Barash (1982) thusly:

Barash, however, is incorrect. Predictability is the ecological necessity for K-selection. This can occur in either a stable environment or a predictably variable one. What has apparently been misunderstood is that subtropical savannahs, where humans evolved, because of sudden droughts and devastating viral, bacterial, and parasitic diseases, are less predictable for long-lived species than are temperate and especially Arctic environments. Although the Arctic climate varies greatly over one year, it is highly predictable, but harsh, over many years (Rushton & Ankney 1993). (p. 299)

There are many things wrong with this formulation. First, there are no citations from the ecological, life history, population, or environmental literature that support his claim that Arctic environments are more predictable than tropical environments. There is absolutely no reason to believe this assertion. The problem here is that Rushton compared apples to oranges. All environments contain both biotic and physical components (these, of course, interact). To compare the general predictability of an environment (and here I am talking about relative to sources of human mortality or factors that influence fertility) we would need to have accurate information about both the biotic and physical sources of variability for comparison. In this paragraph, Rushton compared biotic sources of mortality (viruses, etc.) to nonbiotic sources in the Arctic. This comparison is made without reference to either. Finally we would have to be able to establish causal relations between these sources of variability and their relation to variations in fitness. None of this is provided in this analysis, and neither are relevant studies of this problem provided. Finally, r- and K-selection never explicitly dealt with environmental predictability. This is more in the domain of "bet-hedging" hypotheses (as described in Stearns, 1992). Bet-hedging theory generally does not yield the same predictions concerning the evolution of life histories as r- and K-selection. Again, Rushton simply had these concepts confused.

In his Table 10.1 of r- and K-life history differences Rushton (1995) gracefully ignored some of the major assumptions intrinsic to r- and K-theory, such as the whole issue of density dependence. If K-selection happens in high-density conditions, it is unlikely to occur in a newly colonized area. He also contended that K-selected species should have a low infant mortality rate, when, in fact, it should be the opposite according to the literature. If Rushton had a scientific reasoning behind this disagreement with the prior literature, he would have provided an explanation, as he did with the assigning of r- and K-labels. The absence of such an explanation seems suspect. One could just as well argue that if K-selected species live near the asymptote of the logistic growth curve and competition is severe, the rates of early mortality are going to be high due to the difficulty of initial establishment. On the contrary, it is r-selected organisms that exist in the ecological vacuum where there is little competition, and early mortality rates should be low. Rushton (1995) also neglected to mention that K-selection should predict large body size in his table of r- and K-correlates. Body size is a critical assumption of r- and K-selection due to its energy allocation implications. He suggested that there is a negative correlation between body size and reproductive allocation, but then contradicted this by his own data and citations (e.g., Hegmann & Dingle, 1982). According to his interpretation of his Table

6.4 (p. 122), large size is negatively correlated with total reproductive allocation. The table shows that, in the U.S. Army, Negroid women have an average height of 163 cm and weight of 62.2 kg and Mongoloid women have an average height of 158.1 cm and weight of 58.6 kg (sample for enlisted, 1,206 and 116, respectively). In his Table 8.1 (p, 166) he then rates Blacks consistently highest and Asians consistently lowest in reproductive potential. His own analysis suggests that because the Negroids are larger than Mongoloids they should have lower reproductive values. These data do not explain the blatant contradiction that his findings purport that Africans have higher reproductive allocations. These are also inconsistent with comparisons of modern birthrates per 1,000 in Africa and Asia. These data show that Mongoloid and Caucasian figures exist that are as high as those exhibited in Africa and higher than those shown by U.S. Blacks (Argawala, 1972; China Financial and Economic Publishing House, 1988; Murdoch, 1980).

Worse still is the fact that Rushton (1995) made his entire argument about the nature of selective forces that lead to racial differentiation in life history features utilizing hypothetical arguments about the nature of the predictability of Pleistocene temperate versus tropical environments. The argument proceeds that the environments that existed in Europe and Asia required greater intelligence to survive than those in the tropics. Hence genotypes with greater intelligence left more progeny than those without. This in turn would lead to directional selection for greater intelligence at the cost of reproductive values. This, of course, is not an r- and K-selection argument in reality. It simply asserts that intelligence is negatively genetically correlated with reproduction. He then went on to test his version of differential r- and K-selection theory in early humans, utilizing data he gathered from modern human populations. Thus, in reality, he is asserting with this method that all features of human life history patterns were fixed in the Pleistocene. This formulation is essentialist (as is the Linnaean conception of race he relied on in this argument). For this procedure to make any sense whatsoever, it is necessary for density-dependent selection regimes facing human racial groups to have remained constant, both temporally and spatially, over the range of years our species has existed (for *Homo erectus* and *sapiens*, about 1 million years). Such a proposition is absolutely ludicrous. In evolutionary terms, if we assumed 30-year generation times (15 years to age of first reproduction and 15 years to raise offspring), we could calculate that more than 33,000 generations have passed since the Pleistocene environments Rushton utilized to found his thesis. What do we know about the long-term evolution of life history features?

In a now classic experiment, Mueller et al. (1993) were able to modify life history features in *Drosophila melanogaster*, utilizing both density-dependent and age-specific selection regimes in a dozen generations. In addition, Service, Hutchinson, and Rose (1988) showed that reverse selection would return populations selected for differential patterns of age-related fecundity back to those of the original stocks (e.g., Rose, 1984) within a dozen generations. The study of Lenski, Rose, Simpson, and Tadler (1991) is the longest one of experimental evolution in existence. This study has examined the response to various clones of the bacterium *E. coli* that have adapted to the use of glucose over 2,000 generations in the laboratory. An extremely powerful feature of this study is the fact that Lenski et al. could directly compare the fitness and genetic variation of the evolved progeny with the original strains preserved in liquid nitrogen. An interesting result is that various adaptations have emerged in these clones, even though they have been kept under the same selective conditions for the course of the experiment (the only source of new genetic information is mutation). Thus there was no a priori means to predict the outcome of adaptation, even if selective conditions remain constant. Of course, one could raise the objection that this result may be limited to bacteria; however Leroi, Chippendale, and Rose (1994) demonstrated similar results in long-term laboratory evolution of a genetic trade-off in *Drosophila melanogaster*. This and other laboratory results with *Drosophila* (Cohan & Hoffman, 1986, 1989) demonstrate that even under conditions of uniform selection populations can diverge genetically.

It is fundamentally clear, however, that human populations have not faced uniform demographic regimes throughout their history as a species (thus different density-dependent selection regimes; e.g., data from Population Reference Bureau). These differences were also manifested spatially, so that patterns even within Africa, Asia, and Europe would not have been uniform at any given point in history. Rushton's analysis also lumped comparisons of intelligence and reproductive potential of several African populations, and African Americans, even though these groups have very different population growth and genetic histories. Not only do these populations have different genetic composition (e.g., African Americans are a hybrid population with about 20% to 30% European and about 10% American Indian admixture), they also have lived in a broad range of environments. In reality, Rushton implicitly accepted the socially constructed rule of genetic hypodescent (the one drop rule) as the basis of a biologically valid racial classification scheme. This is tantamount to saying that the six to eight loci responsible for skin pigmentation are also the repository for all important genetically based life history variation. However, we know that this cannot be true, because skin pigmentation also shows discordant geographic variation (melanic populations exist within the so-called Caucasian, Asian, and Australoid races also). Neither do we have any idea what genetic loci are truly related to any substantial normal genetic variation in life history (or intelligence) in humans. Thus Rushton's project, even if *r*- and *K*-selection theory were valid (and remember it is not), would simply not be testable. The type of information concerning the nature of population densities, life history, and behavioral variables simply does not exist at a sufficient level of detail to test the properly formulated hypothesis. Studies that relate to the early history of world population all agree that insufficient data exist to accurately measure birth and death rate statistics (China Financial & Economic Publishing House, 1988; Cipolla, 1978; Murdoch, 1980; Vinovskis, 1976). Finally in fossil data, genetic and environmental sources of variation are almost impossible to disentangle (Erwin, Valentine, & Sepkokski, 1987; Jablonski & Bottjer, 1990; Wagner, 1996).

For example, one could propose a test of the correspondence between the intelligence scores reported for African Americans in Rushton's (1995) Table 6.8 (p. 136) and selection regimes responsible for life history traits. To do so, we would need information concerning the nature of selection regimes individuals faced during American chattel slavery and Jim Crow (Pleistocene tropical environments would simply be irrelevant). We would also need the same data for the European American, and Asian American comparison groups. Finally, we would also need information concerning the correspondence of the environments that these individuals lived in over this time. For example, we know the age of first menarche in populations of European origin has been declining steadily since 1800. In 1800 the average age of menarche for these samples was about 17.5 years; the value recorded in 1980 was about 13.5 years (Moffet, Moffet, & Schauf, 1993). The most likely explanation of this earlier age of sexual maturity is greater nutrition of modern populations, as fertility in women is strongly tied to body fat percentage. Direct comparisons of phenotypes require that environmental sources of variation contributing to the traits in question be equivalent. We know that this was not so for African American and European American populations (e.g., Bryant & Mohai, 1992; Graves & Johnson, 1995). The data referring to African Americans in this table were collected between 1929 to 1988.

African American populations spent, in the main, about nine generations in slavery and about four generations more under Jim Crow conditions (utilizing 15 years to first reproduction and 15 years to raise offspring, a generation equaling 30 years). This would have been ample time to set life history features, assuming some minimal heritability. From 1790 to 1860, the African American slave population in the United States grew from 657,327 to 3,838,765. Most of this growth was due to reproduction of indigenous slaves, as the immigration of African slaves had been effectively ended in 1808. This rate of population growth is one of the highest observed in the history of world populations to that point $r = .017$); compare this to the average rate of increase for industrialized countries $r = .0050$) and the average rate for nonindustrialized countries in 1825 $r = .0050$; United Nations Department of International Economic Studies, 1987).

Even more illustrative is the variation in the rates of population growth that can be shown from existing records. For example, for England and Wales from 1760 to 1831, this rate was .011 (calculated from data in Rotberg & Rabb, 1986), very similar to the African slave rate in America, but in an area much smaller. Taken alone, the naive observer might suspect that the high r- for African slaves in North America is support for Rushton's views. However, the English data are just as capable of being viewed as a high intrinsic rate of increase. Why are the slave data considered r-selected, whereas the English data are not? In addition, if one examines the variation in intrinsic rates of increase by country for the years 1905 to 1909 and 1950, there is no clear pattern attributable to the race of that country. This is illustrated in the calculations of intrinsic rates of increase by country in Table 3.5.

It is notable that every country listed in the 1905 through 1909 data had a higher intrinsic rate of increase than African Americans. The African American data were

TABLE 3.5
Birth, Death, and Intrinsic Rates of Increase for Selected Countries

Country	Birth	Death	Intrinsic (r)
Years 1905–1909			
Egypt	.0452	.0265	.0187
U.S. (total)	.0300	.0096	.0146
African Americans	—	—	.0100
Mexico	.0460	.0329	.0131
Argentina	.0400	.0201	.0199
Chile	.0446	.0332	.0114
Venezuela	.0436	.0298	.0138
Japan	.0319	.0209	.0110
Denmark	.0284	.0141	.0143
England	.0267	.0151	.0116
Finland	.0310	.0177	.0133
Germany	.0323	.0183	.0140
Netherlands	.0300	.0147	.0153
Norway	.0267	.0141	.0126
Sweden	.0256	.0146	.0110
Russia	.0455	.0294	.0161
Year 1950			
U.S. (total)	.0235	.0096	.0139
African Americans	—	—	.0220
Mexico	.0455	.0162	.0293
Venezuela	.0426	.0109	.0317
China	.0450	.0250	.2000
Japan	.0282	.0109	.0173
Germany	.0162	.0103	.0059
USSR	.0265	.0096	.0169
South Africa (whites)	.0251	.0087	.0164

Note. Data from C. M. Cipolla (1962). *The Economic History of World Population,* pp. 84–85. Harmondsworth, UK: Penguin. Copyright ©1962 by Penguin Books. Used with permission.

estimated from the amount of population increase in those classified as Negroes from the U.S. Census data between 1900 and 1910. At this time there was virtually no immigration of Africans or Caribbeans of African ancestry to the United States, so the assumption that the increase represented birth and death rate processes is well founded. Of course, if significant immigration had occurred it would actually make the calculation of indigenous African American intrinsic (r) even smaller. These data show that all of the Nordic (Denmark, Finland, Germany, Netherlands, Norway, and Sweden) and Asian (Japan) populations (reputed by Rushton to be characterized by large brains and small reproductive investments) had larger intrinsic population increases than African Americans in this period. Even if we attempt to compare the hybrid populations to African Americans (e.g., Egypt, Caucasian–African mixture; Mexico and Venezuela, Asian, Caucasian, and African mixture; and finally Argentina and Chile, Asian–Caucasian mixture) they also show much greater intrinsic population increases than African Americans. An examination of the 1950 data in Table 3.5 shows that in two generations, the African American intrinsic rate of increase had become one of the highest in the world. However, again the data suggest that there is no straightforward racial ordering of these data. Again the "large-brained" Chinese and Japanese are near the top of the intrinsic rates of increase. The Chinese and Japanese data are particularly revealing in comparison to the German and the Russian data. All four of these countries had suffered extensive industrial and agricultural damage in World War II, along with high civilian and military casualties. Yet the Asian countries ranked amongst the highest in population growth in this period, in complete contradiction to Rushton's ordering of human races on the r- and K-continuum.

Clearly, density-dependent selection is not determined by the size of r-alone, but rather occurs as a response of populations to density (relative to the carrying capacity). Because we have no way of determining what the carrying capacity meant for slaves or the English and Welsh (the market value of slaves or the number of jobs in the English economy) we have no way of interpreting these data. In addition, much of slave reproduction was involuntary, as evidenced by the 20% admixture of European genes found in African Americans. Thus, for the most part, slave women were not making behavioral decisions on the size of optimal families. On the other hand, the populations of England and Wales were "free." In addition, African populations, at the same time that African-derived slaves were being forcibly bred, themselves exhibited very low rs (e.g., the value cited previously for nonindustrialized nations).

There are also ancient estimates for the growth of China's population (recorded history in China extends 4,000 years before present). Table 3.6 gives some estimates for the intrinsic rate of increase for the Chinese population in different historical periods.

On the face of these numbers, one might think that Rushton's thesis may be supported. After all, for the vast majority of written Chinese history, the intrinsic rates of increase have been low (never as high as African Americans during the period of slave breeding).

TABLE 3.6
Growth of Chinese Population in Recorded History

2140 BC–771 BC	Xia Dynasty to Western Zhou Dynasty; slave society: $r = .0003$
2140 BC–475 BC	All slave society, characterized by high mortality: $r = .0025$
221 BC–129 AD	Warring states period to Western Han Dynasty: $r = .0019$
752 AD–1840 AD	Tang Dynasty to Qing Dynasty: $r = .0015$
1840 AD–1949 AD	Opium Wars to People's Republic: $r = .0025$
1949 AD–1984 AD	People's Republic: $r = .187$

However, these low intrinsic rates of increase were always due to high death rates amongst the peasantry (China Financial and Economic Publishing House, 1988). Throughout the feudal period, large families were considered beneficial, and these led to the popular Chinese myths (more children means greater fortune; China Financial and Economic Publishing House, 1988). The fact that Chinese fertility patterns were probably always high can be seen by the radical shift in intrinsic increase shown by the social revolution caused by the People's Republic. Finally, modern Asian populations have of some the highest rs reported in human history. East Asia, excluding Japan, showed $r = .017$; South Asia showed $r = .027$ from 1965 to 1985 (Agarwala, 1977), and the Chinese postfeudal value was $r = .187$. These estimates are derived from Asian populations classified by some as Mongoloid or Caucasian populations. The values reported are much higher than those ever exhibited by any African population, and cannot be accounted for by a genetic change in life history features because they occur in only two generations. Murdoch (1980) summarized massive evidence that historical demography is most strongly influenced by what parents perceive is economically rational under various social systems. He demonstrates that under economic conditions such as widespread poverty and large variance in income, large families are favored (across racial or ethnic groups). He also showed that changing these conditions favored small families, and that these changes occur on ecological and not evolutionary time scales. The bottom line is that the demographic and environmental history of human beings is too complicated to submit to the sort of simple-minded life history analysis presented in Rushton's (1995) book.

Misrepresentation of Legitimate Research

Correlation of Body Size, Brain Size, and Life History Variation. In the legitimate research Rushton (1995) did cite, he reinterpreted the findings and often the information to suit his agenda. In an effort to support his race differential r–K selection hypothesis, he displayed a table from Bonner (1965) with size (length) of an organism logarithmically plotted against the generation times of various organisms (Fig.

10.1, p. 201). In the same manner in which he subverted the *r*- and *K*-descriptions into evolutionary mechanisms, he claimed that the increase in body size leads to longer life spans. He extended his argument to say, "Larger bodies lead to lower reproductive capacities ... [and] with fewer offspring comes increased parental care and social organizational skills and a concomitant increase in brain size" (Rushton, 1995, p. 200). This he concluded from one descriptive figure. Nowhere did he cite any empirical evidence or data to support the mechanistic interpretation of the figure. To explicitly measure a macroevolutionary trade-off (e.g., large body–reduction in reproduction) there must be a comparative analysis of variance among independent phylogenetic events (Garland & Carter, 1994; Stearns, 1992). The organisms used are not independent due to the presence of many members of various phyla. Within this chapter, "Life History Theory," his ignorance of the literature or his disregard for scientific integrity becomes even less subtle. Remember that Rushton suggested there is a causal relation between reproductive effort and brain size, quoting Lovejoy (1981): "More brains, fewer eggs, more 'K'" (p. 199). Further on in chapter 10, Rushton stated:

> Brain size, even more than body size, is the key factor, acting as the biological constant determining many variables. These include the upper limit on the size of the group cohesively maintained through time (Dunbar, 1982). It also includes other variables like speed of physical maturation, degree of infant dependency, and maximum recorded life span (Hofman, 1993; pp. 205–206)

It is useful to examine what these authors actually reported concerning the relation among body weight, brain weight, and life history variation. One of the best known allometric relations in physiology is the correlation between body weight and brain weight. That is, an organism with a bigger body weight is likely to also have a bigger brain weight, simply because the neural control of a larger body would be more difficult with the same amount of neural tissue. Thus, the real question is to explain organisms that deviate from a predicted allometric relation for body and brain mass, either above or below. Pagel and Harvey (1988) examined 117 species for brain and body weight and calculated an allometric increase of 0.22 in brain weight relative to body weight. The allometric calculations for the relation of body weight to brain weight differed depending on the taxonomic levels utilized in the analysis. They also showed that controlling for factors such as differential diets between taxonomic groups removed that effect. Read and Harvey (1989) examined the relation between brain weight and life history variation in mammals (a central component of Rushton's thesis). They demonstrated that once the effect of body weights was controlled for, there was no significant relation between life history variation (gestation, age at weaning, period of maternal investment, period as independent juvenile, age at maturity, interlitter interval, maximum recorded life span, maximum reproductive life span, number of offspring per litter, annual fecundity, neonatal weight, litter weight, annual biomass production) and brain weight. The authors concluded:

Elsewhere (Harvey and Read, 1988), we have criticized the analyses used as evidence in support of hypotheses postulating a role for brain weight in the determination of life history variation. We add another criticism to those already catalogued: life history variation that exists among orders is not associated with either adult brain weight or litter brain weight independently of body weight effects. Thus brain weight has no greater power to explain life history variation than has weight. *We know of no good reasons for considering litter brain weight or adult brain weight to have a causal role in the determination of life history variation among orders of mammals.* (pp. 342–343)

Rushton also reported that Smith (1989) correlated the timing of primate tooth eruption with life history data from Harvey and Clutton-Brock (1985). She found the life history parameters of body weight, length of gestation, age of weaning, birth interval, sexual maturity, and life span and brain size correlated with tooth eruption .89, .85, .93, .82, .86, .85, and .98, respectively. He then stated that "brain size [is] acting as the biological constant determining factors" (Rushton, 1995, p. 205). For any statistician or scientist to explicitly state that a correlation implies causation, no matter how high the correlation may be, is a blatant sham. He did not even entertain an obvious alternate hypothesis that high correlation may be confounded by age. If brain size increases with age, it is an insignificant correlation that early tooth eruption is correlated with small brains and late eruption is correlated with large brain size. However, it is nontrivial to interpret that brain size is the determining factor in the timing of tooth eruption.

Perhaps the most disturbing of the examples is a clear exaggeration of the conclusions of Taylor and Condra (1980). Rushton used the results of their study as strong support for r- and K-selection. Although he did mention the contrary results, it was done in a quick dismissive manner that gave a clear impression the study supports r- and K-selection. However, the most important contribution that this study made to the r- and K-literature was the contrary results. There were no differences in the parameters in which r- and K-selection makes specific predictions. The authors stated:

> The main predictions of this theory were weakly met.... There were, however, no differences for several traits about which the theory is quite explicit; these include the intrinsic rate of increase, carrying capacity, body size, fecundity, and timing of reproduction (semelparity-iteroparity).[3] (p. 1192)

To downplay this strong statement by the authors is clearly an attempt to mislead. In addition, Rushton (1995) cited a classic experiment by Hegmann and Dingle (1982) concerning the phenotypic and genetic correlations among life histories features in the milkweed bug (*Oncopeltus fasciatus*) as part of his support for the validity of r- and K-selection regimes. First this study was never designed to examine r- and K-selection mechanisms. In addition, the results are inconsistent with the verbal theory of r- and

---

[3]Semelparity and iteroparity refer to singular versus repeated episodes of reproduction.

K-selection as stated by Pianka and utilized by Rushton. Hegmann and Dingle (1982) showed that body length (which is equivalent to body size in these insects) is positively correlated with clutch size and hatchability (Table 10.3, p. 183; phenotypic clutch size, .10, .15, and .09, and for hatchability, .05, .06, and .04; the genetic correlations are even higher, clutch size: .91, 1.2 [The methods used to estimate genetic correlations often return values greater than 1.0; and any number greater than 1.0 is taken to be equivalent to 1.0.], and .69; hatchability: .77, .50, .27). Clutch size and percentage of eggs hatching would determine the value of intrinsic increase (*r*) for this species, the larger the clutch and the greater hatching, the higher rate of increase (*r*). In addition this table shows that clutch size and percentage hatchability are also positively correlated in this insect. Remember, however, that the verbal theory of *r*- and *K*-selection would predict a negative correlation between body size and intrinsic increase (*r*) and between size of clutch and hatchability (see Table 3.1). Once again, Rushton either misrepresented or falsified his report of the significance of Hegmann and Dingle (1982).

Statistical Misinterpretations

Rushton (1995) presented a large amount of data that he suggested demonstrates the *r*-selected character of Negroids. It is not possible in the space allotted here to examine all of his arguments. However, I present some problems with his interpretations of some of the major points he made in this work. The problems are illustrative of his general treatment of the problem of life history evolution and race.

IQ and Brain Size.   In humans the brain is large relative to body size. Gross correlations of the body size to brain size allometry seem to predict the relative behavioral difference at the species level well. However, there is no direct evidence that such data accurately reflect anything within species. One of the fundamentally unresolved questions in research concerning early hominid evolution is how much brain size is necessary to control how much intelligent behavior. We know that large areas of the human brain can be destroyed without altering human behavior in any way. Thus, there seem to be many reserve neurons in the human brain that we can normally do without. We know nothing for certain about how selective pressures in early hominids might have led to increasing brain capacity. We also know nothing for certain about the significance of individual neural capacity and its relation to intelligence (e.g., classic discussion on natural selection and the mental capacity of mankind; Dobzhansky & Montagu, 1947; Purves, 1994). Even if we were willing to accept the validity of standardized testing as a means for assessing innate cognitive ability (and remember, I do not!), there has never been a scientifically acceptable study that supports the hypothesis that intelligence (i.e., IQ scores) is dependent on brain size (Gould, 1996; Montague, 1974; Tobias, 1970). Even allowing Rushton's assertion that there is a different allometry between races, this would imply that on average within any race people with larger heads have greater cognitive abilities, and therefore score higher on IQ tests. Taken a step farther, this analysis suggests that within races, the average-sized man is endowed with greater innate cognitive ability than women simply due to sexual dimorphism in size. Rushton cited and dismissed Tobias (1970) concerning the inadequacy of studies of brain anatomy and measures of intelligence. A more objective analysis of this study shows that such a flippant dismissal is unwarranted. Tobias first reviewed the racist history of brain measures and intelligence. Throughout this study he pointed to inconsistencies of the racial data concerning cranial volume, body weight, height, brain weight, calculations of excess neurons, and so on. Table 3.7 gives Tobias's calculation of the number of excess neurons in various human groups normalized by body size.

These results are inconsistent with Rushton's views of intelligence and race (American Negroes > American Whites, French, and English). Again these calculations are not cited by Rushton, even though he cited figures that are consistent with his analysis in chapter 6. Tobias (1970) also cited a number of environmental conditions that affect brain size that could not have been controlled in all the previous studies of brain size (nutritional state, disease condition, environmental stimuli, occupational group, etc.). Finally, he also discussed a number of artifacts of preparation of brain samples for analysis that are not easily dismissed (cause of death, lapse of time after death, treatment of brain after death, anatomical level of severance, presence or absence of meninges, presence or absence of blood vessels). He concluded that all existing studies of brain size and intelligence were meaningless due to the abundance of these errors in procedure and interpretation.

The statistics Rushton used throughout to support his argument for brain size and intelligence support all of Tobias's criticisms. For example, his Table 2.2 (Rushton, 1995, pp. 38–39) reports the Pearson's correlation coefficients (a statistic symbolized as r,) of 32 studies relating standardized test scores to estimates of brain size. Part A of the table relates external measures of head measurement to tests of supposed "intelligence" or IQ for children. Part B is the same relation for adults, and Part C is the use of magnetic resonance imaging (MAI) to estimate the size of the brain in vivo and

TABLE 3.7
Excess Neurons in Various Populations

Group	Excess Neurons (in Millions)
Kenya Negro	8,400
American White	8,500
French	8,600
English	8,600
American Negro	8,700
Japanese	8,900
Korean	8,900
Swedish	8,900

correlate to various IQ metrics. In Part A, the mean correlation coefficient reported is .23 (a weak correlation, with studies). In reality this analysis is even weaker than it looks. If one examines the way these studies were constructed, only two of these studies can be considered legitimate. Only Osborne (1992) which examined a reasonable sample of white girls and boys and black girls and boys controlled for age, height, and weight in the analysis. The correlation coefficients reported for these are .29 and .28, respectively. These were higher than the average Rushton cited, but the interpretation of these studies is compromised by the small sample size and the fact that both were carried out by the same researcher. The values reported for the external measurements of the adults in Part B are even worse $r = .15$). These studies are actually useless in that none are controlled for differences in height and weight.

The only data in this table that are at all suggestive are the MRI data on IQ test scores, with a mean of $r = .39$. The reason MRI should be a more accurate analysis of brain size is that it provides an in vivo picture of the brain (free from the artifacts described earlier). However, again, three of the four studies do not control for height and weight differences, although the one remaining study that did control for height and weight, reported $r = .35$ for a sample of 40 European American males and females. Again, it must be cautioned that this was one study.

The MRI data more accurately reflect brain size, which could have some rational mechanistic relation to cognitive function in a way that head size would not . Tobias (1970) summarized data suggesting that epigenetic events strongly influence the anatomy of the brain in mammals. Poliakova (1960) showed that different geographic races of the field mouse had different brain weights (agile, climbing red field mouse > sluggish grey field mouse). Herre (1958) showed that domestication of dogs, pigs, rabbits, rats, guinea pigs, cats, and ducks caused a 20% to 30% loss in brain weight. M. C. Diamond (1988) summarized a series of eloquent experiments utilizing genetically identical strains of rats. The rats were raised in control groups that received the normal amount of environmental stimulation, toys, and access to littermates and parents. The experimental group received subnormal exposure to environmental stimuli. The experimental and control groups were subjected to measures of rat cognitive and emotional function. The controls functioned well within the range reported for this genetic strain, however the experimental group illustrated subnormal cognitive function. The rats were sacrificed and the anatomy of the cerebral cortex was examined (this is a well-established procedure for rats; e.g., Purves, 1994). M. C. Diamond found that the environmentally stimulated rats had a more well-developed cortex. The number of cells was the same (remember these were genetically identical stocks), but the volume of cells and the number of dentritic connections between cells was markedly greater in the stimulated rats. M. C. Diamond also showed that these results were reversible; that is, rats from the unstimulated environment could be rescued by giving them the same experimental treatments as the controls, if this occurred at an early enough age. This work, along with a huge volume of research summarized in Purves (1994), strongly suggests the notion that architecture of mammalian brains is strongly influenced by epigenetic factors in development, and even into adulthood. Thus it is entirely possible that brain mass may have some relation to cognitive performance. However, one must take a statement like this with extreme caution (as the psychometricians do not). It is one thing to suggest that differences in brain mass may influence some aspects of cognitive performance, it is another to suggest that any observed differences in this trait result from solely genetic factors. It is even a greater leap to then claim that differences in reported cognitive performances between human subpopulations result from such a purported mechanism. The work concerning the neural basis of human intellect is in its infancy.

Rushton (1995) demonstrated exactly how this type of analysis should not proceed in his Table 2.3 (p. 40). He reported data on head circumference at different ages correlated to IQ score for "whites" and "blacks." The values in this table have been transformed and thus do not correspond to the values reported in the original study (Tables 6.10, 9.28, 9.34, 9.41, and 9.54; pp. 220, 104, 226, 233, and 161 respectively in Broman, Nichols, Shaughnessy, & Kennedy, 1987.) Rushton did not describe in this table or in the text how he performed the transformation. Table 3.8 shows Rushton's figures compared to the actual values for normal IQ children reported by Broman et al. 1987).

The data in his Table 2.3 are the result of lumping all of the IQ cognitive classes for each race reported in the original study (J. P. Rushton, personal communication). The children in this study were assigned to the following cognitive classes: severely retarded, mildly retarded, borderline, average, and above average. The figures in his Table 2.3 were calculated from tables 6.10, 9.28, 9.34, 9.41, and 9.54; pp. 104, 220, 226, 233, and 161 respectively in Broman, Nichols, Shaughnessy, & Kennedy, 1987. While on the surface, lumping all the children by socially identified race may seem reasonable, it is an error in statistical reasoning that favors his thesis of the greater head size of "whites." He arrived at figures shown in Table 3.8 by using a weighted average for all of the cognitive classes at each of the age groups shown. An examination of the original data shows that for each of the age groups the "blacks" in the study had 2–3 times more children assigned to the severely retarded, mildly retarded, and borderline groups. For example, these figures at birth were for whites: 26, 167, and 2,331; and for blacks: 58, 825, and 8,079 respectively.

TABLE 3.8

Comparison of Rushton's Reported Figures and the Published Values in Broman et al. (1987)

| | Rushton (1995) Table 2.3 | | Broman et al. (1987) | |
	Whites	Blacks	Whites	Blacks
Birth	34.0 +/– 1.5	33.4 +/– 1.7	Same	33.5 +/– 1.6
4 months	40.9 +/– 1.4	40.4 +/– 1.6	Same	40.6 +/– 1.5
1 year	45.8 +/– 1.5	45.6 +/– 1.5	Same	45.8 +/– 1.5
4 year	50.1 +/– 1.5	49.9 +/– 1.6	Same	50.1 +/– 1.6
7 year	51.5 +/– 1.5	51.2 +/– 1.6	Same	51.4 +/– 1.6

Thus, the weighted means of the white sample were equivalent to the means of the average cognitive group, but the weighted mean of the black group became less than the mean of the average cognitive group for each age category. It is not an appropriate statistical operation to calculate a weighted mean from groups that have not been drawn from the same population (Zar, Biostatical Analysis, 4th ed., 1999, p. 130). Therefore it makes no sense to lump the categories of children classified as severely retarded, mildly retarded, borderline retarded, normal, and above average into the same group. Finally, the equating of head size alone to intelligence is compromised when no analysis is presented of the relationship of head to body size in the two populations in question. Interestingly enough, Broman et al. (1987) did report data that suggested that the body sizes of the "black" and "white" children in this study were not equivalent. Rushton did not mention this in his discussion of the study. For example, when head size is normalized by body weight in the data for 4-month-old children, the black head circumference/body weight ratio is actually larger than that for white children in all the cognitive classes (head circumference Table 6.10, p. 104; body weight, p. 109; black ratio 7.03, 7.01, 6.672, 6.50, 6.25 and white ratio 6.86, 6.66, 6.51, 6.33, 6.23 respectively.) A similar pattern emerges when we examine body size data from the other age groups reported in this study. Thus, the head circumference data reported in Rushton's Table 2.3 are misleading, particularly if they don't take into account body size differences.

Finally, Broman et al. (1987) is an exhaustive study of biological, social, and cultural variables associated with mental retardation. These variables include socioeconomic variables, such as housing density, prenatal socioeconomic conditions, maternal occupations, mother's marital status, education, and pregnancy intervals; and some biological variables such as age of mother, and disease conditions. Rushton did not report the fact that many of these variables had much higher correlations (r values) with IQ than with head circumference (Table 3.9). These include: prenatal socioeconomic status (SES), .41 and .26; maternal occupation, .32 and .18; maternal education, .43 and .24; 7-year SES

TABLE 3.9

Head Circumference of Above-Average IQ Groups From Broman et al. (1987)

	Rushton (1995) Table 2.3		Broman et al. (1987)	
	Whites	**Blacks**	**Whites**	**Blacks**
Birth	nr	nr	34.2 +/− 1.4	34.0 +/− 1.6
4 months	nr	nr	41.3 +/− 1.4	41.2 +/− 1.6
1 year	nr	nr	46.3 +/− 1.4	46.2 +/− 1.3
4 years	nr	nr	50.7+/− 1.5	50.8+/− 1.4
7 years	nr	nr	52.1 +/− 1.4	52.1 +/− 1.6

Note. Data are extracted from Tables 6.10, 9.28, 9.34, 9.41, and 9.54; pp. 220, 104, 226, 233, and 161, respectively, in Broman et al. (1987).

index, .43 and .24 (Tables 9.16, 9.19, 9.25, 9.46, pp. 207, 210, 216, and 238 for whites and blacks respectively). Again, interestingly enough, the life history variables that were included in this study generally showed weak correlations with IQ in both groups: pregnancy-free interval, .04 and .10; maternal age, .01 and .06 (Tables 9.25, 9.46). Again, these data would indicate that there are strong gene × environment and covariances of gene-environment effects influencing these correlations (e.g., discussion in Graves & Johnson, 1995). Furthermore it can be effectively argued that we have never seen genetically based, "racial" differences in any phenotypic categories in America. In reality, we have been witnessing how physical differences in the environments of the socially constructed races influence genetic predispositions for general health. In fact, these influences are large, historic, and complex in their effect. For example, 10.7% of toxic waste sites within 1 mile of public housing are 50–75% minority occupancy, and 53% of toxic waste sites within 1 mile of public housing are > 75% minority occupancy, and these communities often have elementary schools located by hazardous waste dumps (Graves, 2001.) If members of one "race" have been historically poorer than another, then they would have seen greater exposure to a number of environmental toxins and other sources of biotic stress. It is now known that social status influences predisposition to substance abuse (Morgan et al., 2002.) Substance abuse influences normal development: for example, offspring of alcoholic mothers show fluctuating asymmetry (FA) in their teeth, and FA has been linked to lower performance on IQ tests in college students (Shackelford and Larsen 1997). Finally, a study of breast cancer risk in women from New York City found that organochloride toxins were highest in minority women: DDE levels were highest in African Americans and Hispanics; DDT was highest amongst Hispanics; HPCB's were highest in African Americans; and trans-nonachlor was highest in African Americans (Wolff, et al. 2000). If any of these women were pregnant, these mutagens could affect the development of their children, and they would be concentrated by breast-feeding during their children's infancy. The differences in environmental conditions between Euro-Americans and racial minorities have been so large, it is amazing that anyone ever advanced genetic arguments to describe the physical disparities between them! The questionable analysis of the data from the Broman et al., 1987 study and the selective discussion of its context raise questions about both the validity and interpretation of any of the topics discussed in Rushton's book.

Another clearly questionable technique of which Rushton (1995) was fond is the inclusion of tables based on ranking the various races in personality traits without any mention of how data were collected. Some of the tables report results as high, medium, and low, whereas others are ranked numerically (e.g., Table 8.1, p. 166). In the numerical ranks he even reported that some of the results were significant to $p < 0.05$ without mentioning how such data were analyzed. In much of the numerical data he reported there is no sample size or measure of variance to accompany the data.

Hormonal Values. Rushton's treatment of hormonal values and their relation to reproductive behavior and aggression is also problematic. Citing studies like Ellis and Nyborg (1992) he claimed that black males have higher levels of circulating androgens, and that this makes them more sexually aggressive, violent, and lawless. These androgen differences are again related to the overarching theme of differential r- and K-selection.

The proper interpretation of Ellis and Nyborg (1992) is not straightforward. First, the study examined men that had been discharged from the U.S. Army between 1965 and 1971. The sample size was 3,654 non-Hispanic (whites), 525 blacks, 268 Hispanics, 24 Asian/Pacific Islanders, and 49 native Americans. The hormonal assays were obtained from men at about 38 years old. The raw data reported geometric means for the groups in this order: Asian/Pacific Islander 689 ng/dl > Black 658 ng/dl > White 637 ng/dl > Hispanic 633 ng/dl > Native American 631 ng/dl. These data are adjusted for the age differentials of the samples (testosterone levels are negatively correlated with age) and the rankings remain the same. However, when the samples are adjusted for both age and weight differentials of the groups, the order changes to Black 659 ng/dl > Asian Pacific Islander 647 ng/dl > Native American 645 ng/dl > White 637 ng/dl > Hispanic 623 ng/dl. Ellis and Nyborg (1992) provided no rationale in the work for the specific age and weight relations used to account for the final figures. They simply stated that testosterone levels are negatively associated with weight and provided no allometric equation that could be used to follow their calculations of the new figures. This is problematic. The specific assumptions one uses to calculate these values not only are important in the calculation but also in its biological interpretation. For example, if androgen level secretions were generally constant across weight, and body weight somehow provided a dilution factor, then androgen levels would be negatively correlated with weight. Thus, biologically, men with smaller body weights would in reality be facing higher functional concentrations of androgen. This means that for the purposes of Ellis and Nyborg (1992) and Rushton (1995) the uncorrected figures are the most relevant. These uncorrected figures are, of course, not consistent with their racial r- and K-continuum.

Even with the "corrected" figures we find that, although black men were highest in their study, Asian men were in between them and whites. Even if such data were interpretable in a genetic context, this result is also in opposition with Rushton's continuum. Nor does Rushton's androgen hypothesis of criminality and reproduction do well with the Hispanic figures of Ellis and Nyborg (1992). The two most rapidly growing groups in both reproductive and crime rates in the United States are African Americans and Hispanics (the characteristics of individuals currently in the criminal justice system can be obtained from http://www.ojp.usdoj.gov). Many scholars have argued that the increase of Hispanics and African Americans in the criminal justice system is due to ongoing discrimination, particularly resulting from the "war on drugs." Despite that however, the androgen studies in this sample have Hispanic men lowest in the "corrected" data, again demonstrating a violation of the predictions of the r- and K-continuum and of the androgen level–criminality hypothesis.

Finally, Rushton's assertions about the function of the human endocrine system in this argument are entirely fallacious. It is well known that testosterone levels influence sex drive in male primates, but this influence is markedly modified by learning (Jones, 1991). In experiments in which additional testosterone was given to males, their sex drive did not increase above normal levels, and testosterone levels are strongly influenced by daily and seasonal rhythms (Jones, 1991). Bronson (1995) reviewed extensive literature that shows strong environmental determination of female hormones also. In addition, transient aggression also influences testosterone titers in human males; such things as tennis matches, stress, collegiate exams, army basic training, and so on can decrease titers (Kreuz, Rose, & Jennings, 1972; Mazur & Lamb, 1980; Morberg, 1985; Nelson 1995). In general, studies that used psychological rating scales to quantify levels of aggression and hostility found no relation to androgen levels in human males (Doering et al., 1975; Monti, Brown, & Corriveau, 1977; Persky et al., 1977). Thus, unless all the participants in these testosterone measurements had been kept under the same environments and had displayed the same psychological responses to them, such studies are literally meaningless.

Rushton's analysis of the sex hormone data is crucial to his attempt to claim that r-selected people, Africans, are predisposed to criminality. He characterized these particularly victimizing crimes as the opposite of "altruism" (a K-selected trait). He reprised Ellis's (1987) argument, saying that "across societies, blacks had higher rates of victimizing crime rates than whites, and in turn, whites had higher rates that Orientals" (Rushton, 1995, p. 215). Ellis concluded that the same underlying neurohormonal mechanisms that regulate the racial difference in reproductive strategies are mediating the difference in crime rate also. This assertion ignores the historical and present racism of the U.S. criminal justice system. His theory has a severe problem explaining the Japanese rape and enslavement of Korean women during World War II, the very high rate of Chinese opium addiction following the Opium Wars, and the European perpetration of kidnap, confinement, rape, and murder of Africans during U.S. slavery. The general problem here is attempting to ascribe a genetic basis to a behavior (criminality or law abidingness) that is socially defined (and hence plastic).

CONCLUDING REMARKS

Rushton's view of human evolution suffers from the use of antiquated and simplistic theoretical models concerning life history evolution. In addition his methods of data analysis, results, and data sources call into question the legitimacy of his research. Within the book, Rushton (1995) claimed "to have reviewed the international litera-ture on race differences, gathered novel data and found a distinct pattern" (p. xiii). This is fallacious on many accounts. The scope of the literature is international, to an extent; the data are hardly novel; and the pattern he "found" is hardly distinct from common racist stereotypes. The technical reasons for his failure are once again:

1. That Rushton failed to grasp the history and formulation of density-depend-ent selection theory.
2. That Rushton failed to review the critical experiments that falsified the cen-tral predictions of r- and K-selection theory.
3. That Rushton incorrectly applied r- and K-theory to explain human life his-tory evolution.
4. That Rushton's data are woefully inadequate to test any specific hypothesis concerning the evolution of human life histories.

Having grasped the relatively elementary nature of Rushton's technical failings, it is now proper to ask if there is a larger ideological predisposition that drives his research agenda. Rushton sees himself in the tradition of the London school of psychometry founded by Sir Francis Galton (Rushton, 1995). He and his colleagues, Lynn, Jensen, Herrnstein, and others, were all proud of their association with this "intellectual" tradition. Galton took it without any kind of scientific proof whatsoever that Negroids were intellectually inferior to other races. He even went so far in *Hereditary Genius* (Galton, 1869) to rank the intelligence of various breeds of dogs higher than that of some Englishmen and most Africans. Galton's tradition is also that of Gobineau, Davenport, Laughlin, and other eugenicists who thought that U.S. democracy could not withstand the untrammeled reproduction of the genetically unworthy types (Chase, 1977). I have discussed the allegiance of Herrnstein and Murray to this pseudoscientific tradition elsewhere (Graves & Johnson, 1995; Graves & Place 1995). Rushton's work on race and life history fits well within the racist political agenda that now seeks to reverse the democratic gains made by African Americans, Hispanics, and Native Americans over the last half-century. The new philosophers of race attempt to disguise their assault behind objective scholarship and race neutrality (Ladd, 1997, p. 212). To this end, they rely heavily on work like that of Rushton (1995). What I hope I have accomplished here is, at least, the dismissal of this work as reasoned objective science. Unfortunately, the history of the philosophy of race in the United States has shown that adherence to scientific methodology was not required when one reified the inferiority of blacks to the U.S. public. One can observe the use of Rushton's work to influence popular opinion by visiting www.duke.org, the web site of the former Louisiana Klansman David Duke. The use of pseudoscientific justifications for racist policy will probably continue for some time. As long as it does there will be reason to write chapters such as this. If this piece has changed the mind of at least one person that might have otherwise thought Rushton's work was scientifically validated, then it has served its purpose.

ACKNOWLEDGMENTS

The ideas for this chapter were strongly influenced by a presentation on Rushton's use of life history theory at the 1996 meeting of the American Association for the Advancement of Science by Dr. Paul Turner, Department of Ecology and Evolution, University of Maryland; Charles Richardson, graduate student, Department of Biology, Indiana University; and myself. Margaret Hayes aided in providing library references for this chapter. A. R. Templeton gave many helpful comments on an earlier draft. I would like to dedicate this chapter to the memory of my brother, Dr. Warren A. Graves, MD (December 14, 1957–March 8, 1998).

REFERENCES

Agarwala, S. N. (1977). *India's population problems* (2nd ed.). New Delhi: Tata McGraw-Hill.

Barash, D. P. (1982). *Sociobiology and behavior* (2nd ed.). New York: Elsevier.

Barclay, H. J., & Gregory, P. T. (1981). An experimental test of models predicting life history characteristics. *American Naturalist, 117,* 944–961.

Bierbaum, T. J., Mueller, L. S., & Ayala, F. J. (1988). Density-dependent evolution of life history traits in *Drosophila melanogaster. Evolution, 43*(2), 382–392.

Bonner, J. T. (1965). *Size and cycle.* Princeton, NJ: Princeton University Press.

Brace, C. L. (1995). Region does not mean "race": Reality versus convention in forensic anthropology. *Journal of Forensic Sciences, 40*(2), 29–33.

Broman, S. H., Nichols, P. L., Shaughneessy, P., & Kennedy, W. (1987). *Retardation in young children.* Hillsdale, NJ: Lawrence Erlbaum Associates.

Bronson, F. H. (1995). Seasonal variation in human reproduction: Environmental factors. *Quarterly Review of Biology, 70*(2), 141–164.

Brown, W. M. (1980). *Polymorphism in mitochondrial DNA of humans as revealed by restriction endonuclease analysis.* Proceedings of the National Academy of Sciences USA, *77*(6), 3605–3609.

Bryant, B., & Mohai, P. (Eds.). (1992). *Race and the incidence of environmental hazards: A time for discourse.* Boulder, CO: Westview.

Burn, W. L. (1951–1952) The population of Ireland, 1750–1845. *Economic History Review, Second Series, IV,* 256–257.

Cann, R. L., Brown, W. M., & Wilson, A. C. (1987). Mitochondrial DNA and human evolution. *Nature, 325,* 31–36.

Cavalli-Sfroza, L., Menozzi, M. & Piazza, A. (1994). *The history and geography of human genes.* Princeton, NJ: Princeton University Press.

Chase, A. (1977). *The legacy of malthus: The social costs of the new scientific racism.* New York: Knopf.

China Financial and Economic Publishing House. (1988). *New China's population.* New York: Macmillan.

Cipolla, C. M. (1962). *The economic history of world population.* Harmondsworth, UK: Penguin.

Cipolla, C. M. (1978). *Economic history of world population* (7th ed.). Sussex, UK: Harvestor.

Cody, M. L. (1966). A general theory of clutch size. *Evolution, 20,* 174–184.

Cohan, M. C., & Hoffman, A. A. (1986). Genetic divergence under uniform selection: II. Different responses to selection for knockdown resistance to ethanol among *Drosophila* species. *Genetics, 114,* 145–163.

Cohan, M. C., & Hoffman, A. A. (1989). Uniform selection as a diversifying force in evolution: Evidence from *Drosophila. American Naturalist, 134*(4), 611–637.

Darwin, C. (1859). *On the origin of species by means of natural selection or the preservation of favoured races in the struggle for life.* London: Encyclopedia Britannica.

Darwin, C. (1871). *The descent of man and selection in relation to sex.* Princeton, NJ: Princeton University Press. (Original work published 1871)

Devlin, B., Fienberg, S. E., Resnick, D. P., & Roeder, K. (1997). *Intelligence, genes, and success: Scientists respond to the bell curve.* New York: Springer.

Diamond, J. (1994). Races without color. *Discover, 15*(11), 82–91.

Diamond, M. C. (1988). *Enriching heredity: The impact of the environment on the anatomy of the brain.* New York: The Free Press.

Dobzhansky, T. (1950). Evolution in the tropics. *American Scientist, 38,* 209–231.

Dobzhansky, T., & Montagu, A. (1947). Natural selection and the mental capacities of mankind. *Science, 105,* 587–590.

Doering, C. H., Brodie, H., Kramer, H., Moos, R., Becker, H., & Hamburg, D. A. (1975). Negative affect of plasma testosterone: A longitudinal human study. *Psychosomatic Medicine, 37,* 484–491.

Eisenberg, J. F. (1981). *The mammalian radiations.* Chicago: University of Chicago Press.

Ellis, L. (1987). Criminal behavior and r- and K- selection: An extension of gene-based evolutionary theory. *Deviant Behavior, 8,* 149–176.

Ellis, L. (1989). *Theories of rape.* New York: Hemisphere.

Ellis, L., & Nyborg, H. (1992). Racial/ethnic variations in male testosterone levels: A possible predictor of group differences in health. *Steroids, 57,* 72–75.

Erwin, D., Valentine, J. W., & Sepkokski, J. J. (1987). A comparative study of diversification events: The paleozoic versus the mesozoic. *Evolution 41,* 1177–1186.

Falconer, D. S., & MacKay, T. (1996). *Introduction to quantitative genetics* (4th ed.). London: Longman.

Galton, F. (1869). *Hereditary genius: An inquiry into its laws and consequences.* London: Macmillan.

Garland, T., & Carter, P. (1994). Evolutionary physiology. *Annual Review of Physiology, 56,* 579.

Gould, S. J. (1996). *The mismeasure of man* (2nd ed.). New York: Norton.

Graves, J. L. (in press). *The emperor's new clothes: Biological theories of race at the millennium.* New Brunswick, NJ: Rutgers University Press.

Graves, J. L. (1993). Evolutionary biology and human variation: Biological determinism and the mythology of race. *Race Relations Abstracts, 18*(3), 4–34.

Graves, J. L., & Johnson, A. (1995). The pseudoscience of psychometry and the *Bell Curve* [Special issue: Myth and realities: African Americans and the measurement of human difference]. *The Journal of Negro Education, 64*(3), 277–294.

Graves, J. L., & Mueller, L. D. (1993). Population density effects on longevity. *Genetica, 91,* 99–109.

Graves, J. L., & Place, T. (1995). Race and IQ revisited: Figures never lie, but often liars figure. *Race Relations Abstracts, 20*(2), 4–50.

Graves, J. L., & Rose, M. R. (1989). Population genetics of senescence in *Drosophila. Life Sciences Advances: Fundamental Genetics, 8,* 45–55.

Guo, P., Mueller, L. D., & Ayala, F. J. (1991) Evolution of behavior by density dependent natural selection. *Proceedings of the National Academy of Science USA, 88,* 10905–10906.

Harvey, P. H., & Clutton-Brock, T. H. (1985). Life history variation in primates. *Evolution, 39,* 559–581.

Harvey, P. H., & Pagel, M. D. (1991). *The comparative method in evolutionary biology.* Oxford, UK: Oxford University Press.

Harvey, P. H., Read, A. F., & Promislow, D. E. L. (1989). Life history variation in placental mammals: Unifying the data with the theory. *Oxford Surveys in Evolutionary Biology, 6,* 13–31.

Hegmann, J. P., & Dingle, H. (1982). Phenotypic and genetic covariance structure in milkweed bug life history traits. In *Evolution and genetics of life histories* (pp. 177–186). New York: Springer-Verlag.

Herre, W. (1958) The influence of the environment on the brain of mammals. *Deutsche Medizinische Wochenschrift, 83,* 86.

Herrnstein, R. J., & Murray, C. R. (1994). *The bell curve: Intelligence and class structure in American life.* New York: The Free Press.

Hollocher, H., & Templeton, A. R. (1994). The molecular through ecological genetics of abnormal abdomen in *Drosophila mercatorum*: VI. The nonneutrality of the Y-chromosome rDNA polymorphism. *Genetics, 136*(4), 1373–1384.

Horowitz, I. L. (1995). The Rushton file. In Jacoby & Glauberman (Eds.), *The bell curve debate: History, documents, opinions.* New York: Random House.

Huntington, E. (1925). *The character of races: As influenced by physical environment, natural selection and historical development.* New York: Charles Scribner's Sons.

Jablonski, D., & Bottjer, D. J. (1990). The ecology of evolutionary innovations: The fossil record. In M. H. Nitecki (Ed.), *Evolutionary innovations* (pp. 258–288). Chicago: University of Chicago Press. Chicago.

Jensen, A. R. (1969). How much can we boost IQ and scholastic achievement? *Harvard Educational Review, 39,* 1–123.

Jones, R. E. (1991). *Human reproductive biology.* San Diego, CA: Academic Press.

Joshi, A., & Mueller, L. D. (1989). Evolution of higher feeding rate in *Drosophila* due to density-dependent natural selection. *Evolution, 42,* 1090–1093.

Joshi, A., & Mueller, L. D. (1993). Directional and stabilizing density-dependent natural selection for pupation height in *Drosophila melanogaster. Evolution, 47*(1), 176–184.

Kerfoot, W. C. (1977). Competition in cladoceran communities: The cost of evolving defenses against copepod predation. *Ecology, 58,* 303–313.

Kreuz, L. E., Rose, R. M., & Jennings, J. R. (1972). Suppression of plasma testosterone levels and psychological stress. *Archives of General Psychiatry, 26,* 479–482.

Ladd, J. (1997). Philosophical reflections on race and racism. *American Behavioral Scientist, 41*(2), 212–222.

Lauder, G. V., Leroi, A. M., & Rose, M. R. (1993). Adaptation and the comparative method. *Trends in Ecology and Evolution, 8*(8), 294.

Law R., Bradshaw A. D., & Putwain, P. D. (1977). Life history variation in Poa annua. *Evolution, 31,* 233–246.

Lenski, R., Rose, M. R., Simpson, S. C., & Tadler, S. C. (1991). Long term experimental evolution in *Escherichia coli*: I. Adaptation and divergence during 2,000 generations. *American Naturalist, 138,* 1315–1341.

Leroi, A. M., Chippendale, A. & Rose, M. R. (1994). Long-term laboratory evolution of genetic life-history trade-off in *Drosophila melanogaster*: I. The role of genotype-by-environment interaction. *Evolution, 48*(4), 1244–1257.

Leroi, A. M., Rose, M. R., & Lauder, G. V. (1994). What does the comparative method reveal about adaptation? *American Naturalist, 143*(3), 381–402.

Lovejoy, C. O. (1981). The origin of man. *Science, 211,* 341–350.

Luckinbill, L. S. (1979). Selection of the r/K continuum in experimental populations of protozoa. *American Naturalist, 113,* 427–437.

Luckinbill, L. S. (1984). An experimental analysis of life history theory. *Ecology, 65,* 1170–1184.

MacArthur, R. H., & Wilson, E. O. (1967). *The theory of island biogeography.* Princeton, NJ: Princeton University Press.

Mazur, A., & Lamb, T. A. (1980). Testosterone, status, and mood in human males. *Hormonal Behavior, 18,* 249–255.

McNaughton, S. J. (1975). r- and K-selection in Typha. *American Naturalist, 109,* 251–261.

Moffet, D., Moffet, S., & Schauf, C. (1993) *Human physiology: Foundations and frontiers.* St. Louis, MO: Mosby.

Montagu, A. (1974). *Man's most dangerous myth: The fallacy of race.* Oxford, UK: Oxford University Press.

Monti, P. M., Brown, W. A., & Corriveau, D. P. (1977) Testosterone and components of aggressive and sexual behavior in man. *American Journal of Psychiatry, 134,* 692–694.

Morberg, G. P. (Ed.). (1985). *Animal stress.* Bethesda, MD: American Physiological Society.

Morgan, D., Grant, K. A., Gage, H. D., Mach, R. H., Kaplan, J. R., Prioleau, O., Nader, S. H., Buchheimer, N., Ehrenkaufer, R. L., & Nader, M. A. (2002). Social dominance in monkeys: dopamine D-2 receptors and cocaine self-administration. *Nature Neuroscience, 5*(2), 169–174.

Mueller, L. D. (1988). Evolution of competitive ability in *Drosophila* by density dependent natural selection. *Proceedings of the National Academy of Science USA, 84,* 1974–1977.

Mueller, L. D. (1991). Ecological determinants of life history evolution. *Philosophical Transactions of the Royal Society of London, B, 332,* 25–30.

Mueller, L. D., & Ayala, F. D. (1981). Trade-off between r selection and K selection in *Drosophila melanogaster* populations. *Proceedings of the National Academy of Sciences USA, 78,* 1303–1305.

Mueller, L. D., Graves, J. L., & Rose, M. R. (1993). Interactions between density-dependent and age-specific selection in *Drosophila melanogaster. Functional Ecology, 7*, 469–479.

Mueller, L. D., Guo, P. & Ayala, F. J. (1991). Density-dependent natural selection and trade-offs in life history traits. *Science, 253*, 433–435.

Mueller, L. D., & Sweet, V. F. (1986). Density dependent natural selection in *Drosophila*: Evolution of pupation height. *Evolution, 40*, 1354–1356.

Murdoch, W. W. (1980). *The poverty of nations: The political economy of hunger and population.* Baltimore: John Hopkins University Press.

Nei, M., & Livshits, G. (1989). Genetic relationships of Europeans, Asians, and Africans and the origin of modern Homo sapiens. *Human Heredity, 39*, 276–281.

Nelson, R. J. (1995). *An introduction to behavioral endocrinology.* Sunderland, MA: Sinauer.

Orzack, S. H., & Sober, E. (1994). Optimality models and the test of adaptationism. *American Naturalist, 143*(3), 361–380.

Osborne, R. T. (1992). Cranial capacity and IQ. *Mankind Quarterly, 32*, 275–280.

Pagel, M., & Harvey, P. H. (1988). Recent developments in the analysis of comparative data. *Quarterly Review of Biology, 63*, 413–440.

Parry, G. D. (1981). The meanings of *r*- and *K*- selection. *Oecologia*, 260–281.

Persky, H., O'Brien, C., Fine, E., Howard, W., Khan, M. & Beck, R. (1977). The effect of alcohol and smoking on testosterone function and aggression in chronic alcoholics. *American Journal of Psychiatry, 134*, 621–625.

Pianka, E. R. (1970). On "r" and "K" selection. *American Naturalist, 104*, 592–597.

Poliakova, R. S. (1960). Interspecial differences in brain size. *Arkh. Anat. Gistol. I. Embriol, 39*, 58–64.

Promislow, D. E. L., & Harvey, P. H. (1990). Living fast and dying young: A comparative analysis of life history variation among mammals. *Journal of Zoology, London, 200*, 417–437.

Purves, D. (1994). *Neural activity and the growth of the brain.* Cambridge, UK: Cambridge University Press.

Raven, P. H., & Johnson, G. B. (1996). *Biology* (4th ed.), Dubuque, IA: Wm. C. Brown Publishers.

Read, A. F., & Harvey, P. H. (1989). Life history differences amongst the eutherian radiations. *Journal of Zoology, London, 219*, 329–353.

Reznick, D. (1985). Cost of reproduction: An evaluation of the empirical evidence. *Oikos, 44*, 257–267.

Ricklefs, R. E. (1977). On the evolution of reproductive strategies in birds: reproductive effort. *American Naturalist, 111*, 453478.

Roff, D. (1992). *The evolution of life histories: Theories and analysis.* New York: Chapman & Hall.

Rose, M. R. (1984). Genetic covariation in *Drosophila* life history: Untangling the data. *American Naturalist, 123*, 565–569.

Rose, M. R., Graves, J. L. & Hutchinson, E. W. (1990). The use of selection to probe patterns of pleiotropy in fitness characters. In G. Francis (Ed.), *Genetics, evolution, and coordination of insect life cycles* (pp. 29–40). Berlin: Springer-Verlag.

Rotberg, R., & Robb, T. K. (Eds.). (1986). *Population and history: From the traditional to the modern world.* Cambridge, UK: Cambridge University Press.

Rushton, J. P. (1995). *Race, evolution and behavior: A life history perspective.* New Brunswick, NJ: Transaction.

Rushton, J. P. (1998). The new enemies of evolutionary science. *Liberty, 2*(4), 31–35.

Service, P. T., Hutchinson, E. W., & Rose, M. R. (1988). Multiple genetic mechanisms for the evolution of senescence in *Drosophila. Evolution, 42*, 708–716.

Shackelford, T. K., & Larsen, R. J. (1997). Facial asymmetry as an indicator of psychological, emotional, and physiological stress. *Journal of Personality and Social Psychology, 72*, 456–466.

Skutch, A. F. (1949). Do tropical birds rear as many young as they can nourish? *Ibis, 91,* 430–455.

Smith, B. H. (1989). Dental development as a measure of life-history in primates. *Evolution, 43,* 683–688.

Snell, T. W., & King, C. E. (1977). Lifespan and fecundity patterns in rotifers: The costs of reproduction. *Evolution, 31,* 882–890.

Solbrig, O. T., & Simpson, B. B. (1974). Components of regulation in a population of dandelions in Michigan. *Journal of Ecology, 63,* 473–486.

Stearns, S. C. (1977). The evolution of life history traits: A critique of the theory and a review of the data. *Annual Review of Ecology and Systematics 8,* 145–171.

Stearns, S. C. (1992). *The evolution of life histories.* New York: Oxford University Press.

Taylor C. E., & Condra, C. (1980). *r-* and *K-* selection in *Drosophilia pseudoobscura. Evolution, 34,* 1183–1193.

Templeton, A. R. (1983). The evolution of life histories under pleiotropic constraints and K-selection. In H. I. Freedman & C. Strobeck (Eds.), *Population biology* (pp. 64–71). Berlin: Springer-Verlag.

Templeton, A. R., Hollocher, H., & Johnson, J. S. (1993). The molecular through ecological genetics of abnormal abdomen in *Drosophila mercatorum:* V. Female phenotypic expression on natural genetic backgrounds and in natural environments. *Genetics, 134,* 475–485.

Templeton, A. R., & Johnson, J. S. (1982). Life history evolution under pleiotropy and K-selection in a natural population of *Drosophila mercatorum.* In J. S. F. Barker & W. T. Starmer (Eds.), *Ecological genetics and evolution: The cactus-yeast-Drosophila system* (pp. 225–239). Sydney, Australia: Academic Press.

Tobias, P. V. (1970). Brain size, grey matter, and race-Fact or Fiction? *American Journal of Physical Anthropology, 32,* 3–26.

United Nations Department of International Economic Studies. (1987). *Fertility behavior in the context of development: Evidence from the world fertility study.* New York: United Nations.

Vinovskis, M. A. (1976). *Demographic history and the world population crisis.* Worcester, MA: Clark University Press.

Wagner, A. (1996). Does evolutionary plasticity evolve. *Evolution, 50*(3), 1008–1023.

Wilson, E. O. (1975). *Sociobiology: The new synthesis.* Cambridge, MA: Harvard University Press.

Wolff, M. S., Berkowitz, G. S., Brower, S., Senie, R., Bleiweiss, I. J., Tartter Pace, P. B., Roy, N., Wallenstein, S., & Weston, A. (2000). Organochloride exposures and breast cancer risk in New York City women. *Environmental Research, 84*(2), 151–161.

Zar, J. H. (1999). Biostatical Analysis (4th ed.), p. 130. Upper Saddle River, NJ: Prentice Hall.

4

Folk Heredity

Jonathan Marks

The overarching theme I would like to develop here is the conflict between different theories of heredity that coexist in modern society. There is, on the one hand, genetics, a 20th-century science, with modern literature that can generally be recognized through a vocabulary of "blots," "bands," "gels," and "probes."

On the other hand, there exists a set of commonsense theories of heredity, generally expressed in adages such as "like begets like" and "blood will tell." These are, of course, much older than the science of genetics, and although they are somewhat diverse, they can be conveniently grouped as a set in contrast to genetics, as theories of folk heredity.

Folk heredity comprises a belief in the importance of inherited constitutions in everyday life, in explaining social relationships, in applying formulas for interpreting and improving our world, in the taint of "blood," and in the condemnation of large groups on the basis of qualities inscribed in their natures. These beliefs form the justifications for hereditary aristocracies, for example, and the justification for "isms" of many kinds—although most notably racism.

Importantly, however, contemporary folk heredity draws legitimacy from genetics. Genetics speaks with cultural authority on matters of heredity in the modern world, and consequently its sanction is important. Thus, instead of an archaic phrase like "inherited constitution," we frequently see the same thought expressed with the technical term *gene*, although there is usually little or no overlap between the gene as material, transcriptional entity studied by molecular geneticists and the gene as commonsense explanation of "why-you-are-such-a-jerk" (Marks & Lyles, 1994).

Reciprocally, however, genetics derives popular support by validating popular wisdom, particularly as the science may provide an origin myth for the distribution of modern social power. To the extent that genetics relies on popular support for funding priority, for example, it is in the interests of geneticists to promote folk ideologies insofar as they may imply support for the science itself.

It is consequently crucial to explore their points of contact and to point out the potential conflict of interests. For example, when James Watson was quoted in *Time* magazine a few years ago saying "We used to think our fate was in the stars. Now we know, in large measure, our fate is in our genes," it could raise a number of questions (Jaroff, 1989):

- Do we actually have fate, in any common sense of that term?
- Has it actually been localized to our cellular nuclei?
- Is genetics merely high-tech astrology, although presumably more accurate?

The statement is brilliantly polysemic. Vested with the authority of one of the parents of molecular genetics, this illustrates the conflict of interest that pervades human genetics. Maybe it is merely articulating the manner in which genetic instructions can produce a range of health problems, like diabetes, Huntington's chorea, or sickle-cell anemia. On the other hand, the reference to astrology suggests a broader implication. Perhaps then, it is a general scientific statement, a testable hypothesis about the force of heredity on destiny. But it is at the same time an articulation of political substance. If we have fates and they are in our genes, then by implication the differences between a Harvard professor, a grocery store checkout clerk, a Bosnian Serb, and an urban teenage gang member are explicable by recourse to bands and blots and gels. If we identify Balkan genocide and urban teenage crime as social problems requiring solutions, the statement encodes a social political philosophy. The only hope to change their life trajectories would be by gene therapy (which does not exist) or by extirpation (which does)—from a benign laissez-faire attitude at least as old as Malthus, through amniocentesis and selective abortion, to the infamous Nazi culmination.

However, even that is an incomplete analysis, for the explicit purpose of Watson's comment was dictated by its context—a cover story on the Human Genome Project, which was attempting to drum up several billion taxpayer dollars for molecular genetic research. Of course it needed to convey that it was the most important thing in people's lives. In addition to encoding the authority of science, and a political philosophy, the statement encodes a grant proposal.

The problem is that once we appreciate that geneticists possess conflicting interests, their authority is undermined. One can no more accept at face value a geneticist's statement on the overriding significance of genetics in life than one can accept at face value an Oldsmobile salesman's statement about their car being the best ones on the road today. However, it is nevertheless crucially important to be able to discriminate sound work and reasoning from quackery. There have to be some standards of intellectual rigor in any scientific field, for a situation where all claims are equally valid, and reactionary, politically motivated studies and racist studies are accorded equal status with open-minded, responsible, and competent scholarship is inevitably a victory for the former.

How, then, do we make sense of the miasma of information and misinformation on human genetics that exists in the public forum? I believe the first step is to identify and isolate four pervasive and archaic fallacies about human heredity in popular ideology, toward the ultimate goal of subtracting them from human genetics. These folk hereditary fallacies are taxonomism, racism, hereditarianism, and essentialism.

TAXONOMISM

The first is the division of the human species into a small number of ostensibly natural, and qualitatively distinct, categories. I call this *taxonomism*, and it is one of the most persistent cultural fallacies, somewhat tragically still occasionally maintained as science even by some physical anthropologists (Gill 1998, Marks, 1998).

It is, of course, universal for cultures to distinguish among groups of people. However, the modern, "scientific" approach to the problem dates only from the late 17th century. Prior to that, Europeans had distinguished peoples locally. The politics of expansionism and colonialism and the economics of slavery introduced an expediency into blurring local heterogeneities that had not existed previously and came to seem entirely natural . Thus in 1684, a French physician and traveler named François Bernier proposed a natural division of humanity into "four or five species or races of men in particular whose difference is so remarkable that it may be properly made use of as the foundation for a new division of the earth" (Bendyshe, 1865, p. 361).

Bernier's first group encompassed Europe, North Africa, the Near East, and India. His second was sub-Saharan Africa, and the third encompassed the Asians. His fourth comprised the Lapps of Norway, "little stunted creatures with thick legs, large shoulders, short neck, and a face elongated immensely ..., they are wretched animals" (Behnyshe, p. 362), and somewhat bear-like as well. Finally, "the blacks of the Cape of Good Hope seem to be of a different species to those from the rest of Africa" (p. 362). As to the native Americans, Bernier did "not find the difference sufficiently great to make of them a peculiar species different from ours" (p. 362). (It should be noted that Bernier wrote before the formalization of the biological concept of species, and thus his use of the term should be taken simply as a colloquialism, not implying the ignominious polygenism of a later era.)

Bernier's innovation was indelibly etched into the scientific canon by Linnaeus, the father of modern biological classification. Classifying the animal, vegetable, and mineral kingdoms in his *System of Nature*, Linnaeus (1735) began the work by classifying humans. He identified four subspecies, corresponding to continental land masses, and color-coded, to boot: white Europeans, red Americans, dark Asians (*fuscus*, later amended to *luridus*, yellow), and black Africans.

Linnaeus's role was to legitimize this approach to human variation as scientific. His system had proven so successful for other organisms and his reputation was so immense that he successfully defined the scientific approach to this problem. A generation later, Blumenbach would observe that all over the world, human populations blend into one another, so drawing formal lines between them is highly arbitrary. Yet posturing as heir to Linnaeus, that is precisely what he had to do. (He found five subdivisions of humans, and provided the coinage "Caucasian," for his belief that the most perfect representations of the European skull were from the Caucasus mountains.)

This approach to human variation began to be challenged only in the mid-20th century. A paper by Ashley Montagu (1941) criticized the race concept "in the light of modern genetics," and Frank Livingstone's (1962) terse and widely cited essay "On the Non-Existence of Human Races" emphasized the continuity of human variation and the arbitrariness of partitioning it, like Buffon and Blumenbach 200 years earlier. Perhaps the most influential paper, however, was geneticist Richard Lewontin's (1972) statistical analysis of "The Apportionment of Human Diversity," which showed that the vast bulk of the genetic differences in the human species occurred within and between populations, the differences between continental regions amounting to only about 6% of the total.

Perhaps the most crucial feature of the taxonomist fallacy, however, lies in the fact that the categories of race are transmitted generationally according to rules that are cultural, not genetic. The child of a mixed marriage is forced to assume a single racial identity (generally that of the socially lower, or marked, race), and is not considered to be an equal participant in both, as their biology might dictate (Davis, 1991). Further, the categories of racial classification do not reflect real patterns of human diversity; consequently marriages between "Asians" can encompass people as different as Koreans and Pakistanis without being formally considered interracial. Finally, the legalities of race necessitate definitions of inclusion. The American miscegenation laws and the German Nuremberg laws specified the definition of "Negro" or "Jew" to include anyone with a single great-grandparent from that group. Apparently seven great-grandparents were not enough to make you "White" or "German"—again in defiance of biological relationships.

The fact is that the human species defies classification into such discrete natural groups. Europeans vary extensively among one another, which is why William Z. Ripley's (1899) analysis of *The Races of Europe* compelled anthropologists to differentiate among the Nordic, Alpine, and Mediterranean races within the European race. Africans, however, have the greatest levels of biological diversity of populations on any continent. Sub-Saharan Africans include the tallest and shortest people in the world, and people of diverse facial form, body build, and skin tones. Clustering them together as a homogeneous group in juxtaposition against a homogeneous "European" race simply does not reflect empirical patterns of diversity.

Even geneticists, however, have difficulty shaking this folk hereditary premise. There is, for example, a body of literature asking which two of the "three great races" are most closely related to one another. In the 1960s and 1970s, Cavalli-Sforza argued (based on genetic data) that Europeans and Africans clustered against Asians, reflecting a primordial East–West division of the human species (Cavalli-Sforza, 1974; Cavalli-Sforza & Edwards, 1965). On the other hand, Nei and Roychoudhury (1981) found a different pattern from the same data, namely, that Europeans and Asians clustered against Africans. More recently, however, the meaning of these trees generated from genetic distances has come under scrutiny, for these trees reflect many features aside from simply branching ancestry (Harpending, 1994; Terrell & Stewart, 1996). Programmed to do so, a computer will produce dichotomous trees. However, folk hereditary premises about the data can tint the results.

We now know, after all, that genetically the rest of the human species is a subset of Africans (Merriwether et al., 1991; Tishkoff et al., 1996). Consequently "Africans" do not constitute a valid biological contrast to "Europeans" and "Asians." That would be like contrasting "Mammalia" against "Carnivora" and "Primates." As the latter two are subsumed by the first, the comparison is nonsensical. Thus, the entire corpus of genetic literature on the relations of the three races to one another is largely valueless.

Because the population is now recognized to be the closest thing to a natural unit of the human species (and even that defies precise definition), one must also be particularly skeptical of studies that compare races, for the populations taken to represent the races become synechdoches (metaphors substituting a part for the whole). A study of Kenyan versus Swedish athletes, for example, cannot be relevant to an American black–white comparison, because most American whites are not of Scandinavian ancestry and most American blacks are not of East African ancestry. The claim that "ancestral Europeans are estimated to be an admixture of 65% ancestral Chinese and 35% ancestral Africans" (Bowcock et al., 1991, p. 840) shows how difficult it is to escape the cultural biases of racialized science, especially when accompanied by the information that Africans in this study refers to two populations of central African pygmies.

As we now know, both phenotypic and genetic variation in humans are structured as a series of gradients. We find simply that peoples are similar to those nearby and different from those far away. However, that no more tells us that there are 3 kinds of humans, than it tells us there are 5 or 12 or 31. Thus, a "Caucasoid" Iranian and a "Negroid" Ethiopian are more similar on any biological axis to one another than the Iranian is to a "Caucasoid" Swede or the Ethiopian is to a "Negroid" Senegalese.

The basis for juxtaposing the former two peoples as Caucasoid and the latter two pairs as Negroid reflects a judgment call, the erection of discrete boundaries in defiance of nature. The judgment is a poor one, for it is not justified by their bodies or by their genes. We cluster and divide populations by cultural rules, not by any natural breaks. We can certainly compare populations stemming from different parts of the world, but we have no indications of the number, nature, or existence of any primordial subdivisions. We cluster and segregate populations by fiat, not biology. The basis on which we decide that African people, exceedingly biologically heterogeneous, comprise a single unit to juxtapose against an equivalent single European unit, is cultural, not natural. Again, it constitutes a folk idea about diversity.

RACISM

It is important to distinguish the fallacy of classifying humans into groups, misrepresented as natural, from the denial of rights to people based on how they are classified. The judgment of individuals on the basis of characteristics assigned to their group is the folk hereditary fallacy of racism, although obviously independent of the existence of natural taxonomic categories of people. At root, it reflects two simple beliefs: (a) The properties assigned to groups exist in microcosm in the constitutions of the people composing the groups; and (b) those properties form the basis for assessing individual worth and conferring rights.

When Carleton Coon (1962) published *The Origin of Races* and argued that the economic and political subjugation of dark-skinned peoples was the natural expression of their not having been members of *Homo sapiens* for very long, the thesis was quickly taken up by anti-integration activists (Putnam, 1967). Challenged by liberal scientists to repudiate the odious invocation of his work, Coon refused, on the grounds that his work was merely value-neutral science, and he was not responsible for its citation (Coon, 1968; Dobzhansky, 1968). While both political sides recognized the value-ladenness of the work, only its author (whether out of naiveté or malice is irrelevant) maintained the fiction that the work lay outside a system of values.

That was a defining moment for American anthropology, with two consequences for the field. First, anthropologists began to think far more self-consciously about the political responsibilities they carried in pronouncing authoritatively on basic human differences. Second, biological anthropologists began to shy away from talking at all about race. The latter consequence was almost as tragic as the fiasco that inspired it.

Whether or not group-level properties exist in the makeups of individuals is to some extent an empirical question. A group of dark-skinned people and a group of light-skinned people, after all, differ both at the group and at the individual level. However, the judgment of individual worth and the conferral of rights are political and social issues, not biological issues. Because racism is not derived from scientific knowledge in the first place, it is difficult to imagine that science can help to refute it. One must be vigilant, however, for science can easily naturalize racism.

In *The Third Chimpanzee*, biologist Jared Diamond asserted that xenophobia (a highfalutin neologism referring to fear and loathing of others) and its radical manifestation genocide are biological endowments of the human species, indeed inherited from a common ancestor with chimpanzees. What the biologist neglected, however, is that "otherness" is culturally constructed. The people who hate each other the most, of course, are generally biologically the most similar. Whether they are Nazi and Jew, Huron and Iroquois, Muslim and Hindu, Serbian and Bosnian, Hutu and Tutsi, Irish and English, or Harvard and Yale, the xenophobia, or racism, or simple animosity, is not based on natural differences between the groups. It is based, rather, on constructed identities. Thus, if indeed we are programmed toward group hatred, it is evident that whom we choose to hate, why we hate them, and what we should do about it are entirely culturally programmed. To the extent that biology or genetics may be involved, it would have to be in a very trivial sense.

Racism is thus not predicated on biological races; it is predicated on folk notions of heredity and difference, and it is a social, political, and cultural problem independent of biology and of any class of biological data. class of biological data. The history of science being used to justify racism is well known, from Josiah Nott and George Gliddon (1854) through Carleton Coon (1962) up to J. Philippe Rushton (1995).

It may be interesting to note, however, another genetical approach to the problem, in the assertion that genetics will help put an end to racism. Thus, accompanied by a liberal political bent, the Human Genome Diversity Project acknowledged the equality of the races, even while reifying them. This Project was "expected to undermine the popular belief that there are clearly defined races [and] to contribute to the elimination of racism" (http://www.stanford.edu/group/morrinst/hgdp/summary93.html). Not only is the appeal to eliminate racism ridiculous (as if racism were a biological problem, instead of a political one), but their very own flagship literature presented color-coded maps of the world in which "Four major ethnic regions are shown. Africans are yellow, Australians red, [Mongoloids blue], and Caucasoids green" (Cavalli-Sforza, Menozzi, & Piazza, 1995; Piazza, 1997; Subramanian, 1995).

In other words, they have just showed you in different colors the "clearly defined races" that they say do not exist! However, the scientists failed to appreciate that this is all unrelated to racism. If there were no natural taxonomic units of the human species (which indeed there are not), there would still be group-level identifications and the possibility of prejudice and discrimination on that basis—as the experiences of Jews and Hispanics show. This is based on constructed differences, not on patterns of natural biological variation. The science of genetics cannot eliminate racism, for it is not a biological problem; it is a cultural problem.

HEREDITARIANISM

Hereditarianism is the idea that heredity is a crucial determinant of particular human thoughts and behaviors. One can draw on any number of examples of hereditarian thought in modern society, and that is the theme of a very fine recent book, *The DNA Mystique* by sociologist Dorothy Nelkin and historian Susan Lindee . This is where the conflict of interests described earlier is most evident. It is simply not in a geneticist's best interests to deny the importance of genetics in everyday affairs, so we do have to be cautious about accepting uncritically the pronouncements of geneticists in this area.

In a presidential address to the American Society of Human Genetics, David Comings (1989) contrasted two models of the development of antisocial personality. He eschewed the soft science model in favor of another possibility. "A genetic viewpoint is different," he wrote, "and would suggest that a disinhibition-disorder gene carried by a parent could result in marital chaos and separation and that it is this inherited gene—not the fact that the parents separated—that causes antisocial personality in the child" (Comings, 1989, p. 456).

Well, it may be comforting to blame your "marital chaos and separation" on a divorce gene in the innate constitution of your ex-spouse, but certainly divorce rates have been changing quite independently of the gene pool.

Being a geneticist should mean studying heredity scientifically, not postulating that genes are at the root of everything.

Certainly brains and minds are, at some level, "coded for" by genes. However, it is the variations among them that are of central interest, and that have little, if anything, to do with genetics. One can argue that tuberculosis is genetic, in that the human body is programmed to respond in specific ways to infection by the appropriate bacillus; but why one person got tuberculosis and another did not is far more a function of the circumstances of their lives (e.g., in crowded urban ghettos vs. farms or country estates) versus that of their genes.

The analogous question here is understanding the distribution of variation in thoughts, ideas, and behaviors in the human species. Consequently, it is crucial to distinguish between the causes of mental and behavioral variation within and between groups. Generations of immigrants have shown quite strongly that the great bulk of behavioral and mental diversity in our species has always been what we call cultural—located in group-level differences in language, custom, habits, values, ambitions, and conceptualizations. No matter how diverse they may appear, modern Americans constitute an extraordinarily homogeneous behavioral sample of our species. Regardless of the apparent differences among Pat Buchanan, Anita Hill, and Woody Allen, all three regard a particular set of sounds as meaningful; have similar ideas about the responsibilities incurred in different social roles as parent, spouse, or employee; and have similar ideas about appropriate standards of dress, eating, and life in general. Such similarities cannot be taken for granted in the panoply of human history, and they are dwarfed by the differences between either of those two urban Americans and a Hmong, Hutu, or Apache. These cultural differences comprise the raison d'être of anthropology and are not in any discernible sense genetic—the 16th-century ancestors of Pat Buchanan, Anita Hill, and Woody Allen would be unable to communicate with or relate to either their descendants or each other.

Our very homogeneity often forces us to exaggerate the behavioral and mental differences among ourselves. However, the bulk of human behavioral differences, to the extent that they are group differences and therefore the product of divergent histories, are not genetic. The differences within any particular group, of course, may have diverse etiologies. So immediately, we see that the very study of "human behavioral genetics" allots to itself a tiny portion of the spectrum of human behavioral variation (Marks, 1997b).

So what is the argument about? It is about the failure to partition the diversity; to recognize structure in the variation of human mental and behavioral diversity.

Of course, urbanism, development, and telecommunications seem destined to continue to reduce such variation. The peril is that, as in earlier centuries, we will take as "natural" merely what we perceive, for we will have little with which to contrast it.

How, then, can we take seriously cross-cultural studies of beauty (which conclude that the homogeneities uncovered must be genetic), as if the different cultures constituted independent data points? What are appropriate controls on such studies? (Perhaps a question like "Have you ever heard of Marilyn Monroe?"—and if the answer is affirmative, discard the response.)

Or consider the widely cited amazing twin coincidences. The Jim twins have been studied by researchers at the University of Minnesota, under Thomas Bouchard, whose funding initially came from the Pioneer Fund, notorious for sponsoring research of a white supremacist bent (Lane, 1994). You can probably guess what the research is going to show. Separated at birth, the amazing Jim twins were given the same name, married women with the same name, divorced them, took second wives with the same name, named their sons the same, and named their dogs the same.

There you have it. Nature one, nurture zero.

But is this science? Let us think about this scientifically. There is in fact a rather small universe of explanations for the amazing Jim twins. Perhaps their similarities are just coincidental. But the very fact that it comes up in discourse about genetics (e.g., in the introduction to the recent book, *Living With Our Genes* (Hamer & Copeland, 1998) as having specifically "showed that genes not only help determine how we look, but how we act, feel, and experience life," p. 22) implies that it is not intended to be regarded as a mere coincidence. After all, how many people do you know with the same name, married to women with the same name, with the same named kids and dogs, and then it just happens they are identical twins separated at birth? That would certainly beg our credulity. No, this is newsworthy precisely because it is not intended to be interpreted that way.

Perhaps, then, it is a demonstration of the primacy of genetics in human affairs. Fortunately, I can relate that when I asked for a show of hands at the International Congress of Human Genetics in 1996 on whether the name you give your dog may be under genetic control, none went up. No sane geneticist would actually admit to that one.

Well, then, perhaps it demonstrates the psychic powers of identical twins. That is, in fact, precisely the way this story was represented in the popular media, for example, in *Newsweek* (Begley, 1987) and *U.S. News and World Report* (Lang, 1987).

Suddenly, however, we see that here the hereditarian claim to scientific status is being validated not by genetics, but by parapsychology. One would hope that behavioral genetics is on somewhat firmer footing than parapsychology; if it is not, then the field is in some epistemological difficulties. In fact, it need hardly be pointed out that the correlations on these twins' personality tests would now be useless, as it is an underlying assumption of such testing that the answers are being given independently, and that the twins are not exchanging answers psychically.

Of course the twins are not in psychic contact, nor is anyone else. The line between science and pseudoscience is just a lot fuzzier here than it is ordinarily supposed to be.

Therefore the process of elimination leaves one explanation for the amazing coincidences of the twins: There is just something wrong with the story; somebody is lying. How could this possibly happen? Well, as one of my undergraduates, who is an identical twin with no psychic powers, said to me, "I guess we'll never be on *Oprah*." If you are a twin without an amazing story, nobody is interested. The amazing twin similarities are wonderful urban legends that have often been repeated, but never validated. Who may be kidding whom is not a question I can answer. The point is that this work lies outside the realm of genetic discourse; there is no genetic science here. The astonishing twin similarities are reported and rereported but never investigated and hardly ever examined critically.

There are of course differences among the gene pools of the world's populations. Because we have virtually no information on the genetic basis of variation in normal behavior, we do not know whether or how it might vary across the human species. We must keep an open mind on that issue. At the same time, we have positive knowledge (from generations of acculturation studies) that virtually everyone is capable of being a normal participant in virtually any culture, and that consequently all known between-group variation in human behavior is the result of history and upbringing.

We also have positive knowledge that different groups of people are treated unequally and have distinctly different opportunities and expectations. These differences can, and do, have a determinative effect on people's lives.

But why one person becomes a grocery store checkout clerk and another becomes a professor is fodder for astrologers, not scientists. As long as social inequalities, historical and cultural differences, and prejudices exist, we have a host of uncontrollable variables in explaining the course of individual human lives. Our concern as citizens should be to develop a system in which talented people from any social group can become either checkout clerks or professors. Our concern as academicians should be to make sure that our fellow citizens appreciate that social barriers are principally constructs of human agency, not of nature.

ESSENTIALISM

The final aspect of folk heredity is *essentialism*, in its most general form, ignoring diversity in pursuit of a transcendent underlying unitary form, or more commonly, pretending a transcendent form actually exists. In biology it is known as "typology." In a more specific sense, it is to identify your essence, to define you from one small part of what you do, or what you have. It is a pseudo-biological metaphor.

In its most glaring form, this would be represented by the transference of the word "homosexual" from an adjective describing an act, to a noun defining a person, and then the claim to have identified a gene for it (Hamer, Hu, Magnuson, Hu, & Pattatucci, 1993).

In a less charged but equally spurious vein, geneticists found that 54% of self-designated Hebrew priests, many of whom have the surname Cohen, had the same configuration of two genes on the Y chromosome, as opposed to only 33% of

Jews who did not think they were priests. On this basis, the study's authors inferred that this configuration was the real genetic constitution of the Jewish priestly line, inherited directly from biblical Aaron, and by implication reflecting the genetic makeup of his brother, the lawgiver himself (Skorecki et al., 1997).

Of course, people with the same last names are going to be more closely related than people with different last names, reflecting recent common shared ancestry. Anthropologists have long used the sharing of names as a noninvasive estimate of inbreeding. Given the ethnohistory of population crashes in the study population, the recency of surname use, the fictive nature of the Hebrew priesthood in the last few millennia, and the origin myth the authors took literally, it seems unlikely that the Y chromosome would be able to validate the priestly caste.

What is the fallacy? There is no experimental control. Skorecki et al. (1997) simply inferred that the most common configuration in Jews overrepresenting the name Cohen, present at 54% rather than 33%, is authentic and primordial, in the absence of information on the distribution of Y chromosome haplotypes of a sample of Horowitzes or Steinbergs. The most common form becomes the official form of the highlighted group, and all other forms become spurious.

More important, the authors of that report found themselves in the middle of an identity controversy, as people want to know authoritatively if they are "really" Hebrew priests or not (Grady, 1997). Well, as there is no temple or priesthood, nobody is a Hebrew priest. Nevertheless, these genetic data are culturally invested with authority, in spite of the shaky basis for the inference. The construction of identity is a political arena in which geneticists are uniquely unqualified to work, certainly without a great deal of reeducation.

Obviously, it is hard enough to distinguish folk ideologies about heredity from genetics when the geneticists themselves are the ones contributing to the conflation of scientific knowledge and cultural values. The effect of this is to impart the authority of science to cultural folk knowledge that is not actually validated by scientific knowledge itself. This is, however, the framework for understanding *The Bell Curve* (Herrnstein & Murray, 1994).

MODERN FOLK HEREDITY

The stream of modern folk heredity, within which *The Bell Curve* resides, owes much of its tenacity to a seductive and brilliant formulation by the geneticist Charles Davenport (1911) and his book, *Heredity in Relation to Eugenics*.

Genes, argued Davenport, are what make the brain. The brain is the locus of the mind, and the mind is composed of thoughts. It follows, then, that bad thoughts are ultimately caused by bad genes. The power of this materialist logic is such that it can be found in editorials in the leading science journal in the United States from just a few years ago. In 1990, *Science*'s editor Daniel Koshland (1990) took the bully pulpit to remind us that brains are coded by genes, and can be miscoded by genes: "[I]t is time the world recognized that the brain is an organ and that it can go wrong ... because of hereditary defects .... [T]he irrational output of a faulty brain is like the faulty wiring of a computer" (p. 189).

A few years later, he criticized the German courts for their lack of scientific knowledge in releasing Gunther Parche, assailant of Monica Seles: "We need more understanding of diseases of the brain so that judges with an inadequate knowledge of elementary science do not release criminals who have stabbed a tennis star in the back" (Koshland, 1993, p. 635). Now, nobody is against studying the brain or studying hereditary diseases. However, the train of thought here is very dubious: The assailant had never been diagnosed as having a diseased brain, much less a constitutionally miswired one, only bad thoughts and deeds. And bad thoughts and deeds are far more likely to come from other sources than from a genetically broken brain.

What we have here is the old bait-and-switch. We would like to study minds, but they are metaphysical. Brains are physical—we can study them, but they do not express what we are interested in. But we can pretend they do—hence the fascination with cranial volume in the classical anthropological literature.

The Bell Curve does something very similar, expressed in its key phrase, "cognitive ability." What is cognitive ability? The book uses it in a colloquial sense; cognitive ability is some kind of innate scalar brain force. We are all born with it, and some more than others. School and standardized tests are as good a measurement as we have, and those who do well at them have more of that force than those who do not. That is why doctors earn more than cab drivers, and why they should. Q.E.D.

The academic response to *The Bell Curve* focused on the interpretation of data, as if the statement of the problem were scientifically meaningful, and thus had to be debated on scientific turf. The result is that it looked like a scientific disagreement—"you say potay-to, I say potah-to"—which gives the appearance of two legitimate scientific sides to the issue.

But there aren't. Only one legitimate scientific side exists to that discussion: We do not have the slightest idea how to measure anyone's intrinsic ability, cognitive or otherwise. We can neither affirm nor deny that people have different abilities, much less groups of people, because we do not know what the domains of human abilities are, how they vary, what they require for their development, nor what their genetic underpinnings are.

Ability is thus a metaphysical concept; it is unmeasurable and imperceptible. It can be detected only in the context of the life that has already been lived by the subject. It lies outside the domain of scientific inquiry.

What we have are performances. We can compare them between people and between groups of people, but then we must validate the measurements and comparisons with an argument bridging what we can measure and what we are interested in.

That is precisely what *The Bell Curve* failed to do, and what generations of social scientists have failed to do before it—to establish that expressed performances are reliable guides to innate abilities. The reason is that the relevant issues to this problem are not ontological or scientific (in the common sense of the term, referring to the study of the nature of things), they are epistemological or meta-scientific (in the nature of knowledge). In studying the variation in human ability, we are beyond the limits of the domain of science.

The fallacy is not that we have positive knowledge that different people (or groups) have identical abilities. Rather, it is that we have no way to know what their abilities are, except in retrospect, after those abilities have been cultivated to some extent. This results in a basic asymmetry in the relation between performances and abilities.

The discussion of innate abilities is another example of the folk hereditary fallacy of essentialism. It defines a person, and delimits them, on the basis of a quality that is supposed to be a fundamental aspect of their nature—their essence—and yet is based on no data from the recognizably modern scientific realm of genetics.

This brings us back to *The Bell Curve* and "cognitive ability." The fact that some people and groups perform better than others may be due to differences in ability, or it may not be. If anthropology has shown anything in the 20th century, it is that the simple observation of a consistent difference between groups of people is not a sufficient basis on which to infer that the observed difference is rooted in the constitutions of the members of those groups.

If you examine 1,000 Danes and 1,000 Nigerians, you will find a consistent difference in their skin color, which is genetic; a consistent difference in their language, which is not genetic; and a consistent difference in their body build, which we don't know if it's genetic or not (Marks, 1996).

Without a way to study innate potentials and how they vary in human beings, we can only speculate about them. The issues raised by *The Bell Curve*—whether consistent differences in mental testing results are due to innate differences—thus lie outside the domain of modern scientific inquiry (Marks, 1997a). It is an interesting topic for after hours in a bar, but not fodder for constructive scientific debate. There is, of course, evidence of a humanistic nature that bears on it—that historically, populations derided for their abilities in one time have performed admirably in another, with little concomitant change evident in their gene pool. And the more social variables you control, the more similar the test performances across populations become.

The issue is consequently not whether there are native abilities, but rather, whether at present we can know anything scientifically about them. In the absence of a scientific approach to human potential, though, we are left with two poles of social action: On the one hand, we can argue about the ways of optimizing performances or accomplishments among individuals and among groups. We can try to identify and cultivate diverse talents as widely as possible (by investing our resources in education, day care, and children's enrichment programs). On the other hand, we can condemn large groups of people on the basis of their poor performance, denying their right to be judged as individuals, and denying as well the possibility of society at all benefitting from the innate gifts with which they are endowed.

Neither alternative is particularly scientific, but the first is at least humanitarian.

CONCLUSION: THE VALUE OF HISTORY

The Bell Curve of its era was a book by a wealthy New York lawyer bearing the names of two presidents, Madison Grant. It was called *The Passing of the Great Race*, and it was about the social problems of the day, the prolific poor. This was 1916, so the problem was not welfare, it was immigration, and specifically the immigration of the inferior racial stocks from southern and eastern Europe—code for Italians and Jews. Grant was preoccupied with keeping them out, and 8 years after his best-seller appeared, there was Congressional legislation in place to do just that. Ultimately its effect was to deny asylum to many who would ultimately perish in Europe in the 1940s. But what about the immigrants already here?

Grant (1916) held that America's social problems are biological in nature and linked that to a formula for alleviating them: sterilization. He wrote that it "can be applied to an ever widening circle of social discards, beginning always with the criminal, the diseased, and the insane, and extending gradually to types which may be called weaklings rather than defectives, and perhaps ultimately to worthless race types" (pp. 46–47).

First the handicapped and marginalized, and then the undesirable races. Perhaps it sounds familiar.

But you cannot call him a Nazi; in 1916 there were no Nazis. Yet his book was praised by a spectrum of politicians—from former President Theodore Roosevelt, who served with him on the board of the New York Zoological Society, to Adolf Hitler, an aspiring demagogue, who read and admired the German translation of 1925.

More important, it was reviewed in the journal *Science*, as science, and praised there as well, by a geneticist from MIT (Woods, 1918). Grant's ideas reflected mainstream folk wisdom about heredity, and geneticists of the 1920s were largely unable or unwilling to identify *The Passing of the Great Race* for the pseudoscientific bigotry it was.

In 1929, alongside Madison Grant on the Board of Directors of the American Eugenics Society, were Charles Davenport, who founded the genetics laboratory at Cold Spring Harbor, E. G. Conklin of Princeton, and C. C. Little, founder of the Jackson Laboratories in Bar Harbor. On its large advisory council, alongside the demagogues Albert E. Wiggam and Lothrop Stoddard, were the geneticists Castle and East of Harvard, Guyer of Wisconsin, Holmes of Stanford, Shull of Michigan, Herbert Walter of Brown, Frederick Adams Woods of MIT, and Horatio Hackett Newman and Sewall Wright of Chicago. When Madison Grant was a leader of the American Eugenics Society, those serving with him and under him constituted a veritable Who's Who of the American genetics community. If there were those who muttered about Grant (and some did, such as physical anthropologist Aleš Hrdlička), they posed no major opposition.

In the United States, what was lacking was the invocation of scientific authority to expose and debunk the pseudo-science. Those critiques were consequently obliged to come from nongeneticists. Thomas Hunt Morgan worked in the same building as

Franz Boas, who had been criticizing the movement publicly for over a decade, but limited his own criticisms to a few mildly sarcastic comments in articles published in the mid-1920s. Morgan, interestingly, was a notable holdout from the membership rolls of the American Eugenics Society. However, the first public criticism of the eugenics movement by a biologist was published by Raymond Pearl of Johns Hopkins in a literary magazine in 1927.

German geneticists of the 1930s and 1940s adopted the ideas of their U.S. counterparts enthusiastically. As historians are now showing (e.g., Kuhl, 1995; Paul, 1996) it is surprisingly difficult to distinguish the Nazi geneticists from the non-Nazi geneticists. Who could have known that when geneticists were agreeing that the poor and socially marginalized were not biologically good enough to reproduce, the Germans would have taken them so seriously?

This raises a good question: What is an adequate response to that recognition? "Whoops?" "Hey, we didn't say to kill them, we only said to sterilize them?"

The reason for bringing up the eugenics movement is not to bash the scientific study of heredity, but to analyze it and learn from our mistakes. It would be unfair to judge the scientists of another era with our hindsight, but we may acknowledge a debt accrued by their descendants, payable in the recognition of a responsibility. The key feature is this: Genetics was corrupted in the 1920s by the confusion of folk knowledge with scientific inference. For whatever reasons, outsiders who recognized it were shunned, and insiders were, as they say, a day late and a dollar short. The fairly obvious lesson to be learned is that where science appears to validate folk beliefs, it needs to be subjected to considerably higher standards of scrutiny than ordinary science.

On the other hand, when information about human heredity is at issue, who else can we rely on? In spite of its interest conflict, it is the responsibility specifically of the genetics community to distinguish for the rest of us between folk heredity and scientific knowledge in this area. Unfortunately, it is not part of the training of geneticists generally to deal with this. Geneticists are trained to carry out science, to utilize technology, but not to reflect on the political prejudices intruding into a previous generation's science, much less into their own. That burden is currently being borne by 5% of the Human Genome Project's budget, allocated for Ethical, Legal, and Social Implications of human genome research and whose very establishment is a great credit to the HGP's first director, James Watson.

What ELSI has to say about *The Bell Curve* is significant: "Neither Herrnstein nor Murray are geneticists nor have they carried out studies themselves on the genetic basis of behavior .... [W]e deplore *The Bell Curve*'s misrepresentation of the state of genetic knowledge in this area and the misuse of genetics to inform social policy" (Andrews & Nelkin, 1996, pp. 13–14).

In other words, they crucially identify the book properly for occupying a locus outside the scientific study of heredity. Geneticists did not make that observation in the days of Madison Grant, until it was too late. It is nice to know that progress is being made, but it has to be more widely disseminated, both within the genetics community and the scientific community at large.

Applied to human issues, genetics becomes a humanistic and social science, and it has a poor track record. The first generation of modern human geneticists failed to appreciate the fundamental civil liberties and human rights we take for granted now. If the postmodern world is a better place now, it is unfortunately in spite of, not because of, the genetics and geneticists of that era.

The challenge for scientists of this era is to unharness folk heredity from the science of genetics, to repudiate and resist exploiting the popular prejudices about heredity. That requires a bit of rethinking about science education, and works like *The Bell Curve* regularly make that necessary.

ACKNOWLEDGMENTS

I wish to thank Jeff Fish and Mark Nathan Cohen for their comments on an early version of this chapter. Some of the discussions in this chapter overlap material presented in essays in the *Anthropology Newsletter.*

REFERENCES

Andrews, L., & Nelkin, D. (1996). The bell curve: A statement. *Science, 271,* 13–14.

Begley, S. (1987, November 23). All about twins. *Newsweek,* pp. 58–69.

Bendyshe, T. (1865). The history of anthropology. *Memoirs of the Anthropological Society of London, 1,* 360–364.

Bowcock, A. M., Kidd, J. R., Mountain, J. L., Hebert, J. M., Carotenuto, L., Kidd, K. K., & Cavalli-Sforza, L. L. (1991). Drift, admixture, and selection in human evolution: A study with DNA polymorphisms. *Proceedings of the National Academy of Sciences USA, 88,* 839–843.

Cavalli-Sforza, L. L. (1974). The genetics of human populations. *Scientific American, 231,* 81–89.

Cavalli-Sforza, L. L., & Edwards, A. W. F. (1965). Analysis of human evolution. In S. J. Geerts (Ed.), *Genetics today: Proceedings of the XI International Congress of Genetics* (pp. 923–933). Oxford, UK: Pergamon.

Cavalli-Sforza, L. L., Menozzi, P., & Piazza, A. (1995). *The history and geography of human genes.* Princeton, NJ: Princeton University Press.

Comings, D. (1989). Presidential address: The genetics of human behavior—Lessons for tow societies. *American Journal of Human Genetics, 44,* 452–460.

Coon, C. S. (1962). *The origin of races.* New York: Knopf.

Coon, C. S. (1968). Comment on "bogus science." *Journal of Heredity, 60,* 154.

Davenport, C. B. (1911). *Heredity in relation to eugenics.* New York: Holt.

Davis, F. J. (1991). *Who is black?* University Park: Pennsylvania State University Press.

Diamond, J. (1992). *The third chimpanzee.* New York: HarperCollins.

Dobzhansky, T. (1968). More bogus "science" of race prejudice. *Journal of Heredity, 59,* 102–104.

Gill, G. (1998, March). The beauty of race and races. *Anthropology Newsletter,* 1, 4.

Grady, D. (1997, January 19). Father doesn't always know best. *The New York Times.*

Grant, M. (1916). *The passing of the great race.* New York: Scribner's.

Hamer, D., & Copeland, P. (1998). *Living with our genes: Why they matter more than you think.* New York: Doubleday.

Hamer, D., Hu, S., Magnuson, V. L., Hu, N., & Pattatucci, A. M. L. (1993). A linkage between DNA markers on the X chromosome and male sexual orientation. *Science, 261,* 321–327.

Hannaford, I. (1996). *Race: The history of an idea in the west.* Baltimore: Johns Hopkins.

Harpending, H. (1994). Gene frequencies, DNA frequencies, and human origins. *Perspectives in Biology and Medicine, 37,* 384–394.

Herrnstein, R. J., & Murray, C. (1994). *The bell curve: Intelligence and class structure in American life.* New York: The Free Press.

Jaroff, L. (1989, March 20). The gene hunt. *Time,* pp. 62–67.

Koshland, D. E. (1990). The rational approach to the irrational. *Science, 250,* 189.

Koshland, D. E. (1993). Frontiers of neuroscience. *Science, 262,* 635.

Kuhl, S. (1994). *The Nazi connection.* New York: Oxford University Press.

Lane, C. (1994, December 1). The tainted sources of the bell curve. *The New York Review of Books,* pp. 14–19.

Lang, J. S. (1987, April 13). The gene factor: Happiness is a reunited set of twins. *U.S. News and World Report,* pp. 63–66.

Lewontin, R. C. (1972). The apportionment of human diversity. *Evolutionary Biology, 6,* 381–398.

Livingstone, F. B. (1962). On the non-existence of human races. *Current Anthropology, 3,* 279–281.

Marks, J. (1996). Science and race. *American Behavioral Scientist, 40,* 123–133.

Marks, J. (1997a, February). Limits of our knowledge: Ability, responses and responsibilities. *Anthropology Newsletter, 38*(2), pp. 3, 5.

Marks, J. (1997b). Skepticism about behavioral genetics. In M. S. Frankel (Ed.), *Exploring public policy issues in genetics* (pp. 159–172). Washington, DC: American Association for the Advancement of Science.

Marks, J. (1998). Replaying the race card. *Anthropology Newsletter, 39*(5), 1, 4–5.

Marks, J., & Lyles, R. B. (1994). Rethinking genes. *Evolutionary Anthropology, 3,* 139–146.

Merriwether, D. A., Clark, A. G., Ballinger, S. W., Schurr, T. G., Soodyall, H., Jenkins, T., Sherry, S. T., & Wallace, D. C. (1991). The structure of human mitochondrial DNA variation. *Journal of Molecular Evolution, 33,* 543–555.

Montagu, M. F. A. (1941). The concept of race in the human species in the light of genetics. *Journal of Heredity, 32,* 243–247.

Nei, M., & Roychoudhury, A. K. (1981). *Genetic relationships and evolution of human races: Evolutionary Biology* (Vol. 14). New York: Plenum.

Nelkin, D., & Lindee, M. S. (1995). *The DNA mystique: The gene as cultural icon.* New York: Freeman.

Nott, J. C., & Gliddon, G. R. (1854). *Types of mankind.* Philadelphia: Lippincott.

Paul, D. (1996). Genetics and the swastika. *Dimensions, 10,* 23–28.

Piazza, A. (1997). Un concept sans fondement biologique [A concept lacking a biological basis]. *La Recherche (Paris), 302,* 64–68.

Putnam, C. (1967). *Race and reality.* Washington, DC: Public Affairs Press.

Ripley, W. Z. (1899). *The races of Europe.* New York: Appleton.

Rushton, J. P. (1995). *Race, evolution, and behavior: A life-history approach.* New Brunswick, NJ: Transaction.

Skorecki, K., Selig, S., Blazer, S., Bradman, R., Bradman, N. W., Ismajlowiscz, P. J. M., & Hammer, M. (1997). Y chromosomes of Jewish priests. *Nature, 385,* 32.

Subramanian, S. (1995, January 16). The story in our genes. *Time,* pp. 54–55.

Terrell, J. E., & Stewart, P. J. (1996). The paradox of human population genetics at the end of the twentieth century. *Reviews in Anthropology, 25,* 13–33.

Tishkoff, S., Dietzsch, E., Speed, W., Pakstis, A. J., Kidd, J., Cheung, K., Bonnie-Tamir, B., Santachiara-Benerecetti, A., Moral, P., Krings, M., Paabo, S., Watson, E., Risch, N., Jenkins, T., & Kidd, K. (1996). Global patterns of linkage disequilibrium at the CD4 locus and modern human origins. *Science, 271*, 1380–1387.

Woods, F. A. (1918). The passing of the great race (review). *Science, 48*, 419–420.

The Myth of Race[*]

Jefferson M. Fish

The most important feature of Latin American lowland race relations since the abolition of slavery is the absence of sharply defined racial groupings ... one is obliged to conclude ... that there is no such thing as a Negro group or a white group.... One of the most striking consequences of the Brazilian system of racial identification is that parents and children and even brothers and sisters are frequently accepted as representatives of quite opposite racial types. (Harris, 1964, pp. 54–57)

The notion of mental illness [or, one might substitute in the current context, race] has outlived whatever usefulness it may have had and it now functions as a myth ... the myth of mental illness [race] encourages us to believe in its logical corollary: that social intercourse would be harmonious, satisfying, and the secure basis for a good life were it not for the disrupting influences of mental illness [race].... Mental illness [race] is a myth whose function it is to disguise and thus render more palatable the bitter pill of moral conflicts in human relations. (Szasz, 1970, pp. 21–24)

---

*This chapter is a revision, major expansion (including partial folk taxonomies of "race" from an additional six cultures), and substantial reshaping of the article *Mixed Blood* (Fish, 1995a) that appeared in *Psychology Today*. Because the chapter is about race, it uses mainly racial terms, like *black* and *white* (in lowercase, following common practice in anthropology), rather than cultural terms, like *African American* and *European American*. The term American is also used to refer to the people and culture of the United States because that is our folk term, even though other inhabitants of the New World also think of themselves and their cultures as American.

WHAT IS RACE?

D espite all the talk—including President Clinton's national dialogue—about race, race relations, and racial differences, people rarely stop to ask themselves "What is race?" If race in the biological sense happens to be a nonexistent entity, like phlogiston, then we have to do some rethinking about who we are, how we have been understanding ourselves, and how we have been viewing others and relating to them.

The question of what race is can be divided into two more limited ones. The answers to both questions have long been known by anthropologists, but seem not to have reached other social or behavioral scientists, let alone the public at large (Fish, 1995b). Both answers imply a conceptual world strikingly different from what Americans think of as race, and this chapter explores that world.

The first question is "How can we understand the variation in physical appearance among human beings?" It is interesting to discover that Americans (including some researchers who should know better) view only a part of the variation as "racial," whereas other equally evident variability is not so viewed.

The second question is "How can we understand the kinds of racial classifications applied to differences in physical appearance among human beings?" Interestingly, different cultures label these physical differences in different ways. Far from describing biological entities, American racial categories are merely one of numerous culture-specific schemes for reducing uncertainty about how people should respond to other people. The fact that Americans believe that Asians, blacks, Hispanics, and whites constitute biological entities called races is a matter of cultural interest rather than scientific substance. It is misinformation that tells us something about American culture, but nothing about the human species. In short, the answer to the question "What is race?" is "There is no such thing. Race is a myth."

Etics and Emics

The two questions—regarding variations in appearance and variations in classification—deal with, respectively, the etics and emics (Pike, 1954, 1967) of human physical variation. *Etics* refers to abstract categories or other elements that can be studied objectively and compared across cultures, such as skin color or height. (The word *etics* comes from the ending of *phonetics*, the study of the actual physical sounds of speech and their production.) *Emics* refers to elements of cultural meaning that must be studied within each culture separately, as systems of meaning vary from one culture to another. Thus, as we shall see, different cultures classify the same range of people into different "racial" categories, just as different languages group different sets of sounds produced by the same vocal apparatus into different units of meaning. (The word *emics* comes from the ending of *phonemics*, the study of units of meaning, or phonemes, in different languages.)

Unfortunately, many Americans, including many American scientists, inaccurately assume that American emic categories of "race" are etic biological categories of human physical variation. This ethnocentric confusion of American culture with objective reality underlies many of the inaccurate and misleading assertions that abound in discussions of race. Cross-cultural psychologists recognize that it is possible to operationally define a particular concept (e.g., race) that comes from a particular culture (e.g., the United States) in such a way that it can be imposed on other cultures of which it is not a part for the purposes of gathering comparative data. Such a concept is referred to as an *imposed etic* (Berry, 1969).

HUMAN PHYSICAL VARIATION

Let us begin by considering human physical variation. Human beings are a species, which means that people from anywhere on the planet can mate with others from anywhere else and produce fertile offspring. (Horses and donkeys are two different species because, even though they can mate with each other, their offspring—mules—are sterile.)

Our species evolved in Africa from earlier forms and eventually spread out around the planet. Over time, human populations that were geographically separated from one another came to differ in physical appearance. The three main reasons for these differences are mutation, natural selection, and genetic drift. Because genetic mutations occur randomly, different mutations will occur and accumulate over time in geographically separated populations. Also, as we have known since Darwin, different geographical environments select for different physical traits that confer a reproductive advantage. Finally, the largest proportion of variability among populations may well result from purely random factors. This random change in the frequencies of already-existing genes is known as *genetic drift.*

If an earthquake or disease kills off a large segment of a population, those who survive to reproduce are likely to differ from the original population in many ways. Similarly, if a group divides and a subgroup moves away, the two will, by chance, differ in the frequency of various genes. Even the mere fact of physical separation will over time lead two equivalent populations to differ in the frequency of genes. These randomly acquired population differences will accumulate over successive generations along with any others due to mutation or natural selection.

A number of the differences in physical appearance among populations around the globe appear to have adaptive value. For example, people in the tropics of Africa and South America came to have dark skins, presumably through n   ¬¹ selection, as darker skins conferred the survival advantage of protection agai areas, like northern Europe or northern North America, whic periods of time, and where people covered their bodies for wai have light skins that maximize use of sunlight to produce vitar

The indigenous peoples of the New World arrived about 15 the last ice age, following game across the Bering Strait. (7 enough to create a land bridge because so much water was in the form of ice.) Over time, they spread throughout the New World, implying that the dark-skinned Indians of the South American tropics are descended from much lighter skinned ancestors, similar in appearance to the Eskimo. In other words, even though skin color is the most salient feature thought by Americans to be an indicator of race—and race is assumed to have great time depth—it is subject to relatively rapid evolutionary change. Meanwhile, the extra (epicanthic) fold of eyelid skin, which Americans also view as racial, and which evolved in Asian populations to protect the eye against the cold, continues to exist among South American native peoples in hot as well as cold climates because its presence (unlike a light skin) offers no reproductive disadvantage. Hence, skin color and eyelid form, which Americans think of as traits of different races, occur together or separately in different populations.

There are other physical differences that Americans do not think of as racial, but that also appear to have evolved through natural selection. For example, some populations in very cold climates, like the Eskimo, developed rounded bodies. This is because the closer an object is to a sphere, the less surface area it has to radiate heat. In contrast, some populations in very hot climates, like the Masai, developed lanky bodies. This is because—like the tubular pipes of an old-fashioned radiator—the high ratio of surface area to volume allows people to radiate a lot of heat.

In terms of Americans' thinking about race, lanky people or rounded people are two kinds of whites or blacks. However, it is equally reasonable to view light-skinned people and dark-skinned people as two kinds of "lankys" or "roundeds." In other words, our culturally specific categories for the racial classification of people arbitrarily include certain dimensions (e.g., light vs. dark skin) and exclude others (e.g., rounded vs. elongated bodies). There is no biological basis for classifying race according to skin color instead of body form—or according to any other variable, for that matter. All that exists is (a) variability in what people look like and, as discussed later, (b) the ways different cultures classify that variability. There is no "third thing" left over that can be called race. This is why race is a myth.

Skin color and body form do not vary together; this observation can also be made regarding the facial features Americans think of as racial—eye color, nose width (actually, the ratio of length to width), lip thickness (evertedness), hair form, and hair color. They do not vary together either. If they did, then a "totally white" person would have very light skin color, straight blond hair, blue eyes, a narrow nose, and thin lips; a "totally black" person would have very dark skin color, black tight curly hair, dark brown eyes, a broad nose, and thick lips. Those in between would have—to a correlated degree—wavy light brown hair, light brown eyes, and intermediate nose and lip forms.

People of mixed European and African ancestry who look like this do exist, but they are the exception rather than the rule. Anyone who wants to can make up a chart of facial features, go to a location with a diverse population (e.g., the New York City subway), and verify that there are people with all possible combinations of facial features. One might, for example, see someone with tight curly blond hair, light skin, blue eyes, a broad nose, and thick lips, whose features are half "black" and half "white." That is, each of the person's facial features occupies one end or the other of a supposedly racial continuum, with no intermediary forms (like wavy light brown hair). Such people demonstrate that supposedly racial features do not vary together.

Because the human species spent most of its existence in Africa, different populations in Africa have been separated from each other longer than east Asians or northern Europeans have been separated from each other or from Africans. As a result, there is remarkable physical variation among the indigenous peoples of Africa that goes unrecognized by Americans, who view them all as belonging to the same race. In contrast to the very tall Masai, the diminutive stature of the very short Pygmies may have evolved as an advantage in moving rapidly through tangled forest vegetation. The Bushmen of the Kalahari desert have very large (steatopygous) buttocks (presumably to store body fat in one place, for times of food scarcity, leaving the rest of the body uninsulated to radiate heat) and "peppercorn" hair. (Hair in separated tufts, like tight curly hair, leaves space to radiate the heat that rises through the body to the scalp; straight hair lies flat and holds in body heat, like a cap.) By viewing Africans as constituting a single race, Americans ignore their greater physical variability, assigning racial significance to lesser differences between them and others.

Although it is true that most inhabitants of northern Europe, east Asia, and central Africa look like Americans' conceptions of one or another of the three purported races, most inhabitants of south Asia, southwest Asia, north Africa, and the Pacific islands do not. Thus, the 19th-century view of the human species as comprised of Caucasoid, Mongoloid, and Negroid races, still held by many Americans, is based on a partial and unrepresentative view of human variability. In other words, what is now known about human physical variation does not correspond to what Americans think of as race. (Readers interested in understanding human physical variation in greater detail than can be presented here—or in other chapters of this book—are referred to the work of Alland [1971], Marks [1995], and other physical anthropologists.)

FOLK TAXONOMIES

In contrast to the question of the actual physical variation among human beings, there is the question of how people classify that variation. Scientists classify things in scientific taxonomies—for example, chemists' periodic table of the elements, or biologists' classification of life forms into kingdoms, phyla, and so forth.

In every culture, people also classify things along culture-specific dimensions of meaning. For example, paper clips and staples are understood by Americans as paper fasteners, and nails are not, even though, in terms of their physical properties, all three consist of differently shaped pieces of metal wire. The physical variation in pieces of metal wire can be seen as analogous to human physical variation. The categories of cultural meaning, like paper fasteners versus wood fasteners can be seen as analogous to races. Anthropologists who study these kinds of classifications refer to them as folk taxonomies.

Consider the avocado—is it a fruit or a vegetable? Americans would say it is a vegetable. We eat it in salads with oil and vinegar. Brazilians, on the other hand, would say it is a fruit. They eat it for dessert with lemon juice and sugar. How can we explain this difference in classification?

The avocado is an edible plant, and the American and Brazilian folk taxonomies, although containing cognate terms, classify some edible plants differently. The avocado does not change. It is the same biological entity; but its folk classification changes, depending on who is doing the classifying. A botanist would say that it is a fruit, but this does not mean that Brazilians are correct and Americans are wrong. It merely means that botanists happen to use the same word—with a different meaning —in their scientific taxonomy that Brazilians use in their folk taxonomy.

Human beings are also biological entities. Just as we can ask if an avocado is a fruit or a vegetable, we can ask if a person is white or black. When we ask race questions, the answers we get come from folk taxonomies. Terms like white or black applied to people—or vegetable or fruit applied to avocados—do not give us biological information about people or avocados. Rather, they exemplify how cultural groups (Brazilians or Americans) classify people and avocados.

American "Races"

Hypodescent is the name that anthropologists use for the way in which the American folk taxonomy classifies race according to "blood." According to hypodescent, (a) the various purported racial categories can be arranged in a hierarchy along a single dimension, from the most prestigious (white), through intermediary forms (e.g., Asian), to the least prestigious (black); and (b) when a couple come from two different categories, all their children (thus, the descent in hypodescent) are classified as belonging to the less prestigious category (thus, the hypo). Hence, all the offspring of one white parent and one black parent—regardless of the children's physical appearances—are called black in the United States. One curious result of the American folk taxonomy is that a white woman can give birth to a black child, but a black woman cannot give birth to a white child.

The folk term for the quality carried by members of so-called races, that places all offspring—regardless of their physical appearance—in the less prestigious category, is *blood*. For example, an American "native language" sentence might be, "Because Mary's father is white and her mother is black, Mary is black because she has black blood." (American researchers who think they are studying racial differences in behavior would, like other Americans, classify Mary as black.) In American folk terms, the use of blood as the key to classifying people according to hypodescent is known as the *one drop rule*: Someone with one drop of black blood is black.

The American folk concept of blood does not behave like genes. Genes are units that cannot be subdivided. When several genes jointly determine a trait, chance decides which ones come from each parent. For example, if eight genes determine a trait,[1] a child gets four from each parent. If a mother and a father each have the hypothetical genes BBBBWWWW, then a child could be born with any combination of B and W genes, from BBBBBBBB to WWWWWWWW. In contrast, the folk concept blood behaves like a uniform and continuous entity. It can be divided in two indefinitely—for example, quadroons and octoroons are said to be people who have one quarter and one-eighth black blood. Oddly, because of hypodescent, Americans consider people with one-eighth black blood to be black rather than white, despite their having seven-eighths white blood.

Hypodescent, or blood, is not informative about the physical appearance of people. For example, when two parents called black in the United States have a number of children, the children are likely to vary in physical appearance. In the case of skin color, they might vary from lighter than the lighter parent to darker than the darker parent. However, they would all receive the same racial classification—black—regardless of their skin color.[2]

All that hypodescent tells you is that, when someone is classified as something other than white (e.g., Asian), at least one of his or her parents is classified in the same way, and that neither parent has a less prestigious classification (e.g., black). That is, hypodescent is informative about ancestry—specifically, parental classification— rather than physical appearance.

There are many strange consequences of our folk taxonomy. For example, someone who inherited no genes that produce African-appearing physical features would still be considered black if he or she has a parent classified as black. The category "passing for white" includes many such people. Americans have the curious belief that people who look white but have a parent classified as black are really black in some biological sense, and are being deceptive if they present themselves as white. Such examples make it clear that race is a social rather than a physical classification.

From infancy, human beings learn to recognize very subtle differences in the faces of those around them. Black babies see a wider variety of black faces than white faces, and white babies see a wider variety of white faces than black faces. Because they are only exposed to a limited range of human variation, adult members of each "race" come to see their own group as containing much wider variation than others. Thus, because of this perceptual learning, blacks see greater physical variation among themselves than among whites, whereas whites see the opposite. In this case, however, there is a clear answer to the question of which group contains greater physical variability—blacks are correct.

Why is this the case? Take a moment to think about it, before reading on. This is a good opportunity to play amateur anthropologist and briefly try to step out of American culture.

It is often difficult to get white people to accept what at first appears to contradict the evidence they can see clearly with their own eyes—but that is really the result of a

---

[1]The hypothetical number eight was chosen for illustrative purposes because of the tradition in places like New Orleans of classifying people according to their proportion of black blood as mulatto (½), quadroon ($^1/_4$), or octoroon ($^1/_8$).

[2]A number of identity-related issues facing Americans of mixed ancestry were discussed by Fish and Newton (1998).

history of perceptual learning. However, the reason that blacks view themselves as more varied is not that their vision is more accurate. Rather, it is that blacks also have a long history of perceptual learning although it differs from that of whites. (In addition, during their early years, they have been observers of a larger range of human variation.)

The reason there is greater physical variation among blacks than among whites in the United States goes back to the principle of hypodescent, which classifies all people with one black parent and one white parent as black. If they were all considered white (i.e., if hypodescent were redefined so that anyone with one drop of white blood was white), then there would be more physical variation among whites. In other words, what appears to be a difference in biological variability is really a difference in cultural classification.

Brazilian Tipos

Perhaps the clearest way to understand that the U.S. folk taxonomy of race is merely one of many—arbitrary and unscientific like all the others—is to contrast it with a very different one, that of Brazil. The Portuguese word in the Brazilian folk taxonomy that corresponds to the American *race*, is *tipo*. *Tipo*, which is a cognate of the English word *type*, is a descriptive term that serves as a kind of shorthand for a series of physical features. Because, as we have seen, people's physical features vary independently of one another, there are a lot of *tipos*.

As *tipos* are descriptive terms, they vary regionally in Brazil, in part reflecting regional differences in the development of colloquial Portuguese, but in part because the physical variation they describe is different in different regions. Because the Brazilian situation is so complex, I limit my description of *tipos* to some of the main ones used in the city of Salvador, Bahia, to describe people whose physical appearance is understood to be made up of African and European features.[3] (I use the female terms throughout; in nearly all cases the male term simply changes the last letter from *a* to *o*.)[4]

---

[3]I am omitting terms for Brazilian Indians (e.g., *india*), and for people whose appearance is thought to reflect Indian–white (e.g., *mameluca*) or Indian–black (e.g., *cafuza*) mixtures to avoid excessive complexity. Terms for some such people do appear, however, where they are relevant for illustrative purposes, in presentations of folk taxonomies from other cultures later. I should also mention that some Brazilian terms have more than one meaning. For example, in addition to referring to a specific physical appearance, the term *morena* is sometimes used as a vague descriptor, especially when referring to oneself, to indicate a (usually lighter) classification between *branca* and *preta*.

[4]There is no consistently satisfactory way of referring to categories from gender-marked Romance languages in English. I have chosen in this chapter to use the female forms for Portuguese and Spanish terms (even though the male form is grammatically the general one) because the race-related English terms *blonde* and *brunette* refer to women and because *a* comes before *o* in the alphabet. In the case of French, however, the feminine ending is often attached as a suffix to the masculine one, so use of the masculine form makes for a simpler visual presentation—for example, *mulâtre(sse)*. My apologies for the occasional feminine–masculine inconsistencies in the presentations of folk taxonomies that follow. Unfortunately, different choices on my part would only have led to different inconsistencies.

This information was gathered initially while I was living in Brazil from 1974 to 1976, and was supplemented during subsequent visits there and through contacts with Brazilians in the United States.

Proceeding along a dimension from the "whitest" to the "blackest" *tipos*, a *loura* is whiter than white, with blond straight hair, blue or green eyes, light skin color, narrow nose, and thin lips. Brazilians who come to the United States think that a *loura* means a blonde, and are surprised to find that the American term refers to hair color only. A *branca* has light skin color, eyes of any color, hair of any color or form except tight curly, a nose that is not broad, and lips that are not thick. *Branca* translates as "white," although Brazilians of this *tipo* who come to the United States—especially those from elite families—are often dismayed to find that they are not considered white here, and, even worse, are viewed as Hispanic despite the fact that they speak Portuguese.

A *morena* has brown or black hair that is wavy or curly but not tight curly, tan skin, a nose that is not narrow, and lips that are not thin. Brazilians who come to the United States think that a *morena* is a brunette and are surprised to find that brunettes are considered white but *morenas* are not. Americans have difficulty classifying *morenas*—many of whom are of Latin American origin: Are they black or Hispanic? (One might also observe that *morenas* have trouble with Americans for not just accepting their appearance as a given, but asking instead "Where do you come from?," "What language did you speak at home?," "What was your maiden name?," or even, more crudely, "What are you?")

A *mulata* looks like a *morena*, except with tight curly hair, and a slightly darker range of hair colors and skin colors. A *preta* looks like a *mulata*, except with dark brown skin, broad nose, and thick lips. To Americans, *mulatas* and *pretas* are both black, and if forced to distinguish between them, Americans would refer to them as light-skinned blacks and dark skinned blacks, respectively.

If Brazilians were forced to divide the range of *tipos*, from *loura* to *preta* into kinds of whites and kinds of blacks (a distinction they do not ordinarily make), they would draw the line between *morenas* and *mulatas*. Americans would draw the line between *brancas* and *morenas*.

The proliferation of *tipos* and the difference in the white–black dividing line do not, however, exhaust the differences between the Brazilian and American folk taxonomies. There are *tipos* in the Afro-European domain that are considered to be neither black nor white, an idea that is difficult for Americans visiting Brazil to comprehend. The example that I alluded to earlier, of a person with tight curly blond (or red) hair, light skin, blue (or green) eyes, broad nose, and thick lips, is a description of a *sarará*. The opposite features—straight black hair, dark skin, brown eyes, narrow nose, and thin lips—are those of a *cabo-verde* (Cape Verde). *Sarará* and *cabo-verde* are both *tipos* that are considered by Brazilians in Salvador, Bahia, to be neither black nor white.

The partial Brazilian folk taxonomy just described is summarized in Table 5.1.

As you can see, there are many differences between the Brazilian and American folk taxonomies of race. The U.S. system tells you about how people's parents are

TABLE 5.1
Partial Folk Taxonomy from Salvador, Bahia, Brazil
of Tipos in the Afro-European Domain

loura/o

branca/o

(American division between "kinds of whites" and "kinds of blacks")

morena/o

sarará ——————————(neither "black" nor "white") ——————————cabo-verde

(Brazilian division between "kinds of whites" and "kinds of blacks")

mulata/o

preta/o

Note. The vertical dimension, from *loura/o* to *preta/o* can be understood by Americans as gradations from white to black. (*Loura* and other *a* endings—except for *sarará* and *cabo-verde*, which apply to both sexes—are the feminine form, and *louro* is the masculine form. The horizontal dimension of contrast, from *sarará* to *cabo-verde*, consists of people considered by Bahians to be neither black nor white. Degler (1971) and Harris (1964, 1970) discussed Brazilian *tipos* in greater detail.

classified but not what they look like; the Brazilian system tells you what they look like but not the classification of their parents. When two parents of intermediate appearance have many children in the United States, their children are all of one race; in Brazil they are of many *tipos*.

Americans believe that race is an immutable biological given; but it is easy to see that many people can change their race by getting on a plane and going from the United States to Brazil—just as, if they take an avocado with them, it changes from a vegetable into a fruit. In both cases, what changes is not the physical appearance of the person or avocado, but rather the way they are classified.

ANCESTRY AND PHYSICAL APPEARANCE
IN OTHER FOLK TAXONOMIES

I have gone into some detail about the Brazilian folk taxonomy for a number of reasons. To begin with, it is the most elaborate system (containing the greatest number of classifications, many more than appear in Table 5.1) and the most different from American hypodescent. Furthermore, it is something I can write about with some confidence, having lived in Brazil, experienced it in practice, interviewed Brazilians about it, read about it, and discussed it with anthropologist colleagues. Thus, despite regional differences in Brazil and changes over time, I can feel some assurance that the presentation in this chapter gives American readers a good sense of the way Brazilians think about what Americans call race.

However, there is another reason. In examining superficially a number of other systems of classification, it seems to me that the U.S. and Brazilian systems represent two general principles of classification that can be found in other cultures in differing ways and to differing degrees.[5]

For the sake of simplicity, we can call these ancestry (e.g., American race) and physical appearance (e.g., Brazilian *tipo*[6]).

It should be pointed out in passing that, within each culture, there are behavioral assumptions and stereotypes associated with the various categories. Thus, people assume that they know something of social relevance by observing an individual's physical appearance. What it is that they know—or infer or assume—is the result of historical and other social circumstances within the culture. Nevertheless, the social usefulness of these category systems is one of the reasons for their persistence over time.

Over the years, I have been curious about what different folk taxonomies for classifying people might be like in other cultures.[7] When I have traveled, I have asked locals what they call different kinds of people, and have volunteered information about

---

[5]In the presentations of New World folk taxonomies that follow, it is evident that physical appearance is a more widely used principle than ancestry—making the U.S. system appear deviant by comparison. Perhaps a study of the "racial" folk taxonomies of European cultures—especially those of northern Europe—would reveal more widespread use of the principle of ancestry and demonstrate significant cultural variations in its application.

In particular, whereas both Europeans and Americans have a concept of nationality, there is an important meaning for the term in Europe that Americans do not have. This European use of nationality, which is similar to our concept of blood (and, indeed, is often referred to as blood) may be especially important to understanding the various European "racial" folk taxonomies. Nationality, like the social classification of race, is an emic concept. As such, its meaning can be expected to vary from culture to culture—especially when language barriers impede cultural interchange. (Naturally, geographical, political, religious, historical, and other etic and emic separations also contribute to differentiation in cultural meanings.)

Differences between this European use of nationality and the American concept of race become evident in the way that Bosnian, Croatian, and Serbian immigrants to the United States all find themselves classified together as members of the same racial category (white). This is similar to the way in which Indian and Pakistani immigrants, despite differences in the category of religion that is salient for them, also find themselves lumped together in an American racial category (Asian, or whatever other designation develops over time; see the discussion following).

[6]As with nationality, *tipo* in Portuguese and Spanish and *type* in French is a word with multiple meanings, many of which are shared with the English word *type*. The "racial" use of the word, to refer to a culturally constructed category of physical appearance, however, is not found in American English.

[7]Clearly, there is at least one doctoral dissertation here for an anthropologist, or possibly a sociologist or even a psychologist, who wants to do a more thorough and rigorous description of and comparison among a number of different "racial" folk taxonomies of immigrant groups in the United States. Such a study could also examine the effects of these folk taxonomies on people's identities (including generational differences among immigrants and their children and grandchildren), on intergroup perceptions (including stereotypes), and on intergroup relations. Anyone who wants to do such a dissertation and is looking for an outside reader is encouraged to contact me.

the United States in return. For example, at a psychology convention in England a few years ago, I discovered that the English term for south Asians (Bangladeshis, Indians, Pakistanis, and Sri Lankans) is *black*. This was an interesting finding for two reasons. First, the English seem to have a view of race (based on ancestry or blood) much like our own—understandably, because race is a social rather than a biological classification. That is, because the United States was originally a colony of theirs, both current systems are descended from a common past. Second, south Asians as relatively new immigrants to the United States still have an ambiguous racial identity in this country.

For example, in a class discussion a few years ago (and with her permission), I asked a student who was the daughter of Bangladeshi immigrants what race she was. She paused, looked perplexed, and said "That's a good question." She and the class were able to see, after some discussion, that the problem was not hers but came from the inadequacy of the inaccurately presumed-to-be-biological American folk taxonomy. Recent signs suggest that south Asians are becoming Asian in the United States (a term that has generally been applied only to east Asians). Hence, an American-born descendant of south Asian immigrants may soon be able to change race from Asian to black by flying from New York City to London, just as other Americans flying from New York City to Salvador, Bahia, Brazil can now change from black to (depending on what they look like) any of the *tipos* listed in Table 5.1, as well as many others.

In addition to asking, while traveling abroad, how people classify one another, I have also done so in my teaching—mainly in my cross-cultural psychology course, but occasionally in other courses in which it was relevant. Fortunately, my university is located in Queens, New York City, the most culturally diverse county in the United States. As a result, over the years I have had the opportunity to get information about folk taxonomies in a number of other cultures, especially those in Latin America and the Caribbean.

In the discussion that follows, highlights of this information from a few additional cultures are presented to further illustrate how widely folk taxonomies of race can vary. Because of space limitations and relevance to understanding U.S. race relations growing out of our history of slavery, the terms presented refer mainly to the Afro-European domain. That is, they are thought by those who use them to denote people whose ancestors come from Europe and/or Africa. (I have included additional terms from other cultures when they seemed important to understanding those systems.) My goal in presenting these partial folk taxonomies is not to swamp the reader with details—with the exception of the American and Brazilian systems, I also have trouble remembering many of the terms. Rather, it is to use these widely varying organizations of categories and subcategories to make overwhelmingly clear the point that racial folk taxonomies are cultural constructions. The American understanding of race does not reflect, and cannot reflect, biological divisions into subspecies because *Homo sapiens* has no subspecies. This important insight, that there is no universal understanding of race, makes comprehensible what would otherwise appear to be conceptual chaos outside of our borders.

A discussion of how and why different cultures evolved different racial folk taxonomies is beyond the scope of this chapter. Suffice it to say—as a sweeping and in many ways inadequate generalization—that groups of individuals, finding themselves in varying cultural, economic, geographical, historical, legal, linguistic, political, and social circumstances, did their best to work out solutions to novel problems. Over time, these social solutions achieved the status of implicit categories of what was understood to be biological reality. For example, under slavery, the legal status of children of slaves fathered by slave owners had to be defined, and after slavery the stratification of society into new groups had to be worked out. It is easy to understand how different social realities in different cultures led to different solutions that expressed themselves in different sets of racial categories.

I should also mention in passing that two terms for people considered intermediate between black and white, that come up in one or another cognate form in different languages and cultures, have revealing derivations. *Mulatto*, which can be found in English, French, Portuguese, and Spanish, comes from mule,[8] and reflects an earlier historical time when the difference between cultural groups and biological species—like horses and donkeys—was not understood. *Moreno* appears in Portuguese and Spanish, is derived from *Moor*, and reflects the long Moorish occupation of the Iberian peninsula.

I find these folk taxonomies fascinating—every new class interview with a bicultural student gives a glimpse of a new world of racial classifications, identities, and intergroup relations.[9] Despite limitations, I believe the following information is worth presenting

---

[8]This chapter deals with a variety of racial terms from a variety of cultures that are used to refer to different kinds of people, as defined by those cultures. My intent has been to include descriptive terms and to exclude pejorative terms or epithets. The history of racism being what it is (albeit differing in each culture), many descriptive terms carry some negative semantic baggage as well—except, of course, terms for whites. For example, *mulatto* in the United States is a term that can be used either descriptively (someone with one white parent and one black parent) or with a negative connotation (e.g., a "half breed" or "tragic mulatto"). Emotional meanings and stereotypes associated with the various terms are not a subject of discussion in this chapter.

[9]I want to make the limitations of these data explicit. I got my initial information from classroom exercises in New York City rather than in everyday settings elsewhere, and from immigrants or children of immigrants who are bicultural Americans rather than from unicultural informants answering questions about their own systems. Thus, my students' cultural knowledge may have been incomplete, or distorted by American filters, or modified to fit the classroom setting. The interviews rarely lasted more than 30 minutes, and were conducted in English—hardly an adequate sample. Often they concerned countries I have never visited. Even when I spoke the relevant language (French, Portuguese, and Spanish—but not Capeverdean, Haitian, or Martinican creole) I had no familiarity with racial terminology or the state of race relations, so I might have omitted important questions that could have altered my presentation here.

In preparing the presentations that follow I consulted in greater detail with additional people who could confirm, clarify, and supplement the information I already had; often the changes were substantial. (When my sources were willing to let me do so, I have acknowledged their contributions.) Nevertheless, these presentations remain suggestive rather than authoritative. People from different geographical locations, of different social class or ethnic backgrounds, of different physical appearance, or different in some other culturally significant way might have provided different information. Should there be any inaccuracies, responsibility for them remains with me.

for a number of reasons. As indicated earlier, by "fleshing out" the range of variation, these examples make clear how profoundly folk taxonomies of race can vary. In addition, the examples illustrate the point that folk taxonomies from different cultures speaking the same language and with common historical elements are more similar to one another than they are to folk taxonomies in some other language and with a more different history. Because language and historical continuity are central aspects of culture, we can see once again that variations in folk taxonomies reflect cultural differences of classification rather than biological subdivisions of the human species. Even within a given language, cognate terms in different cultures often refer to people of different appearances and ancestries, suggesting that they result from divergent processes of cultural evolution. Furthermore, these examples highlight the complexity of the varying experiences of race of American immigrants, as people who understand human variation in terms of a variety of folk taxonomies unexpectedly confront the social reality of our own folk taxonomy—not to mention the varying folk taxonomies of other immigrant groups they encounter.

Haiti

Haiti's folk taxonomy, for example, makes use of elements of both physical appearance and ancestry, and even includes the amazing term (for a foreigner [*un blanc*] of African appearance [*noir*]) *un blanc noir*—literally, "a black white." Furthermore, the Haitian French words *race* and *type* appear to have somewhat different implicit meanings from those we have encountered thus far.

Highlights of the Haitian folk taxonomy are presented in Table 5.2. The two *races*, *blanc*, and *noir*, are classified by both physical appearance and, in the case of *blancs*, ancestry. That is, even if a Haitian's physical appearance is entirely European, if he or she has a parent or sibling whose skin color or other features are considered to reflect African ancestry, the person would be considered a *mulâtre(sse)* rather than a *blanc(he)*. This classification is analogous to the American situation of someone who could "pass for white" but still would not be considered white, and contrasts with Brazil, where the person would be a *branca* or *branco* based on physical appearance alone. In contrast, a Haitian whose physical appearance is *noir* but who has a European-appearing parent or sibling would still be considered *noir*. Thus, the classification of people as *blanc* or *noir* has an element of hypodescent to it.

Between the two *races* are a number of *types*, made up of people considered neither *blanc* nor *noir*. *Types* (like *tipos* in Brazil) are composites of physical features, and terms refer only to physical appearance. The varied appearances of the different *types* are thought to be mixed (*métis*) resulting from the "mixed blood" of the two *races* (*du sang mêlé*). In the sense of being intermediate between, or mixtures of, the two *races*, they can be considered neither white (*blanc*) nor black (*noir*). However, there are no Haitian terms for people who are "neither white nor black" in the sense that Brazilian *sararás* and *cabo-verdes* can be implicitly understood to be on a different dimension of classification from black–white.

TABLE 5.2

Partial Folk Taxonomy of Haitian Races and types

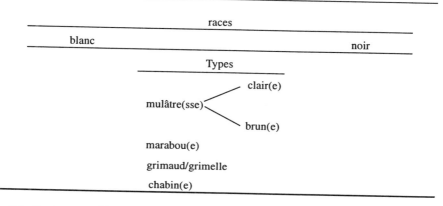

races		
blanc		noir

Types

mulâtre(sse)
— clair(e)
— brun(e)

marabou(e)

grimaud/grimelle

chabin(e)

Note. The two *races*, *blanc* and *noir*, are listed in their masculine forms only; the *types* are listed in masculine forms followed by feminine endings (e.g., a *mulâtre* is a man, a *mulâtresse* is a woman; *grimelle* is the feminine form of *grimaud*). There are two kinds of *mulâtres*, *mulâtre clair* and *mulâtre brun*.

As regards the appearance of different *types*, a *mulâtre* has light skin color; straight black, brown, or light brown (*châtain*) hair; a straight (*pointu*) nose; thin lips; and eyes of any color. Among *mulâtres*, a *mulâtre brun* has darker skin than a *mulâtre clair*. A *marabou* has dark skin color, dark straight hair, a straight nose, thin lips, and brown eyes. The term includes but is not limited to south Asian Indians. A *grimaud* has light skin color; tight curly black, brown, or light brown hair; a broad nose; lips of variable thickness; and brown or green eyes. A *chabin* is similar to a *grimaud*, except with coppery (*peint roux*) skin color and "frizzy" (*frisés*) brownish hair.

I could try to point out similarities between these descriptions and Brazilian or American terms, but my main reaction is one of fascination—"Someone has to study this in greater detail!" Naturally, this fascination comes from my dual American–Brazilian ethnocentrism. The fact that the terms in some other folk taxonomies presented here seem similar to those I am already familiar with, whereas this is not the case with Haitian terms—which therefore pique my curiosity—is a comment on my limited range of experience, not on Haitian categories, which seem normal to Haitians. (Perhaps it is the difference between the French colonial influence and that of England or the Iberian cultures that is responsible for the distinctiveness of the Haitian folk taxonomy.) Clearly, American or Brazilian categories would seem "wrong" or "odd" to Haitians because they would appear arbitrarily to misclassify people. This is the key point about any folk taxonomy—Within a given culture it seems to be a description of reality. For example, Americans believe that blacks and whites are races in some biological sense. However, from outside the culture, it is easy to see that the folk taxonomy is a social construction.

Here are two reasons that the Haitian folk taxonomy strikes me as a really different set of racial categories. First, the *grimaud* is viewed as being closer to *noir* than the *marabou*, even though the *marabou* has a darker skin color. Apparently, Haitians view hair form and facial features as more determinative of blackness than skin color. At least insofar as south Asian *marabous* are concerned, this classification is indeed closer to known genetic relatedness. This is because prehistoric migrations of people from the same central Asian area—located to the north of the Black Sea—into both south Asia and the European peninsula have contributed to the physical appearance of the peoples of both areas.

Second, attempts to translate Haitian *types* into Brazilian *tipos* (e.g., in illustrative examples) require one to pile on a lot of qualifying adjectives. The effect of these adjectives is to indicate that the categories do not really correspond in the first place. For example, to say that a particular *grimaud* looks like a *mulato claro de olhos verdes* (literally, a light *mulato* with green eyes), is really to say that the Haitian *type* category of *grimaud* is a different kind of concept, and does not correspond to the Brazilian *tipo* category of *mulato*.

Perhaps differences between the geographical origins of the groups of people who make up Haiti's population, as compared to those in Brazil or the United States, actually resulted in different constellations of physical appearance. Or perhaps Haitians have simply grouped together different features in their categories from those assembled by Brazilians or Americans in what is, after all, just another set of arbitrarily chosen socially constructed categories. In any event, the sharp contrast between Haitian categories and those of both Brazil and the United States illustrates once again the protean nature of the concept of race.

Martinique

Martinique is a French-speaking island in the Caribbean with a different history from Haiti. Martinique remained a French colony until 1946, when it became a part of France, whereas Haiti has been independent for two centuries—thus providing ample time, along with geographical and political separation, for the two "racial" folk taxonomies to diverge.

As with Haiti, the Martinican folk taxonomy makes use of elements of both physical appearance and ancestry—but it does so in a markedly different way. Both cultures use the terms *race* and *type*, and both view whites (*blancs*) and blacks (*noirs*) as *races*.[10] As in Haiti, *types* are seen as intermediate between the two *races*; but in Martinique *types* are also understood to refer to kinds of *noirs*, as well as to some other people who are neither *blanc* nor *noir*. In addition, although some of the words for different *types* are the same in Haiti and Martinique and some differ, the meanings for a given term are not the same in the two cultures. First, the meanings differ because in

---

[10]In the presentation that follows, I have done my best to follow Martinican practice regarding the capitalization of terms.

Haiti they refer to people who are intermediate between *blanc* and *noir*, whereas in Martinique they refer to a wider range of people. Second, the meanings differ because the same word in the two cultures refers to people of differing physical appearance. In addition, Martinique makes clear distinctions among different kinds of *blancs*, but these are social distinctions based on ancestry and other cultural information—they do not refer to differences in physical appearance. That is, there is a tendency in the Martinican folk taxonomy to make social distinctions among kinds of *blancs*, and distinctions of physical appearance among other people.

Among the *blancs*, the *békés* are the ruling *blanc* elite, descended from the original French colonists, who control the great majority of the economy. The *Métropolitains* are *blancs* who come from continental France to work in Martinique. Others, whose ancestry and geographical origins are unknown, are simply *blancs*.

Among those *types* between *blanc* and *noir*, the *mulâtre* is considered closest to *blanc*. The Martinican *mulâtre* is similar to the Haitian *mulâtre*, with light skin, dark straight hair, and dark eyes (nose form and lip form are not relevant). The Martinican *chabin* is similar to the Haitian *grimaud*, with light skin color and hair and eyes that can also be light in color, but with African hair texture (*cheveux volumineux*—literally voluminous hair). The Martinican *chabin* is sometimes referred to as *un noir blanc* (literally, a white black)—a fascinating contrast to the Haitian term for an African appearing foreigner, *un blanc noir* (a black white).

The Martinican *câpre* is darker than the *chabin*, and similar in appearance to the Haitian *chabin*. Thus, we see that the same term, *chabin*, used by both Martinicans and Haitians, denotes people of different physical appearance, whose appearance is understood to exemplify different meanings of *type*, and who therefore fit into different overall cultural organizations of "racial" concepts. To use the airplane metaphor, a Haitian *grimaud* can change into a *chabin* by flying from Port-au-Prince to Fort-de-France.

The darkest of the Martinican *types*, the *Nègre*, is similar in appearance to the Haitian *noir*, and is considered *noir* in Martinique as well. However, in Martinique there are different *types* of *Nègre*, all of whom are *noir*. This contrasts with Haiti where *noir* is a *race* and does not contain *types*; and the term *type* is understood as referring to admixtures of the two *races*, *blanc* and *noir*, and thus as intermediate between them. In other words, in Martinique the term *type* applies not only to people who are between *blanc* and *noir*, but also to those who are *noir*, as well as to some others who are neither *blanc* nor *noir*. The *types* of *Nègre*, from least to most African appearing in skin color and hair color and texture, are *Nèg Rouge* (red black), *Nèg*, and *Nèg Congo* (Congo black). A *Nèg Rouge* has curly hair that is not black, perhaps having turned reddish from the sun and salt water, and dark skin color with a brownish or reddish cast. A *Nèg* has black hair that is more tightly curled and darker skin color. A *Nèg Congo* is viewed as in some sense pure African, with the darkest skin color and most tightly curled black hair. The term *Nèg Congo* is applied mainly to men.

Finally, mention should be made of the *Coolies*—the descendants of Indians (south Asians) who came to Martinique as laborers following the abolition of slavery, were discriminated against, and had a social status below that of *Nègres*. In addition, those whose physical appearance suggests admixture with descendants of Europeans and/or Africans are known as *chapé-coolies*. (From *échapper*, to escape. The derivation of the term would suggest that *chapé-coolies* are people whose physical appearance allows them to avoid the stigma of looking like a laborer.) Both *Coolies* and *chapé-coolies* are *types* in Martinique, although they would be viewed as other than *blanc* and *noir*. (This is similar to the way Asians in the United States are seen as other than black and white.) Many *Coolies* and *chappé-coolies* would be considered *marabous* in Haiti—a *type* falling between *blanc* and *noir*. This indicates once again the difference in conceptual organization between Haiti's and Martinique's folk taxonomies, as well as the different terms used in each culture.

The preceding partial description of Martinique's folk taxonomy of *races* and *types* is presented in Table 5.3.

Puerto Rico

In contrast to the Haitian and Martinican folk taxonomies, the Puerto Rican folk taxonomy is more like that of Brazil—based on physical appearance—but with fewer terms, and none in the Afro-European domain that would be considered neither black nor white. As in Brazil, a Puerto Rican family with many children of varying appear-

TABLE 5.3
Partial Folk Taxonomy of Martinican Races and Types

races			
blanc		noir	
Social Categories		types	
(not types)	(between blanc and noir)	(noir)	(other than blanc and noir)
béké	mulâtre(sse)	<u>Nègre(sse)</u>	Coolie
Métropolitain(e)	chabin(e)	Nèg(resse) Rouge	chapé-coolie
blanc(he)	câpre(sse)	Nèg(resse)	
		Nèg(resse) Congo	

Note. The two *races, blanc* and *noir,* are listed in their masculine forms only; the *types* are listed in masculine forms followed by feminine endings (e.g., a *mulâtre* is a man, a *mulâtresse* is a woman). The *type* concept does not apply to *blancs*. *Nègre* is a type, and there are three *types* of *Nègre*: *Nèg Rouge, Nèg,* and *Nèg Congo*. *Coolie* and *chapé-coolie* are *types*, and are included in part for purposes of comparison with the Haitian *marabou type* in Table 5.2. The assistance of Valerie Vulcain and Muriel Wiltord of the Martinique Promotion Bureau in preparing this table and the accompanying discussion is gratefully acknowledged.

ance would categorize them by many different terms based on what they look like. Table 5.4 presents some of the main Puerto Rican terms, many of which are cognates (with different meanings) of Brazilian ones presented in Table 5.1. It is important to remember that cultural terms are defined by use, so there are bound to be areas of difference between cognate or similar terms used by different cultures—only field work in those cultures can clarify the areas of overlap and difference. Some of these differences in the meaning of cognate terms are alluded to in the presentation that follows.

In looking at the partial Puerto Rican folk taxonomy, we can see that the first classification that is made, based on physical appearance, is whether the individual belongs to one of three superordinate groups—*blancos, indios,*[11] or *negros.* In the Afro-European domain, that classification is made in a manner reminiscent of America's one drop rule, but unrelated to ancestry—if the person has any African-appearing physical features, he or she is seen as a kind of *negro.*

The following descriptions are my best guesses of intercultural comparisons to give readers a feel for the cultural meanings of terms that I understand only imperfectly. Among *blancos,* a *rubia* is similar in appearance to an American blonde, and a *colorá* is similar to an American redhead. Among *negros,* a *jabá* is similar to an American high yellow, a *trigueña* (wheat colored) is similar to a Brazilian *morena clara* ("light" *morena*), a *mulata* is similar to a Brazilian *morena,* a *morena* is similar

TABLE 5.4
Partial Puerto Rican Folk Taxonomy

blanco	indio	negro
rubia/o	india/o	jabá/jabao
colorá/colorao		trigueña/o
blanca/o		mulata/o
		morena/o
		negra/o
		prieta/o

Note. The vertical dimension, from *jabá/jabao* to *prieta/o* might be viewed by non-Puerto Rican Americans as gradations from light-skinned black to dark-skinned black. (*Blanca* and other *a* endings is the feminine form, and *blanco* is the masculine form.) The assistance of Denise Belén Santiago in preparing this table and the accompanying discussion is gratefully acknowledged.

---

[11]Because Puerto Rican folk terms reflect physical appearance rather than ancestry, *indios* are people whose physical appearance corresponds to what Puerto Ricans believe Indians look like. Because the indigenous peoples of the island were annihilated by the mid-1500s, whatever may constitute the genetic makeup of *indios,* we may be sure that contributions from the original Native Americans are insignificant. This is yet another striking illustration of the way in which racial categories are emic social constructions (and not etic biological classifications).

to a Brazilian *mulata*, a *negra* is similar to a Brazilian *mulata escura* ("dark" *mulata*), and a *prieta* is similar to a Brazilian *preta*.

These comparisons, especially the reversal in position of the terms *morena* and *mulata* between Brazil and Puerto Rico, are a striking illustration of the variability of folk taxonomies even within Latin America. They make clear that the use of cognate terms in different cultures does not imply that they have similar cultural meanings.

Interestingly, these terms are applied only to inhabitants of Puerto Rico. Foreigners are referred to by their country of origin—for example, *alemán* (German) or *francés* (French)—regardless of physical appearance.

Ecuador

Ecuador is similar to Puerto Rico in that Spanish is spoken and the terms in its folk taxonomy are based on physical appearance rather than ancestry. On the other hand, as Ecuador is an Andean country whose population is descended mainly from indigenous populations, its most important distinctions are those that indicate European admixture. Thus, *chola* in the Alteplano and *montúvia* on the Pacific coast refer to people whose physical appearance is believed to reflect a mixture of Indian and European physical traits. (These terms are counterparts of the term *mestizo*, used elsewhere in the Alteplano.) A partial Ecuadorian folk taxonomy is presented in Table 5.5.

Interestingly, in Ecuador, nearly all of these terms seem to be pejorative—or at least impolite. That is, in the course of a discussion no one would say of himself, "I am a *cholo*," or of the person being spoken to to, "You are a *chola*." Rather, the terms would be used *sotto voce* to describe a third party—for example, "Juan is a *cholo*."

Perhaps because the terms are considered negative, the term *blanco* (white) does not appear in everyday discourse. Instead, Ecuadorians of European appearance are referred to by social class terms, such as *de una família aristocrática* (from an

TABLE 5.5
Partial Ecuadorian Folk Taxonomy

blanco	chino	indio		negro
		Andes	**Coast**	
(social class terms)	china/o	chola/o	montúvia/o	mulata/o
gringa/o		india/o	india/o	negra/o
turca/o				
morena/o = trigueña/o	——	morena/o = trigueña/o		morena/o = trigueña/o

Note. Chola and other *a* endings is the feminine form, and *cholo* is the masculine form. The assistance of Lina Norona in preparing this table and the accompanying discussion is gratefully acknowledged.

aristocratic family), *de una muy buena família* (from a very good [i.e., rich] family), or *de una família modesta* (from a family of modest means). As in Puerto Rico, foreigners of any appearance are referred to by their country of origin (e.g., *el francés*), with two exceptions. A person with very light skin and blond hair—usually from northern Europe or the United States—is called a *gringa* or *gringo*. This is not a pejorative term, but rather is similar to the American blonde. Also, the term *turca* or *turco* (literally, Turk) is applied to Arabs, Lebanese, Syrians, Turks, and others of Middle Eastern origin who have tan skin and dark hair.

The category *chino* (literally, Chinese) is used to encompass all east Asians (Chinese, Japanese, and Philippinos) who are referred to as *chinos* rather than by their country of origin. Thus, the term *china*, like *turca*, refers to physical appearance, rather than to ancestry, citizenship, or nationality.

Unlike other terms, *trigueña* and *morena* are complimentary, and refer to an attractive person from any of the groups *blanco*, *indio*, or *negro* (but not *chino*) who has dark straight hair and dark skin. In addition, *trigueña* and *morena* can be used interchangeably—in contrast to Puerto Rico, where they refer to people of different physical appearance.

Jamaica

The contrasts between Haiti and Martinique, and between Puerto Rico and Ecuador, naturally make one want to compare the American set of racial categories with that of another English-speaking New World culture. Like the United States, Jamaica was also a British colony with a slave economy, but its history is very different from U.S. history. Thus, based on cultural reasoning, one would expect it to have developed a different folk taxonomy from ours. Its categories would, however, be expected to show greater similarity to American ones than to those of Haiti, Martinique, or Puerto Rico. That is, despite Jamaica's geographical proximity in the Caribbean to the latter three and similarity in climate, small size, and insular form, one would predict that the British cultural influence would predominate in the formation of racial categories. This is, in fact, the case, despite Jamaican categories being based primarily on physical appearance rather than ancestry.

Social class is very important in Jamaica—money counts more than color. With regard to physical appearance, however, African and European ancestry predominate, and there has been considerable mixture among people from these backgrounds over the years. Although other groups are present, most Jamaicans view their physical appearance as resulting from both African and European traits—a common, expected, and nonproblematic state of affairs. Variation in physical appearance within a family is the norm, and terms exist to refer to some of these differences.

Unlike the situation in the Latin cultures discussed previously, the main physical trait used to classify people in the Afro-European domain is skin color. Facial features, hair texture and color, and eye color are not usually used. Furthermore, because intermediate shades are seen as the norm, the terms *black* and *white* apply to extremes, and are rarely used for Jamaicans. Instead, distinctions are made primarily in the midrange of skin colors, as fair (or light or red), brown, and dark. Thus, it would not be uncommon for a couple to have a fair child, a brown child, and a dark child, and for them and other Jamaicans to describe them that way if asked to do so.[12] This is in contrast to the United States, where all three would be considered black.[13] It also contrasts with the other cultures described earlier, where, as in Jamaica, they would receive different classifications—but where skin color alone would provide insufficient information to categorize them.

For Jamaicans in the United States, our folk taxonomy seems both impoverished and wrong. It seems impoverished because it offers only the two options of black and white, where Jamaicans routinely make more distinctions. It seems wrong because it misclassifies people as white or black (usually just black) when they are actually something in between. Another way of putting this is to say that although both Americans and Jamaicans use the English words *white* and *black* in their folk taxonomies, the words refer to different overlapping groups of people, and thus have different meanings in the two cultures. In the airplane example, someone who gets on as black in New York City can disembark in Kingston as fair (or brown, or dark).

On the other hand, a Brazilian, Haitian, or Puerto Rican might well ask "Why just skin color? Why do English speakers omit all the other obvious variations in facial features, hair texture and color, and eye color (and one could add height or body type) when making up their folk categories?" That is, although the Jamaican system emphasizes an aspect of physical appearance—skin color—in contrast to the American focus on ancestry, the near-exclusive determination of categories in both by skin color forms a contrast to the more elaborate folk taxonomies of physical appearance in Latin cultures.

Outside of the Afro-European domain, Jamaicans have a number of other categories, but for the purposes of this brief presentation only two are mentioned here. These are Chinese and Indian (i.e., south Asian, not Native American). These labels are usually assigned based on physical appearance. When the appearance or known ancestry of a person classified as belonging to one of these groups also suggests representation from the Afro-European domain, he or she is referred to as half Chinese or half Indian.

The preceding partial description of Jamaica's "racial" folk taxonomy is presented in Table 5.6.

---

[12]Jamaicans expect a range of skin colors, and the fact that children might be described differently within a family does not mean that they would be treated differently.

[13]Americans in the 1950s listening to Harry Belafonte's (1956) popular *Calypso* album would doubtless have been surprised to learn that the "Brown Skin Girl" in his song would not have been considered black in Jamaica, nor would the blue-eyed baby left behind with her by the American sailor.

TABLE 5.6
Partial Jamaican Folk Taxonomy

Skin Color	Chinese	Indian
(white)	Chinese	Indian
fair = light = red	half Chinese	half Indian
brown		
dark		
(black)		

Note. Black and white are in parentheses because they are applied to relatively few Jamaicans. This table does not include other Jamaican groups, such as the Maroons, Syrians (a category that includes others from the Middle East), and Germans. Brice-Baker (1996) discussed the Jamaican folk taxonomy briefly, lumping intermediate skin color terms together as *colored*—perhaps in an attempt to make the Jamaican understanding of race easier for Americans to comprehend. The Jamaicans I spoke with, however, indicated that the term *colored* is not used.

Cape Verde

In completing this presentation of two cultures from each language, the last "racial" folk taxonomy I discuss is from Cape Verde (*Cabo Verde*, in Portuguese). This comparison with Brazil is of particular interest because of the *tipo cabo-verde* referred to in Table 5.1 and described earlier. As is easy to comprehend, Capeverdeans view themselves as of varying appearance, understand *Cabo Verde* as their country and not a *tipo*, and would be surprised to know that it is a northeastern Brazilian category.[14]

The Cape Verde islands, where Capeverdean creole and Portuguese are spoken, lie off the northwest coast of Africa, and present a complex contrast both to Brazil and to other island cultures. Unlike the societies of Haiti, Jamaica, Martinique, and Puerto

---

[14]Dictionary definitions of "racial" terms often have a bizarre quality because lexicographers use authoritative and even scientific-sounding language in defining folk categories. This quality is exaggerated in two-language dictionaries, where words are used to communicate concisely the essence of one culture's folk category to members of another culture unacquainted with it. Thus, an authoritative Brazilian Portuguese–English dictionary defines *cabo-verde* as "a half-breed of Negro and Indian" (*Novo Michaelis*, 1973, p. 199).

Leaving aside the question of whether the lexicographer was aware of the pejorative meaning of "half-breed," one is bewildered by the well-known absence of Brazilian Indians from Cape Verde. The following is my attempt—with little confidence—to reconstruct for an American audience the cultural assumptions underlying this amazing definition.

The Brazilian concept of *tipo* as a set of physical features means that the term *cabo-verde* is used to refer to people who look a certain way. These individuals, whose ancestors often include both Brazilian Indians and Africans, resemble some Capeverdeans in appearance, hence the choice of the term.

Rico, each of which is on a single island, Cape Verde consists of 10 islands, 9 of which are inhabited.

Not surprisingly, there is considerable cultural variability among islands, with the major cultural differentiation existing between the northern *Barlavento* (Windward) and southern *Sotavento* (Leeward) island groups. This variation extends to linguistic differences between the Portuguese-based creoles spoken on the *Barlavento* and *Sotavento* island groups. Thus, we can expect significant cultural differences in ways of conceptualizing what Americans call race from one island or island group to another. This means that, in addition to the caveats raised earlier about the provisional nature of the information in these presentations, it should also be pointed out that the partial Capeverdean folk taxonomy discussed here may reflect the categories of some of its islands more than others.

As with the other six non-U.S. systems discussed already, Capeverdean classifications are based on physical appearance. These terms are not used in everyday conversation, as they might be in Brazil, but rather are used to refer to or describe someone who is not present. Although fewer in number, the terms resemble those of Brazil. As is the case there, they are called *tipos* and can be arranged along the white-to-black dimension *branca–morena–mulata–preta*—the same order in which these terms are used in Brazil. This similarity of usage in two Portuguese-based systems, contrasting with usage in the other Romance languages of French (especially *mulâtre*) and Spanish (both *morena* and *mulata*) is yet another confirmation that racial terms reflect culturally constructed categories rather than biological ones.

In contrast to Brazil and as indicated earlier, however, there is no *cabo-verde tipo*. In addition, there is no *sarará tipo*, nor is there a neither-white-nor-black dimension comparable to the *sarará-cabo-verde* one indicated in Table 5.1.

Unlike Brazilian *tipos*, which refer to a constellation of physical—mainly facial—features in addition to skin color, Capeverdean *tipos* give information only about skin color. To communicate more information when describing someone, a Capeverdean might go on to describe the person's eye color or facial features, but these do not constitute part of his or her *tipo*. This striking contrast with Brazil means that the Capeverdean classificatory concept of *tipo* has a very different meaning (skin color) from its Brazilian meaning (skin color + physical features). As a result, each of the *tipos*—*branca, morena, mulata,* and *preta*—refers to a different, larger, and more heterogeneous range of physical appearances in Cape Verde than it does in Brazil. Put another way, depending on what they look like, people flying from Rio de Janeiro to Praia or vice versa can change their *tipo* despite the fact that *tipo* refers to physical appearance in both places, and that their physical appearance does not change. This is because the meaning of *tipo* as well as the meanings of *branca, morena, mulata,* and *preta*, are different in Brazil and Cape Verde.

The Capeverdean classificatory emphasis on skin color is further highlighted by the concept of *cor* (color). There are two *cores*—*clara* (light) or *branca* (white), and *escura* (dark) or *preta* (black).[15] The *cor clara* includes both the *tipos branca* and *morena*; the *cor escura* includes both the *tipos mulata* and *preta*. In other words, Capeverdeans distinguish between light-skinned and dark-skinned people, and each of these ranges of skin color encompasses more than one *tipo*. Although Capeverdeans, like Brazilians, do not ordinarily distinguish between kinds of whites and kinds of blacks, and although the meanings of *morena* and *mulata* are different in the two cultures, the fact that *morenos* are considered *claro* whereas *mulatos* are considered *escuro* suggests that both Portuguese-influenced cultures tend to see some sort of division in a roughly similar place. Both of these contrast with the United States, which would put the dividing line between whites and everyone else.

One example of the way in which the Capeverdean color categories contrast with the more detailed Brazilian ones can be seen in the sentences *"Ela é escura com feições finas"* (She is dark with European features [e.g., straight hair, narrow nose and thin lips]) or, more specifically, *Ela é uma mulata com feições finas* (She is a *mulata* with European features). In northeastern Brazil, one might say *Ela é uma morena escura."* (She is a dark *morena.*) or even Ela é uma *cabo-verde.*

This partial description of Cape Verde's folk taxonomy of *cores* and *tipos* is presented in Table 5.7.

TABLE 5.7

Partial Capeverdean Folk Taxonomy of Cores and Tipos

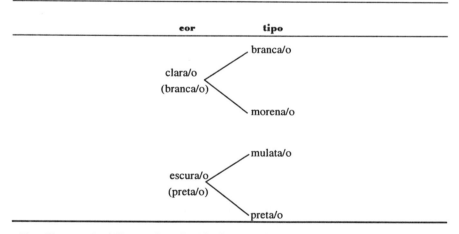

cor	tipo

Note. These are "racial" terms from the Afro-European domain, and do not refer to culturally or geographically defined Capeverdean groups like the Badius and Sampajudos or to foreigners from Europe (especially Portugal) or Africa. (*Clara* and other *a* endings are the feminine form, and *claro* is the masculine form.) De Andrade (1997) and Sanchéz (1998) discussed issues of race and identity among Americans who are immigrants from or trace their ancestry to Cape Verde. The assistance of Gunga T. Tavares in preparing this table and the accompanying discussion is gratefully acknowledged.

---

[15]In any given language, words often have more than one meaning. In Cape Verde, to avoid confusion, we have to remember that the words *branca* and *preta* might refer to either a *cor* or a *tipo*.

THE MYTH OF RACE: IMPLICATIONS

We have seen that "race" is a word, rather than a thing. It is a cultural concept, like ghost or unicorn—or, for more scientific examples, phlogiston or ether—that does not refer to empirically observable phenomena. Those cultures that have the word define it differently and use it differently. Not surprisingly, definitions from different cultures using the same language are more similar than those from cultures speaking different languages. However, even within a given language, the sets of concepts used vary considerably in meaning and organization.

More specifically, the American concept of race does not correspond to the ways in which human physical appearance varies. The American understanding of race in terms of blood (hypodescent) is, as was spelled out in great detail, just one among many folk taxonomies, that differ from one another along linguistic and other cultural dimensions. None of these folk taxonomies corresponds to the biological facts of human physical variation. This is why race is a myth and why races as conceived by Americans (and others) do not exist.

Research

Studies of differences in behavior between U.S. "populations" of "whites" and "blacks," which seek to find biological causes rather than social ones, make an ethnocentric assumption. They assume that blacks and whites are populations in some biological sense, as subunits of the human species. (Most likely, the researchers make this assumption because they are American and understand race in terms of the American folk taxonomy [Fish, 1997].) In fact, however, the groups are sorted by a social rule for statistical purposes. This can be demonstrated by asking researchers "How do you know that the white individuals are really white and the black individuals are really black?" There is no biological answer to this question, because race as a biological category does not exist. All that researchers can do is say "The tester classified them based on their physical appearance," or "Their school records listed their race," or otherwise give a social rather than a biological answer. Although it is logically conceivable that a group of people with large ears and small feet might differ on a test of visual memory from a group of people with small ears and large feet, it would be absurd to conduct such a study, and even more misguided, if differences were found by some bizarre happenstance, to seek a biological explanation for them. This is why, when U.S. researchers study racial differences in behavior, in search of biological rather than social causes for differences between socially defined groups, they are wasting their time. Computers are wonderful machines, but we have learned the expression "garbage in, garbage out." Applying complex computations to bad data yields worthless results. In the same way, the most elegant experimental designs and statistical analyses, applied flawlessly to biologically meaningless racial categories, can only produce a very expensive waste of time.

Immigrants

As immigrants of varied physical appearance come to the United States from countries with racial folk taxonomies different from our own, they are often perplexed and dismayed to find that the ways they classify themselves and others are irrelevant to the American reality. Brazilians, Capeverdeans, Ecuadorians, Haitians, Jamaicans, Martinicans, Puerto Ricans, and others may find themselves labeled by strange, apparently inappropriate, and even pejorative terms, and grouped together in a social category with people who are different from and sometimes unreceptive to them. This can cause psychological complications (e.g., a Brazilian immigrant—who views himself as white—being treated by an American therapist who assumes that he is not). I address some of these issues in *Culture and Therapy: An Integrative Approach* (Fish, 1996).

Immigration has increased, especially from geographical regions whose people do not resemble U.S. images of blacks, whites, or Asians. Intermarriage is also increasing, as the stigma associated with it diminishes. These two trends are augmenting the physical diversity among those who marry each other—and, as a result, among their children. The American folk taxonomy of race (purportedly comprised of stable biological entities) is beginning to change to accommodate this new reality. After all, what race is someone whose four grandparents are black, white, Asian, and Hispanic? As of today, the answer is black, but it is beginning to appear inadequate to increasing numbers of people.

The Census

Currently, the most rapidly U.S. growing census category is "Other," as more and more individuals fail to fit the available options. Changes in the census categories every 10 years reflect the government's attempts to grapple with the changing self-identifications of Americans—even as statisticians try to maintain the same categories over time to be able to make demographic comparisons.

The 2000 census contains categories for both race and ethnicity, inaccurately implying that race is biological and ethnicity is cultural. This system perplexes many individuals who try to make their self-identifications conform to the options offered to them. For example, the census considers Korean a race, but Mexican an ethnicity. Clearly these categories were chosen for political rather than scientific reasons; and they pose awkward questions for the demographers and social scientists who must make sense of the data.

Although the classification system in the 2000 census may have created more confusion than clarity, its very existence is a demonstrations that traditional categories of race are being strained by cultural diversity. Not only the census, but many universities, corporations, and other institutions are now including an option to "check as many as apply" when asking individuals to classify themselves on a list of folk descriptors. Perhaps in the next census the government will drop the term *race* altogether, recognizing that the categories are all social constructions. Then they could either list the categories they need to collect information about without characterizing them in any way, or settle for a single nonbiological term like *ethnicity*.

IN CONCLUSION

Clarifying our thinking to separate the etics of physical appearance from the emics of folk taxonomies illuminates the emotionally charged but confused topic of race. Understanding that different cultures have different folk taxonomies suggests that we respond to the question "What race is that person?" not by "black," or "white," but by "where?" and "when?"

ACKNOWLEDGMENTS

Thanks to Robert Ghiradella and Dolores Newton for their helpful comments on the chapter as a whole and to Dolores Augustine, Clover Hall, Louise McKenzie, Lina Norona, Denise Belén Santiago, Gunga T. Tavares, Valerie Vulcain, and Muriel Wiltord for their assistance with various parts of the chapter.

REFERENCES

Alland, A. (1971). *Human diversity*. New York: Columbia University Press.
Belafonte, H. (1956). Brown skin girl. On *Calypso* [33 rpm record, LPM-1248]. Camden, NJ: Radio Corporation of America.
Berry, J. W. (1969). On cross-cultural comparability. *International Journal of Psychology, 4*, 119–128.
Brice-Baker, J. (1996). Jamaican families. In M. McGoldrick, J. Giordano, & J. K. Pearce (Eds.), *Ethnicity and family therapy* (2nd ed., pp. 85–96). New York: Guilford.
De Andrade, L. L. (1997). The question of race: Cape Verdean Americans talk about their race and identity. *Cimboa, 2*(4), 23–25.
Degler, C. N. (1971). *Neither black nor white: Slavery and race relations in Brazil and the United States*. New York: Macmillan.
Fish, J. M. (1995a). Mixed blood. *Psychology Today, 28*(6), 55–61, 76, 80.
Fish, J. M. (1995b). Why psychologists should learn some anthropology. *American Psychologist, 50*(1), 44–45.
Fish, J. M. (1996). *Culture and therapy: An integrative approach*. New York: Aronson.
Fish, J. M. (1997). How psychologists think about "race." *General Anthropology, 4*(1), 1–4.
Fish, J. M., & Newton, D. (1998). Review of the book *Black, Jewish, and interracial: It's not the color of your skin but the race of your kin, and other myths of identity. American Anthropologist, 100*(3), 23–24.
Harris, M. (1964). *Patterns of race in the Americas*. New York: Walker.
Harris, M. (1970). Referential ambiguity in the calculus of Brazilian racial identity. *Southwestern Journal of Anthropology, 26*(1), 1–14.
Marks, J. (1995). *Human biodiversity: Genes, race, and history*. New York: Aldine de Gruyter.

Novo Michaelis Dicionário Ilustrado, Volume II, Português-Ingles (13th ed.). (1973). São Paulo, Brazil: Edições Melhoramentos.

Pike, K. (1954). *Language in relation to a unified theory of the structure of human behavior* (Vol. 1). Glendale, CA: Summer Institute of Linguistics.

Pike, K. L. (1967). *Language in relation to a unified theory of the structure of human behavior.* The Hague, Netherlands: Mouton.

Sanchéz, G. (1998). Between *Kriolu* and *Merkanu*: Capeverdean diaspora identities. *Cimboa, 3*(5), 22–25.

Szasz, T. S. (1970). *Ideology and insanity: Essays on the psychiatric dehumanization of man.* Garden City, NY: Doubleday Anchor.

PART

II

Racial categories are developed to serve social ends, including the justification and perpetuation of inequality. IQ testing has been a part of this process of stratifying groups.

CHAPTER
6

Science and the Idea of Race: A Brief History

Audrey Smedley

Since the beginning of the Age of Discovery in the 15th century when some Western Europeans ventured out and encountered new worlds with their strange flora and fauna, and peoples alien and exotic to them, there has been a tremendous expansion of knowledge. So massive has been this increase that it is very difficult for scholars at the beginning of the 21st century to place themselves in the positions and minds of those early explorers. However, from the records they left we can trace some of what they experienced, their shock at the discovery of other societies, and the development of their attitudes toward other human beings. In doing so, we can achieve some comprehension of how great this historical transformation has been.

In this regard the emergence of the idea of race and its grounding in the sciences of the last 200 years has been perhaps the most critical development in the history of human social interaction and in the history of science. All of the human sciences —biology, psychology, anthropology, and sociology—in their early stages were predicated in some fashion on what is identified here as the racial worldview. This was a way of perceiving the world's peoples as being divided into exclusive and discrete groups, called races, that are ranked hierarchically vis-à-vis one another. Consciously or not, the racial worldview was a subtle ingredient in the growth of these disciplines and still remains a sometimes aggravating aspect of the social sciences in the United

States. This chapter deals with some of the ways the historical development of the sciences and the idea and ideology of race were intertwined. Although space prevents it from being comprehensive, it provides the necessary background for understanding the emergence of mental testing and the extraordinary focus on, or obsession with, IQ tests in this country.

In the first half-century or so of exploration, the information that found its way back to the learned men of Europe raised numerous new questions about the world and its peoples. Some scholars were looking into the mysteries of the human body, and others were collecting data on the different kinds of human beings and their strange lifestyles. The discovery of hitherto unknown peoples naturally led to questions about who they were, the cause of their divergence from the European "norm," and how they fit into the scheme of world history as different Europeans had understood it.

Educated men had long been conditioned to look to the Bible for answers to profound questions about the nature of man, the relationships between various known groups of humans, their origins, and histories. The scriptures, particularly the book of Genesis, was the premier source of information about human groups, and all known peoples of the Old World had been fitted into schemes of descent from the time of creation. God had created humankind in a single act, and Adam and Eve were thought to have been the progenitors of all human groups. This was the theory of monogenesis (or monogeny) that not only focused on the single origin of all human beings, but underscored the unity of the human family in the Judeo-Christian world. Whatever linguistic, cultural, or physical diversity existed could be traced back to, or otherwise explained by, the events of the Bible, particularly the story of Noah and his three sons (Ham, Shem, and Japheth), their eventual repopulation of the earth after the flood, and the scattering of their descendants from the tower of Babel.

This was all very well for the known peoples of Europe, North Africa, and the Middle East, but what was the origin of the indigenous peoples of the New World? How did they get to such remote regions? If God had made man in his own image,[1] how do you account for the great varieties of humankind, the diversity of skin colors, body sizes and shapes, hair textures, nose shapes, and so on? How do you explain the cultural differences, and sometimes peculiar similarities, among these peoples?

The Bible did not provide many direct clues, so intellectuals of the 16th century throughout Western Europe conjectured fanciful stories based on whatever interpretations they could glean from the scriptures and the newly discovered writings of the Ancients (Greco-Roman). Some said they were the lost tribes of Israel; others claimed that they were descendants of roving Phoenicians, Norsemen, Chinese, Tartars, or other Asians.[2] Alternative ideas about the origins and identities of indigenous peoples also began to appear early in the 16th century. Questions had been

---

[1]It is important to remember that until the latter part of the 20th century the term *man* was inclusive of women who were largely seen merely as mates to men. When discussing perceptions of the world in earlier centuries, I use the historical term only to convey the meanings of the period.

[2]For brief descriptions of these varied theories, see Hallowell (1960).

raised about the human status of some of the natives of the Americas shortly after contact. Were they truly human beings and descendants of that original creation? Did they have souls? Were they rational beings? Most often these questions were raised by men who were directly involved in the conquest, who had decimated the Indians, or who had coerced them into slave labor. To justify their often brutal treatment, some conveyed back to Europe the belief that Indians were not fully human, but animals that could legitimately be forced to work or be exterminated. The information that drifted back to Europe on the exotic and bizarre habits and customs of indigenous peoples often exaggerated or misrepresented these cultures (Jones, 1964).

Intellectuals in Europe were quick to utilize this new information and to pose hypotheses to explain these unexpected realities. Paracelsis (1493–1541), as early as 1520, speculated that the New World native peoples might even be offspring of a different, separate act of creation, and that the Biblical story only referred to the Jews and Christians. It was not necessary to prove that all people found in remote areas were descended from Adam. In 1655, Isaac de la Peyrere, in another rare moment of original thinking, again suggested that there might have been separate origins for Indians, Africans, and Asians, with Adam the progenitor of only the Jews. However, the idea of more than one creation (the theory of polygenesis) was a minor voice hardly acceptable to the world of men deeply steeped in the scriptures or to the political powers that held sway. Polygenist thinking was considered antithetical to the teachings of the Bible. It meant that if they were not fully human, attempts to save the souls of the Indians would be futile. Few scholars entertained the theory seriously because it contradicted not only the holiest of sources of information, but basic tenets of Christian theology. Peyrere's work was condemned, he was forced to recant, and he spent the rest of his life in a monastery.

Judging from the records they left, all the great colonizing powers became engaged in a race to save the souls of the heathens. Portugal in Africa, and Spain (and later Portugal) in the New World began campaigns to bring native peoples under the sway of the Roman Catholic Church. Within a short time, their success was tangible. They succeeded in transporting much of Latin Catholic culture to the New World, where it was synthesized with elements of Indian and African cultures. It also brought these vast new territories within the colonial empires of these European nations and facilitated the exploitation of their wealth. Within a century the Protestant British, the Dutch, and the French entered the race with nearly as much vigor and verbalized intent to save native souls for the benefit of their variations of the Christian faith.

Among all Christians, the single origin theory of the universe governed both learned and popular thought. It provided an image of the world that at least potentially unified all humans and made them equally significant in the eyes of God, the father of all. Because within a few years of the conquests it was obvious that savage men could be made civilized (i.e., savages were capable of converting to the true religion, learning the language, values, and mores of Christianity, and thus eventually behaving like their Christian masters), the debate over origins became muted. The question of whether the natives of the New World were truly human was answered definitively in

1537 by a papal bull (formal order) issued by Pope Paul III. However, the theory of multiple origins (or multiple creations) remained as a minor theme echoed by few writers until it reemerged in the late 18th century, dominated American thought in the 19th century and became part of a major scientific controversy.

EARLY ENLIGHTENMENT ATTITUDES TOWARD HUMAN DIFFERENCES

In England, particularly, a rising sense of individual freedom of inquiry, curiosity, rationality, and increasing private support of scholarly works had created an atmosphere conducive to empirical research. This was due in part to the rebirth of learning, arts, and literature known as the Renaissance (14th–17th century), and in part to the breakaway of the English from the Roman Catholic Church during the Reformation. During the Renaissance, scholarly men had begun the custom of collecting information and materials from around the world and studying the new flora and fauna found in remote areas. Collecting, organizing, and cataloguing materials reflected the beginnings of scientific inquiry. Science and rationalism were being fostered by learned societies, and there were significant advances. Newton formulated the laws of gravity, Lavoisier discovered oxygen, and Harvey was the first European to describe the circulation of the blood.

The study of humankind was also becoming a viable and appropriate field for scholars. Direct research, albeit rudimentary, into the human condition became part of the activities of inquisitive men, like Edward Tyson who, in 1699, became the first Western scientist allowed to compare the anatomy of a human with that of an ape.[3] His work was sponsored by the Royal Society for the Advancement of Science, and it shocked the world of learned men by demonstrating the great similarities in the physical structure of humans and apes.

Tyson's work took place at the dawn of that era of tremendous growth in naturalistic knowledge known as the Enlightenment that began around the time of the Glorious Revolution in England (1688) and ended roughly 100 years later with the Revolutionary Wars of the United States and France (1780s–1790s). During the early part of the Enlightenment, philosophers, historians, essayists, physicians, and other learned men developed a perspective on the human condition that was secular, humanistic, and pragmatic. They also formulated a methodology for the objective study of all natural phenomena that became the basis for modern science. It was the philosophers of the Enlightenment who provided the most sophisticated understanding of the human species, posing many ideas that even today sound very modern.

The major philosophical themes of this period stressed human beings as social animals, as rational beings, and as capable of learning and progress. Enlightenment writers questioned authority and were skeptical of, if not inimical to, the powers of

---

[3]The "pygmy" was in fact a chimpanzee, but the similarities in the anatomical characteristics of the higher primates is such that, given the probable condition of the corpse, Tyson would not have recognized the error.

tradition and religion. They believed that behavior was learned, not inborn, an idea vividly expressed by John Locke, who claimed that at birth the human mind was an empty cabinet. Each human being was thus a product of his society, his social and natural environment. The idea of what we now call culture as external to the human being and acquired in the process of socialization was widely expressed by many other writers such as Montesquieu, Turgot, Count d'Holback, and La Mettrie. So also was a sense of human destiny as something positive and progressive and under the rational control of humankind.

Looking at the range of peoples and cultures known to them, many writers emphasized not only the biological unity of the human species, but a commonality of mental processes, the psychic unity of humankind. They concurred with the French essayist Michel de Montaigne (1533–1592), who a century earlier had taken strikingly advanced and modern positions on the nature of humans and their cultures, claiming "all men are of one species and are provided with the like tools and instruments for judging and understanding" (cited in Slotkin, 1965, p. 61). Man's nature is plastic at birth; each human being is molded by the force of custom, habit, and laws. Montaigne decried prejudice against the different customs of others, and argued for a relativistic position rather than a judgmental one. He delighted, he said, in the varieties of customs and traditions discovered in his travels, saying that nothing found in other societies offended him as all customs have their reasons.

Many of the Enlightenment writers were concerned with social and political changes taking place in their own societies in Europe. They were caught up in the thrust to free their societies from the bonds of archaic feudal tradition and rigid theological dogma. They promoted individualism; human rights; freedom of thought, religion, and expression; as well as the rights of property. Most of all, they provided some of the rallying cries of the late 18th century revolutionary era: freedom, equality, fraternity, and the pursuit of happiness (Anchor, 1967). Their values became part of the political traditions and ideals of North America, echoed in the Revolutionary War era documents, including the Constitution and the Bill of Rights. Their apparent acceptance, at least in theory, of human equality represented a progressive, even radical way of thinking.

By the latter half of the 18th century, however, a new ideology was to emerge, take hold, and eventually supersede these progressive stances. This was an ideology of natural inequality that, although it had been periodically manifest in European history in various forms, emerged almost simultaneously in the 18th century as a powerful new way of looking at human group differences. When it appeared in the context of new historical circumstances, it had to do not immediately with political events in Europe but with the social realities of colonialism, slavery, and imperialism in the New World. By the end of the century, this new ideology had been fabricated in North America into the worldview we call race. In the 19th century, the racial worldview totally consumed popular and scientific thought about human differences and various versions of it were spread around the world. How this came about is best shown when we look at the history of colonialism in North America.

POPULAR PERCEPTIONS AND INTERPRETATIONS
OF HUMAN DIFFERENCES

With new discoveries of peoples in the South Pacific, Australia, New Guinea, and New Zealand, interest in the varieties of human beings expanded. As early as the mid-17th century, large collections of data on different populations were being accumulated and some learned men, called *naturalists*, began to organize and classify these data into orderly and logical categories. Some of the first classifications, like those of Jean Bodin (1530–1596), were based on obvious physical characteristics, especially skin color and hair form. Most were rudimentary and simplistic and derived from information gleaned from the writings of travelers, missionaries, traders, sailors, merchants, and others. Their descriptions, usually for entertaining readers back home, were too often products of fanciful imaginations.

There were other writers, philosophers, ethnologists, geographers, and essayists who explored the customs and traditions of indigenous peoples with the serious intent of ascertaining their ways of life. They collected data on religious beliefs, on hunting and fishing practices, social and political organization, tools and implements, house types, art and decoration, and many other aspects of material culture.

These early anthropological researches did not occur in a historical, social, and political vacuum. It is essential to understand that the subjects of all these researches and professional attention were people who had been conquered and/or enslaved by various European powers, or who had come under the political domination of empire builders of Western Europe. They had been deliberately made and kept subordinate by their rulers and masters; their low status was indicative of their powerlessness in the political, economic, and cultural arenas.

Like peoples everywhere, each European society had an ethnocentric sense of the superior worth of its own customs, habits, religion, arts, technology, foods, laws, morals, and other cultural features. A long tradition dating at least back to the Greeks had divided the world's peoples into those who were civilized (i.e., like themselves) and those who were "savages" or "barbarians." Although some of the Enlightenment scholars were self-consciously more objective or compassionate than others, the majority operated with a sense of their own ethnic superiority. They were civilized, after all, and most of the people who elicited their curiosity were savages or barbarians. Many European writers looked to scholars of the ancient Greco-Roman world for information, theories, and insights into the nature of savages. They also saw in the artifacts from ancient Europe very similar tools and weapons, and some of them observed that there were similarities between ancient Europeans and modern primitive folk.

Two kinds of beliefs about primitive societies emerged in the 16th century. One was the perspective that historians identify as *primitivistic*, a general tendency to see some of the most dramatically different groups (small scale and with hunting and gathering technology) as benign, gentle folk, innocent, uncorrupted, and without guile. This was the "noble savage" who was sometimes amenable to the ministrations of Christian efforts. The other was an antiprimitivistic mode of thought that developed almost simultaneously and that saw in these hunting and gathering peoples, and small-scale horticulturalists, a much more sinister creature. This was the vicious savage: evil, aggressive, cruel, irrational, and sinful.

The version of savagery that dominated the late 16th and 17th centuries was manufactured for a very different time and circumstances than that expressed in earlier writings. It reflected the need for a foil against which Europeans could measure themselves, and a justification for policies and practices that were becoming unacceptable to the wider Christian world. Many Europeans identified all peoples who were not Christian in negative ways; all heathens or pagans were potentially, if not actually, given to savagery, knowing no religion worthy of the title, no laws or morality, no private property, and no government. Savages were naked and bestial, bloodthirsty and violence-prone; they lacked the intelligence of normal men and were morally degraded. These characteristics came to be seen as intrinsic to some alien peoples. In contrast, writers of the ancient world for the most part had understood that savagery was an external condition and that such people could learn the Greek or Latin languages and be transformed into civilized citizens of these states. In other words, ethnic characteristics were acquired, not inborn. This was one of the crucial differences between earlier understandings of human differences and those subsumed under the ideology of race.

ENGLISH EXPERIENCES WITH HUMAN VARIATION IN THE NEW WORLD

The image and role that the savage played in European thought varied considerably in different cultures and at different times, but all scholarly works were affected by popular thought on these matters. English intellectuals developed an extremely negative view of savage life only in part from reading the works of the ancients. Their most immediate source of information about savages stemmed from a long-standing conflict with the Irish. This was to have a profound effect on their attitudes toward the natives of North America and later the Africans they brought into the colonies as slaves. Beginning as early as the 12th century, the English made numerous attempts throughout the next centuries to conquer the pastoral Irish and impose on them a civilized English lifestyle. Irish resistance led to a stalemate and frustration so that by the 16th century, hatred of the "wild Irish" had reached furious heights, particularly among the Protestant nobility. Many members of the English elite had planned to establish agricultural plantations in Ireland and to use the Irish as forced labor, following a pattern established by the Spanish in the Mediterranean. However, the stubborn refusal of the Irish to capitulate and persisting guerilla warfare blocked this goal. During the reign of Elizabeth I (1559–1603), some Englishmen expressed the belief that the Irish would forever be unruly savages and were incapable of civilization. It followed that if savagery were innate or intrinsic, there was no need to attempt to civilize such peoples. The failure to establish plantations in Ireland led in large part to the desire in the early

17th century to settle colonies in the New World, using native Indians as slave labor, again emulating the Spanish.

The idea of the savage was enhanced and institutionalized in English thought through literature and essays by popular and scholarly writers. It was transmitted to the New World when the English established colonies at Jamestown and in Massachusetts Bay; ultimately in both areas it was applied to the indigenous peoples. Some of the same men who had been engaged in warfare to pacify the "wild Irish," such as Sir Walter Raleigh, Sir Francis Drake, Lord de la Warre, and the Earl of Southampton, were also participants in the colonizing of the New World and/or helped to establish colonial policies toward the native Americans. The irredeemable savage image became deeply embedded in the thought and consciousness of colonists after the first conflicts, the massacre at Jamestown in 1622, and continuing episodes of warfare in 1639, 1644, and later. The more the Indians were conquered or died out and their land taken over, the more heinous was the characterization of their savagery.[4]

By the latter part of the 17th century, the colonists faced a massive labor problem. Some form of cheap labor, in increasingly larger numbers, was seen as absolutely essential for the success of the colonies. The Indians had not made good slave laborers; if they did not die in wars with the Europeans, they died of imported diseases to which they had no immunities. Others were weakened by strife with the colonists and ran away, disappearing forever into the hinterlands. Attempts to utilize European labor were also frustrated. Beginning in the 1620s a new strategy of obtaining cheap labor had resulted in the development of indentured servitude under which poor young men and women were conscripted into serving for 4 to 7 years free for masters who had paid their passage from Europe. Such servants were heavily exploited; they were provided with minimum food and housing, and often were brutally punished for running away or other misdeeds. It was rumored in Europe that they were treated like slaves, and many died before achieving freedom.

However, as more servants survived the rigors of servitude toward the middle of the century, they began to demand land and equipment to establish themselves as free men of property. Wealthy landowners, who were also the leaders of the colony and owners of vast tracts of land not under Indian control, resisted the demands of a growing class of poor people. Servant dissatisfaction grew and led to widespread resistance and a series of revolts that culminated in the infamous Bacon's Rebellion of 1676, in which servants and the freed poor threatened the destruction of the colony. Although the rebellion was put down by colony leaders, with the aid of military forces from England, it became very clear that better control over the laboring poor was mandatory.[5]

---

[4]Robert F. Berkhofer (1978), Gary Nash (1982), and Roy Harvey Pearce (1953), among many other historians, have documented this transformation of native Americans into savages in the American mind.

[5]See Allen (1997) for his analysis of the consequences of Bacon's rebellion. Also see P. D. Morgan (1998) for a detailed account of the relationships among blacks and whites in the early colonial period (17th and 18th centuries) and E. Morgan (1975) for his analysis of the process by which slavery was institutionalized and its relation to the American conception of freedom.

For nearly 100 years the Spanish had been directly importing Africans as slaves and their colonies were wealthy and thriving. Many English planters had already perceived that Africans made better workers: They had knowledge of growing crops in tropical lands and many skills and crafts; they also had immunities to many Old World diseases and they had nowhere to run and hide once placed into slavery in North America. Some Africans had been in the Virginia colony since 1619 and had been generally treated as other indentured servants. Blacks constituted at least one fourth of the servants and poor freedmen who became followers of Nathaniel Bacon.

Between 1660 and 1705, the advantages of having a totally controllable, permanent slave labor force comprised of peoples from Africa became very real to the North American colonists. English slave ships entered the direct trade from Africa and ultimately dominated it. Africans and their descendants were vulnerable to growing policies that treated them differently from European bondsmen or freedmen. They could not claim the rights of even the poorest Englishmen who, by virtue of their citizenship, could not only demand their rights but call on the force of English law and the judicial system to support their claims.

Virginia and Maryland began to pass laws gradually restricting the rights of African servants and their descendants, reducing them to permanent and perpetual slavery, encountering no political opposition and few moral restraints. By the first quarter of the 18th century slavery was institutionalized through hundreds of restrictive laws nearly everywhere in the southern and in some northern colonies, and these societies thrived.

English colonists rationalized their purchasing and use of new African slave labor, even though slavery had not been legal in England for centuries, by focusing on the heathenism of the Africans. It was better, they argued, to bring the Africans into Christian slavery than to leave them steeped in their "brutishness," their savagery, sloth, and wickedness in their native lands. Besides, they were already slaves. Christian charity would improve their conditions and their manners and provide them with knowledge of the true God. To save their souls was a godly deed, even though it meant keeping their bodies in slavery. Most of all, however, it was the desire for wealth, and the need for their labor, that led to the institutionalization of slavery only for Africans (Jordan, 1968; E. Morgan, 1975).

The colonial worlds everywhere structured hierarchical societies in which Europeans stood at the top, and the conquered and enslaved peoples had various positions below. It was fortuitous that both the conquered and enslaved peoples were physically distinct from their colonial masters. Those in power soon realized that status could be reflected in the physical differences, especially color, of these various groups interacting in colonial settings. The rigidity of a system based on features that were visible and inherited would allow power, prestige, and wealth to accrue to, and remain with, only the original European colonizers and their descendants.

In the Latin American colonies, long-standing and wide-ranging intermixtures of Europeans, Africans, and Native Americans blurred divisions among individuals and groups and delayed or inhibited such a rigid scheme. However, in North America, early customs and laws preventing intermixture and the separation of Indians onto reservation lands away from white and black contact made it possible for the physical differences to be maintained relatively intact. Indeed, the 18th-century English colonial world focused on and emphasized physical differences more firmly than the early decades of colonialism.[6] The visible physical characteristics of Africans, especially their color, were increasingly being perceived as symbols of their slave status.

The number of slaves increased rapidly during the 18th century. Their value as labor creating enormous wealth for their owners was widely recognized. Their identification in law as primarily property obstructed any humanistic tendencies in planter society. They were defined increasingly as different and of questionable humanity, and this made it easy to treat them merely as property and to give the property rights of masters priority over the human rights of slaves (Smedley, 1999).

In this way, an inegalitarian world comprised of what were seen as biophysically exclusive, distinct, and unequal groups was socially constructed, which in the 18th century came to be perceived and interpreted as normal and natural.

The English colonizers, consciously or unconsciously, selected the term *race* to refer to these groups, although they could have chosen other such terms as *stock*, or *breed*, which had been used as classificatory terms before the 18th century. In the late 16th and 17th centuries, some English literary figures had used the word *race* as a categorizing term with much the same meaning as type, kind, or group. John Bunyon (see Smedley, 1999), for example, spoke of a "race of saints" in his 1678 work *Pilgrim's Progress*. However, by the late 18th century, *race* had become the most common term designating the different peoples interacting in the colonies and it already conveyed a magnified sense of human group differences (Smedley, 1999, chaps. 5–9). It also later became part of the language of science as scientific developments increasingly focused on the nature and meaning of these differences.

In Europe some learned men by the end of the century had reinvigorated an older model of the world whose authority rested in the works of ancient scholars. That was the Great Chain of Being, or "scale of nature" (*scala naturae*). A semiscientific and widely held vision of all of nature, this image became a perfect paradigm for the social inequality that had been created in the New World colonies. It seemed to explain and justify not only the divisions of peoples by their physical features, but also their unique placement in the social system. It made the social ranking based on color and physiognomy appear to be natural and God-given.

A related and even more critical element of social thought was anchored into this growing belief system. In a reaction against an increasingly powerful antislavery movement both in England and in the northern states in the late 18th century, a new rationalization for preserving slavery had begun to appear in popular discourse and

---

[6]Jordan (1968) noted this in passing. He also claimed that the suddenness of English contact with people so different from themselves was a major cause of their willingness to reduce them to slaves (see chaps. 1 and 2).

writings. This was the argument that Africans should be kept in slavery because they were natural slaves, an inferior form of human being whose moral character, intellect, temperament, and other behavior traits were fixed and unalterable. African-American slaves could not be re-created into civilized beings like whites, but were doomed to remain in a state of savagery, unless saved and subsequently cared for by the good graces of white slave owners. Winthrop Jordan (1968) noted that "It was not until the slave trade came to require justification, in the eighteenth century, that some Englishmen found special reason to lay emphasis on the Negro's savagery" (p. 27). Thomas Jefferson, hailed toward the end of the 18th century as one of America's first great intellectuals, was also one of the first public figures to raise this issue and echo this rationale. In doing so, he helped to make the idea of black inferiority part of public consciousness. He was also a very wealthy slave owner, with two plantations with more than 250 slaves on them.

Historians have long documented the denigration and dehumanization of Africans as slaves during this period, although the trend had been slowly growing since the beginning of slavery. What has not been well demonstrated is the degree to which this new ideology, now expressed in the form of superior and inferior races, influenced the works of scientists and scholars, who in turn set about to prove with empirical evidence the differences between races that society had created. It was Jefferson who first called on science to confirm and provide credibility to the expanding popular belief.

Thus, the term *race* from its inception reflected a worldview of unequal groups, ranked not merely on the basis of their physical differences, but also in terms of their presumed behavior and capacity for civilization. European colonists, as a way of protecting the institution of slavery now under attack from powerful forces, decreed that Africans and Indians were innately inferior beings intellectually, morally, physically, and temperamentally. Their physical variations, thought to mirror inherent behavior tendencies that were as unalterable as their bodies, made it impossible for them to ever become assimilated as equals in civilized white society. Thus race represented an ideology created to stratify colonial society so that unequal social divisions appeared to be based in nature. As a new social ideology, it proclaimed that "negroes" and their descendants would forever be relegated to the lowest ranks, and native Americans would eventually disappear with the advance of white civilization.

CLASSIFICATIONS OF HUMAN GROUPS IN THE 18TH CENTURY

It was in this social and historical context that the first modern scientific classifications of human groups based on physical differences were formulated in the 18th century in Europe. There had been a number of attempts to categorize human societies, by John Ray, Bernard Varen, Giordano Bruno, Bernier, and others as we have seen. By the middle of the century, Linnaeus (in various editions, from 1735–1755) published one of the earliest classifications that for the first time placed human beings within the animal world and classified humans with primates (Slotkin, 1965). Linnaeus's comprehensive taxonomy of all known animal forms identified all humans as members of one species, a fact that had been long acknowledged among scholars and scientists. He established the binomial nomenclature that is still used today for identifying distinct species of animals and plants.

The species concept, originating among ancient Greeks, had been well established among scholarly men during the 16th through 18th centuries, with the general understanding that species were separated from one another by reproductive isolation. That is, all members of a common species were able to breed together and produce viable offspring. Populations were separate species, regardless of physical similarities, if they did not or could not mate naturally together and produce fertile children. The recognition that all humans belonged to a common species was highly compatible with the scriptures and especially with the idea of a single divine creation. Most researchers and theorists assumed that all species had been created in the same condition and with the same physical features with which they were found, that species were fixed and unchangeable through time, and that no two or more species occupied the same position or status on the Chain of Being. Under the influence of men like the great naturalist Louis LeClerc (Count de Buffon), 18-century writers explained variations in the physical characteristics of humans as caused by geographical differences, climate, foods, and other habits. In other words, such differences as existed were products of the environment and of the different historical experiences of human groups as they migrated around the world. Greek and Roman writers had also explained human physical variation in terms of environmental features, geography, climate, temperature, diseases, and so forth.

Linneaus classified the human species into four varieties: Asiaticus, Africanus, Europaeus, and Americanus. The groupings were based on physical features, but also were associated with geographical location. In this he showed greater sophistication than Bernier (1684), who also identified four varieties of humans: Europeans, Africans, Asians, and Lapps whom he described as "little stunted creatures with thick legs" (cited in Slotkin, 1965, p. 95). Buffon (1749) published his *Histoire Naturelle*, in which he posed six varieties of humankind: Laplander (or Polar), Tartar (or Mongolian), Southern Asiatic, European, Ethiopian, and Malay. Hunter (1728–1793) suggested seven major subgroups of humans. Finally, toward the end of the 18th century (in 1775), the most important of the classifiers, Johann Blumenbach (1752–1840), proposed the division of the human species into five varieties associated with the major regions of the world. He gave them the names Caucasian, Mongolian, Ethiopian, American, and Malay. He also maintained that it was difficult to establish fixed boundaries around human groups, for "one variety of mankind does so sensibly pass into the other, that you cannot mark out the limits between them" (cited in Slotkin, 1965, p. 189). This sense of the fluid, overlapping, and blending nature of human physical characteristics diminished and became lost in popular and scientific thought with the rise of the racial worldview.

In the 10th edition of his work, published in 1758–1759, Linnaeus expanded on the characteristics of the varieties within the human species and added such features as dress and body decorations, differences of behavior, and personality characteristics. He described indigenous Americans as obstinate, merry, free, and regulated by customs. Europeans were gentle, acute, inventive, and governed by laws. Africans were crafty, indolent, negligent, and governed by caprice, whereas Asians were severe, haughty, miserly, and ruled by opinions (Slotkin, 1965). This reflected a growing tendency to accept what we would consider to be cultural or learned forms of behavior as connected in some way with the biological characteristics of groups. Literature, especially of the latter part of the 18th century (the end of the Enlightenment), shows an unmistakable trend toward explicating differences in behavior among human societies as a function of biology. All of the systematists of the 18th century in fact manifested a subtle acceptance of much of popular judgments about the different groups of humans. Some were civilized, others were savages; thus a ranking, or inequality, of varieties of humans was implicit in virtually all of the taxonomies. Some features of these classifications were openly subjective. Blumenbach used the term *Caucasian* for all Europeans because he thought the skull of a woman of the Caucasus area of southern Russia was the most beautiful.

Several consequences of these classificatory schemes can be discerned in subsequent historical events. First, such classifications gave an aura of permanence and rigidity to social conceptions of human group differences. These were static conceptions of human beings that did not allow for subtle nuances, individual variations, intergradations among groups, or biological change. Second, the descriptive materials fused together both physical characteristics and such behavior traits as temperament, disposition, moral character, and intellectual acumen. They helped to usher in an inexorable linkage between biology and behavior that has remained solidified in the popular mind even until modern times. Third, as we have seen, the categories lent themselves to ranking and were thus consistent with, and clearly influenced by, the status differences already present in the social systems. Finally, because they derived from the hands of learned scholars, the taxonomies made humans part of nature and legitimized as "natural" the inferior qualities of non-Europeans. In other words, they accorded scientific sanctions and credibility to popular social images, justifying the lower positions of non-Europeans in the natural order of things.

Scholarly acceptance thus exhibited the same culturally prescribed tendencies that had already been put into motion as part of wider social realities. This was the evolving ideology of race and race differences, and the extreme exaggeration of all human group differences. So conditioned were the learned men of Europe to focusing on human differences that several of the great philosophers and jurists of the late 18th century, men like Voltaire and Lord Kames, even concluded, like their polygenist forebears, that Africans and Europeans must be separate species. Now, however, conditions were such that the reactions of scholars, scientists, philosophers, legal minds, and the wider public gave evidence that they were prepared to accept such a preposterous claim.

Some of the naturalists who developed these taxonomies, notably Buffon and Blumenbach, posed an explanation for the accepted state of savagery of the inferior groups that was compatible with the belief in monogeny. They suggested that, although all men started from the same condition of life at the time of creation, as some migrated into different regions of the world they began to degenerate as a result of changes in climate, geographical factors, and such things as food habits and disease. Most monogenists ultimately found that degeneration was an acceptable explanation for the increasingly vast differences postulated between civilized man with his wealth and expanding technology and savage man, who retained degraded customs.

After the invention of the cotton gin in 1795, the importance of slavery reached new heights. Cotton promised enormous wealth, but its production required large numbers of workers. Wars had been instigated in many parts of Africa as a way of providing enough "goods" for the growing demands of Europeans in the New World. Hundreds of thousands of people were displaced every year and the trajectory of original development of African societies was disrupted, a process dating from the 16th century on, never again to gain its momentum until the end of the 20th century. So ghastly and brutal was the trade that social and political opposition to it grew, especially in England where the ideals of human freedom had a long history among ordinary people. In the United States, the Quakers were the first religious group to voice open public opposition to the slave trade and to slavery. By the end of the 18th century, organized abolitionists began massive campaigns to bring about an end to the institution.

The conflict over slavery precipitated increasingly more defensive arguments that focused on myths of African savagery and natural inferiority. The American public turned increasingly to learned men and to science to provide documentation and objective confirmation of what was emerging as widespread and deeply entrenched dogma about human differences. Edward Long (1734–1813), a former judge and plantation owner in Jamaica, was one of the first to proffer a description of African "savages" in a scholarly work. In his *History of Jamaica*, he characterized "The Negro" as "brutish, ignorant, idle, crafty, treacherous, thievish and superstitutious" (Cited in Slotkin, 1965, p. 209). "In general," he said, "they (Africans) are devoid of genius and seem incapable of making any progress in civility or science" (p. 209). They have no system of morality among them. All people have at least some good qualities, he proclaimed, except the Africans. He concluded that the Negro must be a separate species of the human genus. On the Chain of Being, he placed the Negro and the Orangutan as intermediate between man and the lower primates. The utmost limit of perfection, he declared, is "in the pure white" (Slotkin, p. 210).

Long's work, published originally in 1774 with excerpts reprinted in the United States in the 1790s, was clearly designed as a proslavery document. By the end of the century, such descriptions of blacks were becoming widely disseminated in North America through numerous publications. They became part of the public imagery of blacks that was to last into the 20th century. Charles White, a Manchester physician, in 1799, published "An Account of the Regular Gradation in Man," one of the first works that attempted to use scientific details relating to anatomical differences to argue that Africans, Europeans, Asians, and Native Americans were separate species. "The Negro" in particular had smaller brains, apelike odors, larger sex organs and were immune to pain, among other things. He also classified the Negro as closer to apes than to Europeans on the Chain of Being and saw degeneration as the cause of black inferiority (Gossett, 1965).

19TH CENTURY DEVELOPMENTS IN THE IDEOLOGY OF RACE

Because of his reputation, White's work helped to reinspire further research and expressions of polygenist beliefs. Within a few decades, there arose a major controversy between monogenists and polygenists in scientific and popular circles. At the core of the controversy was the question of the status of "the Negro." Was he human like other men, or was he so different as to require classification as a separate species of man? This controversy dominated scholarly circles in the middle of the 19th century, both here and in England. It engaged some of America's outstanding physicians, educators, and scientific researchers. A central figure was a Philadelphia physician, Samuel Morton (1799–1851), the founder of craniometry, whose research and measurements of crania (skulls) gave definitive confirmation to the idea that science could provide answers to questions of human identity. Believing that brain size correlated with intelligence, he acquired the largest collection of skulls in the world and developed techniques for measuring the internal capacity of the crania. His research showed that Negroes had the smallest brains, those of Indians were larger, and whites had the largest brains of all. His documentation of differences in brain size among different racial populations seemed to affirm the notion of the intellectual inequality of the races. Morton's scientific works were published in the 1830s and 1840s when the debate over slavery was at its height. Some of his supporters were very much aware of how strongly his declarations on race supported the proslavery cause.[7]

One of Morton's collaborators and colleagues was Louis Agassiz who arrived in the United States to teach at Harvard in 1846. In 1847, after seeing his first blacks, Agassiz converted from a monogenist to a polygenist. The founder and promoter of Harvard's biological sciences programs, museums, and research, Agassiz taught his theory to untold numbers of students who became America's most prominent men of science, transmitting their racial views well into the 20th century. Agassiz argued that there were several species of men and they had been specifically created for adaptation to different regions of the world. Like other polygenists he deplored miscegenation, believing that "hybrids" or children of parents of different races, like the mule, were infertile.

Most of Morton's statistical data, measurements, and conclusions were brought together in a book, *Types of Mankind*, published in 1854, that became the definitive resource for scientific discussions of race. It was edited by Josiah C. Nott, an Alabama physician and friend of Morton, and by George R. Gliddon, a collaborator who had

---

[7]See Gould's (1981) work, *The Mismeasure of Man*, for a critique of Morton's clearly biased research and his conclusions. Morton was praised for the support that he gave to the Southern cause.

helped to supply Morton with Egyptian skulls. The book contained a long chapter by Agassiz, among other writers. *Types of Mankind* was widely read, going through nine editions before the end of the century. It provided the intellectual basis and most comprehensive scientific evidence for the polygenist position.[8] People read it, however, for its documentation of white superiority and its arguments against the possibility that the nonwhite races could ever be civilized. Those with limited education who could not read it received its fundamental "truths" from writers who simplified the concepts and popularized them in journals and other books (Fredrickson, 1987).

Morton left important legacies. His work set a precedent for all future anthropological research for more than a century to come. It made race studies—the ascertaining of the number and identification of human races—the dominant activity of physical anthropology in the United States. The methods and techniques were those of anthropometry and craniometry, the measuring of various body parts and especially the skulls. The accumulation of enormous numbers of quantitative data and their statistical treatment led to the "scientific" expression of race differences in mathematical terms. Races were defined by the averages of their measurements; the aggregate averages taken together reflected the racial type. Thus, typological models of races were formed that were static and unchanging. Such racial characterizations were seemingly sound and unambiguous because of their grounding in the science of the day.

This debate over single or plural origins, revealed in journals, newspapers, speeches, and pamphlets, was both spurious and an anachronistic diversion from the reality of the worldview that had been created in the U.S. Many Southern proslavery proponents, steeped as they were in biblical ideology, would not subscribe to a polygenist point of view even though it best supported their arguments for slavery. So most adhered to monogeny with degeneration as an explanation for the lowered state of civilization of non-Europeans, especially blacks. However, as Fredrickson (1987) noted, Southern politicians did not hesitate to use polygenist arguments and materials from the scientific findings of Morton, Nott, and Gliddon in public forums. Both sides had long concurred on the "fact" of Negro inferiority. Both accepted the tremendous magnification of differences between blacks and whites, regardless of their beliefs in race origins. And both accepted social practices, customs, and laws that continued to degrade the negro, and, after the Civil War, to separate negroes from interaction with whites. It really did not matter whether one viewed black Americans as a separate species or not. The entire society by the end of the 19th century understood that science had proved "the Negro" to be inferior and a separate order of being. The reality was that polygenist thinking had already insinuated into every element of U.S. society as part of the racial worldview (Haller, 1971; Stocking, 1968). Race was now equivalent to species in all but name.

---

[8]One should compare this 800 page volume to *The Bell Curve* (Richard Herrnstein & Charles Murray, 1994) another voluminous work that had some of the same objectives, premises, beliefs, and conclusions.

Charles Darwin's evolutionary theories, published in 1859 and 1871, provided in time a new mechanism and theoretical model for claiming the negro not only to be naturally inferior, but fundamentally different, at the species level. One could argue that the negro was the last human type to evolve, or one could argue, as some did, that the negro had evolved first but had stagnated, and the superior whites had surpassed all other races on the evolutionary trajectory. Either theory could be used to "prove" negro inferiority (see chap. 27 in Gould, 1977). If anything, the Darwinian contribution strengthened the notion of advanced and less advanced human groups, but now the arguments could be more scientifically expressed in the language of evolutionary theory.

It was Herbert Spencer who, prior to Darwin, suggested some of the ideas, the language, and the expressions, that were to be applied to the development of human groups. This Englishman, a premier exponent of capitalism, thought human groups and individuals, like other animals, were in a state of competition out of which only the "fittest" would survive. However, it was economic success that determined who were the fittest. Spencer opposed any kind of government help for the poor and disabled because he thought it would prevent these unfit from dying out. The lower races were clearly among the unfit. His ideas, much more complex than expressed here, came to be known as Social Darwinism.

It is important to understand that Darwin's original studies related specifically to changes in the biophysical features of animal forms as such populations underwent adaptation to specific environments. Those individuals with minor biophysical variations who left the most offspring were seen to be the most fit, reflecting reproductive success. That evolutionary theory and Social Darwinists used some of the same language, such as struggle for existence, survival of the fittest, and so forth, should not obscure the fact that social Darwinism was about a human condition and the realities of an economic system predicated on a market ideology, whereas biological evolution related only to reproductive success. Darwin himself subscribed to both sets of beliefs.

The social and economic realities after the Civil War and Reconstruction precluded any possibility that an egalitarian ideology could prevail when it came to human differences. Race was entrenched as a new mechanism for structuring society based on a conception of naturally fixed, inherited, and immutable status categories. It should be emphasized that the idea of natural inequality was a central component of race from its inception, although virtually no one recognized it as a mere analog of social position transformed into myth. Race continued after the Civil War as an ordering system deeply embedded in the American consciousness. It structured all American thought and behavior regarding human differences. It persisted primarily because it was a useful mechanism for determining who should have access to wealth, privilege, respect, loyalty, and power, and who should not. Race became a generic entity, flexible, comprehensive, and infinitely expandable to any and all human groups of varying degrees of cultural or physical diversity, depending on the objectives of those with the power to establish the race classifications.

Thus, Chinese immigrants who had begun to arrive in the United States in the 1850s and took a major part in the building of the railways in the West were also separated out, denied citizenship, and forced to live in segregated communities. The expressed fear was that they would pollute white racial purity and thus diminish white culture. After 1882, Chinese people were excluded from immigration. In the last two decades of the century, some Japanese migrants began to arrive in the United States, only to be met with a racial antagonism that reached a crescendo with the Gentleman's Agreement of 1908 (Takaki, 1989, 1993).

In the 1840s, also, Irish immigration increased dramatically because of famine conditions in Ireland. Settling on the East coast, they too were subject to some of the elements of the racial worldview, in large part because of their long history of hostility with the English. However, they were physically similar to the original European immigrants, and in fact many Irish had arrived as indentured servants during the colonial period. As they became acculturated to American cultural patterns and lost much of their distinctive Irish ways, their European cultural and historical background, their use of the English language, and "whiteness" made them more easily assimilable.[9]

An even more significant use of race for 20th-century developments was occurring in Europe. In the mid-19th century, some European scientists had turned their scholarly attentions and anthropometric techniques to the study of their own populations. They soon constructed racial theories specific for Europe, concluding on the basis of physical differences that there were three different races in Europe: Nordics, Alpines, and Mediterraneans. Famous racialist thinkers like Count de Gobineau, a French aristocrat, and H. S. Chamberlain, an Englishman enamored of all things German, taking advantage of the capacity of race ideology to justify economic and social inequalities, ranked these races along an inferior–superior continuum. Nordics (or Aryans as they were called by some later) were tall, blond, blue-eyed, long-headed descendants of great German warriors who were born to rule over others; Alpines were shorter, brunette, round-headed, heavy-shouldered ordinary folks of the middle regions of Europe, the Celts, Gauls, and others who were workers and followers. The shorter, darker, Mediterraneans (Italians, Greeks, Armenians) were sensual and unintelligent, morally decadent, and emotional. Beliefs about the different abilities of European races were woven into European history to account for the differential achievements of varying peoples. Chamberlain, some of whose strongest diatribes were against Jews as a "morally defective" race, wrote a two-volume history published in 1899 (*Foundations of the Nineteenth Century*) that was widely read in Germany and became the basis for Nazi propaganda against Jews and others in the 20th century.

Race ideology was so convenient and functional that its components literally spread around the world, often displacing older understandings of ethnic and class differences, especially where there were major conflicts. It is useful to delineate

---

[9]For a fascinating exploration of this process, see Theodore Allen (1994) and Noel Ignatiev (1995).

analytically its salient features as they developed in the United States and to summarize the fully mature ideology at the end of the 19th century. The following elements were integral to the ideology of race in the United States. They can be seen as fundamental beliefs constituting a worldview, often unconsciously held, that provides guidelines to public behavior at all levels of American society.

1. The world's peoples are divided into separate, discrete, and exclusive biological units called races, each of which are, or were, homogeneous.
2. Each race has its own peculiar physical, behavioral, intellectual, moral, and temperamental traits; the biophysical features that distinguish races are but surface manifestations of these inner realities.
3. Races are unequal physically, morally, intellectually, and in terms of their potentialities and capabilities; they must therefore be ranked, with white Europeans at the top, black Africans at the bottom, and others arbitrarily identified at varying positions in between.
4. The distinctive qualities of each race are *inherited* and *natural*, both the physical features and forms of behavior.
5. Each race was created unique, different, and unequal by nature or God, so that the imputed differences, believed fixed and unalterable, can never be bridged or transcended.

In the 19th century, the growing power of an expanding science had confirmed the existence of races and validated the social parameters and constraints imposed on all human beings. Historian John S. Haller, Jr. (1971) showed that the influence of race ideology was so pervasive in the latter part of the 19th century that no one questioned either the existence of races or their presumed inequality.

A continuing output of scientific studies aimed at identifying and documenting racial differences characterized the late 19th and early 20th centuries in the United States. Anthropometric studies expanded as new techniques for measuring various parts of the human anatomy were developed. Many physicians, biologists, anatomists, and scholars in other fields were actively engaged in elucidating the significance of race differences. More laws against race mixture and intermarriage were passed based on the belief that such mating was unnatural; it was the union of two separate species that produced abnormalities or disharmonies in the offspring and led to decadence and immorality. The image of most white Americans was that each race should stay in its own place (i.e., on the Chain of Being), having its own community and customs, marrying its own kind, and functioning within its own institutions. Science had helped to create this image.

IQ: HEREDITARIAN IDEOLOGY AND THE MEASURING OF INNATE MENTAL PROCESSES

Scientists continued and refined their anthropometric activities in the 20th century. Human biologists joined a growing field of anatomists and physical anthropologists trained to measure body parts and their differences. The subdiscipline of physical anthropology was consolidated in the first few decades of the century. Reigning over the field were two men, Aleš Hrdlička and Earnest Albert Hooton, whose main interests were in morphological research and its refinements. Hrdlička founded the *American Journal of Physical Anthropology* and Hooton taught at Harvard for 40 years. An intellectual and philosophical descendant of Agassiz, he trained nearly all of the first generations of physical anthropologists in the United States. He also transmitted to them his scientific expression of the racial worldview, "that the physical characteristics which determine race are associated, in the main, with specific intangible and non-measurable, but nevertheless real and important, temperamental and mental variations" (cited in Barkan, 1992, p. 103).

As usual, whatever differences were found between any group of blacks and whites were interpreted to reflect the inferiority of blacks. However, there were limits to the meanings that could be extrapolated from body measurements. Thomas F. Gossett (1965) observed that by the 1880s it was clear that measurement of crania could not provide a foolproof method of determining racial identity and ranking. There were enormous individual variations within so-called racial populations and these were found to be greater than the average differences between them. The legacy of the craniometrists was a need for some way to demonstrate scientifically the intellectual inferiority of blacks, by measuring processes taking place in the mind. It was in this arena where racial social practices and policies could find their greatest source and sustenance.

The brain had long been determined to be the seat of all mental, emotional, and spiritual activities. Character and temperament were also functions of the brain, and, of course, all forms of learning took place within the brain. As it evolved, racial ideology had asserted strongly that all of these processes were hereditary, just as the physical property of the brain was inherited. Any questions raised about individual or group behavior, capacities, abilities, or tendencies of specific races were answered by what became a grand theory of causality, racial heredity. Heredity as the cause or source of human behavioral traits was a simple, highly acceptable, and ultimately useful explanatory device.

From this 19th-century legacy, and well into the 20th century, the theme of heredity pervaded all of the developing sciences of humankind, anthropology, human biology, psychology, and sociology. Its application was not limited to its role as a mechanism for ascribing racial differences. For many scientists, it could be applied to other forms of behavior, especially among those individuals within the dominant race who deviated from what was accepted as the normal standards.

In the late 19th century, some educated Europeans had begun to suggest that poverty, criminal behavior, prostitution, alcoholism, diseases like tuberculosis, and mental defects were all inherited within family lines. The clear implication was that these traits were fixed and unchanging. Therefore society planners need not attempt to intercede by changing the external conditions of these families. This frame of thought, which came to be known as *biological determinism*, was insidious and seductive. It allowed those in power, the elite, to blame virtually every social disaster or problem on the heredity of "the unfit."

At the roots of this trend were certain publications of the nineteenth century that purported to demonstrate the intellectual superiority of some individuals and classes over others. In 1869, Francis Galton published a major work called *Hereditary Genius*, in which he "proved" by analyzing the genealogies of a selected group of eminent men that only a limited number of families in England provided the geniuses and professional elite, the lawyers, physicians, scientists, statesmen, military leaders, and literary and musical giants. Galton came from this elite class (he was a cousin of Charles Darwin) and was obsessed with its abilities, its seemingly hereditary talents, skills, and general intelligence. His assertion that genius was inherited in an elite class was inherently contradictory to the ideals of equality and liberty on which the English political system was predicated (but all human societies have learned to live with many inconsistencies and contradictions as part of the nature of culture). To the British power establishment, such scholarly evidence of superior heredity hardly went unnoticed. The "natural" inequality of the social classes in England was given a boost by this and many other publications.

This was not the first example of the English sense of inequality, as we have seen. Throughout much of the 18th century, writers had promoted the notion that England was dominated by one superior group, the Anglo-Saxons, whose laws, love of liberty, militarism and aggression, ambition, and energy made them masters of all other groups (Celts, Franks, and others). Their skills and abilities were derived historically from a Germanic background (the German "noble savage" as described by the Roman writer Tacitus in ancient times). By the end of the 18th century, Anglo-Saxonism had become interpreted as a quality carried in the blood; it was both biological and innate. This development in English thought, not surprisingly, coincided with the rise of racial ideology in the United States, each acting synergistically on the other to buttress the themes of racial differences, heritability, and inequality.

Galton had based his study on complex statistical methods. He assumed that intelligence was a quantifiable entity that could also be measured and subjected to statistical manipulation to reach certain scientific truths about intellectual abilities. Therefore, he invented a number of tests designed to identify levels of intelligence. He believed that there were general laws governing heredity, and that on discovering them he would be able to express them mathematically. Thus, he was a "pioneer (in the) quantitative approach to the psychology of individual differences" (Kevles, 1985, p. 77). Many of his tests did not so much tap mental activity but physiological reaction time to certain stimuli. Galton also persuaded the British Association for the Advancement of Science to conduct a survey of the mental abilities of English schoolchildren. In the 1880s he published two other books on the subject of human heredity, *Human Faculty* (1883) and *Natural Inheritance* (1889). All of his works appeared before anyone knew anything about genes, chromosomes, or DNA.

Galton had an almost fanatical concern with heredity and the reproduction of superior people (although he never fathered a child). He coined the term *eugenics* to denote efforts to improve "racial stock" by breeding a better quality people based on the selected marriages of only those "most fit." Lower quality people, largely the uneducated and the poor, would be encouraged not to reproduce, or to be sterilized. Galton gave many lectures and published books and pamphlets for the general educated public. As an advocate of controlled (eugenic) breeding, he devoted time and money to organizations and projects that shared his philosophy. With his many studies, tests and publications, he developed a reputation as a great man of science and became the intellectual and spiritual founder of the Eugenics movement early in the 20th century, which had a major impact on American thought.

Galton's advocacy of breeding only the best quality people struck a rich vein in the United States. His idea of measuring intelligence as an indicator of best quality was also obviously one whose time had come. At the turn of the century, the French government had asked Alfred Binet, a pioneer psychologist, to develop means of testing variability in the capabilities of French school children, especially to detect those who were mentally deficient. Working with a colleague, Theodore Simon, Binet developed a series of tests that were later thought by others to measure degrees of intelligence. Known as the Binet–Simon tests, they were introduced into the United States in 1908 by psychologist Henry H. Goddard, who used a revised version at his Training School for Feeble-Minded Boys and Girls in New Jersey. With these tests, Goddard was able to classify the children in categories that he called "morons," "imbeciles," and "idiots." Goddard is perhaps best known, however, for his publicly recognized work on the Kallikak family, in which he demonstrated, or so he thought, that feeblemindedness had been transmitted through three generations of one family.

The Binet–Simon tests were given to inmates in prisons and reformatories and yielded the conclusion that these persons had a high rate of mental deficiency. A few years later, Lewis Terman, a psychologist at Stanford University, revised the tests (called the Stanford–Binet tests) and used William Stern's concept of *intelligence quotient* (IQ) for the numerical findings. During World War I, a group of psychologists under Robert Yerkes developed tests for military recruits to ascertain the abilities of these young men for different tasks. In all, more than 1,700,000 recruits were tested by the Army Alpha and Beta tests which set a major precedent for future testing by schools, government agencies, and businesses. Goddard also used the tests on immigrants at Ellis Island.

The Army tests and their results were widely disseminated and for generations constituted the basic evidence for racial differences in intelligence. Books such as psychologist Carl Brigham's *A Study of American Intelligence* (1923) concluded exactly what the eugenicists had predicted. As Kevles (1985) observed, "The average intelligence of black Americans, apparently, was just as low as most white Americans had long liked to think it" (p. 83). The "average" black had the mental age of a 10-year-old and disproportionately more blacks were feebleminded. But that was not all: Alpine and Mediterranean races were inferior intellectually to Nordics, who always scored highest on intelligence tests. Yet, the average white American, as extrapolated from the Army findings, had the mental age of a 13-year-old. The results of all these early tests solidified the notion in the public mind that intelligence was a unitary entity that could be expressed in a number, that people from southern and eastern Europe were intellectually inferior to Nordics, and that blacks and Indians were lowest of all.

As Gossett observed, these tests provided a field day for racists whose views were now substantiated and confirmed by an "objective" scientific instrument. From then on, numerous studies were conducted on race differences in intelligence. Social policymakers could now argue that it was useless to try to improve the conditions of the blacks, Indians, and poor whites because their condition was a product of their limited heredity. In the public mind, race became an even more homogeneous, concrete phenomenon, with racial groups now scientifically documented as having different levels of intelligence.

The social contexts in which such studies were done provides an understanding of the visceral needs of some whites and why these kinds of conclusions were so widely accepted. Hatred, fear, and contempt for black Americans reached an extreme level in the early decades of this century. Massive immigration of Europeans from the 1880s through the 1920s threw them into competition for jobs with blacks, most of whose ancestors had already been in the United States since before 1800. The immigrants soon acquired the social values of "white" native-born Americans, and took the position that they as white men had rights to the better jobs, schooling, and training that were increasingly being denied to blacks. Blacks with skilled jobs were removed to make room for whites without skills. The negro's place was to be the "mudsills," to do the dirty and onerous work of society and be content with their low status (Steinberg, 1989). Conflicts ensued as both native-born and white immigrants attacked blacks for refusing to be satisfied with the crumbs of the socioeconomic system. They attacked each other out of competition for the most desirable jobs. The Ku Klux Klan renewed its strategies of intimidation and brutality against blacks and Jews. Race riots and lynchings increased, especially during the 1920s, and by 1923 an estimated 6 million whites held membership in the Ku Klux Klan.

Complicating all of this were intractable economic problems and rising enmity among native-born white Americans toward the new European immigrants, especially those of Jewish and Catholic backgrounds. Southern and Eastern Europeans were perceived as being "racially" different, although not as drastically so as negroes and Indians. Nevertheless, anti-Semitism reached new heights in part because of the role of some Jews in organizing labor unions. It was also affected by the continuing anti-Jewish sentiments in Europe that had intensified in the latter part of the 19th century. For many people, the post-World War I period was an anguishing one of open hostility and violence in which race served too often as a catalyst because of its scapegoat functions and the ease with which it provided excuses for brutality against others.

Consciously or not, the spiritual impetus for so much of the hatred came from American scientists and those who popularized their conclusions. Many of the major writers were members of, or sympathetic to, the eugenics movement, which derived its racist philosophy from Spencer and Galton. At the end of World War I, Madison Grant and biologist Charles B. Davenport, whom Barkan (1992) has called the most prominent racist among American scientists, founded the Galton Society, dedicated to the active promotion of eugenics research and policies. Members included anthropologists like Clark Wissler and Earnest Hooton of Harvard, and psychologists like Edward L. Thorndike, G. Stanley Hall, and Carl Brigham. There were social scientists, including economists like Irving Fisher, and other men from a wide range of the political spectrum, socialists, and capitalists. All were convinced that heredity was more important than factors in the environment in determining a person's character and behavior. In fact, there were few voices favoring external environmental explanations to oppose the strongly dominant hereditarians. Criminals, prostitutes, the feebleminded, paupers, epileptics, and those addicted to alcohol had been deemed to be products of inferior "germ plasm" even before the rediscovery of Mendel's experiments and the introduction of the idea of genes as units of heredity.

Eugenics and the hereditarian ideology flourished during the first three decades of the 20th century (Haller, 1963). With the rise of the field of genetics, more sophisticated understanding of the role of genes, and the patterns of genetic transmission of known traits, most of the scientists involved in the eugenics movement received some training in genetics. Courses in genetics were introduced in many major universities. Textbooks appeared on an increasingly frequent basis with titles that revealed the heavy imprint of eugenics philosophy in the fields of genetics and biology, like William E. Castle's *Genetics and Eugenics* (1916), for several decades the most widely used college text in the field (see Barkan, 1992; Chase 1980).

Some of the eugenics devotees promulgated their hereditarian philosophies with much political vigor, hoping to influence popular thought and public policies. They were actively engaged in influencing immigration policies during the early 1920s when new immigration laws (1921, 1924) were passed, structured to prevent or restrict immigrants not originating from Western and Northern Europe. Many also actively advocated sterilization for the mentally defective or feebleminded. The result was that several states passed compulsory sterilization laws for people in mental institutions and for poor people on welfare who often were summarily rounded up, as was the case in Virginia, and carted to state hospitals for the operation. Although there were some British scientists actively advocating such policies, the British public was generally opposed to involuntary sterilization. The policy of sterilizing the "unfit" reached its most bizarre and brutal state in Germany, where in 1933 a Eugenic Sterilization Law was passed and within 3 years more than 225,000 people had been subjected to the operation (Kevles, 1935). Adolf Hitler's passion for breeding a "super race" prompted ruthless policies such as those establishing special breeding hospitals for "Aryan" women who bore children to SS officers. Worst of all, during World War II, such policies led to euthanasia and massive genocide on a scale that the world could hardly comprehend.

It did not matter that there was not a shred of evidence for genes that caused poverty, or criminality, or feeblemindedness or, for that matter, intelligence or biological race. In fact, little knowledge of genes per se was known, although researchers had discovered the patterns of transmission of some of the blood groups (e.g., the ABO blood system, MN group, Rhesus factor), and even some abnormalities, like phenylketonuria, a metabolic liver disease known to be hereditary. The hereditarian component of race ideology did not require empirical proof. It had, however, facilitated the continuing transference of this form of causality onto the wider public consciousness. And, as the poor have often been ignored, mistreated, and maligned in Western culture (the "let-them-eat-cake" phenomenon), it became almost a middle-class convention that the social pathologies of the poor and uneducated were their own "inherited" fault.

THE SCIENTIFIC REACTION AGAINST RACE IDEOLOGY

Even as hereditarian beliefs were being reified and broadly implanted in American culture and consciousness, and race ideology dominated all aspects of society, some social forces were already spawning a reaction against the idea of race and the components of this ideology. The sources of opposition to the idea of race were not originally products of American thought and values. As Gossett (1965) pointed out, "Virtually all of the systematic critics of racism in the nineteenth century were Europeans" (p. 412; see also Hannaford, 1996). Although most of them were unknown and often ignored by their contemporaries, he added, the fact is that they brought an element of logic into a domain overwhelmed with illogic.

There were at least three major arenas in which change in attitudes toward human differences began to take place. One was the world of science where new technologies and discoveries generated vast amounts of new information about the nature of heredity and the reproduction of biophysical traits. A second was the growth of cultural anthropology, which revealed the complexity of human sociopolitical systems everywhere and ways of understanding different cultures that had nothing to do with human biology. A third arena had to do with liberalizing transformations in the political consciousness of European scholars, the rise of fascism in Europe, and the social and political changes that led to the emergence of Nazi Germany under whom race ideology found its most extreme expression.

Most scientists had accepted the folk race ideas of their times because they were culturally conditioned to them, and the self-serving nature of race superiority was very comfortable to those in high-status race categories. However, as early as 1848, John Stuart Mill had asserted, "Of all the vulgar modes of escaping from the consideration of the effect of social and moral influences on the human mind, the most vulgar is that of attributing the diversities of conduct and character to inherent natural differences" (cited in Gossett, 1965, pp. 411–412). Here he questioned the hereditarian component of race ideology, making clear that it was external factors, "social and moral" influences, that determined conduct and character.

Some European scholars had also expressed skepticism about dividing the world's populations so precisely into biologically distinct groups. They pointed out that human physical traits are not finite and discrete, but continuous from one extreme to another, blending into one another as Blumenbach, Buffon, and even Darwin had recognized. This posed great difficulty in drawing dividing boundaries around many populations, especially where there was any degree of propinquity. The most damming aspect of the biological race concept, however, was its elusiveness. Experts could not agree on the definition of race, the number of human races thought to exist, or the physical criteria by which race status was supposed to be determined. The result was a cacophony of theories about race differences, numerous schemes for identifying biological races, and no consensus whatsoever on the number of races in the world. Ever since the mid-19th century, a debate on these points has been quietly, sometimes vigorously, taking place. As we have seen, Blumenbach had identified five basic varieties (races), Linnaeus named four, Buffon counted six, Hunter claimed there were seven, Agassiz had named eight, and various other scholars going into the 20 century had selected anywhere from 16 to 68 as the correct number of naturally identifiable human races. The criteria for identifying races have been as varied as the numbers. Scientists today are no closer to agreement on definitions and numbers of races in the world than they were at the end of the 18th century.

Some historians of science have observed that a gradual and subtle revolution began to take place in the biological sciences in the 1930s, and alternative perspectives on human physical variability emerged. Although historians differ somewhat on the causes of this shift in thinking, the evidence clearly indicates a growing skepticism in Europe about the reality of race and somewhat later in the United States, although the point may be debated. The typological approach to the understanding of human biophysical differences had assumed that races were permanent, rigid, and unchanging. Biologists began to realize that this made race a sterile and rather nonproductive concept; the mere classifications of and labeling of races were not conducive to greater understanding of the nature, range, and causes of human physical variability. Moreover, it seemed to contradict the evidence of change that geneticists and biologists were finding, as well as the theory of evolution that assumed or suggested more or less constant small alterations in biological species. Not only the reality, but the usefulness of the concept of race was called into question. A renewed interest in biological evolutionary changes and the mechanisms of change appeared in the 1930s. By the 1950s, evolutionary theory was perhaps the dominant paradigm in physical anthropology, but now it had solid data and increased understanding of the genetic basis for heredity.

The rise of the science of genetics, stemming from the rediscovery of Mendel's experiments by three independent researchers, transformed not only evolutionary theory, but the whole scientific perspective on biogenetic variation. Some research-oriented scientists, generally unimpacted by the controversies over eugenics and the racial and class biases expressed in them, began to try to understand in greater detail the processes of Mendelian reproduction, experimenting with plants, fruit flies, mice, and bats. With new and advanced techniques, they soon discovered the internal structure of cells, chromosomes, and genes and their role in the transmission of physical traits. Their findings supported Mendel's particle theory of inheritance and his law of independent assortment, showing that each trait had its own distinct mode of transmission. Studies from the 1930s on revealed the complexity of the combinations and recombinations of genetic traits manifest in such simple forms as fruit flies.

Attempting to be able to predict the outcome of certain manipulations of cell nuclei, genetics researchers found that heat and radiation affected the ways in which certain traits, whose mode of heredity was known, came to be expressed. They brought about *mutations*, subtle changes in the genetic materials, and their biological manifestations, that could be transmitted to the next generations. The discovery of mutations was a major event that had implications for the understanding of all evolutionary change. Most importantly, Thomas Hunt Morgan of Columbia University discovered from his experiments on fruit flies that the environment and genes worked together in relationships far more complicated than had been assumed under Mendelian laws.

When the ABO blood group system was discovered, and later other elements in the blood (MN system, Rhesus system, PTC tasters, etc.) of unmistakable genetic basis, these were perceived as major breakthroughs in finally having techniques for ascertaining race group differences based on variations in gene frequencies in different populations. After the 1950s, the definitions of race could now be expressed in terms of the different frequencies of known genetic features, like the ABO blood groups. However, each of these features varied independently of one another, so that no consistent patterns of race differences could be ascertained. Morever, there were no genes, held exclusively in one group, that definitively identified a person or group as Negro, Japanese, or European.

By the middle of the 20th century, numerous human genetic features had been identified, some of them based on only a single gene or its alleles. Most of the hereditary features have been deleterious, causing abnormalities or diseases. With perhaps several thousand such disorders, geneticists have given up looking for "black" genes or "white" genes. Most now are challenged by known genetic disorders and have worked to find a cure or some mechanism of dealing with the abnormalities. Others have looked for patterns of transmission of particular features whose heredity is suspect, but the mechanism or mode of inheritance is not known. Such research does not require the use of racial categories, although certain maladies, like sickle-cell anemia and Tay–Sachs disease have been found predominantly in limited breeding populations who could not possibly constitute racial populations otherwise.

Arguments about racial differences in IQ diminished for a while between the 1960s and the 1980s as critics of IQ tests demonstrated their uselessness, their many weaknesses, and their failure to actually measure anything more definitive than the educational and personal experiences of students. Scientists no longer think of intelligence as a single monolithic entity. Much evidence suggests that there are numerous domains in which competence can be expressed, and intelligence most likely constitutes multiple different kinds of abilities that can only be realized (or not realized) through cultural conditioning (see, e.g., Gardner, 1985, and other works by this author).

In the late 19th century some European scholars had begun to pay increasing attention to cultures and how they differed. They began the first field trips to study "primitive" societies in their natural settings. It soon became clear that variations in cultural patterns were due to geographical, historical, economic, and other extrinsic factors. Some groups who seem to belong to the same race, or were similar physically, were found to have widely different cultures and languages. Seemingly savage peoples who inhabited tropical forests were found not only to have complex cultures and languages, but to bear striking cultural similarities to those occupying similar habitats in other parts of the world, despite having few phenotypic (physical) similarities. A rising anthropological establishment paid much more attention to behavior as it was learned in the context of a sociocultural system. As anthropologists on both sides of the Atlantic became more sophisticated, it made sense to study cultures on their own without regard to the physical characteristics of the people associated with them. As early as 1871, E. B. Tylor (1871/1958), one of the founders of modern cultural anthropology, had defined *culture* as "that complex whole which includes knowledge, belief, art, morals, law, custom and any other capabilities and habits *acquired by man as a member of society*" (p. i). An emphasis on culture as external and learned was also a part of the growing field of sociology under Emile Durkheim, who had a large following among some British social scientists, especially the anthropological establishment.

The person most closely linked with changes in scientific views of race in the United States was Franz Boas, the Dean of American anthropologists, and the dominant influence in the growth of this discipline in the first five decades. European-born, Boas came into the study of anthropology after a visit to Baffinland, where he interacted with the native Eskimos and became intrigued by their culture. By the end of the 19th century he had arrived in the United States and became involved in museum studies, somatology, and ethnological studies. He became professor of anthropology at Columbia University in 1896 and remained there for more than 40 years, teaching most of the first generations of trained cultural anthropologists in the United States.

In keeping with the trends being established in anthropology, Boas worked in all of the subdisciplines. He became an expert on American Indian languages, did research in physical anthropology, and collected and published ethnographic information on the customs and traditions of Eskimo and Northwest Coast Indian groups. An indefatigable worker, he and his students built American anthropology from the ground up, setting many precedents for later trends (Harris, 1968). His early work in physical anthropology, primarily anthropometric studies of immigrants, in retrospect, helped to revolutionize the field. This work revealed that the children of immigrants had physical measurements that differed significantly from their parents. Round-headed parents from central Europe, for example, had children who were long-headed. And second-generation children were taller on average than their parents. Boas posed the explanation that it was the change in environment, including food habits and diet, that was responsible. These studies demonstrated that physical traits, even in a single population, are not permanent and unalterable, that seemingly hereditary features of human morphology could be modified by external conditions and influences. Average anthropometric findings in one generation may yield totally different results in the next generation, thus discrediting the notion that races were permanent types.

Boas and his students questioned the linkage of biology and culture in the premises of most scholarship. They argued that race should refer only to the biophysical characteristics of a people and should not be confused with language and culture. Culture and language are learned forms of behavior; they are not inherited like skin color and body build. Any normal member of any human race is capable of learning and functioning within any culture. An even stronger statement of the extrasomatic, superorganic nature of culture appeared in an article published by his first student, A. L. Kroeber (1917), who went on to gain eminence in the field himself.

By the 1930s comparative studies of different cultures were well on their way and anthropology took on new significance in the scholarly world. Around the same time, some psychologists and sociologists of progressive social persuasion began to argue that it was nurture, not nature, that was the primary determinant of human behavior. In their opposition to biological determinism (as we have seen, a major tenet of the idea of race), they attacked IQ studies, arguing against the notion that races have innate differences in levels of intelligence and that these differences could be accurately measured by tests. A young disciple and student of Boas, psychologist Otto Klineberg (1935) in a major study of the claims of proponents of IQ tests, demonstrated the bias in such tests.[10] Following Kroeber, he also showed the close relationship between amount of schooling and performance on the tests. Revealing that negroes in four Northern states scored higher on the IQ tests than did whites from the four Southern states where funding for education was lowest, he gave a devastating refutation of IQ tests as a measure of innate racial intelligence (see Chase, 1980).

With the rise of Hitler and Nazism in the 1930s and 1940s, the antagonism of an enlarged liberal scientific establishment in the United States was extended to the growing racism in Germany. It was the racial theories, policies, and practices of this fascist regime that gave a major blow to racial ideology everywhere. Nazi practices revealed the extremes to which the myth of race differences could be taken. The world could not tolerate such inhumane acts; so the consciousness of most Americans turned against prejudice and discrimination, at least overtly. Social policies and government propaganda proclaimed not only liberty, equality, and justice for all, but freedom of blacks and other nonwhite minorities from discrimination in any form.

Progressive scientists at the end of the 20th century have gone further than any public institution in their positions against folk racial ideology. Some have argued that human races in the biological sense do not exist; there is no scientific basis for them and we should eliminate the term from our lexicon (Lieberman, 1968; Montagu, 1971). Others have recognized that the term itself will remain with us for decades to come because its real meaning reflects a social ideology deeply embedded in our culture.

---

[10]In this and other publications, he refuted the rationalization that Northern negroes performed better on IQ tests because they represented the brightest (i.e., selected few) who left the South for better opportunities.

History shows that race ideology is about inequality in access to privilege, power, and position. In our calculations of what features are salient in our identities, variations in skin color, hair form, and physiognomy may well continue to operate because these have long been clues to high-status and low-status races. In a highly competitive society such as the United States, some people will continue to use such physical markers as guides to their conduct.

However, cultural beliefs do change; future generations will not be as uptight about race status as the generations before. New immigrants and the continual intermixture of people around the world will render physical markers less certain as guides to racial identity. In certain contexts some people may well become raceless, that is, they will be able to function, work, and carry on their lifestyles independent of a racial label.

The demand by some individuals who consider themselves "biracial" for a separate "mixed race" category on the U.S. Census forms has brought the reality of the increasingly complicated biological ancestry of modern populations to the forefront of public policy. However, the spokespersons for this movement should understand that there have always been mixed races from the beginning of human group interactions (in North America as elsewhere) and that race is really not about biology. Their advocacy at this time reflects the continuing powerful influence of the racial worldview. It also complicates our understanding of the reality of race in our society. To advocate for a mixed race category on the census forms further advances the myths that distinct races are biological realities and have behavioral concomitants. Most important, it preserves the notion that our basic identities are, or should be, predicated solely on this biology, rather than on other aspects of our social selves (education, occupation, interests, ethnicity, geography, and etc.). The very phrase "mixed race" conjures up the idea that pure races once existed, a myth that has long been contradicted by modern science.

Historical circumstances always change, however, and the ideological components of race appear to have outlived their usefulness in a very different kind of society. Some sociologists are prognosticating the declining significance of race as a social category in the future. As we move into the 21st century, the increasingly sophisticated understandings of the modern sciences about human biophysical variations, heredity, and the reality of socially determined behavior, notwithstanding attempts to resuscitate biological determinism (as in *The Bell Curve*), may play a significant role in bringing this about.[11] We need to educate the public about the real facts of human biological variability, particularly the ecological and adaptive bases for the superficial physical variations that have too long been used to structure an unequal society. At the same time, historians and other social scientists must understand that

---

[11]There is a large and growing body of literature on evolution and the development of adaptive physical characteristics of human populations everywhere. Evidence from the study of DNA clearly indicates that diversity in the human species can only be understood if we abandon homogenizing people into racial groups. It is unfortunate that these scientific findings have not yet found their way into the literature of high schools and other institutions of learning. Some suggested readings include L. L. Cavalli-Sforza and F. Cavalli-Sforza (1995), Lewontin (1995), Marks (1995), and Stringer and McKie (1997).

the persistence of the racial worldview in large sectors of American society can and will occur in tandem with a decline in racism in other sectors. The ideological components of race will only disintegrate, if at all, when greater real equality has been achieved, and individuals everywhere, regardless of their biological characteristics, find social race status irrelevant in their daily lives.

REFERENCES

Allen, T. W. (1994). *The invention of the white race* (Vol. 1). New York: Verso.

Allen, T. W. (1997). *The invention of the white race* (Vol. 2). New York: Verso.

Anchor, R. (1967). *The enlightenment tradition.* Berkeley: University of California Press.

Barkan, E. (1992). *The retreat of scientific racism.* New York: Cambridge University Press.

Berkhofer, R. F., Jr. (1978). *The white man's indians.* New York: Knopf.

Cavalli-Sforza, L. L., & Cavalli-Sforza, F. (1995). *The great human diasporas: The history of diversity and evolution.* Reading, MA: Perseus.

Chase, A. (1980). *The legacy of Malthus.* Urbana: University of Illinois Press.

Fredrickson, G. M. (1987). *The black image in the white mind.* Middletown, CT: Wesleyan University Press.

Gardner, H. (1985). *Frames of mind.* New York: Basic Books.

Gossett, T. F. (1965). *Race: The history of an idea in America.* New York: Schocken.

Gould, S. J. (1977). *Ever since Darwin.* New York: Norton.

Gould, S. J. (1981). *The mismeasure of man.* New York: Norton.

Haller, J. S., Jr. (1971). *Outcasts from evolution: Scientific attitudes of racial inferiority, 1859–1900.* Urbana: University of Illinois Press.

Haller, M. H. (1963). *Eugenics: Hereditarian attitudes in American thought.* New Brunswick, NJ: Rutgers University Press.

Hallowell, A. I. (1960). The beginnings of anthropology in America. In F. de Laguna (Ed.), *Selected papers from the American anthropologist, 1888–1920.* Evanston, IL: Row Peterson.

Hannaford, I. (1996). *Race: The history of an idea in the west.* Baltimore: John Hopkins Press.

Harris, M. (1968). *The rise of anthropological theory.* New York: Crowell.

Herrnstein, R. J., & Murray, C. (1994). *The bell curve: Intelligence and class structure in American life.* New York: The Free Press.

Ignatiev, N. (1995). *How the Irish became white.* New York: Routledge.

Jones, H. M. (1964). *O strange new world.* New York: Viking.

Jordan, W. D. (1968). *White over black: American attitudes toward the negro, 1550–1812.* Baltimore: Penguin.

Kevles, D. J. (1985). *In the name of eugenics.* New York: Knopf.

Klineberg, O. (1935). *Race differences.* New York: Harper.

Kroeber, A. L. (1917). The superorganie. *American Anthropologist, 19,* 163–213.

Lewontin, R. (1995). *Human diversity.* New York: Scientific American Library.

Lieberman, L. (1968). The debate over race: A study in the sociology of knowledge. *Phylon, 29,* 127–141.

Marks, J. (1995). *Human biodiversity: Genes, race, and history.* New York: Aldine de Gruyter.

Montagu, A. (1971). *Man's most dangerous myth: The fallacy of race.* New York: World. (Original work published 1964)

Morgan, E. S. (1975). *American slavery, American freedom.* New York: Norton.

Morgan, P. D. (1998). *Slave counterpoint: Black culture in the eighteenth-century Chesapeake and lowcountry.* Chapel Hill: University of North Carolina Press.

Nash, G. (1982). *Red, white, and black: The peoples of early America* (rev. ed.). Englewood Cliffs, NJ: Prentice Hall.

Pearce, R. H. (1953). *The savages of America.* Baltimore: John Hopkins University Press.

Slotkin, J. S. (Ed.). (1965). *Readings in early anthropology.* New York: Wenner-Gren Foundation for Anthropological Research.

Smedley, A. (1999). *Race in North America: Origin and evolution of a worldview* (2nd ed.). Boulder, CO: Westview.

Steinberg, S. (1989). *The ethnic myth* (2nd ed.). Boston: Beacon.

Stocking, G. (1968). *Race, culture, and evolution.* New York: The Free Press.

Stringer, C., & McKie, R. (1997). *African exodus: The origins of modern humanity.* New York: Holt.

Takaki, R. (1989). *Strangers from a different shore.* New York: Penguin.

Takaki, R. (1993). *A different mirror: A history of multicultural America.* Boston: Little, Brown.

Tylor, E. B. (1958). *Primitive culture.* New York: Harper and Row. (Original work published in 1871)

CHAPTER 7

The Bell Curve and the Politics of Negrophobia

Kimberly C. Welch

Richard Herrnstein and Charles Murray (1994) have produced a controversial and extensive study about human differences, the sources of these differences and how we should respond to them. The early reactions to the book in the popular press concentrated on the authors' discussion of racial disparities and the genetic bases for these differences (Heckman, 1995). In his defense of his work, Murray consistently denied that the book centers around the subject of race, as only 1 of its 21 chapters focuses on arguments regarding African American "intellectual inferiority." *The Bell Curve*, however, limits the eight chapters of Part Two to a discussion about whites alone, indicating that over half the book remains organized around the question of race, unless one considers the notion that whiteness is not a racial category (Giroux & Searls, 1996). The two principal premises in *The Bell Curve* are these: First, measured intelligence (IQ) is largely genetically inherited, and second, IQ is correlated positively with a variety of measures of socioeconomic success in society that are inversely correlated with criminality and other social failures. The authors conclude that socioeconomic successes and failures are largely genetically caused (Devlin, 1995). This chapter discusses the impact of Murray and Herrnstein's observations regarding African Americans and IQ, as exemplified in chapter 13, within the context of a brief historical background on race and eugenics in the West. It concentrates on qualitative, not quantitative, issues regarding Murray and Herrnstein's findings on the subject.

In this chapter, moreover, I examine the public debate regarding the conclusions of *The Bell Curve* within the context of the pervasiveness of *Negrophobia*, the irrational antiblack fear that traditionally influenced U.S. society, especially during the last 20 years. I define Negrophobia as the antipathy toward black people expressed by those whites who regard the former as a political and socioeconomic threat to their notions of racial superiority and privileged status (Winant, 1997). The politics of Negrophobia, therefore, represented the evolution of repressive measures created to deprive African Americans of the same political rights, social mobility and economic opportunities enjoyed by many white Americans.

The historical antecedents of Negrophobia originated from colonial laws and customs that relegated enslaved and free African Americans to subordinate status. In the Virginia colony, the repressive 1680 slave statute forebade frequent meetings by dozens of African Americans, prevented blacks from carrying a weapon instituted pass laws for slaves traveling outside the plantation, and permitted severe corporal punishment if a black person raised his hand against any white Christian (Higginbotham, 1978). Moreover, in Pennsylvania, the legal rights and mobility of free blacks were restricted by a 1725–1726 ordinance that described them as inherently "slothful" and a great public "burden" to the colony (Higginbotham, 1978, pp. 283–284).

However, the emphasis on biological determinism within Negrophobia emerged after the American Revolution. In his 1787 *Notes on the State of Virginia*, Thomas Jefferson stated that it was impossible to assimilate blacks into white society because they were, in his view, innately inferior to Europeans and their descendants. In his occasional public statements on race, Jefferson articulated the attitudes expressed by the majority of whites during that era (Horsman, 1981). President John Adams (1797–1801), for example, believed strongly that the republicanism of a new nation must be ruled by "natural law" that justified the control of "backward peoples," such as African Americans and Native Americans, by the "civilized" white population. Slavery, according to Adams, was morally "unjust," yet crucial for the United States to successfully deal with "uncivilized" nonwhites (Saxton 1990, p.42).

During the 19th century, upper and middle-class whites rationalized the politics of Negrophobia by underscoring their superior, evolutionary "racial" traits within the context of scientific racism. Lacking the intellectual context to distinguish between physical morphology and cultural traits, educated whites in Victorian America felt scientifically justified in asserting that racially primitive men, despite their best efforts, could never evolve to the high level of civilization of white people (Berderman, 1995). The Swiss-born naturalist Louis Agassiz (1807–1873) became the leading spokesperson for the U.S. theory of polygeny during the antebellum period. *Polygeny* specified that human races represented separate biological species, emphasizing that African Americans represented an inferior breed. Agassiz regarded African Americans as a shiftless, passive, and childlike race that remained incapable of social equality with whites. Although opposed to slavery, Agassiz strongly believed that the separation of races after the emancipation of slaves remained necessary to prevent the white race from being "diluted" through interracial sexual relations. Although Agassiz's polygenist position lost support among some U.S. scientists during the 1860s and 1870s, Agassiz's support for de jure racial segregation prevailed within the U.S. public. Agassiz offered no data to support his findings, but Samuel George Morton, a wealthy Philadelphia doctor, collected nearly 1,000 skulls to prove his polygenic ideas that ranked the races according to the measurement of the average sizes of their brains. His research reinforced popular racist sentiments regarding African Americans by purporting to show that whites were superior, and blacks and Indians were regarded as dispensable (Gould, 1981).

Before 1865, Northern and Western state constitutions explicitly placed free and enslaved African American men and women, in the category of "dependents." They were forbidden to exercise "manhood rights," such as voting, electoral office holding, and jury service, which supposedly pertained only to white men. Furthermore, working-class white men demanded that they had a legitimate claim to those political rights that blacks and white women lacked. The consequences of this political disenfranchisement of African Americans underscored the notion that black people, in comparison, with white men, were subhuman (Berderman, 1995).

In the North and the Midwest, whites' reaction to the 19th-century Southern lynching news reports reflected their extreme distrust of the African American population. Regarding most lynchings as justified punishment for alleged rapes, journalists from Northern and Midwestern newspapers frequently represented black lynching victims as "savage" and "cowardly" and they portrayed white lynch mobs as models of discipline and self-restraint. Many of these editorials, however, criticized such lynch mobs as "unmanly" because their actions resembled the unruly nature of primitives such as blacks and Native Americans. Still, these anti-lynching statements described these white participants as defenders of civilization, and their barbarous African American victims as deserving their fate (Berderman, 1995). Such justifications of lynching by Northern and Midwestern whites continued into the 20th century. In his book *Pure Sociology: A Treatise on the Origin and Spontaneous Development of Society*, sociologist Lester Frank Ward (1903) stated that the biological law of self-preservation compelled angry whites to lynch what he labeled the "negro rapist" (Newby, 1973, p. 48).

Notwithstanding the harsh nature of Negrophobia before 1945, its contemporary phase exploited racial fears and hostilities experienced by many middle- and working-class whites in the aftermath of the socioeconomic and political reforms of the civil rights movement (Lipsitz, 1995). Although these measures achieved only partial success over the years, the white neoconservative response to such moderate changes remained antagonistic. These individuals reinterpreted the social justice articulated by the movement as an imminent danger to "white identity," the "color-blindness" of the U.S. legal system, and individual socioeconomic mobility (Winant, 1997). For instance, the Republican Party utilized race-tinged issues and code words such as busing, states' rights, "welfare queen," and affirmative action quotas to capitalize on conservative middle- and lower class whites' political, social and economic insecurities during the Reagan–Bush era (Piliawsky, 1994). In 1990, when President George Bush vetoed an antidiscrimination bill, he labeled it "quota" legislation.

In the South, the manipulation of white fears of African Americans remained a key factor in building a strong Republican constituency. Ultraconservative Jesse Helms capitalized on the anxieties of whites, who blamed African Americans for their economic precariousness, through his televised campaign ads. During the 1990 North Carolina Senate race, one of Helms's campaign commercials featured a white worker subjected to employment rejection because of a racial quota. This campaign ad was especially vitriolic because Helms's opposition during this election was the liberal African American politician Harvey Gantt, the mayor of Charlotte and the first black student admitted to Clemson University (Guillory, 1992).

In addition to their defense of psychometric IQ assessment, Herrnstein and Murray (1994) justified the neoconservative argument of black cultural depravity that blamed the negative social facets of African American life on its own cultural traditions. The historical antecedents of this polemic originated in the negative interpretation of African American life offered by 19th-century scientific racism. In an 1854 speech entitled "The Claims of the Negro Ethnologically Considered," African American abolitionist Frederick Douglass charged that scientists always exaggerated the cultural contributions of whites at the expense of blacks. He emphasized that they invariably depicted European-American society as the epitome of knowledge, artistic beauty, and philosophy whereas African American culture exemplified imbecility and degradation (Brotz, 1966).

Methodist-minister-turned-novelist Thomas Dixon characterized African American traditions as banal and licentious in his popular stories such as *The Leopard's Spots, A Romance of the White Man's Burden* (1902) and *The Clansman* (1905). *The Clansman* later served as the basis for director D. W. Griffith's commercially successful epic film *Birth of a Nation* (1915), the first movie that attracted a nationwide boycott led by the National Association for the Advancement of Colored People (NAACP). The white American public, supportive of existing conditions of legal and customary segregation, generally accepted the racial extremism expressed in Dixon's crude portrayal of African Americans as vicious and depraved animals (Newby, 1973). Moreover, conservative white intellectuals such as economist Emory Q. Hawk (1934) echoed Dixon's sentiments in *The Economic History of the South*, which asserted that blacks, unlike "Anglo Saxons," never underwent a long evolutionary process of cultural creativity and inquiry (Newby, 1973, p. 24).

Theologian Cornel West (1993) maintained that conservative white behaviorists like Herrnstein and Murray continue this historical distortion of African American cultural contributions in their study. They represent African American culture as the product of victimization without a comprehensive analysis of black history or the significance of white supremacy in the United States. Although *The Bell Curve*'s theme regarding African American mental deficiency depends on an analysis of IQ scores, in reality the book's interpretive power relies on the presumption that African Americans traditionally remain, on average, intellectually inferior to whites (Jorgensen, 1995).

Herrnstein and Murray (1994) asserted that, because IQ is genetically determined, it remains impervious to educational and environmental interventions. They argued that U.S. society is becoming more stratified into a "cognitive caste system" with the cognitively disadvantaged trapped at the bottom of society. In their view, this lower caste includes a large portion of the African American population characterized by growing numbers of impoverished single female-headed households filled with children of "lower cognitive ability" (Herrnstein & Murray, 1994, p. 522).

Financial investment and legal reforms aimed at improving this inequality will be wasted, because IQ is biologically determined. Moreover, according to Herrnstein and Murray (1994), the "genetic capital" determining IQ is eroding, mostly due to the greater reproduction of low-IQ individuals and, to a smaller extent, due to immigration primarily from Mexico, Central America, India, China, Vietnam, Africa, and the Caribbean (Devlin, 1995). Herrnstein and Murray (1994) commented that the U.S. government maintains demographic policies that favor the "wrong women" whose offspring contribute to the "dumbing of America." The government "subsidizes" births among poor women who represent the "low end" of the intelligence distribution. To reduce the number of children by these women, they recommended an extensive network of cash incentives and services to encourage "voluntary" sterilization for them (Herrnstein & Murray, 1994). The authors proposed that to raise the IQ in the United States as a method of combatting social ills and creating economic prosperity, "smarter" women should be encouraged to have children. To dissuade low-IQ women from having children, the authors proposed making safe and effective birth control more available to poor women, a disproportionate number of whom are African American (Herrnstein & Murray, 1994).

The arguments presented in *The Bell Curve* were not, for the most part, original. The origin of the authors' ideas was in the work of Sir Francis Galton (1822–1911), the British naturalist and mathematician who introduced the term *eugenics* to the vocabulary of science. Galton became a central figure in the establishment of the eugenics movement. According to him, eugenics was "the study of agencies under social control that may improve or impair the racial qualities of future generations, either physically or mentally" (Allen, 1995, p. 441). Although he never fathered a child, Galton maintained a lifelong obsession with the concept of superior heredity through selective mating to improve a racial stock, as evidenced in his two famous works, *Human Faculty* (Galton, 1883) and *Natural Inheritance* (Galton, 1889). As a first cousin of Darwin, Galton represented the same aristocratic British pedigree that produced a disproportionate number of scientists and intellectuals in the 19th century (Smedley, 1993, p. 266).

Galton's interests in human races led him to join the Ethnological Society of London in 1862, where he encountered the monogenist, antislavery views of Darwin, biologist Thomas Henry Huxley, and naturalist John Lubbock. After reading *On the*

Origin of Species (Darwin, 1859), Galton envisioned the opportunity to "improve" what he regarded as the "miserably low standard of the human race" (Tucker, 1994, p. 41) by guiding the evolutionary process. Moreover, through his active participation in the Royal Geographic Society, Galton also became acquainted with the racialist and semipolygenist opinions of the explorer Sir Richard Burton. Influenced by Darwin's theory of evolution and Burton's racialist ideas, Galton believed that human evolution would be accelerated through eugenics (Stepan, 1982): "What Nature does blindly, slowly and ruthlessly, man may do providently, quickly and kindly" wrote Galton (Devilin, 1995, p. 1483).

Through the use of statistics, Galton attempted to comprehend the laws of inheritance by using limited data to establish the distribution of talent in the British population in 1860. Galton (1869) published *Hereditary Genius*, a landmark volume designed to convince all but the most irascible skeptics of the superior hereditary endowment of certain eminent British families. Galton proved his argument by using complex statistical methods that emphasized the use of a bell-shaped curve to demonstrate the "normal distribution" for what he regarded as "intelligence" (Smedley 1993, p. 266). To further his scientific investigation, Galton created an anthropometric laboratory and collected detailed measurements on families. By collecting meteorological, botanical and human physical data, Galton looked for statistical relations. In 1888, Galton formulated what is known as the *correlation coefficient* to obtain such relations. Although he did not offer any mathematical proofs or solve the problem of the heritability of talent, he did recognize the importance of statistics to the study of intelligence (Devlin 1995).

Although Galton did not define the notion of race precisely, he classified certain races in terms of geography, such as Africans or as a local subdivision, as in the case of lowland Scots, whom he regarded as intellectually superior to the average Englishmen. Although he acknowledged the outstanding mental abilities of a few people of African descent, such as Haitian leader Toussaint L'Overture, Galton believed it was self-evident that white men were inherently superior to blacks (Stepan, 1982).

In his research, Galton successfully incorporated evolutionary, racialist, and eugenic concepts into a coherent synthesis. With his own funds, he created the First Research Fellow in Eugenics in 1905 and in 1907 established the Eugenic Laboratory at University College in London, which his friend mathematician Karl Pearson (1857–1936) directed. On his death in 1911, Galton bequeathed money in his will to endow a Chair of Eugenics, with Pearson as its first incumbent. The founding of the Eugenics Education Society in 1908 in London, meanwhile, institutionalized the study of eugenics as a social and political movement. Its journal, *The Eugenics Review,* became an outlet for the political agenda of the eugenics movement (Stepan, 1983).

Herrnstein and Murray's (1994) ideas embodied the influence of Pearson, the intellectual disciple of Galton. Both Pearson and Galton based their views of heredity on *biometry*, the statistical analysis of biological traits measured for large samples; however their analysis encountered difficulty when applied to individual families or descent lines. The rediscovery of Mendel's laws of heredity in 1900 gave new insights to eugenics. By 1910, with the exception of a few, most biologists agreed that Mendel's theory was applicable to all sexually reproducing forms (Allen, 1995). As the founder of modern statistical methods, including the theory of multiple correlation and regression, Pearson shared Galton's concern with the low procreation rates of the elite and high reproduction among the "unfit." He characterized the unfit as, "the habitual criminal, the professional tramp, the tuberculous, the insane, the mentally defective, the alcoholic, the diseased from birth or excess" (Pearson, 1905, 10–11). In an early discussion of the nature versus nurture controversy, Pearson argued that "We have placed our money on Environment, when Heredity wins in a canter." The human reproduction of intelligent people, contended Pearson, can never be trained or educated. "You must breed it," he wrote (Devlin, 1995).

In 1901, to concentrate more fully on the relation of heredity and evolution in animals and plants and to promote the development of statistical theory applicable to biological problems, Pearson, biologist Walter Weldon and Galton founded the journal *Biometrika*. In the editorial of the first issue, *Biometrika* stressed that the "problem of evolution is a problem in vital statistics of the population" and that the evolutionist must become "a registrar-general for all forms of life" (Stepan, 1982, p. 120). With half its subscribers American, this journal devoted more attention to the subject of eugenics than to statistical methods (Devlin, 1995).

Following in the tradition of Galton and his fellow British eugenicists, Pearson referred to a large assortment of social, religious, and other groups as races in his writings, without much regard for consistency. For example, Africans, Jews, English, Anglo Saxons, Nordics, Orientals, Russians, and Mediterraneans were classified as races in the *Eugenics Review* (Stepan, 1983). In 1925, Pearson established another journal, *Annals of Eugenics*, which in its first issue featured his exhaustive eugenic study, "The Problem of Alien Immigration Into Britain." In this article, Pearson cited IQ test scores and the anthropometric measurements of heads of Jewish children living in London as scientific proof that Jewish emigration posed a grave threat to British civilization (Chase, 1977). Pearson used his publications to lobby the British Parliament to enact anti-immigration laws similar to the 1927 U.S. Immigration Act, which was supported by American eugenicist Henry Herbert Goddard. Goddard claimed that Binet test results obtained from immigrants on Ellis Island in 1912 "proved" Galton's theory that Jews, Catholics, and Southern and Central Europeans were "inferior races" (Chase, 1977, p. 233).

The intellectual foundations of *The Bell Curve* reflect the classical tradition of eugenics, formulated by Galton and Pearson, that stressed the existence and measurability of general intelligence as a core expression of human mental ability (Richardson, 1995). Herrnstein and Murray (1994) reinforced Galton and Pearson's assertions that ethnic and racial IQ differences were real, measurable, and dangerous to the "stability" of the West (Zenderland, 1997). *The Bell Curve* represented a reiteration of 19th century scientific racism, presented as scientific truth, which explained differences in behavior, real and imagined, in terms of heredity (Alland et al., 1996).

The Bell Curve, moreover, incorporated the research of Goddard and psychologist Charles Spearman into its analysis of the innate nature of cognitive ability and the measurability of the *g* factor (general intelligence). As the enterprising director of research at the Vineland Training School for Feeble-Minded Boys and Girls in New Jersey, Goddard believed that the tests of French psychologist Alfred Binet represented measures of a single, innate entity, despite the fact that Binet himself refused to define his test results as indicators of "intelligence." Goddard strongly believed that Binet's tests identified people below the normal range, those he regarded as "high grade defectives" or "morons" (a term Goddard borrowed from a Greek word meaning foolish). As a firm supporter of a unilinear development of evolution, Goddard established a classification of mental deficiency, ranging from imbeciles to morons, which stressed that intelligence remained innate and inherited through family lines (Gould, 1981).

His notorious 1912 study of the Kallikak family (a pseudonym for a poor clan from the New Jersey pine barrens), Goddard's genealogical investigation of the two branches of the descendants of Martin Kallikak, remained a significant contribution to the myth of the "menace of the feeble-minded." One branch purportedly descended from an illicit relationship between Martin Kallikak and a mentally retarded tavern woman, supposedly produced generations of paupers, criminals, prostitutes, and alcoholics (Ryan, 1997). Goddard employed visual means, not standardized intelligence tests, to identify them as feebleminded individuals who represented prime examples of the social dangers that emanated from bad heredity (Zenderland, 1997). In altered photographs of the "degenerate" Kallikak family produced in Goddard's book, heavy dark lines were inserted on the subjects' eyebrows and mouths to make them appear menacing and lethargic. Only the photograph of Deborah, the sole "bad" Kallikak saved from "depravity" by confinement in Goddard's institution, depicted an attractive and calm young woman dressed in white, with a cat lying comfortably on her lap (Gould, 1981). The other lineage conceived law-abiding, respectable citizens from Martin's marriage to a Quaker. The real Kallikak family never resembled a strict dichotomy between good and degenerate members. In fact, they possessed a more varied social and economic makeup than Goddard described in his research (Smith, 1993). The basic social message of Goddard's examination of the Kallikak family emphasized that a considerable proportion of Americans, especially people of color and recent European immigrants, lacked the innate intelligence to control their predisposition toward crime and poverty.

Goddard, however, was not content merely to publish his "scientific" findings. As an activist, he proclaimed that the "hereditary" feebleminded constituted the root cause of socioeconomic problems in U.S. society. He offered a plan of attack that encompassed two proposals. First, the U.S. government should administer intelligence tests to all children so it could identify what he regarded as morons. Then, these mental defectives should be "colonized" in state institutions where they would be prohibited from procreating. Goddard felt strongly that, because it had become impossible to rehabilitate adult morons, the state must place children under its parental control (Ryan 1997). Like Herrnstein and Murray (1994), Goddard adopted a patronizing, elitist attitude toward working-class life and accentuated the deep socioeconomic divide between "us" (respectable, upper and middle-class citizens) and "them" (a large body of lower class troublemakers). Furthermore, he calmly assured his audiences, as Herrnstein and Murray did in *The Bell Curve*, that most scientists and politicians agreed on the major points regarding heredity and intelligence (Zenderland, 1997).

The studies of eminent British psychologist and statistician Spearman, who created the notion of the g (general intelligence) factor in 1904, establishes the only promising theoretical justification those hereditarian theories of IQ ever had (Gould, 1981). Spearman's g remains a scientific construct, not a real component that resides in the brain. It explains an observable phenomenon known as the "positive manifold," the empirical fact that the correlations between tests of cognitive ability are almost always positive (Kranzler, 1995). Spearman believed that he had discovered the essence of intelligence, the elusive entity that makes psychology a "true science." Although Spearman held conventional views regarding the source of differences in intelligence between the races and national groups, he never stressed the inevitability of these discrepancies. In fact, he ascribed sexual differences to training and social traditions and provided few comments about social classes.

Moreover, when discussing racial differences, Spearman associated his hereditarian claim about average scores with a contention that the range of variation within any racial group greatly exceeds the small average difference between groups. This indicates that many members of a so-called "inferior" race will surpass the average intelligence of a "superior" group. Although his concept of the g factor supplied the hereditarian school with its basic argument, Spearman applied his work to studying the structure of the human brain, not as a guide to measuring differences between groups and individuals (Gould, 1981). Herrnstein and Murray (1994), however, went farther than most hereditarians in discussing implications in individual and racial differences in the g factor as the basis for educational and social policies. They regarded the g factor as the sine qua non of success in American life (Kranzler, 1995).

In addition to their orthodox hereditarian interpretation of Spearman's g factor, Herrnstein and Murray (1994) incorporated the controversial ideas of psychologist Arthur Jensen into their arguments about the measurability of intelligence. Jensen's (1969) article in the *Harvard Educational Review*, entitled "How Much Can We Boost IQ and Scholastic Achievement," revived the eugenics movement, which had become identified by many academics in the West with racism, given the revelations of the Holocaust. In their textbook, *Human Heredity*, Neel and Schull (1954) warned against the extremes of the eugenics movement of the past. Endorsing "reform eugenics," which emphasized contraceptives for global population control, they insisted that eugenics should continue promoting the science of human genetics. Although Jensen renewed an old debate concerning IQ and race, his eugenic rationale for what he considered the innate inferiority of African Americans appeared during a period of social activism regarding race and racial equality in the United States

(Duster, 1990). He claimed that the social, economic, and political agendas of the civil rights movement, which addressed the racial inequality in education, housing, employment, and health care, forced scientists to examine all possibilities for such inequities (Tucker, 1994).

Trained under Cyril Burt, the British hereditarian psychologist whose twins studies were recently discredited due to revelations of fraud (Zenderland, 1997), Jensen stated in his 125-page article that the average differences in IQ scores between blacks and whites indicated a highly probable average difference in native intelligence (Kelves, 1985). In his investigation, Jensen claimed that African Americans demonstrated the lowest intelligence scores, 15 IQ points or 1 *SD* below the scores of whites. Because Jensen believed that IQ was genetic, the racial stratification in U.S. society resulted from African Americans' inferior genetic cognitive potential rather than from historic patterns of socioeconomic and political discrimination against them. He concluded that early intervention social welfare programs, such as Head Start, were useless because they could not have any permanent effect on the genetically limited intelligence of African Americans and other racial minorities (Graves & Johnson, 1995).

In the volatile era of the 1960s, when few would argue in the public arena or publish in scholarly journals about the "genetics" of intelligence, crime, or occupational performance, Jensen's ideas provoked intense notoriety in the popular media and academe (Duster, 1990). The timing of Jensen's article, moreover, did not go unnoticed by some conservative and moderate lawmakers on Capitol Hill, who saw in his work a justification for curtailment of compensatory programs in education, employment, and housing. Although Jensen's name was not mentioned, President Richard Nixon's first major statements on education, delivered after his veto of an education appropriation bill, were highly critical of compensatory efforts. Nixon, moreover, emphasized the need for additional research on why some students learned more easily than others before investing more federal aid in projects that he regarded as failures (Tucker, 1994).

Jensen's article unleashed fierce debates on the hereditarian view of intelligence, including a minority of its supporters who were concerned with race. As a psychology professor at Harvard, Herrnstein supported Jensen publicly. In an article in *The Atlantic Monthly* entitled "IQ," Herrnstein (1971) suggested that there were considerable data that suggested that there existed an occupational hierarchy in U.S. society that was strongly correlated to grades of intelligence (Chase, 1977). According to Herrnstein, there existed in the United States a deeply held belief in equality of opportunity, where status was decided by merit. He asserted that differences in social status among Americans in this meritocracy were attributable to the innate characteristics of individuals and, by inference, to the racial or ethnic groups to which they belonged (Kincheloe & Steinberg, 1996).

Herrnstein then contended that the most important catalyst of success in U.S. society was general intelligence or IQ. In his worldview, the smartest people naturally ascend to the top and the dull-witted ones drop to the bottom of society (Graves & Johnson, 1995). Likewise, Herrnstein even speculated that unemployment might have a genetic foundation (Duster, 1990). He argued that, assuming intelligence to be strongly heritable, the United States was slowly turning into a hereditary meritocracy, a prospect that he initially found troublesome (Kelves, 1985). Later, in *The Bell Curve*, Herrnstein and Murray (1994) refined the former's concept of a meritocracy into the conception of a cognitive elite who would become indispensable for the future of American "civilization" (Kaplan & Kaplan, 1997).

Jensen coupled black–white genetic differences with the high inner-city birthrate to raise the most sensitive of traditional eugenic issues—the possibility of dysgenic trends in urban slums. In a U.S. News and World Reports article, engineer William Shockley (1965) argued that the failure to explore the subject of race and intelligence kept U.S. society ignorant of the knowledge to combat such trends, an argument later explored by Jensen (Chase, 1977). In October 1969, Shockley urged the National Academy of Sciences (NAS) to encourage research into the possibility that the quality of the U.S. population was deteriorating genetically. The NAS considered Shockley's proposal, but eventually refused to endorse it in its entirety. Instead, the NAS recommended greater interdisciplinary cooperation between behavioral genetics and such fields as psychology and education (Kelves, 1985).

Despite the initial scholarly rejections of his ideas, Shockley continued to expound on his eugenic notions in the popular press. He eventually became a familiar fixture on television talk shows and the college lecture circuit, where he repeatedly stated he did not promote racism but "raceology," a term derived from 19th-century scientific race studies. He continually cited Armed Forces Qualifying Test (AFQT) scores as statistical evidence of the "inferiority" of African Americans and promoted his sterilization bonus plan. Under the Shockley Plan, he proposed to offer bonuses for sterilization, although taxpayers would receive none. Others, regardless of gender, race, or welfare status, would earn these bonuses contingent on the best scientific estimates of so-called hereditary factors in liabilities such as diabetes, epilepsy, and substance and alcohol abuse. Moreover, Shockley envisioned his sterilization plan as an economic incentive for the unemployed and the working poor, whose low wages failed to support their families. After he went public with his agenda, however, Shockley learned he had been anticipated by similar proposals offered by political commentator H. L. Mencken in 1937 and birth control advocate Margaret Sanger in 1926 (Chase, 1977). Sanger, a committed eugenicist, commented in a 1919 article in the journal *Birth Control Review* that "More children from the fit, less from the unfit—that is the chief issue of birth control" (cited in Larson, 1995, p. 105).

Shockley's controversial ideas regarding the forced sterilization of people of color also found historical precedent in the eugenic sterilization movement in the midwestern and southern United States. During the 1890s, campaigns for the castration of both the mentally retarded and criminals gained public support. The Michigan legislature in 1897 discussed the merits of a bill that required the castration of the feebleminded and certain criminals; however, the bill was ultimately defeated. At the Kansas State Institution for Feeble Minded Children during this era, for example, Dr. F. Hoyt Pilcher castrated 44 boys and girls before strong public criticism forced him to discontinue the practice. In 1907 Indiana became the first state to promulgate an involuntary sterilization law based on eugenic principles. It allowed the sterilization of inmates at state institutions who were insane, mentally retarded, convicted rapists, or repeat offenders (Garver & Garver, 1991).

In the South, there existed strong support among scientists, health professionals, and social reformers for compulsory sterilization of the feebleminded, criminals, alcoholics, epileptics, and African Americans. Southern eugenicists like William Partlow supported voluntary birth control that overlapped with compulsory sterilization. Southern forced sterilization programs targeted poor whites, the mentally ill, alcoholics, drug addicts, criminals, and African Americans. As superintendent of Alabama Home for the mentally retarded, Partlow was empowered by the institution's 1919 legislative provision to sterilize any inmate; the only limitation imposed was the concurrence of the nearby superintendent of the Alabama Insane Hospitals. As a strong advocate of eugenic sterilization, Partlow authorized hundreds of sterilizations of the mentally retarded and delinquent boys. He also instituted a liberal discharge policy that would allow a patient to leave on the condition of sterilization. Not until his death in 1951 did the Alabama state government cease its eugenic sterilization mission (Larson, 1995).

Throughout the 1920s and 1930s, Southern states such as Louisiana, Georgia, Mississippi, Virginia and South Carolina enforced compulsory sterilization programs within their mental hospital systems. During the 1940s and the 1950s, South Carolina intensified its forced sterilization of African Americans at its state mental hospitals, reaching a high of 43 procedures in 1956 before dropping into the single digits during the 1960s (Larson, 1995). Southern eugenicists' obsessive preoccupation with the deterioration of their genteel communities by the reproduction of mental degenerates, poor whites, and African Americans influenced their decision to support state-sponsored eugenic programs (Smith, 1995).

Notwithstanding the draconian raceology solutions proposed by Shockley, the ideas and solutions put forth by Herrnstein and Murray (1994) in *The Bell Curve* represents the insidious rise of what sociologist Henry Giroux and literary critic Susan Searls called the new racism. According to Giroux and Searls (1996), it presents a two-sided argument that first refuses to acknowledge that race remains at the center of its policymaking, as exemplified in welfare "counterreform," tough crime bills, and anti-immigration legislation. Second, it devises justifications for policy changes that purport to be color blind, for example, the elimination of affirmative action and racial gerrymandering in congressional districts. However, this new racism exemplifies and legitimizes a range of ideologies and practices that reinforce the socioeconomic and political privileges that buttress the construction of whiteness and increase racial inequality (Giroux & Searls, 1996).

Herrnstein and Murray's (1994) assumptions about intelligence epitomized the historical continuum of Western eugenic fundamentalism (Semali, 1996). Psychologist Herrnstein persuaded conservative environmentalist Murray, whose antiwelfare monograph *Losing Ground* (Murray, 1984) became the intellectual cornerstone for the Reagan administration, to apply his ideas in the genetic realm and join him in a remake of his earlier works such as *I.Q. in the Meritocracy* (Herrnstein, 1973; see Scott, 1994). The most controversial part of their book is chapter 13, which deals with IQ differences across races, reflecting this continuing eugenic debate. Herrnstein and Murray (1994) stressed that their notion of cognitive ability resided on a single dimension and could be expressed as the single number of the IQ (Meyers, 1996). They presented six conclusions regarding tests of cognitive ability that include these premises:

1. Intelligence test scores correspond to whatever people ascribe to the word *intelligent*.
2. IQ test scores remain constant, albeit not always perfectly, throughout a person's lifetime.
3. Intelligence tests, when conducted appropriately, are not necessarily biased against ethnic, racial, or socioeconomic groups.
4. Cognitive ability is markedly heritable, presumably no less than 40% and no more than 80% (Herrnstein & Murray, 1994).

Educational expert Howard Gardner (1995) commented that Herrnstein and Murray's (1994) emphasis on the supposed links between genetic inheritance and IQ, as well as between IQ and social class, remained much too weak to support the conclusion that genes determine an individual's ultimate status in society. According to Gardner, nearly all the reported correlations between measured intelligence and societal outcomes explained at most 20% of the variance. Moreover, at least 80% of the factors that contributed to socioeconomic status existed beyond measured intelligence.

Social scientist Barton Meyers (1996) observed that, even if intelligence yielded to a consensual definition, the task of specifying actual genes for such an esoteric trait as intelligence within an organism as complex as humans would remain daunting and well beyond the reach of microbiology (Gardner, 1995). Herrnstein and Murray (1994), however, discounted the importance of environmental influences in the definition of intelligence and IQ differences among ethnic groups (Meyers, 1996). Although they admitted that not all ethnic diversities were heritable, they chided social scientists who believed environmental factors account for the majority of ethnic variations as not being "tough-minded enough" (Herrnstein & Murray, 1994, p. 299) to realize the fallacies within their arguments.

Jim Holt (1995), a science reporter for *The New York Times*, pointed out that Herrnstein and Murray (1994) contended that the IQ scores of black children correlated with the scores of their parents, thus inferring that intelligence must be partly governed by genes. He stated that the authors concluded that the IQ difference between blacks and whites had a genetic component that could not be eliminated by society. Herrnstein and Murray's assertion that racial differences between white and African American educational achievement remained genetically determined provided public support for racial discrimination in social and educational policies

(Muntaner, Neto, & O'Campo, 1996). Biologist Stephen Jay Gould (1995) noted that the well-documented 15-point average differences in IQ scores between African Americans and whites, with substantial heritablity of IQ in family lines within each group, permitted no automatic conclusion that truly equal opportunity might not raise the African American average to equal or surpass the white mean. Sociologist Nicholas Rescher (1995) argued that this bell curve discrepancy between white and African American IQ scores should not imply an educational public policy that requires black children to attend racially segregated and poorly funded public schools. Psychologist Robert Sternberg (1996) contended that if Herrnstein and Murray's views of African American intellectual abilities became part of educational public policy, then the failure of school administrators and teachers to recognize the diversity and talents of their students lacking high IQs would result in a waste of the country's most precious resource—its human talent.

In his review of *The Bell Curve*, historian Daryl Scott (1994) noted that, in recent years, the average African American IQ rose by 3 points, suggesting that more Blacks "had crossed the threshold of intelligence necessary to lead productive lives in a complex society" (p. 56–57). Nevertheless, during the same period, the impoverishment of blacks continued to worsen (Scott, 1994). For instance, Herrnstein and Murray (1994) observed some indication that the gap between white and African American IQ scores was narrowing, but they found little reason to expect this trend to continue. They admitted that the historical legacy of racism had influenced, to a certain degree, black cognitive development. Herrnstein and Murray considered, however, the possibility that it might have "lessened" for the new generations, accounting for some of the reduction of the IQ gap between African Americans and whites.

On the other hand, Herrnstein and Murray (1994) reluctantly admitted that, after controlling for IQ, the African American poverty rate remains almost twice as high as that for whites. They were unable, nevertheless, to explain why gaps between the educational attainment of African Americans and whites had diminished during the same period. However, they avoided any implication that this difference was exclusively genetic, although many reviewers accused them of doing so. However, the strong case that they provided for genetic explanations for the definition and measurability of IQ overshadowed the ambiguity of this statement. Herrnstein and Murray believed that transformation of cognitive ability through environmental interventions remained extraordinarily difficult. They agreed with Jensen that government programs such as Head Start failed to maintain the improvement of the IQs of their participants after they entered elementary and high school. However, Herrnstein and Murray never considered the possibility that the educational achievement for some of these students was affected by the poor quality of the educational environments they attended after Head Start. Furthermore, educational psychologist Linda Darling-Hammond (1995) pointed out that Herrnstein and Murray refused to examine the research of the Follow Through program, which found that those Head Start children who continued in high-quality educational institutions maintained the educational gains they had secured. She also criticized them for using a data set that was more than 15 years old, and whose informants had been young adults in 1979. The authors refused to incorporate the educational experience of African Americans who entered school after 1970, when most of the lawsuits to enforce equality in education were initiated.

Moreover, Herrnstein and Murray (1994) strongly rebutted the critics of IQ and aptitude tests who claim these examinations are racially biased and unrelated to actual productivity in schools or in the workplace. They discussed the well-documented disparities among the distributions of IQs for blacks and whites, as well as other ethnic groups, such as Latinos and Asians. Journalist Roger Hernández (1995) noted that the authors, who did not consider Latinos a race, described Latin Americans as highly culturally diverse peoples stemming from a multitude of racial stocks. Hernández contended that although, some Latinos might accept such an observation, many argue that language difficulties and "diverse" socioeconomic backgrounds make generalizations about IQ for Latinos imprecise at best. Furthermore, Hernández stated that Herrnstein and Murray's conclusion regarding the intelligence of Hispanics remains based on a premise that has become so problematic as to be unsustainable.

Similar to Goddard's dire warnings that feebleminded people represent vessels of criminality that must be removed from society, Herrnstein and Murray (1994) applied their social science of intelligence to prove that there exists a causal relation between low IQ and criminal behavior by demonstrating how AFQT scores are related more specifically to crime than social class, with age controlled in their analysis. Their methodological approach, however, considers such factors as family structure and educational background in a rather haphazard manner. Moreover, critics emphasize that Herrnstein and Murray's reliance on data from the National Longitudinal Survey of Youth fails to yield conclusive results because this test is not designed to examine the major psychological or sociological theories of criminology. The authors, nonetheless, refused to categorize the known predictors of crime and then clarify how IQ might explain variations above and beyond certain criminological risk factors. Because they limited their analysis to primarily three factors (IQ, socioeconomic status, and age), Herrnstein and Murray exaggerated the significance of IQ in their study (Cullen, Gendreau, Jarjoura, & Wright, 1997).

Herrnstein and Murray's (1994) biological explanation for crime in U.S. society resonates with a public that regards crime and race as intertwined. For them, the motives of criminality emanate from the individual differences in inherited intelligence. They insisted that criminals are psychologically and biologically unique, in addition to possessing low intelligence test scores. While Herrnstein and Murray admitted that white men commit serious crimes, they claimed these men carry out only a fraction of the serious felonies in this country. In the aftermath of the insider trading and savings and loan scandals of the 1980s, however, they failed to investigate the relation of intelligence, class and crime in reference to the high participation of educated, middle-class white men in white-collar crime (Scott, 1994).

Although Herrnstein and Murray (1994) did not mention African Americans in the chapter on crime, they implied that white male violent offenders are the exception, not the rule, within the total criminal offender population. They did however, point out that because blacks possess lower intelligence than whites, they are 3.8 times more likely to be arrested to their relative numbers in the general population. They used Herrnstein's (1985) study on crime, co-authored with neoconservative political scientist James Q. Wilson, to argue that social, cultural, and economic indicators of crime are ambiguous and not dependable variables for determining criminal behavior. By identifying African American men as genetically predisposed criminals, Herrnstein and Murray (1994) could legitimize the repression of black youth. In the "virtuous society" constructed by Herrnstein and Murray, only ignorant people who violate the law become imprisoned (Cullen et al., 1997).

Herrnstein and Murray's (1994) empirical work argues for the role of IQ in accounting for a considerable proportion of ethnic differences in socioeconomic outcomes, and demonstrates a high concentration of low IQ people, within all races, in a variety of pathological categories. They argued that employment tests banned by the courts as discriminatory at least partly predict productivity and are, if anything, biased in favor of minorities. For Herrnstein and Murray, race-normed adjustments of test scores misclassify workers, create tokenism in the workplace, and often stigmatize the intended recipients of government beneficence. They endorsed a nonracial policy of treating persons as individuals rather than as members of racial groups (Heckman, 1995).

Herrnstein and Murray (1994) condemned the federal government's use of affirmative action in hiring and the famous 1971 Supreme Court case, *Griggs v. Duke Power*, that eliminated the use of educational test requirements for applicants when the employer could not show that such requirements are clearly job related. They believed that IQ defined the essence of job requirements; and the Court's actions and its attendant legal regulations simply led to gross inefficiencies without changing the realities of what the U.S. workplace needs (Devlin, 1995). Herrnstein and Murray declared that if a disproportionate number of whites dominate a particular occupation, then government intervention that fosters racial and ethnic balance that would be counterproductive. Federal, state, and local governments, according to Herrnstein and Murray, subverted the original goal of affirmative action, which was to ensure that people who possess equal qualifications for a job should have an equal chance to be hired.

Herrnstein and Murray (1994) then proceeded to call for the elimination of affirmative action. Their declaration against it constitutes part of a larger, concerted effort by conservatives, moderates, and some liberals to abolish affirmative action. Under fierce attack from the courts, politicians, the media, academics, and local, state, and federal officials, affirmative action received rough treatment in *The Bell Curve* (Devlin, 1995). Anthropologist K. Anthony Appiah (1995) noted that Herrnstein and Murray's comments on affirmative action exploited the economic insecurity that many middle-class whites feel about their own futures. He observed that the authors regarded any form of government aid as an obstacle to a white person obtaining a particular job. Appiah also contended that given the prevailing conservative political climate, neoconservatives like Herrnstein and Murray grant the "naturalness of social differences or social inequality" (p. 307) by stressing heredity. He then stated that Herrnstein and Murray were mistaken about the immutability of heritablity and the effects of an individual's environment.

Herrnstein and Murray (1994) supported the establishment of a stable meritocracy in which the self-appointed cognitive elite dominate over the so-called cognitively disadvantaged. Despite Murray's well-known disdain for government intervention, he and Herrnstein advocated more government funds for gifted children, thereby swelling the ranks of the cognitive elite. Those at the bottom of society, however, remain at the mercy of their intellectual superiors, who ultimately decide their socioeconomic and political fate. Curiously, the authors failed to address middle-class economic concerns regarding the ways in which the material, political, and social privileges enjoyed by the cognitive elite endanger their own survival (Kaplan & Kaplan, 1997).

The peaceful, color-blind universalism envisaged by Herrnstein and Murray (1994) for U.S. society in *The Bell Curve* strengthens and intensifies the prevailing racial, ethnic, and class inequities. In many ways, the book represents a manifesto for antidemocratic movements in the United States that use pseudoscience and racial fears as justifications for white supremacy. According to Herrnstein and Murray, valuable social, economic, and political agency becomes reserved only for those who are white and privileged. Low wages, grueling jobs, poor educational facilities, and lack of access to political representation are allotted to the cognitively disadvantaged—African Americans, Latinos, and the less intelligent whites. Government intervention becomes irrelevant because low IQ is linked causally with social pathology (Giroux & Searls, 1996). The milieu conceived by the authors reflects the historical moment in late 20th-century U.S. society, exemplified by antigovernment sentiment, coupled with the resurgence of racial discrimination, violence, and bigotry.

Although Herrnstein and Murray (1994) claimed publicly that they were not "racist," many of their solutions mirrored the agendas of the new violent proponents of the politics of Negrophobia such as the Church of the Creator, National Association for the Advancement of White People (NAAWP), and the White Aryan Resistance. The Church of the Creator, founded by the late Ben Klassen in 1973, espoused violent antiblack and anti-Semitic views. A former Florida Republican state legislator, Klassen argued that the laws of nature placed white people at the apex of the biological heap. Before his suicide in 1993, Klassen predicted a "holy war" in which whites would fight African Americans, Jews and other nonwhites for control of the planet (Daniels, 1997). Neo-Nazi and former Ku Klux Klan member David Duke founded the NAAWP in 1980 as part of his electoral strategy to dissociate himself from the Klan to participate in mainstream U.S. politics. A former Louisiana legislator and congressional candidate, Duke envisioned NAAWP as a largely middle-class white rights lobby organization and a racial movement (Moore, 1992). Like his former colleague David Duke, former California Klan organizer and congressional candidate Tom Metzger established the White American Political Association in 1984 after he became disillusioned with the Klan's inability to broaden its southern-based membership (Daniels, 1997). Later, Metzger changed the organization's name to White Aryan Resistance, a movement he envisaged as a part of a global struggle of whites against blacks, thus creating a fortress of the white race to combat the influx of Third World immigrants in Europe and North America (Langer, 1990).

Like Herrnstein and Murray (1994), the leadership within these white supremacist movements strongly believes that African Americans are biologically inferior to whites and pose a grave threat to the survival of U.S. civilization. As part of his demand for the "racial improvement" of the U.S. population, David Duke, for example, has advocated for years eugenics programs such as tax incentives for people with high IQs to bear more children. Echoing *The Bell Curve*'s caustic critique of welfare, Duke accuses welfare programs of encouraging low-IQ women to produce large families (Langer, 1990). Klassen's biological determinism reflects Herrnstein and Murray's contention that the black underclass remains destined by nature to occupy the lowest level of U.S. society. Metzger's pan-Aryan alliance against nonwhite immigration incorporates *The Bell Curve*'s assertions that Latino, Asian, and African immigration undermine the social and economic welfare of white Americans (Steinberg, 1995). Despite the organizational and ideological differences among various white supremacist and neo-Nazi groups, these movements share a broad ideological commitment that the historical construction of the white race remains an essential identity, rooted in biological and scientific fact. Moreover, by skillfully manipulating white Americans' racial fears, anti-Semitism, and bigotry, these groups reinforce the concept of the immutability of racism in U.S. society (Daniels, 1997).

Furthermore, these white racist movements insisted that blacks must be controlled through violent intimidation, imprisonment, and, in some cases, genocidal warfare (Daniels, 1997). One of the most violent groups, the small, tightly knit Silent Brotherhood (*Bruden Schweign*) was established in 1983 by the late Robert Matthews with the goal of promoting a campaign of guerrilla terror against African Americans, Jews, Latinos, and other nonwhites to overthrow the U.S. government. Matthews molded his faction on the sadistic *Turner Diaries*, a fictionalized memoir serialized by neo-Nazi and former physics professor William Pierce between 1975 and 1978. In the *Turner Diaries*, a small, fascist insurgency called The Organization, led by its eponymous hero Earl Turner, expelled nonwhite people in southern California during its war against the U.S. government. Hoping its violent activities would encourage a massive white reactionary uprising, The Silent Brotherhood (sometimes referred to as The Order) culminated its fanatical actions with the murder of Jewish Denver talk-show host Alan Berg in 1984 (Barkun, 1997). Although Herrnstein and Murray (1994) never openly sanctioned violent racial repression, their study justified the preservation of white privileges in such areas as education and employment. In many ways, *The Bell Curve* legitimized and encouraged the social, political, and physical repression of millions of people of color in the name of "biological determinism" (Hacker 1995).

The popularity of *The Bell Curve*, moreover, epitomizes the racial antagonism that the politics of Negrophobia disseminates throughout the white middle and working classes. In an era of growing economic and social polarization, it has become fashionable for white elites, neoconservative and moderate politicians, and intellectuals to stress individual merit as determined by IQ, impudence, hard work, and motivation. They attribute the absence of African Americans, Latinos, and Native Americans in many high-level corporate, government, educational, and cultural positions not to the extrinsic advantages of wealthy white Americans but to the hereditary defects of nonwhite people, with the exception of a few wealthy and well-educated Asian Americans. Underscoring the biological determinism arguments made by Herrnstein and Murray (1994), these whites argue that socioeconomic disadvantages suffered by blacks, Latinos, and Native Americans originate from their mental inferiority, which accounts for their inherent inability to succeed in U.S. society (Lind 1995). In his latest attack on government educational and social aid, Jensen (1998) pointed out that psychological and educational techniques to raise IQ among nonwhite children rarely increased scores by more than 5 or 10 points. Emphasizing that such IQ modifications remain temporary at best, Jensen argued that the evolution of mental development should not be left to the mercy of unpredictable environmental coincidence. He then concluded that the genetic and evolutionary nature of human intelligence protects human beings from the vagaries of the environment.

The Bell Curve embodies not only the neoconservative agenda, but encompasses liberal and moderate concerns involving affirmative action, crime control, and welfare reform (Scott, 1994). The political and social mobilization of African Americans, Latinos, Native Americans, women, gays, and lesbians since the 1960s has effectively questioned the social and gender construction of "whiteness" (Daniels, 1997). The recent public support for initiatives to end affirmative action, abolish bilingual education, encourage involuntary sterilization of poor women, and enact immigration restrictions, however, signifies a growing polarization within U.S. society (Feagin & Vera, 1995). Although it remains unlikely that *The Bell Curve* will be used as a direct justification for conservative legislation or court decisions, it serves as a powerful subtext for nearly every policy decision about race, class, and social welfare that leads to the elimination of social programs for impoverished and disadvantaged groups (Scott, 1994). Despite its timing, the ideas presented in *The Bell Curve* reflect the continuity of racial bigotry and prejudice that have legitimized the socioeconomic, cultural, and political oppression of people of African descent.

REFERENCES

Alland, A., Blakely, M., Brace, C., Goodman, A., Molnar, S., Rushton, J., Sarich, V., & Smedley, A. (1996). The eternal triangle: Race, class and IQ. *Current Anthropology, 37,* S143–S181.

Allen, G. (1995). Eugenics comes to America. In R. Jacoby & N. Glauberman (Eds.), *The bell curve debate* (pp. 441–475). New York: Times Books.

Appiah, K. (1995). Straightening out the bell curve. In R. Jacoby & N. Glauberman (Eds.), *The bell curve debate* (pp. 311–313). New York: Times Books.

Barkum, M. (1997). *Religion and the Racist Right: The origins of the Christian Identity Movement.* Chapel Hill: University of North Carolina.

Berderman, G. (1995). *Manliness and civilization: A cultural history of gender and race.* Chicago: University of Chicago Press.

Brotz, H. (1966). *Negro Social and Political Thought, 1850–1920.* New York: Basic.

Chase, A. (1977). *The legacy of Malthus: The social costs of the new scientific racism.* New York: Knopf.

Cullen, F., Gendreau, P., Jarjoura, G., & Wright, J. (1997). Crime and the bell curve: Lessons from intelligent criminology. *Crime and Delinquency, 43,* 387–411.

Daniels, J. (1997). *White lies: Race, class, gender and sexuality in white supremacist discourse.* New York: Routledge.

Darling-Hammond, L. (1995). Cracks in the bell curve: How education matters. *Journal of Negro Education, 64,* 340–351.

Darwin, C. (1859). *On the origin of species by means of natural selection, or, the preservation of favoured races in the struggle for life.* London: Murray.

Devlin, B. (1995). Galton Redux: Eugenics, intelligence, race and society: A review of *The Bell Curve. Journal of the American Statistical Association, 90,* 1483–1488.

Dixon, T. (1905). *The Clansman: An historical romance of the Klu Klux Klan.* New York: Grosset & Dunlap.

Duster, T. (1990). *Backdoor to eugenics.* New York: Routledge.

Feagin, J., & Vera, H.(1995). *White racism: The basics.* New York: Routledge.

Galton, F. (1869). *Hereditary genius: An inquiry into its laws and consequences.* London: Macmillan.

Galton, F. (1883). *Inquiries into human faculty and its development.* London: Macmillan.

Galton, F. (1889). *Natural inheritance.* London: Macmillan.

Gardner, H. (1995). Cracking open the IQ box. In S. Fraser (Ed.), *The bell curve wars: Race, intelligence and the future of America* (pp. 23–35). New York: Basic.

Garver, K., & Garver, B. (1991). Eugenics: Past, present and future. *American Journal of Human Genetics, 49,* 1109–1118.

Giroux, H., & Searls, S. (1996). Race talk and the bell curve debate: The crisis of democratic vision. *Cultural Critique, 34,* 5–27.

Gould, S. (1995). Curveball. In S. Fraser (Ed.), *The bell curve wars: Race, intelligence and the future of America* (pp.11–22). New York: Basic.

Gould, S. (1981). *The mismeasure of man.* New York: Norton.

Graves, J., & Johnson, A. (1995). The pseudoscience of psychometry and the bell curve. *Journal of Negro Education, 64,* 277–294.

Griggs v. Duke Power (1971). 401 U.S. 424.

Guillory, F. (1992). David Duke in southern context. In D. Rose (Ed.), *The emergence of David Duke and the politics of race* (pp.1–11). Chapel Hill: University of North Carolina Press.

Hacker, A. (1995). Caste, crime and precocity. In S. Fraser (Ed.), *The bell curve wars: Race, intelligence and the future of America* (pp. 97–108). New York: Basic.

Hawk, E. (1934). *Economic history of the South.* New York: Prentice Hall.

Heckman, J. (1995). Cracked bell. *Reason, 26,* 49–56.

Hernández, R. (1995). On not getting it. In R. Jacoby & N. Glauberman (Eds.), *The bell curve debate* (pp. 314–316). New York: Times Books.

Herrnstein, R. (1971, September). IQ. *Atlantic Monthly, 43*–64.

Herrnstein, R. (1973). *IQ in the meritocracy.* Boston: Little, Brown Company.

Herrnstein, R., & Murray, C. (1994). *The bell curve.* New York: The Free Press.

Herrnstein, R., & Wilson, J. (1985). *Crime and human nature.* New York: Simon and Schuster.

Higginbotham, A. (1978). *In a matter of color: Race and the American legal process: The colonial period.* New York: Oxford University Press.

Holt, J. (1995). Skin-deep science. In R. Jacoby & N. Glauverman (Eds.), *The bell curve debate* (pp. 57–60). New York: Times Books.

Horsman, R. (1981). *Race and manifest destiny: The origins of American racial Anglo Saxonism.* Cambridge, MA: Harvard University Press.

Jensen, A. (1969). How much can we boost IQ and scholastic achievement? *Harvard Educational Review, 39*(1), 1–123.

Jensen, A. (1998). *The limited plasticity of human intelligence* [Online]. Retrieved July 7, 1998 from the World Wide Web: www.duke.org/library/intelligence/Jensen/htm

Jorgensen, C. (1995). The African American critique of White Supremacist science. *Journal of Negro Education, 6*(3), 232–242.

Kaplan, L., & Kaplan, C. (1997). Democracy, meritocracy and the cognitive elite: The real thesis of the bell curve. *Educational Theory, 47*, 425–431.

Kevles, D. (1985). *In the name of eugenics: Genetics and the uses of human heredity.* New York: Knopf.

Kincheloe, J., & Steinberg, S. (1996). Who said it can't happen here? In A. Gresson, J. Kincheloe, & S. Steinberg (Eds.), *Measured lies: The bell curve examined* (pp.3–47). New York: St. Martin's.

Kranzler, J. (1995). Commentary on some of the empirical and theoretical support for the bell curve. *School Psychology Review, 24*, 36–41.

Langer, E.(1990, July 16–23). The American neo-Nazi movement today. *The Nation, 251*, 82–107.

Larson, E. (1995). *Sex, race and science: Eugenics in the deep south.* Baltimore: Johns Hopkins Press.

Lind, M. (1995). To have and to have not: Notes on the progress of the American class war. *Harper's Magazine, 290*(1741), 35–47.

Lipsitz, G. (1995). The possessive investment in whiteness: Racialized social democracy and the white problem in American studies. *American Quarterly, 47*, 369–387.

Meyers, B. (1996). The bell curve and the new social Darwinism. *Science and Society, 60*, 195–204.

Moore, W. (1992). David Duke: White Knight. In *The emergence of David Duke* (pp. 41–58). Chapel Hill: University of North Carolina Press.

Muntaner, C., Neto, F., & O'Campo, P. (1996). The bell curve: On race, class and epidemiologic research. *American Journal of Epidemiology, 144*, 531–536.

Murray, C. (1984). *Losing ground: American social policy, 1950–1980.* New York: Basic.

Neel, J., & Schull, W. (1954). *Human heredity.* Chicago: University of Chicago.

Newby, I. A. (1973). *Jim Crow's defense: Anti-Negro thought in America, 1900–1930.* Baton Rouge: Louisiana State University Press.

Pearson, K. (1905). *National life from the standpoint of science.* London: A. and C. Black.

Piliawsky, M. (1994). Racism or realpolitik? The Clinton Administration and African Americans. *Black Scholar, 24*(2), 2–10.

Rescher, N. (1995). The bell curve revisited. *Public Affairs Quarterly, 9*, 321–330.

Richardson, T. (1995). The window dressing behind the bell curve. *School Psychology Review, 24*, 42–44.

Ryan, P. (1997). Unnatural selection: Intelligence testing, eugenics and American political cultures. *Journal of Social History, 30*, 669–684.

Saxton, A. (1990). *The fall of the white republic.* New York: Verso.

Scott, D. (1994). Cognitive conceit: A review of *The Bell Curve. Social Policy, 25*, 50–59.

Semali, L. (1996). In the name of science and of genetics and of the bell curve: White supremacy in American schools. In A. Gresson, J. Kincheloe, & S. Steinberg (Eds.), *Measured lies: The bell curve examined* (pp. 161–175). New York: St. Martin's.

Shockley, W. (1965). Is the quality of the U.S. population declining? *U.S. News and World Report,* 68–71.

Smedley, A. (1993). *Race in North America: Origin and evolution of a worldview.* Boulder, CO: Westview.

Smith, J. (1993). *The eugenics assault on America: Scenes in red, white and black.* Fairfax, VA: George Mason University Press.

Smith, J. (1995). The bell curve and Carrie Buck: Eugenics revisited. *Mental Retardation, 33,* 60–61.

Steinberg, S. (1995). *Turning back: The retreat from racial justice in American thought and policy.* Boston: Beacon Press.

Stepan, N. (1982). *The idea of race in science: Great Britain, 1800 to 1960.* Hamden, CT: Archon Books.

Sternberg, R. (1996). The school bell and the bell curve: Why they don't mix. *NASSP Bulletin, 80,* 46–56.

Tucker, W. (1994). *The science and politics of racial research.* Urbana: University of Illinois Press.

Ward, L. (1903). *Pure sociology: A treatise on the origin and spontaneously development of society.* New York: Macmillan.

Winant, H. (1997). Behind blue eyes: Whiteness and contemporary US racial politics. In M. Fine, L. Weis, L. Powell, & L. Mun Won (Eds.), *Off-White: Readings in race, power and society* (pp. 40–53). New York: Routledge.

Zenderland, L. (1997). The bell curve and the shape of history. *Journal of the History of Behavioral Sciences, 33,* 35–139.

PART

Cultural content, values, and assumptions are an inherent part of IQ tests. Formal schooling teaches people new ways of thinking, which are then measured by the tests. Access to schools, school quality, modes of instruction, attitudes toward formal education, and educational values vary cross-culturally.

An Anthropologist Looks at "Race" and IQ Testing

Mark Nathan Cohen

All science, indeed all thought, begins with assumptions that frame the task at hand—things taken to be true without proof that provides a starting point for any analysis. In good science, such assumptions are explicit and can easily be verified or rejected. Too often, however, assumptions are not verified, are unspoken, or are even unconscious. They may also reflect the unspoken biases and habits of the culture of a particular group, which are themselves arbitrary but are embedded very deeply in the minds of members of the group. The biases and habits of any culture may appear to be absolutely true (because one's neighbors share them and because most people have little experience outside their first culture) so they are assumptions that are not consciously held much less articulated.

Verified or not, the assumptions direct the analysis. Bad assumptions produce bad results no matter how careful the resulting work. Sophisticated statistics may be important to good research design, but the results they provide are no better than the assumptions they serve. Unfortunately, in far too much science, the focus is on sophisticated research strategies rather than on careful analysis of underlying assumptions.

The use of IQ tests to measure the genetically endowed "intelligence" of individuals on a linear scale demands a large number of assumptions. To rank "races" on this basis demands more assumptions.

I offer a partial list of these assumptions. Several are of questionable value or demonstrably wrong. However, only one needs to be wrong to destroy the chain of reasoning. To assume that all are correct involves an enormous act of misplaced faith.

1.   To make comparative cross cultural judgments about the relative intelligence of individuals or groups we must assume that what we measure has a basis in nature and biology rather than being an arbitrary cultural amalgam of varied skills or scores on certain tests. We must assume that it is not merely an arbitrary mathematical construction based on a narrowly defined range of tasks that would vary with local custom and need. Jensen (1969, 1998) and Herrnstein and Murray (1994) argued for the existence of such a general intelligence factor (g). The assumption is that g can be found in any person anywhere, and assigned a specific number permitting all individuals regardless of their origins to be assigned an intelligence rating on a linear scale. Other recent reviewers have discussed a hierarchical model of intelligence in which a general factor "g" contains subsets of abilities at two further levels of specificity (Brody, 1994; Carroll, 1993; Sternberg, 1994) I maintain that if g exists at all it must have a different composition in each culture because the g we usually measure is so closely bound to American culture and values.

A good case has also been made against the idea that "intelligence" is a single thing (Cohen, 1998; Gardner, 1983; Gould, 1996). Rather than measuring a single natural entity, g may be an artificial mathematical concoction that disguises varied patterns of abilities that could more fruitfully be identified and nurtured individually rather than being combined and ranked and that might well vary from group to group. Assigning "intelligence" a single number is like assigning health a number. One could obtain a "score" and "ranking " from one's doctor, but the ranking would have no meaning except to prevent diagnosis and correction of specific problems. Many psychometricians are falling into this trap.

g can be identified mathematically and assigned a number and a rank (at least within certain tightly controlled populations). However, it is a matter of interpretation whether those values have real meaning. Many scholars have pointed out that calculating a number does not establish the reality of what is being measured because mathematical computations will not provide an answer whether or not anything real is being calculated.

I believe that the things Americans test are demonstrably so arbitrary and observable patterns of thought in other cultures are so varied (discussed later) that g cannot possibly be anything other than an arbitrary amalgam of things we choose to test. If newer IQ tests have some limited ability to predict success in American-style institutions it may not reflect the value of the tests for measuring natural "intelligence" so much as the fact that tasks and tests come from the same arbitrary culture code. At best the tests measure the degree to which one is prepared to function in one's culture.

Moreover, the very idea of unitary "intelligence" and the idea of linear ranking of people are both American constructions that most other cultures do not share (contrary to the vacuous opening assertion of *The Bell Curve* [Herrnstein &

Murray, 1994]). Members of many other cultures see diversity and specialized skills without rank, turning temporarily to different individuals for leadership and honor when their particular skills are called for, without assuming that one person's skills are "best" overall. This is the very definition of egalitarian politics (Fried, 1967) that characterizes the smallest human groups and probably characterized all human groups for more than 90% of our history. If genetic evolution is invoked to explain human intelligence, it seems that the model for the evolution of the brain must reflect this diversity.

Larger societies may recognize formal social hierarchies and may consider them the natural order of things, but most such hierarchies (those "ascribed") are not based on personal qualities at all. In others, individuals gain "achieved" status by their individual accomplishments (not their potential). However, such hierarchies rarely if ever embody a ranking of overall mental ability on a single scale. Because linear ranking and unitary intelligence are American cultural perceptions, not objective assessments of the real world, we should be particularly cautious in applying them.

2.   We must assume that intelligence is the same thing in all cultures and sub-cultures, that American categories of intellectual functioning represent and exhaust the natural categories of thought, and that American choices of what to measure and how to measure it are shared by other people.

Yet, we define intelligence based only on a narrow slice of Euro-American experience and skills, using mostly European or American test populations and test questions. Then we simply postulate that our definition applies to others (See, e.g., Carroll, 1993; Sternberg, 1994). Proponents of g assume that it will have the same composition in any culture and in the face of any task. To an anthropologist, it seems clear that even if g can be measured meaningfully from the array of skills employed in any culture, the definition will differ from (sub)culture to (sub)culture because the mix of necessary skills and abilities—and the ways certain problems are solved—will differ in different contexts. Whatever the outcome of the IQ debate, it is enormously important that we move the whole discussion beyond the closed system of American variables and recognize that ours is only one arbitrary system of cognition among innumerable human systems, just as our language is only one of many. If a valid universal definition of intelligence is ever to emerge, it must reflect a very broad range of cognitive functioning in different cultures.

American definitions of how to assess "intelligence" are demonstrably imperfect and incomplete. Americans do not consider facility in foreign languages a sign of intelligence even though many other cultures value it highly and it makes an obvious contribution to success in real life. Language acquisition is clearly a very important skill for success in a multilingual world (which has been the human norm). In addition, for most of human history, survival demanded understanding the trajectory of a thrown object, the ability to orient oneself in complicated terrain, and the capacity to understand the habits of animals, the growth patterns of plants, or the patterns of specific diseases. ("Primitive" people are commonly superb naturalists, with intricate knowledge of resources and natural cause and effect, even if their IQs, measured by our tests, are low.) This, not manipulating figures on paper, would be the kind of intelligence honed by genetic evolution. As sociobiologists have pointed out, evolution is likely to have honed individual skills in calculating costs and benefits in interpersonal relations (Hamilton, 1970; Trivers, 1971). Social skills are critical to success in every culture we know of.

Moreover, the style of many or most American-designed tests (including IQ tests and commonly used surrogates such as the Armed Forces Qualifying Test [AFQT] or Scholastic Assessment Test) contradicts assumptions about ability in many cultures. Most cultures do not consider speed an essential element of mental ability: They may denigrate speed as a sign of a simple mind. Most do not see the value of simple "right or wrong" answers (rather than thoughtful judgments), or of working competitively as individuals in isolation rather than as teams. (Immigrant children are often surprised by the requirement that they work alone.) Our IQ tests also assume that problems must be solved the way Americans solve them, but individuals elsewhere may solve complex quantitative problems without knowledge of Western mathematics (Powell & Frankenstein, 1997).

Measuring innate intelligence with paper-and-pencil tests misrepresents the realities of our history and evolution. Only the last 5,000 years have involved literacy in any part of the world, and most human populations (including most Europeans) were not literate until the 20th century. To suggest that human intelligence is genetic but can be measured through literate means ignores this history.

3.   Even if we focus only on Americans, we have to assume that IQ tests and their surrogates provide a valid measure of American intellectual needs—an assumption that is manifestly not true in many cases. Speed (of the type tested) is not essential to most jobs. Individuals rarely work alone. Important questions rarely have simple answers. Social skills are often more important than problem solving. The problems we face as adults are complex, involving cooperation, judgment, partial truths, and competing values, not simple answers. (The very concepts of simple "truth" and "falsehood," and "correct" or "incorrect" answers derives more from Western scholasticism and our testing methods than from human experience.) In fact, even some of our own models of education (e.g., Perry, 1968) emphasize the need to lift students from simple dualistic right-and-wrong thinking, which they have been taught, to consideration of more complex and subtle answers. We use standard tests to measure "intelligence" because they provide a practical format for mass testing and scoring—and because they favor those we intend to favor—not because they reflect the most important intellectual skills. The tests in fact place an artificially narrow hurdle in our paths, and therefore force us to work in the real world with an artificially narrowed range of problem-solving skills and the unrealistic expectation of clear, simple answers. Dropping the tests would probably enhance the range and quality of job performance by letting in a wider variety of people who could bring a different set of perceptions and understandings to any problem. Black baseball players, once considered unfit to

play in the major leagues, did not only increase the pool of major league talent; they added new dimensions of competition and changed the way the game was played by all. Female college professors have had a similar effect on higher education. We have a lot to gain by more open minded acceptance of alternate styles.

4.   We have to assume that intelligence is under genetic control. To show genetic influence is not enough. We must show that genes exert sufficient control to account for very minor variations in intelligence. Arguments about the immutability of intelligence of individuals (Herrnstein & Murray, 1994) must depend on almost total genetic determination of intelligence. Much of the argument of *The Bell Curve* quietly assumes nearly 100% determination of intelligence by genes, not the mere 60% the authors postulated (and which many critics [e.g., Daniels, Devlin, & Roeder, 1997] consider far too high). If society has a malleable 40% or more to work with, it can easily reverse any cognitive disadvantage of birth if it makes the investment.

Given the enormous range of mental abilities that all normal human beings display, the differences in "intelligence" we measure with IQ tests surely represent only a tiny fraction of an individual's abilities, the tip of an iceberg. Differences in IQ may seem large, but measured against the total of human abilities they are trivial. Therefore, to assume that genes control IQ, we have to assume that genes exert very fine-tuned control over our capabilities—far more control than genes maintain with, say, height. As a parallel example it may be possible to argue that genes contribute to the difference between someone 5 feet tall and someone 7 feet tall; however, to assert that genes control measured IQ is the equivalent of asserting that genes control the difference between heights 5'7" and 5'7½".

In fact, genetic fine tuning of mental performance seems unlikely. Genes usually establish the broad outlines or limits of a chemical process, but they often leave a history of environmental action to refine the outcome. Genes may make organisms "selfish," for example, but experience dictates how selfish ends are achieved (Dawkins 1976). Given the constant change of the natural world, fine genetic tuning of problem-solving ability would be counterproductive and would be selected against. Organisms need flexibility to respond to changing environments, but such flexibility implies that there is slippage between an organism's unalterable genes and its developing capabilities.

The evolutionary process itself is not about perfection or even rankable linear improvement. Fitness involves a complex balancing act that changes rapidly as the environment changes. Fitness results from being in the right place at the right time with the right equipment, not overall superiority. For the most part, one animal's body is not better or worse than another although it may be better suited to certain specialized, temporary conditions. Evolution produces variety and (particularly in the primate line) flexibility. If mental capabilities are defined by genes they must involve a fluid body of abilities that can adapt to changing circumstances. The "intelligence" one measures must therefore also depend on circumstances including local needs and cultural variation.

Biological evidence for genetic control of (as opposed to possible influence on) intelligence is actually extremely weak. Genes produce chemical sequences, and they cannot produce an abstraction or promote an ability or a behavior except through a chemical–physical pathway, yet to be demonstrated in the case of intelligence. No variation in the structure or chemistry of the brain., including its size, is known to affect differential intelligence within the normal range. There is no known bit of DNA that creates a protein, leading to a chemical pathway that affects fine variations in ability. There is one (but only one) recent report of possible and fairly minor correlation of DNA and IQ in a particular population (Chorney and associates, 1998). The effect of the allele identified by Chorney et al. (1998) represented about 4 IQ points or 1.5% of the observed variance.

However, proving a causal connection between a specific gene and a particular outcome, as Chorney et al. (1998) acknowledged, involves more than finding a correlation, and it is a more rigorous challenge than many proponents of genetic theories of IQ seem to realize. The mere existence of a pattern to the distribution of IQ or even a correlation between IQ and some gene does not prove the case. A correlation of the kind the authors described (in which a certain gene was found with higher frequency, but not universally, in a high-intelligence group) might be explained without any reference to genetic effects on intelligence. For example, the high-IQ sample might include many Ashkenazi Jews (my example) or any other group (including a group more subtly defined) who share a gene by virtue of shared genetic history, but whose "superior intelligence" results only from a shared cultural tradition valuing education.

A demonstration that IQ correlates negatively with presence of African genetic markers would not prove a causal connection between the two, because there is no biochemical link between gene and outcome and there is more than one plausible explanation for the correlation, including obvious cultural–environmental links. For example, if the degree of one's pigmentation affects the racism one encounters, as it obviously does, then African racial markers might correlate with low IQ (as one hypothesis argues) for purely social reasons.

There are probably no genes for "intelligence" any more than any gene directly and uniquely contributes to any other single complex trait. It is quite likely that most genes that exert an influence on "intelligence" (if any) are not "intelligence" genes per se, but exert their influence in very indirect ways that might be specific to local circumstances. A gene might, for example, contribute to intelligence by contributing to growth and health. (The allele identified in the Chorney et al. [1998] study was in fact insulin like growth factor 2.) A version of Leibig's law of the minimum applies here. A particular environment might lack a certain nutrient or contain an excess of a certain toxin. A certain gene might enable its bearer to grow and develop body and mind more successfully than its peers in those particular conditions. The gene would appear to contribute to the development of intelligence. However, in another environment, with a different toxin or nutrient shortage, the same gene might have no importance; a different gene might contribute to growth and development and therefore intelligence. by overcoming different environmental shortcomings. If the environment changed, a gene indirectly conferring "intelligence" on a parent in the rigors of one environment might have no value to the offspring. This model is more probable than the assumption that uniquely dedicated genes for universal intelligence have accumulated historically in certain individuals or groups.

Most anthropologists would not accept a hypothesis linking genes to traits based only on correlation. In studies of sickle-cell anemia, perhaps the best studied human genetic trait, specific known variations in DNA at the hemoglobin locus correlate with the disease; in addition they have been shown to create proteins of known but differing composition from the "normal" and to control the variant chemical pathways that result. The gene–protein–function sequence is well established. Blood cells containing a particular version of the protein can be shown to produce the sickling, anemia-promoting effects that define the symptoms of the disease. The proteins also help prevent malarial parasites from attacking red blood cells. Natural selection on the basis of differences in the gene–protein trait can be demonstrated and shown to account reasonably for the historic distribution of the trait.

All of the steps applied to sickle cell anemia are necessary to establish a causal connection between a gene and a trait, including intelligence.

One must also show that alternate hypotheses are inadequate. (The latter challenge never ends.) The genetic and environmental influences on physical variations such as stature or nose shape—traits far better defined than intelligence—still have not been sorted out to the satisfaction of most scientists. Traits as obviously biological as length of limbs or shape of heads, once considered genetic, racial traits, are known to be at least partly plastic responses to development in different environments. In contrast, the way in which some scientists readily embrace a presumed genetic basis of intelligence, ignoring both the complexities of definition and proof and the need to consider and disprove competing hypotheses, seems facile and shallow.

There is little if any other evidence unequivocally linking intelligence to genetic factors (which is not to deny that genetic factors might be involved; cf. review of the methods of estimating heritability by Brody, 1994.) Familial transmission of intelligence may be partly genetic but it is also cultural, like wealth or religion. Cultural transmission is more reliable than genetic transmission. Plomin, Fulker, Corley, and DeFries (1997) reported that the IQs of children come to resemble those of their natural parents whether or not they have been adopted, suggesting that genetic inheritance plays a major role (ignoring the possible role of prenatal environmental influences or other biological and health variables only indirectly related to intelligence). However, for a complex trait displaying continuous variation, each parent must have a mixed assortment of genes if there is something like a smooth distribution to the trait and if genes are involved at all. If, as in the Chorney et al. (1998) study, a particular allele is related to variation of only about 4 IQ points, the number of alleles involved must be fairly large. Parents pass on random samples of their genes to each offspring. Sexual recombination of genes, a shuffling device, produces variety among offspring; it does not automatically perpetuate "good" traits. Parents mix samples of their genes that then affect one another in unpredictable ways. (I know one natural family in which with great certainty the same two parents produced one black-haired child, one brown-haired child, one blonde/light-brown-haired child, and three redheads. One son was 6'4", another 5'8".) Just as parents of moderate height or color will have some children taller and shorter or darker and lighter than they are (who resemble them on average but not individually), so should they have children with a wide range of intelligence who resemble them only on average. If children routinely get their natural parents' intelligence, it cannot be genetic. In any case, the alternative hypothesis—environmental factors in family transmission (health, wealth, practice, outlook, investment, education)—is so obvious that genetic transmission cannot be assumed to be the primary factor.

Identical twins do not demonstrate that intelligence is inherited, either, although they are still considered the primary evidence for the role of genes (Daniels et al., 1997). Heritability is measured by the difference in concordance between identical and fraternal twins or other siblings. Greater concordance in intelligence between identical twins than between fraternal twins is explained by their the greater genetic similarity (discounting postnatal influences) because all twins share a common prenatal environment.

However, the two types of twins do not have the same experience in the womb. Many (but not all) identical twins share an environment that fraternal twins do not share—a common placenta (Phelps, Davis, & Schartz, 1997). Fraternal twins have separate placentas, whereas identical twins may have one or two. Tests comparing monoplacental and diplacental identical twins suggest that sharing a placenta increases concordance in development in significant ways (it also decreases concordance in some ways). The results suggest that concordance observed between identical twins (when mono- and diplacental identical twins were not distinguished) could reflect a common placenta, not just common genes.

The environment of the womb is different for identical and fraternal twins in another more basic way. The prenatal environment is defined not only by maternal nutrition or other factors that all inhabitants of the womb experience. It is also defined by chemical similarities and differences (and potential incompatibility, sometimes lethal) between the mother and a particular fetus and between fetuses occupying the womb simultaneously.

Fetal incompatibility (as in the Rh factor and some differences in ABO blood groups) is a well-established principle not yet thoroughly explored. There are at least 15,000 to 20,000 ways (the *minimum* estimated number of polymorphic gene loci in the human genome—the number is growing rapidly) in which a fetus may differ genetically and chemically from its mother or its siblings, potentially causing an immune reaction by the mother or the other siblings. It seems quite likely that other forms of chemical incompatibility can kill a fetus too early to detect, although as reported by Holman, O'Connor, and Wood (in press), this is not a major cause of fetal death. However, lethal incompatibilities must represent only the tip of an iceberg of sublethal, subclinical, or very subtle reactions affecting development.

Identical twins, for better or for worse, share common genes and proteins and they experience the chemical environment created by the mother's chemistry and one another in an identical fashion. Fraternal twins or other siblings, whose genes and proteins differ from one another, do not. They may have very different chemical experiences in the same womb. Being identical twins may be as much a statement about the level of environmental similarity in the womb as it is about genetic similarity. The greater similarity of intelligence in identical twins could, quite plausibly, be entirely environmental. The significant genes may not be (and clearly are not entirely) genes for intelligence, but in this case genes that control chemical similarity or dissimilarity with one's mother and one's sibling. Both mechanisms just described suggest that we are clearly overestimating the importance of "genes for intelligence" per se.

In addition, as has been pointed out many times—dating back to its original formulation (Hirsch, 1997; Jacquard, 1983, cited in Hirsch, 1997; Lush, 1940, cited in Hirsch, 1997)—but ignored just as often (see, e.g., Wade, 1998), heritability, the concept usually referred to in these discussions, simply does not measure inherent genetic control of any organic outcome including intelligence (cf. Brody, 1994, for estimates of heritability of intelligence ranging from 50%–80%) In fact, heritability, a statistical concept, cannot accurately be conflated with biological heredity in any simple sense. It is a statistic describing a population, not a statement of genetic control in individuals (Hirsch, 1997). Moreover, because it is the reciprocal of environmental effects, heritability is influenced heavily by how much environmental variety is introduced. The more uniform the environment of those compared, the higher heritability will appear. Heritability is not an inherent property of genes; it is only a measure of the importance of genes in explaining differences between particular individuals or groups compared under any particular set of circumstances.

A dramatic enough difference in the environment can clearly reduce heritability to almost nothing, no matter how great the genetic similarity. Imagine, for example, identical twins, one of whom receives a brain-damaging injury or is starved as a child. The marked differences in their test performances result entirely from environmental influences. Genetic inheritance is defeated. Clearly then, differences in intelligence of genetically similar beings can be caused by significant environmental differences. These might include less dramatic but significant factors such as poor health and nutrition, neglect, or being raised in a different or discriminated "race" or class. One needs no genes at all to explain groups' differences in behavior or intelligence.

Our standard estimates of heritability all come from measurements among individuals where environmental differences are very limited, providing an unrealistic picture of the power of genes. This principle applies not only to intelligence, but also to many other inherited conditions such as various diseases. Both diabetes and hypertension appear significantly to follow genetic lines in the environment of the late 20th century. It appears that both are highly heritable. However, the substantial increase in prevalence of both diseases in the United States between 1850 and 1990, when significant changes in the environment occurred, is almost entirely the result of environmental change. There has not been time for genetic change. The heritability of each disease appears high in one test and much lower in the other. Estimates of heritability depend significantly on what question is asked and what population(s) are studied. Heritability has no predictive power from one situation to the next and results from measuring twins cannot be extrapolated even crudely from group to group.

A similar observation can be made about the degree to which fostered children come to resemble their natural parents in IQ. Clearly, as Plomin et al. (1997) acknowledged, they will not approximate their parents' IQs if major environmental factors (e.g., the aforementioned brain damage, starvation, discrimination etc.) are involved. Therefore, children only come to resemble their biological parents if the environmental differences introduced by their foster homes are small enough. In fact, because of our formal and informal rules, adopted children are most often placed with families that are not very different from their birth families. Once again heritability appears high only because environmental variation is tightly controlled. It says nothing at all to help explain differences across larger environmental gaps such as racial identity.

Each time we change the circumstances we get a different figure for heritability. Heritability measures of intelligence in twin and family or fostering studies, or even within one socially defined "race," no matter how often replicated, cannot be extrapolated to explain "race" differences, class differences, geographical differences, "school track" differences or any differences that involve environmental disparity greater than that in the original tests and the original test population. To say that the heritability of intelligence or any other trait is inherently 40%, 60%, or 80% and that that figure can be used as a general tool is completely spurious. We cannot even assume that heritability across "races" will hover somewhere near the results obtained from twins. Changing the populations and circumstances compared can change the apparent heritability quite drastically as my diabetes example shows.

5. To associate IQ with "races" we must assume that "races" exist (as clearly defined and sharply bounded groups of people with known clusters of correlated biological traits) such that skin color can be expected to correlate with other features, visible and invisible, including one's "intelligence". We also have to show that differences observed between politically defined races (the usual basis for "racial" identification) are genetic rather than environmental. (The black "race" is clearly a political construct.) Yet, many "racial" traits like shape of head and limb length turn out to depend partly on environment as I have indicated. Others, like differences in fecundity and fertility at the group level, reflect environmental and behavioral factors and cultural choices (breast-feeding, nutrition, birth control) almost entirely. The differences we see (or simply assume) in reproductive habits are cultural choices based more than anything else on social class.

Almost all anthropologists (e.g., Boyd & Silk, 1997; Cavalli-Sforza et al., 1994; Cohen, 1998; Marks, 1995; Molnar, 1998; Relethford, 1997) agree that races in the popular sense do not exist and never have. The human species is a growing, branching family with a great deal of interbreeding, its distinctions as gradual, multifaceted, and subtle as the divisions of any family. Cavalli-Sforza, Menozzi, and Piazza (1994) demonstrated the difficulty of attempting to define the branches of the human family even by the most careful genetic analysis. They showed that obvious racial traits have very little to do with finding out who is actually related to whom. (Dark and light skin each seem to have evolved several times, independently, in different branches of the family so color is not a good cue.) They pointed out also that skin color and nose shape, used in "race" classifications, are superficial traits that evolve fairly rapidly to match regional climates and therefore present a misleading picture of regional uniformity, family ties, and the distribution of other genes. Under the skin, there is very little order to real human genetic variation.

Specific colors, noses, eyes, hair, and body shapes that make up our racial stereotypes do not "go together" partly because a great deal of evolution is random and because various features are adapted to distinct (although often overlapping) features of the natural environment: heat, cold, ultraviolet radiation, humidity, altitude, malaria and other possible diseases, and so forth. We, therefore see an enormous array of combination of features in indigenous populations around the world. Dark skin can come with blond, wavy hair, with long or short limbs, and broad or narrow noses. These patterns are easy to verify through travel or merely by consulting back issues of *National Geographic*, usually devoted to the most isolated, least cosmopolitan, and least "mixed" of human populations.

More important, of the more than 15,000 to 20,000 gene pairs (a minimum estimate) that create the differences between people, few seem to be correlated with skin color (which is controlled by only an estimated six pairs or 0.03% of all variable genes—not to mention the number of genes for which only one allele or variant is known within the human species). Most genes that come in various forms do not differ among populations as much as they differ among individuals within any population. In a "multiracial" group, one cannot reliably tell by looking which individuals are most similar biologically. One cannot pick a person to provide a safe blood transfusion based on appearances. Blood type is just one trait among thousands that do not correspond to skin color.

Even the sickle cell trait is not correlated with black skin in the way our stereotypes imply. In fact it can be used to disprove the existence of races. In Africa the trait occurs in only a very small fraction of the individuals (generally less than 15%) in those groups that have it, centered primarily in one area of west central Africa where malaria was common. It did not occur or occurred very rarely among dark-skinned people in other regions of Africa, and very rarely in dark-skinned people elsewhere but it did occur in malarial areas of southern Eurasia from Spain to India among individuals, many of whom are now considered "white." If the Americas had been colonized from southern Europe and Africans had been brought from north, east, or southern Africa, the sickle-cell trait might be associated in our minds with white skin—and blackness would be associated in our minds with narrow noses, not broad ones.

There is no reason to assume that intelligence is an exception to this pattern of independent variation of most human traits, even if it is found in genes. To assume that intelligence genes go with skin color is to argue against enormous odds.

The existence of a contemporary black–white difference in test scores is hardly sufficient to make the case for genetic superiority and inferiority, because "races" as politically defined, have profound effects on how people are treated by others. One would have to be able to show that differences in treatment cannot explain intelligence, leaving only genes as a possible explanation. In fact, however, many observations suggest that "racial" differences in intelligence can be explained by health, discrimination, and other social and educational factors (the list of which is much broader than what is defined as socioeconomic status, the usual correction applied to make groups comparable for testing; Cohen 1998).

6. We have to eliminate poor education or lack of exposure to a specific culture or language (including slang, nuance, dialect, etc.) as a source of poor performance on measures of intelligence. We must assume that knowledge of the necessary cultural content, even the part that is unspoken, is uniformly available to all and not affected by ethnicity, wealth, social class, schooling, geography, or language. This is manifestly not true. There is no such thing as a culture fair or culture-free test. Most tests do not even try to approach that ideal.

I have reviewed a variety of IQ tests and surrogate tests from the last 30 years, including the Otis Quick Scoring Mental Ability Tests for Children, an old Wechsler Adult Intelligence Scale (Wechsler, 1955), a Woodcock–Johnson PS battery, the McCarthy Scales of Children's Abilities, a respected textbook on psychometrics (Anastasi, 1988), a practice booklet for a MENSA (UK)-designed test for 11 to13-year-olds to which I could obtain access (Russell & Getting, 1994), 10 SAT exams (the College Board, 1997), 27 Graduate Record Exams (Educational Testing Service, 1996), and more than 30 practice tests for the Miller Analogy Test (MAT; Bader, Burt, & Steinberg, 1991; Barron's, 1986; Psychological Corporation, 1994). I am seriously disturbed by the degree to which familiarity with English vocabulary, American cultural assumptions about knowledge and logic, American choices about what is significant, American styles of categorizing things or representing them in two dimensions and knowledge of American or European culture per se pass as measures of "intelligence" or ability.

Not all of these tests are recognized IQ tests. However, the very fluidity of the definition of an IQ test protects IQ testing from criticism. A test can be disowned while its results are used to stand for IQ. The authors of *The Bell Curve* (Herrnstein & Murray, 1994) relied on the AFQT and the SAT to measure intelligence, but the AFQT is not designed to measure intelligence or cognitive ability; it measures school achievement, which is substantially a social variable, not a measure of innate ability (Fischer et al., 1996). The College Board (1997) pointed out clearly that success on SATs is related to preparation, familiarity, and practice. It clearly states that vocabulary, which is so important to the tests, is acquired knowledge. Yet despite some vocal critics, neither the use of the SAT or the AFQT as surrogate IQ tests nor the specific conclusions of Herrnstein and Murray have been generally disavowed by psychometricians.

The real question, however, is not whether a test officially measures IQ; it is whether it is used to test "innate ability" to determine school tracking, and fair admission and hiring policies.

THE ITEM CONTENT OF THE TESTS

Tests discriminate against groups and individuals (in the common not the technical sense of the word) if they utilize items that are less familiar to some people than to others. Some of the most egregious examples—such as tennis courts—have been eliminated. However, working with city children as I have makes it clear that such seemingly innocuous objects as thread, household tools, freestanding single-family houses, cows, pigs, corn, oak trees, and acorns, or puzzles that still appear on tests are not always familiar nor are their properties understood. Many children have never seen such "familiar" childhood items as picture puzzles, alphabet blocks, toy sailboats or trains, or toy xylophones. Doing puzzles is a learned skill. Many may know household objects under different names or with different ideas of proper use. (See Brown [1965] for a description of trying, as a child, to fry shrimp in Vaseline, because he had been told to cook with grease.) Using any of these items on a test puts such children at a disadvantage. So does asking them to name as many items of food or clothing as they can in a limited time (McCarthy Scales of Children's Abilities). The latter is a test of exposure, not intelligence, especially if the items the child does name—and does use—are dismissed as incorrect because the testers do not wear or eat them and do not know the vocabulary used in the child's home. Asking children to recognize incomplete pictures of red wagons, alphabet blocks, Raggedy Ann dolls, and old-fashioned kites (Woodcock–Johnson PS battery) also tests exposure to those items. If children are asked to fill in the missing sounds from the middle of words (Woodcock–Johnson PS battery), success obviously depends on vocabulary (including having no vocabulary the tester does not have) and on pronouncing words as the tester does. An Australian child given the word *coo ... ie* (cookie) to complete might "incorrectly" say that there was no missing sound, because *cooey* is a well known word in Australian English.

Mere exposure to or awareness of objects may be insufficient; real working familiarity is required. One can "know" an object without having thought much about it—to think about the fact, for example, that a single-family house typically has a chimney, or that an isolated farmhouse (which city children never see) casts a sequence of shadows in all directions (Anastasi, 1988).

Many tests rely heavily on knowledge of fairly obscure vocabulary tilted heavily toward classical education. Examples from the various tests include *rook*, *minstrel*, *apocryphal, didactic, heinous, mesmeric, toady, evanescent, elliptical* (speech), *panegyric, malapropism, fusillade, chanteys, apostrophe* (figure of speech) *emollient,* and *contumacious.* In fact, many of these words are so uncommon in normal use and so peculiar to one subculture that they could be considered upper class white slang. However, there is no attempt to balance these with the slang of other groups. Taking the MENSA (UK) test demonstrates the problem of taking a test in a different dialect of one's language because the needed vocabulary includes *Dorset* (a county) and *Mid-off* (a position in cricket).

The worst offender is the MAT, which is heavily skewed to sophisticated English vocabulary, to the point that it seems quite forced. These tests provide upper middle-class white Americans an enormous advantage at the expense of the working class, minorities, and immigrants (even if the latter have obtained an equivalent practical education but at a public college instead of a private one). They claim to test ability and are used as a basis for "fair" or "merit-based" admissions to graduate programs, but they are a parody of such a test.

Among the MAT practice tests, I found more than 40 words that I, a college professor in my 50s with the benefit of a first-class education had never seen (*diapason, houyhnhnm, peccatophobia*). Many other words represented obscure, formal, upper class written English, not normal usage.

The tests also focus heavily on upper class mainstream knowledge to the almost complete exclusion of popular or ethnic culture of any kind: Husserl, Mazarin, Daumier, Valjean, Merseault, and Anchises.

Supporters of the test argue that some vocabulary and knowledge has to be obscure to permit fine distinctions in scores at the upper end of the scale. However, this fine discrimination is based on exposure to cultural items, not logical ability.

Bias (in the common, nontechnical usage of the word) exists not only in the specific items used, but also in other less obvious aspects of culture. Culture is more than an aggregate of facts and items. It is a conventional learned structure, analogous to the grammar of a language, which affects how people behave, think, and categorize; how they develop logical principles; how they are motivated; how they learn; what they value; what forces of cause and effect they recognize; what they see and hear selectively from an array of stimuli; how they represent and recognize ideas artistically, and so forth. As with any other culture, the structure of American thought and perception is largely an arbitrary convention that other people—even people within our own political boundaries—may not share. The tests reflect this arbitrary convention, using common mainstream American items, but also culturally defined logic and categories, graphics, perceptions, and ways of knowing.

We fail to recognize that people get information in different ways: oral stories, pictures, books, or television. A person trained by oral stories may know a famous person well, although not by sight. We fail to understand that cultural content, like language, cannot simply be translated item for item from one culture or minority to another to produce comparable result because the same items have different significance, meaning, clusters of meaning, and nuances in different cultures even after translation. (The word *machismo* or *macho*, adopted from Spanish to English, does not refer to exactly the same behaviors in the two languages.) (One implication of this is that there is no meaning whatsoever to comparisons of U.S. and Japanese IQ scores (or comparisons of white Americans and minority Americans) because there is no way to know that people in two cultures are actually taking identical tests. Test questions, with or without translation, may not have equal salience and equal difficulty for different groups.)

Problems often involve arbitrary value judgments. One has to know what the culture prefers not what is logical. An item on the Otis Quick Scoring Mental Ability Tests for Children reads: "A soldier who dies in battle has made a great _____ (effort, honor, reputation, sacrifice, mistake). The "correct" (patriotic) answer is sacrifice, but the answer should really be "mistake." Another item asks, "Is it safest to judge a man's character by his: deeds, voice, clothes, wealth?" The "correct" answer is presumably deeds, (that is actually an English aphorism), but the real answer in our culture is "wealth." An SAT item asks the test-taker to pick a pairing analogous to *lawyer:client* on the assumption that everyone shares the proper idealized cultural model of the lawyer–client relationship. However, many Americans view lawyers as just one more element in the white power structure to be circumvented. Another SAT item asks for an analogy to the pair *libertarian:tyranny*, despite the fact that that relation involves an outdated sense of the meaning of libertarian or implies a highly politicized perspective on the people who now call themselves libertarians. Takers of the MAT are asked to recognize that *mongrel:pedigree::boor:manners* on the highly spurious assumption that good breeding makes good manners or that manners means superficial stylistic mannerisms of the upper class, not more important human qualities.

Questions that ask what is the best version of an underlined portion of a sentence or the "best way to revise it" (e.g., on the SAT) often involve grammatical principles or even stylistic preferences that few people recognize and to which even fewer people actually adhere.

Questions may involve arbitrary cultural ways of putting things in categories. A question on the Otis Quick Scoring Mental Ability Tests for Children asks whether a fox most resembles a pig, a goat, a wolf, a tiger, or a cat. The correct scientific answer is "wolf," but a much more logical classification for a child or anyone else without knowledge of Linnaean classification would be a "cat."

Problems may involve the presumption of certain cultural standards, as in this item from the Otis tests: "A party consisted of a man and his wife, his four sons and their wives and three children in each son's family. How many people were involved?" The correct answer (22) assumes that all sons are married but no son has a polygynous marriage.

One may have to share the testers' knowledge and ignorance to answer this question from the Otis tests: "Which pair of words is least like the others: run–fast, large–big, loan–lend, buy–purchase." The answer (run–fast because the other pairs are synonyms) assumes that loan is a synonym for lend. However, many of us were taught that in "proper" English, loan can only be used as a noun. This is finicky, but that is just the point. If one is not bound by "correct" English then most questions can be answered in a variety of ways. Do we use words only with utmost precision according to some dictionary (which one?) or the way they are actually used (by whom?)? How is the individual being tested supposed to know where the testers draw any particular line unless he or she is privy to their particular style?

PERCEPTUAL EXPECTATION

We fail to understand that people of different cultures see and hear different things, selectively, from the same flow of information. Different cultures (or even different social roles) teach one different patterns of selectivity. Not all people see or consciously register the same things, so children from different groups who have presumably had the "same" experiences may bring very different sets of knowledge and may see different things in the same problems. (Take a foreign friend to a baseball game and later discover what he or she saw that you did not see because you had learned to tune it out.) We have all had the experience that young children are observant of things that adults ignore. However, what adults choose to ignore is a function of socialization in a particular culture. If the color of clothing has no meaning in a culture, most people will not remember it; if it signifies important status differences, people will focus on it. Therefore, success on test questions may depend on whether one has the same selective perception and focus as the tester.

Children or adults of one culture may be at a disadvantage when asked to identify what is wrong in a picture, or which item is different, or when asked to identify the trend in a series of figures or identify the missing one, because they focus on different things and because "missing," "difference," and "wrong" reflect arbitrary cultural standards.

If we ask a child to copy a drawing, as on the McCarthy Scales of Children' Abilities, and then assign various points for varying degrees—and different kinds—of exactitude, we are assuming that the child "should" focus on and replicate the same salient points as the tester. (Deciding what is the most important thing to get right—size, straightness of lines, intersection of lines, rotation of figure, number of lines, etc., is a cultural choice.) For example, in copying the shape of a backward L (straight vertical and horizontal lines meeting at a right angle), should one get more credit for making the corner pointed and the lines straight than for having the proper orientation, angle or size?

DRAWING CONVENTION

Many tests from the simplest children's test to the culture-free progressive matrices involve drawings. On the McCarthy Scales of Children's Abilities, test takers are asked to draw a child, assuming that a "more intelligent" person will draw something more in the nature of a Western sense of realism, even though many cultures would not expect or train that style. We assume that a child who departs from that standard is less intelligent, even though we know that great artists often depart intentionally from realistic portrayal because they have something else to express. Might not a child, particularly one of a different culture, also wish to express something different from what a tester wants (After all, similar tests are used to identify emotional problems)? We are asked to interpret drawings, identify time sequence, or point to what is missing with apparent disregard for the fact that such interpretations depend on familiarity with drawing conventions and knowledge of the items, not just logic or perception. We must know what a cartoonlike line drawing represents, and what, among all the things that are inevitably missing in any line drawing, is not supposed to be missing. That is, we have to know the cultural convention determining what aspects of an object are necessary and sufficient to convey an object's identity and therefore cannot be left out. (Bugs Bunny has rabbit ears, teeth and tail so we know what the cartoon stands for, even if the rest of him is not very rabbitlike and may lack the details of rabbit that other cultures consider definitive.)

We also have to know the arbitrary Western conventions that "up" means "background" and "down" means foreground and that larger is near and smaller is far away. Some questions involve the rotation of a geometrical figure, a highly unusual skill involving familiarity with two-dimensional rendering, mechanical drawing, machine-oriented thinking. This reflects our conventions for representing a solid object in two dimensions, which many cultures do not share.

We can understand drawing conventions and the problems of defining what is "missing" or "wrong" more clearly if we look at drawings in other cultures. In historic Persian paintings, for example, the artists do not try for perspective; they tell a story with various episodes depicted in the same drawing. The spatial relations of the scenes does not describe geography so much as sequence; relative size indicates not distance but importance. A mystic quality to an individual is conveyed by fire coming out of his or her head (which would appear "wrong" to an American) and the fact that his or her face may be left blank (it would appear "missing" to a Westerner). An important person may be depicted larger than other figures, in profile, or with a halolike disk behind his or her head, the "halo" conveying a very different meaning from what it does in Western art. Interpreting the picture involves knowing a whole set of rules unfamiliar to almost all Americans.

Finally, because there is such an emphasis on sameness, similarity, and symmetry or logical sequence in our tests, a clear statement is made of cultural values. Individuals who focus on regularity and symmetry will do well; individuals whose art and thought are more creative and less restricted by patterns will do poorly.

CONSTRUCTION OF CATEGORIES

What we consider the basic logic of analogies is also largely a product of culture. Analogies are based on putting items into categories. However, the rules for categorization are arbitrary conventions themselves (see Cole, Gay, Glick, & Sharp, 1971.) The cultural categories in which things are placed may not seem obvious or even correct to someone trained in another culture, particularly when the classification is based on purely cultural or even mystical qualities. One cannot, for example recognize that a large leather glove, a ball, and a thick wooden rod go together unless one knows baseball. One would not know that the paraphernalia of any religion belong together without being exposed to the religion. People who see other ways to categorize or who rank various kinds of categorization in a different order (there are usually many possibilities) will do badly on our analogy problems even if their logical facilities are perfectly developed. The hot–cold classification system of Mesoamerica that cross-cuts most of our categories is completely foreign to most of us and we would find solving analogy problems in those cultures very difficult, although members of those cultures do it almost without thinking.

The correct answer to an analogy problem may involve the very obscure principles of categorization chosen by the tester. Thus the analogy television:distance ::anarchy:leader on the MAT (because each pair is related by the Greek root of one syllable), or Jackson:Van Buren::Wilson:Tyler because the first two were both widowed and remained single in the White House and the second two remarried. Or 4:baseball::10:football because each number "marks an episode in its sport after which the game continues, with the same team in possession of the ball." The following analogy is offered ping pong:badminton::tennis: ?. "Lacrosse" is the correct answer (because all use rackets), but one cannot give the answer "handball" (because all involve alternately hitting an object and trying to make the other person miss). If some questions involve obscure, arbitrary answers why can't similar answers apply to other questions?

Often the analogy exists only because English combines different meanings in the same word. Every language combines somewhat arbitrary clusters of meaning in each word to limit the number of words that have to be used. However, different languages combine meanings into words differently, which is why verbatim translation is so difficult. Can we really say (logically rather than semantically) that tweezers: bleach::pickpocket:eraser because all "remove" something, as five on the MAT? Is it really useful to say cow catcher:locomotive::climax:denouement because a cow catcher "precedes" a locomotive as a climax ""precedes" a denouement? Is it really an analogy to say that a fall:china::spring-recess:semester (one might add felon:law: :innovator:precedent::an emotional person:down::marriage:up::prisoner:silence: :car:down::man:wind) because in each case the first breaks the second? People from different (sub)cultures who do not cluster all those actions in one word will have a profound disadvantage.

Despite the supposed emphasis on logical skills, knowledge of vocabulary and esoteric facts is often the only challenge: The analogies themselves may be trivial if you know the facts. For example it is not logically challenging to figure out that Anchises: Aeneas::Jocasta:Oedipus (parent:child::parent:child) if you know the names of the Greek gods and know their relationships. That, like many MAT questions, is a test of social class, not logic.

In fact, the whole presentation of analogies in the tests abuses the real meaning of analogy. Analogies are levers we use to expand our thinking by comparing things to one another to gain new insights. Analogies are not right or wrong or good or bad: They are more useful … less useful in particular situations. The premium ought to be on seeing as many analogies as possible (or even seeing one that nobody else has seen) and then distinguishing the significant from the trivial. However, the tests measure and teach the trivial.

RIDDLES

Many questions, particularly on the MAT, are actually riddles—that is, questions for which the correct answer is defined not by knowledge or logic but by an unspoken, arbitrary subset of cultural rules to which you must be privy before you can get them right. In *Culture of Intolerance* (Cohen, 1998) I quoted a question supposedly disseminated by MENSA: "What English word has the letters 'kst' in the middle, in the beginning, and at the end?" Getting the answer right (*inkstand*) involves knowing that you are allowed to break the rules of serious inquiry and utilize tricks in the wording of the question to frame your answer. Once you realize that you can put aside normal rules, the answer is not hard. However, knowing which rules you can bend (some are always sacred even as others are bent) is a matter of initiation into a special culture, not intelligence. The analogy Arizona:Hawaii::Maine:Cuba, given on the MAT, is really a riddle because you have to know that for this particular question, you can and must go beyond the implied geographical grouping and find other meanings for the words. Arizona and Maine are not places but battleships.

7. The final assumption necessary to use IQ tests to rank individuals and "races" in terms of intelligence is the assumption that all participants in the exam are equally healthy and well-nourished, and equally willing and able to bring their full intellect to bear—that all are equally limited (or not limited) by their own emotional reactions to the exam itself or to the school or the society.

There can be no question (because it is borne out by a wealth of public health statistics) that the poor and discriminated minorities, particularly blacks, Native Americans, and Hispanics, are far more likely than middle-class whites to be struggling with health problems, to be under stress when they approach the tests, or to have suffered damage to their cognitive abilities through earlier ill health or poor nutrition. Moreover we have to distinguish the biological effects of poverty from those of politically defined "race." Members of physically distinct minority groups are likely to have suffered repeated challenges to their self-esteem as well as tensions in social interactions of a kind that even poor whites do not experience. In addition, poor minorities are commonly supported by community networks that are less capable than those of whites to prepare them for success in white culture. Many other factors are involved as well. As noted earlier, these problems are far broader than what is usually measured as socioeconomic status, so controlling for SES is not adequate to make comparisons meaningful.

Aside from problems of an individual's other limits, a test format that is unfamiliar or the use of unfamiliar items or a testing situation that is threatening can cause anxiety and delay even if the underlying logic of the question is perfectly clear. Most of us experience such situations repeatedly in everyday affairs.

One of the problems of IQ tests is that many are so different from real-life problems that they require suspension of disbelief, the willingness to put aside one's skepticism and play along. Aside from vocabulary that most of us will never use except on the tests, mathematical principles are applied that most of us will never need again until we prepare our children for their SATs. The style of answering, the speed, and the simple answers further extend disbelief, and the test situation itself is highly artificial. Middle-class Americans are socialized to suspend disbelief and try their best, knowing that test scores will help them get ahead, no matter how meaningless the actual content or context of the tests. Members of minorities who are not so socialized, whose parents do not understand the game—or who assume correctly that their chances of getting ahead are small in any case—might find it hard to give the tests serious attention.

The College Board recognizes the importance of various comfort and emotional factors in test performance. They talk about the need to be relaxed and confident, to concentrate and to focus. We know that an opponent can always be "put off his game" by various kinds of "psyching" or induced stress. Moreover, social and personal stresses are virtually certain to skew performance, and it seems obvious that members of discriminated minorities have more than their share of social stresses. Any number of social theorists from Durkheim (1951) to Memmi (1991) have pointed out that much of the behavior of colonialism, racism, or mistreatment of minorities, both intentionally and not, has had the effect of keeping minority individuals in a state of anomie. Therefore, it seems fairly likely that a member of an involuntary minority group will arrive at the tests—which are, after all bastions of white supremacy—carrying more than a fair share of ambivalence and stress.

We know, moreover, that people focus their abilities on different targets, partly as a conscious choice but partly for subconscious reasons that even they cannot describe. We are all taught where to focus by our parents and our culture, but we also direct our own focus based on any number of accompanying emotions, and our focus may contribute more to our success than our intelligence. Surely psychologists know that. If they do not, psychiatrists, counselors, parents, lovers, anyone with introspection, anyone who reads great literature, and a host of other people know it. Ogbu (Fordham & Ogbu, 1986) in fact developed a compelling theory suggesting that reluctance or resistance—refusal to focus where they are told—may be a major hallmark of minority group status, particularly for those included in the fabric of the state involuntarily. Much of this reluctance is vividly demonstrated in overt behavior; much of it is likely to be more subtle.

Finally, cultural literacy has another meaning, beyond knowledge of test material. It means that a person is literate in the nonverbal cues and body language a society uses constantly and is able to "read" the exam situation or classroom culture and the tester or teacher both as a matter of comfort and as a matter of obeying implicit or unspoken instructions. Part of doing well on tests or in classrooms is a matter of understanding the proper nonverbal cues or understanding when words are being used literally and when a figure of speech is being employed. An individual also has to give off the proper behavioral, verbal, or postural cues.

When we measure ability on the job we similarly have to assume that objective measurement of job performance is not marred by interpersonal or cultural differences in style of work, presentation of self, or interpersonal interactions. We tend to ignore this problem. Yet Rabin (1997), describing the famous nanny trial (the trial of a British *au pair* in the United States charged with the murder of a child in her care) from the point of view of an Englishman long resident in the United States provided a humorous but very graphic account of how body language was interpreted very differently, providing very different emotional reactions, by members of two cultures as similar as American and British. Imagine then, how easy it is for members of the majority and the minority to misunderstand (and fear) one another and how much that is likely to affect both the reality and the evaluation of minority performance.

CONCLUSION

The use of IQ tests to measure the innate, genetically determined ability or intelligence of individuals, particularly individuals from different social classes, ethnic groups, or races, involves a long string of assumptions, each of which can be shown to be highly improbable if not completely spurious. To continue to classify individuals in this way, and to use such tests to provide an "unbiased" way to measure ability for college entrance or for jobs not only perpetuates a scientific fiction; it imposes an enormous, unwarranted burden on individuals who, as a result of prior exclusion, do not participate fully in the mainstream culture. (Crouse & Tusheim, 1988 in Hirsch 1997; Hartigan & Wigdor, 1989, cited in Hirsch, 1997). In fact it provides very dramatic "affirmative action" for upper middle class white individuals. To use these tests without compensating for this enormous advantage, as the United States now appears intent on doing, is unconscionable, making a mockery of our protests of equal opportunity.

REFERENCES

Anastasi, A. (1988). *Psychological testing* (6th ed.). Upper Saddle River, NJ: Prentice Hall.

Bader, W., Burt, D., & Steinberg, E. (1991). *MAT.* Upper Saddle River, NJ: Prentice Hall.

Boyd, R., & Silk, J. (1997). *How humans evolved.* New York: Norton.

Brody, N. (1994). Cognitive abilities. *Psychological Science, 5,* 63–68.

Brown, C. (1965). *Manchild in the promised land.* New York: Macmillan.

Carroll, J. B. (1993). *Human cognitive abilities: A survey of factor-analytic studies.* New York: Cambridge University Press.

Cavalli-Sforza, L. L., Menozzi, P., & Piazza, A. (1994). *The history and geography of human genes.* Princeton, NJ: Princeton University Press.

Chorney, M. J., Chorney, K., Seese, N., Owen, M. J., Daniels, J., McGuffin, P., Thompson, A., Detterman, D. K., Benbow, C., Lubinski, D., Eley, T., & Plomin, R. (1998) A quantitative trait locus associated with cognitive ability in children. *Psychological Sciences, 9*(3), 159–166.

Cohen, M. N. (1998). *Culture of intolerance.* New Haven: Yale University.

Cole, M., Gray, J., Glick, J. A., & Sharp, D. W. (1971). *The cultural basis of learning and thinking.* New York: Basic.

Crouse, J., & Trusheim, D. (1988) *The case against the SAT.* Chicago: University of Chicago Press.

Daniels, M., Devlin, B., & Roeder, K. (1997). Of genes and IQ. In B. Devlin, S. E. Feinberg, D. P. Resnick, & K. Roeder (Eds.), *Intelligence genes and success* (pp. 45–70). New York: Springer-Verlag

Dawkins, R. (1976). *The selfish gene.* Oxford, UK: Oxford University Press.

Durkheim, E. (1951). *Suicide: A study of society.* Glencoe, IL: The Free Press.

Educational Testing Service. (1996). *GRE big book.* Princeton, NJ: Author.

Fordham, S., & Ogbu, J. U. (1986). Black students school success: Coping with the burden of "acting white." *Urban Review, 18*(3), 1–31.

Fried, M. (1967). *The evolution of political society.* New York: Random House.

Gardner, H. (1983). *Frames of mind: The theory of multiple intelligences.* New York: Basic.

Gould, S. J. (1996). *Mismeasure of man.* New York: Norton.

Hamilton, W. D. (1970). Selfish and spiteful behavior in an evolutionary model. *Nature, 228,* 1218–1220.

Herrnstein, R., & Murray, C. (1994). *The bell curve: Intelligence and class structure in American life.* New York: Free Press.

Hirsch, J. (1997). Some history of heredity-vs-environment, genetic inferiority at Harvard and *The* (incredible) *Bell Curve. Genetica, 99,* 207–224.

Holman, D. J., O'Connor, K. A., & Wood, J. W., (in press). Age and female reproductive function. In A. Hill, N. Mascie-Taylor, & C. Sauvain-Dudgeril (Eds.), *Age: Between nature and culture.* Oxford, UK: Oxford University Press.

Jensen, A. R. (1969). How much can we boost IQ and scholastic achievement. *Harvard Educational Review, 39,* 1.

Jensen, A. (1998). *The g factor: The science of mental ability.* Westport, CT: Greenwood.

Marks, J. (1995). *Human biodiversity.* New York: Aldine.

McCarthy, D. (1972). *Scales of children's abilities.* New York: Psychological Corporation.

Memmi, A. (1991) *The colonizer and the colonized.* Boston: Beacon.

Molnar, S. (1998). *Human variation.* Upper Saddle River, NJ: Prentice Hall.

Otis, A. S., & Lennon, R. T. (1967). *Otis Lennon Mental Ability Test* (Form J, Advanced level, grades 10 through 12). New York: Harcourt Brace.

Perry, W. G., Jr. (1968). *Forms of intellectual and ethical development in the college years: A scheme.* New York: Holt Rinehart.

Phelps, J. A., Davis, J. O., & Schartz, K. M. (1997). Nature, nurture and twin research strategies. *Current Directions in Psychological Science, 6,* 117–121.

Plomin, R., Fulker, D. W., Corley, R., & DeFries, J. C. (1997). Nature, nurture and cognitive development from 1 to 16 years: A parent-offspring adoption study. *Psychological Science, 8,* 442–447.

Psychological Corporation. (1994). *MAT candidate information booklet.* New York: Harcourt Brace.

Rabin, J. (1997, November). What the nanny trial tells us about transatlantic body language. *The New Yorker, 73,* 55.

Relethford, J. (1997). *The human species.* Mountain View, CA: Mayfield.

Russell, K., & Carter, P. (1994). *Getting better at IQ tests.* London: Foulsham.

Sternberg, R. J. (1986). *How to prepare for the MAT.* New York: Barron's Educational Series.

Sternberg, R. J. (1994). 468 factor analyzed data sets: What they tell us and don't tell us about human intelligence. *Psychological Science, 5*(2), 63–66.

Trivers, R. L. (1971). The evolution of reciprocal altruism. *Quarterly Review of Biology, 46*(4), 35–57.

Wade, N. (1998, May 14). First gene to be linked with high intelligence is reported found. *New York Times,* p. A16.

Wechsler, D. (1955). *Wechsler Adult Intelligence Scale.* New York: Psychological Corporation.

Wilson, E. O. (1975). *Sociobiology.* Cambridge, MA: Harvard University Press.

Woodcock-Johnson, R. W. (1989–1990). *Tests of cognitive abilities: WJR education, standard battery revised.* Allen, TX: DLM Teaching Resources.

African Inputs to the IQ Controversy, or Why Two-Legged Animals Can't Sit Gracefully

Eugenia Shanklin

My subtitle for this chapter, "Why Two-Legged Animals Can't Sit Gracefully," is taken from an Igbo proverb Chinua Achebe quoted in a 1996 talk at the New York Public Library on racism. The full proverb is, "A two-legged animal never learns how to sit gracefully but a four-legged animal knows." In other words, the animals in power never understand either their own capacities or the capacities of the "other" animals that watch them. It is as though a four-legged animal is watching a two-legged (human) animal, so Achebe says, "those who are given all the facilities [i.e., bottoms for sitting] don't know how to use them but those who don't have all the facilities [bottoms] struggle and master the problem nonetheless" (C. Achebe, personal communication, October 8, 1998).[1] Borrowing a prac-

---

[1] I am indebted to Chinua Achebe for clarifying the deeper meanings of this proverb for me. I also assume full responsibility for any interpretive errors. Achebe seems not to have published this proverb anywhere; for a full discussion of the use of proverbs in Igbo culture and Achebe's use of them in his writings, see Lindfors (1997).

tice from African orators, I parse the proverb in several ways, to review both African inputs to the IQ controversy and perspectives on ranking groups intellectually. First, I take up the IQ tests that have been carried out in Africa since 1915 and used to demonstrate the "inferiority" of Africans. Second, I discuss responses amongst educated Africans to such tomes as *The Bell Curve*, specifically the subscribers to an online discussion group, CAMNET, and the Cameroonians who are the majority of its participants. These responses illustrate the differences between American and African critiques of the issues, and point up the different categories and assumptions that Africans and Americans use in formulating their arguments. Finally, I contrast the 19th-century evolutionary racist notions espoused in *The Bell Curve* with the symbolic racist ideas that were gaining acceptance in the last decade of the 20th century and suggest what I believe to be appropriate social science responses to the issues raised by the history of IQ testing.

AFRICAN TESTING

Since 1915, IQ tests have been administered to Africans, both as a way of "proving" hereditarian or biological determinist theses and as a means of demonstrating that third-world populations are "deficient in the ability to abstract." Mensh and Mensh (1991) pointed out that IQ testing has been carried out in Africa since 1915, when it was first experimented with by A. L. Martin, who administered tests to South African "youths and children" and came to two conclusions: First, those tested were deficient in the requirements for "abstract thought;" and second, the Binet test should be revised for use on "uncivilized children and adults" (p. 109).

Mensh and Mensh (1991) went on to review the history of IQ testing in Africa. For example, in 1929, in South Africa, comparisons were made among test scores of 10,000 children using South African categories of black, Indian, "coloured," and white. At about the same time, other testing projects were conducted to support a biological determinist thesis known as *early arrest*, which holds that an African's mental development stops earlier than that of a white, making an African adult the mental equivalent of a white child.

From the 1930s on, most of the colonial nations—Portugal, Britain, France, Belgium, and Spain—tested their colonized subjects, comparing them with soldiers in the Portuguese case, English schoolboys in the British case, and, in the French case, testing Africans of various age groups, including adults and teenagers, against French 3-year-olds.

Between 1960 and 1975, the period in which African independence was achieved, more testing was done in Africa than ever before, partly because the South African government—then under the control of the Afrikaners—was supporting and encouraging the tests. Another impetus for increased testing was Western curiosity about whether Africans would be able to lead their countries after independence. Cryns (1962), for example, concluded that Africans would be unable to lead their countries because they lacked both abstracting ability and well-developed brains. Two methods were used for the tests: In one, the same test was given to an indigenous population and a control group of Europeans or people of European descent. In the other, a special test, said to be "conceptually equivalent," was given to the indigenous group and the control group. These latter tests may have required formal logical skills that the indigenous group had little or no opportunity to acquire. Because formal logical skills are equated with the human ability to reason, the tests always yielded data that supported the claim that third-world populations are deficient in the ability to abstract. Further, in all the tests, there were items that required agreement with designated social values (items that originated with IQ tests) or that required some specialized cultural knowledge not available to many South Africans; for example, one of the test items asked children to draw a tennis court (Cohen, 1995).

Mensh and Mensh (1991) proceeded to a discussion in which they contrasted anthropological theories, especially those of Lévy-Bruhl and Boas, that supported or challenged concepts included in the testing procedures. Lévy-Bruhl (1925) characterized the mental processes of the colonized as "prelogical" and although late in his life he rejected this theory (at least partly as a result of Boas's refutations), Mensh and Mensh believed that the arrested development notion continues at the core of the IQ method. Boas (1911/1963), who disagreed with Lévy-Bruhl's prelogical argument from the outset, made the point unequivocally in his book, *The Mind of Primitive Man*: "There is no fundamental difference in the ways of thinking of primitive and civilized man" (p. 17). Boas also said that what different people think differs, but not the way they think. The second part of his argument was that the primitive mind assumption is a product of bias on the part of the observers, who then take their own biases and misinterpretations as evidence of the inferiority of the observed but, because Boas's examples are a bit dated, I use contemporary ones of which he would have approved. First, the point that what people think differs but not the way they think: Fish (chap. 5, this volume) gives a nice example when he points out that in North America, avocados are considered vegetables and eaten in salads with oil and vinegar and salty items, whereas in South America, avocados are considered fruits and eaten as desserts, with sugar and lemon juice. In a similar vein, Barrett (1984) made the point that on the English side of the Atlantic, mussels are considered highly edible and enjoyed, whereas clams are considered inedible; on the American side, the reverse was true until recently. All societies make distinctions between categories of edible/inedible or vegetable/fruit; however, which species is in which category may vary from one society to the next.

Second, in support of the Boasian idea that notions of arrested development were a product of observer bias and misinterpretation, Mensh and Mensh (1991) cited Gladwin's 1960s study of navigation in Puluwat, an island in the western Pacific. Gladwin chose to study in Puluwat to gain insight, he said, into the academic problems of poor children in the United States. His formal logic system was this: Poor U.S. children do badly on IQ tests; the same could be expected of Puluwatans; therefore cognitive qualities that handicap poor U.S. children could be discovered among the Puluwatans. Gladwin contrasted navigational systems in Puluwat and in the West, and discovered that the Puluwatan system was complex, rational, and efficient; it was based on a body of theory that was taught as a logically coherent system. There were superficial differences, but "they cover the same things for the same reasons," he decided. However, when it came to considering the implications of this finding, he reverted to his own way of thinking and did not assume that there might be something wrong with the distinction between middle class children's capacity for abstract thought and poor children's limitation to concrete thought. Instead, his conclusion was—not that schools provide superior and inferior educations along class and color lines—the speculation that there was some other cognitive peculiarity that handicaps poor children (Mensh & Mensh, 1991).

Therefore, whether the question is edible and inedible shellfish, avocados as vegetables or fruits, or the implications of one's theory when it turns out that navigational systems function on the same or similar principles, we seldom suspect our own categories of being faulty or constrictive. Instead we easily conclude that those "Others" are different or perhaps inferior. The contemporary descendants of such dichotomous concepts as logical and prelogical still haunt anthropology, at least to the extent that ideas such as traditional versus modern or primitive versus civilized are considered valid distinctions, worthy of inclusion in anthropological textbooks (Shanklin, 1994).

The major lesson to be learned from the foregoing has to do with the equality or universality of cognitive capacities. In the 19th-century scientific literature, this equality was first asserted by Wallace, Darwin's codiscoverer of natural selection or evolution. Wallace became aware of it when he was collecting information about plants from Brazilian natives who, he discovered, had a taxonomic system of their own for classifying plants; in most instances their classifications were more fine-tuned than those of the European scientists.

The same principle was asserted by Franz Boas (1911/1963), who said—on different grounds—that cognitive capacities in humans are all the same. Research in social anthropology in this century and particularly in the works of Lévi-Strauss and his followers has confirmed this over and over again—there are universal oppositions, such as hot–cold, left–right, up–down, raw–cooked, and nature–culture, and there are cultural specificities about where things are placed.

So what we might have learned from the last century of testing of IQs among Africans is more about the universal cognitive capacities of humans and, even perhaps, a little about cultural specificities other than our own, but what we have learned is more about how we reinforce and reify our own cultural categories and protect our own spurious dichotomies. In other words, the two-legged animal does not think it necessary to learn how to sit gracefully because it already "knows" how sitting should be done, and any animal that does not know this is automatically inferior, an inferiority that can be proved either by a glance or by a standardized test.

CAMNET AND *THE BELL CURVE*

CAMNET is an electronic listserver set up by Cameroonians studying in various parts of Europe and the United States. It operates from Italy and its purpose is to allow discussion of (largely but not exclusively) Cameroonian issues. In 1994, there were about 200 participants in the discussions, including myself. By my informal count, based on the people I know on the list and those who have non-Cameroonian names, I would say that there were about 30 Europeans (i.e., non-Africans) on the list, roughly one out of seven. Mainly the discussions are of political issues relating to African matters but in the case of *The Bell Curve*, the discussion began when one Camnetter wrote to this effect:

> There is a furor in the press ... recently about a book entitled "The Bell Curve".... The controversy arises from a proposition that blacks score low in IQ tests because of inferior genes and that this has translated itself into poor performance in society and low socio-economic status.... What these people have done is to articulate what white people generally carry around in silence and use in their interactions with black people. It is an important matter because it must be factored into our interactions with non-Africans in business, foreign affairs and at all other levels. (CAMNET, October 29, 1994, 9:15:05)[2]

Within 2 hours, protests began pouring in from Europeans and from Cameroonians. The first protester had a European name and he said:

> I vehemently object to this attempt to categorize the 'general thoughts' of white people towards blacks. I'm sure that there is a substantial number of white people who do think this way, but the mere fact that it [the book] has generated controversy suggests that this is NOT an attitude that can be ascribed to whites in general. (CAMNET. October 29, 1994, 11:14:18)

The next to respond—within 3 hours—was a Cameroonian woman, a graduate student at a major Canadian university:

> We all should know better than to be consumers or readers of such profusely racist-infested material. (CAMNET, October 29, 1994, 15:55:12)

Then, the next day, came a revisionist version of Cameroon history, put together by a Cameroonian but phrased in the terms of *The Bell Curve*:

> The BELL CURVE debate is not so alien and strange after all, that it is not just a white vs. Black thing, but one that has been at the center of Cameroon's "bal-

---

[2] I do not want to identify Camnetters by name, and thus have identified them by the time of their posting. Specific characteristics (e.g., "graduate student at ...") are based on my personal knowledge of the individuals at the time of their postings.

anced development policy" debate since the 60's; ... I can see some netters shaking their head and saying this has never been a Cameroonian affair, that we are racist-free, though democratically impaired nation. (CAMNET, October 29, 1994, 19:19:42)

There followed a lengthy discussion of policy toward Northerners, Southerners, and Easterners in Cameroon politics, and because most readers will not have heard much about these groups, I summarize the arguments. In the North, the Fulanis were said to have been the beneficiaries of a benevolent state because they were of the same group as the then-reigning president, Ahmadou Ahidjo. Northerners, however, were born with an IQ well below the national average so they had to have different, looser academic standards in public exams. In the East, the Pygmies, more recently called the Baka, should simply be abandoned to their primitive state, along with the monkeys. The Southerners, but especially a group called the Bamilekes, were the main or major victims of this IQ policy because the Bamilekes were born with superior IQs and so would survive in any event; therefore, they should be deprived of positions in government and professional schools. This author concluded by urging:

> So while we rant and rave (and rightly so) against two guys who argue in the Bell Curve that blacks are intellectually inferior to whites, let us take some time off and take a closer look at the situation in our own country. Let us ask ourselves whether Cameroon's warped quota system—largely based on a dangerously flawed and outright racist analysis of ethnicity and IQ—should be pursued. (CAMNET, October 29, 1994, 19:19:42).

The next to respond was another Cameroonian woman, a graduate student at the University of Wisconsin. She concluded:

> Hey! GENETICISTS, get to work. Let those genes responsible for IQ be determined and cloned. The nucleotide sequence should indicate differences amongst races, tribes, and sexes, etc. (if any). (CAMNET, October 30, 1994, 10:37:11).

Next to write was a Cameroonian studying at the University of Dundee in Scotland. His response was brief and best typified by his first and last statements:

> I see all this talk about IQ, Bell Curve, and IQ genes, etc. simply as POWER GAMES .... So folks, lets ignore all these people talking about inherited low and high IQs. It is, in my opinion, a defensive approach in the power and hence survival struggle. (CAMNET, October 30, 1994, 16:41:16)

These were the main points about which the Camnetters argued—whether "all whites" think in a racist way; whether Cameroonian history could be recast in these terms (but with a geographic and ethnic distinction, not a "black" and "white" one), whether the way to fight "scientific" racism's evidence was with scientific evidence of their own. What was most interesting to me was that (except for the last argument) these were not the terms in which the debate that raged over *The Bell Curve* and the U.S. academic reviews were phrased. The person who asserted that "all whites" think this way was immediately told that he had learned too much racist thinking from his European education, that generalizing about all whites was as stupid as generalizing about all blacks. He was also asked where he got the idea that there was a correlation between skin color and thought processes, a question emphatically not raised in most of the U.S. reviews of *The Bell Curve,* as seen shortly.

The recasting of Cameroonian history in terms of correlations between geography and IQ was jumped on by most commentators and the consensus was unmistakable. One man said "what is the correlation here? Race? Skin pigmentation? ... for someone to attempt to parallel the findings [of *The Bell Curve*] with a situation in Cameroon is a dangerous step towards intellectualism." He concluded, "This has never been a Cameroonian affair; we are a racist-free though democratically-impaired nation." Another critic said, "If low IQ is the question, this has never been attributed to skin color. It has been a question of accusations of backwardness because of poor and inadequate schooling. I see no correspondence between this racist book ... and the situation in Cameroon and it is less than honest, indeed a disservice, to use this book to revive ethnic tensions in Cameroon." A third critic, a Cameroonian who is a Stanford professor, sent along a nice piece titled "How To Tell An African From An African." This began, "It comes as something of a surprise to many Africans to discover that all Africans look the same to non-Africans." Then it goes on with African stereotypes about Africans: "Surely everybody knows that the loud and cocky ones are the West Africans; ... the East Africans always say yes even when they disagree violently. If you want to be more specific, the Camerounians will borrow money to buy Champagne whilst the Ghanaians think they invented politics .... When a cabinet minister is caught in a corruption scandal, he commits suicide in Southern Africa; in West Africa he's promoted after the next *coup d'etat.*" The conclusion: "It's got to be something in the water .... But when it comes to skin colour, surely all Africans are black, all black?"[3]

To emphasize the differences in African and American categories in discussing the IQ controversy, I turn now to a cursory review of the U.S. critics of *The Bell Curve* (Herrnstein & Murray, 1994). Most of *The Bell Curve* reviewers took issue with the book's premises; only a few voiced respect for the authors and the issues they were trying to raise. One such was Malcolm Browne (1994), science reporter for *The New York Times,* who reviewed *The Bell Curve* together with two other books. He called Murray and Herrnstein (as well as Rushton and Itzkoff) "serious scholars" but then

---

[3]Compare Shreeve's (1994) article, in which he said that genetic diversity may be greatest in Africa, so that there may be several African "races," and one that encompasses all the peoples of all other continents. Others suggest that if there were such a thing as racial groups, geneticists would identify five such groups, all of them in Africa.

equivocated by suggesting that some of the questions raised may be unanswerable. He concluded that the four authors were pleading for "freedom of debate and an end to the shroud of censorship imposed upon scientists and scholars by pressure groups and an acquiescing society" (p. 45).

Few reviewers agreed with Browne (1994) about either the authors' standing or the need to reopen debates about the inferior capacities of certain groups. In one of the best of many fine reviews of *The Bell Curve*, Gould (1994) made the point that the book is based on two sequential arguments. First, four shaky tenets of early 20th-century social Darwinism are invoked to conclude that "intelligence ... must be depictable as a single number, capable of ranking people in linear order, genetically based, and effectively immutable" (p. 139). If any of these premises is false (and, critics generally agree, almost all are false), their argument collapses. Second is the "claim that racial differences in IQ are mostly determined by genetic causes" (p. 139). Gould took issue with both arguments: "Disturbing as I find the anachronism of '*TBC*,' I am even more distressed by its pervasive disingenuousness. The authors omit facts, misuse statistical methods, and seem unwilling to admit the consequences of their own words" (p. 140). He concluded:

> "*TBC*" is scarcely an academic treatise in social theory and population genetics. It is a manifesto of conservative ideology; the book's inadequate and biased treatment of data displays its primary purpose—advocacy. The text evokes the dreary and scary drumbeat of claims associated with conservative think tanks; reduction or elimination of welfare, ending or sharply curtailing affirmative action in schools and workplaces, cutting back Head Start and other forms of preschool education, trimming programs for the slowest learners and applying those funds to the gifted. (pp. 147–148)

Most critics lambasted Murray and Herrnstein for the book's conservative agenda and its pseudo-scientific claims. *The Nation*'s editorial of November 7, 1994, announced:

> *The Bell Curve* is ... the most recent in a long line of American paranoid literature—the threat of communism now replaced with the threat of a brutish underclass. Such apocalyptic visions ... have often fueled vicious national ideologies, from the Know-Nothings through McCarthyism. It's tempting to shrug *The Bell Curve* off as a momentary blip on the country's racial radar. But it will be so only if its ideas are engaged and hooted out of respectable forums. ("Inequity Quotient," 1994, p. 516).

In *Time*, Lacayo (1994) suggested that *The Bell Curve* would be remembered for "some dubious premises and toxic conclusions" (p. 67).

Ryan (1994), writing in *The New York Review of Books*, observed:

> There is a good deal of genuine science in *TBC*; there is also an awful lot of science fiction and not much care to make sure the reader knows which is which

.... Fewer readers will notice the authors' throwaway admissions that these predictions are highly speculative, and only loosely rooted in the data they assemble. (p. 8)

Ryan concluded: "In short, *TBC* is not only sleazy; it is, intellectually, a mess" (p. 11). Nisbett (1994), writing in *The New Republic* asked:

What has happened to the black–white gap after decades of concerted effort to improve black ability and achievement test scores? Murray and Herrnstein review the evidence and correctly note that the studies range from showing a slight convergence of black and white scores in the past twenty to twenty-five years to indicating that as much as one-half of the difference has been eliminated .... Yet they summarily dismiss this extraordinarily hopeful evidence: "too soon to pass judgment."

Such coolness about evidence that contradicts their position together with uncritical warmth shown toward supporting evidence is found throughout the painful sections of the book dealing with race and the modifiability of IQ This is not dispassionate scholarship. It is advocacy of views that are not well supported by the evidence, that do not represent the consensus of scholars and that are likely to do substantial harm to individuals and to the social fabric. (p. 15)

Reed, reviewing the book in both *The Progressive* (1994a) and *The Nation* (1994b) characterized *The Bell Curve*'s point as "to advance a reactionary, racist and otherwise anti-egalitarian ideological agenda by dressing it with a scientistic patina. Beneath the mind-numbing barrage of numbers, this book is really just a compendium of reactionary prejudices" Reed (1994b) also noted:

TBC is committed to *racial* inequality. Admitting that they can't isolate biologically pure racial categories, Herrnstein and Murray opt to "classify people according to the way they classify themselves." But this destroys the possibility that their statistical hocus-pocus does any of the hereditarian work they claim for it. What they describe at most is race as a category of common social experience.

To conclude this section on African discussions versus U.S. reviews, then, I believe it illustrates the major point that while Africans and Cameroonians are well aware of the ways in which Europeans construe the concept of race, Europeans themselves are not so aware. Throughout the U.S. reviewers' discussions of *The Bell Curve*, as in *The Bell Curve* itself, race and ethnicity are equated with skin color (black and white almost entirely) taken as the distinguishing characteristic. However, when Cameroonians discuss race, they make the distinction that race means skin color to Europeans and Americans (those who did not mention it just put race in quotes and skin color in parentheses behind it) and then move on, in their own discussions, to geographic or national ethnic distinctions.[4] The four-legged animal watches, sees, and understands very well what and how the two-legged animal thinks, but is not convinced that something is so just because the two-legged animal thinks it is. Camnetters are mostly Africans who are or have been educated in our Euro-American system and I know from personal experience how difficult it is to unteach the race = skin color equation to Americans, for whom it is a nearly unconscious premise. Therefore I am reasonably certain that the Camnetters learned this equation from their own observations, not from our educational system, in which the race = skin color equation is seldom mentioned because it is almost universally assumed. I believe the Camnetters learned from observation and from beginning with different premises. They came to different conclusions about the meaning or nonmeaning of *The Bell Curve* from their own perspectives, observing from the perspective of being differently abled animals, according to the categories of the fully equipped animal.

CONCLUSIONS

To conclude the issue of why two-legged animals can't sit gracefully, first, two-legged (Western) animals perceive themselves as whole, fully developed, and perfectly empowered. Any deviation from their (Western) norm is a sign of inferiority or incapacity. Second, unlike the four-legged (other or African) animals who watch them, the two-legged (Western) animals tend to be unaware of their own assumptions, as are the Americans debating the issues raised in *The Bell Curve*. Now we must ask what else we can learn from inputs to the IQ controversy that might contribute to questioning and understanding our assumptions. First, what is race as we begin the 21st century and a new millennium? Second, why do we still think race matters and why do we still debate its terms and putative outcomes? As Hitchens (1994) observed, "Linguistics, genetics, paleontology, anthropology: All are busily demonstrating that we as a species have no objective problem of 'race'" (p. 640). But, he noted, "What we still do seem to have are all these racists" (p. 640). Third, what can social scientists do about racism and what, in particular, can social scientists contribute to the refutation of racist thinking?

I begin with an analogy similar to one used by Kuhn in *The Structure of Scientific Revolutions*. As an anthropological concept, race is much like the 18th-century physicists' concept of "ether" as the substance that filled the earth's atmosphere. Lord Kelvin, the English physicist, and others in the 19th century, developed a number of mechanical models of ether and its effects, but all subsequent attempts to verify its properties failed and shortly thereafter Einstein's formulation of the theory of

---

[4]A similar discussion took place in June 1998 about a Hungarian referee's decision in a World Cup game, a decision that caused Cameroon to be eliminated from the competition; this time CAMNET had 840 participants, some of whom were considerably more bloodthirsty than in previous discussions and inclined toward assassination of the referee, but a majority of the Camnetters systematically refuted charges of racism and disallowed the race = skin color equation.

relativity eliminated these speculations (*Encyclopedia Britannica,* 1997). Like race, ether was a useful category when theories about the earth's atmosphere were in their infancy, but as scientific knowledge advanced, physicists discarded ether as irrelevant, as race was discarded by most anthropologists in the 1950s.

The nonanalogical social science answer to the question of what race is is that the notion of race is part of our (Western or Euro-American) commonsensical understanding of the world—what is usually termed ideology—and that "ideology is a product of elite intellectuals who picked up the biased notions of the ruling class and turned them into theories" (Carr, 1997, p. 155). Race as a category was picked up from the ruling class by elite intellectuals (mainly 19th-century anthropologists) and turned into theory. This theory is now termed *evolutionary racist* thinking, and its premises, advanced in the 19th century, are these: The major races (first identified by appearance, later by genetic markers) had progressed at different rates throughout prehistory and history; "Caucasians" had made the most strides forward (reiterated by Coon, 1950); and the mental condition of a group was connected to its material development (Tylor, 1891). In the logic of this position, it followed that arrested development could account for failure to advance, either materially or, more recently, in IQ scores. Although these ideas have now been discarded by most anthropologists (Lieberman & Jackson, 1995; Littlefield, Lieberman, & Reynolds, 1982; Shanklin, 1994), they are regularly revived in popular discourse, most recently by contemporary psychologist J. Philippe Rushton (cf. Fish, 1998) and, prior to that, by Jensen. As a scientific concept, race in its evolutionary racist formulation was discredited from the 1950s on (Shapiro, 1952) but discussions continue in some, often obscure, places; for example, the Internet anthropology discussion group, ANTHRO-L, where Coon's data and suppositions are endlessly debated by anthropologists and others, including, on occasion, Rushton himself.

Meanwhile, race in its late 20th-century symbolic form, as now debated in public discourse, is newer, meaner, and much more difficult to extirpate. Why do we now think race matters? Although the existence of race was discredited in science, its by-product—racism—was harder to eradicate because racism continues to serve the interests of those who benefit from its existence and its excesses. Crudely put, it is in the interests of the haves to keep the have-nots at bay, both by quietly discriminating against the have-nots and by keeping high the tensions among have-not groups.

The symbolic racist position is one that seldom uses the term *race* (or uses it as sloppily as Herrnstein and Murray [1994] did in *The Bell Curve,* to mean either race or skin color or someone's self-identification with a group based on some vague definition or understanding of those ideas). A symbolic racist is one who has "a negative affect toward African American people that [is] not expressed in traditional ways, but as an irrational opposition to things such as affirmative action and busing" (Carr, 1997, p. 171). Further, the position is highly correlated with "an updated, multidimensional measure of anti-African American prejudice" (p. 171).

This is how the tenets of the new, symbolic racism (sometimes known as the *modern* or *color-blind* racism) play out: Certain groups, although they may have been underprivileged in the past, must now rely on their own indigenous characteristics without expecting favoritism. In other words, third-world countries have only themselves to blame for their failure to develop, and should not expect to be bailed out by first-world countries. Or, in Herrnstein and Murray's (1994) terms, U.S. "blacks" should content themselves with excellence in the proven strengths of their own race or ethnic group (e.g., sports and music). They should not try to compete against the strengths of other races or ethnic groups in their strong areas (e.g., medicine or investment banking). Nor should anyone expect costly measures like Head Start programs to correct their "inherent" IQ deficiencies. This is a more sophisticated argument than the evolutionary racist one, in part because it blurs the distinction between the outmoded concept of race and the term *ethnic group*, even allowing self-selection as its criterion of membership. It denies to the members of certain groups (i.e., "blacks") any remedial help whatsoever, because in its (quasi-evolutionary) terms, deficiencies are not correctable. The logic of this argument is similar to that of the evolutionary racists but it uses the (sometimes admittedly faulty) statistics of scientific racism to underpin its theories, and it uses quasi-liberal language (i.e., ethnic groups, level playing fields, individualism and democratic ideals) to persuade its audience that all efforts to change inherent characteristics of groups are futile.[5]

The arguments against evolutionary racism do not work well against symbolic racism, as we have seen earlier in the U.S. critical response to *The Bell Curve*. In my opinion, what is needed in contemporary discourse is more discussion of the moral flaws and antidemocratic stances of a book such as *The Bell Curve*, not more reviews of its statistical faults. Only a few of the critics approached the book in these terms, especially Reed (1994a, 1994b), and most of the blows the reviewers struck were glancing sideswipes, not body blows.

This is where I think the American Left and social science professionals have a major contribution to make: They are in the best position to evaluate the moral, social, and political outcomes of acceptance of racist doctrines. Their contributions must be phrased in terms of their understanding of how people think, their focus on the universality of the way people think, and the policy implications of racist attitudes and institutions. We must drive home the point that all humans have the same tools for thinking and think in the same ways (i.e., with binary categories), although we know they do not put the same objects into the same categories.

Since Boas's time, anthropologists have gathered a great deal of information on the subject of how people think or the ways in which people categorize their cultural universes, but most of that information has been buried in jargon-ridden professional journals, often inaccessible because it is incomprehensible or, if not incomprehensible, devalued in anthropology because of its "popular" slant. I believe that

---

[5]I hope, for example, that Winant (1997) was wrong when he said that the American Left has fallen apart, that the arguments for affirmative action have been made to seem as specious as those against it.

anthropology's data on universal cognitive capacities could be used to considerable advantage in countering the symbolic racist approach.[6]

The major opposition in U.S. society, the black–white dichotomy, has received little attention from social scientists generally, and anthropologists especially. I have written elsewhere (Shanklin, 1999) about why this is so; here I concentrate on what the effects might be of subverting this opposition, of breaking down our major fallacious opposition between black and white, that has plagued U.S. society for centuries.

There is precedent in the anthropological literature that helps to understand the effects of denying or discarding a major binary opposition. Decades ago, anthropologist Ralph Linton (1959) told a story about a Hawaiian group whose twin institutions of *mana* (sacred power, used for accomplishment) and *taboo* (forbidden power, used for destruction) had rendered their society almost unworkable. The opposition between *mana* and *taboo* was especially manifest in the person of the king, who was so sacred he could not be touched by ordinary people in any context. Thus the king was severely hampered in all his activities and so he decided to suspend the *taboos*. Linton (1959) said, "successive rulers and a well-organized priesthood imposed more and more taboos until the commoners were reduced to poverty and desperation" (p. 55). The struggle between church and state continued until one day:

> The king himself broke the taboo by eating publicly from the same dish with his queen. When it was seen that nothing happened to either one of them, word spread like wildfire. The entire institution collapsed. The commoners rose, overthrew the priests and destroyed the temples, so that Hawaii was without an official religion when the first missionaries arrived. (pp. 55–56)

One can imagine the trepidation that accompanied this meal—someone likened it to sitting down to a meal in which there is a live atom bomb on the table—but nothing untoward happened at the meal. The Hawaiians might not all have lived happily ever after, but one surmises that life became considerably easier for most. This kind of radical break with the past is what I believe is needed in the United States: We must abandon our binary opposition between black and white. Doing so will not cause the overthrow of our institutions; instead, it should lead to some necessary realignments. In the United States, we should be focusing on bettering the lot of all our citizens, in terms not of skin color but of educational achievement, financial status, and comparable measures that enhance life chances.

---

[6]In psychology, Freudians, Jungians and all the rest may be divided about the particulars but they seem to agree about the generalities of human thought processes. Malinowski, a turn-of-the-century anthropologist, was determined to demonstrate that Freud was wrong about the universality of the Oedipus complex and adduced evidence that the matrilineal Trobrianders had entirely different concepts of biological, moral, and familial "fatherhood." However, he never proved his point to his own satisfaction, which suggests that Freud may have been right about the universality of the Oedipus complex or, more broadly, parent–child tensions as part of the socialization process.

This is what social scientists must do about racism—help defang and defuse the black–white binary opposition that causes so much tension and friction in our society. Anthropologists and anthropology teachers need to come up with their own definitions, in Carr's (1997) terms, of an "updated, multidimensional measure of anti-African American prejudice," and publicize those definitions, making sure that their audience understands the distinctions between the old, evolutionary racist formulations and the new, symbolic racist thinking. We must recognize the recurrence of racism in its newer, more virulent forms and denounce both racism and its effects, wherever found. In another context, I asked how one sets about dissolving a harmful opposition.

> First, by recognizing if for what it is—not black and white, but pink and brown, humanity's shades, not those of our monstrous creations; and then by taking steps to insure that the wider public understand not only the oppositions's fallacious nature but its harmful consequences. Second, by insisting that scholars and the general public recognize the inconsistency between their own egalitarian ideals and their discriminatory institutions/acts. The task remains for anthropologists to take up these questions in serious comparative ways, lest we find the next generations asking nineteenth-century questions (eugenics) and answering with twenty-first century technology (cloning). If we anthropologists do not want to see repeated the racist predicates of the twentieth century, we must explain, clarify, and reiterate the non-racist ideals we hope will guide the future (Shanklin, 1999, p. 677).

REFERENCES

Barrett, R. A. (1984). *Culture and conduct: An excursion in anthropology.* Belmont, CA: Wadsworth.

Boas, F. (1963). *The mind of primitive man.* Westport, CT: Greenwood Press. (Original work published 1911)

Browne, M. W. (1994, October 16). What is intelligence, and who has it? [Review of *The bell curve*, J. Philippe Rushton's *Race, evolution, and behavior*, and Seymour W. Itzkoff's *The decline of intelligence in America*]. *New York Times Book Review*, pp. 3, 41, 45.

Carr, L. G. (1997). *"Color-blind" racism.* Thousand Oaks, CA: Sage.

Cohen, M. N. (1995). Anthropology and race: The bell curve phenomenon. *General Anthropology, 2*(1), 1–4.

Coon, C. S. (1950). *Races: A study of the problems of race formation in man.* Springfield, IL: CI Thomas.

Cryns, A. G. J. (1962). African intelligence: A critical survey of cross-cultural intelligence research in Africa south of the Sahara. *Journal of Social Psychology, 47*, 283–284.

Encyclopedia Britannica. (1997). Optics [cd version; EB/_3.htm#].

Fish, J. (1998). Politically correct red herring. *Anthropology Newsletter, 39*(6), 2.

Gould, S. J. (1994, November 28). Curveball. *The New Yorker*, 139–149.

Herrnstein, R. J., & Murray, C. (1994). *The bell curve: Intelligence and class structure in American life.* New York: The Free Press.

Hitchens, C. (1994, November 28). Minority report; intelligence and race. *The Nation, 259*(18), 640.

Inequity quotients. (1994, November 7). [Editorial]. *The Nation,* p. 517.

Lacayo, R. (1994). For whom the bell curves. *Time,* pp. 66–67.

Lévy-Bruhl, L. (1925). *How natives think.* (L. A. Clare, Trans.). London: G. Allen & Unwin.

Lieberman, L., & Jackson, F. L. C. (1995). Race and three models of human origin. *American Anthropologist, 97*(2), 231–242.

Lindfors, B. (Ed). (1997). *Conversations with Chinua Achebe.* Jackson: University Press of Mississippi.

Linton, R. (1959). *The tree of culture.* New York: Vintage Books.

Littlefield, A., Lieberman, L., & Reynolds, L. T. (1982). Redefining race: The potential demise of a concept in physical anthropology. *Current Anthropology, 23,* 641–655.

Mensh, E., & Mensh, H. (1991). The testers, South Africa, and the third world. In *The IQ mythology: Class, race, gender and inequality* (pp. 107–134). Carbondale: Southern Illinois University Press.

Nisbett, R. (1994, October 31). Blue genes. *The New Republic,* p. 15.

Reed, A., Jr. (1994a, December 15). Intellectual brown shirts. *The Progressive, 58*(12), 15–17.

Reed, A., Jr. (1994b, November 28). Looking backward. *The Nation, 259*(18), 654–662.

Shanklin, E. (1994). *Anthropology and race.* Belmont, CA: Wadsworth.

Shanklin, E. (1999). The profession of the color-blind: Sociocultural anthropology and racism in the 21st century. *American Anthropologist, 100*(3), 669–679.

Shapiro, H. (1952). Revised version of the UNESCO statement on race. *American Journal of Physical Anthropology, 10,* 363–368.

Shreeve, J. (1994, November). Terms of estrangement. *Discover, 15*(11), 57–102.

Tylor, E. B. (1958). Primitive culture (Vol. 2). New York.

Winant, H. (1997). The new international dynamics of race. In C. Hartman (Ed.), *Double exposure: Poverty and race in America* (pp. 45–54). Armonk, NY: Sharpe.

CHAPTER 10

Cultural Amplifiers of Intelligence: IQ and Minority Status in Cross-Cultural Perspective

John U. Ogbu

My overall objective in this chapter is to explain why Black Americans and similar minorities have lower IQ test scores than the dominant group in society. My explanation is based on two assumptions. One is that IQ test scores reflect culturally acquired skills and behaviors. The other is that there are different types of minority status with different implications for IQ test performance.

The chapter is divided into six parts. In the first part I consider conventional definitions of intelligence, propose an alternative definition, and argue that IQ test scores reflect a part of the adaptive intellectual skills in the ecocultural niche of the Western middle class. I distinguish several levels of analysis necessary to comprehend the nature and meaning of intelligence in cross-cultural perspective: (a) *cultural amplifiers* of intelligence or activities in the ecocultural niche that give rise to people's intellectual skills; (b) *cultural transmitters* of adaptive intellectual skills (i.e., the cultural agencies responsible for transmitting preexisting adaptive intellectual skills);

and (c) *the cultural formulae* or processes whereby the adaptive intellectual skills are transmitted and acquired.

Minority status is the subject of the next part. I discuss two major types of minorities in the United States, namely, immigrant or voluntary minorities and nonimmigrant or involuntary minorities. I explain why immigrant minorities do relatively well on IQ tests. Then in the next part I use Black Americans an example to explain why involuntary minorities, as a group, do not perform well on IQ tests. Two examples of involuntary minorities in Japan who also perform low on IQ tests are discussed. I then discuss the relation between epistemology and paradigms of the study of Black–White differences in IQ test scores and with that discussion respond to critiques of my approach. Although the chapter is not about policy or programs, I conclude with some observations about what could be done.

INTELLIGENCE IN CROSS-CULTURAL PERSPECTIVE

Conventional Definitions

Psychologists equate intelligence with IQ but do not agree about what intelligence or IQ means. Some (Jensen, 1969) say that IQ is a technical term used to label whatever intelligence tests test. Others believe that IQ reflects a "global ability to absorb complex information, or grasp and manipulate abstract concepts" (Travers, 1982, p. 235). Still other psychologists define IQ or intelligence as information processing; that is, how people interpret or process the information they receive (Kyllonen, 1994). One thing that some psychologists from the three persuasions agree on is that intelligence or IQ can be measured. So when they refer to intelligence, they mean IQ, which is what they measure. As Jensen (1969) put it, intelligence (i.e., IQ) is what intelligence tests test.

An Alternative Intelligence?

I propose an alternative definition of intelligence based partly on some speculations of Baumrind (1972) and Vernon (1969) and partly on the findings of cross-cultural researchers of the Piagetian and Vygotskian schools.[1]

From a cross-cultural or comparative perspective, intelligence is a cultural system of thought, a cultural or group repertoire of adaptive intellectual (or cognitive) skills. Let me explain with Vernon's distinction of three levels of intelligence: genotypic intelligence (Intelligence A), phenotypic intelligence (Intelligence B) and measured intelligence or IQ (Intelligence C). See Fig. 10.1.

Intelligence A, the genotype, is the innate capacity or potential (i.e., genetic endowment for intelligence) that individuals inherit from their parents. Intelligence A

---

[1]It is not necessary for these authors and researchers to agree with my interpretation of their work or for them to continue to maintain their earlier points of view. The important thing is that I find their ideas useful in formulating my own ideas on the problem.

determines the level of intellectual abilities possible for individuals under given conditions. Similarly, the genetic potential of a population, Intelligence A, determines the extent of the intellectual skills of its members. Intelligence A is a hypothetical construct that cannot be directly observed or measured by psychologists, behavioral geneticists, or anyone else. However, it can be inferred or estimated from behavior, such as from test scores (Jensen, 1994; Plomin, 1994; Vernon, 1969; see also Ogbu, 1978, 1994a, 1994b). Intelligence A is what Greenfield (1998) called *panhuman genotypic intelligence*. She defined it as the ability in all normal members of the human species to acquire competence in technology, linguistic communication, and social organization.

Intelligence B, the phenotype, is the observable behavioral manifestation of intelligence. It refers to everyday observed behaviors of individuals considered intelligent or not intelligent by members of their population. The intelligent behaviors reflect the adaptive repertoire of intellectual or cognitive skills in a population.

Intelligence B is a product of both genetic potential (Intelligence A or nature) and environment. By environment I mean the cultural activities in the ecocultural niche of a population that require and enhance cognitive or intellectual skills in the population. It is not the environment as used in conventional environmental theory of IQ. Intelligence B is often different for different populations partly because the cultural activities that amplify it may be different and partly because it is culturally defined. For

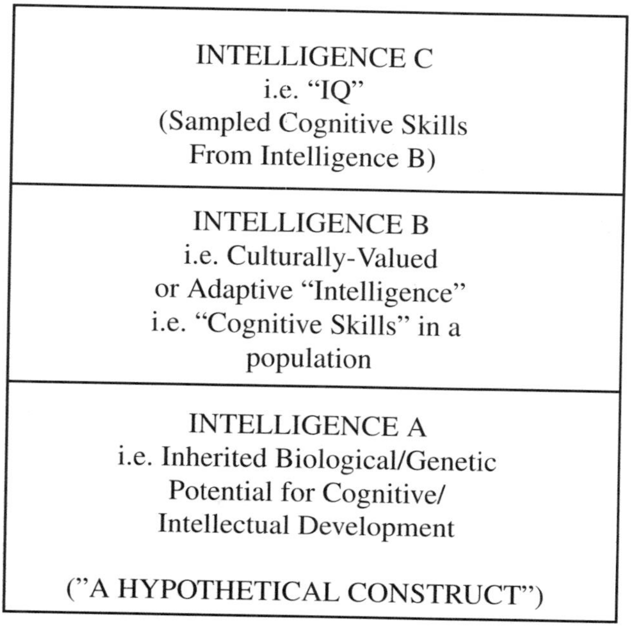

FIG. 10.1.   Intelligences A, B, and C.

example, the kinds of behaviors considered intelligent, required, and valued in the ecological niche of White middle-class Americans are to large degree different from behaviors considered intelligent, required, and valued in the ecocultural niche of Igbo farmers of Nigeria. However, the extent and form of expression of Intelligence B in any population are determined by the same biological potential or Intelligence A, the panhuman genotype.

On the basis of my own experience, born to nonliterate parents in an Igbo village and now a professor at a major U.S. university, I agree with Vernon that Intelligence B is not fixed. It changes when the ecocultural niche of an individual or a population changes. My Intelligence B changed when I moved from my Igbo village to be educated at a university in the United States. My experience is not unique; I have observed countless others in similar and varying situations. Intelligence B of a population changes, for example, when its members begin to participate in formal schooling. What is important to bear in mind is that any normal individuals and a whole population can acquire any intellectual skills because they possess the panhuman genotype.

Intelligence C, the IQ test scores or measured intelligence, refers to the behavioral manifestation of intellectual skills selected from the adaptive intellectual skills in the ecocultural niche of the White middle class. The selected skills are a part of Intelligence B of the White middle class. Thus, one difference between IQ and intelligence B is that IQ is only a part of Intelligence B. IQ is not synonymous with intelligence. IQ is also different from intelligence in another way. The intellectual skills included in IQ tests are selected for specific purposes, such as to predict academic achievement or job performance.

CULTURAL AMPLIFIERS OF INTELLIGENCE

Cultural Amplifiers

What I call *cultural amplifiers* of intelligence are those activities or tasks in an ecocultural niche that require and enhance intellectual skills.[2] The activities are cultural because they are things people do as a way of life in their ecocultural niche; they are amplifiers of intelligence because they require, stimulate, increase, or expand the quantity, quality, and cultural values of adaptive intellectual skills (see Fig. 10.2). Cultural amplifiers in the Western middle-class ecocultural niche include handling much complex technology, participating in and managing a large-scale economy, bureaucratic roles, and urban life. These cultural activities require and enhance intellectual skills that include abstract thinking, conceptualization, grasping relations, and sym-

---

[2]Previously I used the terms *effective environment* (Ogbu, 1981a) or *macro-environment, ecological niche* (Ogbu, 1994a, 1994b) for the wider societal environment where activities or cultural tasks generated the cognitive problems for members of a population. In this chapter I have chosen to use the concept of *ecocultural niche* from Greenfield's (1998) work on the problem of culture and cognitive skills, as a better descriptive term.

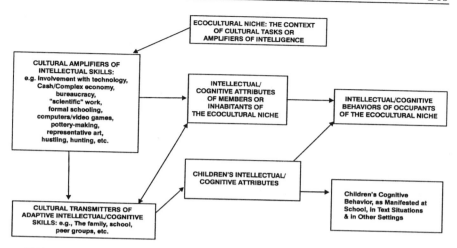

FIG. 10.2.   Cultural amplifiers of intellectual skills. Source: John U. Ogbu (1978). Miority *Education and Caste: The American System in Cross-Cultural Perspective* (p. 35). New York: Academic Press. (Originally adapted from B. B. Whiting (Ed.), 1963, *Studies of Child Rearing*, (p. 5). New York: Wiley.

bolic thinking; these skills eventually permeate other aspects of life (Vernon, 1969). Other examples of cultural amplifiers of specific intellectual skills are pottery-making, trading, formal schooling, working with computers, and playing video games.

Pottery Making and Conservation Skills.   Pottery making is a cultural task that amplifies the skills of manipulating matter, such as clay materials of different sizes and weights. In a comparative study in Mexico, researchers found that children from pottery-making villages were superior in conservation of matter to children from other villages (Price-Williams, 1961; Price-Williams, Gordon, & Ramirez, 1969).

Hunting-Gathering and Spatial and Perceptual Skills.   Hunting and gathering are cultural activities that demand and enhance perceptual and spatial skills. As a result, hunters and gatherers are good at such skills, value them and emphasize them in raising their children. Thus, Dasen (1974) found that Australian Aborigine children appeared to develop spatial concepts before logico-mathematical concepts, in contrast to White Australian children.

Commerce and Mathematical Skills.   One may expect that mathematical skills are usually more prevalent and valued in a culture whose economy is based on commerce rather than in a farming culture. This was found to be the case in a comparative study of a merchant population (the Dioula) and an agricultural people (the

Baoule) in West Africa (Posner, 1982; Saxe & Dioula, 1983). Dioula culture provided children with many opportunities to acquire these skills. When tested, Dioula children who had no Western-type schooling were superior to similar Baoule children in mathematical skills.

Schooling and Cognitive Skills.   Formal schooling changes how members of a population remember, improves their ability to reason "logically" (in the Western sense), and alters how they use language (Cole & Scribner, 1974; Scribner & Cole, 1973; Stevenson, 1982). These suggestions seem reasonable because I have observed differences in these intellectual skills of my fellow Igbo villagers who have attended Western-type schools compared to other villagers who have not. The way schooling influences intellectual skills is described later.

Cultural Transmitters of Adaptive Intellectual Skills

Cultural transmitters are the societal institutions responsible for transmitting the preexisting adaptive skills to children. These societal institutions include the family, school, peer groups, and other agencies performing this function. The cultural transmitters themselves do not originate the intellectual skills children acquire; they merely transmit those in existence.

Cultural Formulae or How Cultural Transmission Works

Another necessary distinction is between cultural transmitters and the formula or process by which preexisting adaptive intellectual skills are transmitted and children acquire them. That is, I suggest that we treat the family, schools, and so on as cultural institutions for transmitting adaptive skills separate from the way they function: the process of transmission and acquisition. The process of transmission and acquisition of preexisting intellectual skills lies in the formulae that have evolved in the history of a population to be used by the cultural transmitters for these purposes. The formulae are not the same in all populations. A comparative study may show that two populations use different formulae to transmit the same intellectual skills. For example, Australian Aborigines and White Australians may use different formulae to transmit perceptual and spatial skills. One can also imagine that the formulae used by the Dioula and White middle-class Americans to transmit mathematical knowledge and skills will be different. Furthermore, a comparative study may reveal that similar cultural transmitters in two populations differ in using the same formulae (e.g., childrearing practices) to transmit the same intellectual skills. We see this later when discussing the childrearing practices of White middle-class American and Chinese families in Hong Kong. The important thing to bear in mind in the study of the process of development is that we are dealing with how cultural transmitters transmit and how children acquire the preexisting adaptive intellectual skills of their ecocultural niche. There are usually many formulae in a given ecocultural niche for this purpose (see Ogbu, 1979, 1981a, 1982). The following section provides three examples of the formulae.

Family Childrearing Practices.   Family childrearing practices constitute one formula for transmitting adaptive intellectual skills to children. Differences among populations in this formula can be seen by comparing the childrearing practices of White middle-class Americans with those of Chinese families in Hong Kong. U.S. researchers often conclude that children whose parents emphasize *self-direction* (responsibility, consideration of others, curiosity) perform better on IQ tests than children whose parents emphasize *conformity* (obedience, neatness, good manners, and appropriate sex-role behaviors; (Sameroff, Seifer, Baldwin, & Baldwin, 1993). In contrast, Chinese parents in Hong Kong stress social control, are intolerant of deviancy, and pressure their children to conform. They also stress impulse control in early childhood and discourage boisterous and high verbal behaviors. Yet, Chinese children score as high as White American children on IQ tests and score higher than White American children on math tests (Ho, 1994).

Schooling.   Another cultural formula for transmitting adaptive intellectual skills is formal schooling. The process of transmission and acquisition through schooling is best observed where schooling is newly introduced. Schooling acts on people's Intelligence A to expand and change their Intelligence B. An important feature of this formula is an increased role for language. Teaching and learning before the advent of schooling are primarily by demonstration and observation. With schooling come explicit verbal formulations of what is to be learned and how it is to be learned. The linguistic formulations and other features of school teaching and learning have important cognitive consequences described by Scribner and Cole (1973) and summarized here:

1. *Enhanced language skills*: Explicit linguistic formulations that make it possible for learning to proceed from verbal description to empirical referents have several cognitive consequences. First, the learner develops a scientific approach to learning; that is, the student learns to understand and accept generalized rules and verbal definitions of problems. He or she learns to start with the verbal definition of a problem and proceed to find the answer. Second, the student acquires competence in using language to describe behavior, classify, and describe operations and rules for solution to problems. Finally, the student acquires the ability to describe things and situations more accurately.

2. *Ability to learn out of context*: Formal schooling enhances people's ability for decontextualized learning. People develop an ability for decontextualized learning when they learn to understand the meaning or significance of materials or ideas in a different way than in their everyday, natural, or cultural context. An example is learning to manipulate numbers qua numbers.

3. *Acquisition of new symbols for learning*: Students acquire symbol systems as tools for learning (e.g., using numbers to learn math). They also learn infor-

mation processing as instrumental techniques for further learning (e.g., how to read, how to write, how to figure). These techniques mediate future learning.

4. *Acquisition of a new learning system*: Students acquire a new learning system or learning ability, namely, *learning to learn*. This is the ability to apply the same solution to different problems. The ability to apply a common operation to many different tasks is probably one of the reasons why people who have attended school can generalize rules and operations to several problems when taking IQ tests.

Video Games and Nonverbal Cognitive Skills.   Games and play constitute another formula for the development of children's adaptive intellectual skills. Greenfield (1998) presented several examples from experimental studies and made a convincing case that video games, films, and computers influence perceptual and spatial skills in the contemporary United States. Video games require and enhance the development of "skills in visual–spatial representation and iconic imagery, and these are important skills for performance in the nonverbal portions of IQ tests" (p. 99). She illustrated the effects of video games on perceptual and spatial skills with studies of Tetris, a puzzle game. This game involves putting together pieces of puzzle that fall from the top of a computer screen. In one study it was found that, after playing this game for 6 hours, participants' performances "on several paper-and-pencil tests that are similar to nonverbal IQ measures" (p. 92) were enhanced. She suggested that playing Tetris would also enhance performance on block design tests, included in the Wechsler Intelligence Scales for adults and children and the Stanford–Binet children's intelligence scale, because they require skills in assembling puzzles similar to the skills enhanced by Tetris.

A cross-cultural study of cultural amplifiers of intelligence and the formulae for their transmission and acquisition leads to some conclusions. First, prevalent intellectual skills are not the same in all populations, but depend on the cultural amplifiers in the ecocultural niche. Second, normal members of all human populations can acquire new intellectual skills, including those of the Western middle class, because they have the Intelligence A (panhuman genotypic ability) to do so. This is what happens when members of a population begin to participate in Western-type schooling.

Ecocultural Context of IQ Tests

IQ tests measure intellectual skills adaptive for and valued by White middle-class Americans. Psychologists brought up in the White middle-class ecocultural niche acquire these skills, valued in that niche. When they make up IQ tests they include verbal or nonverbal intellectual problems from the White middle-class ecocultural niche that require White middle-class knowledge to solve. The questions or tasks they use to elicit the intellectual skills in IQ tests are those that are familiar to the Western middle class. They are knowledge or skills that have become an ingrained part of the thinking of the White middle class. The psychologists who design the tests are probably not aware of this; nevertheless that is the case.

Greenfield (1998) illustrated the culture-specific nature of the knowledge for solving even nonverbal tasks on the IQ tests with an item from the Guilford–Zimmermann Aptitude Survey. This nonverbal task measures not only the spatial ability of the test taker but also his or her ability to shift perspective. According to Greenfield, "the test-taker is first asked to identify an upside-down alarm clock: second, to rotate it mentally a quarter turn to the right, before matching the resulting visual perspective with one of five different drawings" (p. 110). Greenfield concluded that this task is "extremely culture-specific." She continued:

> Note that it requires knowledge of what the back of an alarm clock looks like. It also requires knowledge of the arrow as a visual symbol as well as even more specific knowledge that the arrow as portrayed does not symbolize a horizontal direction on a flat plane but rather represents rotation in the third dimension. (pp. 110–111)

A number of cross-cultural researchers have pointed out that it is erroneous for those who design or use IQ tests to assume that they are measuring universal human abilities and that performance on the tests is determined by genes or a narrowly defined environment, such as the home. On the other hand, as with Intelligence B, all normal individuals in any human population can acquire the intellectual skills that are measured in IQ tests because they have the panhuman genotype (Cole & Cole, 1993; Greenfield, 1998; Ogbu, 1978; Vernon, 1969).

MINORITY STATUS AND IQ

Minority Status, Not Race, Causes Low IQ Test Scores

One conclusion from cross-cultural research is that differences in IQ test scores are not caused by racial differences. The gap also exists where there are no racial differences. Thus we find them in IQ when we compare pairs of groups belonging to the same "race": Hasidic Jews and Yeshiva Jews in New York, Bedouin Arabs and urban Arabs in the Middle East (Dennis, 1970), Oriental Jews and the Ashkenazi Jews in Israel (Ortar 1967); Burakumin and Ippan in Japan (DeVos, 1973; Osaka Prefecture, 1979), and Koreans and Ippans in Japan (DeVos, 1973).

IQ Tests and Minority Status

Another conclusion from cross-cultural research is that IQ test scores seem to depend on minority status. IQ tests measure intellectual skills adaptive for and valued by White middle-class Americans. As a result, the tests inevitably discriminate against all minorities. Yet, some minorities do well on these IQ tests and others do not. Why?

Minority Types And IQ Test Performance

There are different types of minority status with different implications for IQ test performance. The two major types I wish to discuss are immigrant or voluntary minorities and nonimmigrant or involuntary minorities. The distinction between voluntary and involuntary minorities is not based on race. Thus, Afro-Caribbeans, Asians, Jews, and Latinos are voluntary minorities; Black Americans, Chicanos, Native Americans, and native Hawaiians are involuntary minorities. Voluntary or involuntary minority status is determined by history—the way a group became a minority in the United States (Ogbu & Simons, 1998).

Voluntary or immigrant minorities are people who have come to the United States by choice because they expected better opportunities (better jobs, more political freedom, etc.) than they had in their homelands or place of origin. People in this category may be different from one another in "race" or ethnicity, religion, or language. Voluntary minorities in the United States include immigrants from Africa, the Caribbean, China, India, Japan, Korea, Mexico, the Philippines and South America. The important thing to bear in mind is that the people classified as voluntary minorities chose to move more or less permanently to and become minorities in the United States because they expected a better future. Immigrants do not interpret their presence in the United States as forced on them by White Americans.

Why Voluntary Minorities Have Higher Test Scores

Immigrant minorities in the United States generally do well on IQ tests (Suzuki & Gutkin, 1994a; Vernon, 1982; Vraniak 1994). I suggest the following reasons for their good performance.

Preemigration Experience.   Some minorities do well because prior to emigration they participated in cultural tasks requiring the skills used in IQ tests.

Cognitive Acculturation.   Some do well because they acquired the intellectual skills and know-how when they began to participate in White middle-class cultural tasks, in school and the economy.

History and Incentive Motivation.   Immigrant minorities are strongly motivated to maximize their performance on IQ tests, other standardized tests, and in school in general by three factors. The first is *preemigration expectation*. The immigrants believe that high test scores and school success are necessary to achieve the goal of their emigration. Their strong motivation is a product of their history. The immigrants chose to become minorities with the belief that they would become successful in the United States by getting a good education. They tend to equate a good education with good classroom grades and high scores on IQ and other standardized tests. The second factor is a *positive frame of reference*. The immigrants are motivated to maximize their test scores and school performance by their positive dual frame of reference. The immigrants see their chances of becoming successful or becoming somebody through education (test scores) as better in the United States than back home. Furthermore, the immigrants have an option to reemigrate or return to their homeland if things do not work out in the United States. The immigrant who reemigrates can still benefit from his or her American education, which is often considered better than the education back home. The third factor is the *folk theory of getting ahead in the United States*. The immigrants not only believe that their chances of success are better in the United States than back home; they also believe that the key to success in the United States is a good education. As already noted, they usually equate this education with good grades and high test scores, including high IQ test scores. Immigrants complain about employment discrimination, but they more or less think that it is a temporary problem that they can overcome through education and hard work, learning to speak good English, and having their children become citizens (Ogbu 1998).

Pragmatic Trust.   The test performance of the immigrants is also enhanced by the pragmatic trust they adopt toward U.S. schools and White people who control them. Immigrant minorities do not necessarily think that U.S. school personnel like them. However, they think of teachers and other school personnel as useful experts who can provide them with the skills and knowledge they need to succeed in the United States. They rarely question school authority, the curriculum, language, or IQ and other standardized tests.

Willingness and Ability to Accommodate.   Immigrants are willing to accommodate or adopt White ways of behaving and talking because they are aware that the cultural and language differences they encounter are partly due to their foreign cultures and languages. Before they emigrated they expected to learn new ways of behaving and talking. Once they arrive, they believe that this is necessary to succeed. The immigrants are able to accommodate because the differences between their ways and the White ways are not oppositional, as the differences predated emigration and they did not emerge under oppression. Because they are nonoppositional, the immigrants do not imagine that accommodating to "White ways" or "White language" threatens their own ways and language. Rather, they consider learning the White ways, like speaking good English, as acquiring new and necessary instrumental skills. Therefore, they are willing to do whatever is necessary to succeed or get high test scores (Ogbu 1991, 1994b; Ogbu & Simons, 1998).

Involuntary Minorities

Involuntary minorities are people who are a part of the United States because they were conquered, colonized, or enslaved. They have been made a part of the U.S. society permanently against their will. Involuntary minorities may differ from one another in race, ethnicity, religion, or language. Involuntary minorities in the United States include Native Americans and Alaskan Natives, native Hawaiians, Black Americans, early Mexicans in the Southwest, and Puerto Ricans. The important thing is that these minorities did not choose but were forced against their will to become part of U.S. society.

Involuntary minorities possess the panhuman genotype, the ability to acquire the intellectual skills used in the IQ tests. However, as a group, they experience greater difficulty than the immigrants and have low IQ test scores (Brand, 1996; Jensen, 1994; Suzuki & Gutkin, 1994b; Valencia & Aburto, 1991). The reasons for the greater difficulty and low IQ test scores include (a) a longer history of mistreatment by White Americans, (b) an absence of incentive and motivational factors that help the immigrants, and (c) the ways they as involuntary minorities respond to their mistreatment. I use the case of Black Americans to illustrate the difficulties of involuntary minorities.

BLACK AMERICANS, INVOLUNTARY MINORITY STATUS, AND IQ

Black Americans score low on IQ tests because of (a) mistreatment by White Americans, (b) lack of historically induced incentive motivation, and (c) their responses to involuntary minority status.

Societal Treatment and Low IQ Test Scores

I discuss four types of White mistreatment that affect IQ test scores of Black Americans: (a) exclusion from cultural amplifiers of White middle-class intellectual skills; (b) confinement to segregated and inferior education; (c) job ceilings; and (d) expressive discrimination.

Exclusion From Cultural Amplifiers.   Jensen (1972) reported to a U.S. Senate Committee that, unlike other ethnic groups, Black Americans had not achieved their expected representation in occupations requiring the intellectual skills of the White middle class. His explanation was that Blacks lack the adequate genetic endowment (i.e., the panhuman genotype) for such mental abilities. I will discuss Jensen's explanation in detail later. Suffice it here to note, with respect to cultural amplifiers of intelligence, that the problem with Jensen's explanation is threefold. First, it erroneously assumes that the passage of the legislation to eliminate employment barriers immediately ended the barriers in practice (see Carnoy, 1994). Second, it fails to consider the length of time it would take Blacks to "catch up" with Whites because of generations of exclusion as a group from White middle class education and occupations. Third, it fails to consider the cognitive impacts of excluding generations of Black Americans from education and occupations that serve as amplifiers of middle-class intellectual skills.

Segregated and Inferior Education.   For generations after slavery, Blacks were relegated to segregated and inferior education. The inferior schooling enhanced for Blacks the intellectual skills required in those portions of the IQ tests that Jensen labeled as Level 2 intelligence.

Job Ceiling.   Before the mid-1960s, Blacks were largely relegated to menial jobs by a job ceiling. This had the same effects as relegation to inferior and segregated education.

Expressive Discrimination: Cultural, Linguistic and Intellectual Denigration.   Expressive discrimination includes (a) White Americans' belief that Black Americans are inferior to them in culture, language, and intelligence; and (b) White refusal to acknowledge and reward Black intellectual and other accomplishments. These mistreatments have adverse effects on Black performance on IQ tests partly because Blacks internalize the White beliefs. Later I describe the perceptions of this belief and their impact on attitudes toward IQ tests within the Black community. Here I want to present data to support the allegations by Blacks that White Americans claim that to be superior and that their behaviors and speech are correct or proper whereas Black behavior and speech are incorrect.

Johnson (1939/1969) provided one of the earliest detailed summaries of the negative portrayal of Blacks by White authors. A few years later, Myrdal (1944) gave an even more elaborate account of the denigration of Blacks by "ordinary White Americans," including the White belief about the "in-born (and) indelible inferiority" (p. 100) of Blacks. Others more recently have also written about the historical existence of the same problem (Fredrickson, 1971; Pieterse, 1992). These beliefs are reflected in the way Whites treat Blacks in general, in White jokes, and in their oral and written stories about Blacks, as well as in their scientific studies. The belief that Blacks are inferior arouses aversions that result in another denigrating belief, namely, that Black Americans are unassimilable. Contrary to contemporary misinterpretation of the concept of *assimilation*, White Americans do not mean that Black people cannot acquire the education, economic status, and lifestyle of the White middle class. What White Americans mean is that it is not desirable to assimilate or accept Blacks, or their mixed offspring as a part of White people because Blacks belong to an inferior race. It is largely for this reason, not simply for economic gains, that Whites instituted residential and social segregation against Blacks. Residential and social segregation was (and is) an attempt to "quarantine what is evil, shameful and feared in society" (Myrdal, 1944, p. 100).

Many White Americans no longer believe or openly admit that Blacks are inferior to Whites but the residue of the beliefs remains. A poll conducted by *Newsweek* in 1978 found that one quarter of the White respondents (25%) still believed that Blacks were less intelligent than Whites, and about 15% thought that they were inferior to White people ("How Whites Think About Blacks," 1979; see also Campbell, 1971).

The publication of *The Bell Curve* by Herrnstein and Murray (1994) is a reminder that beliefs in the inferiority of Blacks still exist even in White scientific minds. The belief that Blacks are intellectually inferior is used to rationalize their exclusion from desirable jobs and positions in the larger society.

Associated with the beliefs that Blacks are intellectually inferior is White people's refusal or reluctance to recognize intellectual and other accomplishments by Blacks. Myrdal (1944) suggested that it would make White people uncomfortable to acknowledge Black accomplishments. I have documented in my research in the United States during the past 30 years or so instances of White people's refusal to recognize Black accomplishments; instead, they sometimes attributed Black accomplishments to other Whites. For example, during my research in Stockton, California (1968–1970) there were occasions when exemplary work by Black craftsmen was reported in the local newspaper, the *Stockton Record*, to have been done by White craftsmen. This kind of treatment in Stockton was first brought to my attention by a high school student who was present during an interview with his mother (Ogbu 1989). I later found several examples when I examined documents presented at public hearings and other articles in the *Stockton Record*.

Expressive discrimination is not limited to lower class Blacks. It exists in schools and colleges, as I show from interviews with middle-class Blacks. Writing in the case of professional Blacks, Cose (1993) suggested that racism is sustained against middle-class Blacks by the fear of White people that justifies negative stereotypes of Blacks. Consciously or unconsciously, the beliefs lead Whites to treat professional and middle-class Blacks as inferior. Expressive discrimination generates self-doubts and frustrations that could affect the mood of Blacks in test-taking situations.

Black Responses and the Low IQ Test Scores: History and Absence of Incentive Motivation

Prior to being forced into minority status, Blacks did not expect to become successful in life by getting White education or high IQ test scores. Blacks do not have the "back home" situation to compare to, as immigrants do. They compare their situation to that of White Americans and usually conclude that they are worse off than White people because of discrimination. Furthermore, they lack the opportunity to benefit else-where from their American education if things do not work out for them in the United States. Black Americans wish they could get ahead in the United States through high test scores and good education; however, as we shall see later, they know from individual and group experience that they cannot. They see little or no connection between doing well on IQ tests and job opportunities and other social benefits. This situation has existed for so long that they have come to perceive the barriers as more or less institutionalized and permanent. Thus, unlike the immigrants, they are not sure that education is the key to success in the United States. For these reasons there is no strong motivation to perform well on the IQ tests.

The Problem of Change

The ecocultural niche to which generations of Blacks were confined did not provide them with the chance to develop the intellectual skills for performing like Whites on IQ tests. However, some Blacks were involved within their segregated ecological niche with amplifiers of intellectual skills similar to those of the White middle class. For example, some Blacks held professional jobs in segregated educational and health institutions. Some others, such as preachers and hustlers, also engaged in activities that require and enhance forms of operational intelligence or smartness similar to the intellectual skills of the White middle class. However, it does not appear that their superior intellectual skills or smartness serve to raise their IQ test scores. Current studies suggest that, as a group, Blacks still score 1 SD lower than White Americans on IQ tests. Furthermore, "when Blacks and White groups are matched for education, socioeconomic status (SES), and residence, differences in intelligence test scores are only slightly reduced" (Gordon & Bhattacharya, 1994, p. 896; see also Jensen, 1994).

It appears, then, that involvement in activities requiring and enhancing intellectual skills similar to those of White people or even possessing such intellectual skills does not necessarily mean that Blacks will perform like their White counterparts on IQ tests. Many preachers, hustlers, and other "smart" Black people probably do poorly on IQ tests and drop out of school. As some psychologists have observed, the scores Black children obtain on IQ tests like the Wechsler Intelligence Scale for Children (Wechsler, 1991) do not represent their true intellectual ability or the best they can do (Naiven, Hoffmann, & Bierbryer, 1969, cited in Dreger, 1973). Dreger (1973) added that this view is

In line with the experience of many psychologists who have dealt with youngsters, especially from deprived Black culture. In non-test situations (psychologists) observe the youngster communicating with his peers, solving problems, and utilizing conceptualizations that they are accustomed to associate with IQ of a Binet type ten to fifteen points higher than the youngster actually gets on a formal test. (p. 207)

I concur with this interpretation based on my own observations of Black youngsters in the community and my discussions with teachers, parents, students, and other adults in the Black community. My conclusion is that the IQ test scores of Black Americans do not reflect their true ability or the best they can do. In addition to the reasons for lack of historically derived incentive motivation discussed earlier, I now offer three reasons why Blacks who are as intelligent or as smart as their White peers do not necessarily perform like them or show their "smartness" when taking IQ tests. I focus on the people's perceptions of their experience with IQ test scores rather than with education in general. What I want to emphasize is the importance of the cultural meaning of IQ tests, not the meaning assigned to them by the psychologist.

How the Black Response Affects IQ Test Scores

The Missing Link: IQ Test Performance and Getting Ahead.   Black Americans did not become minorities in the United States with the expectation that they would have to get high test scores on IQ or other tests to become successful in life. Furthermore, for many generations after they became wage earners Blacks did not experience any real connection between how well they did on IQ tests and their ability to get good jobs, earn decent wages, achieve social recognition, and gain other benefits. This lack of connection between performance on IQ tests and self-betterment continues today in some segments of the Black population.

From my ethnographic research in the Black community, it seems that the individual and collective experience of not getting ahead through IQ test scores has not fostered the motivation to strive for the highest test scores. It has also not enhanced good performance on IQ tests as a cultural value. In fact, it has sometimes resulted in a rejection of the test scores as a criterion for employment or school admission. Of course, when questioned Blacks say that good test scores and school credentials are important for getting ahead in the United States. However, because of their experience, they also believe that for them, Black Americans, test scores and school credentials are not sufficient; at least, they are not sure. Some Blacks even interpret the test scores as a "White-made" rule unfair to Black people. Some also suspect that IQ tests are designed to keep Black people from getting ahead. Partly for these reasons, they attack test requirements for hiring and promotion and try to change them, rather than work to meet them.

The following cases from my ethnographic research in the community show that Black Americans see a dismal connection between their performance on IQ tests and their chances to get ahead. The first incident was a dispute over the use of IQ test scores in hiring civil employees in Stockton, California.

At several city council meetings in 1969, Blacks and Mexican Americans complained that they were systematically excluded from city jobs. Specifically, they complained that, by requiring candidates for hiring or promotion to pass biased IQ tests, the city effectively excluded them. They noted that in 1969 only 30 out of 886 city employees were Black and just about the same number were Mexican Americans because of the tests.

Because of repeated allegations, the city council set up a workshop in equality to study the problem. Verbal and written presentations at the workshop indicated that the city charter stipulated in 1935 that candidates could be tested for physical or mental abilities, but the tests should be job related. The mental or IQ test was the revised Army Alpha Test. Those wishing to take the test for consideration for civil service positions were expected to have attained a level of formal education required for the position. To be interviewed for the position a person had to score at least 95 points on the IQ test. By 1969 these requirements had been modified: The Army Alpha had been replaced with another test; only the written version was administered; candidates needed to obtain 70 points on each part of the examination and on the overall test to be eligible for interview; and war veterans were eligible for interview with scores of 60 to 65 points. In spite of the lowered minimum test scores, few Blacks made the interview list or were employed by the city for positions above manual labor.

Whites and Blacks had different views about using IQ test scores for hiring and promotions and different explanations for low test scores of minorities. City officials (who were White) justified using the test scores by saying that they provided an objective way to select the best qualified people for city jobs, placed civil service above politics, and ensured high standards in city civil service. City officials explained that Blacks and Mexican Americans scored lower than Whites on the test because of their disadvantaged cultural and family background. The officials promised to establish remedial programs to prepare minorities to get higher scores on the tests.

Blacks and Mexican Americans insisted that the test was culturally biased and the required minimum test score to become eligible for interviews excluded the average resident from city jobs. They pointed out that minorities who failed the test obtained and performed well at similar jobs in the private sector. Finally, they alleged that both city and county officials used prisoners (many of them minorities) who had not taken or passed the civil service tests to do some city jobs that minorities as ordinary citizens were denied because they failed the IQ tests.

In my subsequent interviews in the community, there seemed to be a general feeling that IQ tests for civil service jobs were used to exclude Blacks. Furthermore, getting high scores on the test did not guarantee employment because Black candidates generally failed the oral interviews. Knowing that one would fail the oral interview did not encourage people to try harder on the written test. The following informant, a school counselor, described the feeling of many Blacks in Stockton about the civil service examinations:

> The civil service test consists of a written IQ test, … a written examination area test, and it consists of an oral interview test. Now, unless they have changed it, the oral interview counts as much as the written. So, if three people would go down and take the test, see, you go take the IQ examination, the written examination, the oral examination. You pass 'em in that order. Now, we have eliminated and weeded out up to the oral examination; now 4 or 5 people go in for this oral examination. You're sitting down in front of 5 other, … White middle class people for your oral examination. How would you feel? Would you feel that you would be on equal terms as the lily White boy that went up there and sit down in front of these five people for an oral examination? And that oral examination is counting as much as the written examination. You're gonna tell me that in the history of Stockton not one Black man has ever qualified and passed a fireman's examination. A Black man don't qualify on a fireman's test? Hell! I can't take a water hose and put out a fire. Not one has ever passed a fireman's test, oral examination!!

Based on their own experience, some Black parents did not believe that taking or passing the IQ tests helped Black people get ahead. Here is how one parent described her experience with an IQ test for employment. She believed the test was intended to screen out Blacks:

> In my case they didn't allow me the opportunity. I went to the employment office (and) I passed this test. I made eighty, the man (told me) when I came downstairs. He said, "Oh, you didn't make it," he says, "you just made eighty." So, what is the passing mark? They didn't tell me. He told me, he said, "You made eighty, but you didn't pass it." Well, I went on and forgot it because, see, this White man had told me this. I then began to think about this. I said, "Eighty?" And the more I thought about (it). Then one day I decided I would ask one of the men in the employment office. He said, "You passed that test." He told me I passed but I didn't get no job. Because at that time they only hired a White person, the Mexican and two or more Negroes to make it look good and that was all .... This was only a gimmick to keep the Negro out of a job and he didn't really know what was really going on. That is one reason I didn't believe in this paper business when you go and look for a job.

The next account, from a Mexican American parent in the same neighborhood, embodies the perceptions and feelings of many Black and Mexican American residents. This parent said that he got a high score on the IQ test for a civil service job but was not hired. As one can infer from the interview excerpt, this parent was very smart and learned: He studied Greek, Latin, Spanish, and so forth. Like other minorities in his neighborhood, he felt that it is not knowledge and qualifications (including IQ test scores) that really count but whether an applicant is White:

> This was about 1950–51. There was about 40 or 50 people (who) took the test. It was pretty easy for me because I always did like to study and read. At that time I had just completed four years of Spanish, two years of Greek; just recently, four years of Latin. So, consequently even though I can't use a word because I don't really mingle with people who use words such as absolute.... I can comprehend just about everything I read. At that time the stuff was fresh in my mind. So they had this how much you can retain. Say that you read a paragraph and they ask you questions. Well, I remember everything. Then they gave you a vocabulary test. Well, I know a lot of the roots, so consequently, I knew Spanish before I ever took this stuff, I always studied pretty good and due to all the translations I had in Latin; well, I beat them all, see. I got a real nice score on that; I hardly missed anything. So I went to the oral, this oral test. They thought I was Japanese. They asked me why I wanted the job. Well, I said it sounds like it pays pretty good.... They asked me another question, what my plans were and all that and they were going to call me back in a couple of weeks. It never happened .... So, subsequently, I know who got the job and she ... barely passed. *So it isn't your knowledge that does it, it's your presence.*

Over the years I have interviewed many Black parents and other adults who described similar experiences of their own, of their friends, or their relatives. Some parents would report getting high scores in civil service IQ tests or other employment tests, but they were not hired. Others claimed that apprenticeship examinations in their cities were used to exclude Blacks, written tests were used to screen out Blacks, and test score cutoffs were used to deny Blacks promotions on the job. Some informants gave examples of White people who were hired or promoted without taking IQ or employment tests. Children were often present during my interviews. Older children joined in the discussions of Black experiences with tests in school and for employment. They, too, reported on their own experiences with unfair tests and grading.

One incident I recorded in Los Angeles in 1969 serves as an example of the perception of a White-made criterion as a screening device. This concerns the use of standard English. The incident was reported by one of my teachers during a summer workshop on Black history and culture at the University of California at Los Angeles. My teacher was an accomplished actress. In the late 1960s she was helping Black youths to enroll in apprenticeship programs for positions as technicians in the Hollywood movie industry. She reported that on one occasion, one of the Black applicants was rejected after an oral interview because she did not speak standard English. However, my teacher and other Blacks had a different interpretation of the rejection: They said it was discrimination. My teacher noted that before the 1960s there were Blacks who spoke "perfect standard English" but could not get jobs in Hollywood and could not rent or buy homes in Westwood. She said that the problem was not that Black people did not speak like White people; rather, it was that even when they spoke like White people, they were still denied equal opportunity for employment.

In the experience and perception of the people in the community, the lack of connection between good performance on IQ tests and education on the one hand, and getting ahead, on the other, is not entirely a matter of history. In 1996 I recorded several incidents involving Black professionals—lawyers, doctors, and school administrators—who claimed they could not get jobs or were not paid appropriate salaries in spite of their qualifications; they did not have the same chance as their White peers (see also Benjamin, 1991; Dill, 1982; A. Fashokun, personal communication, January 1996; Matusow, 1989).

As a result of their experience with IQ testing it appears that many Black Americans I studied in Stockton and elsewhere do not see good performance on IQ tests and, indeed, on almost all other tests given by White people, as helping them get good jobs or get ahead. One also gains the impression from interviews and discussions with Black students, parents, and other members of the Black community that they have an ambivalent attitude about the instrumental value of the tests. In this situation it is difficult to imagine that parents encourage their children to maximize their IQ test scores. Some school counselors have reported that students do not seem to be aware of the significance of the tests and so do not try to maximize their performance. Some school counselors even reported that some Black students fall asleep during group IQ tests or other standardized tests.

Internalization of White Beliefs About Black Intelligence.   White beliefs that Black Americans are intellectually inferior are all too well known among Blacks. The beliefs have also become internalized or an ingrained part of the thinking of many Blacks. Evidence of the internalization shows up explicitly or implicitly during formal and informal interviews with Black school personnel, students, parents, and others. One school counselor, for example, told me that White intellectual denigration of Blacks was prevalent in the school district where he worked just as it was in the college he attended in Arizona:

> If a kid is doing any work (in this school district), he gets a C. If he does not do enough work he gets a C. And this isn't only found in elementary school. It's found in the junior and (senior) high schools. It's even found in our colleges. When I went to Arizona State, there were many teachers that said, "The most a Black person can get in my class is a C. I don't care what kind of work you do." … You know, the thing is, why it's just outright stereotypes of Black people. They feel there is no such a thing as an "A" Black person, a superior person. What does the grade "A" mean, superior. You can't grade a Black person a superior grade when he's not a superior person. I've heard teachers say that. "I teach in North Stockton (mostly White area). (Therefore) I teach superior kids. I'm a superior teacher. You teach in South Stockton (mostly minority area). (Therefore) you teach below-normal kids and you're a below-normal teacher." This is a status symbol that they attach to where they teach and where you work. In other words, White is good, Black is bad. Anyway it goes.

My own study of the grading of one cohort of Black and Mexican American children in one elementary school in the same school district lent some support to the counselor's suggestion that teachers refused to reward minorities according to their intellectual accomplishments. I examined the records of 17 children over a 6-year span, from first to sixth grade. Every year the children were given the same grade, C, regardless of their academic improvements or lack of it, all noted by teachers in the children's files (Ogbu 1977).

In my research I have come across some Black parents and other adults who live with the sense of intellectual inferiority because they were labeled as "mentally retarded" in their school days. Take the case of this mother in the following excerpt:

> When I was a kid, it must have been in the 3rd or 4th grade, I was given a test. This White psychologist had come to the school to test the students …. The test she gave me was like a little puzzle, another was a chart … I asked her, was I doing fine? She said I was doing fine …. And so, then, a month later, my mother get the results and it said I was retarded … and it has affected me from my childhood, until adulthood, until now.

Black children become aware quite early in life and begin to internalize the belief of White Americans that Black Americans are intellectually inferior to Whites. In my study of more than 1,300 precollege Black students in Oakland, California, 82% reported that people in their families and community thought that White Americans did not believe that Black Americans were as intelligent as White people (Ogbu, 1998). In contrast, only 14% of the immigrant Chinese and 50% of the semi-immigrant Mexican Americans in the same study reported similar thinking in their families and communities (Fig. 10.3). Further insight into Black students' sensitivity to the issue of intelligence is shown in their response to other questions in the study. Black students wished they could prove to White Americans that they are wrong. Thus when asked why minorities went to school, Blacks asserted nearly three times as often (18%) as the Chinese (7%) and twice as often as Mexican Americans (9%) that they went to school to show Whites that they are smart (Ogbu & Simons, 1994).

One incident at a preschool/afterschool class during a Black history month program in February 1996 illustrates just how early children begin to internalize the belief that Black people are not as intelligent as White people. Three Black Americans from the San Francisco Health Department had gone to make a presentation on health to the 4- to 10-year-olds. One of the three public health officials was a doctor who talked about what she and other doctors do. Asked what they wanted to be, many of the children replied that they wanted to be doctors, architects, dentists, and lawyers. Asked what they would do to achieve their goals, they responded almost in unison, "Get good education." Finally, when questioned about what might make it difficult to attain those career goals, a 7-year-old said that Black people cannot be doctors because they are not good (i.e., not intelligent) enough. Several other children agreed.

In a discussion among the health officials and day-care staff later, these adults repeatedly noted that in their communities children begin as early as 3 or 4 years of age to understand that White people discriminate against Black people and do not believe

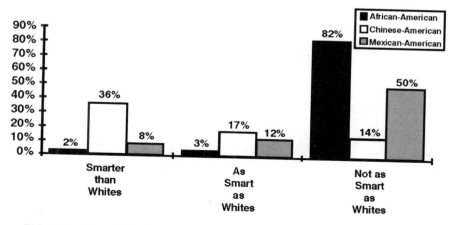

FIG. 10.3.   Minorities' perceptions of the beliefs of White Americans about their intellectual abilities vis-à-vis White intellectual abilities.

that Blacks are as smart as Whites. To further illustrate the seriousness of the internalization problem, the doctor described a visit to her health center by a 3½ year-old boy. The social worker who brought the boy had told him that it would be a good experience for him to see a Black doctor. The boy replied that there were no Black doctors. When the social worker introduced him to the narrator, the doctor, the boy repeatedly asked her if she was a real doctor. The basis of the child's skepticism became obvious when he said, "All doctors are supposed to be White."

One consequence of the internalization is self-doubt, coupled with resignation in situations requiring intellectual performance. The phenomenon of self-doubt can be seen in this excerpt from my interview with a Black school administrator:

> The Black kids do not pay any attention to the test scores. They're resigned to the idea that (White) kids are smarter than they are. They've been told that they can't achieve and they accept it .... The (Black) kids will say, talking about math and all, they'll say, "You know, we're not as smart as they (i.e., White students) are." When a girl made this statement, and we were talking about how smart they are in math, "You know, we aren't as smart as they are. They don't have any muscles, we have muscles (for sports and athletics)."

Self-doubt is also widespread among parents and other adults. Luster (1992) found this to be the case in her study in San Francisco. Most of the women in her study were parents with children in public schools. They were attending a community school to prepare for their general equivalency diplomas (GEDs). Luster described her own effort and the effort of the school personnel to convince the women that they could pass their GED tests. Here is her description of one incident that illustrates the extent of self-doubt of these parents:

> One day a woman who had been studying several months for the GED social studies test was in the lounge arguing with her instructor. The instructor was urging her to take the test, telling her she had studied enough, she had scored well on the pre-tests, she was ready and should go to the testing center and take the test. The woman kept insisting that she was not ready, that she did not know enough to take the test. This exchange turned into a shouting match—the teacher insisting, "You can!," the woman insisting, "I can't!" While the vehemence of the exchange may not have been typical, the essence was. (pp. 240–241)

It is partly because they have internalized the White belief that they are less intelligent than White people and partly because of their intellectual treatment in school based on IQ test scores that some Blacks are highly suspicious of IQ tests and the motives of those who give them. It is also partly for the same reasons that they develop self-doubt or come to feel that they cannot do well on these tests. One can imagine that under this circumstance many Black parents would have difficulty effectively encouraging their children to perform well on IQ and other tests. Telling children to do well is not sufficient to undo the negative effects of the actual texture of the parents' or Black collective experience with the IQ tests. One can also imagine that the children themselves have difficulty striving to maximize their IQ test scores.

Group Identity and IQ Test Scores.   The phenomenon of group identity also contributes to the low IQ test scores. As an involuntary minority group, the culture, dialect, and group identity of Black Americans have, to a large extent, been forged in opposition to those of White Americans. Partly for this reason, Blacks perceive accommodating to White ways as a subtractive process: They think that this requires them to give up their own ways of behaving and communicating and their collective identities. It is significant that some Black intellectuals consider it "assimilation" for Black children to learn standard English (Steele 1992). This is precisely the attitude that I found among some people in the community. This interpretation results in opposition by peer groups to those who are accommodating to White ways and White language; the latter are suspected of abandoning their Black identity and threatening racial solidarity in favor of the Whites, their oppressors. Some individuals avoid adopting White ways because they fear that they may, indeed, be losing their Black identity and leaving the Black community (see DeVos, 1984).

The target areas of opposition are those historically defined as White prerogatives, first by White people and then conceded to by minorities. These are areas in which it has long been believed that only White people could perform well, and in which few Blacks were given the opportunity to perform or were adequately rewarded when they succeeded. These are also areas where the criteria for evaluation of performance and rewards are established and controlled by White Americans or their minority representatives. The criteria for evaluation involve demonstration of the right behavior, proper language or speech, and the right skills, which Blacks interpret as White behaviors, White language or speech, and White skills. Performance on intelligence (IQ) tests, scholastic achievement tests, and in high-status jobs in the mainstream economy are examples of such areas. Good performance in the target areas tends to acquire the secondary meaning of a symbol of affiliation with White oppressors and a loss of one's Black collective identity. As a result, Black persons manifesting behaviors conducive to good performance in the target areas or adopting "White ways" are criticized by their peers or community and their bona fide identities are questioned. For the same reasons, some individuals consciously or unconsciously resist striving for good performance. In my research in Stockton (Ogbu, 1974) and Oakland (Ogbu, 1998), Black students reported that some who are smart do not show their smartness in class because they are afraid of being rejected by other Black students.

EPISTEMOLOGY AND EXPLANATIONS OF THE BACK–WHITE GAP

The explanation of the Black–White gap in IQ test scores outlined earlier was criticized by Jensen (1994, 1998), who dismissed it as ad hoc because it is not based on a "detailed pattern of psychometric differences." He also asserted that there is no way to test our explanation scientifically (Jensen, 1994). Jensen's criticisms and claims for the superiority of the psychometric approach raise a fundamental question as to what constitutes scientific method in the study of the Black–White gap in IQ test scores. Apparently, Jensen is not aware that his lifelong endeavor to attribute Black–White differences in IQ test scores to genetic differences is based on a particular epistemology about the social and biological realities of Black Americans. Other researchers hold other epistemologies or assumptions about the social and biological realities that shape their own scientific studies of the IQ test gap. To put Jensen's criticisms and claims in perspective, I discuss briefly the role of epistemology in the study of the racial differences in IQ test scores. Differences in our assumptions about what we study (theory) and how we study it (method) are due to differences in epistemology. The concept of paradigm is a useful tool to explain these differences without asserting that one's approach is superior to another's.

Paradigms and Research Approaches

A theoretical paradigm is a way of thinking about the world, about society, about people, about IQ, or about any phenomenon we are studying (Bailey, 1987; Kuhn, 1962). As Bailey put it, a research paradigm is a particular way of understanding whatever we are studying. A given paradigm is distinguished by (a) basic assumptions the researcher holds about the phenomenon (e.g., IQ), (b) the concepts the researcher uses to describe the phenomenon, (c) the questions the researcher asks about it, (d) the methods used to study the problem, and (e) the researcher's explanations of the problem when the study is completed (Bailey, 1987). How differences in paradigms shape research approaches and results can be seen among those studying the problem of overpopulation. One group of researchers, following Malthus, assumes that population grows on a generational basis at a geometrical rate, but food production grows at an arithmetic rate. From their point of few, starvation is inevitable if population growth is not controlled. Malthus (1798) called this the natural law of population growth and said that it is not subject to a particular form of political system. His recommendation for controlling population growth included delaying marriage, moral restraint, refraining from extramarital sex, positive checks, and the like. When researchers with this theoretical paradigm study the overpopulation problem, the concepts guiding their data collection, analysis, and explanations include arithmetic rate, geometric rate, positive check, preventive check (e.g., age of marriage), vice, and so on.

   In contrast, Marxist researchers employ a different paradigm. According to Marxism, there is no natural law of population growth. The law of population growth varies, depending on whether the control of food production is socialist or capitalist. Overpopulation is caused in capitalist societies because capitalism needs surplus labor to exploit. Overpopulation would disappear if capitalism were replaced with socialism. When Marxists study overpopulation, the concepts that guide their data collection, analysis, and explanations include class struggle, means of production, surplus labor, exploitation, and the like.

These two groups of researchers, Malthusians and Marxists, study the same phenomenon (overpopulation) with greatly different paradigms or from vastly different perspectives, collect different kinds of data, and reach different conclusions. There is and probably will never be an agreement between the two groups as to the causes of overpopulation or what to do about it. One cannot, a priori, claim that one approach is better or more scientific than another.

Paradigms and the Study of the Black–White Gap in IQ

A similar situation exists with regard to the study of "racial" differences in IQ test scores. There are many competing paradigms here, but I have selected three, represented in Fig. 10.4, for discussion. We may label the researchers subscribing to the theoretical paradigms as *hereditists*, *environmentalists*, and *cultural ecologists*. All three are studying the same phenomenon, Black–White difference in IQ test scores; the three paradigms differ in their theoretical assumptions, their definitions of social and biological realities as reflected in the concepts that guide their data collection, and their methods of collecting and analyzing data.

Hereditists believe that the intelligence (IQ) of an individual is largely determined by genetic endowment; that 80% of the variance in IQ is due to genetic differences and the remaining 20% due to environmental differences; and that both individual differences in IQ within the White populations or within the Black population, as well as mean differences between the White and Black populations in the United States, are caused by genetic differences. That is, because heritability of IQ is high within the

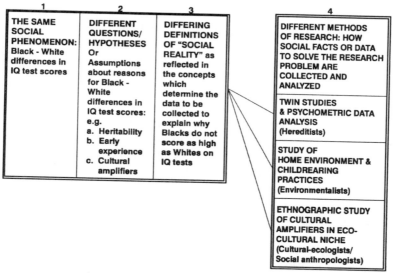

FIG. 10.4.   Relationship between researcher's epistemology or research paradigm and the study of Black–White differences in IQ test scores.

White population (and almost as high within the Black population), it is plausible that the differences between Blacks and Whites are also primarily caused by genetic differences (Jensen, 1969, 1973, 1998; Ogbu, 1986a). The methodological paradigm that follows calls for sampling, testing, and psychometric analyses of test scores. On the basis of this the IQ of each population is inferred and the gap between the IQs of Blacks and the Whites is observed and explained.

Environmentalists assign a greater weight to environmental factors. They claim that the socioeconomic status of the parents determines the quality and quantity of interaction with the child as well as the material resources available to him or her. Both the interaction and the resources influence a child's cognitive development (Hunt, 1969). It follows that some children develop more intelligence or cognitive skills (IQ) than other children because they come from a rich environment and receive more and better stimulation in early childhood. A fundamental environmentalist assumption has been termed the *critical period hypothesis* (Williams, 1972). Some environmentalists believe that there is a period in a childs' life when he or she must receive a particular form of stimulation, or permanent damage will be done to his or her cognitive and social development (see White, Kaban, & Attanucci, 1979). The environmentalists believe that the differences in the IQ test scores of Blacks and Whites lie in the differences in the early experience of the two populations. Black children do not receive adequate stimulation from their parents during the early years of life because Black parents do not have the childrearing capabilities of White middle-class parents.

The methodological paradigm of environmentalists leads to sampling and collection of data on childrearing practices, including language interactions between children and their parents.

The theoretical position of the cultural ecologists has been outlined in this chapter. They trace the origins of intelligence or cognitive skills not to genes or childrearing practices or home environment during early childhood but to the cultural tasks in an ecocultural niche that act as amplifiers of the intellectual skills in a population. To explain the pattern of Black test scores in ethnographic study, data are collected on opportunities and barriers to participation in cultural amplifiers, on cultural transmitters of intellectual skills (including family childrearing practices, schooling, games and play, etc.), as well as Blacks' perceptions, beliefs, and interpretations of their experiences with IQ tests. Black American test behaviors are not determined only by genes or early childhood experiences in the family. Their test behaviors are also influenced by access to cultural amplifiers of the cognitive skills measured by IQ tests, as well as their perceptions of and beliefs about the tests.

Research Paradigms and Jensen's Criticisms

In addition to placing Jensen's psychometric analysis in proper perspective, the discussion of paradigms leads us to assess Jensen's understanding of the cultural ecological approach he criticized. His specific criticism is that the lower IQ test scores of Black Americans cannot be attributed to slavery, discrimination, caste status, and involuntary minority status (Jensen, 1998). On close examination, Jensen's understanding of these factors seems doubtful.

Effects of Slavery on IQ Test Performance.   Jensen argued that past history of slavery cannot account for Black–White mean differences on psychometric tests because these differences occur in non-Black societies where Blacks have never been slaves. The first point to raise about Jensen's assertion that a past history of slavery has no impact is that nowhere is there evidence in Jensen's work that he is familiar with the vast literature on the cultural, social, and psychological consequences of slavery. Second, his theory does not explain why African immigrants in the United States are usually more academically successful in the same schools than are U.S.-born Black Americans. For example, in a recent study in the Miami–Dade County public schools, Johnson (1999) found that African immigrants, whether English-speaking or not, did better than Black Americans. The study consisted of a random sample of 366 10th-grade students who were classified as high achieving (3.5 grade point average) and low-achieving (1.5 grade point average or lower). Johnson conducted a chi-square analysis to see if there was a difference between the immigrant and native-born Blacks as well as between English-speaking and non-English-speaking students. Her analysis showed that Blacks born outside the United States, whether English-speaking or not, were more likely to be high achieving: $X_2 = 12.77, p = .001$, and those whose first language was not English were also more likely to be high achieving than low achieving, $X_2 = 6.41, p = .011$. As for the test scores of Black people in non-Black societies where they were never slaves, there are no citations.

Minority Status, Discrimination, and IQ Test Scores.   The Black–White mean differences on psychometric tests are not caused by discrimination because other minorities who also suffered discrimination do better than Blacks. As Jensen (1998) put it, other minorities (e.g., Asians—Chinese, Japanese, East Indians) and Jews, or "physically identifiable" minorities who have experienced discrimination and even persecution, "perform as well or better in *g*-loaded tests and *g*-loaded occupations" (p. 110) as White Americans or "the majority population of any of the countries in which they reside" (p. 111). He therefore concluded that "social discrimination *per se* obviously does not cause lower levels of *g*" (p. 111). He even suggested that discrimination causes minorities to score higher than dominant group members on IQ tests. I disagree that discrimination causes immigrant minorities to do well on IQ tests and have already explained why the immigrants, regardless of their racial background, do well. Unlike Jensen, I leave Jews out of this analysis and debate because Jensen cannot seriously classify them as a "non-White" or "physically identifiable" minority.

Involuntary Minorities and IQ Test Scores.   I began to classify minorities as immigrants (voluntary minorities) or nonimmigrants (involuntary minorities) to avoid lumping together, as Jensen did, groups with different histories and experiences.

The classification was based on an extensive comparative study of minorities in the United States and other societies. It was found that there are many significant differences between voluntary and involuntary minorities, including differences in educational and occupational experiences, attitudes, and strategies (Gibson & Ogbu, 1991; Ogbu, 1987, 1998). Jensen (1998) did not believe that such differences exist to explain Black–White differences in IQ test performance. He rejected involuntary minority status as a contributing factor because I did not explain why voluntary or immigrant minorities are able to do well on IQ tests that are based on "a narrow set of Western specialized cognitive abilities and skills" (p. 510), whereas Black Americans who live in Western (i.e., U.S.) societies do not. Whereas I argue that Black Americans were for centuries excluded from cultural tasks (White middle-class occupation and education) that enhance the development of those cognitive abilities and skills, Jensen contended that Blacks have been unable to pursue such education and those occupations because they lack the g factor, which is a prerequisite. The immigrants are able to pursue White middle-class education and attain occupations requiring the g factor because they possess this attribute.

A brief review of Jensen's work on Black occupational history reveals an a priori belief that Black Americans (and perhaps Black people in general) are biologically and intellectually inferior. He asserted in his well-known paper on race, IQ, and scholastic achievement (Jensen, 1969) that the reason Blacks have not achieved their expected proportion in professional and high-level occupations is that they lack the g factor for education and occupations requiring it. He further noted that they had not made it in spite of the fact that all barriers to their attaining such positions had been eliminated through civil rights legislation (see also Herrnstein, 1973, for similar conclusions). Jensen (1972) repeated his explanation for the underrepresentation of Blacks in high-level occupations in his presentation to a U.S. Senate Committee. That time he compared Blacks to other groups, saying that unlike other American ethnic groups, Black Americans had not achieved their expected representations in occupations requiring the intellectual skills of the White middle class. He repeated the explanation that Blacks lack the adequate genetic endowment (g factor) for the mental abilities required for such occupations. The occupations Jensen listed included accounting, architecture, college professorship, engineering, law, natural sciences, proprietorship, and technical jobs. The evidence supporting the opposite conclusion for why Blacks are underrepresented in the high-level occupations is well documented in the works of Hill (1968), Myrdal (1944), Norgren and Hill (1964), Ogbu (1979, 1981a), and Wallace (1976).

Jensen is wrong for two reasons. First, almost every study of the occupational history of Blacks through the periods covered by Jensen's report concluded with indisputable evidence that Black underrepresentation in high-level occupations was caused by racial discrimination. Our own study of Black occupational history from the period of slavery to 1974 provides no support for Jensen's claims. Moreover, in 1969 when Jensen was reporting that barriers to equal opportunity had been removed, the people of Stockton, California, were holding the workshop in equality described earlier in this chapter in response to allegations by Blacks and Mexicans of generations of discrimination. In 1972, while Jensen was giving a U.S. Senate Committee a list of occupations that Blacks did not possess the *g* factor to perform, investigators from the California Fair Employment Practices Commission were reporting to the Stockton City Council their findings on employment discrimination against Blacks and Mexican Americans in the city. It found that one of the reasons for the lack of representation of Blacks and Mexican Americans in high-level occupations was that intelligence tests used in civil service employment were not valid and were used to screen out minorities (1972). To summarize, until the civil rights legislation of the 1960s, Black Americans were excluded from those occupations on Jensen's list by law in some parts of the country and by custom in other parts (Ogbu, 1978). Furthermore, the exclusion persisted after the civil rights legislation, as can be seen in the case of Stockton, California. In contrast to Jensen, we must conclude that the underrepresentation of Blacks in high-level occupations is due to discrimination, not to a lack of the *g* factor.

Jensen is also wrong in another way: His failure to understand the difference between voluntary and involuntary minorities leads him to expect that involuntary minorities and voluntary minorities would share the same epistemology toward learning the *g* factor and the spatial factor that represent specialized Western cognitive skills. Although both groups can learn these cognitive skills, acquiring these abilities and skills has different affective meanings for immigrant (voluntary) and nonimmigrant (involuntary) minorities. However, as explained earlier, learning the Western abilities and cognitive skills depends on more than the *g* factor. It also is affected by how the minorities perceive and interpret the cognitive skills and abilities. Voluntary and involuntary minorities differ in this respect.

Caste Status and IQ Test Scores.   I have suggested since 1978 that caste status has an adverse effect on the IQ test scores and general academic performance of the lower castes, not only in the United States, but worldwide (Ogbu, 1978). Jensen cited no studies and provided no data to challenge this conclusion, but rather asserted that there is no way of testing it scientifically. What needs to be emphasized here is that the IQ test performance of lower caste groups is more depressed when the tests are interpreted as the property of the dominant caste and less depressed when the tests are seen as "foreign" to both the dominant and the lower caste groups. Thus, in Japan, where the lower caste Buraku interpret IQ tests as coming from the dominant Ippan caste, and in the United States, where the subordinate caste of Blacks interpret or identify IQ tests as the property of the dominant White caste, the test scores of the lower castes are depressed beyond what might be expected from differences in socioeconomic status. In contrast, in India, Nigeria (Igbos), and Rwanda, where IQ and academic tests were introduced by "foreigners," chiefly the British and the French, the performance of the lower castes is not depressed beyond what might be expected from their lower socioeconomic status (Ogbu, 1986a; Ogbu & Stern, in press).

A matter of serious concern is that Jensen bases his criticisms of nonpsychometric approaches on a superficial knowledge of those approaches and unsubstantial evidence. I, as well as others (e.g., Alland, 1973), have noticed this since the publication of his article on IQ and scholastic achievement (Jensen, 1969). It is not surprising that in his latest book, *The g Factor* (1998), Jensen's criticisms of my alternative approach and explanation are based on two of my publications, *Minority Education and Caste: The American System in Cross-Cultural Perspective* (Ogbu, 1978) and "Culture and Intelligence" (Ogbu, 1994a). In *Minority Education and Caste*, I showed with comparative data that Jensen's (1969) hypothesis about the Black–White gap applied to subordinate castes even where there were no racial differences. I have since published other papers specifically devoted to Black–White castelike stratification in the United States and its implications for mental development and IQ test performance (see Ogbu, 1986a, 1986b). Jensen cited none of these later works. The second work he cited, "Culture and Intelligence" was an encyclopedia entry in which I was specifically asked by the editor not to discuss race.

Completely absent from Jensen's references are any of my publications specifically dealing with minority status and schooling or minority status and intelligence. Yet I have several publications on how and why immigrant (voluntary) and nonimmigrant (involuntary) minorities differ in general, with respect to schooling or IQ tests (see Gibson & Ogbu, 1991; Ogbu, 1983, 1987, 1991; Ogbu & Simons, 1998). Jensen's discussion of involuntary minority status and the *g* factor in education or occupation should be dismissed as having no foundations in the literature or empirical reality.

INVOLUNTARY MINORITY STATUS AND IQ IN CROSS-CULTURAL PERSPECTIVE

Analysis of the IQ test performance of minorities in other societies shows involuntary minorities have low test scores. Lower performance on IQ tests of involuntary minorities has been reported in India (Chopra, 1966; Gaur & Sen, 1989) Europe and North America (McShane & Berry, 1988; Verma, 1988), New Zealand (Ogbu, 1978), and Japan (DeVos, 1973). It is instructive, however, to observe the performance of the same minority group in one society where they are an involuntary minority and in another where they are a voluntary minority. I use the Burakumin and Koreans in Japan to show that it is type of minority status, not race, that affects IQ test scores.

The Burakumin

The Burakumin are an involuntary minority group in Japan. There are no racial differences between them and the dominant Ippan Japanese. They usually score lower than the dominant Ippan on the Tanaka–Binet IQ test. The lower test scores have been reported in the Osaka region (DeVos 1973; DeVos & Wagatsuma, 1967; see Fig. 10.5). *Time* magazine had the following to say about the Buraku–Ippan gap in IQ test scores in 1973:

> The state proclaimed the outcaste system illegal in 1871, but prejudice did not yield to government fiat. On the average, Burakumin are less well educated than their countrymen, and their children test 16 IQ points lower than other Japanese.

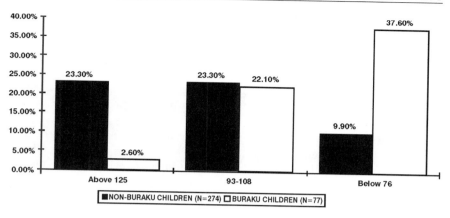

FIG.10.5.   Buraku IQ test scores. From *Japan's Outcasts: The Problem of the Burakumin* by G. A. DeVos, 1973, p. 9. Copyright © 1973 by Minority Rights Group. Reprinted by permission.

(Remarkably similar to the average 15-point difference between U. S. Blacks and Whites, which most experts attribute to environment influences). ("Japan: The Invisible Race," 1973, pp. 31–312)

The gap in IQ test scores persists even though the Japanese government has spent about $60 billion to improve the economic and social conditions and education of the Buraku since 1979 (Shimahara, 1991). On the other hand, the discrimination and prejudice against the Burakumin by the Ippan majority persists (Kegard Prefecture, 1989). During my visit to Osaka in the summer of 1999 I found that both discrimination against the Buraku and the low academic performance of the latter continue in 42 neighborhoods for which data were available. In one elementary school I visited, the gap in school performance between Buraku and non-Buraku widens as the children progress into higher grades.

As voluntary minorities, the Burakumin in the United States perform well. Or, to put it differently, there is no evidence that they do less well on IQ tests and in school than other Japanese immigrants. In fact, the only study of Japanese immigrant school performance in the United States that identified them indicates that they do slightly better in school than other Japanese immigrants (Ito, 1967).

The Korean Case

Koreans are an involuntary minority group in Japan. They were taken to Japan as forced laborers when Korea was colonized by Japan. In other words, Koreans did not choose to go to Japan expecting better economic well-being or political freedom, but were forced to become minorities in Japan. Having been separated from Korea for more than half a century, many Koreans in Japan do not feel that they can return to Korea, although they are now free to do so. Most were born in Japan, but they are still treated as foreigners by the Japanese and are required to get fingerprinted and to carry an identification card at all times. Job and school discrimination as well as other forms of discrimination are common among them. They have an oppositional collective identity and cultural frame of reference vis-à-vis the majority Ippan Japanese and they deeply distrust the Ippan majority.

We do not have IQ test scores of Japanese Koreans. However, the results of other standardized tests indicate that they do not perform as well as the dominant Ippan Japanese. For example, in 1976, 29.4% of the Ippan high school graduates and 18.7% of the Burakumin graduates, but only 12.7% of Koreans in Hyogo Prefecture qualified to enter a university (Fig. 10.6; see Lee, 1991).

Koreans in Japan and the United States are racially, culturally, and linguistically identical. However, Koreans in the United States are immigrants, or a voluntary minority group. In the United States, the immigrant Koreans perform as well as or better than mainstream White Americans on standardized tests (Fig. 10.7; Lee, 1991). The test performance of the Burakumin and Koreans in Japan is instructive in light of the conventional view of Asians in the United States as "model minorities" who are academically successful. Their academic success in the United States is often attributed to their "Asian cultures" that, according to some, promote academic success more than other cultures, and to Asians being more intelligent than other groups. If these two factors were responsible for the performance of Asians in the United States,

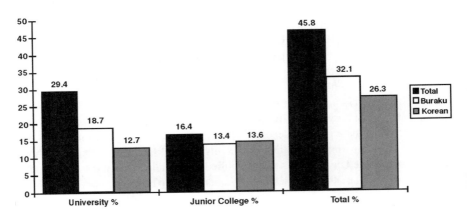

FIG. 10.6. Korean school performance in Japan. From "Koreans in Japan and the United States," by Y. Lee, 1991. In M. A. Gibson & J. U. Obgu (Eds.), *Minority Status and Schooling: A Comparative Study of Immigrant Involuntary Minorities* (pp. 131–167). Copyright © 1991 by Garland Press. Reprinted by permission.

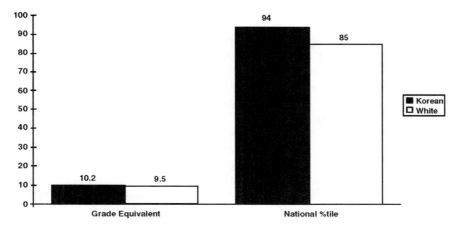

FIG. 10.7.   Korean school performance in the United States. From "Koreans in Japan and the United States," by Y. Lee, 1991. In M. A. Gibson & J. U. Obgu (Eds.), *Minority Status and Schooling: A Comparative Study of Immigrant Involuntary Minorities* (pp. 131–167). Copyright © 1991 by Garland Press. Reprinted by permission.

the Koreans and the Burakumin who live in Japan should be as successful as their fellow Koreans and Burakumin who live in the United States.

It is also instructive to compare Koreans in Japan, where they are involuntary minorities with Koreans in China, where, as in the United States, they are voluntary minorities. Koreans in China are also portrayed as a model minority out of China's 56 minority groups, in educational and professional accomplishments. We have no IQ test scores from China; however, Koreans in China have the highest rate of literacy among the minorities (89.55% vs. 57.37%) and a higher rate than the dominant Han group (89.55% vs. 68.81%; C. L. Lee, 1986).

CONCLUSION

IQ tests measure culturally valued intellectual skills. Because the tests are based on a sampling of the intellectual skills valued by middle-class Americans, they inevitably discriminate against members of minority cultures. The minorities have the biological potential to develop the required intellectual skills and they usually do. However, the minorities that have the most difficulty performing well on the IQ tests, even when they have the intellectual skills, are involuntary minorities. Involuntary minorities perform poorly on IQ tests not only because of discrimination by the dominant group or because they are not familiar with the tasks in the tests, although these are important. Additional barriers faced by involuntary minorities include a lack of incentive motivation, self-doubt arising from the internalization of intellectual denigration, and the conscious or unconscious opposition to adopting White ways that are associated with good IQ test performance because doing so threatens their collective identity. For involuntary minorities, cultural bias in IQ tests means not just that they are not familiar with the intellectual tasks in the tests or with how to perform those tasks. For them, the bias extends to the instrumental, relational, and expressive meanings of the tests.

One prerequisite for increasing the IQ test scores of involuntary minorities is to recognize that the tests are a part of White American culture and intellectual attributes, and that they are perceived to be such by involuntary minorities. A second prerequisite is to recognize that Blacks belong to a distinct type of minority group whose experiences and interpretations of the tests may lead them to resist the tests consciously or unconsciously. Finally, residue of various forms of discrimination should be eliminated and programs should be developed so that the minorities will develop nonthreatening interpretations of the tests and test-taking.

ACKNOWLEDGMENTS

The preparation of this chapter was supported by the University of California, Berkeley, faculty research fund. The research was supported by a grant from the National Institute of Education (NIE Grant G-80-0045). I am grateful for the institutional support. However, the opinions expressed in the chapter are solely mine.

Earlier versions of this chapter were presented at a colloquium in the Department of Anthropology, University of California, Berkeley; at the University of Toronto, Canada; and at the New York Academy of Sciences conference on race and intelligence: "The Bell Curve Reconsidered: Multidisciplinary Perspectives on Race and IQ."

REFERENCES

Alland, A. (1973). *Human diversity.* Garden City, NY: Doubleday.

Bailey, D. K. (1987). *Methods of social research* (2nd ed.). New York: The Free Press.

Baumrind, D. (1972). Subcultural variations in values defining social competence: An outsider's perspective on the Black subculture. Unpublished manuscript. Institute of Human Development, University of California, Berkeley.

Benjamin, L. (1991). *The Black elite: Facing the color line in the twilight of the twentieth century.* Chicago: Nelson-Hall.

Bock, R. D., & Kolakowski, D. (1973). Further evidence of sex-linked major gene influence on human visualizing ability. *American Journal of Human Genetics, 25,* 1.

Brand, C. (1996). "g," genes and pedagogy: A reply to seven (lamentable) chapters. In D. K. Detterman (Ed.), *Current topics in human intelligence: Vol. 5. The environment* (pp. 113–120). Norwood, NJ: Ablex.

Campbell, A. (1971). *White attitudes toward Black people.* Ann Arbor: University of Michigan.

Carnoy, M. (1994). *Faded dreams: The politics and economics of race in America.* New York: Cambridge University Press.

Chopra, S. L. (1966). Relationship of caste system with measured intelligence and academic achievement of students in India. *Social Forces, 44,* 573–576.

Cole, M., & Cole, S. R. (1993). *The development of children.* New York: Scientific American Books.

Cole, M., & Scribner, S. (1974). *Culture and thought: A psychological introduction.* New York: Wiley.

Committee of Correspondence on the Future of Public Education. (1984). *Education for democratic future: A manifesto.* New York: Author.

Cose, E. (1993). *The rage of the privileged class: Why are middle-class Blacks angry? Why should America care?* New York: HarperCollins.

Dasen, P. (1974). The influence of ecology, culture and European contact on cognitive development in Australian Aborigines. In J. W. Berry & R. P. Dasen (Ed.), *Culture and cognition: Readings in cross-cultural psychology* (pp. 381–408). London. Methuen.

Dennis, W. (1970). Good enough scores, art experience, and modernization. In A. I. Al-Issa & W. Dennis (Ed.), *Cross-cultural studies of behavior* (pp. 134–152). New York: Holt.

DeVos, G. A. (1973). Japan's outcasts: The problem of the Burakumin. In B. Whitaker (Ed.), *The fourth world: Victims of group oppression.* New York: Schocken Books.

DeVos, G. A. (1984, April). *Ethnic persistence and role degradation: An illustration from Japan.* Paper presented at the American–Soviet Symposium on Contemporary Ethnic Processes in the USA and the USSR, New Orleans, LA.

DeVos, G. A., & Wagatsuma, H. (Eds.). (1967). *Japan's invisible race.* Berkeley: University of California Press.

Dill, K. (1992, December). "Getting good skills": Racism and the employment of African-American hospital workers. Paper presented at the annual meeting of the American Anthropological Association, San Francisco, CA.

Dowa Mondai Research Institute. (1989). *Discrimination against Buraku in Osaaka prefecture.* Unpublished manuscript. Osaka City University, Osaka, Japan.

Dreger, R. M. (1973). Intellectual functioning. In K. S. Miller & R. M. Dreger (Eds.), *Comparative studies of Blacks and Whites in the United States* (pp.185–229). New York: Seminar Press.

Fredrickson, G. M. (1971). *The Black image in the White mind: The debate on Afro-American character and destiny, 1817–1914.* New York: Harper & Row.

Gaur, P. D., & Sen, A. K. (1989). A study of deprivation among non-scheduled castes, scheduled castes and mentally retarded children. *Journal of Applied Psychology, 26,* 26–34.

Gibson, M. A., & Ogbu, J. U. (Eds.). (1991). *Minority status and schooling: A comparative study of immigrants and involuntary minorities.* New York: Garland.

Gordon, E. W., & Bhattacharya, M. (1994). Race and intelligence. In R. J. Sternberg (Ed.), *Encyclopedia of intelligence* (pp. 889–899). New York: Macmillan.

Greenfield, P. (1998). The cultural evolution of IQ. In U. Neisser (Ed.), *The rising curve: Long-term gains in IQ test scores and what they mean* (pp. 81–122). Washington, DC: American Psychological Association.

Herrnstein, R. J. (1973). *IQ in the meritocracy.* Boston: Little, Brown, & Co.

Herrnstein, R. J., & Murray, C. (1994). *The bell curve: Intelligence and class structure in American life.* New York: The Free Press.

Hill, H. (1968). Twenty years of fair employment practices commissions: A critical analysis with recommendations. In L. A. Ferman, I. L. Kornbluh, & J. A. Miller (Eds.), *Negroes and jobs* (pp. 496–522). Ann Arbor: University of Michigan Press.

Ho, D. Y. F. (1994). Cognitive socialization in Confucian heritage cultures. In P. A. Greenfield & R. R. Cocking (Eds.), *Cross-cultural roots of minority children* (pp. 285–313). Hillsdale, NJ: Lawrence Erlbaum Associates.

How Whites think about Blacks. (1979, February 26). *Newsweek,* p. 48.

Hunt, J. M. (1969). *The challenge of incompetence and poverty: The role of early education.* Urbana: University of Illinois Press.

Ito, H. (1967). Japan's outcasts in the United States. In G. A. DeVos & H. Wagatsuma (Eds.), *Japan's invisible race.* Berkeley: University of California Press.

Japan: The invisible race. (1973, January 8). *Time,* pp. 311–312.

Jensen, A. R. (1969). How much can we boost IQ and scholastic achievement? *Harvard Educational Review, 39,* 1–123.

Jensen, A. R. (1972). *Statement of Dr. Arthur R. Jensen, Senate Select Committee on Education.* Unpublished manuscript.

Jensen, A. R. (1973). *Educability & group differences.* New York: Random House.

Jensen, A. R. (1994). Race and IQ scores. In R. J. Sternberg (Ed.), *Encyclopedia of intelligence* (pp. 899–907). New York: Macmillan.

Jensen, A. R. (1998). *The g factor: The science of mental abilities.* Westport, CT: Praeger.

Johnson, C. (1999, November). *An assessment of African descent from their own set of normative behaviors in Miami–Dade County public schools.* Poster presented at Stanford Conference on Race: African Americans: Research and Policy Perspectives at the Turn of the Century, Stanford, CA.

Johnson, G. B. (1969). The stereotype of the American negro. In O. Klineberg (Ed.), *Characteristics of the American negro* (pp. 1–22). New York: Harper. (Original work published 1939)

Kegard Prefecture. (1989). *The present situation of discrimination against Buraku: Research on the conditions of Buraku.* Unpublished manuscript.

Kuhn, T. S. (1962). *The structure of scientific revolutions.* Chicago: University of Chicago Press.

Kyllonen, P. C. (1994). Information processing. In R. J. Sternberg (Ed.), *Encyclopedia of intelligence* (pp. 580–588). New York: Macmillan.

Lee, C.-L. (1986). *China's Korean minority: The politics of ethnic education.* Boulder, CO: Westview.

Lee, Y. (1991). Koreans in Japan and the United States. In M. A. Gibson & J. U. Ogbu (Eds.), *Minority status and schooling: A comparative study of immigrant and involuntary minorities* (pp. 131–167). New York: Garland.

Luster, L. (1992). *Schooling, survival, and struggle: Black women and the GED.* Unpublished doctoral dissertation, Stanford University, Stanford, CA.

Malthus, T. (1798). *An essay on the principles of population, as it affects the improvement of society.* London.

Matusow, B. (1989, November). "Alone together: What do you do when the dream hasn't come true, when you're Black and middle-class and still shut out of White Washington, when it seems to quit trying? *The Washingtonian,* pp. 153–159, 282–290.

McShane, D. A., & Berry, J. (1988). Native North Americans: Amerindians and Inuit abilities. In S. H. Irvine & J. W. Berry (Ed.), *Cultural context of human abilities* (pp. 385–426). London: Oxford University Press.

Myrdal, G. (1944). *An American dilemma: The Negro problem and modern democracy* (Vol. 1). New York: Harper.

Naiven, B., Hoffmann, J., & Bierbryer (1969). The effects of subject's age, sex, race and socioeconomic status on psychologists' estimate of "True IQ" from WISC scores. *Journal of Clinical Psychology, 25,* 271–274.

Norgren, P. H., & Jill, S. E. (1964). *Toward fair employment.* New York: Columbia University Press.

Ogbu, J. U. (1974). *The next generation: An ethnography of education in an urban neighborhood.* New York: Academic Press.

Ogbu, J. U. (1977). Racial stratification and education: The case of Stockton, California. *ICRD Bulletin, 12*(3), 1–26.

Ogbu, J. U. (1978). *Minority education and caste: The American system in cross-cultural perspective.* New York: Academic Press.

Ogbu, J. U. (1979). Social stratification and socialization of competence. *Anthropology and Education Quarterly, 10*(1), 3–20.

Ogbu, J. U. (1981). Origins of human competence: A cultural-ecological perspective. *Child Development, 52,* 413–429.

Ogbu, J. U. (1982). Socialization: A cultural ecological perspective. In K. Borman (Ed.), *The socialization of children in a changing society* (pp. 251–265). Hillsdale, NJ: Lawrence Erlbaum Associates.

Ogbu, J. U. (1983). Minority status and schooling in plural societies. *Comparative Education Review, 27,* 168–190.

Ogbu, J. U. (1986a). Castelike stratification and mental retardation in the United States. In D. C. Farran & J. D. McKinney (Ed.), *The concept of risk in intellectual and psychological development* (pp. 83–119). New York: Academic Press.

Ogbu, J. U. (1986b). The consequences of the American caste system. In U. Neisser (Ed.), *The school achievement of minority children: New perspectives* (pp. 19–56). Hillsdale, NJ: Lawrence Erlbaum Associates.

Ogbu, J. U. (1987). Variability in minority school performance: A problem in search of an explanation. *Anthropology and Education Quarterly, 18*(4), 312–334.

Ogbu, J. U. (1989). Cultural boundaries and minority youth orientation toward work preparation. In D. Stern & D. Eichorn (Eds.), *Adolescence and work: Influences of social structure, labor markets, and culture* (pp. 101–140). Hillsdale, NJ: Lawrence Erlbaum Associates.

Ogbu, J. U. (1991). Low school performance as an adaptation: The case of Blacks in Stockton, CA. In M. A. Gibson & J. U. Ogbu (Eds.), *Minority status and schooling: A Comparative study of immigrant and involuntary minorities* (pp. 249–286). New York: Garland.

Ogbu, J. U. (1994a). Culture and intelligence. In R. J. Sternberg (Ed.), *The encyclopedia of intelligence* (Vol. 1, pp. 228–238). New York: Macmillan.

Ogbu, J. U. (1994b). From cultural differences to differences in cultural frame of reference. In P. M. Greenfield & R. R. Cocking (Eds.), *Cross-cultural roots of minority child development* (pp. 365–391). Hillsdale, NJ: Lawrence Erlbaum Associates.

Ogbu, J. U. (1998). *Community forces and minority education strategies: The second part of the problem.* New York: Russell Sage Foundation.

Ogbu, J. U., & Simons, H. D. (1994). *Final report: Cultural models and school achievement.* Unpublished manuscript. National Center for the Study of Writing, University of California, Berkeley.

Ogbu, J. U., & Simons, H. D. (1998). Voluntary and Involuntary minorities: A cultural-ecological theory of school performance with some implications for education. *Anthropology and Education Quarterly, 29*(2), 155–188.

Ogbu, J. U., & Stern, P. (in press). Caste status and intellectual development. In R. J. Sternberg (Ed.), *Environmental effects on intellectual functioning.* Mahwah, NJ: Lawrence Erlbaum Associates.

Ortar, G. R. (1967). Educational achievements of primary school graduates in Israel as related to their socio-cultural background. *Comparative Education, 4,* 23–34.

Plomin, R. (1994). Nature, nurture and development. In R. J. Sternberg (Ed.), *Encyclopedia of intelligence* (pp. 754–764). New York: Macmillan.

Posner, J. K. (1982). The development of mathematical knowledge in two West African societies. *Child Development, 53,* 200–208.

Price-Williams, D. R. (1961). A study concerning concepts of conservation of quantities among primitive children. *Acta Psychological, 18,* 293–305.

Price-Williams, D. R., Gordon, W., & Ramirez, M. (1969). Skills and conservation: A study of pottery-making children. *Developmental Psychology, 1*, 769.

Sameroff, A. J., Seifer, R., Baldwin, A., & Baldwin, C. (1993). Stability from pre-school to adolescence: The influence of social and family risk factors. *Child Development, 64*, 80–97.

Saxe, G. B., & Posner, J. (1983). The development of numerical cognition: Cross-cultural perspectives. In H. P. Ginsburg (Ed.), *The development of mathematical thinking* (pp. 291–317). New York: Academic Press.

Scribner, S., & Cole, M. (1973). Cognitive consequences of formal and informal education. *Science, 182*, 553–559.

Shimahara, K. N. (1991). Social mobility and education: Burakumin in Japan. In M. A. Gibson & J. U. Ogbu (Eds.), *Minority status and schooling: A comparative study of immigrant and involuntary minorities* (pp. 342–353). New York: Garland.

State of California. (1972). *City of Stockton: Affirmative action survey.* Sacramento: California Fair Employment Practices Commission.

Steele, C. (1992, April). Race and the schooling of Black Americans. *The Atlantic Monthly,* 68–75.

Stevenson, H. W. (1982). Influences of schooling on cognitive development. In D. A. Wagner & H. W. Stevenson (Eds.), *Cultural perspectives on child development.* San Francisco: Freeman.

Suzuki, L. A., & Gutkin, T. B. (1994a). Asian Americans. In R. J. Sternberg (Ed.), *Encyclopedia of intelligence* (pp. 140–144). New York: Macmillan.

Suzuki, L. A., & Gutkin, T. B. (1994b). Hispanic. In R. J. Sternberg (Ed.), *Encyclopedia of intelligence* (Vol. 1, pp. 539–545). New York: Macmillan.

Travers, J. R. (1982). Testing in educational placement: Issues and evidence. In K. Heller, W. H. Holtzman, & S. Messick (Eds.), *Placing children in special education: A strategy for equity* (pp. 230–261). Washington, DC: National Academy Press.

Valenchia, R. R., & Aburto, S. (1991). The uses and abuses of educational testing: Chicanos as a case in point. In R. R. Valencia (Ed.), *Chicano school failure and success* (pp. 203–251). New York: Falmer.

Verma, G. K. (1988). Educational adaptation and achievement of ethnic minority adolescents in Britain. In S. H. Irvine & J. W. Berry (Eds.), *Human abilities in cultural context* (pp. 509–533). Cambridge, UK: Cambridge University Press.

Vernon, P. E. (1969). *Intelligence and cultural environment.* London: Methuen.

Vernon, P. E. (1982). *The abilities and achievements of Orientals in North America.* New York: Academic Press.

Vraniak, D. A. (1994). Native Americans. In R. J. Sternberg (Ed.), *Encyclopedia of intelligence* (Vol. 2, pp. 747–754). New York: Macmillan.

Wallace, P. A. (Ed.). (1976). *Equal employment opportunity and the AT&T case.* Cambridge, MA: MIT Press.

Wechsler, D. (1991). *Manual for Wechsler Intelligence Scale for Children* (3rd ed.). San Antonio, TX: Psychological Corporation. Original work published in 1949

White, B. L., Kaban, & Attanucci. (1979). *The origins of human competence.* Lexington, MA: Heath.

Williams, T. R. (1972). *Introduction to socialization: Human culture transmitted.* St. Louis, MO: Mosby.

Biological-sounding concepts, especially heritability, have been misused to imply a genetic basis for group differences in IQ scores. There are many cognitive abilities—a single general factor of intelligence is inadequate to account for current knowledge in psychological measurement or cognitive science.

CHAPTER
11

How Heritability Misleads About Race

Ned Block

According to *The Bell Curve*, Black Americans are genetically inferior to Whites. Herrnstein's and Murray's (1994) book also argued that there is something called general intelligence that is measured by IQ tests, socially important, and 60% heritable within Whites. (I explain heritability later.) However, my target here is their claim about Black genetic inferiority. It has been subject to wide-ranging criticism since the book was first published. Those criticisms, however, have missed its deepest flaws. Indeed, the Herrnstein and Murray argument depends on conceptual confusions about the genetic determination of human behavior that have not been fully addressed—in fact have been tacitly accepted to some degree—by many of the book's sharpest critics.

Before getting to the confusions, let us first be clear about the conclusion itself. In a recent article, "The Real Bell Curve," Murray (1994) grumbled about critics, such as Gould (1994), who read the book as saying that racial differences in IQ are mostly genetic. Murray answered by quoting from the book:

> If the reader is now convinced that either the genetic or environmental expla-
> nations have won out to the exclusion of the other, we have not done a suffi-
> ciently good job in presenting one side or the other. It seems highly likely to us
> that both genes and the environment have something to do with racial differ-
> ences. What might the mix be? We are resolutely agnostic on that issue; as far

as we can determine, the evidence does not yet justify an estimate. (Herrnstein & Murray, 1994, p. 311)

In this passage, Herrnstein and Murray (1994) were "resolutely agnostic" about whether bad environment or genetic endowment is more responsible for the lower IQs of Blacks. However, they indicated no agnosticism at all about whether part of the IQ difference[1] between Blacks and Whites is genetic; and given their way of thinking about the matter, this means that they are not at all agnostic about some Black genetic inferiority.

THE SIMPLE ARGUMENT

The Herrnstein–Murray argument for genetic IQ differences is based on two facts: IQ is 60% heritable within the White population and there is a stable 15-point difference between average IQs of Whites and Blacks. With IQ largely genetic in Whites, it is natural to conclude—according to Herrnstein and Murray—that the Black–White difference, too, is at least partly genetic. Their argument has more to it; they raised issues about the pattern and magnitude of the differences that I get to later. However, the most important flaws in the more complex version are fully visible in this simple argument.

Herrnstein and Murray's argument depends on thinking of the 15-point IQ difference as divisible into a genetic chunk and an environmental chunk. This picture suggests the following three alternatives:

- *Extreme Environmentalism*: Blacks are genetically on par with Whites, so the IQ gap is all environmental.
- *Extreme Geneticism*: Blacks are environmentally on par with Whites, so the IQ gap is all genetic.
- *The Reasonable View*: Blacks are worse off both genetically and environmentally: so some of the gap is genetic, some environmental.

The 60% heritability of IQ is thought to exclude extreme environmentalism. Well-known environmental effects on IQ, together with differences between Black and White environments acknowledged by Herrnstein and Murray, exclude extreme geneticism. Thus we are left with the reasonable view, which postulates *some* Black genetic inferiority.

Notice, however, that the statement of alternatives blots out a crucial possibility: Blacks are much worse off than Whites environmentally and better off genetically. Allowing this option, we get a different set of alternatives: Genetically, Blacks are worse off, better off, or equal to Whites. I do not say that it is likely that Blacks are genetically better off than Whites, but it is possible, and—a very important point—what you consider possible affects what you think is an extremist position.

---

[1]I am going along with a dangerous way of thinking here. As I point out in the last section of this chapter, this talk of part of an IQ difference is deeply problematic.

And what you think is an extremist position affects your estimate of the *probabilities*. Moreover, the critics of Herrnstein and Murray have tended to trip over this possibility. For example, in a *New York Times* op-ed critique that describes *The Bell Curve* as "bogus" and "nothing but a racial epithet," Herbert (1994) insisted that "the overwhelming consensus of experts in the field is that environmental conditions account for most of the disparity when the test results of large groups are compared" (p. 250). In effect, he used known environmental effects on IQ to argue for a low degree of Black genetic inferiority: in effect, he accepts a version of The Reasonable View. Even Gould (1994), in his otherwise excellent article in *The New Yorker*, misstepped here. Apparently accepting *The Bell Curve*'s way of conceiving the issue, he complained that Herrnstein and Murray wrongly minimized the large environmental malleability of IQ. He said that they turn "every straw on their side into an oak, while mentioning but downplaying the strong circumstantial case for substantial malleability and little average genetic difference" (p. 7). Gould did not do enough to guard against the natural interpretation of "little average genetic difference" in the context of discussion of *The Bell Curve* as little average genetic inferiority of Blacks. Several critics in *The New Republic* (Gates, 1994), in turn, wondered about the size of the "genetic component of the Black–White difference" (p. 10), thereby buying into the same way of thinking.

If you accept *The Bell Curve*'s way of putting the options, then the idea that environmental differences between Blacks and Whites are big enough to account for 15 IQ points looks like extremism. However, given the actual alternatives—that Blacks are genetically on par with Whites, or worse off, or better off—zero genetic difference does not seem extremist at all.

However, isn't the idea of Black genetic superiority in IQ a desperate and pathetic attempt to exploit a mere logical possibility? Consider a parallel case. Number of toes is genetic in sloths and humans, and humans are observed to have five toes whereas diurnal sloths are observed to have three. Is there any real possibility that the genetic toe difference between humans and sloths goes in the opposite direction from the observed toe-number gap? It could be that the three-toed sloth evolved six toes, but we observe only three because of a thalidomide-like chemical that has polluted their food during the years in which we have observed them. However, this possibility is only worth mentioning as an example of something extremely unlikely. This example suggests a fundamental principle that, although never articulated, underlies all of Herrnstein's and Murray's thinking on genes and IQ: If a characteristic is largely genetic and there is an observed difference in that characteristic between two groups, then the genetic difference between the two groups is very likely to go in the same direction as the observed difference.

Applying this principle to the case of IQ: given the substantial heritability of IQ (recall, 60% within the White population), if East Asians are superior in measured IQ, then, according to the fundamental principle, they are highly likely to be genetically superior. If Blacks are inferior in measured IQ, then they are likely to be genetically inferior in IQ.

Although the fundamental principle seems intuitively plausible, it is either irrelevant to the Herrnstein–Murray argument or simply false. To see the problem, we need first to understand a crucial ambiguity in the term *genetic*. That term has two senses, and in the next section, I describe those senses in some detail. To put the point schematically for now: the claim that a trait is genetic can mean either that the trait itself is fixed by a person's genes—the trait is genetically determined—or that differences in the trait in some populations can be traced to genes—the trait shows a high degree of heritability. Once that distinction is in place, the problems for the principle follow. Again, to put the point schematically for now: if "genetic" is used to mean genetically determined, then IQ is not genetic because it is not fixed by a person's genes, and the principle is therefore irrelevant. If "genetic" is used to mean heritable, then IQ is genetic but the principle is false because heritability within one group implies nothing about what is likely in explanation of differences between groups. In neither case, however, does the principle support *The Bell Curve*'s claim about genetic differences in IQ.

TWO SENSES OF "GENETIC"

To understand *The Bell Curve*'s fallacy, we need to distinguish the ordinary idea of genetic determination from the scientific concept of heritability, on which all of Herrnstein and Murray's (1994) data rely. Genetic determination is a matter of what causes a characteristic: Number of toes is genetically determined because our genes cause us to have five toes. Heritability, by contrast, is a matter of what causes differences in a characteristic: Heritability of number of toes is a matter of the extent to which genetic differences cause variation in number of toes (that some cats have five toes, and some have six). Heritability is, therefore, defined as a fraction: It is the ratio of genetically caused variation to total variation (including both environmental and genetic variation). Genetic determination, by contrast, is an informal and intuitive notion that lacks quantitative definition, and depends on the idea of a normal environment. A characteristic could be said to be genetically determined if it is coded in and caused by the genes and bound to develop in a normal environment. Consequently, whereas genetic determination in a single person makes sense—my brown hair color is genetically determined— heritability makes sense only relative to a population in which individuals differ from one another—you cannot ask "What's the heritability of my IQ?"

For example, the number of fingers on a human hand or toes on a human foot is genetically determined: The genes code for five fingers and toes in almost everyone, and five fingers and toes develop in any normal environment. However, the heritability of number of fingers and toes in humans is almost certainly very low. That is because most of the variation in numbers of toes is environmentally caused, often by problems in fetal development. For example, when pregnant women took thalidomide some years ago, many babies had fewer than five fingers and toes. If we look at numbers of fingers and toes in adults, we find many missing digits as a result of accidents. However, genetic coding for six toes is rare in humans (although apparently not in cats). Therefore, genetically caused variation appears to be small compared to environmentally caused variation. If someone asks, then, whether number of toes is genetic or not, the right answer is: "it depends what you mean by genetic." The number of toes is genetically determined, but heritability is low because genes are not responsible for much of the variation.

Conversely, a characteristic can be highly heritable even if it is not genetically determined. Some years ago, when only women wore earrings, the heritability of having an earring was high because differences in whether a person had an earring were "due" to a genetic (chromosomal) difference. Now that earrings are less gender specific, the heritability of having an earring has no doubt decreased. But neither then nor now was having earrings genetically determined in anything like the manner of having five fingers. The heritability literature is full of cases like this: high measured heritabilities for characteristics whose genetic determination is doubtful. For example, the same methodology that yields 60% heritability for IQ also yields 50% percent heritability of academic performance and 40% heritability of occupational status (Plomin et al., 1990, p. 393). Obviously, occupational status is not genetically determined: Genes do not code for having a blue-collar job.

More significantly, a child's environment is often a heritable characteristic, strange as this may seem. If degree of musical talent is highly heritable and if variation in the number of music lessons a child gets depends on variation in musical talent, then the number of music lessons that a child gets may be heritable, too, despite not being genetically determined. In fact, recent studies of heritabilities of various features of children's environments show substantial heritabilities for many environmental features—for example, the "warmth" of the parents' behavior toward the child. Even number of hours of TV watched and number and variety of a child's toys shows some heritability (Plomin & Bergman, 1991; Scarr & McCartney, 1983). If this seems unintelligible, think of it this way: Variation in these environmental properties is in part due to variation in heritable characteristics of the child, and so the environmental characteristics themselves are heritable. Readers of *The Bell Curve* often suppose that a heritable characteristic is one that is passed down in the genes, but this identification is importantly flawed. The number and variety of a child's toys is not passed down in the genes. Heritability is a matter of the causation of differences, not what is passed down.

THE CASE OF IQ

I have given examples of traits that are genetically determined but not heritable and, conversely, traits that are heritable but not genetically determined. Do these weird examples have any relevance to the case of IQ? Maybe there is a range of normal cases, of which IQ is an example, for which the oddities that I have pointed to are simply irrelevant.

Not so! In fact, IQ is a great example of a trait that is highly heritable but not genetically determined. Recall that what makes toe number genetically determined is that having five toes is coded in and caused by the genes so as to develop in any normal environment. By contrast, IQ is enormously affected by normal environmental variation, and in ways that are not well understood. As Herrnstein and Murray (1994) conceded, children from very low socioeconomic status backgrounds who are adopted into high socioeconomic status backgrounds have IQs dramatically higher than their parents. The point is underscored by what Herrnstein and Murray called the Flynn Effect: IQ has been rising about 3 points every 10 years worldwide. Since World War II, IQ in many countries has gone up 15 points, about the same as the gap separating Blacks and Whites in this country. In some countries, the increase has been more dramatic. For example, average IQ in Holland rose 21 points between 1952 and 1982 (Flynn, 1987). In a species in which toe number reacted in this way with environment (imagine a centipedelike creature that added toes as it ate more) I doubt that we would think of number of toes as genetically determined.

It is worth emphasizing the strength of the data about the large IQ increases in Holland. The 21-point increase reported by Flynn (1987) is based on comprehensive testing of all Dutch 18-year-olds who pass a medical exam (and there has been no change in the passing rate). The test used is Raven's Progressive Matrices, a widely respected "nonverbal test that is an especially good measure of [general intelligence]" (p. 273). Even Lynn (1992), the arch-Jensenist who is the source of much of *The Bell Curve*'s data on race, conceded this point. He said:

> The magnitude of the increase has generally been found to be about three IQ points per decade, making fifteen points over a fifty-year period. There have, however, been some larger gains among 18-year-old conscripts in The Netherlands and Belgium amounting to seven IQ points per decade.

Lynn also mentioned that similar results have been found in France (Lynn, 1992). Herrnstein and Murray (1994) conceded that "In some countries, the upward drift since World War II has been as much as a point per year for some spans of years" (p. 308). In an area where the facts are often contested, it is notable that this set of facts seems to be accepted by both sides.

One very important conclusion from the Flynn data is that no one understands very much about how environmental variation differentially affects IQ. The cause of the large increases in Holland is simply unknown. Even Herrnstein and Murray conceded that "relatively little [of the environmental variation in IQ] can be traced to the shared environments created by families. It is, rather, a set of environmental influences *mostly unknown at present*, that are experienced by individuals as individuals" (p. 108, italics added). Indeed, the crucial factor that has enabled the research that Herrnstein and Murray reported to exist at all is the fact that one can measure the heritability of a characteristic without having much of an idea of what the characteristic is. To calculate the heritability of IQ, we do not need to know what IQ tests measure; we need only to be able to measure IQ—whatever it is—in various circumstances.

A few additional observations about heritability and IQ underscore the need for great caution in drawing any inferences about the sources of differences in IQ. A common method for measuring heritability relies on comparisons of the correlations of IQ among one-egg twins raised by their biological parents compared with two-egg twins raised by their biological parents. Suppose you give IQ tests to two children and they get the same score. One has a one-egg (identical) twin; the other has a two-egg (fraternal) twin. Suppose that you can predict the score of the one-egg twin reliably, but that your prediction of the score of the two-egg twin is much less reliable. This difference would be an indication of high heritability of IQ because one-egg twins share all their genes, whereas two-egg twins share half their genes.

Heritability studies of IQ within White populations in the United States and northern Europe have tended to yield moderately high heritabilities: Herrnstein's and Murray's (1994) 60% is a reasonable figure. However, it is important to note that no one would do one of these heritability studies in a mixed Black–White population. The reason is straightforward: If you place a pair of Black one-egg twins in different environments "at random," you automatically fail to randomize environments. The Black twins will bring part of their environment with them; they are both Black and will be treated as Black.

Moreover, heritability—unlike genetic determination—can be very different in different populations. For example, the heritability of IQ could be decreased if half the population were chosen at random to receive IQ-lowering brain damage: By damaging the brains of some people, you make the environmentally caused variation larger. Or suppose we could make a million clones of Al Gore, raising them in very different environments so there would be some variation in IQ, all environmentally caused. Heritability in that population would be zero because the ratio of genetic variation to total variation is zero if the genetic variation is zero. To take a real example, the heritability of IQ increases throughout childhood into adulthood. One study gives heritability figures of under 20% in infancy, about 30% in childhood, 50% in adolescence, and a bit higher in adult life.[2] Studies of older twins in Sweden report an 80% heritability figure for adults by age 50 as compared to 50% heritability for children (Pedersen et al., 1992). One possible reason for the rise in heritability is that although the genetic variation remains the same, environmental variation decreases with age. Children have very different environments; some parents do not speak to their children, others are ever verbally probing and jousting. Adults in industrialized countries, by contrast, are to a greater degree immersed in the same culture (e.g., the same TV programs). With more uniform environments, the heritability goes up. I hope these points remove the temptation (exhibited in *The Bell Curve*) to think of the heritability of IQ as a constant (like the speed of light). Heritability is a population statistic just like birthrate or number of TVs and can be expected to change with changing circumstances. There is no reason to expect the heritability of IQ in India to be close to the heritability of IQ in Korea.

These issues are pathetically misunderstood by Murray (Wright, 1995). In a CNN interview reported in *The New Republic*, Murray declared "When I—when we—say

---

[2]Plomin (1990) noted that the results are not a consequence of increasing reliability of IQ tests.

60 percent heritability, it's not 60 percent of the variation. It is 60 percent of the IQ in any given person." Later, he repeated that for the average person, "60 percent of the intelligence comes from heredity," and added that this was true of the "human species," missing the point that heritability makes no sense for an individual and that heritability statistics are population relative. In a letter to the editor in which Murray complained about being quoted out of context (Murray, 1995), he quoted more of what he had said: "Your IQ may have been determined overwhelmingly by genes or it may have been—yours personally—or overwhelmingly by environment. That can vary a lot from individual to individual. In the human species as a whole, you have a large genetic component." *The Bell Curve* itself does not make these embarrassing mistakes. Herrnstein, the late co-Author, was a professional on these topics. However, the upshot of part of this chapter is that the book's main argument depends for some of its persuasive force on a more subtle conflation of heritability and genetic determination. Murray's confusion serves to underscore just how difficult these concepts can be, even for someone so numerate as Murray.

What is the upshot of the distinction between genetic determination and heritability for the argument of *The Bell Curve*? Recall the sloth example: Toe number is genetic in sloths and in humans; there is a difference in toe number; therefore the toe number difference is genetic. This is a good argument: It strains the imagination to suppose that the genetic toe difference between sloths and humans goes in the opposite direction from the observed toe difference. It is ludicrous to suppose that our genes code for two, despite the five we see at the beach. In this sense the Herrnstein and Murray (1994) argument works for the concept of genetic determination. However, the data on genes and IQ are about heritability, not genetic determination.

Is IQ genetically determined as well as heritable? No! As I already pointed out, IQ is very reactive to changes in environments in the normal range. Recall the example of the large increase in scores Holland. Further, the claim that IQ is genetically determined is not the kind of quantitative claim on which Herrnstein and Murray (1994) would want to base their claims about genes and race.

If "genetic" means genetically determined, then IQ is not genetic in Whites or anyone else (and in any case the issue is not quantitative), so the fundamental principle is irrelevant. If "genetic" means heritable, however, then IQ is largely genetic (among Whites in the United States at least). However, in the next section I show that in this sense of genetic, the argument does not work because the fundamental principle is false.

HERITABILITY AND RACE DIFFERENCE

In an article in the *Harvard Review*, Jensen (1969) started off the current controversy by arguing from heritability within Whites to the genetic difference between Whites and Blacks. Lewontin (1970) responded a year later with a graphic illustration of why this is a mistake. Suppose you buy a bag of seed corn from a hardware store. Grow one handful of it in a carefully controlled environment in which the seeds get uniform illumination and uniform nutrient solution. The corn plants will vary in height, and because the environment is uniform, the heritability of height will be 100%. Now take another handful of corn from the same bag, and grow it in a similarly uniform environment but with a uniformly poor nutrient solution. Again, the plants will vary in height, but all will be stunted (see Fig. 11.1). Once more the heritability of height is 100%. Despite the 100% heritabilities of height within each group, the differences in height between the groups are entirely environmentally caused. Therefore, we can have total heritability within groups, substantial variation between groups, but no genetic difference between groups.

The application to race is obvious: Heritability is high within Whites. However, as Lewontin's example shows, high heritability within groups licenses no conclusion about how to explain differences between groups—none, in particular, about genetic explanations of the differences. Nor does it dictate the direction of any genetic difference between groups. The stunted corn could have been genetically taller, with the genetic advantage outweighed by the environmental deprivation.

In Lewontin's (1970) example, it is assumed that there is no genetic difference between the two groups of corn. But suppose we knew nothing about the two groups of people except that they differed by 15 points in IQ and that IQ had some heritability in both, and we had to guess the causes. For all I have said so far, it would make sense to guess that the lower scoring group was disadvantaged both genetically and environmentally. In the next section, I show that even this weak principle is wrong. However, the principle has no application to the racial question because we know lots more than nothing: We know that the environment can have huge effects on IQ (e. g., the Flynn Effect of 3 points per decade and the 21-point increase in Holland), and that Blacks are environmentally disadvantaged in a way that has been shown to count. However, without being able to measure the effect of being treated as subnormal, and of a historical legacy of slavery and discrimination, how do we know whether its average effect is sufficient to lower Black IQ 15 points, or less than that—or more than that? Our

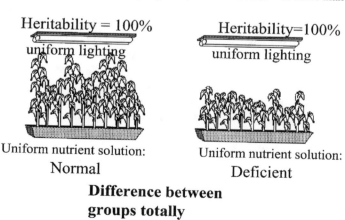

FIG. 11.1.   Heritability can be high within each of two groups even though the difference between the two groups is entirely environmental.

understanding of how the environment affects IQ is not sufficient to make any one of these three alternatives any more likely than the others.

Herrnstein and Murray (1994) have heard appeals to the legacy of slavery and discrimination, and they have a response that appeals both to the pattern of racial differences and their magnitude.

First, the pattern: They remind us that the Black–White IQ difference is smallest at the lowest socioeconomic levels. This leads them to ask:

> Why, if the Black/White difference is entirely environmental, should the advantage of the White" environment compared to the "Black" be greater among the better off and better educated Blacks and Whites? We have not been able to think of a plausible reason. An appeal to the effects of racism to explain ethnic differences also requires explaining why environments poisoned by discrimination and racism for some other groups—against the Chinese or the Jews in some regions of America, for example—have left them with higher scores than the national average. (Herrnstein & Murray, 1994, p. 299)

However, these facts are not hard to understand. Blacks and Whites are to some extent separate cultural groups, and there is no reason to think that a measure like socioeconomic status means the same thing for every culture. Herrnstein and Murray (1994) mentioned the work of Ogbu, an anthropologist who has distinguished a number of types of oppressed minorities (Ogbu, 1986). A key category is that of castelike minorities who are regarded by themselves and others as inferior, and who, if they are immigrants, are not voluntary immigrants. This category includes the Harijans in India, the Burakumin and Koreans in Japan, and the Maori in New Zealand. He distinguished them from groups like Chinese and Jews who are voluntary immigrants and have a culture of self-respect. If higher socioeconomic status Blacks still are to some extent part of a castelike minority, then they will be at an environmental disadvantage relative to higher socioeconomic status Whites. However, low-status Blacks and Whites are more likely to share a caste background. As Gates (1994) pointed out, affirmative action has had the effect of quadrupling the size of the Black middle class since 1967. Most middle-class Blacks have arrived in the middle classes relatively recently, many of them under less than ideal conditions for the development of self-respect. It would be surprising if children of these newly middle-class Blacks were to have fully escaped their caste background in so short a time.

Ogbu (1986) noted that where IQ tests have been given, "the children of these caste-like minorities score about 10–15 points ... lower than dominant group children." He noted further that differences remain "when minority and dominant group members are of similar socioeconomic background." But when "members of a caste-like minority group emigrate to another society, the twin problem of IQ test scores and low academic achievement appears to disappear." Data suggest that the Burakumin who have immigrated to this country do "at least as well at school and the work place" (pp. 32–33) as other Japanese.

As to the magnitude: Herrnstein and Murray (1994) calculated that "the average environment of blacks would have to be at the sixth percentile of the distribution of environments among whites ... for the racial differences to be entirely environmental" (p. 299). They believed that "differences of this magnitude and pattern are implausible" (p. 299). That is, 94% of Whites would have to have an environment that is better for the development of IQ than the environment of the average Black—if the 15-point difference is to be explained environmentally. Herrnstein and Murray believed this is implausible because when you look at environmental measures—for example, parental income and school quality—you do not find that 94% of Whites have a better environment than the average Black. However, this calculation ignores the effect of being in Ogbu's category of a castelike minority. Compare the Dutch 18-year-olds of 1982 with their fathers' cohort, the 18-year-olds of 1952. The difference is entirely environmental despite the probable substantial heritability within each group. Using the same procedures as Herrnstein and Murray, Flynn (1987) calculated that 99% of the 1982 group had to have a better environment for the development of IQ than the average member of the 1952 group. Given differences of this magnitude among people of a uniform culture who are separated only by a single generation, is it really so implausible that 94% of Whites have an environment better than a Black at the 50th percentile?

Environmental differences, then, including the sort that affect Black Americans, are known to have large effects on IQ. Moreover, we currently have no way to quantify these effects, so we should draw no conclusion about the probability of any Black genetic IQ advantage or disadvantage. As applied to the case of IQ, then, the fundamental principle is false: The combination of high heritability within the White population and persistent Black–White differences does not support a case for probable genetic differences.

INDIRECT HERITABILITY

Earlier, I commented that if we knew nothing at all about two groups except that they differed by 15 points in IQ and that IQ is heritable in both, and we had to guess the causes, it might seem sensible to guess that the lower scoring group was disadvantaged both genetically and environmentally. I have been emphasizing that in the case of Black–White IQ differences, we know much more than "nothing at all." In particular, we know that environmental differences affect IQ in ways that we do not understand (the Flynn Effect) and that American Blacks are environmentally disadvantaged, but we do not know the magnitude of the disadvantage. So we do not have any way of judging the probability that Blacks are genetically worse off than Whites, genetically better off, or genetically equal. I now want to show that even if we knew nothing, any such guess would be misguided, for reasons that go to the heart of the notion of heritability.

Let us start with an example (Jencks et al., 1972). Consider a culture in which red-haired children are beaten over the head regularly, but all other children are treated well. This effect will increase the measured heritability of IQ because red-haired identical twins will tend to resemble one another in IQ (because they will both have low IQs) no matter what the social class of the family in which they are raised. The effect of a red-hair gene on red hair is a direct genetic effect because the gene affects the color via an internal biochemical process. By contrast, a gene affects a characteristic indirectly by producing a direct effect that interacts with the environment so as to affect the characteristic. In the hypothetical example, the red-hair genes affect IQ indirectly. In the case of IQ, no one has any idea how to separate out direct from indirect genetic effects because no one has much of an idea how genes and environment affect IQ. For that reason, we do not know whether or to what extent the roughly 60% heritability of IQ found in White populations is indirect heritability as opposed to direct heritability.[3]

The methodology used to measure heritability obscures this ignorance by counting differences in characteristics as caused by genetic differences whenever there is a genetic difference, even if there is also an environmental difference. This distorts the ways we normally think about causation. For instance, the heritability methodology focuses on the difference between the red-hair genes and genes for other hair colors, not on the fact that red-haired children—unlike blond children—are beaten.

Earlier I said that wearing earrings used to be highly heritable because differences were "due" to the XY–XX difference. I put quotes around "due" because it is a by-product of the methodology for measuring heritability to adopt a tacit convention that genes are taken to dominate environment. When virtually only women were wearing earrings, variation in earrings was as much social as genetic, but counted as highly heritable. If there is a genetic difference in the causal chains that lead to different characteristics, the difference counts as genetically caused even if the environmental differences are just as important. If we adopted the opposite convention—concluding from any environmental difference in two causal chains that the differences are environmentally caused—then we could not use current methodology for measuring heritability, because we have no general method of detecting indirect genetic effects using current techniques. Heritabilities using the two different conventions would be radically different if there are substantial indirect genetic effects.

Recall the examples mentioned earlier about the measured heritabilities of such quantities as number of hours watching TV. No one should suppose that there is variation in genes *for* watching TV; this is a case of indirect effects. Consider further the fact that no one would do a heritability study on a mixed Black–White population. I mentioned earlier that if you place a pair of Black one-egg twins in different homes, you automatically fail to randomize environments, because the Black twins will bring part of their environment with them; they are both Black and will be treated as Black. This is an indirect genetic effect par excellence. Implicitly, everyone in this field recognizes that, yet more subtle possibilities of indirect effects are typically ignored.

Recall that heritability is defined as a fraction: variation due to genetic differences divided by total variation. The measure of variation that is always used (although alternatives are available) is a statistical quantity known as *variance*. One factor that raises variance is a positive correlation between genetic and environmental variables.

---

[3]I coined the term *indirect heritability* many years ago (Block & Dworkin, 1974), but it is now sometimes called *reactive heritability* (Tooby & Cosmides, 1990).

Suppose that children whose genes give them an advantage in musical talent tend to have parents who provide them with an environment conducive to developing that talent—music lessons, concerts, a great CD collection, musical discussion over dinner, and so on. Suppose further that other children who have a genetic disadvantage also have an environment that stultifies their musical talents. The correlation between genes and environment will move children toward the extremes of the distribution, increasing the variance in musical skills.

Variance due to gene–environment correlation (gene–environment "covariance") should not be counted in the genetic component of the variance, and there are a variety of attitudes toward separating out such variance. It is common in behavior genetics to distinguish among a number of different types of covariance (Loehlin & DeFries, 1987; Plomin, 1990; Plomin, DeFries, & Loehlin, 1977). The kind just mentioned, in which parents provide genes for musical talent and an environment that develops it, is called passive covariance because it does not depend on what the child does. Reactive covariance is a matter of the environment reacting to the child's qualities, as when a school gives extra music classes to children who exhibit musical talent. With active covariance, the child creates a gene–environment correlation, as when a musically talented child practices musical themes in the imagination or pays attention to the musical environment. Passive covariance can be controlled in heritability calculations by attention to adoption studies in which the double advantage or double disadvantage does not exist. However, reactive and active covariance cannot be measured without specific hypotheses about how the environment affects IQ. As I observed, little is known—as all parties to the disagreements about genetics and IQ agree—about how the environment affects IQ. Therefore, distinguishing reactive and active covariance is, on the whole, beyond the reach of the empirical methods of our era's "behavior genetics," for those methods do not include an understanding of what IQ is—whether it is information-processing capacity, or whether it has more to do with how information-processing capacity is deployed.

These points about covariance assume that there are genes for IQ and that these genes may affect the environment so as to produce effects on IQ that are correlated with the ones that the genes themselves produce. However, this way of presenting the issue seriously underestimates its significance. For as the red-hair example illustrates, indirect genetic effects need not work through anything that should be thought of as IQ genes.

Because we do not know much about how variation in the environment differentially affects IQ, we can only guess about how variation in genes differentially affects IQ indirectly, via the environment. Suppose that a child's perceived attractiveness and self-confidence strongly affects how adults interact with a child in a way that largely accounts for the variation in IQ.[4] Of course, adults could give some

---

[4]Scarr and McCartney (1983), for example, said "It is quite likely that smiley, active babies receive more social stimulation than sober, passive infants. In the intellectual area, cooperative, attentive preschoolers receive more pleasant instructional interactions from the adults around them than uncooperative distractible children. (p. 427) ... The social psychology literature on attractiveness ... would seem to support our view that some personal characteristics evoke differential responses" (p. 433).

children more attention than others without producing IQ differences, but differences might result from variations in adult attention. Suppose further that personal attractiveness and self-confidence are highly heritable. Then we would have an indirect effect par excellence, and such an effect could, for all we know, largely account for the heritability of IQ. Without an understanding of how the environment affects IQ, we simply have no way of determining how much of the variance in IQ is indirect genetic variance of this sort. Of course, if we knew that some specific adult behavior that is triggered by some specific heritable property of children was responsible for a large component of IQ variation, then we could measure that behavior. However, there is no theory of intelligence or IQ that would allow us to have any real grip on such factors.

The upshot is that there may be a large component of heritability due to indirect genetic effects, including (but not limited to) gene–environment correlation, that is outside the boundaries of what can be measured given the mainly atheoretical approach available today. Where does the gene–environment covariance show up in heritability calculations? Answer: active and reactive effects that we do not know how to measure inevitably are included in the gene component. This is often regarded by behavior geneticists as perfectly okay (e.g., Roberts, 1967). In practice, if researchers were to actually identify an "unmeritocratic" effect such as the red hair indirect effect mentioned earlier, they would undoubtedly count the variance produced by the effect as covariance rather than genetic variance. An adoption study involving both black and white adopted children would be recognized by all to be a study in which the adopted children bring part of their environment with them into the adoptive family. However, we have no idea how much of the 60% of the variance in IQ that is said to be genetic involves genes that change the environment in this way. So in practice, covariance due to indirect effects that people know how to measure—at least if it is flagrantly nonmeritocratic—is not counted in the heritability; but other indirect effects are counted as genetic. So what counts as genetic variance (inflating heritability) is a matter of value judgements and of what effects we know about. Surely this makes heritability a lousy scientific concept.

In effect, the field has adopted an axiom that heritability of IQ can be measured by current methods. Without this assumption, the right conclusion would be that because we cannot separate indirect genetic effects (including certain kinds of gene–environment covariance) from pure genetic variance, no heritability estimate can be made. Why does the field adopt this axiom? I cannot help thinking that part of the explanation is that behavior genetics is a young field, struggling for acceptance and funding, and heritability is a flag that attracts attention to it (Plomin, 1990).

Let us return to the speculation that the 60% heritability of IQ (within Whites) is entirely indirect and due to differential treatment of children on the basis of heritable characteristics. Then the direct heritability of IQ would be zero and we would have no reason to think that anything that could be called genes for IQ (e.g., genes for information-processing capacity) vary in the White population, and no reason to look for genetic differences to explain the 15-point difference between Blacks and Whites. Instead, we would have reason to look for differences in the ways adults interact with children to explain the Black–White IQ difference. So indirect heritability suggests an environmental hypothesis about the measured Black–White IQ difference, one that could perhaps be the object of social policy. Are there reasons to expect indirect genetic effects in the Black–White difference? I mentioned the obvious example of genes for skin color earlier, but there may be less obvious indirect effects as well. There are many more low-birth-weight Black babies than White babies. Nothing known appears to rule out a genetic explanation (Lieberman, 1995). Low birth weight correlates negatively with IQ. If Blacks are more likely to have genes for low-birth-weight babies, perhaps the effect could be neutralized by diet or by drug intervention in pregnancy. Certainly, no one should think of genes for low birth weight as IQ genes.

The points I have just made about indirect heritability show why, as I said at the beginning of this section, any inferences from heritability statistics to genetic disadvantage would be misguided. Such inferences seem plausible if we assume that the heritability of IQ within Whites reflects differences in IQ caused by differences in IQ genes. However, the points about indirect heritability show that we do not know whether any of the variation within Whites is due to variation in IQ genes. If we have no real grip on the kinds of causal mechanisms that produce the 60% heritability within Whites, we can have no confidence in any extrapolation to Blacks.

Let us call a person's genome (his or her total set of genes) genetically inferior with respect to IQ if that genome yields low IQ in any normal environment. But what is to count as a normal environment? In the example discussed earlier, genes for red hair yield low IQ within environments that are normal in the environment of the hypothetical society, but in environments that we would consider normal, the red-hair genes are irrelevant to IQ. What if the heritabilities observed for IQ are a result of indirect effects that can be changed by changing social practice? Then phrases like "genetically inferior in IQ" and "genetic disadvantage in IQ" will only apply to genomes such as that of Down's syndrome that yield low IQ no matter what the social practices.

The same points apply to recent reports of a gene for homosexuality—for example, a *New York Times* article headlined "New Evidence of a 'Gay Gene.'" Brothers who are both gay turn out to be more likely to share some genetic material on their X chromosomes. However, the shared genetic material could code for physical or psychological characteristics that interact with our highly contingent social structures in a way that increases the probability that its possessor will be gay. Perhaps the shared material makes both brothers more attractive to gays, or perhaps it increases their interest in bodily fitness, which puts them in contact with a gay culture that also values fitness. Or perhaps it is a gene for early puberty, causing boys to mature at an age at which it happens to be socially acceptable for boys to be friends with other boys but not with girls. If the effect is indirect, it might disappear in another cultural setting.

The point about indirect heritability also casts doubt on Herrnstein and Murray's (1994) ideas about genetic social stratification among Whites. If the 60% heritability does not reflect IQ genes, then there is no reason to suppose that social classes differ at all in genuine IQ genes even if there are any. Herrnstein and Murray worried about pollution of the gene pool by immigrants and by large numbers of children of low-IQ parents. However, if the heritability of IQ is mainly indirect, their emphasis on genes is misdirected. If we lived in a culture that damaged the brains of red-haired children, it would be perverse to complain about genetic pollution when large numbers of red-haired immigrants arrived. Instead, we should try to change the social practices that deprive those with certain genes of an equal chance.

ACKNOWLEDGMENTS

This article is adapted from one that originally appeared in *The Boston Review, 20*(6), January 1996, pp. 30–35, under the title "Race, Genes, and IQ." Thanks to Holly J. Zack for her editorial assistance.

REFERENCES

Block, N., & Dworkin, G. (1974). IQ, heritability and inequality, part II. *Philosophy and Public Affairs, 4*(1), 40–99.

Flynn, J. R. (1987). Massive IQ gains in 14 nations: What IQ tests really measure. *Psychological Bulletin, 101*(2), 171–191.

Gates, H. L., Jr. (1994, October 31). Why now? *The New Republic, 211,* 10.

Gould, S. J. (1994). Curveball. *The New Yorker,* 139–149.

Herbert, B. (1994, October 26). Throwing a curve. *The New York Times.*

Herrnstein, R. J., & Murray, C. (1994). *The bell curve: Intelligence and class structure in American life.* New York: The Free Press.

Jencks, C., Smith, M., Acland, H., Bane, M., Cohen, D., Gintis, H., Heyns, B., & Michelson, S. (1972). *Inequality: A reassessment of the effect of family and schooling in America.* New York: Basic Books.

Jensen, A. R. (1969). How much can we boost IQ and scholastic achievement? *Harvard Educational Review, 39,* 1–123.

Lewontin, R. (1970). Race and intelligence. *Bulletin of the Atomic Scientists, 26*(3), 2–8.

Lieberman, E. (1995). Low birth weight—not a Black-and-White issue. *New England Journal of Medicine, 332*(2), 117–118.

Loehlin, J., & DeFries, J. (1987). Genotype-environment correlation and IQ. *Behavior Genetics, 17*(3), 263–277.

Lynn, R. (1992). Lynn replies to Flynn. In J. Lynch et al. (Eds.), *Cultural diversity and the schools.*

Pedersen, N. L., Plomin, R., Nesselroade, J., & McClearn, G. (1992). A quantitative genetic analysis of the cognitive abilities during the second half of the life span. *Psychological Science, 3*(6), 346–353.

Plomin, R. (1990). *Nature and nurture.* Pacific Grove, CA: Brooks-Cole.

Plomin, R., & Bergman, C. (1991). The nature of nurture: Genetic influence on "environmental" measures. *The Behavioral and Brain Sciences, 14*(3), 373–386.

Plomin, R., DeFries, J., & McClearn, G. (1990). *Behavior Genetics: A primer.* New York: Freeman.

Plomin, R., DeFries, J., & Loehlin, J. (1977). Genotype-environment interaction and correlation in the analysis of human behavior. *Psychological Bulletin, 84*(2), 309–322.

Roberts, R. C. (1967). Some concepts and methods in quantitative genetics. In J. Hirsch (Ed.), *Behavior-genetic analysis* (pp. 214–257). New York: McGraw Hill.

Scarr, S., & McCartney, K. (1983). How people make their own environments: A theory of genotype (environment effects. *Child Development, 54,* 424–435.

Tooby, J., & Cosmides, L. (1990). On the universality of human nature and the uniqueness of the individual: The role of genetics and adaptation. *Journal of Personality, 58*(1), 17–67.

Wright, R. (1995, January 2). Has Charles Murray read his own book? *The New Republic,* 6.

Selections of Evidence, Misleading Assumptions, and Oversimplifications: The Political Message of *The Bell Curve*

John L. Horn

PROLOGUE

Those who think the ethnic differences are readily explained by environmental differences haven't been tough-minded enough about their own argument.... At this complex intersection of complex factors, the easy answers are unsatisfactory ones. (Herrnstein & Murray, 1994, p. 299)

T he tumult surrounding *The Bell Curve: Intelligence and Class Structure in American Life* has died down. However, the main ideas it expressed are still with us, widely and sincerely proclaimed. They are not new: they seem always to have been with us. But judging from the news media coverage—major articles in *Newsweek*, *The Wall Street Journal*, *The New Republic*, and radio and TV reports—*The Bell Curve* appears to be a particularly appealing and compelling statement of these ideas.

What would make it so? First, the book gives clear voice to widely held beliefs: people come in types and races, some inferior, some superior; not much can be done, or should be done, to improve the lot of the "inferior." This accounts for some of the book's appeal, but what makes it compelling is its ring of authority. It stamps beliefs with a seal of scientific approval. It claims to be "tough-minded," based on the most valid, up-to-date scientific evidence, agreed on by all well-informed scientists. It is big and complex—884 pages, 22 chapters, 1,034 references, 108 pages of footnotes, 110 pages in 7 appendixes. The size and complexity of the book—the time and effort needed to produce it—suggest that it must be correct.

The book is written to be accessible to a wide audience. It has a clear message that comes across early and is drumbeat steadily through the chapters. It intones that our society is a meritocracy and increasingly is developing into a system of hereditary castes. This results because: (a) general intelligence is primarily genetically determined, and (b) differences in general intelligence produce differences in social class status—wealth and possessions, occupational level, prestige, and influence on the high end; poverty, welfare dependency, illegitimacy, and crime at the other end. The argument proceeds as follows.

Our culture is complex and becoming more complex. The work of maintaining that culture requires people of high intellectual capability. People in the lower part of the distribution of general intelligence are genetically ill-equipped to reach these high levels, and thus are not able to help maintain the culture. They are not needed. Only the benevolence of welfare maintains them. As the culture becomes more complex, the level of intelligence required to maintain it increases and the proportion of people not needed increases for this reason, as well as because the lower classes overreproduce. Increasingly, therefore, people in the lower part of the distribution of intelligence become a burden on society. On the other hand, people at the high end of the distribution of general intelligence, well endowed by genetic inheritance, able to reach the high levels of capability needed to maintain the culture, are precious and therefore will get, and deserve to get, the high status, influence, and rewards of the society. They are selected through education for further education, which brings them into proximity with each other for purposes of breeding. The lower classes are deselected, and this also creates conditions for interbreeding. Thus, increasingly people will be separated by their genetically determined intelligence into attainment classes, segregated by schools attended, consequent wealth, residence, and associated ethnic, geographic, and lifestyle factors, all setting up inbreeding castes. These conditions are now before us and can be seen. *The Bell Curve* was presented to show this. It forecasts that in societies such as that of the United States, increasingly rigid social stratification will develop. At the top will be a class of people equipped by their inheritance to maintain and advance the culture. At the bottom will be a class of the not needed and unwanted, ordained by their heredity to be forever locked in this condition, reproducing more of their kind than is desired.

The *Bell Curve* authors, Herrnstein and Murray (1994) argue that they will not take a position on whether ethnic group differences in test performances (that indicate the genetically determined intelligence that underlies segregation into castes) are mainly genetically or environmentally determined. They recognize that both genes and the environment have something to do with these differences, but as concerns just what the mix might be, they claim to be "resolutely agnostic."

This disclaimer is disingenuous—an example of what Gardner referred to as a technique of "rhetorical brinkmanship"—protesting that they do not intend to say X (e.g., that blacks are lacking in intelligence) but presenting information and structuring statements in such a way as to lead the reader to the X conclusion. For example, they urge the reader to clearly understand that intelligence is largely genetically determined, that Blacks score 15 points lower than whites on IQ tests (which they say are measures of intelligence), that this difference is essentially the same across all socioeconomic classes, that these results are not due to bias in the tests, and that they believe that neither Blacks nor Whites need be affected by knowledge that a group difference in measured intelligence is genetic instead of environmental. They describe Rushton's (1995) theory of the intellectual inferiority of Blacks, but assure the reader that they are not saying the theory is correct. Thus it is that they say they are resolutely agnostic about ethnic group differences, but present observations, information, suggestions, arguments, and criticisms well calculated to plant the thought that, indeed, Blacks are inherently lacking in intelligence.

I refer to these main arguments of *The Bell Curve* as Herrnstein and Murray's thesis, acknowledging that these ideas are not original with them and have been around for some time—at least, since the 1910s and 1920s, for example, in Brigham's (1923) "scientific justifications for restrictive immigration quotas" and Yerkes's (1921) essays on racial differences; since Jensen's (1969) writings in the 1960s on the immutability of race differences in intelligence and the futility of Head Start, and somewhat later, accompanying this, in Shockley's (1971) advocacy of sterilization for people of low IQ to do away with the problems of social welfare, and in Herrnstein's (1973) writings on meritocracy determined by IQ.

These earlier presentations of the thesis were accompanied by flurries of criticisms that would appear to strike it down. But then, after a time, the thesis would reappear. Perhaps the need to express it is always there, lurking in needs to justify social inequalities, waiting for an eloquent voice to give it affirmation. More troublesome, perhaps the thesis is fundamentally correct, and the repeated efforts to express it, accompanied by critiques, are simply iterations along a path converging toward a correct statement of a principle of human culture.

Perhaps, but probably not. Individual differences are inevitable, societies and cultures becoming more complex may be inevitable, and merit will probably always tend to be rewarded, but segregation into inbreeding classes based on inherent individual differences in intelligence does not follow necessarily from these conditions.

Even if the thesis is correct, it is not shown to be so by the data and arguments of *The Bell Curve*. The book lacks the necessary evidence and reasoning to prove the case.

Contrary to claim, it is not tough-minded, based on only the facts of science. It is argument that uses selections of scientific evidence to make a case in support of opinions.

This should be understood because the book is put forth as, and has been proclaimed to be, the ultimate in sound argument from the evidence of the social sciences. Instead, it is a good example of how to mislead with selections from science. It should not persuade. This should be understood by those who would champion the book's thesis, as well as by those who do not like it.

There are thus good reasons to study the book carefully, to identify why it is incorrect, and see how, nevertheless, it can be convincing.

BOOK LAYOUT

There are three main parts to the book: the text, the footnotes, and the appendixes. In the text the main arguments are presented forcefully, but also in a manner structured to be diplomatic, balanced, and reasonable. In the footnotes the arguments become more strident, the assumptions underlying the arguments are made more nearly clear, and one can gain some understanding of the particular literature to which Herrnstein and Murray attended and the particular authoritative statements they selected for their arguments. The appendixes provide a principal reason for the book. These contain a report of an empirical study Herrnstein and Murray carried out on a large sample of youth. The principal arguments of the book are said to derive from the results of this study.

Three major claims are put forth. First, it is claimed that valued outcomes indicated by job status, wealth, and so on, on the one hand, and poverty, criminality, and so on, on the other hand, are determined primarily by differences in genetically based IQ—general intelligence—not by environmental factors. Results from the empirical study are advanced to support this claim. As part of this argument it is claimed, second, that IQ is not biased, and does not incorrectly favor one class over another. As part of the claim that individual differences in general intelligence are mainly genetically determined, it is argued that group levels and individual differences in IQ are not notably changed by intervention programs. There are other parts to the book—an argument against welfare and affirmative action, a chapter attempting to reconcile increases in norms for IQ tests, the Flynn (1987) Effect, with the authors' concerns that population IQ is declining—but the main thrust of the book is along the lines of the three claims just outlined.

PLAN OF THIS REVIEW

Herrnstein and Murray's (1994) major claims are evaluated in the order listed. It is found that their empirical study demonstrates what is already well known—that school achievement is related to other such achievements and to socially valued outcomes—but does not indicate the extent to which these achievements are related to environmental or innate factors. The extant evidence questions their claim that there is a single, genetically determined attribute of general intelligence. Herrnstein and

Murray's argument that IQ tests are not biased omits consideration of bias in the criteria. Their argument from genetics is not well qualified, misrepresents the evidence, and derives from incorrect conceptualization. Their claim for the immutability of general intelligence omits much of the evidence, and they selectively interpreted such evidence as is admitted. Herrnstein and Murray presented their thesis in the way a lawyer might present a case to win a verdict, rather than in the way a scientist or detective would piece together evidence to get at the truth.

HERRNSTEIN AND MURRAY'S STUDY

To evaluate Herrnstein and Murray's (1994) principal arguments one needs to look carefully at the study the results of which they put forth as support for their thesis. This study is based on a nonminority subsample of the 12,686 14- to-22-year-old youth drawn in 1979 for the National Longitudinal Survey of Youth (NLSY; Baker, Keck, Mott, Quinlan, 1993). The NLSY sample was selected to be census-representative of people and communities in the United States. The information used in Herrnstein and Murray's analyses was gathered over a period from 1979 through 1990. At the time the youth were first measured, information was obtained on the parents and childhood environment. Follow-up information included evidence of the youth's subsequent education, occupational achievement, work history, family formation, and cognitive abilities.

The study can be described in two notably different ways. In Herrnstein and Murray's description it is a study showing that in comparison with environmental influences, high general intelligence, determined through genetic inheritance, is the primary cause of valued achievement outcomes in our society and low intelligence is the primary cause of failure and undesirable outcomes. Described concretely in terms of variables and analysis, the study is a comparison of the correlates of an ability measure (of academic achievement) with the correlates for a measure of socioeconomic status (SES), designed to show that the former are larger than the latter.

In essence, then, two variables are put in regression analysis competition: an ability measure and SES. To understand Herrnstein and Murray's thesis at its core, it is necessary to have a clear picture of the nature of these two variables

The Ability Measure

This was obtained from subtests of the Armed Services Vocational Aptitude Battery. Four of the 10 subtests of this battery were combined to provide one measure. The four tests are Word Knowledge, Paragraph Comprehension, Arithmetic Reasoning, and Mathematics Knowledge. Herrnstein and Murray (1994) found that these four tests had the largest correlations with the first principal component (FPC) based on all 10 tests. They argued that tests that best measure general intelligence are tests that correlate most highly with other tests in a battery, that the size of the correlation with the FPC indicates this, and, therefore, because the four tests referred to correlate most highly with the FPC, a measure obtained with these tests is "one of the most highly g-loaded tests in use" (Herrnstein & Murray, 1994, p. 583). They occasionally referred to the single measure obtained by summing the scores of the four subtests as the Armed Forces Qualification Test (AFQT), but most often they refer to it as IQ or g or general intelligence.

Herrnstein and Murray's (1994) arguments for what is measured with the AFQT are not sound. An FPC component is not a finding in support of a general attribute of any kind, much less one of general intelligence. It has been well established by mathematical analysis and over 60 years of psychometric research on cognitive tests that the magnitude of the relation between a test and the FPC is determined by the extent to which that which is measured by the particular test is repeated in the measurements of the other tests of the battery. For example, if 8 of 10 tests in a battery are reliable measures of different aspects of sewing ability, and 2 are Paragraph Comprehension and Arithmetic Reasoning, the FPC would be mainly indicative of sewing ability. By Herrnstein and Murray's logic, that which would be proclaimed in this battery to be one of the most highly g-loaded tests in use would be a combination measure of bobbin threading, embroidering, pattern cutting, and tatting.

Herrnstein and Murray used the terms AFQT, IQ, g, and general intelligence interchangeably, suggesting that they are synonyms, and that all refer to a single attribute that represents the connotations of the English word intelligence. They claimed that this usage is supported by the early theory and findings of Spearman (1927) and the findings of research since that time.

It should be acknowledged that Herrnstein and Murray are not alone in this claim. Many quite reputable psychologists accept the argument that there is a g factor in all measures of individual differences in cognitive capacities, that this is what is indicated by the FPC in any battery of ability measures, and that this is what IQ tests measure (Snyderman & Rothman, 1988). Thus, many well-known and respected psychologists readily accept Herrnstein and Murray's claim that general intelligence is measured by the AFQT.

Nevertheless, results from many studies in developmental and cognitive psychology show that the phenomena identified as indicating human intelligence are multidimensional—that several dimensions are required to describe these capabilities. There is no particular combination of the several dimensions that defines a functional unity of general intelligence. No single dimension of general intelligence has been found.

Spearman (1927) proposed a rigorous test of the hypothesis that a single dimension, g, describes all measures of cognitive capabilities that are indicative of what has been described as human intelligence. This test specifies that, ruling out swollen specifics,[1] there is one, and only one, common factor among all such measures, and each measure has a unique factor that is not common and is not shared

---

[1] A term coined by Spearman to represent the fact that simply including repeated versions of a particular kind of measure in an analysis will make what otherwise would be the unique factor for that measure into a common factor, thus rendering it impossible to demonstrate that one and only one common factor will account for the relations among variables.

by other measures. Spearman's hypothesis is testable. This is an important feature of his theory. It is based on a scientifically testable hypothesis.

The Spearman hypothesis has been tested several times in well-designed studies. In every test the hypothesis has been rejected. The results have come back again and again saying that a single common factor is not sufficient to account for the individual differences variation seen in putative tests of intelligence.[2]

As is common in claims that the evidence supports a finding of a single g factor (e.g., Jensen, 1998), Herrnstein and Murray (1994) confuse a prevalent finding of positive intercorrelations among abilities with a finding in support of Spearman's hypothesis. An FPC[3] well represents the positive intercorrelations in a battery of cognitive ability measures, but that FPC is not the only component among the measures and that component in one battery and sample of participants is not the same as the FPC of other batteries and samples. The FPC (or FCF; see footnote 3) is not indicative of Spearman's g or any other particular concept of general intelligence. Different batteries of tests yield different FPCs. Different FPC measures provide different orders of individual differences. People who score high along one FPC are located at lower points along another FPC (see Horn & Goldsmith, 1981, for examples of this in one book by Jensen). An FPC in a particular battery of tests is not a finding indicative of what will be found in principal components analysis in other batteries of tests.

Thurstone (1947) described this arbitrary feature of principal components more than 50 years ago. He used methods to identify more than one stable common factor within a battery of tests when a single common factor could not account for the individual differences.[4]

Thurstone also pointed out that scientific understanding of common factors can not be indicated by psychometric analysis alone, but must derive from what today is called *construct validation*. This requires that researchers establish a network of relations of factors to other variables. Common sets of relations with other variables provide

---

[2]We have reviewed this evidence in several publications (Horn, 1991, 1994, 1998; Horn & Hofer, 1992; Horn & Noll, 1994).

[3]Or, better, the first common factor (FCF), which is devoid of specific factor variance that inevitably enters into the FPC. The FCF represents what is common among abilities of a battery better than the FPC, but it has the same problems when considered as evidence for a g factor—namely, that it is not sufficient to account for the common variance and is not invariant from one battery and sample to another.

[4]The several common factors indicated in batteries of ability tests, referred to as first-order factors, are themselves positively correlated, and common second-order factors among these factors can be calculated. The second-order factors, too, are positively correlated and third-order factors may be calculated. Eventually, in stepping up the orders in this way a single common factor usually is found—the factors never become orthogonal. All this represents the positive intercorrelations among the tests, as such. Not uncommonly, however, it is asserted that the highest order factor indicates g. But this assertion has the same problem as the assertion that the FPC or FCF indicates g—the highest order factor is not invariant across batteries of putative indicators of human intelligence and samples of participants.

evidence of a single unitary influence if one is there, and different sets of relations for different factors provide evidence that the factors measure different attributes.

Construct validation studies have now established that there are at least nine different common factors that indicate what is called intelligence in humans. Among these factors is one referred to as *crystallized knowledge, Gc*, that is most similar to what is measured in the AFQT. A measure of Gc is an estimate of the extent to which an individual has acquired the valued knowledge of the dominant culture of a society. It is an important measure of one aspect of what is referred to as human intelligence. The AFQT, as such, is a rather narrow estimate of Gc obtained with tests of abilities specifically taught in a schooling aspect of acculturation—tests of word knowledge (vocabulary), ability to read and extract meaning from paragraphs written in English, and ability to do arithmetic operations and solve mathematical problems.

Even in its broadest form, Gc is not the sine qua non of all measures of human intelligence; that is, it is not general intelligence. There are other distinct factors among cognitive ability measures that identify capacities that also are regarded as important indicators of human intelligence. Indeed, Herrnstein and Murray's own empirical analysis indicated no fewer than three such distinct factors.

One of these factors resembled a *fluid reasoning dimension, Gf*, that has been described in the findings of construct validation studies as an important form of human intelligence. This set of capabilities indicates the extent to which in encountering novel problems one can comprehend the relations among the fundaments, extract correlates from these relations, and in that sense understand and solve the problems. Gf has more face-validity claim to represent the concept of *g* as this was formulated by Spearman than does Gc: Gf certainly has more claim to indicate Spearman's *g* than does the AFQT of Herrnstein and Murray's analysis.

Gf also is not the sine qua non of all measures of human intelligence. Many ability measures do not fall into this factor. Also, Gf indicators are not in the majority of tests in most batteries of intellectual tests, so Gf tests usually are not among the tests most highly correlated with the FPC among mixtures of different abilities. Gf is not well represented by the AFQT of Herrnstein and Murray's analysis

There is also evidence of a broad common factor of *visual comprehension and processing (Gv)* and one indicating *auditory capabilities (Ga)*, each capturing many of the features of human intelligence. These factors differ from Gf and Gc in their relations with a variety of variables that define their construct validities and thus indicate that they are separate forms of intelligence (Gardner, 1993; Horn, 1991).

Also important in descriptions of intelligence is a common factor of *short-term apprehension and retrieval (Gm)*. This capability is prominent in measures of information processing. It has been studied in much research on learning and neurological functioning, in each case often regarded as indicating the sine qua non of human intelligence. However, its construct validity is different from that of other factors of intelligence. It has a different statistical distribution across members of our society than do Gc, Gf, Gv, and Ga. People who score very high in measures of this factor often do not score equally high in measures of Gc, Gf, Gv, or Ga.

Apart from the structural evidence indicating several different intelligences, there is evidence from research on the development of cognitive capabilities, evidence from research on neurological structure and function, and evidence from genetic analyses that are not consistent with the hypothesis of a unitary concept of intelligence, all suggesting that more than one concept is needed to describe the phenomena of individual differences in what is regarded as indicative of human intelligence. The evidence adds up to indicate that there is no single dimension of general intelligence (or if there is, it has not yet been identified).

Thus, we see that (with the caveat that some prominent scientists agree with Herrnstein and Murray) scientific understanding of the phenomena of human intelligence is different from what is portrayed in *The Bell Curve*. Contrary to Herrnstein and Murray's (1994) claims, the AFQT does not measure general intelligence. It is a narrow estimate of Gc indicating largely schooling achievement. It is an important predictor and correlate of other important achievements, adaptations, and adjustments, but it is not the only or central determinant of such outcomes. *The Bell Curve* is not the authoritative statement on the nature of human intelligence that it purports to be.

The Measure of Environmental Influences

An SES measure was obtained in Herrnstein and Murray's (1994) study by combining young peoples' responses to questions about their mother's and father's education, income, and occupation. Herrnstein and Murray put this variable forward as the measure of the nongenetic influences that could have produced the outcomes they assessed in the youth of their NLSY sample, that is, all the environmental influences operating over the 14 to 22 years proceeding the time when outcome assessments were obtained.

A caveat is called for in this case, too, for there is a sense in which Herrnstein and Murray were correct in arguing that SES should represent environmental influences. Many who argue that the environment is important also often refer to SES as if it represents what is most important about the environment. In fact, it does not. On the one hand, it represents genetic influences to some extent, not simply environmental influences, and on the other hand, it is simply not a good measure of the kinds of environmental influences known to affect the development of cognitive abilities. The Herrnstein and Murray measure of SES is particularly inadequate for this purpose, because it is exceptionally lacking in reliability. Unreliable measures cannot be good predictors of anything.

Herrnstein and Murray's (1994) measure of SES is unreliable for several reasons. First, the measure was obtained from unreliable sources. The youth of the NLSY study often simply would not have the information they were asked to provide for the measure. They would not know about their father's or mother's income or education. They would leave questions unanswered or guess. This is particularly true for youth whose parents were less well educated and more likely to be separated—often the poorer youth.

Herrnstein and Murray replaced missing information about SES with the average for the people who provided such information. Thus, the income level estimated for the father of youth who did not answer a question—often because there was no father, and no father income, in the home—was assumed to be the average of youth who estimated their father's income. This produces bias (as well as unreliability) in analyses. The SES of poor youth who did not answer a question is biased upward. With this bias SES is more likely to appear to be unrelated to outcome variables related to income.

Correcting for this kind of bias in the same data that Herrnstein and Murray analyzed, Hout (1997) found that parents' poverty related to youth outcome variables associated with poverty at levels comparable to or above the level of the relations for the AFQT. This finding is quite contrary to Herrnstein and Murray's claims that g correlates more with poverty than does SES.

SES is also unreliable and invalid because the different components of the index indicate different things. Education and income do not represent a unitary construct. The outcomes that parental education predicts are different from the outcomes family income predicts, particularly as concerns the outcome variables of the Herrnstein and Murray study. The general finding is that education predicts education; financial situation predicts financial situation. For example, the academic achievement (education) of youth is more highly correlated with parental level of education than with family income, and the income levels young people attain (particularly those at levels indicating poverty) are more highly related to parental income than they are to parental education (e.g., Hout, 1997; Jencks et al., 1972).

When parental education and parental income are combined in SES, the low correlation of parental income with youth achievement is averaged with the higher correlation of parental education. The result is a correlation for the composite SES that is lower than the correlation for parental education. On the other hand, the correlation between SES and the income youth attain is decreased relative to the correlation between parental income and youth income by inclusion of parental education in the composite SES. Either way, the correlation of SES with outcome measures is lowered, and thus tends to be low relative to the correlation that other variables, such as the AFQT, have with these same outcome measures.

Analyzing the same data that Herrnstein and Murray (1994) analyzed, Hout (1997) found that in predicting poverty with the separate components of SES, parental income had a weight in the multiple prediction that was nearly eight times as large as the weights for either mother's education or father's education or both considered together (as used in the composite SES measure of Herrnstein and Murray). For other outcome variables of the Herrnstein and Murray study, Hout found that when the separate elements of SES were considered, the relations were over four times as large as those estimated for the SES measure Herrnstein and Murray used to represent environmental influences.

These limitations in Herrnstein and Murray's (1994) use of SES question even the most elementary interpretation of their findings. However, lack of reliability and validity are less a problem with their general argument than the fact that SES simply does not represent what it is assumed to represent—the many environmental influences that determine human cognitive abilities. Such influences on the positive side, related to good development of abilities, are factors of safeness of the home and neighborhood, parental sharing with the child and teaching responsibility, and generally the extent to which intellectual activities are practiced, valued, and encouraged in the child's home, school, and neighborhood. On the negative side, associated with low intellectual development, are stress (before birth, in the prenatal environment, and later), punitive childrearing, physical and sexual abuse, and disruption and violence in the home and neighborhood. These kinds of factors are associated with brain damage, lead poisoning, hyperactivity, aggressiveness, inattention in school, poor motivation, disassociation, and various psychopathologies, conditions that in each case relate to low academic achievement. When the negative factors are present and the positives are not, there is increased truancy and school absenteeism in the early years of schooling, and delinquency, drug abuse, and school dropout in the later years of schooling. In each case these variables are indicative of low academic achievement, poverty, unemployment, being on welfare, births out of wedlock, and criminality. Some of these factors are related to SES, to be sure, but SES is a correlate, not a good measure of the factors, as such, either collectively or individually.

In sum, Herrnstein and Murray selected a poor variable to represent the environmental influences that would have operated in the homes, schools, and neighborhoods to affect the development of cognitive abilities of the 18- to 22-year-old youth of the NLSY study.

The Analysis and Results

Using logistic multiple regression analysis, controlling for age, Herrnstein and Murray (1994) found that the AFQT in adolescence was more predictive of later academic attainment and occupational selection (or level within occupations) than was SES. Similarly, they found that the AFQT, compared with their measure of SES, was more highly related in the negative direction to indicators of poverty, unemployment, idleness, births out of wedlock, welfare dependency, and crime. They summarized their results with an analysis indicating that the AFQT is more highly related than SES to a composite sum of positive outcomes and the absence of negative outcomes—a composite they referred to as the Middle Class Values Index.

Thus, the basic finding is that a fairly reliable measure of academic achievement is a better predictor of subsequent academic achievement and its correlates than is a rather unreliable measure of social class, which even in its most reliable form is not a highly valid indictor of the factors that determine academic achievement and the variables with which it is correlated. Such a finding is not new or surprising. It is indicated by much previous research. It does not indicate that environmental influences amount to very little, or that inherited differences in intelligence cause the outcomes of the Middle Class Values Index.

In the same NLSY sample that Herrnstein and Murray studied, Hout (1997) found that the AFQT correlated .54 with years of education prior to the time of testing and .33 with years of schooling after the testing. If attained education is included among the predictors in analyses such as Herrnstein and Murray conducted, it accounts for virtually all the predictive variance that is otherwise associated with the AFQT (Feinberg, Devlin, Resnick, & Roeder, 1995). These results indicate that the AFQT is an outcome measure of schooling and attained education, and that the attained education at one time is predictive of attained education at a later time. Today's achievement is indicative of tomorrow's achievement. This kind of result is well known from much research conducted prior to Herrnstein and Murray's study. Link this with their findings for race, unemployment, births out of wedlock, and so on, and one might well interpret the findings as providing good reason to value education, good teaching, and good schools.

Viewed from a scientific perspective, the findings of Herrnstein and Murray's (1994) empirical study, if new, would give justification for writing a book or research article to provide fresh evidence. That the findings are not new questions such a decision. The empirical study probably does not meet a rigorous standard for publication of new information in a scientific journal.

However, the book is not a report on scientific findings, much as it claims to be based on such findings. It is an argument that inherited differences in intelligence determine differences in the outcomes Herrnstein and Murray identified in their Middle Class Values Index. It is an argument that social welfare policies, affirmative action, and intervention programs—indeed any effort to improve the conditions and capabilities of the kind of people who have not achieved well in our society—are futile and wasteful. It is a political argument, not a scientific argument.

BIAS IN THE MEASUREMENT OF IQ

Even as Herrnstein and Murray (1994) assured their readers that they remained "reso-lutely agnostic" about reasons for ethnic differences in IQ, they presented data to show that Blacks score lower on IQ tests than do Whites and Asians. This inferiority is not, they argued, artifact, due to oddities of the tests: IQ tests are not measurably biased against socioeconomic, ethnic, or racial subgroups. In support of this view, they cited Jensen (1980): "The definitive assessment of internal evidence of bias is in Jensen 1980" (p. 718). Jensen, they said, could find no statistically reliable evidence of pre-dictive bias against Blacks where cognitive ability tests are the predictor variable for educational achievement or job performance.

A principal problem with this argument is their source: Jensen's (1980) book is a political treatise, similar in this respect to *The Bell Curve*, not a balanced review of the available evidence. This point is made in a review of the book (Horn & Goldsmith, 1981) that Herrnstein and Murray never mentioned. Jensen selected and misused evidence to fit his case. He did not deal with evidence suggesting that both the test predictors and the test criteria are biased in much the same way.

Jensen's argument proceeds as follows: If tests relate to criterion measures in the same way in samples representing different social, economic, ethnic, and gender classifications, the tests are unbiased. More specifically, if the slopes for the regression equations of different groups are not significantly different, then this is proof that the tests are not biased.

This is an important piece of evidence to consider in addressing the question of bias, but it is not the only evidence that is relevant. This evidence alone does not speak to the question of whether the criterion itself is biased. In the studies considered in Jensen's (1980) book, the tests and the criteria measure the same kind of factor—educational achievements that are valued in the dominant culture. IQ tests measure school achievements of the past and predict other school and educational achievements in the future. At a lower level they predict ratings by supervisors that are tied to educational achievements. Under these conditions of prediction, the regression equations for predicting criteria from IQ tests have similar slopes in different social, economic, and ethnic classifications of people. The predictors and the criteria are equally biased or, to put it more neutrally, equally related to factors that bring about the achievement differences of social, economic, and ethnic groupings of people.

There is another way to consider bias that is important for understanding how adverse conditions are perpetuated. Even when the slopes for the regression equations of different groups are not different, and the same regression equation is used in different groups to make selections for, say, educational opportunities, but there are mean differences between groups on the predictor variable, then the differences between the proportions selected with the test and the proportions succeeding on the criterion will be larger for the group that has the lower mean than for the group that has the higher average. This is sometimes referred to as Darlington's (1971) concept of bias. It means that at any selection point in the upper part of a distribution of a predictor measure, the ratio of the number of minority persons selected for a valued opportunity relative to the number who could succeed in that activity if given the chance, is smaller than the comparable ratio for those of the majority group. Such selection thus perpetuates a condition of relatively few minority persons attaining the status (income, etc.) attainable through the valued opportunity.

Jensen (1980) and Herrnstein and Murray (1994) made no mention of this concept of bias. This is an example of ignoring evidence that is not favorable to their thesis.

ARGUMENT FROM GENETICS

Herrnstein and Murray's (1994) claim that others have not been tough-minded in thinking about environmental influences is part of their argument that genetic factors underlie class differences and the increasingly rigid social stratification they said is developing in this country. They cited results from a selected sample of studies to support a claim that individual differences in IQ are mainly genetically determined. They added this to their claim that high general intelligence is the primary cause of success in life, whereas low general intelligence is the cause of poverty, crime, unemployment, and being on welfare. They concluded that these outcomes are genetically determined, and that selection in terms of general intelligence segregates people into inbreeding castes.

This kind of argument is appealing partly because it is simple. It reduces explanation that otherwise would require identifying and linking complex sequences of environmental and genetic influences to merely one kind of determinant, the genes. However, the argument is not tough-minded reasoning from the evidence. It is poorly based on measurement and poorly based on the science of behavior genetics. Herrnstein and Murray do not properly qualify the information they presented, they present wrong information, and they fail to present the most relevant information.

The Measurement Problem

This is the problem (identified earlier) of lack of evidence for a factor of general intelligence. To regard the AFQT configuration of abilities as indicating a genetically determined general intelligence is rather like supposing that a particular configuration of facial features—say, eye color, nose length, and chin structure—represents the genetic basis for a measure of general beauty. In this case, too, no particular configuration is known to represent a quality "beauty in general." It is thus merely opinion to argue that general beauty is inherited.

This does not discount an observation that individual differences in the various separate features of physiognomy are inherited, and that agreed-on definitions of beauty can be defined in terms of these attributes. Various kinds of beauty, not one general beauty, can be specified in this way. If the component attributes are largely inherited, each of these forms of beauty will be largely inherited.

In this same sense various capacities of what is called intelligence might be genetically determined, and particular combinations of these components might be genetically determined, even as it is true that no particular configuration of basic abilities is known to indicate intelligence in general. Each configuration of basic abilities would indicate something different both about what is measured and about the chromosomal partitioning that occurs in genetic transmission.

Consider an example. The genes determining hippocampus structure in the brain, related to discrimination reversal leaning and memory, are not the same as the genes determining the cerebellar cortex, most related to sensory associative leaning and memory (Lavond, Jeansok, & Thompson, 1993; Mauk & Thompson, 1987). A configuration including mostly one of these forms of memory and not much of the other could involve the same degree of heritability as a configuration with the reverse of this allocation of forms of memory, but measures based on the two configurations would order individual differences in different ways and the genetic basis for the two configurations would be different. Also, the components of one configuration could be largely inherited when the components of another configuration were not, so different heritabilities would obtain for the different measures of *g*. There are many possible configurations that might be (or might have been called) general intelligence.

It might seem that this problem could be solved by accepting one configuration of abilities as being intelligence—say Gf—and building Herrnstein and Murray's (1994) theory on this definition. This would narrow the thesis and in that sense would improve the argument. (The book would need to be rewritten, of course.) However, the problem of specifying the genetic basis would not be solved by simply finding the heritability of the Gf measure, because even this narrower conception of intelligence is comprised of different component capacities that may stem from different genes. At this point in time, the components of Gf have not yet been fully described, and it cannot therefore be known that the components of Gf have different genetic bases. It is known that elementary components of other functional systems—for example, the eye and the ear—have different genetic determinants. It seems likely that the components of cognitive capability systems would have somewhat different genetic bases. It is misleading to suggest that current scientific thinking indicates that Gf (or any other factor of intelligence) is largely determined by genetic factors.

Problems With Heritability

Laying aside this fundamental problem with the argument that individual differences in general intelligence are mainly determined by genetic factors, and accepting the in-apt assumption that evidence for heritability can be derived from the study of a measure of IQ (any measure), Herrnstein and Murray's (1994) argument from genetics even in this case is misleading and incorrect. There are different measures of heritability: They use an inappropriate measure that inflates their estimate of the heritability of IQ. Heritability concepts are based on limiting assumptions that should be made clear if statements about heritability are not to be misleading (Loehlin, 1995; Schonemann, 10994). Herrnstein and Murray do not make these assumptions clear.

Assessing Heritability.   Heritability is derived from analysis of two estimates of the variability of (individual differences in) a measure: an estimate based on the variability between the averages for groups of genetically related people and an estimate based on the variability of the measure within such groups. A comparison of the two estimates of variability is described in what is called the *intraclass correlation*, calculated as follows:

$$R_I = (MS_b - MS_w)/[MS_b + (n - 1)MS_w] \qquad (1)$$

in which MS_b is the variability estimate obtained between groups, MS_w is the estimate obtained from within-group variability, and *n* is the number of groups.

In twin data, from which heritability is often estimated, a group is a pair of twins, so $n = 2$, and the intraclass correlation is simply

$$R_1 = (MS_b - MS_w)/(MS_b + MS_w) \tag{2}$$

Here one can first think of the average IQ for each pair of twins, then of the variability among these averages: The MS_b variance estimate is based on that variability. For the MS_w estimate, one can think of how, within each set of twins, the IQs differ: The MS_w variance estimate is based on those differences. One can then see that to the extent that the variability estimated from between sets of twins is larger than the variability estimated from within sets, the intraclass correlation is large. The larger the correlation, the more accurately one can estimate the IQ of one twin with the IQ of the other twin; that is, the less the difference between the two measures.

One can see in this example, also, that R_1 is a function of the heterogeneity of the sample of twins. If the sample is drawn from a wide section of the population (all nationalities, all countries, rural, urban, etc.), MS_b will tend to be large, so R_1 will tend to be large, whereas if the sample is homogeneous, MS_b, hence R_1, will be relatively small.

However, the size of intraclass correlation, in itself, does not indicate heritability. It can be large either because the people of a class have very similar environmental experiences or because they have similar genetic structures or because both of these factors operate. These possibilities are represented in the following theoretical partitioning of R_1 into correlations representing similarities in genetic and environmental influences

$$R_1 = R_G H_B + R_E (1 - H_B) \tag{3}$$

Here H_B represents what is called heritability in the broad sense, R_G represents the part of the intraclass correlation for related persons that is due to the people having similar genes (genetic determinants), and R_E represents the part that is due to the people having similar environments (environmental determinants). H_B is estimated in different samples of related people using this partitioning theory and assumptions about R_G and R_E. It is particularly important to qualify interpretations of heritability with clear statements about these assumptions.

In estimating heritability from samples of identical twins and fraternal twins, there are two versions of Equation 3, one for an identical twin sample, R_{II}, and one for a fraternal twin sample R_{IF}:

$$R_{II} = R_{GI} H_B + R_{EI} (1 - H_B) \qquad \text{and}$$

$$R_{IF} = R_{GF} H_B + R_{EF}(1 - H_B), \tag{4}$$

It is assumed that R_{EI}, the similarity of environmental determinants for identical twins, is equal to R_{EF}, the similarity of environmental determinants for fraternal twins. With this assumption ($R_{EI} = R_{EF}$), the two equations of 4 have only one unknown, H_B, which can be solved for by subtracting the second equation from the first, and dividing through with ($R_{GI} - R_{GF}$), to obtain

$$H_B = (R_{II} - R_{IF})/(R_{GI} - R_{GF}). \tag{5}$$

Here R_{II} and R_{IF} are the observed intraclass correlations for identical and fraternal twins, respectively; R_{GI} represents the similarity of the genetic determinants in the identical twin sample; and R_{GF} represents the similarity of gene determinants in the fraternal twin sample. R_{GI} is assumed to be 1.00 because identical twins have the same genes, and R_{GF} is assumed to be 0.50 because 50% (on average) of the genes of fraternal twins are the same. Substituting for R_{GI} and R_{GF} with these assumptions, the solution for H_B becomes simply

$$H_B = (R_{II} - R_{IF})/(1.00 - 0.50) = (R_{II} - R_{IF})/.50 = 2(R_{II} - R_{IF}) \qquad (6)$$

That is, the estimate of heritability is simply twice the difference between the observed intraclass correlations for identical and fraternal twins. Falconer (1960) presented this as an upper bound estimate of heritability in the broad sense.

H_B is estimated, also, from samples of identical twins reared in different environments. In this case it is assumed that R_E is zero—that none of the observed R_I similarity in twins is due to systematic correlation between their separate environments. With this assumption, Equation 3 becomes

$$R_{II} = R_{GI}H_B \qquad (7)$$

Then assuming R_{GI} is 1.00 (because identical twins have the same genes), the intraclass correlation itself, $R_{II,}$ is the estimate of heritability.

Understanding the Assumptions.   These examples illustrate concretely that heritability estimates are based on assumptions about environmental influences. In estimating heritability from comparisons of fraternal and identical twins (R_{EF} assumed to equal R_{EI}) the similarity of the environmental influences affecting two fraternal twins is assumed to equal the similarity of the environmental influences affecting two identical twins.[5] In the case of identical twins reared apart (R_E assumed to be zero) these influences are assumed to be random, not systematic, across the different environments of the separated twins. In thinking about heritability estimates. one should consider conditions under which these assumptions would be implausible or wrong and what the effect on the heritability estimate would be under these conditions.

The research design for obtaining estimates of heritability is described as quasi-experimental (Campbell & Stanley, 1963) rather than experimental because variables that can be controlled in an experimental design simply cannot be controlled in quasi-experimental studies. In a controlled experiment, a hypothesized causal factor, X, is varied as all other possible causal factors, W, are held constant, which means that W does not vary systematically as X varies. An association between X and an outcome variable, Y, then indicates how Y varies as the causal factor, X, varies, and thus provides a basis for inference that X is a cause of Y. In quasi-experimental designs, however, the putative causal factor and other possible causal factors are confounded—X and W occur together—so that as X varies W also may vary. The possible causal influence of X cannot be disentangled from the possible causal influence of W.

---

[5]Similar assumptions are involved in estimating heritability from samples of other kinds of relatives—mother–daughter, siblings, child–grandparent, and so on.

In the quasi-experiment in which fraternal and identical twins are compared and heritability is calculated with Equation 6, wherein it is assumed that the environmental influences are equally similar for the two kinds of twins ($R_{EI} = R_{EF}$), it is likely that the assumption is not in accordance with reality because environmental influences are more similar for pairs of identical twins than for pairs of fraternal twins. How much more similar (as this would relate to the development of the abilities measured in IQ tests) is not known. However, one can get some idea of the effect of falsely making the assumption by solving Equations 4 for H_B without making this critical assumption. This yields

$$H_{BC} = [(R_{II} - R_{IF}) + (R_{EF} - R_{EI})]/[.5 + R_{EF} - R_{EI})] \tag{8}$$

where H_{BC} (instead of H_B) represents the correct heritability in the broad sense. Here one can see that if indeed $R_{EI} = R_{EF}$, this equation gives the same result as Equation 6—$H_{BC} = H_B$—but if R_{EI} is greater than R_{EF}, then heritability estimated under the false assumption is larger than the correct heritability ($H_B > H_{bc}$). One can see this by trying out possible values of R_{II}, R_{IF}, R_{EF}, and R_{EI} in Equation 8, being careful to use only mathematically and logically reasonable solutions. In each case the estimate is substantially smaller than the .70 estimate obtained under the assumption that there are no relevant similarities in environments of separated identical twins.

For example, assume the obtained difference between R_{II} and R_{IF} is 0.4, so H_B therefore is estimated to be 0.8 (under the condition that $R_{EI} = R_{EF}$), then for instances in which R_{EI} is larger than R_{EF} one can consider ($R_{EI} - R_{EF}$) differences of different magnitudes—say, .39, .35. .30, .25, .20, and .10—and calculate the correct heritability, to find that H_{BC} is .09, .33, .50, .60, .67, and .75, respectively. Each H_{BC} is smaller than H_B, more substantially so the more the assumption is incorrect.

Similarly, for the quasi-experiment of identical twins raised in a different place, the assumption that R_E is zero is questionable if the environmental (W factor) influences of the separated twins are similar. If the twins are placed in the same kinds of homes, for example (even though these homes are clearly different), the W factor influences would be similar. It is difficult to even think of all such influences, much less to estimate the extent to which they are systematically similar across the situations of separated identical twins, but it is clear that separated twins are not randomly assigned to different environments: These assignments are systematic. Typically the placement is designed to keep things similar to what they would have been had the twins not been separated. Often the twins are placed in the homes of relatives—one goes to Aunt Mary, the other to Aunt Ellen. The different homes usually have much the same ethnic, social, religious, economic, and educational composition. It seems likely that some W factor variables are systematically similar across the different environments of separated twins: If R_E is not zero, then R_{II} of Equation 7 does not represent heritability alone; it also represents environmental influences, as are represented in the $R_E(1 - H_B)$ term of Equation 3. For example, if R_I in Equation (3) is .70, and R_E takes on the possible values .65, .60, .50, .40, and .30 then H_B is estimated to be .14, .25, .40, .50, and .54 respectively.

The extent to which the different environments of identical twins reared apart involve systematically similar influences on the development of IQ abilities is not known, just as the extent to which genetic factors influence the development of these abilities is not known. The calculated H_B coefficient can just as well indicate one of these kinds of influence as it can the other. What is called heritability thus is most likely an indication of both kinds of influence, but in proportions that are unknown.

The kinds of qualifications described here are well known among scientists who study behavior genetics data, but they generally are not known in the kind of audience to which *The Bell Curve* was directed. If the aim of Herrnstein and Murray (1994) in this book was mainly to accurately inform that kind of audience, one would think they would have accompanied their presentations of results from heritability studies with a clear statement of these qualifications. That they did not suggests that they were more intent on convincing (that general intelligence is inherited) than on informing.

In studies of separated twins, Bouchard, Lykken, McGue, Segal, and Tellegen (1990) found H_B heritability for religious attitudes to be .49 in samples in which the calculated heritability for an IQ measure was .69. Genetic factors could partly determine religious attitudes, of course, but it seems likely that to a large extent these twin similarities stem from similarities in the homes in which the separated twins were placed and raised, and thus also in the churches, neighborhoods, and school environments wherein religious attitudes are acquired.

Assuming that the heritability estimate for religious attitudes reflects similarities associated with placement of the twins, the difference between this heritability and the heritability for IQ is an estimate of the extent to which individual differences in IQ are associated with genetic determiners that are independent of environmental (placement) determiners. This difference (.69 − .49), taken from the studies of Bouchard et al. (1990), suggests that the heritability of IQ is about .20, a value considerably smaller than the .60 that Herrnstein and Murray (1994) claimed well represents the findings of most studies.

The .20 might be an underestimate. It is not presented as a definitive statement on the heritability of IQ; it is presented merely to reinforce the point that one should consider the assumptions involved in estimating heritability. When one does this, not only can one gain an improved understanding of heritability, one can also see that assumptions somewhat different from the conventional assumptions can be made and lead to results that provide a fresh perspective on the problem of estimating heritability. It is interesting in this regard that the .20 estimate obtained under assumption that heritability for religious attitudes reflects placement similarity is closer to the estimates (average around .30) obtained in several studies (Chipuer, Rovine, & Plomin, 1990) than the .60 estimate that Herrnstein and Murray presented. They did not discuss these other estimates.

Choosing the Right Heritability.   The heritability estimate on which Herrnstein and Murray (1994) based their thesis is probably the wrong kind of estimate. This wrong estimate is inflated relative to the correct kind of estimate.

There are two kinds of heritability. The first is heritability in the broad sense, H_B, as described earlier; the second is heritability in the narrow sense, H_N. Behavior geneticists regard H_N, not H_B, as most indicative of the extent to which a trait is transmitted across generations (Falconer, 1981; Weir, Eisen, Goodman, & Namkoong, 1988). It is this transmission across generations that Herrnstein and Murray spoke of in their prediction of emergence of cognitive castes and the decline of general intelligence in a population.

Broad heritability includes all genetic variance, both an additive component, A, and nonadditive component, N. Narrow heritability includes only the additive part of genetic variance. Expressing heritability as a simple ratio of genetic variance to total variance, G/T, heritability in the broad sense is $H_B = (A + N)/T$, whereas heritability in the narrow sense is simply $H_N = A/T$.

The additive effect on the variance of a trait is the average effects of the individual genes, as such, irrespective of other genes. The nonadditive effect includes dominance and epistatic effects. If dominance occurs, the effect of a gene depends on the interaction of alleles (forms of a gene) at a single chromosomal locus. In epistasis there is interaction among genes at different loci, and the effect of a gene depends on what other genes are present. If the expression of a trait involves a great deal of dominance and epistasis, H_B can be considerably larger than H_N.

The formation of inbreeding castes in accordance with Herrnstein and Murray's (1994) argument is a form selection for a trait. Selection was illustrated in an early study by Tryon (1940) showing that if rats that ran fastest in a maze were selected and bred it was possible over several generations of such selection to obtain a breeding group in which practically all the offspring could run mazes faster than the offspring of descendants of the original group. Such directional selection (as for IQ in Herrnstein and Murray's argument) builds on dominance effects, which, as R. A. Fisher (1930) demonstrated, reduces additive genetic variance relative to nonadditive variance.[6] The nonadditive variance should be removed from the heritability estimate to correctly estimate of the transmission of the trait through selection: H_N is the critical quantity determining the likelihood of Herrnstein and Murray's prediction that cognitive castes are emerging and dysgenic forces are at work.

Epistatic effects on a trait are similar to those of dominance, but can indicate not only how the particular qualities of a trait are transmitted, but also how other qualities are transmitted. The transmission of such other qualities is not a part of what Herrnstein and Murray predicted, and thus should not be included in the heritability estimate. Thus, again it is suggested that H_N, not H_B, is most appropriate for indicating the extent to which general intelligence would be transmitted across generations in accordance with the Herrnstein and Murray argument.

Estimates of broad heritability of IQ have ranged from a low of 0 (Kamin, 1974) to as high as .87 (Burt, 1972), with most centering around a value of about .45. In this context, estimates of narrow heritability typically are .15 to .20 lower, centering around a value of

---

[6]Selection may be manifested in lowered intelligence in offspring from matings of closely related persons—a dysgenic effect, as in Herrnstein and Murray's (1994) argument.

about .30 (Bouchard & McGue, 1981; Chipuer et al., 1990; Feinberg et al., 1995; Loehlin, Lindzey, & Spuhler, 1975; Plomin & Loehlin, 1989; Rao, Morton, Lalouel, & Lew, 1982). Thus, the correct heritability for the kind of argument Herrnstein and Murray (1994) are making is about one-half the value they used. It is not clear that they understood the arguments in favor of using the H_N kind of estimate in their analyses. Whether or not they understood, the effect is the same: The reader is misled.

Thus, even accepting the questionable assumption that different IQ tests indicate a single general intelligence and not correcting heritability estimates for the amounts of environmental variance they include, Herrnstein and Murray's argument for the formation of castes and dysgenic decline of IQ is exaggerated.

There are other problems with Herrnstein and Murray's argument from behavior genetics. The incorrect heritability estimate they used was obtained in homogeneous samples of largely middle-class Whites. Heritability estimates are inflated by such selective sampling, because environmental variability is reduced relative to what it is in the broad population. It is the population environmental variability that should be entered in total variance in the denominator of the $G/T = H_B$ ratio. With an underestimate of variability due to the environment in the denominator of this ratio, even a fairly small genetic component can result in a large H_B. This caution, too, should be provided in presenting an estimate of the heritability.

Early environment may be important for the development of cognitive abilities, but the effects from this source are confounded with genetic effects and inflate estimates of heritability. Again, cautions are called for, but were not supplied by Herrnstein and Murray.

In adoption studies the effects of the environment from the time of birth to the time of adoption could be important. They are not teased out in estimates of heritability. The prenatal environment is known to have large effects in studies of mammals other than humans (Falconer, 1980). The association between fetal alcohol syndrome and various at-birth and postnatal effects suggests that the effects of the prenatal environment may be substantial.

In studies of twins, including separated twin studies, prenatal effects are confounded with genetic effects. Prenatal effects are not confounded with genetic effects in studies in which heritability estimates are obtained from comparisons of relatives that do not share a prenatal environment—ordinary siblings, parent–child comparisons. Comparing heritability estimates obtained from these latter sources with estimates obtained in twin studies, Plomin and Loehlin (1989) estimated that the prenatal effect that is confounded with the genetic effect in twin studies might increase the heritability estimates by about .20. Herrnstein and Murray (1994) did not speak of such possible overestimation in their argument for the high heritability of IQ.

The point of all this is that the arguments Herrnstein and Murray advance are not simply "tough-minded" applications of scientific knowledge. They should be qualified, and they are not. They are based on selective use of some scientific information, not all of it. They are designed primarily to persuade, not primarily to inform.

MALLEABILITY OF ABILITIES

Herrnstein and Murray (1994) suggested that little can be done to improve IQ in groups for which the averages are low. They implied that the group differences result from inherited differences.

Heritability, an indicator of variance, tells us nothing about differences between group averages or the malleability of an attribute. Consider two buckets of wheat from the same bin, having the same average heritability, one planted in fertile, well-watered soil with optimal amounts of nitrogen, the other planted in poor soil that was not well watered. The plants of the first bucket will grow taller and have substantially greater yield than the plants of the second bucket (Lewontin, 1970). Similarly, for groups of humans having the same average heritability, one in which children grow up on a high-protein diet, the other in which protein in the diet is low, the average height for the groups differs substantially (Loehlin et al., 1975). In much the same manner the differences between the IQ averages of different groups (high and low social class, etc.) can be due to differences in conditions for acquiring abilities.

Herrnstein and Murray (1994) acknowledged this possibility, but they argue that it does not happen. As they referred to results suggesting that the abilities that make up IQ can be improved, they emphasized limitations, pointed to failures, and explained away findings of the studies that produced these results. With such rhetorical brinkmanship, they lead the reader to a view that little can be done to change IQ.

Contrary to Herrnstein and Murray's conclusion, there is evidence that the abilities measured in IQ tests can be improved. More important, as concerns outcomes such as crime, birth out of wedlock, unemployment, and other such forms of maladjustment, IQ is probably not the major cause. More likely causes are other factors of the person, such as impulsivity and lack of ego resilience (Block, 1995), coupled with factors operating through the conditions in which a person develops—factors that affect motivation and self-esteem. These factors can be changed. For example, quite a bit is known about how to improve motivation and self-esteem and promote adjustment and adaptation. These factors enable people to realize their genetic potential for ability development (Honig, 1994; Zigler & Trickett, 1978).

The amount of change in abilities and related factors of personality that can be produced by intervention, and the longevity of the effects, depends on the intensity and duration, as well as the kind of the intervention. In studies in which there was early, intensive, and sustained intervention with programs that improved childrearing conditions (involving the parents), as well as the regimen for learning, mean IQ change ranged from between 0.5 to 1.4 SD (8–20 IQ points) and was maintained, at least into early adolescence (Garber, 1988; Honig, 1979; Huston, 1992; Lazar & Darlington, 1982; Ramey, 1993; Ramey & Campbell, 1992; Ramey, Campbell, & Finkelstein, 1984; Ramey & Ramey, 1990; Ramey, Yeates, & Short, 1984; Schweinhart, Barnes, & Weikart, 1993).

In the studies of Ramey and coworkers, intervention for children considered at risk for mental retardation started 1 month after birth (an age at which some nongenetic prenatal and perinatal influences would already have operated). Babies were provided with the program's care for 8 hours a day, 5 days a week, 50 weeks a year. In times when the children were not in the program's care, they were cared for by a relative, usually their mother. The program's care was directed at ensuring a safe environment for the infant and young child. Children need to feel secure if they are to develop intellectually. The program's care also included cognitive enrichment activities. The intervention continued until the children reached 5 years of age, at which time the average IQ for the treated children was 0.5 *SD* above the average IQ of children in the control conditions. Twelve years later, only 13% of the treated children had IQs less than 85 compared to 44% of the children in the comparison group.

The intervention in the Honig (1979) studies began in the third month of life and continued until the children started school. It, too, was directed at children at risk for retardation. The children in the experimental group received day care 5 days a week, 52 weeks of the year. Siblings of the studied children also received child care and their mothers received training in parenting, as well as in job skills. Compared at the time the children entered school, the average IQ for children in the experimental group was 25 points higher than the average for the children of the comparison group. Not all this gain was sustained, but a standard deviation of IQ point difference remained at ages from 12 to 14 years (Garber, 1988).

It has also been found (Johnson, 1994; McArdle, 1998; Messick, 1980) that even as late in development as adolescence and young adulthood, practice and coaching enables people to notably increase scores on the kind of tests that Herrnstein and Murray (1994) equated with IQ and general intelligence—namely, the Scholastic Aptitude Tests (SAT). The largest gains were for the lower scoring students, and the initial and early gains were larger than subsequent gains. On average, individuals improved about 24 points in the math portion of the SAT and about 14 points on the verbal portion (the standard deviation of each test being about 100) over 3 days of intensive coaching. The improvements continued with more coaching, but at a progressively slower rate, up to an average gain of about 29 points on the quantitative and 24 points on the verbal test after 100 hours of coaching. Well-structured coaching, coupled with parental involvement, produced gains of .45 to 1.10 *SDs* for the combined verbal and quantitative scores (Johnson, 1994; Zuman, 1987).

Herrnstein and Murray (1994) argued that such changes are small for the amount of time spent in intervention. They claimed the samples were not large enough to establish the findings. They questioned whether random assignment to conditions was really accomplished.

These points are well taken, but taking them fully into account, the findings still indicate that scores on the SAT can be changed in adolescence and young adulthood. Therefore, if the SAT is a measure of IQ, as Herrnstein and Murray contended, then IQ can be changed as late in development as adolescence and young adulthood. Also, although the interventions might seem to involve a lot of time, they represent only a very small segment of the period of time over which abilities are developed. They represent a very small portion of the environmental influences that can operate to produce cognitive capabilities and determine outcomes such as poverty, crime, and so on.

In sum, a balanced review of the research on interventions to improve the abilities of intelligence suggests that there are intervention programs that will improve the cognitive abilities of IQ. The environmental influences that are most likely to produce the largest and most durable increments in abilities are those that operate early in life—before birth and in the earliest weeks and months of infancy—and continue over the formative years of childhood and young adulthood. There are no quick fixes that produce large and durable changes, but it is incorrect to conclude that group differences in IQ levels are forever set by heredity.

SUMMARY AND CONCLUSIONS

The Bell Curve presents a theory about the causes and consequences of individual differences in humans. It is said to be based on scientific evidence, to be balanced and objective, and to provide a dependable basis for thinking about policies dealing with welfare, education, intervention, and affirmative action. There are reasons to question these claims.

The book purports to show that there is good evidence to support the following conclusions: (a) Individual differences in contributions to maintenance and advancement of our culture are determined primarily by genetically based general intelligence, not by environmental factors; (b) selection for education and occupation is based on general intelligence; (c) this selection is producing a rigid stratification of society into inbreeding castes, and a progressive decrease in the population level of general intelligence; and (d) social policy aimed at improving the intellectual abilities of those in the lower strata is a waste; it is futile to try to put together programs to improve these abilities because they are largely fixed by heredity.

The findings of an empirical study reported in appendixes of the book are interpreted as supporting the first of these claims. However, the results of this study indicate only that a particular (AFQT) measure of academic achievements in adolescence is more related to later academic achievements and, on the negative side, personal maladjustment and social maladaptation, than is a relatively unreliable and invalid measure of socioeconomic class, the SES variable interpreted as representing putative environmental influences.

The first claim is questionable because no single factor of general intelligence has been identified. There are several factors of human intelligence, not one general factor; no single principle uniting the several factors in a single dimension has been found. The AFQT is a narrow estimate of one among several factors. It is no more general intelligence than is any one of the other factors. It does not represent the factor that is conceptually most similar to the attribute Spearman (1927) described as *g*, often regarded as the sine qua non of human intelligence.

The book's major claim thus is based on a scientifically incorrect characterization of a principal variable of the claim—general intelligence. It is also based on an incorrect characterization of a second principal variable—the environmental influences that determine the development of the abilities of human intelligence. The SES measure obtained to estimate these influences is not adequate for this purpose. This would be true even had it been measured with a good level of reliability and validity, and it was not. It is particularly lacking in reliability and validity. Thus, a finding that such a measure correlates at a lower level than the AFQT with measures of achievement, adjustment, and adaptation is not evidence that the environment is of no consequence in determining these outcomes: It is merely evidence that a relatively unreliable measure of a narrow range of environmental influences does not predict as well as a relatively more reliable measure of achievement that is operationally similar to achievement outcomes and to outcomes that stem directly from achievements.

The book's contention that general intelligence is genetically determined is based on a review of results from studies of the heritability of measures of IQ. Different IQ measures involve different combinations of the separate factors of intelligence, and like the AFQT, no one of them has any more claim to representing general intelligence than any other. Estimates of broad heritability of these various measures have ranged from a low of 0 to a high of .87, with most hovering around a value of about .45. The authors of *The Bell Curve* selected an estimate of .60 to support their claims for genetic transmission and decline of general intelligence, social stratification based on this transmission, and the futility of policies aimed at improving the lot of those in the lower social strata.

Not only is .60 a high-end estimate of heritability, it is probably the wrong estimate for the claims of *The Bell Curve*. Heritability in the narrow sense is more appropriate for these claims. Narrow heritability estimates are smaller than broad heritability estimates, typically by about .15. The more nearly correct estimate of heritability for the arguments of *The Bell Curve* is thus about .30. The .30 estimate of heritability, if taken fully at face value, indicates low likelihood of the stratification and dysgenic effects envisioned in *The Bell Curve*.

Estimates of heritability should not be taken at face value. They are based on quasi-experimental research designs in which genetic and environmental influences are inextricably confounded. The estimates are inflated by assumptions in the calculation of heritability that are not fully warranted—assumption of no systematic similarities in the environmental influences of identical twins raised apart, assumption that environmental influences are the same for identical and fraternal twins. The estimates are based on measures obtained after prenatal, at-birth, and early childhood environmental influences would have operated: These influences are treated as if they were genetic influences, which inflates the estimates.

Heritability, no matter how large, does not indicate that differences between groups are genetic or immutable, nor does it indicate that abilities cannot be improved. The authors contended that the results of intervention studies designed to improve the abilities of intelligence indicate little sustained improvement. They suggested that this reinforces the claim that genetic factors, rather than environmental factors, mainly determine the abilities of intelligence and contributions to maintenance and advancement of the culture. This conclusion is hasty generalization from selected bits of evidence.

The results from intervention studies indicate that if programs begin early and are continued over a major portion of childhood development, then substantial improvements in the abilities of intelligence can be realized and maintained. The improvements can be particularly large if intervention effects result in favorable change in the childrearing environment as well as school learning environment. It is not true that the environment is of little consequence in the development of the abilities of human intelligence.

Thus, in general the major claims of *The Bell Curve* are not well based on scientific knowledge. The information the book presents is sometimes incorrect. Other times it is not well qualified. Often it is a selection from the total information, omitting information that is not supportive. Often this information is slanted in interpretation to provide the most favorable arguments in support of the book's claims.

Speculations about genetically based social stratification are not well based on the knowledge of behavioral genetics. Formulation of the arguments for such transmission is incorrect. Social class stratification can also derive from the way wealth makes wealth and economic opportunity as it can from segregation due to individual differences in basic cognitive capabilities. One need not question the increasing importance of education in today's society or the evidence that there is increasing separation of the very rich from the very poor, but these conditions, in themselves, do not support claims of formation of a cognitive elite determined by a particular indicator of human intelligence.

The concluding chapters of *The Bell Curve* present arguments opposing policies of affirmative action and aid to dependent children. The book appears to have been written to justify and supply support for these arguments. It is thus in the end a political treatise, a statement about what should and should not be social policy. Viewed as such, it can well be regarded as forceful and, depending on the reader's political orientation, as eloquent or demagogic. In either case it should not be thought to derive from the authority of science.

ACKNOWLEDGMENTS

I am grateful for suggestions the following people made that helped me improve this chapter: Jack Block, Herb Eber, Howard Gardner, Lloyd Humphreys, John Loehlin, Jeff Long, Jack McArdle, John Newman, and Penelope Trickett.

REFERENCES

Baker, P. C., Keck, C. K., Mott, F. L., & Quinlan, S. V. (1993). *NLSY child handbook (rev. ed.): A guide to the 1986–1990 National Longitudinal Survey of Youth child data*. Columbus: Center for Human Resources Research.

Block, J. (1995). IQ and ego-resiliency: Conceptual and empirical connections and sepa-rateness. *Journal of Personality and Social Psychology, 70*, 349–361.

Bouchard, T. J., Jr., Lykken, D. T., McGue, M., Segal, N. L., & Tellegen, A. (1990). Sources of human psychological differences. *Science, 250*, 223–228.

Bouchard, T. J., Jr., & McGue, M. (1981). Familial studies of intelligence: A review. *Science, 212*, 1055–1059.

Brigham, C. C. (1923). *A study of American intelligence.* Princeton, NJ: Princeton University.

Burt, C. (1972). Inheritance of general intelligence. *American Psychologist, 27*, 175–190.

Campbell, D. T., & Stanley, J. C. (1963). Experimental and quasi-experimental designs for research on teaching. In N. L. Gage (Ed.), *Handbook of research on teaching* (pp. 171–246). Chicago: Rand-McNally.

Chipuer, H. M., Rovine, M. J., & Plomin, R., (1990). LISREL modeling: Genetic and environmental influences on IQ revisited. *Intelligence, 14*(1), 11–29.

Darlington, R. B. (1971). Another look at "cultural fairness." *Journal of Educational Measurement, 8*, 71–82.

Falconer, D. S. (1960). *Introduction to quantitative genetics.* Edinburgh, Scotland: Oliver & Boyd.

Falconer, D. S. (1981). *Introduction to quantitative genetics.* New York: Longman.

Feinberg, S. E., Devlin, B., Resnick, D. P., & Roeder, K. (1995). *Heritability, IQ, and life outcomes.* New York: Springer-Verlag.

Fisher, R. A. (1930). *The genetical theory of natural selection.* Oxford, UK: Oxford University Press.

Flynn, J. R. (1987). Massive IQ gains in 14 nations: What IQ tests really measure. *Psychological Bulletin, 101*, 171–191.

Garber, H. L. (1988). *The Milwaukee project: Preventing mental retardation in children at risk.* Washington, DC: American Association on Mental Retardation.

Gardner, H. (1993). *Multiple intelligences: The theory in practice.* New York: Basic Books.

Herrnstein, R. J. (1973). *IQ in the meritocracy.* Boston: Little, & Brown.

Herrnstein, R., & Murray, C. (1994). *The bell curve: Intelligence and class structure in American life.* New York: The Free Press.

Honig, A. S. (1979). *Parent involvement in early childhood education.* Washington, DC: National Association for the Education of Young Children.

Honig, A. S. (1994). Intervention, infant and preschool. In R. J. Sternberg (Ed.), *Encyclopedia of human intelligence* (Vol. 1, pp. 599–607). New York: Macmillan.

Horn, J. L. (1991). Measurement of intellectual capabilities: A review of theory. In K. S. McGrew, J. K. Werder, & R. W. Woodcock (Eds.), *Woodcock–Johnson technical manual* (pp. 197–246). Allen, TX: DLM Teaching Resources.

Horn, J. L. (1994). The theory of fluid and crystallized intelligence. In R. J. Sternberg (Ed.), *The encyclopedia of intelligence* (pp. 443–451). New York: Cambridge University Press.

Horn, J. L. (1998). A basis for research on age differences in cognitive abilities. In J. J. McArdle & R. Woodcock (Eds.), *Human cognitive abilities in theory and practice* (pp.57–91). Chicago: Riverside Press.

Horn, J. L., & Goldsmith, H. (1981). Reader be cautious: Bias in mental testing by Arthur Jensen. *American Journal of Education, 89*, 305–329.

Horn, J. L., & Hofer, S. (1992). Perspective on the nature of human cognitive capabilities. In R. J. Sternberg & C. A. Berg (Eds.), *Intellectual development* (pp. 44–99). Boston, MA: Cambridge University Press.

Horn, J. L., & Noll, J. (1994). A system for understanding cognitive capabilities. In D. K. Detterman (Ed.), *Current topics in human intelligence.* Norwood, NJ: Ablex.

Hout, M. (1997). *Inequality by design: Myths, data, and politics.* Berkeley: University of California Press.

Huston, A. (1992). *Children in poverty.* New York: Cambridge University Press.

Jencks, C., Smith, M., Acland, H., Bane, M. J., Cohen, D., Gentis, H., Heyns, B., & Michelson, S. (1972). *Inequality: A reassessment of the effect of family and schooling in America.* New York: Harper & Row.

Jensen, A. R. (1969). How much can we boost IQ and scholastic achievement? *Harvard Educational Review, 39,* 1–123.

Jensen, A. R. (1980). *Bias in mental testing.* New York: The Free Press.

Jensen, A. R. (1998). *The g factor.* Westport, CT: Praeger.

Johnson, S. T. (1994). Scholastic assessment tests (SAT). In R. J. Sternberg (Ed.), *Encyclopedia of human intelligence* (Vol. 2, pp. 956–960). New York: MacMillan.

Kamin, L. (1974). *The science and politics of IQ.* Hillsdale, NJ: Lawrence Erlbaum Associates.

Lavond, D. G., Jeansok, J. K., & Thompson, R. F. (1993). Mammalian brain substrates of aversive classical conditioning. *Annual Review of Psychology, 44,* 317–342.

Lazar, I., & Darlington, R. (1982). Lasting effects of early education: A report from the consortium for longitudinal studies. *Monographs of the Society for Research in Child Development, 195*(2–3), 1–151.

Lewontin, R. C. (1970). Race and intelligence. *Bulletin of the Atomic Scientists, 26*(3), 2–8.

Loehlin, J. C. (August 13, 1995). *Genes and environment in The bell curve.* Paper presented at the American Psychological Association Symposium: Perspective on the Bell Curve, Washington, DC.

Loehlin, J. C., Lindzey, G., & Spuhler, J. N. (1975). *Race differences in intelligence.* San Francisco: Freeman.

Mauk, M. D., & Thompson, R. F. (1987). Retention of classically conditioned eyelid responses following acute decerebration. *Brain Research. 493,* 89–95.

McArdle, J. J. (1998). Contemporary statistical models for examining test-bias. In J. J. McArdle & R. W. Woodcock (Eds.), *Human cognitive abilities in theory and practice* (pp. 157–196). Mahwah, NJ: Lawrence Erlbaum Associates.

Messick. S. (1980). *The effectiveness of coaching for the SAT: Review and reanalysis of research from the fifties to the FTC.* Princeton, NJ: Educational Testing Service.

Plomin, R., & Loehlin, J. C. (1989). Direct and indirect IQ heritability estimates: A puzzle. *Behavior Genetics, 19*(3), 331–342.

Ramey, C. T. (1993). A rejoinder to Spitz's critique of the Abecedarian experiment. *Intelligence, 17,* 25–30.

Ramey, C. T., & Campbell, F. A. (1992). Poverty, early childhood education, and academic competence: The Abecedarian experiment. In A. Huston (Ed.), *Children in poverty* (pp. 190–221). New York: Cambridge University Press.

Ramey, C. T., Campbell, F. A., & Finkelstein, N. W. (1984). Course and structure of intellectual development in children at high risk for developmental retardation. In P. Brooks, R. Sperber, & C. McCauley (Eds.), *Learning and cognition in the mentally retarded* (pp. 343–401). Hillsdale, NJ: Lawrence Erlbaum Associates.

Ramey, C. T., & Ramey, S. L. (1990). Intensive educational intervention for children of poverty. *Intelligence, 14,* 1–9.

Ramey, C. T., Yeates, K. O., & Short, E. J. (1984). The plasticity of intellectual development: insights from preventive intervention. *Child Development, 55,* 1913–1925.

Rao, D. C., Morton, N. E., Lalouel, J. M., & Lew, R. (1982). Path analysis under generalized assortative mating: II. American IQ. *Genetical Research, 39,* 187–198.

Rushton, J. P. (1995). *Race, evolution, and behavior.* New Brunswick, NJ: Transaction.

Schonemann, P. H. (1994). Heritability. In R. J. Sternberg (Ed.), *Encyclopedia of human intelligence* (Vol. 1, pp. 528–536). New York: Macmillan.

Schweinhart, L. J., Barnes, H. V., & Weikart, D. P. (1993). *Significant benefits: The High/Scope Perry preschool study through age 27* (Monograph No. 10). Ypsilanti, MI: High/Scope Press.

Shockley, W. (1971). Negro IQ deficit: Failure of a "malicious allocation" model warrants new research proposals. *Review of Educational Research, 41*, 227–248.

Snyderman, M., & Rothman, S. (1988). *The IQ controversy: Media and public policy.* New Brunswick, NJ: Transaction.

Spearman, C. E. (1927). *The abilities of man: Their nature and measurement.* New York: Macmillan.

Thurstone, L. L. (1947). *Multiple factor analysis.* Chicago: University of Chicago Press.

Tryon, R. C. (1940). *Genetic differences in maze-learning ability in rats.* 39th Yearbook of the National Society of Student Education (pp. 111–119). Bloomington, IL: Public School Publishing Company.

Weir, B. S., Eisen, E. J., Goodman, M. M, & Namkoong, G. (1988). *Proceedings of the Second International Conference on Quantitative Genetics.* Sunderland, MA: Sinauer Associates.

Yerkes, R. M. (Ed.). (1921). Psychological examining in the United States Army. *Memoirs of the National Academy of Sciences, 15.*

Zigler, E., & Trickett, P. K. (1978). IQ, social competence, and evaluation of early childhood intervention programs. *American Psychologist, 33*, 789–798.

Zuman, J. P. (1987). The effectiveness of special preparation for the SAT: An evaluation of a commercial coaching school. *Dissertation Abstracts International, 48*, 1749. (University Microfilms No. ADG 87-22714.880.1)

PART

V

A wide variety of data, including reanalyses of data presented in *The Bell Curve*, imply that group differences in IQ are social in origin and can change as the result of changing social circumstances or social interventions.

CHAPTER 13

Test Scores, Education, and Poverty

Michael Hout

In *The Bell Curve*, Herrnstein and Murray (1994) argued that individual differences in intelligence are the main source of inequality in the United States. They base their claim on an analysis of how poverty (and other outcomes) related to test scores in a large national database known as the National Longitudinal Survey of Youth (NLSY). Their interpretation of the test of cognitive abilities that is part of the NLSY rests on the assumption that test scores reflect abilities that are innate, not taught. Evidence presented here contradicts that assumption. They dismissed class origins as a factor in poverty; improved measures of class background contradict that conclusion. They ignored the role of gender and family in poverty and the role of institutions in determining whether individual characteristics matter or not. Patterns in the NLSY show how gender, family circumstances, and other institutional factors are important influences that account for more of the variation in poverty than test scores do. Altogether the results imply a stronger effect of social environment for U.S. poverty than Herrnstein and Murray's analysis implies.

The existence of poverty amidst plenty has raised moral questions for Americans of every era. Troubled souls could at least take some solace in the tendency for poverty to spread only during hard times. Usually good times raised the incomes of the poor as well as the rich, so that poverty abated when the economy turned up. It was possible to entertain the hope that enough sustained economic growth could someday wipe out poverty in the United States. The first 30 years of the postwar era made that hopeful scenario seem plausible. From 1959 to 1974 recession-free prosperity cut the poverty rate in half—from 22% to 11% of families (U.S. Bureau of Census, 1997). That was the first postwar generation. Since 1974, a growth-resistant strain of poverty has appeared. The stagflation—high unemployment accompanied by inflation—of the second half of the 1970s nudged the poverty rate upward even though income per person rose. Recessions raised the poverty rate to 15% in 1982, 1983, and 1993. Subsequent economic recoveries have failed to reduce the poverty rate below 12.8% even though the recoveries of 1985 through 1989 and 1993 onward have been quite robust (U.S. Bureau of the Census 1997). The average poverty rate since 1980 has been 14% (compared to 12% for 1965–1974) despite continued growth of income per capita.

The proximate cause of growth-resistant poverty is income inequality. Between 1959 and 1969 income per person grew for households in all economic classes. Since then, per-capita income of the richest one fifth of households has grown by over $30,000 (standardized to 1989 prices), per-capita income of the middle three fifths of households has grown by $7,000, and per-capita income of the poorest one fifth of households has actually declined by $1,200 (Fischer et al., 1996; Karoly & Burtless, 1995). Thus, economic growth is no longer effective in reducing poverty because the fruits of economic growth are more and more concentrated at the top of the U.S. class structure. However, these statistics simply restate the problem of growth-resistant poverty; concentration of economic resources does not explain why the poor are being left behind.

Most scholars and political writers who have sought explanations for poverty and inequality have zeroed in on social institutions: the family, schools, labor markets, and government actions (e.g., Danziger & Gottschalk, 1996; Jencks, 1992). A controversial exception is *The Bell Curve* by Herrnstein and Murray (1994). They argued that differences in individual abilities are responsible for the growth-resistant poverty and economic inequality of the 1980s and 1990s. Their point is that the poor cannot escape their plight in the 1990s because, unlike the poor of the last generation, today's poor lack the ability to succeed in the new U.S. economy. Herrnstein and Murray acknowledged that every human society has people with limited cognitive ability, but now it is a social problem because employers are putting an ever-higher premium on the cognitive skills of their workers.

Long before *The Bell Curve* appeared in 1994, scholars of social inequality explored the links between ability and success (e.g., Ashenfelter & Mooney, 1968; Duncan, 1968; Griliches & Mason, 1972; Jencks et al., 1972; Sewell, Haller, & Portes, 1970). The consensus of these scholars was that the kind of cognitive abilities measured by paper-and-pencil tests were closely related to success in school and modestly related to success in the labor market (e.g., Jencks et al., 1972). Although Herrnstein and Murray's (1994) results do not contradict this consensus, their rhetoric does. They reported that test scores account for about 10% of the variance in poverty outcomes—a modest effect that is consistent with the consensus reached in the early 1970s. Despite their reading of the economy as newly skill-happy, they presented evidence more consistent with a conclusion of little or no change (see Hauser & Huang, 1997).

How could they sustain an argument that was so inconsistent with the evidence they presented? First, they had some very convincing evidence that their explanatory variable—test scores—had changed. This was actually a bit of a problem for them, though, because the point of citing intrinsic differences among individuals was to explain growth-resistant poverty. If the scores were increasing while poverty persisted, how did test scores solve the puzzle? Had they presented evidence of increasing variance in test scores, they might have had a more relevant piece of evidence. Growing variance around an increasing average would indicate that some students were being left behind as the top (and probably the middle) of the population moved higher. However, they did not present evidence of growing variance in test scores. In fact, their discussion of educational "leveling"—a practice of not presenting the most challenging material to avoid embarrassing dull students at the risk of holding back the smartest students—suggests that they believed that if the variance of intelligence has changed, it decreased (see Herrnstein & Murray, 1994).

Second, their data analysis strategy did not actually address contending explanations of social problems. Instead they posed the question in terms of nature versus environment as the explanation for social problems. Test scores represented nature and socioeconomic background represented environment. The core of their evidence consists of statistical analyses that relate test scores, an index of socioeconomic background, and age to the risk of becoming poor, a high school dropout, unemployed, an unwed mother, on welfare, a neglectful mother, or imprisoned. In almost every one of these analyses, the statistic that represents the effect of test scores on the risk of a bad outcome is bigger than the statistic for the effect of socioeconomic background on that outcome. Thus, they concluded that they dismissed socioeconomic origins as an explanation of growth-resistant poverty and other social problems (see Murray, 1995).

As many critics have pointed out, these analyses are flawed by poor statistical practice and questionable inferences (Fischer et al., 1996; Goldberger & Manski, 1995; Hauser, 1995; Heckman, 1995; Knapp, Kronick, Marks, & Vasburgh, 1996; Korenman & Winship, 1995). In this chapter I review some of the main conclusions of that critical research. The empirical contribution of this chapter is a fuller specification of the factors that affect who becomes poor so that *The Bell Curve*'s explanation of poverty—based on individual variation in ability—can be compared to explanations that emphasize institutional factors like the family, schools, and labor markets.

INSTITUTIONAL EXPLANATIONS OF POVERTY

Individuals do not succeed or fail on their own. There is no social vacuum. The context of peoples' lives makes some things easier and some things hard for them. Important institutions exist to ameliorate the effects of individual fates and fortunes. However, access to these institutions is harder to achieve for some people than for others. The search for a fuller explanation of growth-resistant poverty begins with the observation that families headed by women are far more likely to fall into poverty than are families headed by couples. In 1996, a year with an overall poverty rate of 13.7%, poverty among families with a single female head was five times greater than that of families headed by a man or a couple—35.8% poor compared to 7.3% poor (U.S. Bureau of the Census, 1997).

Single women who head families face a number of economic problems that women with adult men in the house are less likely to face. Most obvious is the problem of numbers; families with more adults have more potential money-earners. The gender gap in wages is also important: Single women who head families have to get by on wages that, despite improvements, still lag 30% behind men's wages (Bianchi, 1995). Finally, single women with children have more complicated child-care problems than women in other families have.[1] Some women in two-adult families have no children who need care; those with children have the option of sharing either labor force participation or child care (or both). Even if both adults in a two-adult family opt for the labor force, they then have two incomes that can be pooled to meet expenses, including child-care expenses.

Growth is less effective in raising female-headed poor families out of poverty than it is in raising male-headed poor families out of poverty because the fruits of growth are spread through the labor force. Male family heads are both more likely to be employed and more likely to earn a living wage than are female family heads (Bianchi, 1995). The proportion of poor persons whose family is headed by a woman (among poor people living in families) grew from 20% to 50% between 1960 and 1974. Thus, according to this explanation, poverty became growth-resistant because a rising share of poor families were isolated from the labor market.

Changes in education may also promote growth-resistant poverty. Schooling differs in quality and quantity. Each has been shown to be an important factor in determining who is poor and who is not (Fischer et al., 1996). The quality and quantity of schooling may be important for growth-resistant poverty if the variance in either one has increased. An increase in the variance of quality would indicate that the highest quality schools have improved while the lowest quality schools have gotten worse. Although many commentators seem to assume that schools are more variable than they used to be, it is very difficult to find data on trends in school quality. An increase in the variance of quantity would mean that although the average worker is as well-qualified as before (perhaps even better), the number of unqualified workers may have increased at the same time.

One of the many appealing features of the data set used by Herrnstein and Murray (1994) was its unusually detailed data on the quality of the schools that the study's participants attended. Herrnstein and Murray made scant use of this information, but this study exploits it more fully.

Finally, the labor force is the key economic institution in the United States. Even before the welfare changes of 1996, most U.S. families' economic fortunes were tied to the wage and salary income of adult members. Thus, the probability of being poor

---

[1]By definition these are families of women and children; women living alone and unrelated women sharing living quarters are not considered "families" in these statistics.

depends in no small measure on the array and quality of jobs available in a local labor market. It also depends on how that market allows a worker to convert skills into cash; that is, on the economic returns to human capital (inherited and acquired). Wages, and consequently the probability of being poor, depend on the extent of racial and gender discrimination as it varies across the country (Farley, 1988; Lucas, 1994). The data set used by Herrnstein and Murray (1994) is not the best for exploring these kinds of effects, but some local labor market conditions are available for analysis.

THE NATIONAL LONGITUDINAL SURVEY OF YOUTH AND THE ARMED FORCES QUALIFYING TEST

Herrnstein and Murray's (1994) original empirical work is an analysis of data from the NLSY. Begun in 1979 with a sample of over 12,500 youths 14 to 22 years old, the panel is still being followed. The most recent data available to Herrnstein and Murray were from the 1991 wave of the panel, so they examined poverty status in the year before that. A key part of the study is the battery of tests that participants took in 1980. The tests are revisions of the components of the Armed Services Vocational Aptitude Battery (ASVAB). A subset of four tests known as the Armed Forces Qualifying Test (AFQT) constitute Herrnstein and Murray's IQ test.

The AFQT consists of four subsections, amounting to 105 questions, within the nearly 3½-hour, 333-question ASVAB: (a) Section 2, Arithmetic Reasoning (30 items with a 36-minute time limit), composed of word problems using arithmetic skills; (b) Section 3, Word Knowledge (35 items in 11 minutes), composed of vocabulary words; (c) Section 4, Paragraph Comprehension (15 items in 13 minutes), composed of questions referring to short paragraphs; and (d) Section 8, Mathematics Knowledge (25 items in 24 minutes), composed of questions testing algebra and higher mathematical skills. The target population for the test is high school students.

Readers will find no examples of the actual AFQT questions in *The Bell Curve*, but Fischer et al. (1996) reprinted a few provided by Bock and Moore (1986). The Appendix to this chapter shows one from each module of the AFQT. These are "simulated" versions of what remain confidential questions. Each example is rated at about average difficulty.

Debates about *The Bell Curve* concern the content and other properties of the AFQT. Herrnstein and Murray (1994) claimed that the AFQT is an excellent measure of intelligence: "The AFQT qualifies not just as an IQ test, but [as] one of the better ones psychometrically" (p. 580). A group of psychometricians who defended *The Bell Curve* in the *Wall Street Journal* (Arvey, 1994) wrote that "while there are different types of intelligence tests, they all measure the same intelligence" (p. A18) implying that the AFQT serves that purpose, too. Critics counter that the AFQT is a measure of how well the test-takers learned and displayed their knowledge of school subjects (as well as their interest, cooperativeness, stamina, and experience in taking tests).

WHAT THE AFQT MEASURES

On face value, the example items from Bock and Moore (1986) look less like measures of test-takers' intelligence—defined as a "deeper capability ... for 'catching on'"—than as measures of test-takers' exposure to curricula in demanding math and English classes. Bock and Moore analyzed the actual AFQT in detail. They described Section 4 (Paragraph Comprehension) as "lean[ing] rather heavily on general knowledge. A well-informed person has a good chance of answering many of the items correctly without reading the paragraph. This means that the better educated ... [have] both the benefit of reading the passages and already knowing many of the facts contained in them" (p. 34). This is an important advantage in a timed test. They said of Section 8 (Math Knowledge) that the answers would be "known only to persons who had some exposure to high school algebra and geometry, or who had studied text books on these subjects" (pp. 35).

Intelligence probably contributes to doing well on the AFQT. Youths who process information better probably learn more in school and so do better on the test, as do youths who sit still, pay attention, and care more. However, if intelligent youths have not been exposed to these subjects—and it matters not whether the deficiency arises because of lousy schools, lousy homes, or lousy attitudes—then they will not do well on these tests.[2]

What does it matter if the test also includes some environmental influences? Herrnstein and Murray (1994) controlled for environment in their statistical analyses. However, their statistical model adds the indirect effects of the environmental influences on test scores to those of intelligence to produce a single coefficient; then Herrnstein and Murray (mis)interpreted that coefficient as if it measured only the effect of intelligence. Here is how that happens: Begin with an equation that summarizes how intrinsic intelligence and environment combine to produce an individual's score on the AFQT:

$$\text{AFQT}_i = q_1 \text{ intelligence}_i + q_2 \text{ environment}_i \tag{1}$$

where i signifies that each individual i has a score on AFQT, intelligence, and environment, q_1 and q_2 are constants that apply to all individuals, and there is no error. Because neither intelligence nor environment can be observed directly, it is necessary to select a scoring system for them. A simple scheme that imposes no loss of generality is one that states that both coefficients are positive ($q_1 > 0$ and $q_2 > 0$), and that they add up to one ($q_1 + q_2 = 1$). The next step is to write the propensity to be poor (y) as a function of AFQT and environment:

---

[2]Moreover, of the subtests, the two math tests—ones that probably most require having taken the right classes, having had good instruction, and having paid attention—are the ones that contribute most to the final score. Paragraph comprehension contributed least. The correlation of number right in the subtest with the final bell-curved score that Herrnstein and Murray (1994) used, zAFQT, were (whites only): Arithmetic Reasoning, $r = .90$; Words, $r = .85$; Paragraphs, $r = .79$, and Math Knowledge, $r = .89$.

$$y_i = a + bAFQT_i + c\,environment_i + e_i \qquad (2)$$

where a, b, and c are constants and e_i is the sum of all influences that are not correlated with AFQT and environment. It is reasonable to expect $b < 0$ and $c < 0$; that is, the propensity to be poor will fall as test scores rise and environments improve. The person i will actually be poor if y_i is greater than 0.[3]

With environment controlled in Equation 2, does b reflect how intelligence affects the propensity to be poor (as Herrnstein and Murray asserted)? Not cleanly. To see what is going on, substitute the right-hand side of Equation 1 into Equation 2, and collect terms:

$$y_i = a + b(q_1 intelligence_i + q_2 environment_i) + c\,environment_i + e_i = \qquad (3)$$
$$a + bq_1 intelligence_i + (c + bq_2)environment_i + e_i.$$

Mathematically, unless $q_1 = 1$ and $q_2 = 0$, the product bq_1 will be closer to zero than b is and $c + bq_2$ will be further from zero than c is. In plain words, the mathematical result in Equation 3 demonstrates that if the AFQT contains even a trace of environmental influences ($q_2 > 0$), the statistic (b) that Herrnstein and Murray (1991) relied on exaggerates the influence of intelligence on the risk of being poor. In a complementary way, their use of c understates the effect of the environment. Even the staunchest defenders of the AFQT have shied away from claiming that it is purely intelligence. They have (mistakenly) thought that its validity depends on the preponderance of influences.[4] However, Equation 3 shows definitively that b is biased unless p_2 is exactly zero. The critic's job is much easier than most defenders and critics of *The Bell Curve* have thought.

The critique I have just presented is perfectly general. That is, although I have cast the dependent variable as poverty, there is nothing in the substance of the critique that makes use of that designation. Thus I could just as easily have said that y represented crime or teen pregnancy or truancy. As far as the mathematical logic goes, I could have simply said that y represents the generic bad outcome. For that reason, my demonstration that Herrnstein and Murray's (1994) inferences rest on the untested assumption that the AFQT is completely free of environmental influences applies to their entire analysis, not just to their analysis of poverty.

Is there any evidence of environmental influences on test scores? The circumstances of the test itself offer an important clue. Because the test was given to

---

[3]It might seem natural to define y_i as the probability that person i is poor. However the limits on probabilities—they cannot get smaller than zero or bigger than one—lead to statistical problems. Over the years statisticians have devised solutions to these problems. The most commonly used solution since the advent of fast computers has been to transform y into something called a *logit* (which is defined by the formula $y = \ln[p / (1 - p)]$, that is, the natural logarithm of the ratio of the probability that an individual is poor to the probability that she or he is not poor) and perform a logistic regression. Herrnstein and Murray and their critics have all adopted this statistical transformation to study the probability of living in poverty and other problematic outcomes.

[4]Mathematically their assumption works out to assuming that p_1 is greater than p_2.

16- to 24-year-olds, the test came at different points in many young peoples' educations. Although most NLSY participants were in school at the time they took the AFQT, some of them had completed their education. Having completed more or less education up until the time of the test is a key environmental influence that could be part of p_2. Of course smart young people are likely to go farther in school than dull young people will, even if schooling has no effect on test scores, so it would be unreasonable to assert that a correlation between schooling prior to the AFQT and score on the AFQT is evidence of environmental effects.

The evidence of environmental influence comes from the comparison between pretest schooling and posttest schooling. If all of the correlation between education and test scores is due to the role of intelligence in determining who will go farther in school, then the correlation between test score and posttest schooling will be the same as the correlation between test score and pretest schooling. If environmental factors are important, then the correlation between pretest schooling and AFQT will exceed that between posttest schooling and AFQT. The data show strong evidence of environmental effects on test scores; the correlation between pretest schooling and AFQT is .52, whereas the correlation between AFQT and posttest schooling is just .29.[5]

This is sufficient evidence to show that p_2 is greater than zero; that is, that environmental influences on test scores led Herrnstein and Murray (1994) to exaggerate the importance of intelligence as a factor in social problems. Further evidence includes a correlation between AFQT and whether the test-taker had college prep courses or was assigned to the academic track in high school ($r = .48$). Regressing the normalized AFQT score on years of education completed at the time the test was taken (education_t), the academic coursework variable (track), and the test-taker's age at the time of the test, reveals

$$zAFQT = -3.85 + .27*(education\_t) + .55*(track) - .15*(zAge); R^2 = .32; n = 5,252.$$

Taking college prep or academic courses raises test scores by .55 normalized units (adding roughly 8 correct answers). More important, the net effect of education at the time of the test (.27) is just about half of its correlation with test scores (.52), indicating that just about half of the influence of schooling on test performance comes about indirectly by way of the kinds of courses that high school students take. This bolsters the case that the tests are sensitive to school-related environmental effects, specifically, opportunities for learning that are available to some youth but not others.

Age is weakly correlated with test scores. In fact, age is negatively correlated with normalized AFQT score once education and track are taken into account. This surprising age pattern is further evidence that the AFQT is a test of school learning; the older test-takers among those with a given level of education had been out of school

---

[5]The correlations presented here are for all persons in the nationally representative NLSY sample. *Inequality by Design* presents the figures for whites only (p. 60). The two sets of correlations are remarkably similar because the correlations for blacks and whites are not significantly different from one another.

longer and had more time to forget what they had learned.[6] The alternative explanation, if one were to assume instead that the AFQT tested basic intelligence, would be that the younger cohorts coming up through school in about 1980 were about 1.2 SDs smarter than the oldest cohorts in the NLSY (.15 × 8years). One sixth of an SD (.15) is an implausibly large difference between people born a year apart; it implies an improvement of 1.2 SDs over these eight cohorts. The environmental arguments seem much more plausible.

The AFQT might actually serve as a reasonable measure of exposure to effective education, rather than intelligence. It captures how much schooling people encountered better than does the conventional years of education measure, incorporating educational quality as well as time in school. Thus it is useful to analysts who care about education. It is nearly useless in the nature–nurture debates.

It is no surprise that youths who do well on tests will usually continue to do well in school. In the test-happy environment of the contemporary United States, doing well on tests will open up more opportunities for schooling, as selective schools award spaces on the basis of these kinds of tests. Nor is it any surprise that doing well in school helps one to do well in life. As every parent with an adolescent is acutely aware, our society today is structured so that even though a diploma may not guarantee success, the lack of one is a serious drawback later in life. That finding is all too familiar, but it reveals the direct consequences of schooling rather than of cognitive ability. The AFQT also reflects mental disabilities, motivation, attitude, and luck (Fischer et al., 1996). These traits, too, influence how well someone does in the labor market—especially those parts of it that require schoollike skills and schoollike discipline.

IQ AND THE CAUSES OF POVERTY

If the AFQT reveals at least as much about peoples' current knowledge of things taught in school as it does about their native intelligence, researchers cannot naively use it to address the basic *Bell Curve* thesis—that lack of innate ability is at the root of social problems, especially growth-resistant poverty. However, as a test of cognitive acuity, the AFQT can be used to consider whether cognitive acuity, whatever its source, is as important as educational credentials, family, and labor market factors in determining who does or does not live in poverty.

Economists, psychologists, and sociologists have reanalyzed the NLSY data and found that many of Herrnstein and Murray's (1994) results are wrong (Fischer et al., 1996; Goldberger & Manski, 1995; Knapp et al., 1996; Korenman & Winship, 1995). The results dramatically reverse Herrnstein and Murray's conclusions. Improving the measurement of social origins revises the estimates of how socioeconomic background affects poverty dramatically upward. In this analysis I add institutional

---

[6]Bock and Moore (1986) used these same data to show that age reduces scores within groups having the same amount of education; they explicitly tie the negative effect of age to forgetting school lessons.

and sociological variables to the analysis: neighborhood and high school context, educational credentials, local labor market conditions, race, gender, marriage, and fertility. Institutional factors dwarf individual differences as determinants of the propensity to be poor. Not only are social origins much more important than Herrnstein and Murray's measure implies, other aspects of the social environment have substantial effects as well.

In limiting their attention to just one environmental variable—the socioeconomic standing of the household a young person grew up in—Herrnstein and Murray (1994) completely overlooked elements of the social environment that exist outside the family of origin but may nonetheless be extremely important for people's life chances. In throwing down a challenge to critics to come up with better measures of environmental influences associated with social origins, Murray (1995) supposed that "a good measure of 'the degree of presence and competency of a father'" or "the degree to which a young male is raised in an environment where high moral standards are enforced consistently and firmly" (p. 29) might strengthen the case for the importance of social origins. This focus on individualist interpretations of the environment pervades both *The Bell Curve* and much of the positive and negative discussion of it. To the sociologist, environment is context, not personality. For example, racial and class segregation are unmistakable features of life in the United States (Massey & Denton, 1993). Yet, Herrnstein and Murray's measures of social origin take none of that reality into account. As more results show, the kind of high schools people attend and the kind of local labor market people live in affect their life chances regardless of their individual ability or other personal factors.[7]

Measurement and Modeling Strategy

Poverty is potentially a subjective phenomenon reflecting the disparity between a person's income and a community's standard of living. Since the 1960s, however, the U.S. government has set an official poverty line based on income and family composition. Most research uses the official definition—or some multiple of it—to code people as poor or not poor. To be precise, people who do not live in families are classified as poor if their personal income falls below the official poverty line for individuals; people who live in families are classified as poor if the combined income of all members of the family falls below the poverty line defined for families with the same composition. I follow prevailing practice and score individuals living alone as poor if their income is below the poverty line and individuals living in families as poor if their family's total income falls below the poverty line.

Socioeconomic background turns out to be a complex construction, too. Herrnstein and Murray (1994) combined four indicators to form a single index of socioeconomic

---

[7]These are standard findings in sociological and economic research; for example, Hogan and Kitagawa (1985), Massey and Eggers (1991), Massey and Denton (1993), Crane (1991), Rosenbaum and Popkin (1991), Wilson (1991), Brooks-Gunn, Duncan, Klebanov, Sealand (1993), and Brewster (1994).

background (parental SES). Indexes are useful in statistical analysis because they can average out errors that mar the variables when they are taken one at a time. Indexes can produce misleading results sometimes, though, if some of the components of the index do not have the same relation to the outcome variable as the others. In the NLSY, mother's and father's education do not significantly affect the respondent's earnings, income, and poverty. That means that the index does not correlate with important outcomes as closely as family income alone or an index formed from just two items—family income and main earner's occupational status—would. Compounding the problem with their index, there are more missing data on parental income than for the other components. Herrnstein and Murray simply substituted the average parental income for the missing cases, a dubious substitution.[8] Fischer et al. (1996) corrected for these errors of misattribution by adding variables that measure difference between the poverty risk for a person with missing data and a person with an average value on each of the components of parental SES.[9] They also supplemented the origin variable by including indicators for farm origins and two-parent families as well as a count of the number of siblings; these are standard components of sociologists' measures of social origins (DiPrete & Grusky, 1990; Duncan, Featherman, & Duncan, 1972; Featherman & Hauser, 1978). The result of these modifications and improvements is a new index of social origins that is more powerful than either Herrnstein and Murray's index or any of the separate indicators alone (Fischer et al., 1996). Its power comes from the way it weights the components according to their importance for poverty, the correction for missing data, and the inclusion of three other aspects (farm origins, two-parent family, and number of siblings). In this chapter there is little need for any index, so I use each component by itself without any combination.

Thus the basic model of who becomes poor among young adults can be expressed this way:

$$y_i = \ln(p_i / (1 - p_i)) = \beta_0 + \beta_1 \mathbf{AFQT}_i + \beta_2 \mathbf{Age}_i + \Sigma_k \beta_k X_{ki} \qquad (4)$$

where p_i is the probability that person i is poor, AFQT_i is his or her score on the test, and the variables X_{ki} (for $k = 3, \ldots 9$) are his or her scores on parental income, parental occupation, mother's education, father's education, farm background, two-parent family, and number of siblings. The model is a logistic regression. This model has many advantages for statistical inference. Unfortunately, its parameters are not easy to interpret. Most challenging is the way that a one-point increase in some X can have a

---

[8]In describing their index, Herrnstein and Murray (1994) stated that they left the missing cases out of the index. This is equivalent to assigning the mean because the mean of a normalized variable is zero and not adding it to the index is the same thing as "adding zero."

[9]Korenman and Winship (1995) used a much more sweeping adjustment. They took advantage of the total household design of the NLSY (all persons 14–22 years old in a sampled household were included in the study) to match siblings. Through a fixed effects approach, they then captured all of the effects of origins, including neighborhood effects, mobility effects, and any other common links among siblings that might turn out to be important for poverty (or any of the other outcomes they explored).

small or large effect on p, depending on the exact combination of p and X.[10] In this application p will almost always be below .5 and b_k will usually be less than zero, so the effect of small changes in X_k will be sharply negative for low values of X_k, modestly negative around the mean of X_k, and negligible for high values of X_k.

To this basic model, I then add several institutional variables. Years of schooling, experience with academic or college preparatory courses, and an index of high school context (composed of racial segregation, percentage of students receiving subsidized lunch, and percentage of students dropping out before graduation; summed and divided by 3)[11] mark the role of the educational system. Three variables capture the broader social environment of the young person's experience: the unemployment rate in the metropolitan area (for metropolitan residents) or state (for nonmetropolitan residents) where she or he lives,[12] the type of community she or he lives in (central city, suburban, or rural residence, implemented as a pair of 0–1 or "dummy" variables with suburban as the comparison category), and region of the country (four regions, implemented as three dummy variables with Midwest as the comparison category). Perhaps the most important addition is gender. Model 3 adds contemporary family circumstances: a dummy variable for marital status (currently married vs. all other), the number of children, and the interaction between marital status and gender.

The modeling strategy is to build up from Herrnstein and Murray's (1994) analysis to a more complete one. To avoid repeating their sins of omission, it is necessary to enter all of the institutional variables at once. However, some reasonable argument could be made that the family variables are endogenous; that is, effects of poverty instead of causes of it. Independent variables have to be causes or correlates, it is not appropriate to include effects among the list of independent variables. In this case the best solution is to present the results both ways—with and without family variables— so that readers can compare them.

All three models are assessed for whites and African Americans separately. Some statistical efficiency could be gained by combining them, but the substantive interest in which of these factors affect racial groups the same and which have different effects for whites and African Americans outweighs this technical consideration.

---

[10]For a continuous X, the rate of change in p for a small increment in X is given by the formula: difference in p relative to difference in $X_k = dp/dX_k = b_k\, p(1 - p)$.

[11]School administrators, not respondents, provided these data, so they are of good quality. Each measure was recoded to have a *Mean* = 0 and *SD* = 1 (the shape of the distribution was not "normalized"). Unfortunately, data are missing for 21% of the sample. The cases with missing context data are not a random sample of the total, so the missing cases got a score of 0 (average), and the logistic regression equations adjust for this with an added a dummy variable coded 1 for missing cases and 0 otherwise. The value of the coefficient for the dummy variable indicates how much these cases differ from the average value imputed to them.

[12]An exact unemployment rate would disclose the identity of some NLSY respondents, so the date file reports this variable in six intervals. I scored the first five intervals to the midpoint of the interval and coded the open-ended top category as 16.5%.

Descriptive Results

Young adults as a whole are not the poorest segment of U.S. society. The poverty rate for the young adults in the NLSY is 7.7% (compared to a national poverty rate of 14% in 1990). Among whites the rate is 7.4%; among young African Americans it is 26.1%—nearly four times higher (see Table 13.1).

The poverty gap between African Americans and whites is so large, in part, because whites have several important advantages. The average white person in the NLSY cohorts grew up in a family that had twice as much money as the average African American's family ($48,000 compared to $24,000). The main earner in a white youth's household had a job that was 1 *SD* better than the one held by the average African American youth's. Whites' mothers had 1 year more schooling than the African Americans' mothers; the gap between fathers' educations is 2 years. Ninety percent of whites grew up in a two-parent household; 66% of African Americans did. Whites attended schools that conferred a 1 *SD* advantage over the schools attended by African Americans and were 20% more likely than African American students to be put in the academic track. With these advantages, it is hardly surprising that whites scored 1 *SD* higher on the AFQT.

Results for the Basic Model

The basic model is incomplete and therefore statistically flawed, so its coefficients should not be taken seriously. However, because it is *The Bell Curve* model, it is of some interest.

From Model 1 it appears that some socioeconomic factors have a strong association with the risk of poverty. The weights on specific factors differ for whites and African Americans, but the sum of socioeconomic influences is about the same for both groups. Family income and family size are the significant socioeconomic factors among whites (–.404 for income and .190 for siblings). Family income and main earner's occupational status affect African Americans' poverty.

Test scores also appear to have a powerful influence on poverty outcomes. The coefficient for AFQT is –.693 for whites and –.691 for African Americans. The similarity between these two coefficients is interesting. However, the coefficients obtained from this simple model contain a mixture of true effects and spurious associations, so it would be premature to render an interpretation (see Table 13.2).

Socioeconomic Background

The results for the several factors that capture the socioeconomic standing of each young person's family origins mean that few people from middle-class origins are poor. If upper middle-class origin is quantified as 1 *SD* above average (for all variables), the coefficients for white youth imply a poverty rate of 3.5% for the upper middle class. At the low end of the distribution a modest increase in family resources

TABLE 13.1
Descriptive Statistics of All Variables by Race

Variable	Whites			African Americans		
	M	SD	N	M	SD	N
Poverty Outcome (1990)						
Poor	.074	.262	3,422	.261	.440	1,920
Test Results						
AFQT (number correct)	71.688	20.505	4,346	46.083	18.469	2,785
zzAFQT[a]	.176	.897	4,346	−.896	.794	2,785
Individual Characteristics and Social Background						
Family income (1978–79)b	48.309	27.165	3,409	24.691	19.486	2,337
Parent's SEIa	.115	.946	4,118	−.583	.980	2,247
Mother's education	11.995	2.433	4,174	10.769	2.636	2,542
Father's education	12.328	3.270	4,067	10.147	3.511	2,043
Siblings (1979)	2.996	1.906	4,344	4.751	2.979	2,776
Two-parent family	.902	.297	4,346	.657	.475	2,785
Farm background	.058	.235	4,346	.029	.167	2,785
Age (1979)	17.557	2.257	4,346	17.496	2.195	2,785
Male	.497	.500	4,346	.493	.500	2,785
Northeast region	.223	.416	4,263	.167	.373	2,747
West region	.143	.350	4,263	.060	.237	2,747
Central region	.375	.484	4,263	.186	.389	2,747
Missing family income	.074	.262	4,346	.064	.245	2,785
Missing parent's SEI	.027	.162	4,346	.050	.218	2,785
Missing mother's education	.040	.195	4,346	.087	.282	2,785
Missing father's education	.064	.245	4,346	.266	.442	2,785
School Background						
High school composition	.182	.651	4,346	−.669	1.022	2,785
Years of schooling pre-AFQT	11.806	1.761	4,346	11.358	1.696	2,785
Years of schooling post-AFQT	1.583	1.968	4,313	1.269	1.594	2,747

Variable	Whites			African Americans		
	M	SD	N	M	SD	N
Academic track in high school	.337	.473	4,234	.276	.447	2,690
Missing school reports	.212	.409	4,346	.333	.471	2,785
1990 Individual Characteristics and Social Context						
Unemployment rate	8.374	5.699	3,850	7.180	5.196	2,469
Central city	.096	.294	3,677	.255	.436	2,437
Rural	.238	.426	3,677	.186	.389	2,437
Children	.909	1.091	4,195	1.086	1.271	2,708
Married	.616	.486	3,980	.327	.469	2,550
Married man (interaction effect)	.279	.449	3,980	.155	.362	2,550

[a]Normalized to *Mean* = 0, *SD* = 1. [b]In thousands, 1990 dollars.

lowers the risk of poverty substantially. For the lowest origins (corresponding to about $8,200 family income), poverty is almost 27%; people 1 *SD* above that (at $12,800 family income) have a 14% poverty rate (still twice the average of 7% among young adults). The logistic regression model has a nonlinear form that results in these precise estimates, but the observed poverty rates also follow a curve that slopes less sharply as income and other advantages rise.

African Americans have much higher poverty but similar socioeconomic differences in poverty rates. For African Americans from households that are 1 *SD* above the mean for all variables combined, the poverty rate is 9.6%; at the overall mean the African American poverty rate is 16%; 1 *SD* below the overall mean (just about the African American average) the poverty rate for African Americans is 23.8%. Of course at any point on the race-specific distribution of social origins the poverty gap is about twice as large as it is when comparing the same dollar amounts because the African American distribution is so sharply disadvantaged to begin with.

These socioeconomic effects are by and large direct. Comparing their magnitude in Models 1 and 2 reveals little difference. Thus, the class advantages and disadvantages associated with parental income and employment do not operate through the schools. Nor do they operate through the marriage market, according to Model 3. Contrary to the research of the 1960s and 1970s, the inheritance of poverty seems all too real for whites and African Americans in the cohorts covered by the NLSY. Poverty persisted

TABLE 13.2

Coefficients That Measure How Much Each Variable Affects the Probability of a Person Being in Poverty in 1990 by Race

	Whites (N = 3,031)			African Americans (N = 1,726)		
	Model 1	Model 2	Model 3	Model 1	Model 2	Model 3
zzAFQT[a]	−.693* (.088)	−.431* (.108)	−.371* (.115)	−.691* (.073)	−.398* (.089)	−.366* (.095)
Family income (1979)[a]	−.404* (.109)	−.373* (.119)	−.338* (.120)	−.277* (.092)	−.273* (.097)	−.246* (.102)
Parent's SEI[a]	−.051 (.083)	.027 (.097)	−.004 (.098)	−.225* (.074)	−.238* (.076)	−.191* (.084)
Mother's education[a]	.005 (.088)	.027 (.093)	.056 (.101)	−.115 (.070)	−.042 (.076)	−.017 (.082)
Father's education[a]	−.057 (.095)	.010 (.103)	−.024 (.111)	.015 (.074)	.074 (.080)	.065 (.086)
Siblings (1979)[a]	.190* (.065)	.149* (.070)	.047 (.077)	−.056 (.063)	−.071 (.068)	−.049 (.072)
Years of schooling, pre-AFQT		−.243* (.077)	−.279* (.083)		−.375* (.059)	−.338* (.063)
Years of schooling, post-AFQT		−.233* (.068)	−.201* (.071)		−.258* (.057)	−.211* (.061)
Academic track in high school		−.461 (.257)	−.202 (.272)		−.391* (.167)	−.359* (.176)
School composition		−.246* (.069)	−.276* (.075)		−.240* (.073)	−.245* (.078)
West region		.875* (.235)	.589* (.257)		.739* (.275)	.617* (.288)
Northeast region		.129 (.287)	−.022 (.309)		.347 (.206)	.199 (.214)
Central region		.528* (.215)	.313 (.233)		.812* (.167)	.578* (.179)
Local unemployment rate (1990)		.029* (.015)	.022 (.017)		.031* (.012)	.031* (.013)

Male	−.866* (.165)	−.998* (.224)			−.993* (.134)	−.676* (.170)
Children (1990)			.724* (.089)			.424* (.061)
Married (1990)			−3.074* (.257)			−2.030* (.226)
Married man (1990)			−.506* (.181)			−.090 (.181)
Intercept	−2.872* (.237)	−.092 (.958)	1.473 (1.077)	−1.325* (.131)	2.977* (.736)	2.529* (.829)
Pseudo R2	.116	.181	.322	.117	.210	.289

Note. Each model includes controls for age, type of residence, family structure, and missing data. Standard errors are given in parentheses.
[a]Normalized to a $M = 0$, $SD = 1$.
*$p < .05$.

across generations for these people, at least into their late 20s and early 30s.[13] In a complementary way, the upper middle class—white and African American—was largely insulated from the risk of poverty (except while in school).

The precise mechanism that allows the intergenerational transmission of advantage and disadvantage is not obvious. First of all, the gifts and loans that parents with means are likely to pass on to their young adult offspring are probably underreported in the NLSY, so even if they lift a young person's financial standing, they are undetected in these data. How many of the respondents thought about the money their parents gave them or the bills their parents paid when they were asked to report their 1990 income (in the 1991 NLSY interview)? Therefore, the mechanism is less tangible than cash yet effective.

Test Scores as a Factor in Poverty

Test scores—and presumably the skills they are designed to measure—predict future poverty as well as or better than many demographic factors do. The controversy over the genetic or environmental determinants of scores has obscured this key result. Regardless of its source, the relation of skills to rewards is important (e.g., Farkas, England, Vicknair, & Kilbourne, 1997). People who do well on tests also do well in avoiding poverty; but not as well as the numbers in *The Bell Curve* suggest. Replicating their model with improved measures of socioeconomic standing (Model 1)

---

[13]Much of that previous research focused on the relation between parent's occupational status and income for whites. As these results show, family income bears a much stronger relation to white young adults' incomes than occupational status does.

yields a coefficient of −.693 for AFQT. Improving that estimate by controlling for relevant factors that are correlated with test scores reduces that coefficient to −.371 for young whites. Whites in the top quarter of test-takers have an expected poverty rate of 4.9%; whites in the bottom quarter of the test distribution have a much higher poverty rate—11.0%.

African Americans do worse on tests than whites do, but test scores have the same effect on African Americans as they do on whites (compare the coefficients of −.371 and −.366 for AFQT in Model 3 for the two groups). So among African Americans in the top quarter of the test score distribution (10% of all young African Americans), the poverty rate is about half the poverty rate of African Americans at the 25th percentile—14% compared to 26%. At each specific score, the white poverty rate is lower than the rate among African Americans.[14]

Education, Test Scores, and Poverty

Education is closely tied to how well people do on tests like the AFQT, as the first part of this chapter made clear. However, test performance does not capture all of the effects of education. For example, employers have access to educational credentials but most of them do not know an applicant's test scores. It is also important to include both education and test scores in the analysis for statistical reasons. To the extent to which education and AFQT are correlated, including one but excluding the other will produce misleading results. If one variable is excluded, the effect of the included variable will be exaggerated. Thus an analysis that includes only AFQT will ascribe to test scores not only the actual effect of this measure but also the unobserved effects of education.[15]

In estimating the effect of education on poverty with the NLSY data, it is necessary to distinguish between two phases of education—that which took place before the AFQT (and thus is presumably part of the test score) and that which has taken place since.[16] Tracking within schools is also important for educational outcomes, so I distinguish between academic secondary education characterized by college preparatory coursework and general or vocational secondary education. The four batteries of the AFQT are more closely tied to the academic subjects taught in a college preparatory curriculum than to the skills taught in some vocational programs (and tested by batteries of the ASVAB that are not included in the AFQT).

The results for Models 2 and 3 show how including education furthers our understanding of poverty and its causes. Staying in school dramatically reduces the risk of poverty for whites and African Americans alike. If anything, African

---

[14]I address the implications of these results at the end of the chapter.

[15]By the same logic, the myriad published results that include education but exclude cognitive skills blend the effects of schooling and ability.

[16]Griliches and Mason (1972) used post-AFQT education to get an unbiased estimate of the returns to education. The NLSY design differs from the design of their study of veterans, so it is not appropriate to interpret the NLSY results exactly as they interpreted theirs.

Americans get more from a year of education than otherwise comparable whites do. Two years of schooling, just a little more than 1 *SD*, is comparable to 1 *SD* on the AFQT as a protection against poverty. For whites the poverty rate falls from 11% to 3% as education increases from 10 years to 16 years; among African Americans high school dropouts can expect a 38% poverty rate, whereas less than 10% of black college graduates can expect to be poor.

Poverty, Neighborhoods, and Segregation

Social origins involve more than simply the spending money and culture inside the home. The neighborhood context also affects the standard of living, regardless of a family's own resources. That simple and obvious fact is part of the reason why Americans of limited means spend so much of their income on shelter (Mayer, 1997; Myers & Wolch, 1995). It is one thing to be poor in a middle-class suburb with parks, low crime, and good schools, and much harder to be poor in an inner-city neighborhood that lacks those supports. The child in a well-endowed neighborhood gets the benefits of the locale regardless of his or her family's own resources, just as the inner-city child bears the burdens of city life even if his or her family might have an average income or more.

Poverty and other social problems are visible because they are concentrated in specific neighborhoods of our biggest cities. Since the publication of *The Truly Disadvantaged* by Wilson (1987), social scientists have taken that neighborhood context more seriously and have found compelling evidence of how segregation exacerbates the consequences of poverty, family breakup, crime, and deterioration (Crane, 1991; Hogan & Kitagawa, 1985; Massey & Denton, 1993). Herrnstein and Murray (1994) completely ignored the social context of social problems. Segregation and other aspects of the neighborhood context affect poverty in three ways. They induce disruptions in public schools that interfere with the educations of able students and "dull" students alike; they put distance between the jobless and jobs; and they restrict social contacts between ethnic groups and across class lines (Massey & Denton, 1993; Wacquant & Wilson, 1989).

Models 2 and 3 add the social context of the individuals in the NLSY to the poverty equation. The data show how school composition interacts with individual abilities and resources and how inner cities and rural areas offer fewer economic opportunities, job prospects, and marriageable partners than suburbs and towns do. The most powerful measure of local economic context is the unemployment rate for the metropolitan area the individual lives in.[17] Rural and inner-city areas do not compare favorably with suburbs.

Local and Regional Labor Markets

If brains were all that mattered in U.S. stratification processes, then the national labor market would eliminate all residual differences. In fact, our results show strong regional

---

[17]The definition of unemployment requires that individuals be looking for work to be counted.

effects that are inconsistent with the individualist perspective. Surprisingly residents of the South are no more poor than people from the Northeast who have the same origins, test scores, and education. Among African Americans, those from the Northeast are actually more likely to be poor. White Midwesterners have a midrange poverty rate, and white Westerners have the highest poverty (net of other factors). Among African Americans the Midwest is the region of highest poverty; the West is third.

Unemployment in the local labor market also increases individuals' risk of poverty slightly—a 1-point increase in the local unemployment rate raises a young person's poverty risk by 2.9% (which works out to one-tenth of a percentage point on average). This a modest but important effect. Perhaps the key to understanding growth-resistant poverty is not to focus on the nation as a whole but on the local and regional labor markets that make up the nation. Regional economies have always differed some, but there are signs that regional differences are more out of sync than they used to be (Kasarda 1995). For example, the recession that gripped most of the United States in the early 1990s persisted almost 2 years longer in California.

Gender and Poverty

From its bulk, it appears that The Bell Curve contains a discussion of every vital subject relevant to poverty. Surprisingly, however, it lacks a serious discussion of how gender relations have affected poverty in recent years. The difference between women's and men's poverty is more fundamental than any other cleavage. Over one fourth of young white women with average origins but test scores 1 SD below the mean are poor. For white men of average origins, poverty does not reach 25% until test scores fall to 2 SDs below the mean. The gender gap in poverty at any combination of origins and test scores is equivalent to the difference between two people of the same sex whose test scores differ by 45 points (out of 105) or whose family incomes differ by $45,000. The gender gap among African Americans is 15% bigger than the gender gap among whites.

Women's and men's poverty differs so dramatically because young women make less money and spend more time caring for children than men their age do. These differences in opportunities and responsibilities are largely mitigated by marriage, so a full discussion of them needs to take the difference between couples and singles into account.

Money, Marriage, and Poverty

Marriage affects poverty more than any other observable variable. Indeed marriage is integral to the huge gender gap in poverty. The married young people in the NLSY are not very likely to be poor; they have a 4% poverty rate whether they are white or African American. Unmarried women have dramatically higher poverty rates unless they have high test scores or come from advantaged origins. Children are an important contingency for women's poverty, but not for men's. The presence of children dramatically raises the risk of living in poverty for unmarried white women. Children also increase the probability of being poor among unmarried African American women, but not as dramatically.

The intricate patterns involving marital status, parenthood, socioeconomic origins, race, and gender are shown in Table 13.3. The percentages in the table refer to high school graduates. People with different educational attainment would have higher or lower poverty rates, but the pattern of differences by marital status, parenthood, socioeconomic origins, race, and gender would be the same. The poverty rates of married, young high school graduates are almost all less than 10%. The exceptions are African American mothers who grew up poor; they have poverty rates of 12% and 17% depending on whether they have one or two children. Married men, regardless of the number of children they have, whether they grew up poor or middle class, or whether they are white or African American, have poverty rates of 9% or less.

Single young people face dramatically higher poverty risks. Young men who grew up poor can expect poverty rates that range from 12% among childless whites to 34% among African American fathers. Women's poverty is even higher. Among women who grew up poor, the rates differ little by race. White and African American women who

TABLE 13.3

Expected 1990 Poverty Rates (From Model 3) as They Vary by Marital Status, Parenthood, Socioeconomic Origins, Race, and Gender

Marital Status	Parenthood	White Women	White Men	African American Women	African American Men
Grew up poor					
Single	Childless	26	12	40	25
	One child	43	21	50	34
	Two children	43	—	39	—
Married	Childless	1	<1	3	2
	One child	2	<1	5	2
	Two children	3	1	8	4
Grew up middle class					
Single	Childless	15	6	21	12
	One child	27	12	29	18
	Two children	43	—	39	—
Married	Childless	1	<1	3	2
	One child	2	<1	5	2
	Two children	3	1	8	4

Note. Expected probabilities for high school graduates living in Midwest suburbs; all other variables set to average values.

grew up poor and graduated from high school have poverty rates that range from 25% (white childless singles) to 60% among single mothers of either race who have two children. Even among women who grew up middle class, the poverty rates are double digits, ranging from 15% to 43% among white women (according to whether they have none, one, or two children). African American single mothers from middle-class origins can expect poverty rates that climb from 21% to 39% for (according to whether they have none, one, or two children).

Why are young women, especially unmarried women and unmarried mothers, so much more exposed to poverty than young men? Low wages and, for the mothers, limitations on the hours they can work account for most of the gender gap in poverty. Women gained significant ground in the economy of the 1980s (Bianchi, 1995). Most of those gains came to full-time workers, older cohorts of workers, and college graduates, however. Few of the young mothers whose experiences make up the NLSY database took part in that change. They may see their prospects improve once their children are old enough that they can become full-time workers. Unmarried men are not as exposed to poverty as women are because their higher wages and lower child-care responsibilities give them higher per-capita income (although some of it presumably goes to the mother's household for child care). Married women are not as poor as unmarried women because they share in their husbands' economic advantages.

These gender-specific marriage and child-care patterns hold throughout the range of test scores and for origins as high as 1 *SD* above average. To understand contemporary U.S. poverty we cannot look to causes in an individual's past. We must look at more proximate causes. The high poverty of unmarried women—especially unmarried mothers—comes from the combination of economic need and economic disadvantage that is peculiar to women in the United States since the mid-1970s. Other societies, even this one in days gone by, have shielded young women, especially young mothers, from the ravages of the economic marketplace. Contemporary U.S. society is unique in its lack of provision for mothers (Fischer et al., 1996). Let it suffice here to note that the combination of low wages and few hours they have available for paid work are the proximate causes of the very high poverty of unmarried women, especially mothers. The more distant causes, whether ability or social origins, are secondary to these more proximate causes.

CONCLUSIONS

Institutionalized inequality—not intrinsic differences in individuals' abilities—account for growth-resistant poverty in the United States. Ability as Herrnstein and Murray (1994) defined it is all too small a factor in economic inequality in the United States. Gender, especially as it interacts with marriage and family, is far more important than ability. Although gender is a characteristic of individuals, its importance for poverty comes from the way in which employers reward men's and women's human capital differently and how that discrimination gets played out in families. The social problems associated with growth-resistant poverty would be more nearly tractable if women faced less discrimination in the labor force. Our estimates indicate that the combination of gender and test score effects imply that a young woman who wishes to reduce her risk of poverty to the lower level of her brother has to score 41 to 55 points higher on the AFQT than he does (out of a possible 105 points). These figures assume that the young woman in question has an average chance of being married or not. Marriage gives a young woman access to her husband's earning power (Waite, 1998). For women married to white men, marriage acts like an antipoverty insurance policy; only 4% of them are poor. For unmarried mothers (African American and white), the risk of poverty is very great indeed—over one fourth are poor.

This analysis has addressed the order of finishing in the U.S. economic game. The rules of the game determine the order of finishing but not the relative sizes of the prizes (a distinction completely obscured by Herrnstein & Murray, 1994). In *Inequality by Design*, Fischer et al. (1996) discussed (a) the prizes, (b) how the distribution of those prizes has changed over time, and (c) how the United States compares with other rich countries in the distribution of them. That discussion provides more evidence of the importance of institutions in U.S. inequality and for the very small role that intrinsic individual differences, including abilities, play.

ACKNOWLEDGMENTS

This research is part of a project that also involves five other members of the Sociology Department at the University of California, Berkeley—Claude S. Fischer, Martín Sanchez Jankowski, Samuel R. Lucas, Ann Swidler, and Kim Voss—and Richard Arum of the Sociology Department at the University of Arizona. Together we published *Inequality by Design: Cracking the Bell Curve Myth* (Princeton University Press, 1996). The Survey Research Center at the University of California, Berkeley, and the Russell Sage Foundation supported the project.

REFERENCES

Ashenfelter, O., & Mooney, J. D. (1968). Graduate education, ability, and earnings. *Review of Economics and Statistics, 50*, 78–86.

Bianchi, S. (1995). Changing economic roles of women and men. In R. Farley (Ed.), *State of the Union: America in the 1990s* (Vol. 1, pp. 107–154). New York: Russell Sage Foundation.

Bock, D., & Moore, E. G. J. (1986). *Advantage and disadvantage: A profile of American youth.* Hillsdale, NJ: Lawrence Erlbaum Associates.

Brewster, K. L. (1994). Race differences in sexual activity among adolescent women. *American Sociological Review, 59*, 408–424.

Brooks-Gunn, J., Duncan, G. J., Klebanov, P. K., & Sealand, N. (1993). Do neighborhoods influence child and adolescent development? *American Journal of Sociology, 99*, 353–395.

Crane, J. (1991). The epidemic theory of ghettos and neighborhood effects on dropping out and teenage childbearing. *American Journal of Sociology, 96*, 1226–1258.

Danziger, S., & Gottschalk, P. (1996). *America unequal.* Cambridge, MA: Harvard University Press.

DiPrete, T. A., & Grusky, D. B. (1990). Structure and trend in the process of social stratification. *American Journal of Sociology, 96,* 107–144.

Duncan, O. D. (1968). Inheritance of poverty or inheritance of race? In D. P. Moynihan (Ed.), *On understanding poverty* (pp. 85–110). New York: Basic Books.

Duncan, O. D., Featherman, D. L., & Duncan, B. (1972). *Socioeconomic background and achievement.* New York: Academic Press.

Farkas, G., England, P., Vicknair, K., & Kilbourne, B. S. (1997). Cognitive skill, skill demands of jobs, and earnings among young European American, African American, and Mexican American workers. *Social Forces, 75,* 913–938.

Farley, R. (1988). After the starting line: Blacks and women in an uphill Race. *Demography, 25,* 477–495.

Featherman, D. L., & Hauser, R. M. (1978). *Opportunity and change.* New York: Academic Press.

Fischer, C. S., Hout, M., Sánchez-Jankowski, M., Lucas, S. R., Swidler, A., & Voss, K. (1996). *Inequality by design: Cracking the bell curve myth.* Princeton, NJ: Princeton University Press.

Goldberger, A. S., & Manski, C. F. (1995). Review article: *The Bell Curve* by Herrnstein and Murray. *Journal of Economic Literature, 33,* 762–777.

Griliches, Z., & Mason, W. (1972). Ability effects as excluded variable bias. In A. S. Goldberger & O. D. Duncan (Eds.), *Structural equation models in the social sciences* (pp. 285–316). New York: Academic Press.

Hauser, R. M. (1995). Review of *The Bell Curve. Contemporary Sociology, 24,* 149–154.

Hauser, R. M., & Huang, M.-H. (1997). Verbal ability and socioeconomic success: A trend analysis. *Social Science Research, 26,* 331–376.

Heckman, J. J. (1995). Lessons from *The Bell Curve. Journal of Political Economy, 105,* 1091–1121.

Herrnstein, R. J., & Murray, C. (1994). *The bell curve.* New York: The Free Press.

Hogan, D. P., & Kitagawa, E. M. (1985). The impact of social status, family structure, and neighborhood on the fertility of Black adolescents. *American Journal of Sociology, 90,* 825–855.

Jencks, C. (1992). Is the American underclass growing? In C. Jencks & P. E. Peterson (Eds.), *The urban underclass* (pp. 28–100). Washington, DC: Brookings Institution.

Jencks, C., Smith, M., Ackland, H., Bane, M. J., Cohen, D., Gintis, H., Heyns, B., & Michelson, S. (1972). *Inequality.* New York: Basic Books.

Karoly, L. A., & Burtless, G. (1995). Demographic change, rising earnings inequality, and the distribution of personal well-being. *Demography, 32,* 379–405.

Kasarda, J. (1995). Industrial restructuring and the changing location of jobs. In R. Farley (Ed.), *State of the union: America in the 1990s* (pp. 28–100). New York: Russell Sage Foundation.

Korenman, S., & Winship, C. (1995). *A reanalysis of The Bell Curve* (NBER Working Paper No. 5230). Cambridge, MA: National Bureau of Economic Research.

Knapp, P., Kronick, J. C., Marks, R. W., & Vasburgh, M. G. (1996). *The assault on equality.* Westport, CT: Praeger.

Lucas, S. R. (1994). *State level discrimination against Blacks and Women.* Unpublished doctoral dissertation. University of Wisconsin, Madison.

Massey, D. S., & Denton, N. (1993). *American apartheid.* Cambridge, MA: Harvard University Press.

Massey, D. S., & Eggers, M. L. (1990). The ecology of inequality: Minorities and the concentration of poverty, 1970–1980. *American Journal of Sociology, 96,* 1153–1188.

Mayer, S. E. (1997). *What money can't buy.* Cambridge, MA: Harvard University Press.

Murray, C. (1995, May). *The Bell Curve* and its critics. *Commentary, 99*(5), 23–30.

Myers, D., & Wolch, J. R. (1995). The polarization of housing status. In R. Farley (Ed.), *State of the union: America in the 1990s* (Vol. 1, pp. 269–334). New York: Russell Sage Foundation.

Rosenbaum, J. E., & Popkin, S. J. (1991). *Why don't welfare mothers get jobs? A test of the culture of poverty and spatial mismatch hypotheses.* Evanston, IL: Northwestern University, Center for Urban Affairs and Public Policy.

Sewell, W. H., Haller, A. O., & Portes, A. (1970). The educational and early occupational status attainment process. *American Sociological Review, 35,* 1014–1027.

U.S. Bureau of the Census. (1997). *Poverty of households, families, and individuals, 1996.* Washington, DC: U.S. Government Printing Office.

Wacquant, L. J. D., & Wilson, W. J. (1989). Poverty, joblessness, and the social transformation of the inner city. In P. H. Cottingham & D. Ellwood (Eds.), *Welfare policy for the 1990s* (pp. 70–102). Cambridge, MA: Harvard University Press.

Waite, L., & Gallagher, M. (in press). *The case for marriage.*

Wilson, W. J. (1987). *The truly disadvantaged.* Chicago: University of Chicago Press.

Wilson, W. J. (1991). Social theory and the public agenda: The challenge of studying inner-city social dislocations. *American Sociological Review, 56,* 1–16.

APPENDIX: EXAMPLES OF AFQT QUESTIONS

Arithmetic Reasoning

If a cubic foot of water weighs 55 lbs, how much weight will a 75½ cubic foot tank trailer be carrying when fully loaded with water?

  (a) 1,373 lbs   (b) 3,855 lbs   (c) 4,152.5 lbs   d) 2,231.5 lbs

Word Knowledge

Solitary most nearly means

  (a) sunny   (b) being alone   (c) playing games   (d) soulful

Paragraph Comprehension

People in danger of falling for ads promoting land in resort areas for as little as $3,000 or $4,000 per acre should remember the maxim: You get what you pay for. Pure pleasure should be the ultimate purpose in buying resort property. If it is enjoyed for its own sake, it was a good buy. But if it was purchased only in the hope that land might someday be worth far more, it is foolishness.

    Land investment is being touted as an alternative to the stock market. Real estate dealers around the country report that rich clients are putting their money in land instead of stocks. Even the less wealthy are showing an interest in real estate. But dealers caution that it's a "hit or miss" proposition with no guaranteed appreciation. The big investment could turn out to be just so much expensive desert wilderness.

    The Author of this passage can best be described as:

  (a) convinced   (b) dedicated   (c) skeptical   (d) believing

Math Knowledge

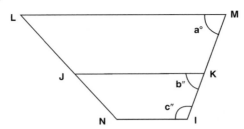

In the drawing above, JK is the median of the trapezoid. All of the following are true EXCEPT

(a) LJ = JN   (b) a = b   (c) JL = KM   (d) a ≠ c

Intelligence and Success:
Is it All in the Genes?

Bernie Devlin, Stephen E. Fienberg,
Daniel P. Resnick, and Kathryn Roeder

O ccasionally, very occasionally, big books appear in the social sciences that make both scholars and the lay public take notice. Richard Herrnstein and Charles Murray's (1994) *The Bell Curve: Intelligence and Class Structure in American Life* was one of those publishing events. *The Bell Curve* is big both in size (more than 850 pages) and in scope. It draws on diverse social science databases and deals with themes of broad social significance. The book became an immediate best-seller, reaching far beyond the community of behavioral and social science researchers. The authors provoked a counterliterature of criticism, qualification, and confrontation that has advanced the enterprise of social research.

In *The Bell Curve*, Herrnstein and Murray (1994) were worried about America's future. Growing inequality has become a major theme of social research in America and *The Bell Curve* has an important place in this literature. In a democracy, social problems seek political solutions. Wise governmental action, in turn, requires focused social research. In our society, since the Progressive period, the social sciences have provided that base of knowledge.

Although *The Bell Curve* set off a hailstorm of controversy about the relations among IQ, genetics, and various social outcomes, including welfare dependency, crime, and earnings, much of this reaction was polemical. It did not focus on the details of the science and in particular on the validity of the statistical arguments that underlie the book's conclusions. A detailed understanding of the arguments in *The Bell Curve* requires knowledge about (a) statistical models for genetic heritability; (b) factor analysis, especially as it has been applied to the analysis of IQ tests; (c) logistic regression and multiple regression analyses; and (d) causal modeling and alternative statistical frameworks for making inferences from longitudinal data.

In this chapter, we revisit the scientific and in particular the statistical underpinnings of the Herrnstein and Murray (1994) arguments and take stock of their implications for public policy. This chapter draws directly on material in a book we have coedited, entitled *Intelligence, Genes, & Success* (Devlin, Fienberg, Resnick, & Roeder, 1997), which contains contributions from a number of social scientists and statisticians addressing specific topics raised in *The Bell Curve*. It also provides a brief epilogue with some commentary on papers and books that have appeared since the publication of this volume. The Appendix to this chapter includes the table of contents for our volume.

THE BELL CURVE'S MAIN ARGUMENT

How do we view the questions raised by Herrnstein and Murray (1994) in *The Bell Curve?* In a review in *Contemporary Sociology*, Taylor (1995) succinctly summarized the main themes of the book via the following syllogism:

- *First premise*: Measured intelligence (IQ) is largely genetically inherited.
- *Second premise*: IQ is correlated positively with a variety of measures of so-cioeconomic success in society, such as a prestigious job, high annual income, and high educational attainment; and inversely correlated with criminality and other measures of social failure.
- *Conclusion:* Socioeconomic successes (and failures) are largely genetically caused.

As a corollary, Herrnstein and Murray (1994) claimed that IQ is resistant to educational and environmental interventions. They argued that American society is becoming increasingly stratified via a cognitive caste system, with the cognitively disadvantaged trapped at the bottom of society. This lower caste includes a large portion of the African-American population. Money spent and laws aimed to ameliorate this inequity will be wasted because IQ is largely genetically determined. Moreover, the genetic capital determining IQ is eroding, in large part due to the greater reproduction of low IQ individuals and, to a smaller extent, immigration.

The Bell Curve's pessimistic argument about declining intelligence in society, isolated ruling castes, and overreproduction of the least able is not new to Western social thought. In the introduction of *Intelligence, Genes, & Success* (Devlin et al., 1997), we outlined the history of this argument. It begins with well-known statistical names such as Galton, Pearson, and Fisher, all of whom were linked scientifically to the eugenics movement, and it has progressed through to the present day.

A quick overview of the evidence Herrnstein and Murray (1994) marshaled on the effects of IQ on income (or wages) can be gleaned somewhat informally in the causal diagram presented in Fig. 14.1. In *The Bell Curve*, Herrnstein and Murray used essentially the same models for all of their societal incomes. Thus, similar diagrams are appropriate (or inappropriate as the case may be) for other outcome variables. Later in this chapter, we present a simple alternative to the causal diagram in Fig. 14.1, consistent with the data and Herrnstein and Murray's analysis, but very different in its implications. The alternative uses income as the dependent variable of interest in a statistical causal model.

In the remainder of this chapter, we address three fundamental issues associated with the Herrnstein and Murray argument for which statistical issues really do matter. We focus on:

- The genetic basis of intelligence.
- The existence of a single factor for intelligence, known as g, for general intelligence.
- The role of intelligence in predicting desirable or successful social outcomes.

In Table 14.1, we link these topics to databases and analytic methods used in *The Bell Curve*. The statistical methods formally involve three quite different statistical tools: variance components, factor analysis, and regression. To cut to the chase, the contributors to Devlin et al. (1997) found the uses of these methods by Herrnstein and Murray (1994) and the authors they cite to be flawed in a consistent fashion. In each case, it is not that there is no evidence for an effect, but rather that the effect is much weaker than Herrnstein and Murray argued. Thus the implications of their findings for public policy have at best a limited scientific basis. In fact, even if we credit the scientific claims in *The Bell Curve*, in many cases they are only loosely linked to Herrnstein and Murray's proposed policies. Consequently we can easily fashion the opposite policy from exactly the same evidence.

DEVLIN ET AL.'s RESPONSE TO THE BELL CURVE

In preparing a critique of an empirical analysis of social science data it is rather easy to decry the lack of control in the gathering of the data, the impact of missing data and attrition, the possible effect of unmeasured variables, and the departures from the assumptions of the underlying statistical model. To a large extent the contributors in

TABLE 14.1
Three Key Scientific Arguments From The Bell Curve

Issues	Data	Methods
1. Genetical basis of intelligence	Twin studies	Factor analysis
2. Existence of singe factor, g, for intelligence	Collections of IQ test results	Factor analysis
3. Role of intelligence in predicting social outcomes	NLSY	Multiple regression: Logistic regression

Devlin et al. (1997) resisted the urge to rest our scientific case regarding the arguments in *The Bell Curve* on such grounds. Instead, we asked hard questions about Herrnstein and Murray's (1994) analyses and conclusions by reexamining with care the very databases that they claimed to have relied on. We also ask hard questions about the models themselves in cases where we believe that alternative perspectives lead to very different types of scientific models and, from them, policy recommendations.

SCIENCE

The Genetics–Intelligence Link

Genetics is an important part of the science that bears on intelligence, even though it receives little direct examination in *The Bell Curve*. There may be close to 100,000 genes in the human system. A substantial fraction of these genes may contribute to measured intelligence, but less than a handful have been characterized. Moreover, the relation among genes, gene systems, and external environment is interactive, defying and challenging the nature–nurture formulation. Where Herrnstein and Murray (1994) saw fixed divisions of genes and environment affecting measured intelligence, most geneticists see no such division and envision considerable malleability in the development of intellectual capacity. Herrnstein and Murray claimed that the literature shows coefficients of heritability in the range of 60% to 80%. This sounds impressive.

Daniels, Devlin and Roeder (1997), in their genetic reanalysis of classic familial IQ studies, found that Herrnstein and Murray's (1994) claim is a gross exaggeration. Their analyses differentiate between two kinds of heritability: broad-sense and narrow-sense. Geneticists distinguish between gene effects that are independent of genetic background and thus shared by parents and their offspring (additive), and gene effects that are dependent on genetic background and thus not shared by parents and their offspring (nonadditive). Broad-sense heritability measures the total effect of genes on IQ, whereas narrow-sense heritability measures the additive effect of genes. Only the narrow-sense heritability matters for Herrnstein and Murray's arguments about IQ's impact on the evolution of American society because only the additive effect is shared across generations. The new analyses show values on the order of 30%. They also find evidence to support potent environmental effects on IQ, namely through the maternal (womb) environment and through the shared family environment. The technical details of this chapter are also of interest. The primary tool is a Bayesian meta-analysis, which fits rather nicely with the variance components notion of heritability and stands in marked contrast with the statistical tools that are the stock in trade of the traditional behavior-genetic literature (e.g., see the papers in the recent volume edited by Sternberg and Grigorenko, 1997, and the description in Jensen, 1998).

In a related chapter, Wahlsten (1997) focused on how environment impacts IQ, arguing for the malleability of intelligence and the need to explore further the interaction between nature and nurture. In a third chapter on this topic, Singer and Ryff

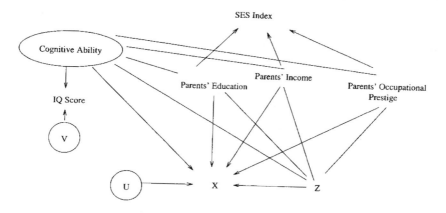

FIG. 14.1.   Careful look at *The Bell Curve* causal model (education is omitted).

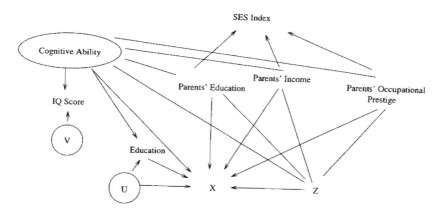

FIG. 14.2.   Alternative to *The Bell Curve* causal model (education is included).

(1997) demonstrated how alternative biological and psychosocial models can be used to explain effects that others have traditionally labeled as genetic inheritance.

Although the analyses and assessments we reported on clearly allow for some genetic component associated with intelligence, other things matter considerably. We concluded that Herrnstein and Murray's (1994) evolutionary arguments have little basis in science. Their argument about the erosion of cognitive capital (IQ dysgenics) is presented without acknowledging its evolutionary framework or its environmental assumptions. When viewed from a more rigorous perspective, sizable IQ dysgenic effects are implausible.

Is there any empirical evidence against IQ dysgenics? Instead of a dysgenic effect, the opposite seems to have occurred during this century. IQ scores have risen 15 to 20 points throughout the world since 1950. This pattern, known as the Flynn Effect (after Flynn, 1987), is widely acknowledged. Of course, the Flynn Effect cannot be due to genetics alone. Genetic changes of this magnitude are virtually impossible in this short of a time span. Many critics of *The Bell Curve* have cited the Flynn Effect as proof that Herrnstein and Murray's (1994) worry about IQ dysgenics is unfounded. However, the Flynn Effect must be largely the result of environmental influence: It tells us nothing about the genetics of populations, as they pertain to IQ, and how that might be changing over time. Hence the presence of the Flynn Effect cannot obviate the possibility of IQ dysgenics. Conversely, in view of the Flynn Effect, how does one estimate the selection differential required for this evolutionary argument? It makes little sense to compare IQs across generations if, in fact, the IQ scale is entirely different for those generations. In that case, what appears to be a drop in IQ by simple subtraction could really be an increase in IQ after adjusting for the scale change inherent in the Flynn Effect. For an extended discussion on rising IQs and their interpretation, including an update by Flynn, see Neisser (1998).

Intelligence and the Measurement of IQ

The Bell Curve sees intelligence as a fixed variable, established at birth and relatively unchanged through life. IQ tests are used as an indicator of this native intelligence. Herrnstein and Murray (1994) took general intelligence—*g*—as a given, rather than discussing its basis in factor analysis. Some, like Gould (1996) in the new edition of *The Mismeasure of Man*, argue that Herrnstein and Murray's reliance on factor analysis is the Achilles heel of their entire effort and have dismissed it accordingly.

Carroll (1997) reviewed our knowledge of the psychometric domain, the history of the search for generalized intelligence, and the relations of more specialized capacities to a general factor. His goal was to explain the measurement process from the analytic perspective, and he offered an internalist view. He found a large consensus within the psychometric community about the existence of generalized intelligence and the ability of IQ tests to measure it, along with evidence of more specialized capacities.

Hunt (1997) presented a far more skeptical evaluation of the existence of *g*. He gave an overview of how intelligence is viewed in modern cognitive theory, pointing to the evidence for and arguments about multiple factors of intelligence. These multiple factors have different implications for societal functioning and they appear, in some senses, in some of the predictive models in Devlin et al. (1997), especially the chapter by Cawley, Conneely, Heckman, and Vytacil (1997).

Thus these psychologists have differing judgments about the unidimensional features of intelligence and reach at most limited conclusions about the implications of *g*, or its multidimensional alternatives, for success in life or for social policy.

Analyzing the Outcomes

Murray and Herrnstein (1994) draw on data from the National Longitudinal Study of Youth (NLSY) to examine some of the societal sequelae of intelligence as measured by *g*. The Devlin et al. (1997) contributors looked a lot harder at the numbers than the typical *The Bell Curve* reader, and they were deeply disappointed.

Alternative analyses of NLSY data can support interpretations far different from the ones made by Herrnstein and Murray. What is the relation of IQ to crime, educational attainment, employment, and income? What do the regression analyses show? Here is some of what the contributors to Devlin et al. (1997) found.

Cawley et al. (1997) reanalyzed the NLSY data related to earnings and they found *The Bell Curve's* argument that *g* predicts differences in wages to be overstated. Other components of ability are also associated with wage levels. However, even lumped with education and experience, ability of all kinds does not predict wage levels very well. The difference in earnings of demographic groups with the same cognitive levels, but of different race and gender, is considerable. Those differences undermine, fundamentally, the claim that the job market is meritocratic.

The Bell Curve's claims for the existence of a meritocratic wage structure and against affirmative action are also challenged by Cavallo, El-Abbadi, and Heeb (1997), who found that race differences in earnings have been masked by Herrnstein and Murray's (1994) statistical procedures. Controlling for ability, they found a sizable gap in the earnings of Black and White men. Education and experience differences may also be affected by racism in ways that are less easily established and not captured in standard regression models.

For Winship and Korenman (1997), *The Bell Curve* fails to deal adequately with the relation between education, family background, and IQ. In their analysis of the NLSY data, every year of school beyond 8th grade is likely to increase IQ by 2 to 4 points. They also faulted *The Bell Curve's* statistical procedure for its treatment of the effects of both family background and years of education. Educational investments would thus appear to be a promising way to impact earnings.

The Bell Curve has revived a favored eugenics argument that IQ is a strong predictor of criminal behavior. Manolakes (1997) challenged Herrnstein and Murray's (1994) view that, controlling for socioeconomic background, people of low IQ are more likely to commit criminal actions. She faulted their explanatory model for the inadequate specification of socioeconomic variables and showed that interactions between race and education are important. Contrary to what *The Bell Curve* argues, IQ and level of parental education have very different effects on criminality for Black and White respondents in the NLSY.

Clearly intelligence plays an important role in many dimensions of human endeavor. We come from a university, and the importance of intelligence is fundamental to our raison d'être. However, based on these and other assessments of Herrnstein and Murray's (1994) core regression and logistic regression analyses of the

NLSY data, we are unpersuaded about the "dominant" role of IQ in determining all important life outcomes.

In Fig. 14.1 we present a causal model adapted from one in a chapter by Clark Glymour (1997), who presented a sweeping discussion of the role of causal models in *The Bell Curve* and in the social sciences more broadly. In discussing his version of our Fig. 14.1, he argued that all of Herrnstein and Murray's analyses presuppose a common causal schema such as that depicted in Fig. 14.1 for the variable income:

> Here X is some social ill—poverty, illegitimacy, or whatever—Z is some covariate, often age. [The error variables, U and V, and Cognitive Ability are unmeasured.] The directed edges indicate hypothetical causal relations, while the undirected edges represent unexplained correlations. The SES Index is a linear function of the variables that are its parents in the graph. In addition, Herrnstein and Murray assume that the variance of V is small, so that IQ score is a good proxy for cognitive ability. The arguments of the book are almost all based on regressions of various X variables on IQ, SES index, and, for each choice of X, some choice of Z.

> The obvious objection is that the regression model leaves out variables that influence both IQ and X. The list of possibilities is endless. Herrnstein and Murray write: "A major part of our analysis accordingly has been to anticipate what other variables might be invoked and seeing if they do in fact attenuate the relationship of IQ to any given social behavior" (p. 123). In fact, however, the only variable they consider is education.

> Adding education or other variables to the set of regressors in *The Bell Curve* would, I am sure, have changed the estimates of the influence of cognitive ability on social ills, but it would have done little to improve the scientific case. Suppose, for example, education is added to the set of regressors. Then, if education is a cause of IQ scores and X, a "spurious correlation" between IQ scores and X, will have been removed. But what if, in addition, unmeasured cognitive ability influences IQ scores and also influences education, and furthermore, there is some other omitted common cause of education and X? (pp. 271–272.)

In Fig. 14.2 we present Glymour's first alternative casual model. We believe that such criticisms of the models presented in *The Bell Curve* are ones social scientists should take seriously, and they would raise questions about the validity of Herrnstein and Murray's (1994) conclusions, even in the absence of the empirical evidence marshaled in the reanalysis described earlier.

Genetics, Race, and IQ

So what is left? Only one chapter in *The Bell Curve* deals exclusively and explicitly with race, but as the book's preface acknowledges, "This book is about differences in intellectual capacity among people and groups and what these differences mean for America's future" (Herrnstein & Murray, 1994, p. xxi). Differences among people, individual differences, quickly become differences of class and caste. Differences among groups, in turn, get resolved to differences between races. The decision of Herrnstein and Murray to move from arguments about individual differences within groups, where the data are abundant, especially for Whites, to theories of race difference, where data are sparse and more contested in meaning, is puzzling. Moreover, there is no mention of the potentially profound implications of racial and ethnic self-identification in the NLSY and in other national surveys and censuses.

There is no disagreement that median IQ scores show a 13-point gap between Blacks and Whites in the United States, but there is a lot of disagreement about what this means. Herrnstein and Murray noted that the gap between Black and White scores may be closing, but they saw little reason to expect this trend to continue. It is surprising to us, however, that they might even consider a dominantly genetic explanation for racial differences for IQ, especially given the dearth of theory supporting this explanation and the wealth of evidence suggesting the difference is, at least in large part, due to differences in environment.

IMPLICATIONS OF THE BELL CURVE FOR PUBLIC POLICY?

Despite their extensive use of the NLSY data, the themes Herrnstein and Murray (1994) explored are not new, their quantification did not proceed at the needed level of sophistication, and their policy recommendations are more the product of a moral persuasion and libertarian ideas than they are of solid statistical evidence. Here are four of their findings, each tied to a policy recommendation:

1. Everyone cannot learn. Efforts to improve the lot of average and below-average students have taken place through the systematic neglect of the cognitively gifted minority. Put public money into programs for the gifted.

2. Affirmative action in the workplace has been tried and found wanting as it produces large "racial" discrepancies in job performance and incurs costs in efficiency and fairness. End attention to equal opportunity in employment and end affirmative action. Market forces will continue to reduce racism.

3. More inequality and social tension are inevitable. Prepare to invest more heavily in internal security: Expect to spend more money for prisons and for the protection of wealthier neighborhoods.

4. Government has failed the citizen. Virtues like respect and self-reliance can be cultivated primarily in the private sphere. Reduce the role of government in public life.

Zigler and Styfco (1997) took up Herrnstein and Murray's charge that little can be done to raise the intelligence of those in the poorest areas of our cities and countryside. They pointed out that the popular Head Start program, which Herrnstein and Murray targeted for criticism because of its failure to raise IQs, was never designed to do so.

However, they noted the benefits in other areas, like school completion, and they made a strong civic case for this investment.

Affirmative action in the U.S. workplace and in higher education is currently under assault—in the media, in Congress, and in the courts. It also comes in for rough treatment in the final chapters of *The Bell Curve*. Herrnstein and Murray's (1994) argument is somewhat philosophical, but largely pragmatic in tone. After all, because IQ is largely genetically determined and resistant to change, and because IQ causes the inequities in educational and social outcomes observed in American society, laws aimed at ameliorating the inequity must fail.

We agree with Herrnstein and Murray about many of the problems in the federal government's attack on racial discrimination in the workplace, especially the naive and potentially misleading uses of statistics. We, too, are against reverse discrimination. However, this does not mean that all of the law and practice that has moved the United States away from its discriminatory past is perverse and inequitable. Nor will simply allowing employers to once again use tests to discriminate in hiring necessarily serve the nation well.

How should we respond to the inequality in our midst? Is it an unfortunate by-product of the otherwise laudable emergence of the cognitive elite? Readers of *The Bell Curve* are asked to celebrate the growth of a more competent America in which those with advanced degrees go to the best schools, intermarry, earn well, live together in enclaves, send their children to good preparatory schools, and manage the nation. We are asked to recognize the rightness and necessity of this kind of development, because a complex United States now requires the services of those with high IQs.

Herrnstein and Murray (1994) argued that efforts to broaden educational and social opportunity by public investment are doomed to failure because of natural limits created by the distribution of IQ, and that great inequality is socially tolerable if the police offer adequate protection to those in wealthy segregated enclaves. Although professing displeasure at growing inequality, Herrnstein and Murray saw no alternative.

However, these views seem to be based more on *The Bell Curve's* nostalgia for Jeffersonian America, small towns, and self-reliance than on the science in the book. Herrnstein and Murray (1994) shared the consensus among social researchers about growing inequality in the United States, but they stand apart in their explanation of why this is happening and what can be done about it. They also stand apart in the tight and directional ties they posited between the smarts that people are born with and the kind of lives that they lead. They stand apart from most Americans in the depth of their hostility to government. For Murray (1997b), this is a principled hostility and it can be seen to drive his views on policy irrespective of empirical evidence. Because of their principled opposition to government, Herrnstein and Murray would deny Americans the support of public institutions in the struggle against rising inequality. Armed with the counterevidence in Devlin et al. (1997), we believe that others might make a strong case to the contrary, in which government is legitimate, and even large and powerful.

Herrnstein and Murray (1994) wrote an interesting book about an important problem, but is the science underlying their arguments correct? Our answer is no! The scientific arguments in *The Bell Curve* are often badly distorted, and this really matters when it comes to tracing the implications for public policy.

EPILOGUE

Since Devlin et al. (1997) went to press early in 1997, papers and books on related topics have continued to appear. The journal *Intelligence* published a special issue (January–February 1997) on intelligence and social policy. The papers in it cover some of the issues raised by the authors in our volume, but, not surprisingly, most of them continue to echo Herrnstein and Murray's (1994) emphasis on the importance of intelligence and its genetic base. Jensen (1998) recently published a volume presenting the evidence in support of the existence of *g*, restating the earlier positions about the heritability of *g*, and in part citing Herrnstein and Murray's analyses as evidence of the causal implications of *g*. His statistical arguments, we believe, are flawed in much the same way that those in *The Bell Curve* are. The book edited by Sternberg and Grigorenko (1997) also contains related papers on the heritability of IQ as well as some from opposing schools of psychological thought. Finally, the book edited by Neisser (1998) presents an update on the issues of rising IQs (the Flynn Effect), the narrowing gap in Black–White test score differentials, and how these empirical results relate to the Herrnstein and Murray claim on dysgenic trends.

Murray continues to write on the topic, first in an article in *The Public Interest* (Murray, 1997a), and more recently in an expanded monograph (Murray, 1998). Like the arguments and the rhetoric in *The Bell Curve*, Murray's latest analyses sound convincing. And, although they are better than those in *The Bell Curve*, they share fatal flaws. In his new work, Murray's thesis is that IQ drives economic success and it will continue to do so in the future. Consequently IQ will form the basis for social stratification, just as he and Herrnstein envisioned *The Bell Curve*. We can quibble about the relative importance of IQ, but let us not get distracted from the fundamental issue. In *The Bell Curve*, Herrnstein and Murray (1994) argued that the impact of genes on IQ, together with assortative mating on IQ, would essentially ensure the transmission of elite status from parents to children and on to grandchildren; likewise, the children and grandchildren of cognitive peasants were doomed to be peasants. In his more recent work, Murray subtly changes the argument by describing the impact of IQ on current-day economic success, a link that is hardly surprising. Even in his current revision, the details of his statistical arguments are not beyond challenge.

Murray's latest approach used sib pairs, a technique he adapted from Winship and Korenman (1997). Because the siblings were raised together, Murray assumed a contrast of their outcome reflects IQ differences unencumbered by environmental influences. To the contrary, although it controls for shared environment of the children, it does not control for nonshared environmental influences or for interactions between environment and other factors, such as genes. (He also examined only a subsample of sib pairs, which raises troubling ascertainment issues that merit close examination.)

Murray also continues to demonstrate assortative mating for IQ, as if this bolsters the genetic argument used in *The Bell Curve*. But there is little doubt that people of similar IQ tend to intermarry, because this fact was established long before *The Bell Curve*. What was remarkable about *The Bell Curve* was the prediction that such patterns would lead to cognitive and economic stratification of society by the force of genes coming together in the children of cognitively elite and dull parents. Perhaps because we pointed out the dubious nature of the argument (Devlin et al., 1997), Murray dropped intergenerational genetics from his argument. Yes, there is social stratification in American society, but there is no genetic justification for its persistence.

Thus we end this chapter as we ended *Intelligence, Genes, & Success* (Devlin et al., 1997), with a healthy skepticism regarding the proffered arguments about and statistical analyses regarding the genetic basis of intelligence and the implications of this for modern society.

ACKNOWLEDGMENT

Parts of this chapter are adapted from materials we wrote originally for *Intelligence, Genes, & Success*. We thank Springer-Verlag for permission to use these materials here.

REFERENCES

Carroll, J. B. (1997). Theoretical and technical issues in identifying a factor of general intelligence. In B. Devlin, S. E. Fienberg, D. P. Resnick, & K. Roeder (Eds.), *Intelligence, genes, & success: Scientists respond to the bell curve* (pp. 125–126). New York: Springer-Verlag.

Cavallo, A., El-Abbadi, H., & Heeb, R. (1997). The hidden gender restriction: The need for proper controls when testing for racial discrimination. In B. Devlin, S. E. Fienberg, D. P. Resnick, & K. Roeder (Eds.), *Intelligence, genes, & success: Scientists respond to the bell curve* (pp. 125–126). New York: Springer-Verlag.

Cawley, J., Conneely, K., Heckman, J., & Vytlacil, E. (1997). Cognitive ability, wages, & meritocracy. In B. Devlin, S. E. Fienberg, D. P. Resnick, & K. Roeder (Eds.), *Intelligence, genes, & success: Scientists respond to the bell curve* (pp. 179–192). New York: Springer-Verlag.

Daniels, M., Devlin, B., & Roeder, K. (1997). Of genes and IQ. In B. Devlin, S. E. Fienberg, D. P. Resnick, & K. Roeder (Eds.), *Intelligence, genes, & success: Scientists respond to the bell curve* (pp. 45–70). New York: Springer-Verlag.

Devlin, B., Fienberg, S. E., Resnick, D. P., & Roeder, K. (1997). *Intelligence, genes, & success: Scientists respond to the bell curve*. New York: Springer-Verlag.

Fischer, C. S., Hout, M., Jankowski, M. S., Lucas, S. R., Swidler, A., & Voss, K. (1996). *Inequality by design: Cracking the bell curve myth*. Princeton, NJ: Princeton University Press.

Flynn, J. R. (1987). Massive IQ gains in 14 nations: What IQ tests really measure. *Psychological Bulletin, 101*, 171–191.

Glymour, C. (1997). Social statistics and genuine inquiry: Reflections on the bell curve. In B. Devlin, S. E. Fienberg. D. P. Resnick, & K. Roeder (Eds.), *Intelligence, genes, & success: Scientists respond to the bell curve* (pp. 257–280). New York: Springer-Verlag.

Gould, S. J. (1996). The *mismeasure of man* (rev. and expanded ed.). New York: Norton.

Jensen, A. R. (1998). *The g factor: The science of mental ability.* Wesport, CT: Praeger.

Herrnstein, R. J., & Murray, C. (1994). *The bell curve: Intelligence and class structure in American life.* New York: The Free Press.

Hunt, E. (1997). The concept and utility of intelligence. In B. Devlin, S. E. Fienberg. D. P. Resnick, & K. Roeder (Eds.), *Intelligence, genes, & success: Scientists respond to the bell curve* (pp. 157–176). New York: Springer-Verlag.

Manolakes, L. A. (1997). Cognitive ability, environmental factors, and crime: Predicting frequent criminal activity. In B. Devlin, S. E. Fienberg. D. P. Resnick, & K. Roeder (Eds.), *Intelligence, genes, & success: Scientists respond to the bell curve* (pp. 235–255). New York: Springer-Verlag.

Murray, C. (1997a). IQ and economic success. *The Public Interest, 128*, 21–35.

Murray, C. (1997b). *What it means to be a libertarian: A personal interpretation.* New York: Broadway Books.

Murray, C. (1998). *Income inequality and IQ.* Washington, DC: EI Press.

Neisser, U. (Ed.), (1998). *The rising curve: Long-term gains in IQ and related measures.* Washington, DC: American Psychological Association.

Singer, B., & Ryff, C. (1997). Racial and Ethnic inequalities in health: Environmental, psychosocial, and physiological pathways. In B. Devlin, S. E. Fienberg. D. P. Resnick, & K. Roeder (Eds.), *Intelligence, genes, & success: Scientists respond to the bell curve* (pp. 89–122). New York: Springer-Verlag.

Sternberg, R. J., & Grigorenko, E. (Eds.). (1997). *Intelligence, heredity, and environment.* New York: Cambridge University Press.

Taylor, H. (1995). Review symposium of *The Bell Curve. Contemporary Sociology, 24*, 153–158.

Wahlsten, D. (1997). The malleability of intelligence is not constrained by heritability. In B. Devlin, S. E. Fienberg. D. P. Resnick, & K. Roeder (Eds.), *Intelligence, genes, & success: Scientists respond to the bell curve* (pp. 71–87). New York: Springer-Verlag.

Winship, C., & Korenman, S. (1997). Does staying in school make you smarter? The effect of education on IQ in the bell curve. In B. Devlin, S. E. Fienberg. D. P. Resnick, & K. Roeder (Eds.), *Intelligence, genes, & success: Scientists respond to the bell curve* (pp. 215–234). New York: Springer-Verlag.

Zigler, E., & Styfco, S. J. (1997). A "head start" in what pursuit? IQ versus social competence as the objective of early intervention. In B. Devlin, S. E. Fienberg. D. P. Resnick, & K. Roeder (Eds.), *Intelligence, genes, & success: Scientists respond to the bell curve* (pp. 283–314). New York: Springer-Verlag.

APPENDIX: TABLE OF CONTENTS OF INTELLIGENCE, GENES, & SUCCESS

Part I: Overview

Part II: The Genetics–Intelligence Link

4. "The Malleability of Intelligence is Not Constrained by Heritability," Douglas Wahlsten

5. "Racial and Ethnic Inequalities in Health: Environmental, Psychosocial, and Physiological Pathways," Burton Singer and Carol Ryff

Part III: Intelligence and the Measurement of IQ

6. "Theoretical and Technical Issues in Identifying a Factor of General Intelligence," John B. Carroll

7. "The Concept and Utility of Intelligence," Earl Hunt

Part IV: Intelligence and Success: Reanalyses of Data From the NLSY

8. "Cognitive Ability, Wages, and Meritocracy," John Cawley, Karen Conneely, James Heckman, and Edward Vytacil

9. "The Hidden Gender Restriction: The Need for Proper Controls When Testing for Racial Discrimination," Alexander Cavallo, Hazem El-Abbadi, and Randal Heeb

10. "Does Staying in School Make You Smarter? The Effect of Education on IQ in *The Bell Curve*," Christopher Winship and Sanders Korenman

11. "Cognitive Ability, Environmental Factors, and Crimes: Predicting Frequent Criminal Activity," Lucinda A. Manolakes

12. "Social Statistics and Genuine Inquiry: Reflections on *The Bell Curve*," Clark Glymour

Part V: *The Bell Curve* and Public Policy

13. "A "Head Start" in What Pursuit? IQ Versus Social Competence as the Objective of Early Intervention," Edward Zigler and Sally J. Styfco

14. "Is There a Cognitive Elite in America?," Nicholas Lemann.

15. "Science, Public Policy, and *The Bell Curve*," Stephen E. Fienberg and Daniel P. Resnick

Compensatory Preschool Education, Cognitive Development, and "Race"

W. Steven Barnett
Gregory Camilli

The extent to which preschool education can improve the long-term cognitive abilities of children in poverty is a question of substantial importance for both social policy and scholarship. Much of the debate over public spending on preschool education programs such as Head Start and other investments in the education of poor children revolves around the issue of whether such investments can produce meaningful improvements in the cognitive abilities of children from low-income families. Those who conclude that preschool education has not and cannot produce such effects tend to conclude that large additional public investments in the education (preschool and otherwise) of poor children are unwarranted (Herrnstein & Murray, 1994; Jensen, 1969). Similarly, estimates over time of the effects of preschool education on the cognitive abilities of children in poverty have implications for our understanding of cognitive abilities and their malleability.

Minority children are much more likely to spend the first years of their lives in poverty. Over 40% of African-American and Latino children under the age of 6 are poor and the vast majority live in families with inadequate incomes (under 185% of the poverty level). By contrast only 13% of non-Latino white children under the age of 6 live in poverty (Li & Bennett, 1998). To the extent that preschool education for children in poverty can improve children's cognitive development and academic performance, it can contribute to closing the gaps in educational and economic success between white non-Latino and minority populations. In addition, studies of the cognitive impacts of preschool programs shed light on the nature and origins of the differences in cognitive abilities by "race" that can inform both the public's views regarding cognitive differences and scholarly research on this topic.

This chapter begins with a review of the evidence regarding the effects of preschool education on the cognitive abilities of children in poverty. It challenges the conventional view that preschool programs have only short-term cognitive effects. This requires an in-depth, critical examination of the evidence, because the conventional view derives from a failure to distinguish important differences between measures of IQ and achievement and common methodological weaknesses in the research. We believe that this in-depth review also provides valuable insights into the nature and limitations of the measures used to assess cognitive development. To aid readers who are not social scientists we have avoided jargon when possible and defined it when necessary, as well as providing summaries of key points throughout the chapter. Finally, we discuss the implications for public policy and further research, recognizing that debates about "race" differences at some level are really debates about the extent and manner in which societies will allocate resources to redress educational and economic inequalities.

SHORT-TERM EFFECTS

Information on the short-term effects of preschool education comes from two largely separate bodies of research: one on the effects of ordinary child care on children generally, and the other on the effects of intensive preschool education programs targeting children in poverty. Child-care research first focused on the question of whether nonparental care of young children was harmful. The consistent finding is that child care per se is not harmful to cognitive development for the general population (Lamb & Sternberg, 1990). Studies find that child care produces small improvements in cognitive development into the first few years of school, especially for children from impoverished homes, and that there is a modest relation between program quality and child care's effects on cognitive development (Caughy, DiPietro, & Strobino, 1994; Lamb & Sternberg, 1990; Phillips, McCartney, & Scarr, 1987; Zaslow, 1991).

Research on intensive preventive or compensatory interventions for children in poverty from the start focused on the potential for positive contributions to cognitive development. Meta-analyses (that summarize the results from multiple studies by pooling data or results across studies and applying statistical tests) of decades of research on intensive preschool programs for children in poverty find immediate effects on IQ and achievement tests of about 0.5 SDs (McKey et al., 1985; Ramey, Bryant, & Suarez, 1985; White & Casto, 1985). These effects are larger than those estimated for ordinary child care for the general population or children in poverty. Consistent with this, the magnitude of effects of targeted preschool interventions appears to vary with program intensity, breadth, and duration (Frede, 1998; Ramey et al., 1985). Moreover, intervention programs that do not provide intensive educational experiences for children do not produce much in the way of immediate or short-term gains in cognitive development (St. Pierre, Layzer, & Barnes, 1998). The number of studies of compensatory preschool programs is much larger than the number of studies of child care's cognitive effects and includes randomized trials, the "gold standard" research design for studies of this type (Barnett, 1998; Ramey et al., 1985).

LONG-TERM EFFECTS

Meta-analyses and traditional literature reviews find that in most studies the estimated effects of even intensive and targeted preschool education programs decline over time and are negligible several years after children leave the programs (Haskins, 1989; Locurto, 1991; McKey et al., 1985; Ramey et al., 1985; Spitz, 1986; White & Casto, 1985; Woodhead, 1988). This pattern leads many to conclude that even intensive preschool programs produce no lasting effects on cognitive development. In this view, initial effects are either artificial (children learn to answer test questions better, but are not really smarter) or do not lead to long-term gains in cognitive ability. Those attending to differences among programs tend to conclude that large-scale public programs for children in poverty (Head Start and public school programs) produce no meaningful improvements in cognitive abilities, whereas more intensive, small-scale (and impractical) programs may produce small gains in cognitive development. For example, Herrnstein and Murray (1994) concluded, "Head Start, the largest program, does not improve cognitive functioning. More intensive, hence more costly, preschool programs may raise intelligence, but both the size and the reality of the improvements are in dispute" (p. 389). They and others contend that to the extent more intensive programs have substantive long-term benefits these are more likely due to socialization than to effects on cognitive functioning (Herrnstein & Murray, 1994; Woodhead, 1988; Zigler & Freedman, 1987). At first glance such a view may seem quite reasonable, but a closer look at the evidence reveals that it is based on uncritical and incomplete reviews of the literature that treat all findings equally regardless of the quality of the study. This chapter looks critically at the research to determine the strength of support for findings and conclusions and finds widespread design limitations and methodological flaws.

GROUND RULES FOR A CRITICAL REVIEW

An extensive search of the literature revealed 37 studies that met the criteria set out for inclusion in this review. These criteria are: (a) children entered the program before age 5, unless kindergarten was unavailable; (b) the target population was children in poor or low-income families; (c) at least one measure of cognitive ability was collected at or beyond age 8, allowing any fade-out to be observed; (d) program participation was known from program records; and (e) the research design attempted to provide a comparable no-treatment group or to statistically adjust for group differences. These 37 studies exceed the number with long-term outcome measures included even in the previous meta-analyses, and many have not been reviewed together previously.

For review, the studies are divided into two categories depending on whether the program studied was a small-scale research model or large-scale public program. In 15 studies, researchers developed model programs to study the effects of controlled treatments. In 22 other studies, researchers investigated the effects of ongoing, large-scale public programs: 10 studied Head Start programs, 8 examined public school programs, and 4 studied a mix of Head Start and public school programs.

Model Program Studies

The 15 studies of model programs are described in Table 15.1, which gives a brief description of the program, ages of program participation, information on the research design (whether it was a randomized trial or used some other method and whether it used school-administered tests), initial and long-term follow-up sample sizes, grade at which last follow-up was conducted, IQ outcomes, and school outcomes including achievement test scores. Attrition rates (loss of sample during follow-up) can be determined by comparing initial and follow-up sample sizes. The model programs were more generously funded and so more intensive and (probably) better implemented than large-scale public programs. In all but one study the majority of children were African-American. The Houston Parent Child Development Center (PCDC) served Latino-American families. The average level of mother's education was under 12 years in all studies, and under 10 years in five studies. Three studies further limited their target populations in ways that could have affected their results. The Harlem Training Project served only boys. The Perry Preschool study selected children based on low IQ scores, and its sample had substantially lower IQs at age 3 than children in other studies. The Milwaukee study selected children whose mothers had IQs below 75.

As shown in Table 15.1, the model programs studied varied in entrance age, duration, services provided, and historical context (1962–1980). Most of the comparison children began formal education at kindergarten, but in the more recent studies significant percentages of the comparison groups are likely to have attended a preschool or child-care program, including Head Start, leading to underestimation of program effects. For example, two thirds of the control group in the Abecedarian study attended a program for 1 year or more by age 5, and this appears to have enhanced the cognitive abilities of the control group (Burchinal, Lee, & Ramey, 1989).

Two of the model program studies stand out because they were randomized trials, began with sample sizes larger than 30 in each group, and had low attrition throughout follow-up—the Abecedarian and Perry Preschool studies. Five other model program studies were randomized trials, but two—Milwaukee and the Early Training Project—began with extremely small samples, and the remaining three suffered serious attrition, raising questions about the representativeness of the final sample and reducing final sample sizes. The other eight model program studies constructed comparison groups, and it is possible that the groups differ in ways that may have biased the comparisons either for or against the program (Barnett, 1998). In randomized trials, children are randomly assigned to the model preschool program or to a control group. This provides an assurance that the two groups do not differ from each other from the start. When randomized trials are not used, it is difficult to distinguish program effects from the effects of preexisting differences between children (and their families) in the preschool group and the comparison group, a problem sometimes referred to as *selection bias*.

Large-Scale Public Programs

The 22 studies of large-scale public programs are described in Table 15.2, which reports ages of participation, study design, initial and latest follow-up sample sizes, grade at latest follow-up, school outcomes, and methodological issues. Most programs served children part-day for one school year at age 4. Four programs served children from age 3. The programs studied are generally representative of public preschool programs for children in poverty. Compared to the model programs, these public programs have larger class sizes and less qualified staff. In nearly all of the studies children moved on to regular public elementary schools. In the Cincinnati Title I study most full-day kindergarten students had attended preschool and most half-day kindergarten students had not. In the Child Parent Center (CPC) studies, the intervention program continued through Grade 3.

All of the large-scale public program studies used quasi-experimental designs. Some constructed comparison groups from waiting lists or other groups of children thought to be similar to program children. Others relied on natural variation in program participation within a target population. Both strategies raise concerns for selection bias in the estimation of program effects due to self-selection and administrative selection. Self-selection occurs when preschool program participation is affected by parental efforts to obtain educational opportunities for their children—for example, some parents expend more effort to find good schools and teachers and to provide good educational experiences at home and in the community. Administrative selection occurs when programs ration enrollment by choosing to serve those with the greatest needs (e.g., the poorest or most disorganized families, or the children who lag farthest behind). When comparison groups are identified later, there are no preprogram measures of children's cognitive abilities to assure that the two groups were the same to start with. Many studies employ family background measures to assess comparability and adjust for initial group differences, but there is always a risk that the adjustments are imperfect and unmeasured differences between groups bias the results.

STUDY FINDINGS

For brevity, only long-term results are reported in Tables 15.1 and 15.2. Outcome measures included are IQ test scores, reading and math achievement test scores, and three

TABLE 15.1
Model Early Childhood Programs

Program Name Description and Sources	Research Design and Methodological Issues	Sample Size[a] and Time of Follow-up	IQ[b], Achievement and School Success[c]
1. Carolina Abecedarian 1972–1985 Full-day year-round educational childcare Entry: 6 weeks to 3 months Exit: 5 years (Campbell & Ramey, 1993 & 1994)	Randomized	Initial E = 57, C = 54 Follow-up ages 8, 12, 15 E = 48, C = 44 (15)	IQ E > C age 12, E = C age 15 E = 95, C = 90 (15) Achievement tests: E > C age 15 Special education: E < C age 15 E = 24%, C = 48% Grade retention: E < C age 15 E = 39%, C = 59%
2. Houston Parent Child Development Center 1970–1980 Home visits & full-day year-round educational childcare, center-based program for parents Entry: 1 to 3 years Exit: 3 to 5 years (Andrews, et al., 1982; Johnson & Walker, 1991)	Randomized; high attrition	Initial E = 97, C = 119 Follow-up grades 2-5 School data: E = 50, C = 87 Achievement data: E = 39, C = 78	IQ not measured Achievement tests: E > C Grades: E = C Bilingual education: E < C E = 16%, C = 36% Special education: E = C grades 2-5 E = 27%, C = 31% Grade retention: E = C grades 2-5 E = 16%, C = 23%
3. Florida Parent Education Project 1966–1970 Twice weekly part-day preschool (ages 2 to 3) & Home visits Entry: 3 to 24 months Exit: 5 years (Jester & Guinagh, 1983)	Initially randomized; added more "control group" members at 24 months; randomization lost when new "controls" added; high attrition; school-administered tests	Initial E = 288, C = 109 Follow-up grades 4-7 E = 83, C = 24	IQ E = C E = 83, C = 80 Reading achievement: E = C Math achievement: E > C Special education: E < C grade 7 E = 23%, C = 54% Grade retention: E = C grade 7 E = 28%, C = 29%

Program	Design	Sample	Results
4. Milwaukee Project 1968–1978 Full-day year-round educational childcare; job & academic training for mothers Entry: 3 to 6 months Exit: 5 years (Garber, 1988)	Groups of 3 to 4 children assigned alternately to E & C groups; small sample	Initial E = 20, C = 20 Follow-up grades 4 & 8 E = 17, C = 18	IQ E > C E = 101, C = 91 Achievement tests: E = C grade 4 (E > C prior to grade 4) Grades: E = C Special education: E = C grade 4 E = 41%, C = 89% Grade retention: E = C grade 4 E = 29%, C = 56%
5. Syracuse Family Research Program 1969–1975 Home visits; year-round educational childcare; transition from half-day to full-day by 18 months Entry: 6 months Exit: 5 years (Lally, Mangione, & Honic, 1988)	Matched comparison group selected at 36 months; not randomized	Initial E = 82, C = 72 Follow-up grades 7-8 Parents E = 52, C = 42 Children E = 49, C = 39	IQ E = C age 5 Teacher ratings: E > C, girls only Attendance: E > C, girls only Grades: E > C, girls only
6. Yale Child Welfare Research Program 1968–1974 Home visits and full-day year-round educational childcare Entry: Prenatal Exit: 30 months (Seitz, Rosenbaum, & Apfel, 1985; Seitz & Apfel, 1994)	Two comparison groups from same neighborhoods for first follow-up Matched comparison group selected for follow-up at 30 months; not randomized; school-administered test	Initial E = 18, C = 18 Follow-up ages 7, 8, 10 Age 7 to 8 E = 17, C1 = 33, C2 = 31 Age 10 E = 16, C = 16	IQ E = C age 10 Achievement tests: E = C Attendance: E > C Teacher ratings: E = C Special education: E = C E = 25%, C = 50%

continued on next page

375

TABLE 15.1 (continued)

Program Name Description and Sources	Research Design and Methodological Issues	Sample Size[a] and Time of Follow-up	IQ[ab], Achievement and School Success[a]
7. Verbal Interaction Project 1967–1972 Home visits Entry: 2 to 3 years Exit: 4 years (Levenstein, O'Hara, & Madden, 1983)	Six groups with three matched comparison groups; not randomized	Initial E = 111, C = 51 Follow-up grade 3 E = 79, C = 49	IQ E > C E = 102, C = 94 Achievement tests: E > C Special education: E < C grade 7 E = 14%, C = 39% Grade retention: E = C grade 7 E = 13%, C = 19%
8. Early Training Project 1962–1967 Home visits and summer part-day preschool Entry: 4 to 5 years Exit: 6 years (Gray, Ramey, & Klaus, 1982, 1983)	Randomized; school-administered tests	Initial E = 44, C = 21 Follow-up post high school E = 36, C = 16	IQ E = C age 17 E = 79, C = 76 Achievement tests: E = C Special education: E < C grade 12 E = 5%, C = 29% Grade retention: E = C E = 58%, C = 61% High school graduation: E = C E = 68%, C = 52%
9. Experimental Variation of Head Start 1968–1969 Part-day preschool Entry: 4 years Exit: 5 years (Karnes, Shwedel, & Williams, 1983)	Post hoc comparison group from same communities; not randomized; school administered tests	Initial E = 116, C = 24 Follow-up post high school E = 102, C = 19	IQ E < C at age 13 E = 85, C = 91 Achievement tests: E = C Special education: E = C grade 7 E = 13%, C = 15% Grade retention: E = C grade 7 E = 10%, C = 16%

Study	Design	Sample	Results

10. Harlem Training Project 1966–1967
One-to-one tutoring or child-directed play
Entry: 2 to 3 years
Exit: 4 years
(Palmer, 1983)
	Comparison group recruited from children born 1 to 2 months later; not randomized; school-administered tests	Initial
		E = 244, C = 68
		
		Follow-up grade
		7 E = 168, C = 51
			IQ E = C at age 12
			  E = 92, C = 89
			Reading achievement: E < C
			Math achievement: E > C
			Grade retention: E < C grade 7
			  E = 30%, C = 52%

11. High/Scope Perry Preschool Project 1962–1967
Part-day preschool & Home visits
Entry: 3 to 4 years
Exit: 5 years
(Weikart, Bond, & McNeil, 1978; Schweinhart, et al., 1993; Barnett, Young, & Schweinhart, 1998)
	Randomized	Initial
		E = 58, C = 65
		
		Follow-up post high school
		E = 58, C = 65
			IQ E = C age 14
			  E = 81, C = 81
			Achievement tests: E > C
			Grades: E > C
			Special education: E = C grade 12
			  E = 37%, C = 50%
			Grade retention: E = C grade 12
			  E = 15%, C = 20%
			High school graduation: E > C
			  E = 67%, C = 49%

12. Howard University Project 1964–1966 Part-day preschool Entry: 3 years Exit: 5 years (Herzog, Newcomb, & Cisin, 1974)	Comparison group from neighboring tracts; not randomized	Initial E = 38, C = 69 Follow-up grade 4 E = 30, C = 69	IQ not measured Grade retention: E = C E = 33%, C = 47%

continued on next page

TABLE 15.1 (continued)

Program Name Description and Sources	Research Design and Methodological Issues	Sample Size[a] and Time of Follow-up	IQ[a,b], Achievement and School Success[a]
13. Institute for Developmental Studies 1963–1967 Home visits, part-day preschool and parent center Entry: 3 years Exit: 9 years (Deutsch, Taleporos, & Victor, 1974; Deutsch, et al., 1983)	Randomized; high attrition; school-administered tests	Initial E = 312, C = 191 Follow-up grade 7 E = 63, C = 34	IQ E = C age 8 E = 97, C = 91 Achievement tests: E = C grade 3 Special education: E = C E = 0%, C = 13% Grade retention: E = C E = 23%, C = 43%
14. Philadelphia Project 1963–1964 Part-day preschool & Home visits Entry: 4 years Exit: 5 years (Beller, 1983)	Matched comparison group from same kindergarten classes; not randomized; school-administered tests	Initial E = 60, C = 53 Follow-up post high school E = 44, C = 37	IQ E > C age 10 E = 98, C = 92 Achievement tests: E = C Special education: E = C grade 12 E = 5%, C = 6% Grade retention: E = C grade 12 E = 38%, C = 53%
15. Curriculum Comparison Study 1965–1967 Part-day preschool program & Kindergarten program Entry: 4 years Exit: 5 or 6 years (Miller & Bizzell, 1983, 1984)	Post hoc comparison group from original pool; not randomized; school-administered tests	Initial E = 214, C = 34 Follow-up post high school E = 134, C = 22	IQ not measured Special education: E = C grade 12 E = 32%, C = 63% Grade retention: E = C grade 12 E = 26%, C = 58% High school graduation: E = C E = 67%, C = 53%

[a]Throughout Table 15.1, E refers to the experimental or intervention group and C refers to the control or comparison group. Outcomes listed as E > C or E < C were statistically significant at the p < .05 level. [b]IQ's were measured using the WISC or WISC–R, unless otherwise noted.

measures of school progress or placement: grade repetition, special education place-ment, and high school graduation. All of these are considered to be indicators of cogni-tive abilities, although the measures have obvious differences. Moreover, it is clear that school progress and placement is not only a matter of cognitive abilities even if these were to be defined broadly to include social cognition and dispositions toward learn-ing. Thus, it is important to consider evidence regarding how long-term effects on these outcomes are produced, as we do at the end of the review.

Intelligence as Measured by IQ

All of the model program studies found positive initial effects on IQ. In most cases IQ effects were sustained at least until school entry. At age 5, 10 studies reported effects between 4 and 11 IQ points, the Milwaukee study reported a gain of 25 points, and the Syracuse study reported no effect. The other three model program studies did not mea-sure IQ at school entry. The two experimental studies that enrolled infants in intensive full-day educational programs reported the largest initial effects (Milwaukee and Abe-cedarian) and found that some IQ gain persisted at least into adolescence. None of the large-scale program studies provided IQ data on Stanford–Binet or Wechsler Intelli-gence Scale for Children (WISC) IQ tests comparable to the data from the model pro-gram studies (Wechsler, 1974). A few administered the Peabody Picture Vocabulary Test (PPVT; Dunn & Dunn, 1981), and the Westinghouse study employed the Illinois Test of Psycholinguistic Abilities (McCarthy & Kirk, 1961). These large-scale pro-gram studies found no effects on these IQ-type measures after school entry.

The evidence that intensive interventions over the first 5 years of life may produce very long-term, possibly permanent, increases in IQ stands out in sharp contrast to the apparent failure of later and more modest interventions to produce lasting IQ gains. It suggests that very early and more intensive interventions may have not just larger, but more fundamental or general effects on the cognitive development of children in poverty. However, the findings of both studies are discounted by scholars advocating the importance of heredity as an explanation for the low cognitive abilities of children in poverty (despite the fact that even the strongest claims for heredity leave sufficient room for the effects estimated in these studies). It is important to consider carefully the validity of their reasons for rejecting the evidence.

The Abecedarian study's results have been rejected on the grounds that differences in IQ scores appear in the first year of life, and, it is argued, this is too early for IQ scores to have been affected by the program (Herrnstein & Murray, 1994; Spitz, 1986). Thus, the groups must have differed in IQ from the start. This argument fails on several counts. First, young children's IQ scores can respond very quickly to educational interventions. Substantial gains are found after even a few months of intervention. The "6-week surge" has been remarked on by researchers working with interventions for children in poverty for decades. Second, the long-term effects of the Abecedarian program on IQ are found even after controlling for maternal IQ and infant home environment, presumably sources of preexisting differences in IQ between the treatment and control groups. Third, the pattern of IQ effects in the Abecedarian sample is consistent with the view that the program produced results through environmental enrichment; the largest gains are for children whose mothers had the lowest IQs.

The Milwaukee study's results have been rejected based on the claim that the apparent IQ effects are not accompanied by improvements in academic performance (Herrnstein & Murray, 1994; Jensen, 1989; Locurto, 1991; Spitz, 1986). Yet, the evidence does not support this claim. Statistically significant and quite large differences in academic achievement were found in the early grades. Special education and grade repetition rates for the control group were twice the rates for the experimental group by Grade 4. These differences in special education and grade repetition and later differences in academic achievement are not statistically significant, but the magnitudes of the estimated effects are quite large. The very small sample size in the Milwaukee study provides such limited statistical power that it is irresponsible to construe lack of statistical significance for longer term academic effects as support for the view that IQ effects occur without meaningful effects on academic success. In fact, an overview of all the evidence from this study contradicts that view.

Achievement

In contrast to the IQ findings, results regarding long-term effects on achievement varied considerably across studies. Five of 11 model program studies with achievement data found statistically significant positive effects on achievement test scores beyond Grade 3. Evidence of achievement effects was strongest in the seven randomized trials. All of these found statistically significant effects on achievement at some point. The two randomized trials with low attrition rates, the Abecedarian and Perry Preschool studies, found effects on test scores persisting into high school. The Houston PCDC study found effects in Grades 2 to 5 (the most recent follow-up). The Florida Parent Education study found effects through Grade 7 for children with at least 2 consecutive years in the program. The Milwaukee study found that effects were statistically significant to Grade 2, and the Early Training Project ceased to find significant effects at Grade 4. However, the last two studies both had extremely small samples for these follow-ups ($n < 50$) so that this may reflect limited statistical power rather than lack of program effects. Of the quasi-experimental model program studies, only the Verbal Interaction Project (VIP) found persistent effects on achievement (and the experimental studies of VIP contradict this evidence), although some found statistically significant effects for earlier years. Nine studies of large-scale programs never found statistically significant effects or lost statistical significance by Grade 3. Twelve studies of large-scale programs found significant positive effects on achievement at least through grade 3. In three of these, significant positive effects were maintained until at least Grade 6.

Much of the variation in findings regarding long-term effects on achievement across programs can be explained by differences in the research methods and procedures. Indeed, the evidence of fade-out in effects on achievement appears to

TABLE 15.2

Large-Scale Public Early Childhood Programs

Program Name Description and Sources	Research Design and Methodological Issues	Sample Size[a] and Time of Follow-up	Outcomes[a]
1. Child-Parent Center 1965–1977 Entry: 3 or 4 years Exit: 9 years (Fuerst & Fuerst, 1993)	Compared former CPC children with non-CPC children from same feeder schools; no pretest; school-administered test	Initial E = 684, C = 304 Follow-up post high school E = 513, C = 244	Achievement tests: E > C grade 2 E = C grade 8 High School graduation: E > C E = 62%, C = 49%
2. Child-Parent Center II 1983–1985 Entry: 4 or 5 years Exit: 9 years (Reynolds, 1994a, 1994b, 1993)	Compared former CPC children with several other groups; no pretest; school-administered test	Initial Unknown Follow-up Grade 7 E = 757, C = 130	Achievement tests: E > C grades K-7 Special E/education: E < C E = 12%, C = 22% Grade retention: E < C E = 24%, C = 34%
3. Cincinnati title I Preschool 1969–1971 Entry: 4 or 5 years Exit: 6 years (Nieman & Gasthright, 1981)	Compared children who attended full-day kindergarten and mostly had preschool with children who attended half-day kindergarten and mostly had no preschool; no pretest; school-administered test	Initial E = 688, C = 524 Follow-up Grade 8 E = 410, C = 141	Achievement tests: E > C grades 1, 5, 8 Special education: E = C, grade 8 E = 5%, C = 11% Grade retention: E = C, grade 8 E = 9%, C = 12%
4. Maryland Extended Elementary Pre-K 1977–1980 Entry: 4 years Exit: 5 years (Eckroade, Salehi, & Carter, 1988; Eckroade, Salehi, & Wode, 1991)	Compared attenders to nonattenders, including only children continuously enrolled in school district (kindergarten to grade 5); no pretest; school-administered test; high attrition	Initial Unknown Follow-up Grade 8 E = 356, C = 306	Achievement tests: E > C grades 3, 5, 8 Special education: E < C, grade 8 E = 15%, C = 22% Grade retention: E < C, grade 8 E = 31%, C = 45%

continued on next page

TABLE 15.2

Program Name Description and Sources	Research Design and Methodological Issues	Sample Size[a] and Time of Follow-up	Outcomes[a]
5. New York State Experimental Prekindergarten 1975–1976 Entry: 3 or 4 years Exit: 5 years (State Education Dept., 1982)	Compared attenders with children in same district on waiting list and in districts with no prekindergarten program; high attrition	Initial 1,800[b] Follow-up Grade 3 E = 1,348, C = 258	Achievement tests: E > C kindergarten E = C grade 1 Special education: E = C E = 2%, C = 5% Grade retention: E < C E = 16%, C = 21%
6. Florida Prekindergarten Early Intervention Cohort 1 1988–1989 Entry: 4 years Exit: 5 years (Ling, Cappellini, & Gravens, 1995)	Compared early intervention children with children from same schools who qualified for free or reduced-price lunch; no pretest; school-administered test; high attrition	Initial Unknown Follow-up Grades 3-4 E = 350, C = 352	Achievement tests: E > C kindergarten E = C in grades 1 to 3, E < C grade 4 Special education: E = C E = 25%, C = 25% Grade retention: E = C E = 3%, C = 3% Disciplined: E < C E = 11%, C = 32%
7. Florida Prekindergarten Early Intervention Cohort 2 1989–1990 Entry: 4 years Exit: 5 years (King, Cappellini, & Rohani, 1995)	Compared early intervention children with children from same schools who qualified for free or reduced-price lunch; no pretest; school-administered test; high attrition	Initial Unknown Follow-up Grades 3-4 E = 983, C = 1,054	Achievement tests: E > C kindergarten E = C grades 1 to 4 Special education: E = C E = 17%, C = 15% Grade retention: E < C E = 9%, C = 13%
8. Florida Chapter I 1985–1986 Entry: 4 years Exit: 5 years (King, Rohani, & Cappellini, 1995)	Compared children screened into Chapter I pre-k with those screened out based on a test (DIAL-R); high attrition; school-administered tests	Initial E = 103, C = 121 Follow-up Grade 8 E = 54, C = 65	Achievement tests: E > C grades 1, 2, 4, 7, 8 E = C grade 5, 6 (no data for grade 3)

Study	Comparison	Sample	Results
9. Detroit Head Start and Title I Preschool 1972–1973 Entry: 4 years Exit: 5 years (Clark, 1979)	Compared children who had attended Head Start or Title I preschool with children who were eligible but did not attend; no pretest; school-administered test	Initial Unknown Follow-up Grade 4 Unknown	Achievement tests: E > C grade 4

10. DC Public Schools and Head Start 1986–1987
Entry: 4 years
Exit: 5 years
(Marcon, 1990, 1993, 1994)
	Compared children who attended public school preschool or Head Start with other children in same kindergartens; high attrition	Initial
		E = 372, C = 89
		
		Follow-up Grades 4-5
		E varies, C varies
			Achievement tests: E = C grades 3-5
			Special education: E = C grade 4
			  E = 10%, C = 9%
			Grade retention: E = C grade 4
			  E = 31%, C = 38%

11. Philadelphia School District Get Set and Head Start 1969–1971 Entry: 4 years Exit: 5 years (Copple, Cline, & Smith, 1987)	Compared children in enriched K-3 program (follow-through) who had and had not attended preschool; no pretest; high attrition; school-administered tests	Initial E = 1,082, C = 1,615 Follow-up Grades 4-8, varies by cohort E = 688, C = 524	Achievement tests: E = C Grade retention: E < C
12. Seattle DISTAR and Head Start 1970–1971 Entry: 4 years Exit: 5 years (Evans, 1985)	Compared children who had attended Head Start and DISTAR with matched children from same school and grades; no pretest; high attrition; school-administered tests	Initial E = 92, C = unknown Follow-up Grades 6, 8 E = 44, C = 20	Achievement tests: E = C
13. Cincinnati Head Start 1968–1969 Entry: 4 years Exit: 5 years (Pinkleton, 1976)	Compared third graders who had attended Head Start with those who had not; no pretest	Initial Unknown Follow-up Grade 3 Unknown	Achievement tests: E = C grade 3

continued on next page

TABLE 15.2

Program Name Description and Sources	Research Design and Methodological Issues	Sample Size[a] and Time of Follow-up	Outcomes[a]
14. Detroit Head Start 1969–1970 Entry: 4 years Exit: 5 or 6 years (O'Piela, 1976)	Compared children who had attended Head Start with children in Title I elementary programs; no pretest; school-administered tests	Initial Unknown Follow-up Grade 4 Unknown	Achievement tests: E > C grade 4
15. ETS Longitudinal Study of Head Start 1969–1971 Entry: 4 or 5 years Exit: 5 or 6 years (Shipman, 1970, 1976; Lee, et al., 1990)	Compared children who went to Head Start with children who went to other preschools or no preschool; high attrition	Initial 1,875 Follow-up Grade 3 852	Achievement tests: E > C grade 1 E = C in grades 2, 3
16. Hartford Head Start 1965–1966 Entry: 4 years Exit: 5 years (Goodstein, 1975)	Compared children who had attended Head Start with those who had not; no pretest; high attrition; school-administered tests	Initial 293 Follow-up Grade 6 E = 148, C = 50	Achievement tests: E = C grade 6 Special education: E = C E = 5%, C = 10% Grade retention: E < C E = 10%, C = 22%
17. Kanawha County, West Virginia Head Start 1973–1974 Entry: 4 years Exit: 5 years (Kanawha board of Ed., 1978)	Compared children who had attended Head Start with low-income children who had not; no pretest; attrition unknown	Initial Unknown Follow-up Grade 3 Unknown	Achievement tests: E = C grade 3
18. Montgomery County, Maryland Head Start 1970–1971; 1974–1975; 1978–1979 Entry: 4 years Exit: 5 years (Hebbeler, 1985)	Compared children who had attended eight or nine months with those who had attended one month or less; no pretest; high attrition; school-administered tests	Initial E = 1,915, C = 619 Follow-up Grade 11 E = 186, C = 112	Achievement tests: E = C, but negative trend in most grades, E > C grade 11

Study	Sample	Results
19. New Haven Head Start 1968–1969 Entry: 4 years Exit: 5 years (Abelson, 1974; Abelson, Zigler, & DeBlasi, 1974)	Compared children who attended Head Start with those who had not; no pretest	Initial E = 61, C = 48 Follow-up Grade 3 E = 35, C = 26	Achievement tests: E > C grade 1, E = C grade 3
20. Pennsylvania Head Start 1986–1987 Entry: 3 to 5 years Exit: 5 to 6 years (Reedy, 1991)	Compared children who attended Head Start with children who had applied but had not been admitted; no pretest	Initial E = 98, C = unknown Follow-up Grade 3 E = 54, C = 18	Achievement tests: E = C, but positive trend grades 2, 3
21. Rome, Georgia Head Start 1966 Entry: 5 years Exit: 6 years (McDonald and Monroe, 1981)	Compared children who attended Head Start with children in first grade in disadvantaged schools in 1966; no pretest; school-administered tests	Initial E = 130, C = 88 Follow-up Post high school E = 94, C = 60	Achievement tests: E > C grade 5, E = C grades 6 and above Special education: E < C E = 11%, C = 25% Grade retention: E = C E = 51%, C = 63% High school graduation: E > C E = 50%, C = 33%
22. Westinghouse National Evaluation of Head Start 1965–1966 Entry: 4 or 5 years Exit: 5 or 6 years (Westinghouse Learning Corp. & Ohio University, 1969)	Compared children who attended Head Start with those who did not (matched within grade); no pretest; matching fails to match cohorts properly	Initial Unknown Follow-up grades 1-3 E = 1,988, C = 1,992	Achievement tests: E > C grade 1, E = C grades 2, 3

[a]Throughout Table 15.2, E refers to the experimental or intervention group, and C refers to the control or comparison group. Outcomes listed as E > C or E < C were statistically significant at the p < .05 level.

[b]The numbers of children in experimental and comparison groups were not reported separately.

result largely from limitations of research methods that biased estimated effects toward and high rates of attrition in achievement test data that decreased the statistical power to detect effects over time. Perhaps the most common source of increased downward bias in estimated effects on achievement over time is reliance on achievement test data from schools' routine testing programs. Although this strategy provided data at low cost, it had several unfortunate consequences. First, the quality and uniformity of test administration is lower when testing is done for entire classes by teachers rather than individually by specialists. Second, schools' testing programs administer tests by grade; children who are held back a grade are not tested with their age cohort and usually are lost to the study as a result. Third, children who perform poorly are systematically excluded from school testing. The use of routine testing to hold schools accountable places pressure on school administrators to remove poor performers from the test pool at each grade level (McGill-Franzen & Allington, 1993). Many schools do not test children in special education classes, for example.

At best, studies relying on school-administered tests measure achievement test effects with lower reliability and increased attrition. Both limitations reduce their ability to detect program effects. At worst, these studies systematically lose the more poorly performing students from year to year as the cumulative percentage of children retained in grade, placed in special education, or otherwise omitted from testing grows. The result is that, in studies relying on school-administered tests, persistent differences between program and comparison groups are gradually hidden as grade level rises. The children who perform most poorly (a larger percentage of the comparison group) are increasingly culled from the pool tested at each grade level as the two groups advance through school.

It may be helpful to consider a stylized example illustrating how the use of routinely administered school tests in a study can produce misleading results that mimic a fade-out. Suppose a study begins with 100 children who attend a preschool program and 100 who do not attend. Both groups enter kindergarten and are tested at the end of kindergarten. At this time, the group that attended preschool is found to have higher test scores. The next year, all of the preschool group goes into regular first-grade classrooms, but due to poor school performance 10% of the comparison group is held back in kindergarten and 10% is placed in special education classes. At the end of first grade, the schools administer another test, but the children who were held back in kindergarten or who are in special education do not participate in the first-grade test. The first-grade test score difference between the two groups is smaller than at kindergarten because the comparison children who would score lowest have been excluded from the test. Moving on to second and third grade, more children are held back and placed in special education, so that by the time the third-grade test is given, 95% of the preschool group, but only 70% the comparison group, is in regular third-grade classes and tested. At this point the children in two groups who are tested have been essentially equated on ability and do not differ in their test scores. However, there is a significant difference between the two groups in the percentage of children retained in grade and in special education. The simultaneous findings of effects on school progress and placement and no effects on achievement is not inconsistent, but an artifact of test data collection procedures.

A review of Tables 15.1 and 15.2 indicates how important a limitation it is to rely on routine testing data. All of the model program studies failing to find lasting effects on achievement relied on school-administered tests. All but one of the model program studies finding lasting effects administered their own achievement tests. Most of the large-scale program studies employed routine school test data, but three that did not had idiosyncratic flaws that led to similar biases in achievement test data. The New Haven Head Start study individually administered achievement tests, but included only children at the expected grade level. As grade repetition was less frequent for the program group, this had the effect of gradually equating the tested program and control groups on achievement over time. The ETS Head Start study tested only children in classes in which at least 50% of the children were study participants, thereby excluding from testing children who repeated a grade or were placed in special education classes. The Westinghouse National Evaluation of Head Start formed its comparison group by matching former Head Start children in Grades 1, 2, and 3 with other children in their grade levels. This had the effect of excluding from the comparison group children who were repeating an earlier grade and including in the comparison group children who were repeating the current grade. Evidence of this is provided by the ages of Head Start and comparison groups in each grade. In first grade, where an effect on achievement is found, the Head Start and comparison groups do not differ in age. In the second and third grade, where achievement effects fade out, the Head Start groups are significantly younger than the comparison groups, and the age gap widens from second to third grade.

School Progress and Placement

School progress and placement were primarily measured by the percentage of children repeating grades, given special education services, and graduating from high school. A few studies employed teacher ratings and grades. Findings on long-term effects on school progress and placement are relatively uniform and constitute overwhelming evidence that preschool education truly can improve school success. All but one of the model program studies reported grade repetition and special education rates, and in all of these the rates were lower for the program group. In five model program studies the effects at last follow-up are statistically significant. In the Head Start and public school studies, statistically significant effects on grade retention or special education were found in 9 of the 11 studies that collected the relevant data. Three model program studies, one Head Start study, and one public school study provide data on high school graduation. All five produced large estimates of effects on the graduation rate, although only in the three with larger sample sizes were these statistically significant.

The estimated effects on grade repetition and special education placements can be combined across studies to produce estimates for the literature as a whole and to investigate the sources of differences across studies. (There are too few studies of high school graduation to make a quantitative analysis of pooled results useful.) The simplest cross-study comparisons were conducted by treating each study's results as a data point. The average effects on grade repetition (special education) were estimated by subtracting the percentage repeating a grade (in special education) in the comparison group from the percentage repeating a grade (in special education) in the preschool group. Table 15.3 presents means and standard deviations of estimated effects for both outcomes by program type (model vs. large-scale public). Note that these estimated effects indicate the percentage of the total population served who no longer are held back or placed in special education. Average effects are substantial for both types of programs, but estimated effects are significantly larger for model programs.

These results in Table 15.3 are consistent with the expectation that more intensive programs would have larger effects, but are not the results of direct comparisons of the two types of programs within a single study. Differences in studies other than the type of program (e.g., the extent of poverty or educational disadvantages in the population served) could affect the results. Thus, it is reassuring that the two studies that directly compared model programs to large-scale public programs serving the same population both found large-scale public programs to be less effective (Burchinal et al., 1989; Van de Reit & Resnick, 1973). Clearly, more such direct comparisons would be valuable.[1]

TABLE 15.3
Long-Term Effects on Grade Repetition and Special Education Placement: Model Versus Large-Scale Preschool Programs

Outcome Measures	Model Program Estimated Effects			Large-Scale Program Estimated Effects		
	M	SD	N	M	SD	N
Reduction in percent repeating at least one grade	14.9*	9.8	14	8.4*	5.4	10
Reduction in percent ever in special education	19.6**	14.6	11	4.7**	5.3	9

*p < .05, two-tailed t test with unequal variances.
**p < .01, two-tailed t test with unequal variances.

---

[1]Although many researchers have considered reasons that model program effects might overestimate the effects that could be produced on a large scale, it is possible that the effects of model programs are underestimated relative to the effects of large-scale programs because model program studies fail to capture "bandwagon effects" that occur when a program implemented on a large scale improves norms for school behavior or produces a more favorable learning environment in the school as whole.

EXPLAINING PATTERNS OF EFFECTS OVER TIME

To summarize our view of the evidence so far, compensatory preschool education for children in poverty improves cognitive abilities during early childhood and academic achievement and school success over the long run. Although many studies fail to find persistent effects on achievement, this is due primarily to flaws in study design and follow-up procedures. Well-implemented randomized controlled trials find persistent effects on achievement. This is not the case with IQ effects; these do seem to genuinely fade out over time in most studies. To some this mixed picture for IQ and achievement presents a paradox. It has led more than a few researchers to conclude that achievement and other academic gains must be the result of such noncognitive effects as increased motivation or socialization, parent involvement, or even teacher expectations (Locurto, 1991; Reynolds, 1992; Woodhead, 1988; Zigler & Freedman, 1987). One recent study provides an alternative cognitive explanation that is consistent with the evidence.

Barnett, Young, and Schweinhart (1998) investigated alternative explanations for the mixed picture by estimating structural models (statistical models in which the same variable can be both a cause and an outcome) for each major alternative and by examining the year-to-year pattern of effects on test scores. Data for these analyses were from the Perry Preschool study, which provided a rich set of measures of cognitive development, academic achievement and school progress, social development, school behavior, motivation, parental attitudes and behavior, and the home environment from age 3 through age 19. Models positing direct effects of the preschool program on motivation, behavior, or parents as the source of early effects on achievement and school success were strongly rejected. The effects of the preschool program on achievement test scores and school success are strongly indicated to begin with cognitive effects as measured by IQ test scores. No direct effects of the preschool program on parental involvement in schooling were found, and measures of home environment showed no evidence of a response to the preschool program. Initial cognitive effects were found to generate a broader set of changes in motivation and classroom behavior that together with early achievement score gains increase later achievement and educational success despite the decline in effects on IQ.

An explanation for this pattern of effects can be found in differences between what achievement and IQ tests measure and the ways in which these change with the child's age. The basic achievement–IQ distinction is that achievement tests measure subject-matter-specific knowledge and abilities, whereas IQ tests measure general intellectual abilities. At best, IQ measures a broadly important general intellectual ability or set of abilities that contribute to the ease with which one learns. Both general intellectual abilities and subject-matter-specific intellectual abilities are important for learning. However, at the preschool level it is difficult to differentiate general intellectual abilities from subject matter-specific-abilities. Thus, it seems likely that IQ and achievement are not easily distinguished in preschool-age children, and the tests increasingly diverge in what they measure as the children tested become older.

From this perspective, the observed pattern of effects can be interpreted as follows. Initial effects on preschool intellectual abilities provide a basis for increased subject-matter-specific learning in school. Subject matter learning is a highly cumulative process, and the child's greater success in school learning leads to greater subsequent subject-matter-specific learning in school both directly and through indirect effects on motivation and behavior (De Corte, 1995; Weinert & Helmke, 1995). There are several possible alternative explanations for the failure of general intellectual abilities, as measured by IQ, to show the same sorts of stable gains over time. One is that home and neighborhood environments are more important to the development of general intellectual abilities and these remain impoverished. By their nature, IQ tests exclude what is readily learned in school, and schooling, the major source of learning resources for poor children, becomes increasingly focused on subject matter as children get older. Another is that the preschool program never improved the general intellectual abilities of children in the sense in which IQ tests measure these for older children (perhaps conceived of as raw information processing or facility in manipulating abstract symbols). However, the inherent constraints on testing young children's intellectual abilities make it difficult to distinguish general intellectual abilities. In some sense the abilities tested later do not even exist in young children.

A slightly different explanation for the pattern of differences between IQ and achievement test scores is that items that are highly likely to be learned in school are eliminated from IQ tests. Test construction assumes that IQ tests measure aptitude and that what is learned in the home and community outside of school reflects aptitude alone rather than aptitude and differential access to learning associated with differences in family economic, social, and human resources. IQ tests have not yet eliminated items responsive to learning in preschool programs because preschool programs were not pervasive when the tests were developed. It will be interesting to see if the tests are revised in this way in the future, although it may prove difficult to do because of the high degree of overlap between what is learned in and out of preschool.

Interestingly, the pattern of effects over time found in preschool studies corresponds to the pattern of correlations over time found in studies linking the IQs of parents and children and the IQs of biological and adoptive children (Plomin & Petrill, 1997). Correlations between parental and child IQ are lower during the preschool years than subsequently. Correlations between the IQs of adoptive siblings are substantial during childhood, but disappear in adolescence and adulthood. This evidence is commonly interpreted as showing that a uniform construct of intelligence is more subject to environmental influence during early childhood and that it is only concurrent ability that is affected. A subtler explanation for this pattern of correlations over time is that intelligence itself (i.e., what it means to be intelligent) changes as the age of the child increases, and the abilities measured during the preschool years are more subject to environmental influence than the abilities measured at older ages. Our argument is somewhat different. We would say that the test measures different abilities at different ages, increasingly focusing on abilities least likely to be influenced by schooling as the child becomes older. Whatever one's view, it is clear that those cognitive abilities of young children that preschool education enhances contribute to early academic achievement and school success, and thereby increase long-term educational and economic success.

To date, structural models have not been estimated for full-day, year-round interventions beginning in infancy and continuing to school entry. However, the pattern of effects for these early and more extensive interventions seems to differ from the pattern for later interventions in that an underlying persistent effect on general intellectual abilities appears to be overlaid by the usual temporary effect on IQ. The result appears to be larger long-term effects on achievement and school success. There are several possible explanations for this difference. One is that the abilities measured by IQ over the long term (or their precursors) are more malleable in the first 3 years of life so that interventions that begin earlier have a qualitatively different impact. Another is that the sheer amount of intervention provides such large increases in cognitive abilities that the child's abilities to learn from the school and long-term increases in subject-matter-specific knowledge are so great as to generate gains in general cognitive abilities later as well. New experimental research with longitudinal follow-ups and adequate sample sizes comparing the effects of highly intensive educational interventions over the first 5 years of life to the effects of comparable interventions beginning at age 3 could contribute a great deal toward our understanding of the nature of such program's effects and the potential gains from very early intervention.

DIFFERENTIAL EFFECTS BY "RACE"

None of the studies reviewed found that program effects on cognitive development and school success differed across ethnic groups. Many of the longer term studies were conducted with samples composed only or primarily of African-American children. Thus, it is to some extent an extrapolation to conclude that long-term effects could be produced for other ethnic groups. However, many studies have found no ethnic differences in short-term effects, and it seemed reasonable to assume no differences in long-term effects, as well. Some confirmation of the validity of this assumption was provided by Johnson and Walker (1991) for Latino children. More recently, this view was challenged in an unexpected way by Currie and Thomas (1995), who asserted that Head Start has long-term effects for white non-Latino and Latino children, but not for African-American children. They suggested that Head Start does not generate sufficient lasting benefits to be judged a cost-effective public investment for African-American children. Although their study does not meet the criteria for inclusion in our review, the study has been so widely reported that a response is required.

Currie and Thomas (1995) based their conclusions on a fixed-effects analysis of data from the National Longitudinal Study of Youth Child–Mother file (NLSCM; Baker, Keck, Mott, & Quinlan, 1993). This approach seeks to avoid the problem of selection bias (children qualify for Head Start based on family poverty and participation is voluntary) by estimating Head Start's effects from within-family comparisons where one child attends Head Start and another does not (for this comparison, the family is fixed). Although this is a seemingly clever approach, it has serious limitations, and, as employed by Currie and Thomas, it produces misleading results. Exploring these problems requires a somewhat technical discussion of the data and analysis. As explained in the following, we doubt that any valid conclusions can be drawn regarding the effects of Head Start from a fixed-effects analysis of the NLSCM data.

Data Limitations

Although the National Longitudinal Study of Youth (NLSY) provides a sample of 6,676 children who were age 3 by 1990, the sample available for the fixed-effects model is a small, unrepresentative fraction of the total. Over 30% of the sample was lost because they could not be found for the interview, they failed to provide a valid answer to the Head Start question, or they lacked a test score. This attrition was hardly random. For example, data were not collected for children who lived apart from their biological mothers. However, the most attrition occurred because the fixed-effects model estimates Head Start effects using only children in families where at least one child attended Head Start and at least one other did not. As a result, the effective sample for estimating Head Start effects is a small fraction of the total, as shown in Table 15.4.

Unfortunately, the residual sample used to estimate Head Start effects is not just small, but it is unrepresentative. Within each ethnic group we compared the cognitive test scores of three groups: (a) Head Start children who were the only child in their family, (b) Head Start children whose siblings all attended Head Start, and (c) Head Start children with a least one sibling who had not attended Head Start (Head Start children in the fixed-effects sample). Comparisons were made on four cognitive tests used as outcome measures: the Peabody Picture Vocabulary Test–Revised (PPVT–R)

TABLE 15.4
Effective Sample Sizes for Fixed-Effects Estimation of PPVT Head Start Effects by Ethnicity

Ethnic Group	With at Least One Head Start and One Other Child		With at Least One Head Start and One No-Preschool Child		
	Families	Children	Families	HS	No-PreK
White Non-Latino	89	214	69	97	84
Latino	68	189	45	70	71
African-American	136	359	96	130	125

Note. HS indicates children reported to attend Head Start. Other indicates children not reported to attend Head Start. No-PreK indicates children not reported to attend Head Start or another preschool program.

(Dunn & Dunn, 1981) and Peabody Individualized Achievement Tests (PIAT) (Dunn & Markwardt, 1970) in math, reading recognition, and reading comprehension. In every comparison, Group A significantly differed Least Significant Difference (Last Significant Difference, LSD test, $p < .05$) from the fixed-effects group (Group C). Group B significantly differed from the fixed-effects Group C on two of four tests for Latinos and on all four tests for whites.

A second data limitation of the NLSCM sample is that the treatment indicator (whether a child attended Head Start or not) contains serious errors because it is based on retrospective parent report. Data from the National Household Education Survey suggest that parents may have difficulties distinguishing Head Start from other types of programs so that Head Start participation is substantially overreported (Nolin, Collins, & Hopper, 1992). Random error in the Head Start variable is a serious problem because it biases estimates of Head Start's effects toward zero (Aigner, 1973; Freeman, 1984; Griliches, 1986; Kmenta, 1986). However, the problem is even more serious because the errors are not likely to be random.

As Table 15.5 shows, substantial percentages of families with relatively high incomes reported sending a child to Head Start, and rates of reported attendance for higher income families are especially high among African-American families. As other studies have found Head Start families to be among the poorest in low-income neighborhoods (Barnett, Tarr, & Frede, 1999; Kresh, 1988; Lee, Brooks-Gunn, Schnur, & Liaw, 1990; McKey et al., 1985), this suggests that the NLSCM sample is either highly unrepresentative or that erroneous reporting occurs frequently. Moreover, the problem is notably worse for African-American families. Error in parental report is likely to be nonrandom in at least one other way. For most children the question was asked years after the event in question (for children over age 15, more than a decade had passed), and accuracy of recall typically declines over time. This pattern of errors could easily result in an apparent fade-out in effects over time.

TABLE 15.5

Percentage Reported to Attend Head Start by Ethnicity and Family Income (1990 Dollars) When the Child Was Age 3

Income at Age 3	White	African-American	Latino
< $10,000	32%	39%	28%
$10,000–14,999	26%	31%	22%
$15,000–19,999	16%	38%	19%
$20,000–29,999	7%	24%	19%
$30,000–39,000	4%	18%	9%
$40,000+	1%	18%	4%
Sample Size (n)	2,222	1,441	894

Some indication of the extent of measurement error in reported Head Start attendance can be obtained directly from the NLSCM data. In both 1988 and 1990, parental report of Head Start participation was available for 242 African-American, 178 Latino, and 318 white children. In each of these groups a number of children were reported as having been in Head Start in 1988, but never having been in Head Start in 1990. As a percentage of children in 1990, the latter error rates for African-Americans, Latinos, and non-Latino whites were 16%, 21%, and 4%, respectively. Once again, it appears that errors in the data are most severe for minority families.

Differential performance of the tests used as outcome measures across ethnic groups also poses a problem for the study. Cognitive abilities were measured by PPVT–R and PIAT test scores. A full discussion of their limitations is beyond the scope of this chapter (see Barnett & Camilli, 1999). However, differences between results on the PPVT–R and the PIAT are important in light of previous discussions of differences in effects as measured by IQ and achievement measures. The PPVT–R is a receptive vocabulary test often used as "quick" measure of IQ, whereas the PIAT is designed to measure achievement. As shown in Table 15.6, mean percentile scores on the PPVT–R are lower than those on the PIAT tests for all groups, but the gap in scores is much larger for minority children, and is most severe for African-American children. Inspection of the PPVT–R percentile data reveals that minimum (floor) scores were obtained much more frequently for African-American and Latino children than for white children. This problem was much less common with the PIAT scores.

The comparisons in Table 15.6 raise questions about the validity of the PPVT–R for minority children and about the use of percentile scores in statistical analyses. Whether the validity problem is unique to the PPVT–R or occurs with other IQ measures is an interesting question, but one that cannot be addressed with the NLSCM data. The use of percentile scores creates problems because it discards information contained in the raw scores on differences in ability at the low end of the distribution (where much of the Head Start effect might be expected) and discards much more information for minority children, especially African-Americans. For example, PPVT–R percentile scores of zero were received by 15%, 10%, and 2% of African-American, Latino, and white children, respectively, in the 1990 NLSCM sample. Given these problems, it is important to conduct analyses on the PIAT as well as the PPVT–R and to use raw scores rather than percentiles.[2] Another reason to include the PIAT is that, as noted earlier, a critical review of the literature leads one to expect persistent effects on achievement measures like the PIAT, but not on IQ-type measures like the PPVT–R.

---

[2]Percentile scores exaggerate group differences near the middle of a distribution, or, alternatively, shrink group differences in the tails. Statistical analysis of raw or scale scores is advocated by leading psychometricians (Anastasi & Urbina, 1997; Cronbach, 1990) because the percentile metric is likely to create nonlinearities and nonhomogenous regressions, as well as heteroskedastic error variances.

TABLE 15.6

Mean PPVT and PIAT Percentile Scores, Standard Deviations, and Sample Size for "Head Start" Children by Ethnicity

Ethnicity	PPVT–R	PIAT M	PIAT RR	PIAT RC
White non-Latino				
Percentile score	41.55	51.32	57.50	58.02
SD	27.44	23.61	24.85	24.96
N	1,759	1,592	1,582	1,309
African-American				
Percentile score	15.23	39.11	49.85	47.68
SD	19.10	22.36	25.03	25.01
N	1,324	1,245	1,234	1,052
Latino				
Percentile score	20.08	39.75	49.05	49.75
SD	24.00	22.41	25.41	25.64
N	735	668	667	530

Note. PIAT M = PIAT math score; PIAT R = PIAT reading recognition score; PIAT RC = PIAT reading comprehension score.

Limitations of the Analysis

The ability of the fixed-effects model to produce accurate estimates of Head Start effects depends on two highly questionable assumptions: One is that children who do not attend Head Start do not benefit from Head Start, and the other is that siblings do not differ systematically in their treatment by the family. The first assumption is completely inconsistent with the program's intentions. Head Start is designed to intervene with the entire family, beginning with maximum feasible participation of parents, and including parenting education and services to siblings (Kracke, 1995; Parker, Piotrowski, & Peay, 1987; Slaughter, Washington, Dyemade, & Lindsey, 1988; Zigler, 1979; Zigler & Muenchow, 1992;). The second assumption is at odds with our knowledge that families respond to differences in children rather than treating each in exactly the same way. This could lead to families selecting children for Head Start based on each child's needs or to families attempting to compensate children who did not attend Head Start for this lost opportunity. Becker (1981) long ago suggested that parent efforts to compensate siblings of Head Start children out of a concern for fairness could lead to flawed estimates of Head Start's effects that mimic a fade-out. Evidence that parents allocate different amounts of family resources based on differences in child needs and that parents compensate siblings of children in interventions has been found in other studies (Barnett & Boyce, 1995; Becker, 1981; Quittner & Opipari, 1994).

Fixed-Effect Results

The finding by Currie and Thomas (1995) that Head Start effects faded out for African-American but not white children was limited to fixed-effects model results for one outcome variable, PPVT–R percentile scores. In these analyses, white non-Latino and Latino children were combined into a single "white" group. No Head Start effects were found on math achievement. Results for PIAT reading scores were reported to be similar to those for the PPVT–R, although weaker. To our knowledge, their fixed-effects study is unique in finding persistent effects on an IQ-type measure, but finding weak or no effects (for math) on achievement measures.

We reestimated the fixed-effects model using raw scores and conducting separate analyses for white non-Latino and Latino children as well as for African-American children. When ethnic differences are at issue, there is no justification for treating white non-Latino and Latino children as a single population, particularly given the differences in their test scores and reported Head Start participation rates. In our analyses, the variables used to explain child cognitive ability are Head Start attendance, other preschool program attendance, an interaction between Head Start attendance and child age (to detect fade-out in effects), child age, whether or not the child was the firstborn, and the Home Observation for Measurement of the Environment (HOME; Caldwell & Bradley, 1979) score when the child was age 3 (a measure of home environment known to relate to cognitive development). Results are presented in Table 15.7 for the PPVT–R and the PIAT reading recognition scale (fewer valid scores were obtained for reading comprehension and results are similar to those for reading recognition, whereas no significant effects were found for math scores).

For African-American children, Head Start was found to have a statistically significant positive initial effect on the PIAT reading recognition score, and a nearly significant initial effect on the PPVT–R. Significant negative coefficients on the Head Start × Age interaction terms indicate a fade-out. For white children, the initial effects do not reach statistical significance and both Head Start × Age interactions are negative, although only for the PIAT is the interaction statistically significant. However, the point estimates for white children are highly similar to those for African-American children, and for the PPVT–R they are virtually identical. For Latino children, we obtained surprising results: no initial effects with a positive Head Start × Age interaction that is statistically significant for the PPVT–R. No theory or previous study has suggested this pattern of effects for Latinos or any other children. In our view, the results are exactly the sort of nonsense one can expect when flaws plague both the data and the analytical model, and no conclusions should be drawn from any fixed-effects estimates based on the NLSCM data.

TABLE 15.7

Coefficients for the Fixed–Effects Model for PPVT–R and PIAT Raw Scores

Independent Variables	African–American		Latino		White Non–Latino	
	PPVT–R	PIAT	PPVT–R	PIAT	PPVT–R	PIAT
Head Start	2.389[†]	3.932***	1.456	−.448	2.236	2.150
	(1.451)	(1.347)	(1.998)	(2.219)	(1.695)	(1.586)
Other preschool	−.539	1.517	−.070	−1.040	.257	.641
	(1.345)	(.992)	(1.788)	(1.325)	(1.165)	(.817)
Head Start by age	−.053**	−.066***	.084**	.026	−.048	−.048*
	(.025)	(.021)	(.042)	(.039)	(.035)	(.029)
Age	.935***	.426***	.862***	.479***	.908***	.467***
	(.020)	(.019)	(.028)	(.029)	(.019)	(.019)
Firstborn	−.375	1.264*	.892	1.395	1.756*	2.611***
	(.905)	(.737)	(1.236)	(1.008)	(.812)	(.648)
HOME score	−.004	.016***	.009	.013*	.033***	.027***
	(.007)	(.005)	(.009)	(.007)	(.007)	(.005)

Note. Standard errors are reported in parentheses. *$p < .10$, **$p < .05$, ***$p < .01$, [†]$p = .1003$.

DISCUSSION

A critical review of the evidence indicates that preschool education for young children in poverty can greatly increase their cognitive abilities and that this leads to long-term increases in achievement and school success. The most far-reaching follow-up demonstrates that increased adult economic success follows (Schweinhart, Barnes, Weikart, Barnett, & Epstein, 1993). Conclusions to the contrary were based on reviews of the evidence that failed to distinguish IQ from achievement or to identify common methodological flaws that led to the appearance of a fade-out in achievement gains over time. Although preschool education generally produces only temporary increases in general cognitive abilities as measured by IQ, it produces long-term increases in the specific abilities measured by standardized achievement tests in reading and math. Moreover, the apparent paradox of long-term reductions in grade repetition and special education placement without gains in achievement turns out to be an artifact of inadequate research methods that produce misleading results for achievement.

Research on how one preschool program produced its long-term effects confirms that educational gains stem from initial cognitive gains.

There is no credible evidence that effects are smaller or less persistent for African-American children or any other ethnic group. Indeed, the strongest evidence for long-term effects comes from studies limited to African-American children. Poverty and the limits it imposes on access to educational resources at home and in the community may explain much of the observed differences in cognitive abilities among ethnic groups, particularly if the role of limited human capital (partially represented by the quantity and quality of parental education) is taken into account. It is clear that family income is strongly associated with the magnitude of the increases in cognitive development obtainable from preschool education. More extensive research is warranted on the ways in which poverty hinders cognitive development and the extent to which there may be other differences in the lives of minority children that limit their access to human capital.

One of our most intriguing findings is that intensive educational interventions beginning in the first year of life and continuing through age 5 might permanently improve the general cognitive development of children in poverty and produce very large improvements in academic achievement and school success. The importance of this finding must not be overlooked. First, it provides a strong indication that IQ can be permanently changed by early experience. Not only does childhood poverty (which is more than a financial condition) stunt the development of general cognitive abilities, but educational interventions can offset some of its effects. Second, early, intensive interventions may be able to close a large part of the gap in educational achievement and school success between rich and poor, minority and majority. It is possible that no other single societal effort could do more to increase equality of opportunity.[3]

Opponents of early compensatory education have rejected this approach as impractical, even if effective. According to Herrnstein and Murray (1994):

> The nation cannot conceivably implement a Milwaukee Project or Abecedarian Project for all disadvantaged children. It is not just the dollar costs that put such ambitions out of reach (though they do) but the impossibility of staffing them. With teacher-to-child ratios as high as one to three and staff-to-child ratios even higher, these programs come close to calling for a trained person per eligible child (p. 415).

They exaggerated, of course. The highest ratios are required only at the youngest ages and Herrnstein and Murray appeared to be unaware that some states already require a ratio of 1:3 for infant care and most states require a ratio of at least 1:4. Thus, the marginal cost over existing programs is not as large as they would have us believe,

---

[3]Intensive enrichment programs that continue into the earlier grades also may yield important cognitive benefits for children in poverty on top of the benefits from preschool programs, but reform of K–12 education is beyond the scope of this chapter (Allington & Walmsley, 1995; Entwisle, 1995).

and the most costly aspect is likely to be increasing the quality of staff, not the quantity. Moreover, whether or not a program is too expensive can be judged only by comparing the costs to the benefits. Barnett's (1993) study of the economic benefits of compensatory preschool suggests that very early, intensive programs might more than pay for themselves in purely economic terms. When one adds their potential value in increasing equality of opportunities between rich and poor, and the vast overrepresentation of minorities among the poor, it is dismaying that such programs have not received more attention.

There is also much to be learned from new research on existing compensatory preschool programs. There have been calls for increased research on the effects of Head Start, including a U.S. General Accounting Office (1997) report concluding that existing studies were inadequate. We agree. However, satisfactory studies will not be easily produced. Methodological weaknesses of past studies to be avoided include the use of cognitive tests without adequate consideration of exactly what, and how well, they measure, and the use of test data routinely collected by schools. The massive statistical studies of Head Start using data from the NLSCM and other large-scale surveys that some have urged (e.g., Shokraii & Fagan, 1998) are unlikely to be productive. Instead, the field should design specialized prospective studies, including randomized trials, that take into account the nature and goals of Head Start. Head Start needs new studies that assess its effects, not just on cognition, but on socialization, nutrition, health, and many other program goals—a list that expands with each revision of its performance standards. Although it has been found that well-designed compensatory preschool programs can produce major benefits in socialization without diluting their cognitive benefits (Schweinhart & Weikart, 1997), it is less clear that efforts outside the classroom do not detract from the primary mission.

Although the evidence supports the view that existing public preschool education programs produce significant long-term cognitive and educational benefits for children, it also appears that they have smaller effects than model programs created by researchers. There are two obvious factors that might account for this difference. One is that existing programs are underfunded, forcing them to trade quality for quantity so that these programs are less intensive (less well-educated teachers with larger classes) and shorter (1 year rather than 2, 9 months of the year rather than 12). The other is that public programs may be less carefully targeted and serve less disadvantaged populations than the model programs. Both may be operative, but whether more precise targeting would be useful in addition to greater intensity can only be determined from cost–benefit calculations for which we do not have the data at present.

Head Start and other public programs target children in poverty because intensive preschool education benefits children in poverty far more than children from more advantaged circumstances. Minority children stand to benefit disproportionately from these programs because they are much more likely than other children to live in poverty. For these programs to fulfill their promise, funding will have to be increased to a level that makes it possible to serve all children in poverty (less than half are served now) and to increase the quality and intensity of these programs. However, the federal poverty guideline may not provide the appropriate cutoff point for public preschool services. It is highly arbitrary, and many families above the poverty line do not have resources that are fully adequate to meet their children's early educational needs. Many African-American and Latino children live in families with incomes not far above the poverty level; yet they are not eligible for services. Public preschool programs that target entire communities where many families have low incomes and where educational failure is serious and widespread or programs that provide access to all families in a state (wealthier parents might pay fees) could prove more cost-effective than current programs.

Enthusiasm for compensatory preschool education and a desire to provide it without much increase in public spending sometimes combine to lead policymakers to seek to use the existing child-care system to provide these services. There is something to be said for this approach. Many children already attend child-care programs, welfare reform has led to an expansion of publicly funded child care for children in low-income families, and it makes sense to take advantage of resources already invested in this system. Unfortunately, few existing child-care programs can provide the quality educational services that produce enduring gains in cognitive development and school success. Building on the existing child-care system will require major investments in program improvement in the form of increased funding for capital and current expenses, professional development, and technical assistance, together with much higher standards.

In sum, compensatory preschool education presents an interesting nexus of research and policy regarding cognitive development and "race" that is of more than academic interest. Research on preschool education has identified important differences among measures of cognitive development. Different tests assess different aspects of cognitive development. The same test assesses different cognitive abilities at different ages. Tests that purport to measure the same thing can differ substantially in their estimates of the relative abilities of different ethnic groups. These findings raise questions about which tests best measure which mental abilities, assumptions about ethnic group differences that underlie test construction, how one might judge the fairness of alternative tests, and the relative importance of various types of mental abilities. Tests could be biased in their assessments of minority populations with respect to both the types of abilities and knowledge assessed (access to these may vary by ethnic group) and the fairness with which specific types of abilities and knowledge are assessed.

Preschool research also has implications for public policies designed to reduce inequalities and improve cognitive abilities. It calls attention to the role of poverty in shaping the cognitive development of young minority children who are much more likely than other children to be poor, to live in deep and persistent poverty, and to live in high-poverty neighborhoods (Duncan, Brooks-Gunn, Yeung, & Smith, 1998; McLoyd, 1998). The malleability of cognitive development during the preschool years provides one obvious explanation for the greater effects of poverty in this period, but it is also relevant that public investment in education is highly limited prior to kindergarten. Children are much more dependent on their families for education in the early years than in the school years. In any case, preschool research not only demonstrates that cognitive development is significantly malleable in the early years, but that preschool education can substantially improve later cognitive development for children in low-income families. This leads us to recommend increased public investments in preschool education as a means to decrease educational and economic inequality. We do not mean to suggest that preschool education could by itself eliminate interethnic inequalities or that it is the only policy that should be pursued for this purpose (policies to increase the incomes of poor families with young children are also obvious candidates). We do believe that this is one avenue to increased equality that is greatly underutilized.

REFERENCES

Abelson, W. D. (1974). Head Start graduates in school: Studies in New Haven, Connecticut. In *A report on longitudinal evaluations of preschool programs* (Vol. I, pp. 1–14). Washington, DC: U.S. Department of Health, Education, and Welfare.

Abelson, W. D., Zigler, E., & DeBlasi, C. L. (1974). Effects of a four-year follow through program on economically disadvantaged children. *Journal of Educational Psychology, 66*, 756–771.

Aigner, D. J. (1973). Regression with a binary independent variable subject to errors of observation. *Journal of Econometrics, 17*, 49–59.

Allington, R. L., & Walmsley, S. A. (1995). *No quick fix: Rethinking literacy programs in America's elementary schools.* New York: Teachers College Press.

Anastasi, A., & Urbina, S. (1997). *Psychological testing* (7th ed.) Upper Saddle River, NJ: Prentice Hall.

Andrews, S., Blumenthal, J., Johnson, D., Kahn, A., Ferguson, C., Lasater, T., Malone, P., & Wallace, D. (1982). The skills of mothering: A study of parent child development centers. *Monographs of the Society for Research in Child Development, 46*(6), Serial No. 198.

Baker, P., Keck, C., Mott, F., & Quinlan, S. (1993). *NLSY child handbook, 1993.* Columbus: Ohio State University, Center for Human Resource Research.

Barnett, W. S. (1993). Benefit-cost analysis of preschool education: Findings from a 25-year follow-up. *American Journal of Orthopsychiatry, 63*(4), 500–508.

Barnett, W. S. (1998). Long-term effects on cognitive development and school success. In W. S. Barnett & S. S. Boocock (Eds.), *Early care and education for children in poverty* (pp. 11–44). Albany: State University of New York Press.

Barnett, W. S., & Boyce, G. C. (1995). Effects of a child with Down syndrome on parents' activities. *American Journal on Mental Retardation, 100*(2), 115–127.

Barnett, W. S., & Camilli, G. (1999). *Estimating Head Start effects.* Unpublished paper, Rutgers University, Graduate School of Education, New Brunswick, NJ.

Barnett, W. S., Tarr, J., & Frede, E. C. (1999). *Early childhood education in the Abbott districts: Children's needs and the need for high quality programs.* New Brunswick, NJ: Rutgers University, Center for Early Education at Rutgers.

Barnett, W. S., Young, J. W., & Schweinhart, L. J. (1998). How preschool education contributes to cognitive development and school success: An empirical model. In W. S. Barnett & S. S. Boocock (Eds.), *Early care and education for children in poverty* (pp. 167–184). Albany: State University of New York Press.

Becker, G. S. (1981). *A treatise on the family.* Cambridge, MA: Harvard University Press.

Beller, K. (1983). The Philadelphia study: The impact of preschool on intellectual and socio-emotional development. In Consortium for Longitudinal Studies (Ed.), *As the twig is bent ... lasting effects of preschool programs* (pp. 133–170). Hillsdale, NJ: Lawrence Erlbaum Associates.

Burchinal, M., Lee, M., & Ramey, C. (1989). Type of day-care and intellectual development in disadvantaged children. *Child Development, 60*, 128–137.

Campbell, F. A., & Ramey, C. T. (1993, March). *Mid-adolescent outcomes for high risk students: An examination of the continuing effects of early intervention.* Paper presented at the biennial meeting of the Society for Research in Child Development, New Orleans, LA.

Campbell, F. A., & Ramey, C. T. (1994). Effects of early intervention on intellectual and academic achievement: A follow-up study of children from low-income families. *Child Development, 65*, 684–698.

Caldwell, B. M., & Bradley, R. H. (1979). *Home Observation for Measurement of the Environment.* Little Rock: University of Arkansas at Little Rock.

Caughy, M. O., DiPietro, J., & Strobino, M. (1994). Day-care participation as a protective factor in the cognitive development of low-income children. *Child Development, 65*, 457–471.

Clark, C. M. (1979). *Effects of the project Head Start and Title I preschool programs on vocabulary and reading achievement measured at the kindergarten and fourth grade levels.* Unpublished doctoral dissertation, Wayne State University, Detroit, MI.

Copple, C. E., Cline, M. G., & Smith, A. N. (1987). *Path to the future: Long-term effects of Head Start in the Philadelphia school district.* Washington, DC: U.S. Department of Health and Human Services.

Cronbach, L. (1990). *Essentials of psychological testing* (5th ed.). Cambridge, MA: Harper & Row.

Currie, J., & Thomas, D. (1995). Does Head Start make a difference? *American Economic Review, 85*, 341–364.

De Corte, E. (1995). Fostering cognitive growth: A perspective from research on mathematics learning and instruction. *Educational Psychologist, 30*(1), 37–46.

Deutsch, M., Deutsch, C. P., Jordan, T. J., & Grallo, R. (1983). The IDS program: An experiment in early and sustained enrichment. In Consortium for Longitudinal Studies (Ed.), *As the twig is bent ... lasting effects of preschool programs* (pp. 377–410). Hillsdale, NJ: Lawrence Erlbaum Associates.

Deutsch, M., Taleporos, E., & Victor, J. (1974). A brief synopsis of an initial enrichment program in early childhood. In S. Ryan (Ed.), *A report on longitudinal evaluations of reports on preschool programs* (Vol. I, pp. 49–60). Washington, DC: U.S. Department of Health, Education, and Welfare.

Duncan, G., Brooks-Gunn, J., Yeung, W., & Smith, J. (1998). How much does childhood poverty affect the life chances of children? *American Sociological Review, 63*, 406–423.

Dunn, L. M., & Dunn, L. M. (1981). *Peabody Picture Vocabulary Test–Revised.* Circle Pines, MN: American Guidance Service.

Dunn, L. M., & Markwardt, F. C. (1970). *Peabody Individual Achievement Test.* Circle Pines, MN: American Guidance Service.

Eckroade, G., Salehi, S., & Carter, J. (1988). *An analysis of the midterm effects of the extended elementary education prekindergarten program.* Baltimore: Maryland State Department of Education.

Eckroade, G., Salehi, S., & Wode, J. (1991, April). *An analysis of the long-term effect of the extended elementary education prekindergarten program.* Paper presented at the annual meeting of the American Educational Research Association, Chicago.

Entwisle, D. R. (1995). The role of schools in sustaining early childhood program benefits. *The Future of Children, 5*(3), 133–144.

Evans, E. (1985). Longitudinal follow-up assessment of differential preschool experience for low income minority group children. *Journal of Educational Research, 78*(4), 197–202.

Frede, E. C. (1998). Preschool program quality in programs for children in poverty. In W. S. Barnett & S. S. Boocock (Eds.), *Early care and education for children in poverty* (pp. 77–98). Albany: State University of New York Press.

Freeman, R. B. (1984). Longitudinal analysis of the effects of trade unions. *Journal of Labor Economics, 2*, 1–26.

Fuerst, J. S., & Fuerst, D. (1993). Chicago experience with an early childhood program: The special case of the Child Parent Center Program. *Urban Education, 28*, 69–96.

Garber, H. L. (1988). *The Milwaukee project: Prevention of mental retardation in children at risk.* Washington, DC: American Association on Mental Retardation.

Goodstein, H. A. (1975). *The prediction of elementary school failure among high-risk children.* Unpublished manuscript, University of Connecticut, Storrs.

Gray, S. W., Ramsey, B., & Klaus, R. (1982). *From 3 to 20: The Early Training Project.* Baltimore: University Park Press.

Gray, S., Ramsey, B., & Klaus, R. (1983). The Early Training Project, 1962–1980. In Consortium for Longitudinal Studies (Ed.), *As the twig is bent ... lasting effects of preschool programs* (pp. 33–70). Hillsdale, NJ: Lawrence Erlbaum Associates.

Griliches, Z. (1986). Economic data issues. In Z. Griliches & M. D. Intriligator (Eds.), *Handbook of econometrics* (pp. 1466–1514). New York: North-Holland.

Haskins, R. (1989). Beyond metaphor: The efficacy of early childhood education. *American Psychologist, 44*, 274–282.

Hebbeler, K. (1985). An old and a new question on the effects of early education for children from low income families. *Educational Evaluation and Policy Analysis, 7*(3), 207–216.

Herrnstein, R. J., & Murray, C. (1994). *The bell curve: Intelligence and class structure in American life.* New York: The Free Press.

Herzog, E., Newcomb, C. H., & Cisin, I. H. (1974). Double deprivation: The less they have, the less they learn. In S. Ryan (Ed.), *A report on longitudinal evaluations of preschool programs* (Vol. I, pp. 69–93). Washington, DC: U.S. Department of Health, Education, and Welfare.

Jensen, A. R. (1969). How much can we boost IQ and scholastic achievement? *Harvard Educational Review, 39*, 1–123.

Jensen, A. R. (1989). Raising IQ without increasing *g*? A review of The Milwaukee Project: Preventing mental retardation in children at risk. *Developmental Review, 9*, 234–258.

Jester, R. E., & Guinagh, B. J. (1983). The Gordon Parent Education Infant and Toddler Program. In Consortium for Longitudinal Studies (Ed.), *As the twig is bent ... lasting effects of preschool programs* (pp. 103–132). Hillsdale, NJ: Lawrence Erlbaum Associates.

Johnson, D., & Walker, T. (1991). A follow-up evaluation of the Houston Parent Child Development Center: School performance. *Journal of Early Intervention, 15*(3), 226–236.

Kanawha County Board of Education. (1978). *Kanawha Count Head Start evaluation study.* Unpublished report.

Karnes, M. B., Shwedel, A. M., & Williams. M. B. (1983). A comparison of five approaches for educating young children from low-income homes. In Consortium for Longitudinal Studies (Ed.), *As the twig is bent ... lasting effects of preschool programs* (pp. 133–170). Hillsdale, NJ: Lawrence Erlbaum Associates.

King, F. J., Cappellini, C. H., & Gravens, L. (1995). *A longitudinal study of the Florida Prekindergarten Early Intervention Program, Part III.* Tallahassee: Florida State University, Educational Services Program.

King, F. J., Cappellini, C. H., & Rohani, F. (1995). *A longitudinal study of the Florida Prekindergarten Early Intervention Program, Part IV.* Tallahassee: Florida State University, Educational Services Program.

King, F. J., Rohani, F., & Cappellini, C. H. (1995). *A ten-year study of a Prekindergarten program in Florida.* Tallahassee: Florida State University, Educational Services Program.

Kmenta, J. (1986). *Elements of econometrics* (2nd ed.). New York: Macmillan.

Kracke, K. (1995). *Head Start parent involvement: Vision, opportunities and strategies* (Paper prepared for the Parent Involvement Institute). Silver Spring, MD: Research Assessment Management.

Kresh, E. (1988). *Families in Head Start.* Unpublished paper, Head Start Bureau, Administration on Children, Youth and Families, Department of Health and Human Services.

Lally, J. R., Mangione, P., & Honig, A. (1988). The Syracuse University Family Development Program: Long-range impact of an early intervention with low-income children and their families. In D. Powell (Ed.), *Parent education as early childhood intervention: Emerging directions in theory, research, and practice* (pp. 79–104). Norwood, NJ: Ablex.

Lamb, M., & Sternberg, K. (1990). Do we really know how day care affects children? *Journal of Applied Developmental Psychology, 11*, 351–379.

Lee, V. E., Brooks-Gunn, J., Schnur, E., & Liaw, F. R. (1990). Are Head Start effects sustained? A longitudinal follow-up comparison of disadvantaged children attending Head Start, no preschool, and other preschool programs. *Child Development, 61*, 495–507.

Levenstein, P., O'Hara, J., & Madden J. (1983). The Mother–Child Home program of the Verbal Interaction Project. In Consortium for Longitudinal Studies (Ed.), *As the twig is bent … lasting effects of preschool programs* (pp. 237–263). Hillsdale, NJ: Lawrence Erlbaum Associates.

Li, J., & Bennett, N. (1998). *Young children in poverty: A statistical update, March 1998 edition.* New York: Columbia University, National Center for Children in Poverty.

Locurto, C. (1991). Beyond IQ in preschool programs? *Intelligence, 15*, 295–312.

Marcon, R. A. (1990). *Early learning and early identification: Final report of the three year longitudinal study.* Washington, DC: District of Columbia Public Schools.

Marcon, R. A. (1993). *Early learning and early identification follow-up study: Transition from the early to the later childhood grades 1990–93.* Washington, DC: District of Columbia Public Schools, Center for Systemic Change.

Marcon, R. A. (1994). Doing the right thing for children: Linking research and policy reform in the District of Columbia public schools. *Young Children, 50*(1), 8–20.

McCarthy, J., & Kirk, S. (1961). *Examiner's manual: Illinois Test of Psycholinguistic Abilities.* Urbana, IL: University of Illinois, Institute for Research on Exceptional Children.

McDonald, M. S., & Monroe, E. (1981). *A follow-up study of the 1966 Head Start program, Rome City Schools.* Unpublished paper.

McGill-Franzen, A., & Allington, R. L. (1993). "Flunk 'em or get them classified: The contamination of primary grade accountability data." *Educational Researcher, 22*(1), 19–22.

McKey, R., Condelli, L., Ganson, H., Barrett, B., Mcconkey, C., & Plantz, M. (1985). *The impact of Head Start on children, families, and communities* (Final Report of the Head Start Evaluation, Synthesis, and Utilization Project, OHDS 90-31193). Washington, DC: Department of Health and Human Services.

McLoyd, V. C. (1998). Socioeconomic disadvantage and Child Development. *American Psychologist, 53*(2), 185–204.

Miller, L. B., & Bizzell, R. P. (1983). The Louisville experiment: A comparison of four programs. In Consortium for Longitudinal Studies (Ed.), *As the twig is bent … lasting effects of preschool programs* (pp. 171–200). Hillsdale, NJ: Lawrence Erlbaum Associates.

Miller, L. B., & Bizzell, R. P. (1984). Long-term effects of four preschool programs: Ninth and tenth grade results. *Child Development, 55*, 1570–1587.

Nieman, R. H., & Gastright, J. F. (1981). *The long-term effects of ESEA Title I preschool and all-day kindergarten: An eight-year follow-up.* Cincinnati, OH: Cincinnati Public Schools.

Nolin, M., Collins, S., & Hopper, N. (1992). *NHES:93 Cognitive laboratory report.* Rockville, MD: Westat.

O'Piela, J. M. (1976). *Evaluation of the Detroit public schools Head Start program, 1975–1976.* Detroit, MI: Detroit Public Schools.

Palmer, F. (1983). The Harlem study: Effects by type of training, age of training, and social class. In Consortium for Longitudinal Studies (Ed.), *As the twig is bent ... lasting effects of preschool programs* (pp. 201–236). Hillsdale, NJ: Lawrence Erlbaum Associates.

Parker, F. L., Piotrowski, C. S., & Peay, L. (1987). Head Start as a social support for mothers: The psychological benefits of involvement. *American Journal of Orthopsychiatry, 57,* 220–233.

Phillips, D. A., McCartney, K., & Scarr, S. (1987). Child-care quality and children's social development. *Developmental Psychology, 23,* 537–543.

Pinkleton, N. B. (1976). *A comparison of referred Head Start, non-referred Head Start and non-Head Start groups of primary school children on achievement, language processing, and classroom behavior.* Unpublished doctoral dissertation, University of Cincinnati, Cincinnati, OH.

Plomin, R., & Petrill, S. A. (1997). Genetics and intelligence: What's new? *Intelligence, 24*(1), 53–78.

Quittner, A. L., & Opipari, L. C. (1994). Differential treatment of siblings: Interview and diary analyses comparing two family contexts. *Child Development, 65,* 800–814.

Ramey, C. T., Bryant, D. M., & Suarez, T. M. (1985). Preschool compensatory education and the modifiability of intelligence: A critical review. In D. Detterman (Ed.), *Current topics in human intelligence* (pp. 247–296). Norwood, NJ: Ablex.

Reedy, Y. B. (1991). *A comparison of long range effects of participation in Project Head Start and the impact of three differing delivery models.* Unpublished paper, Pennsylvania State University, University Park.

Reynolds, A. J. (1992). Mediated effects of preschool intervention. *Early Education and Development, 3,* 139–164.

Reynolds, A. J. (1993). One year of preschool intervention or two: Does it matter? *Early Childhood Research Quarterly, 10,* 1–33.

Reynolds, A. J. (1994a). Effects of a preschool plus follow-on intervention for children at risk. *Developmental Psychology, 30,* 787–804.

Reynolds, A. J. (1994b, February). *Longer-term effects of the Child Parent Center and expansion program.* Paper presented at the annual meeting of the Chicago Association for the Education of Young Children, Chicago.

Schweinhart, L. J., Barnes, H. V., Weikart, D. P., Barnett, W. S., & Epstein, A. S. (1993). *Significant benefits: The High/Scope Perry Preschool study through age 27* (Monographs of the High/Scope Educational Research Foundation, No. 10). Ypsilanti, MI: High/Scope Educational Research Foundation.

Schweinhart, L. J., & Weikart, D. P. (1997). *Lasting differences: The High/Scope preschool curriculum comparison through age 23* (Monographs of the High/Scope Educational Research Foundation, No. 12). Ypsilanti, MI: High/Scope Educational Research Foundation.

Seitz, V., & Apfel, N. H. (1994). Parent-focused intervention: Diffusion effects on siblings. *Child Development, 65,* 677–683.

Seitz, V., Rosenbaum, L. K., & Apfel, N. H. (1985). Effects of family support intervention: A ten-year follow-up. *Child Development, 56,* 376–391.

Shipman, V. C. (1970). *Disadvantaged children and their first school experiences: ETS-Head Start longitudinal study: Preliminary description of the initial sample prior to school enrollment* (ETS Tech. Rep. Series, PR-70-20). Princeton, NJ: Educational Testing Service.

Shipman V. C. (1976). *Stability and change in family status, situational, and process variables and their relationship to children's cognitive performance.* Princeton, NJ: Educational Testing Service.

Shokraii, N., & Fagan, P. (1998). *After 33 years and $30 billion, time to find out if Head Start produces results* (Heritage Foundation Rep. No. 1202). Washington, DC: Heritage Foundation.

Slaughter, D. T., Washington, V., Oyemade, U. J., & Lindsey, R. W. (1988). Head Start: A backward and forward look. *Social Policy Report, 3*(2), 1–19.

Spitz, H. H. (1986). *The raising of intelligence: A selected history of attempts to raise retarded intelligence.* Hillsdale, NJ: Lawrence Erlbaum Associates.

State Education Department, University of the State of New York. (1982). *Evaluation of the New York State experimental prekindergarten program: Final report.* Albany: Author. (ERIC Document Reproduction Service No. ED 219 123)

St. Pierre, R. G., Layzer, J. I., & Barnes, H. V. (1998). Regenerating two-generation programs. In W. S. Barnett & S. S. Boocock (Eds.), *Early care and education for children in poverty* (pp. 99–122). Albany: State University New York Press.

U.S. General Accounting Office. (1997). *Head Start: Research provides little information on impact of current program* (Rep. GAO/HEHS-97-59). Washington, DC: U.S. Government Printing Office.

Van de Reit, V., & Resnick, M. B. (1973). *Learning to learn: An effective model for early childhood education.* Gainesville: University of Florida Press.

Wechsler, D. (1974). *Manual for the Wechsler Intelligence Scale for Children.* Rev. New York: Psychological Corporation.

Weikart, D. P., Bond, J. T., & McNeil, J. T. (1978). *The Ypsilanti Perry Preschool Project: Preschool years and longitudinal results through fourth grade.* Ypsilanti, MI: High/Scope Press.

Weinert, F. E., & Helmke, A. (1995). Interclassroom differences in instructional quality and interindividual differences in cognitive development. *Educational Psychologist, 30*(1), 15–20.

Westinghouse Learning Corporation and Ohio University. (1969). *The impact of Head Start: An evaluation of the effects of Head Start on children's cognitive and affective development* (Vols. 1 & 2, Report to the Office of Economic Opportunity). Athens, OH: Westinghouse Learning Corporation and Ohio University.

White, K., & Casto, G. (1985). An integrative review of early intervention efficacy studies with at-risk children: Implications for the handicapped. *Analysis and Intervention in Developmental Disabilities, 5*, 7–31.

Woodhead, M. (1988). When psychology informs public policy: The case of early childhood intervention. *American Psychologist, 43*, 443–454.

Zaslow, M. (1991). Variation in child care quality and its implications for children. *Journal of Social Issues, 47*(2), 125–139.

Zigler, E. (1979). Project Head Start: Success or failure? In E. Zigler & J. Valentine (Eds.), *Project Head Start: A legacy of the war on poverty* (pp. 495–507). New York: The Free Press.

Zigler, E., & Freedman, J. (1987). Early experience, malleability, and Head Start. In J. J. Gallager & C. T. Ramey (Eds.), *The malleability of children* (pp. 85–96). Baltimore: Brookes.

Zigler, E., & Muenchow, S. (1992). *Head Start: The inside story of America's most successful educational experiment.* New York: Basic Books.

Author Index

T

Subject Index

S